Rick Steves'

PARIS

Rick Steves, Steve Smith
& Gene Openshaw

2010

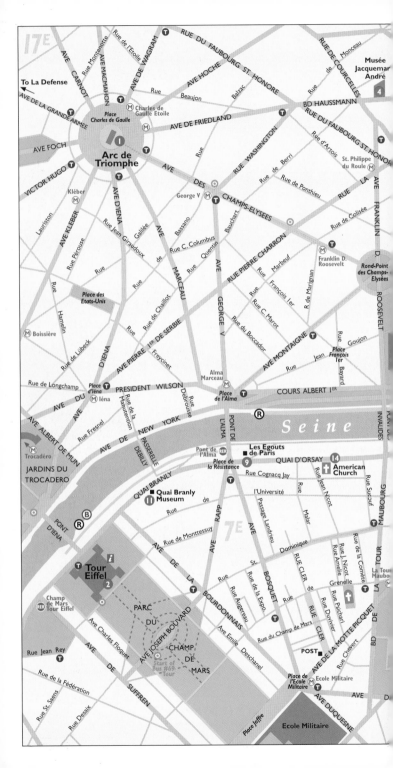

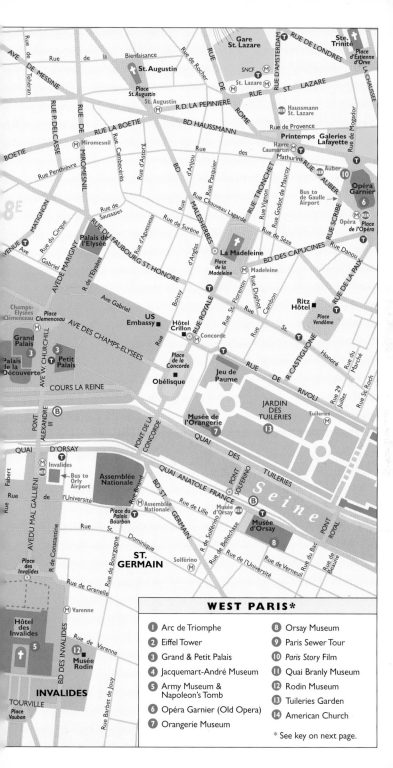

WEST PARIS*

1 Arc de Triomphe
2 Eiffel Tower
3 Grand & Petit Palais
4 Jacquemart-André Museum
5 Army Museum & Napoleon's Tomb
6 Opéra Garnier (Old Opera)
7 Orangerie Museum

8 Orsay Museum
9 Paris Sewer Tour
10 *Paris Story* Film
11 Quai Branly Museum
12 Rodin Museum
13 Tuileries Garden
14 American Church

* See key on next page.

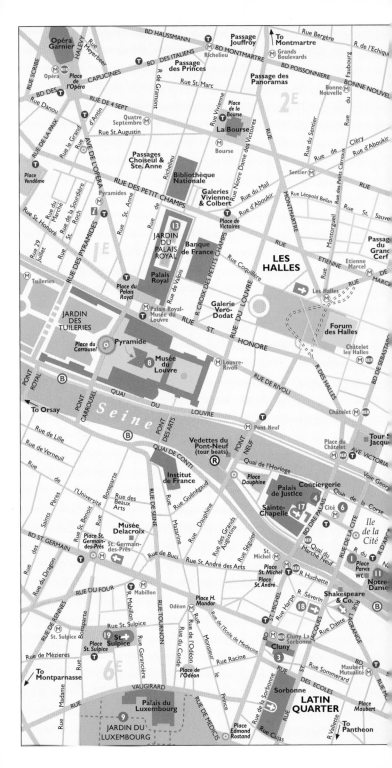

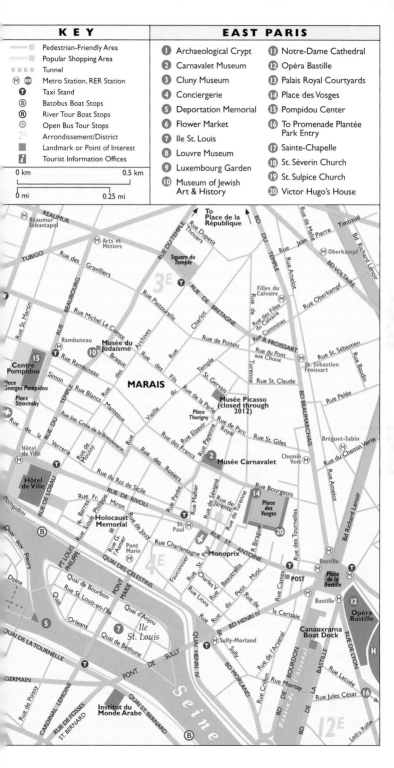

KEY

- ┄┄ Pedestrian-Friendly Area
- ┅┅ Popular Shopping Area
- ▪▪▪ Tunnel
- Ⓜ ⓇⒺⓇ Metro Station, RER Station
- Ⓣ Taxi Stand
- Ⓑ Batobus Boat Stops
- Ⓡ River Tour Boat Stops
- ⊙ Open Bus Tour Stops
- 2ᴱ Arrondissement/District
- ▪ Landmark or Point of Interest
- 𝒊 Tourist Information Offices

0 km ————————— 0.5 km

0 mi ————————— 0.25 mi

EAST PARIS

- ❶ Archaeological Crypt
- ❷ Carnavalet Museum
- ❸ Cluny Museum
- ❹ Conciergerie
- ❺ Deportation Memorial
- ❻ Flower Market
- ❼ Ile St. Louis
- ❽ Louvre Museum
- ❾ Luxembourg Garden
- ❿ Museum of Jewish Art & History
- ⓫ Notre-Dame Cathedral
- ⓬ Opéra Bastille
- ⓭ Palais Royal Courtyards
- ⓮ Place des Vosges
- ⓯ Pompidou Center
- ⓰ To Promenade Plantée Park Entry
- ⓱ Sainte-Chapelle
- ⓲ St. Séverin Church
- ⓳ St. Sulpice Church
- ⓴ Victor Hugo's House

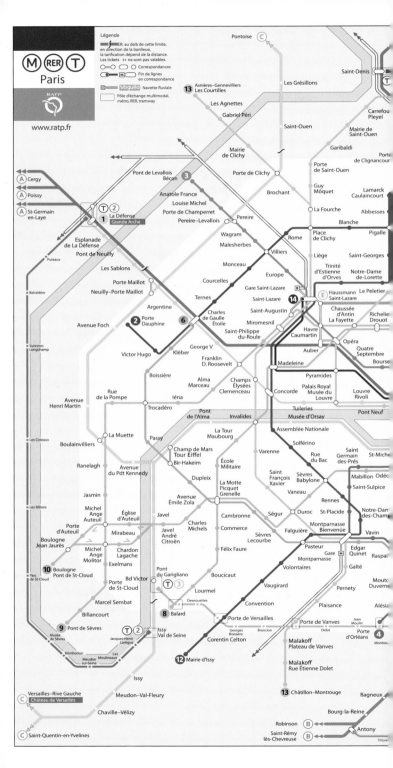

D Orry-la-Ville–Coye

Théâtre Gérard Philipe Marché de St-Denis
1 Gare de Saint-Denis
Basilique de St-Denis
Saint-Denis Porte de Paris
Cimetière de St-Denis Hôpital Delafontaine Cosmonautes La Courneuve 6 Routes
13 Saint-Denis–Université
Hôtel de Ville de La Courneuve
43 CDG Aéroport Charles de Gaulle B
La Courneuve Aubervilliers
Le Bourget B
Stade Géo André
Danton
La Courneuve 8 Mai 1945 Maurice Lachâtre Drancy-Avenir Mitry-Claye B
Stade de France Saint-Denis
La Plaine Stade de France
7 Fort d'Aubervilliers
Hôpital Avicenne
Gaston Roulaud
Escadrille Normandie–Niémen
4 Simplon
Jules Joffrin
Marcadet Poissonniers
Marx Dormoy
12 Porte de la Chapelle
Aubervilliers–Pantin Quatre Chemins
Pantin
La Ferme
Libération
Bobigny–Pantin Raymond Queneau
5 Bobigny Pablo Picasso
Jean Rostand Auguste Delaune
Pont de Bondy
Chelles Gournay E
Petit Noisy
Funiculaire de Montmartre
Château Rouge
Barbès Rochechouart
La Chapelle
Porte de la Villette
Corentin Cariou
Crimée
Riquet
Stalingrad
Église de Pantin
Noisy-le-Sec T 1
Touman E
Anvers
Gare du Nord
Magenta
7 bis Louis Blanc
Ourcq Porte de Pantin Hoche
Laumière
Jaurès
Bolivar
Danube
7 bis Pré St-Gervais
11 Mairie des Lilas
Cadet
Poissonnière
Château Landon
Gare de l'Est
Colonel Fabien
Buttes Chaumont
Botzaris
3 bis Porte des Lilas
Château d'Eau
Belleville
Pyrénées Jourdain Place des Fêtes Télégraphe
Saint-Fargeau
Strasbourg Saint-Denis
Jacques Bonsergent
Couronnes
Ménilmontant
Pelleport
Grands Boulevards
Bonne Nouvelle
Réaumur Sébastopol
Temple
Arts et Métiers
République
Oberkampf
Parmentier
Père Lachaise
Porte de Bagnolet
3 Gallieni B
Sentier
Filles du Calvaire
Rue Saint-Maur
Étienne Marcel
Les Halles
Châtelet Les Halles
Rambuteau
St-Sébastien Froissart
Saint-Ambroise
Philippe Auguste
3 bis Gambetta
9 Mairie de Montreuil
Cité
Hôtel de Ville
Chemin Vert
Richard Lenoir
Voltaire
Alexandre Dumas
Croix de Chavaux
Robespierre
Châtelet
St-Paul
Bréguet Sabin
Charonne
Avron
Porte de Montreuil
Maraîchers
Marne-la-Vallée Parcs Disneyland A
11 Pont Marie
St-Michel Notre-Dame
Bastille
Ledru-Rollin
Rue des Boulets
2 Buzenval
Vincennes A
Cluny La Sorbonne
Sully Morland
Faidherbe Chaligny
6 Nation
Saint-Mandé
Boissy-Saint-Léger A
Maubert Mutualité
Cardinal Lemoine
Gare de Lyon
Reuilly-Diderot
Porte de Vincennes
Luxembourg
Quai de la Rapée
Montgallet
Picpus Bérault
1 Château de Vincennes
Jussieu
Place Monge
Daumesnil
Bel-Air
Port-Royal
Gare d'Austerlitz
10 Gare d'Austerlitz
Bercy
Michel Bizot
Censier Daubenton
Saint Marcel
Dugommier
Denfert Rochereau
Les Gobelins
Campo Formio
Quai de la Gare
Parc de Bercy
Porte Dorée
Saint-Jacques
Corvisart
Place d'Italie
Chevaleret
Cour St-Émilion
Porte de Charenton
Glacière
5 Nationale
Bibliothèque Fr. Mitterrand
Ivry Pont Mandela
Liberté
Cité Universitaire
Tolbiac
14 Bibliothèque Fr. Mitterrand
Charenton–Écoles
École Vétérinaire de Maisons-Alfort
Gentilly
Maison Blanche
Olympiades
Porte d'Italie Porte de Choisy
T 3 Porte d'Ivry
Ivry sur-Seine
École Vétérinaire de Maisons-Alfort
Stade Charléty Poterne des Peupliers
Le Kremlin Bicêtre
Pierre et Marie Curie
Maisons-Alfort Alfortville
Maisons-Alfort–Stade
Laplace
Villejuif Léo Lagrange
Mairie d'Ivry
7
Maisons-Alfort Les Juilliottes
Arcueil–Cachan
Villejuif Paul Vaillant-Couturier
Vitry sur-Seine
Créteil-L'Échat
Créteil-Université
7 Villejuif–Louis Aragon
Le Vert de Maisons
8 Créteil–Préfecture
Les Ardoines
Orly Ouest Orly Sud
42 Orly
Massy–Palaiseau Versailles–Chantiers C
Dourdan C
Saint-Martin-d'Étampes
Malesherbes D
Melun D

Rick Steves'

PARIS

2010

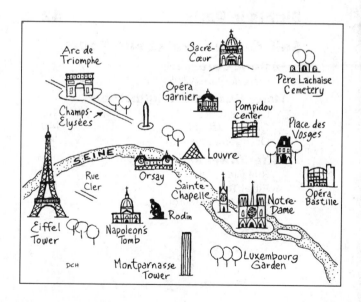

AVALON
TRAVEL

CONTENTS

French History and Contemporary Politics   567

Overview of Maps

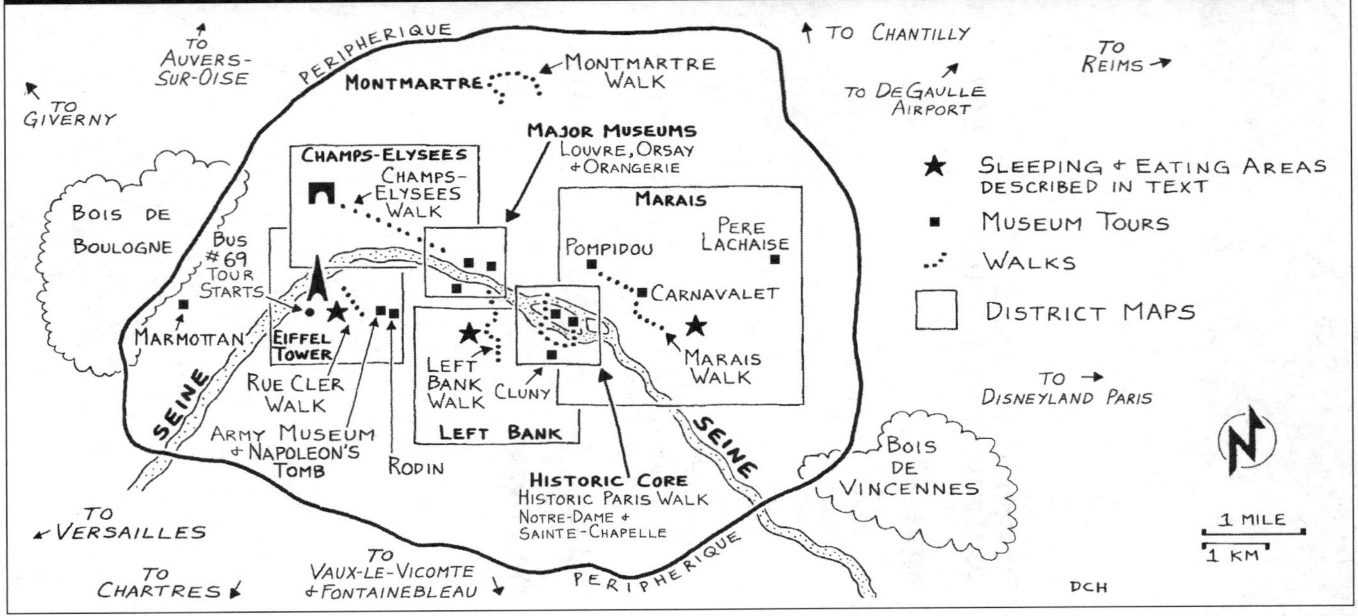

★ SLEEPING + EATING AREAS DESCRIBED IN TEXT

■ MUSEUM TOURS

⋯⋯ WALKS

☐ DISTRICT MAPS

1 MILE
1 KM

TO GIVERNY
TO AUVERS-SUR-OISE
PERIPHERIQUE
BOIS DE BOULOGNE
MARMOTTAN
Bus #69 TOUR STARTS
SEINE
EIFFEL TOWER
RUE CLER WALK
Army Museum + Napoleon's Tomb
RODIN
CHAMPS-ELYSEES
CHAMPS-ELYSEES WALK
MAJOR MUSEUMS
Louvre, Orsay + Orangerie
MONTMARTRE
MONTMARTRE WALK
TO CHANTILLY
TO DE GAULLE AIRPORT
TO REIMS →
MARAIS
POMPIDOU
PERE LACHAISE
CARNAVALET
MARAIS WALK
SEINE
HISTORIC CORE
Historic Paris Walk
Notre-Dame + Sainte-Chapelle
LEFT BANK CLUNY
LEFT BANK WALK
PERIPHERIQUE
TO VAUX-LE-VICOMTE + FONTAINEBLEAU
TO DISNEYLAND PARIS
BOIS DE VINCENNES
TO CHARTRES
TO VERSAILLES

DCH

INTRODUCTION

Paris—the City of Light—has been a beacon of culture for centuries. As a world capital of art, fashion, food, literature, and ideas, it stands as a symbol of all the fine things human civilization can offer. Come prepared to celebrate, rather than judge the cultural differences, and you'll capture the romance and *joie de vivre* that Paris exudes.

Paris offers sweeping boulevards, chatty crêpe stands, chic boutiques, and world-class art galleries. Sip decaf with deconstructionists at a sidewalk café, then step into an Impressionist painting in a tree-lined park. Climb Notre-Dame and rub shoulders with the gargoyles. Cruise the Seine, zip up the Eiffel Tower, and saunter down avenue des Champs-Elysées. Master the Louvre and Orsay museums. Save some after-dark energy for one of the world's most romantic cities.

About This Book

Rick Steves' Paris 2010 is a personal tour guide in your pocket. Better yet, it's actually three tour guides in your pocket: The co-authors of this book are Steve Smith and Gene Openshaw. Steve has been traveling to France—as a guide, researcher, home owner, and devout Francophile—every year since 1985. Gene and I have been exploring the wonders of the Old World since our first "Europe through the gutter" trip together as high school buddies in the 1970s. An inquisitive historian and lover of European culture, Gene wrote most of this book's self-guided museum tours and neighborhood walks. Together, Steve, Gene, and I keep this book current (though, for simplicity, from this point "we" will shed our respective egos and become "I"). For any updates that have occurred since our recent research, see www.ricksteves.com/update, and for a valuable list of reports and experiences—

good and bad—from fellow travelers, check www.ricksteves.com /feedback.

The book divides Paris up into convenient neighborhoods (shown on "Overview of Maps" on previous page spread). In this book, you'll find the following chapters:

Orientation includes specifics on public transportation, local tour options, helpful hints, and tourist information (note that tourist information is abbreviated "TI" in this book). The "Planning Your Time" section suggests a day-to-day schedule for how to best use your limited time.

Sights provides a succinct overview of the most important sights, arranged by neighborhood, with ratings:

▲▲▲—Don't miss.

▲▲—Try hard to see.

▲—Worthwhile if you can make it.

No rating—Worth knowing about.

The **Self-Guided Walks** cover six of Paris' most intriguing neighborhoods: Historic Paris (including Notre-Dame and Sainte-Chapelle), rue Cler (near the Eiffel Tower), the Left Bank, the Champs-Elysées, the Marais, and Montmartre.

The **Self-Guided Tours** lead you through Paris' most fascinating museums and sights: the Louvre, Orsay, Orangerie, Eiffel Tower, Rodin, Army Museum and Napoleon's Tomb, Marmottan, Cluny, Pompidou Center, Carnavalet, and Père Lachaise Cemetery. The Bus #69 Sightseeing Tour gives an inexpensive overview of the city.

Sleeping describes my favorite hotels in four cozy neighborhoods, from budget deals to cushy splurges.

Eating serves up a good range of options, from inexpensive eateries to romantic bistros, arranged by neighborhood, plus a listing of "Grand Cafés."

Paris with Children includes my top recommendations for keeping your kids (and you) happy in Paris.

Shopping gives you tips for shopping painlessly and enjoyably, without letting it overwhelm your vacation or ruin your budget. Read up on Paris' great department stores, neighborhood boutiques, flea markets, outdoor food markets, and arcaded, Old World shopping streets.

Entertainment is your guide to fun activities, including music, bus and taxi tours, and the best night walks and river cruises. You'll also find information on how to easily translate *Pariscope*, the weekly entertainment guide.

Connections lays the groundwork for your smooth arrival and departure, covering transportation by train and plane, with detailed information on Paris' two major airports (Charles de Gaulle and Orly), a minor airport (Beauvais), and Paris' six train stations.

Day Trips covers nearby sights: the great châteaux of Versailles (includes self-guided tour), Vaux-le-Vicomte, Fontainebleau, and Chantilly; Chartres' majestic cathedral (includes self-guided tour); the contemporary Champagne town of Reims; the Impressionist retreats of Claude Monet's Giverny and Vincent van Gogh's Auvers-sur-Oise; and, *finalement*, Disneyland Paris. For those who like to linger, I list accommodations near most of these sights.

French History and Contemporary Politics gives you a quick overview of France from the past to the present.

The **appendix** is a traveler's tool kit, with telephone tips, useful French phone numbers, recommended books and films, a festival list, climate chart, handy packing checklist, hotel reservation form, guide to pronouncing Parisian landmarks, and French survival phrases.

Throughout this book, when you see a ✪ in a listing, it means that the sight is covered in much more detail in one of the tour chapters.

Browse through this book and select your favorite sights. Then have a *fantastique* trip! Traveling like a temporary local, you'll get the absolute most out of every mile, minute, and euro. As you visit places I know and love, I'm happy you'll be meeting my favorite Parisians.

Planning

This section will help you get started planning your trip—with notes on trip costs, when to go, and things to know before you take off.

Travel Smart

Your trip to Paris is like a complex play—easier to follow and really appreciate on a second viewing. While no one does the same trip twice to gain that advantage, reading this book in its entirety before your trip accomplishes much the same thing.

Design an itinerary that enables you to visit the various sights at the best possible times. Make note of festivals, holidays, street market days, and days when sights are closed. You can wait in line at the Louvre, or—with a Paris Museum Pass—zip through without a sweat. Day-tripping to Versailles on Monday is bad, since it's closed—but it's not recommended on Tuesday either, when the Louvre is closed and tourist mobs storm the palace. A smart trip is a puzzle—a fun, doable, and worthwhile challenge.

Sundays have the same pros and cons as they do for travelers in the US. Special events and weekly markets pop up, sightseeing attractions are generally open, banks and many shops are closed, public transportation options are fewer, and there's no rush hour.

Major Holidays and Weekends

Popular places are even busier on weekends...and inundated on three-day weekends. Plan ahead and reserve your accommodations and transportation well in advance.

In 2010, be ready for unusually big crowds during these holiday periods: Easter weekend and the two weeks following it (April 2-18, busiest April 2-11); Labor Day (April 30-May 2); Ascension weekend (May 13-16); Pentecost weekend (May 21-23); Bastille Day (July 14) and the week during which it falls; Assumption weekend (Aug 13-15); and the winter holidays (Dec 19-Jan 2). Note that Christmas week is quieter than the week of New Year's; see "Winter in Paris" on page 457 for information on things to do. The following two holidays are usually quiet, but holidays nonetheless: All Saints' Day (Nov 1) and Armistice Day (Nov 11). For more information, check the list of festivals and holidays near the end of the appendix.

Saturdays are virtually weekdays (without the rush hour).

Be sure to mix intense and relaxed periods in your itinerary. Every trip (and every traveler) needs at least a few slack days. Pace yourself. Assume you will return.

Plan ahead for laundry and picnics. Get online at Internet cafés or at your hotel to research transportation connections, confirm events, and check the weather. Buy a phone card (or carry a mobile phone) and use it to make reservations, reconfirm hotels, book tours, and double-check hours.

Connect with the culture. Set up your own quest for the best café, Eiffel Tower view, or crêpe. Enjoy the friendliness of your Parisian hosts. Slow down and be open to unexpected experiences. Ask questions—most locals are eager to point you in their idea of the right direction. Keep a notepad in your pocket for organizing your thoughts. Wear your money belt, and learn the local currency and how to estimate prices in dollars. Those who expect to travel smart, do.

Trip Costs

Five components make up your trip costs: airfare, surface transportation, room and board, sightseeing/entertainment, and shopping/miscellany.

Airfare: A basic round-trip US-to-Paris flight can cost from $800 to $1,600, depending on where you fly from and when (cheaper in winter). If your trip covers a wide area, consider saving time and money in Europe by flying "open jaw" (into one city and out of another—e.g., into Nice and out of Paris).

Surface Transportation: For a typical one-week visit, allow about $60 for Métro tickets and a couple of day trips. To budget the cost to get between Paris and either airport, add an extra $75 by taxi, $50 by airport van, around $25 for the airport bus, or $15 for the RER train.

Room and Board: You can thrive in Paris on an overall average of $155 a day per person for room and board. This allows $15 for breakfast, $20 for lunch, $40 for dinner, and $80 for lodging (based on two people splitting the cost of a $160 double room). If you've got more money, I've listed great ways to spend it. Students and tightwads can enjoy Paris on $80 a day ($40 per bed, $40 for meals and snacks).

Sightseeing and Entertainment: Get the Paris Museum Pass, which covers most sights in the city (for more information, see page 42). You'll pay about $45 for a two-day pass (4 days/$70, 6 days/$90). While you can buy the pass through some US travel agents, it's easy and cheaper to buy in Paris. Without a Museum Pass, figure on paying roughly $10–15 each for the major sights (Orsay $12, Louvre $13) and $10 for others. Assume that bus tours and splurge experiences (concerts in Sainte-Chapelle) cost about $35.

An average of $30 a day works for most. Don't skimp here. After all, this category is the driving force behind your trip—you came to sightsee, enjoy, and experience Paris.

Shopping and Miscellany: Figure $5 per ice cream cone, coffee, or soft drink. Shopping can vary in cost from nearly nothing to a small fortune. Good budget travelers find that this category has little to do with assembling a trip full of lifelong and wonderful memories.

When to Go

Late spring and fall have the best weather and the biggest crowds. May, June, September, and October are by far the toughest months for hotel-hunting. Summers are generally hot and dry; if you wilt in the heat, look for a room with air-conditioning. It's fairly easy to find rooms in summer, and though many French businesses close in August, you'll hardly notice. Paris makes a great winter getaway (see "Winter in Paris," page 457). Airfares are less, the cafés are cozy, and the city feels lively but not touristy. The only problem—weather—is fixed by dressing correctly. Expect cold and rain, but not snow. For specific temperatures, see the climate chart in the appendix.

Know Before You Go

Your trip is more likely to go smoothly if you plan ahead. Check this list of things to arrange while you're still at home.

You need a **passport**—but no visa or shots—to travel in France. You may be denied entry into certain European countries if your passport is due to expire within three to six months of your ticketed date of return. Get it renewed if you'll be cutting it close. It can take up to six weeks to get or renew a passport. (For more on passports, see www.travel.state.gov.) Pack a photocopy of your passport in your luggage in case the original is lost or stolen.

Book your rooms well in advance, especially if you'll be traveling during peak season and any major **holidays** (see "Major Holidays and Weekends," on page 4).

Call your **debit and credit card companies** to let them know the countries you'll be visiting, so that they'll accept (and not deny) your international charges. Confirm your daily withdrawal limit; consider asking to have it raised so you can take out more cash at each ATM stop. Ask about international transaction fees.

If you're interested in **travel insurance**, do your homework before you buy. Compare the cost of the insurance to the likelihood of your using it and your potential loss if something goes wrong. For details on the many kinds of travel insurance, see www.ricksteves.com/plan/tips/insurance.htm.

If you'll be **traveling with children,** read over the list of pretrip suggestions on page 422.

If you're bringing an iPod or other MP3 player, take advantage of our free downloadable **audio tours** of the Louvre, Orsay, Versailles, and Historic Paris (see page 587 for details).

Also on iTunes you'll find Rick Steves iPhone apps for sale, with interactive, multimedia versions of some of the tours in this book (for details, see www.ricksteves.com/iphonesupport).

If seeing the City of Light at night from a taxi appeals to you, **photocopy the "Floodlit Paris Taxi Tour"** (in the Entertainment chapter) to bring along and give to your cabbie. (You could photocopy it at your hotel, but it can be simpler to have it ready to go.)

If you'll be **renting a car** for travels beyond Paris, bring your driver's license. It's recommended—but not required—that you carry an International Driving Permit (IDP), available at your local AAA office ($15 plus the cost of two passport-type photos; see www.aaa.com).

All high-speed TGV **trains** require a seat reservation—book as early as possible, as these trains fill fast. (For more on train travel, see page 470 and www.ricksteves.com/rail.) If you're taking an overnight train (especially between Paris and Rome or Venice), and you need a *couchette* (overnight bunk) or sleeper—and you *must* leave on a certain day—consider booking it in advance through a US agent (such as www.raileurope.com), even though it may cost more.

Because **airline carry-on restrictions** are always changing, visit the Transportation Security Administration's website (www.tsa.gov/travelers) for an up-to-date list of what you can bring on

Where Do I Find Information On...?

Credit-Card Theft	See page 10.
Packing Light	See the packing list on page 595.
Phoning	See "How to Dial" on page 576.
Language	See page 597.
Making Hotel Reservations	See page 357.
Tipping	See page 11.
Tourist Information Offices	See page 25.
Updates to This Book	See www.ricksteves.com /update

the plane with you...and what you have to check. Remember to arrive with plenty of time to get through security.

Cheap Tricks in Paris

Since hotels take the biggest bite out of your dollar, **book your room early** to land one of my great-value hotels. I list several well-located and comfortable hotels with rooms under €100, but you'll need to beat other travelers to the punch.

Enjoy picnic lunches and dinners regularly. You'll find tasty €4 sandwiches, to-go salads, quiches, and high-quality takeout at bakeries, *charcuteries,* and stands throughout Paris. Scenic picnic sites are everywhere.

Order only a *plat* (main course) for dinner on some nights. And at cafés (as opposed to restaurants), it's fine to order only a soup or salad for dinner.

Visit sights on free days (see "Affording Paris' Sights" sidebar on page 54).

Buy a Paris Museum Pass and use it wisely (see page 42 for advice). For stays of a week or longer, consider getting a Métro pass (see page 28).

Practicalities

Emergency Telephone Numbers: In France, dial 17 for police help or 15 for a medical emergency. Or ask at your hotel for help. They'll know the nearest medical and emergency services.

Time: In France—and in this book—you'll use the 24-hour clock. It's the same through 12:00 noon, then keep going: 13:00, 14:00, and so on. For anything over 12, subtract 12 and add p.m. (14:00 is 2:00 p.m.)

France, like most of continental Europe, is generally six/nine hours ahead of the East/West Coasts of the US. The exceptions are the beginning and end of Daylight Saving Time: Europe "springs forward" the last Sunday in March (two weeks after most of North America), and "falls back" the last Sunday in October (one week before North America). For a handy online time converter, try www.timeanddate.com/worldclock.

Business Hours: In France, most shops are open Monday through Saturday (10:00–12:00 & 14:00–19:00) and closed Sunday, though many small markets, *boulangeries* (bakeries), and street markets are open Sunday mornings until noon. On Mondays, some businesses are closed until 14:00, and possibly all day. Saturdays are like weekdays (but most banks are closed).

Watt's Up? Europe's electrical system is different from North America's in two ways: the shape of the plug (two round prongs) and the voltage of the current (220 volts instead of 110 volts). For your North American plug to work in Europe, you'll need an adapter, sold inexpensively at travel stores in the US. As for the voltage, most newer electronics or travel appliances (such as hair dryers, laptops, and battery chargers) automatically convert the voltage—if you see a range of voltages printed on the item or its plug (such as "110–220"), it'll work in Europe. Otherwise, you can buy a converter separately in the US (about $20).

Discounts: Although discounts aren't listed in this book, seniors (age 60 and over), students with International Student Identification Cards, teachers with proper identification, and youths under 18 or even 26 can get discounts. Always ask. To inquire about a senior discount, ask, *"Réduction troisième âge?"* (ray-dook-see-ohn twah-zee-ehm ahzh). To get a teacher or student ID card, visit www.statravel.com or www.isic.org.

News: Americans keep in touch through the *International Herald Tribune* (published almost daily throughout Europe and online at www.iht.com). Other newsy sites are http://news.bbc.co.uk and www.europeantimes.com. Every Tuesday, the European editions of *Time* and *Newsweek* hit the stands with articles of particular interest to European travelers. Sports addicts can get their daily fix online or from *USA Today*. Many hotels have CNN and BBC television channels.

Money

This section covers how to get cash, using credit and debit cards in Paris, what to do if your card is lost or stolen, and tips on tipping.

Cash from ATMs

Throughout Europe, cash machines (ATMs) are the standard way for travelers to get local currency. As an emergency backup, bring

Exchange Rate

1 euro (€) = about $1.40

To convert prices in euros to dollars, add about 40 percent: €20 = about $28, €50 = about $70. (To get the latest rate and print a cheat sheet, see www.oanda.com.) Just like the dollar, the euro is broken down into 100 cents. You'll find coins ranging from 1 cent to 2 euros, and bills from 5 euros to 500 euros.

several hundred dollars in hard cash (in $20 bills, not hard-to-exchange $100 bills). Avoid using currency exchange booths (lousy rates and/or outrageous fees); if you have currency to exchange, take it to a bank. Also avoid traveler's checks, which are a waste of time (long waits at banks) and a waste of money (in fees).

To use an ATM (known as a *retrait, point d'argent,* or *distributeur)* to withdraw money from your account, you'll need a debit card (ideally with a Visa or MasterCard logo for maximum usability), plus a PIN code. Know your PIN code in numbers; there are only numbers—no letters—on European keypads. It's smart to bring two cards, in case one gets demagnetized or eaten by a temperamental machine.

Before you go, confirm with your bank that your cards will work overseas, and alert them that you'll be making withdrawals in Europe—otherwise, the bank might freeze your card if it detects unusual spending patterns. (Credit-card companies do the same thing—inform them of your travel plans as well.) Also ask about international fees; see "Credit and Debit Cards," below.

When using an ATM, try to take out large sums of money to reduce your per-transaction bank fees. If the machine refuses your request, try again and select a smaller amount (some cash machines limit the amount you can withdraw—don't take it personally). If that doesn't work, try a different machine.

To keep your cash safe, use a money belt—a pouch with a strap that you buckle around your waist like a belt, and wear under your clothes. Thieves target tourists. A money belt provides peace of mind, allowing you to carry lots of cash safely. Don't waste time every few days tracking down a cash machine—withdraw a week's worth of money, stuff it in your money belt, and travel!

Credit and Debit Cards

For purchases, Visa and MasterCard are more commonly accepted than American Express. Just like at home, credit or debit cards work easily at larger hotels, restaurants, and shops, but smaller businesses prefer payment in local currency (in small bills—break large bills at a bank or larger store). If receipts show your credit-card number, don't toss these thoughtlessly.

Fees: Credit and debit cards—whether used for purchases or ATM withdrawals—often charge additional, tacked-on "international transaction" fees of up to 3 percent plus $5 per transaction. Note that if you use a credit card for ATM transactions, it's technically a "cash advance" rather than a "withdrawal"—and subject to an additional cash-advance fee.

To avoid unpleasant surprises, call your bank or credit-card company before your trip to ask about these fees. If the fees are too high, consider getting a card just for your trip: Capital One (www.capitalone.com) and most credit unions have low-to-no international transaction fees.

If merchants offer to convert your purchase price into dollars (called dynamic currency conversion, or DCC), refuse this "service." You'll pay even more in fees for the expensive convenience of seeing your charge in dollars.

Dealing with "Chip and PIN": Some parts of Europe (especially France, Great Britain, Ireland, the Netherlands, and Scandinavia) are adopting a "chip and PIN" system for their credit and debit cards. These "smartcards" come with an embedded microchip, and cardholders enter a PIN instead of signing a receipt. In most cases, you can still use your credit or debit card at the cashier and sign the receipt the old-fashioned way. A few merchants might insist on the PIN—making it helpful for you to know the PIN for your credit card (ask your credit-card company); in a pinch, use cash or your debit card and PIN instead.

Your US credit and debit cards will not work in train- or Métro-ticket machines, at self-service gas pumps, or at freeway tollbooths. But in most of these situations, there's a cashier nearby who can take your credit or debit card and make it work.

Damage Control for Lost Cards

If you lose your credit, debit, or ATM card, you can stop people from using it by reporting the loss immediately to the respective global customer-assistance centers. Call these 24-hour US numbers collect: Visa (410/581-9994), MasterCard (636/722-7111), and American Express (623/492-8427). For another option (with the same results), you can call these toll-free numbers in France: Visa (08 00 90 11 79) and MasterCard (08 00 90 13 87). American Express has a Paris office, but the call isn't free (01 47 77 70 00, English spoken). Diners Club has offices in the US (702/797-5532, call collect) and Britain (from France, dial 00-44-1695-53760).

At a minimum, you'll need to know the name of the financial institution that issued you the card, along with the type of card (classic, platinum, etc). Providing the following information will allow for a quicker cancellation of your missing card: full card number, whether you are the primary or secondary cardholder, the cardholder's name exactly as printed on the card, billing address, home phone number, circumstances of the loss or theft, and identification verification (your birth date, your mother's maiden name, or your Social Security Number—memorize this, don't carry a copy). If you are the secondary cardholder, you'll also need to provide the primary cardholder's identification-verification details. You can generally receive a temporary card within two or three business days in Europe.

If you report your card lost or stolen promptly, you typically won't be responsible for any unauthorized transactions on your account, although many banks charge a liability fee of $50.

Tipping

Tipping *(donner un pourboire)* in France isn't as automatic and generous as it is in the US, but for special service, tips are appreciated, if not expected. As in the US, the proper amount depends on your resources, tipping philosophy, and the circumstances, but some general guidelines apply.

Restaurants: At cafés and restaurants, a 12–15 percent service charge is always included in the bill *(service compris)*, though it's good form to tip 5 percent extra for good service. When you hand your payment plus a tip to your waiter, you can say, *"C'est bon"* (say bohn), meaning, "It's good" (and you don't want any change back). If you order a meal at a counter, don't tip.

Taxis: To tip the cabbie, round up. For a typical ride, round up to the next euro on the fare (to pay a €13 fare, give €14); for a long ride, round to the nearest €10 (for a €75 fare, give €80). If the cabbie hauls your bags and zips you to the airport to help you catch your flight, you might want to toss in a little more. But if you feel like you're being driven in circles or otherwise ripped off, skip the tip.

Special Services: It's thoughtful to tip a couple of euros to someone who shows you a special sight and who is not otherwise paid. Tour guides at public sites sometimes hold out their hands for tips (€1–2) after they give their spiel; if I've already paid for the tour, I don't tip extra, unless they really impressed me. The usher who seats you at a cinema or theater will expect a €1 tip. At hotels, porters expect a euro for each bag they carry (another reason to pack light). Leaving the maid a euro per overnight at the end of your stay is a nice touch. In general, if someone in the service industry does a super job for you, a tip of a couple of euros is appropriate, but not required.

When in doubt, ask. If you're not sure whether (or how

much) to tip for a service, ask your hotelier or the tourist information office; they'll fill you in on how it's done on their turf.

Getting a VAT Refund

Wrapped into the purchase price of your French souvenirs is a Value-Added Tax (VAT) of about 19.6 percent. If you purchase more than €175 (about $245) worth of goods at a store that participates in the VAT-refund scheme, you're entitled to get most of that tax back. Getting your refund is usually straightforward and, if you buy a substantial amount of souvenirs, well worth the hassle. If you're lucky, the merchant will subtract the tax when you make your purchase. (This is more likely to occur if the store ships the goods to your home.) Otherwise, you'll need to do the following:

Get the paperwork. Have the merchant completely fill out the necessary refund document, *Bordereau de Vente a l'Exportation*, also called a "cheque." You'll have to present your passport at the store.

Get your stamp at the border or airport. Process your cheque(s) at your last stop in the EU (e.g., at the airport) with the customs agent who deals with VAT refunds. It's best to keep your purchases in your carry-on for viewing, but if they're too large or dangerous (such as knives) to carry on, track down the proper customs agent to inspect them before you check your bag. You're not supposed to use your purchased goods before you leave. If you show up at customs wearing your chic new French ensemble, officials might look the other way—or deny you a refund.

Collect your refund. You'll need to return your stamped document to the retailer or its representative. Many merchants work with a service, such as Global Refund (www.globalrefund.com) or Premier Tax Free (www.premiertaxfree.com), which have offices at major airports, ports, or border crossings. These services, which extract a 4 percent fee, can refund your money immediately in your currency of choice or credit your card (within two billing cycles). If the retailer handles VAT refunds directly, it's up to you to contact the merchant for your refund. You can mail the documents from home, or, even quicker, from your point of departure (using a stamped, addressed envelope you've prepared or one that's been provided by the merchant)—and then wait. It could take months.

Customs for American Shoppers

You are allowed to take home $800 worth of items per person duty-free, once every 30 days. The next $1,000 is taxed at a flat 3 percent. After that, you pay the individual item's duty rate. You can also bring in duty-free a liter of alcohol (slightly more than a standard-size bottle of wine; you must be at least 21), 200 cigarettes, and up to 100 non-Cuban cigars. You may take home vacuum-packed cheeses; dried herbs, spices, or mushrooms; and canned fruits or vegetables including jams and vegetable spreads. Baked goods, candy, chocolate, oil, vinegar, mustard, and honey are OK. Fresh fruits or vegetables are not. Meats are generally not allowed, though canned pâtés are permitted if made from geese, duck, or pork. Note that you'll need to carefully pack any bottles of wine and other liquid-containing items in your checked luggage, due to limits on liquids in carry-ons. To check customs rules and duty rates before you go, visit www.cbp.gov, and click on "Travel," then "Know Before You Go."

Sightseeing

Sightseeing can be hard work. Use these tips to make your visits to Paris' finest sights meaningful, fun, fast, and painless.

Plan Ahead

Set up an itinerary that allows you to fit in all your must-see sights. For a one-stop look at opening hours, see "Paris at a Glance" (page 48). Remember, the Louvre and other museums are closed on Tuesday, and many others are closed on Monday (see "Daily Reminder" on page 22). Most sights keep stable hours, but you can easily confirm the latest by picking up the booklet *Musées, Monuments Historiques, et Expositions,* available at most museums. You can also find good information on many of Paris' sights online at www.parisinfo.com.

If you'll be visiting during a holiday, find out if a particular sight will be open by phoning ahead or checking its website. And don't put off visiting a must-see sight—you never know when a place will close unexpectedly for a holiday, strike, or restoration.

To get the most out of the self-guided tours and sight descriptions in this book, reread them the night before your visit. The Louvre is much more entertaining if you've boned up on the *Venus de Milo* the night before. When you arrive at the sight, use the overview map to get the lay of the land and the basic tour route.

When possible, visit key museums first thing in the day (when your energy is best) and save other activities for the afternoon. Hit the highlights first, then go back to other things if you have the stamina and time. Going at the right time can also help you avoid crowds. This book offers tips on specific sights. Try visiting the sight very early, at lunch, or very late (evening hours are usually peaceful, with fewer crowds). The Louvre and Orsay museums are open selected evenings, while the Pompidou Center is open late every night except Tuesday (when it's closed all day).

Plan to buy a Paris Museum Pass, which can speed you through lines and saves you money (for pass details, see the beginning of the Sights chapter). For information on more money-saving tips, see "Affording Paris' Sights" on page 54.

At Sights

All sights have rules, and if you know about these in advance, they're no big deal. At churches—most of which offer amazing art (usually free) and a welcome seat—a modest dress code (no bare shoulders or shorts) is encouraged.

Some important sights may have metal detectors or conduct bag searches that will slow your entry, while others require you to check daypacks and coats. They'll be kept safely. If you have something you can't bear to part with, stash it in a pocket or purse. To avoid checking a small backpack, carry it (at least as you enter) under your arm like a purse. From a guard's point of view, a backpack is generally a problem though a purse is not.

If you check a bag, the attendant may ask you (in French) if it contains anything of value—e.g., camera, phone, money, passport—since these cannot be checked.

Photography is banned at most major sights. Look for signs or ask. If cameras are allowed, flashes or tripods usually are not. Flashes damage oil paintings and distract others in the room. Even without a flash, a handheld camera will take a decent picture (or buy postcards or posters at the museum bookstore). Video cameras are generally allowed.

Museums may have special exhibits in addition to their permanent collections. Some exhibits are included in the entry price; others come at an extra cost (which you may have to pay even if you don't want to see the exhibit).

Many sights rent audioguides, which generally offer dry-but-useful recorded descriptions in English (ranging from free to about €6). I have produced interactive iPhone apps as well as free audioguide versions of my tours for the Louvre, Orsay Museum, Versailles, and Historic Paris (see page 587). If you bring along your own pair of headphones and a Y-jack, you can sometimes share one audioguide with your travel partner and save. Guided tours in English (usually about €6, and widely ranging in quality) are most likely to occur during peak season.

Expect changes—artwork can be on tour, on loan, out sick, or shifted at the whim of the curator. Ask museum staff if you can't find a particular painting. Say the title or artist's name, or point to the photograph in this book and ask for its location by saying, *"Où est?"* (oo ay).

Important sights often have an on-site café or cafeteria (usually a good place to rest and have a snack or light meal). The WCs at many sights are free and clean. Key sights and museums have bookstores selling postcards and souvenirs. Before you leave, scan

How Was Your Trip?

Were your travels fun, smooth, and meaningful? If you'd like to share your tips, concerns, and discoveries, please fill out the survey at www.ricksteves.com/feedback. I value your feedback. Thanks in advance—it helps a lot.

the postcards and thumb through the biggest guidebook (or skim its index) to be sure you haven't overlooked something that you'd like to see.

Most sights stop admitting people 30–60 minutes before closing time, and some rooms close early (generally about 45 minutes before the actual closing time). Guards usher people out, so don't save the best for last.

Every sight or museum offers more than what is covered in this book. Use these tours as an introduction—not the final word.

Transportation

Transportation concerns within Paris are limited to the subway (Métro), buses, and taxis, all covered extensively in the Orientation chapter. Connections to day-trip destinations are covered in those chapters. You don't want to drive in Paris. If you have a car, stow it (for suggestions on parking, see the end of the Connections chapter). For information on connecting Paris with the rest of France and with London on the Eurostar train, see page 481.

Traveling as a Temporary Local

We travel all the way to Europe to enjoy differences—to become temporary locals. You'll experience frustrations. Certain truths that we find "God-given" or "self-evident," such as cold beer, ice in drinks, bottomless cups of coffee, hot showers, and bigger being better, are suddenly not so true. One of the benefits of travel is the eye-opening realization that there are logical, civil, and even better alternatives.

Paris is an understandably proud city. To enjoy its people, you need to celebrate the differences. A willingness to go local ensures that you'll enjoy a full dose of Parisian hospitality.

If there is a negative aspect to the image the French have of Americans (apart from our foreign policy), it's that we are big, loud, aggressive, impolite, rich, superficially friendly, and naive.

The French (and Europeans in general) place a high value on speaking quietly in restaurants and on trains. Listen while on the bus, the Métro, or in a restaurant—the place can be packed, but the decibel level is low. Try to adjust your volume accordingly to show respect for their culture.

Although the French look bemusedly at some of our Yankee excesses—and worriedly at others—they nearly always afford us individual travelers all the warmth we deserve. Judging from all the happy feedback I receive from travelers who have used this book, it's safe to assume you'll enjoy a great, affordable vacation—with the finesse of an independent, experienced traveler.

Thanks, and *bon voyage!*

Back Door Travel Philosophy
From Rick Steves' *Europe Through the Back Door*

Travel is intensified living—maximum thrills per minute and one of the last great sources of legal adventure. Travel is freedom. It's recess, and we need it.

Experiencing the real Europe requires catching it by surprise, going casual..."Through the Back Door."

Affording travel is a matter of priorities. (Make do with the old car.) You can eat and sleep—simply, safely, and enjoyably—nearly anywhere in Europe for $120 a day plus transportation costs (although allow more for bigger cities). In many ways, spending more money only builds a thicker wall between you and what you traveled so far to see. Europe is a cultural carnival, and, time after time, you'll find that its best acts are free and the best seats are the cheap ones.

A tight budget forces you to travel close to the ground, meeting and communicating with the people. Never sacrifice sleep, nutrition, safety, or cleanliness to save money. Simply enjoy the local-style alternatives to expensive hotels and restaurants.

Connecting with people carbonates your experience. Extroverts have more fun. If your trip is low on magic moments, kick yourself and make things happen. If you don't enjoy a place, maybe you don't know enough about it. Seek the truth. Recognize tourist traps. Give a culture the benefit of your open mind. See things as different, but not better or worse. Any culture has much plenty to share.

Of course, travel, like the world, is a series of hills and valleys. Be fanatically positive and militantly optimistic. If something's not to your liking, change your liking.

Travel can make you a happier American, as well as a citizen of the world. Our Earth is home to six and a half billion equally precious people. It's humbling to travel and find that people don't have the "American Dream"—they have their own dreams. Europeans like us, but, with all due respect, they wouldn't trade passports.

Thoughtful travel engages us with the world. In tough economic times, it reminds us what is truly important. By broadening perspectives, travel teaches new ways to measure quality of life.

Globetrotting destroys ethnocentricity, helping us understand and appreciate other cultures. Rather than fear the diversity on this planet, celebrate it. Among your most prized souvenirs will be the strands of different cultures you choose to knit into your own character. The world is a cultural yarn shop, and Back Door travelers are weaving the ultimate tapestry. Join in!

ORIENTATION

Many people fall in love with Paris. Some see the essentials and flee, overwhelmed by the big city. With the proper approach and a measure of patience, you'll fall head over heels for Europe's capital city.

This orientation to the City of Light will illuminate your trip. The day plans—for visits of one to seven days—will help you prioritize the many sights. You'll tap into Paris' information sources for current events. Most importantly, you'll learn to navigate Paris by Métro, bus, taxi, or on foot.

Paris: A Verbal Map

Paris (population of city center: 2,170,000) is split in half by the Seine River, divided into 20 arrondissements (proud and independent governmental jurisdictions), circled by a ring-road freeway (the *périphérique*), and speckled with Métro stations. You'll find Paris easier to navigate if you know which side of the river you're on, which arrondissement you're in, and which Métro stop you're closest to. If you're north of the river (the top half of any city map), you're on the Right Bank (Rive Droite). If you're south of it, you're on the Left Bank (Rive Gauche). The bull's-eye of your Paris map is Notre-Dame, which sits on an island in the middle of the Seine. Most of your sightseeing will take place within five blocks of the river.

Paris Arrondissements

Arrondissements are numbered, starting at the Louvre and moving in a clockwise spiral out to the ring road. The last two digits in a Parisian zip code indicate the arrondissement number. The abbreviation for "Métro stop" is "Mo." In Parisian jargon, the Eiffel Tower is on *la Rive Gauche* (the Left Bank) in the *7ème* (7th arrondissement), zip code 75007, Mo: Trocadéro.

Paris Métro stops are used as a standard aid in giving directions, even for those not taking the Métro. As you're tracking down addresses, these words and pronunciations will help: Métro (may-troh), *place* (plahs—square), *rue* (roo—road), *avenue* (ah-vuh-noo), *boulevard* (boo-luh-var), and *pont* (pohn—bridge).

Paris by Neighborhood

Paris is a big, sprawling city, but its major sights cluster in convenient zones. Grouping your sightseeing, walks, dining, and shopping thoughtfully can save you lots of time and money.

The **historic core** centers on the Ile de la Cité ("Island of the City"), located in the middle of the Seine. On the Ile de la Cité, you'll find Paris' oldest sights, from Roman ruins to the medieval Notre-Dame and Sainte-Chapelle churches. Other sights in this area: Archaeological Crypt, Deportation Memorial, Conciergerie, flower market, Paris Plage, and the lovely island, Ile St. Louis, with appealing shops, cafés, and restaurants. Paris' most historic riverside vendors, *les bouquinistes*, line both sides of the Seine as it passes Ile de la Cité.

Just west of the historic core is the **major museums neighborhood,** where you'll find the Louvre, Orsay, and Orangerie. Other sights: the Tuileries Garden, Palais Royal's courtyards, and shopping at place de la Madeleine.

The **Champs-Elysées**—the greatest of many grand, 19th-century boulevards on the Right Bank—runs northwest from the place de la Concorde to the Arc de Triomphe. Other sights: the Petit and Grand Palais, Opéra Garnier, Jacquemart-André museum and Fragonard Perfume museum, La Défense and La Grande Arche, and shopping at Galeries Lafayette and at Passages Choiseul and Ste. Anne.

ORIENTATION

Paris Neighborhoods

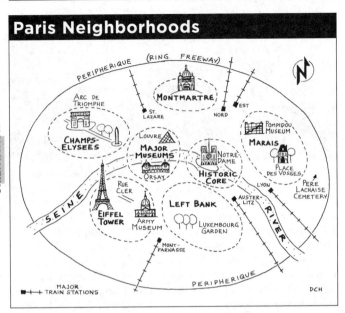

South of the Champs-Elysées, the **Eiffel Tower** neighborhood, which is located in the shadow of that famous monument in the Champ de Mars park, has colorful rue Cler (with many recommended hotels and restaurants), the Army Museum and Napoleon's Tomb, the Rodin Museum, and the thriving outdoor market Marché boulevard de Grenelle (Wed and Sun mornings). Other sights: Quai Branly Museum, National Maritime Museum, and Sewer Tour. The Marmottan Museum is west of the Eiffel Tower on the Right Bank.

The **Left Bank** is home to...the Left Bank. Anchored by the large Luxembourg Garden (near numerous hotels and eateries listed in this book), the Left Bank is the traditional neighborhood of Paris' intellectual, artistic, and café life. Other sights: the Latin Quarter, Cluny Museum, St. Germain-des-Prés and St. Sulpice churches, Panthéon, Montparnasse Tower, Catacombs, Delacroix Museum, and the Jardin des Plantes park. This is also one of

Paris' best shopping areas (see the Sèvres-Babylone to St. Sulpice shopping stroll on page 434).

The **Marais neighborhood** has lots of recommended restaurants and hotels, shops, the delightful place des Vosges, and artistic sights such as the Pompidou Center and Picasso Museum (currently closed for renovation). This area is alive with avant-garde boutiques (see page 439). Other Marais sights: Jewish Art and History and Carnavalet museums, Victor Hugo's House, Holocaust Memorial, Promenade Plantée park, Père Lachaise Cemetery, the traffic-free street market on rue Montorgueil, and markets at Bastille and place d'Aligre.

Finally, hovering on the northern fringes of your Paris map is the hilltop neighborhood of **Montmartre,** which still retains some of the untamed rural charm that once drew Impressionist painters and turn-of-the-century bohemians. Other sights: Sacré-Cœur basilica, Dalí and Montmartre museums, Moulin Rouge, Museum of Erotic Art, Pigalle, and nearby Puces St. Ouen flea market.

Planning Your Time

In the planning sections below, I've listed sights in descending order of importance. Therefore, if you have only one day, just do Day 1; for two days, add Day 2; and so on. When planning where to plug in Versailles, remember that the palace (Château) is closed on Mondays and especially crowded on Sundays and Tuesdays—try to avoid these days. For other itinerary considerations on a day-by-day basis, check the "Daily Reminder," next page.

Paris in One, Two, or Three Busy Days

If you want to fit in Versailles on a three-day visit, try the afternoon of the second day (easier) or the third day.

Day 1

Morning: Follow this book's Historic Paris Walk, featuring Ile de la Cité, Notre-Dame, the Latin Quarter, and Sainte-Chapelle.

Afternoon: Tour the Louvre.

Evening: Enjoy the Trocadéro scene and a twilight ride up the Eiffel Tower.

Day 2

Morning: Follow this book's Champs-Elysées Walk from the Arc de Triomphe down the grand avenue des Champs-Elysées to Tuileries Garden.

ORIENTATION

Daily Reminder

Sunday: Many sights are free on the first Sunday of the month, including the Louvre, Orsay, Rodin, Cluny, and Delacroix museums, the Arc de Triomphe (Oct–March only), and Pompidou Center. These free days at popular sights attract hordes of visitors.

Versailles is more crowded than usual on Sunday—but on the upside, the garden's fountains are running (April–Sept).

Look for organ concerts at St. Sulpice and possibly other churches. The American Church often hosts a free concert (often classical piano and vocals, generally Sept–June at 17:00—but not every week). Summer brings puppet shows to Luxembourg Garden and Champ de Mars park.

Most of Paris' stores are closed on Sunday, but shoppers will find relief in the Marais neighborhood's lively Jewish Quarter, where many stores are open. Many recommended restaurants in the rue Cler neighborhood are closed for dinner.

Monday: These sights are closed today: Orsay, Rodin, Marmottan, Carnavalet, Catacombs, Petit Palais, Victor Hugo's House, Montmartre Museum, Quai Branly, and Paris Archaeological Crypt. Outside of Paris, these sights are closed: all sights in Auvers-sur-Oise, and the Château and Domaine de Marie-Antoinette at Versailles. The Louvre and Eiffel Tower are more crowded because of these closings. The Army Museum (and Napoleon's Tomb) is closed the first Monday of every month. Some small stores don't open until 14:00.

Midday: Cross the pedestrian bridge from the Tuileries Garden, then tour the Orsay Museum.

Afternoon: Tour the Rodin Museum, or the Army Museum and Napoleon's Tomb.

Evening: Cruise the Seine River, take Paris Vision's nighttime Illumination bus tour, or follow this book's "Floodlit Paris Taxi" Tour (see the Entertainment chapter; if you're staying more than two days, save this for your last-night finale).

Day 3

Morning: Ride the RER suburban train out to Versailles (tour the château and sample the gardens).

Afternoon: Take this book's Marais Walk.

Evening: Follow this book's Montmartre Walk, featuring the Sacré-Cœur basilica.

Street markets such as rue Cler and rue Mouffetard are dead today. Some banks are closed. It's discount night at many cinemas.

Tuesday: Many sights are closed today, including the Louvre, Orangerie, Cluny, Pompidou, National Maritime, and Delacroix museums, as well as the Grand Palais, the châteaux of Chantilly and Fontainebleau, and lesser sights in Auvers-sur-Oise. The Eiffel Tower, Orsay, and Versailles are particularly busy today.

Wednesday: All sights are open (Louvre until 21:45). The weekly *Pariscope* magazine comes out today. Most schools are closed, so many kids' sights are busy, and in summer the puppet shows play in Luxembourg Garden and Champ de Mars park. Some cinemas offer discounts.

Thursday: All sights are open except the Sewer Tour. The Orsay is open until 21:45. Some department stores are open late.

Friday: All sights are open (Louvre until 21:45) except the Sewer Tour. Afternoon trains and roads leaving Paris are crowded; TGV train reservation fees are higher.

Saturday: All sights are open except the Jewish Art and History Museum and the Holocaust Memorial. The fountains run at Versailles (April–Sept), and Vaux-le-Vicomte hosts candlelight visits (early-May–early-Oct); otherwise, avoid weekend crowds at area châteaux and Impressionist sights. Department stores are jammed. The Jewish Quarter is quiet. In summer, puppet shows are held at Luxembourg Garden and Champ de Mars park.

Paris in Five to Seven Days Without Going In-Seine
Day 1

Morning: Follow this book's Historic Paris Walk, featuring Ile de la Cité, Notre-Dame, the Latin Quarter, and Sainte-Chapelle. If you enjoy medieval art, visit the Cluny Museum.

Afternoon: Tour the Opéra Garnier (English tours available), consider the *Paris Story* film (for a video orientation), and end your day enjoying the glorious rooftop view at Galeries Lafayette department store.

Evening: Cruise the Seine River.

Day 2

Reversing the morning and afternoon activities on this day works well because the Champs-Elysées Walk leaves you near the Louvre—but most people have more energy for museums in the morning.

Morning: Tour the Louvre (arrive 20 min before opening). Have coffee or lunch at Café le Nemours.

Afternoon: Follow this book's Champs-Elysées Walk from the Arc de Triomphe downhill along the incomparable avenue des Champs-Elysées to the Tuileries Garden, and possibly the Orangerie Museum.

Evening: Enjoy dinner on Ile St. Louis, then a floodlit walk by Notre-Dame.

Day 3

Morning: Tour the Orsay Museum (arrive 15 min before opening).

Midday: Tour the Rodin Museum (café lunch in gardens).

Afternoon: Visit the Army Museum and Napoleon's Tomb, then take this book's Rue Cler Walk and relax at Café du Marché.

Evening: Take this book's Montmartre Walk, featuring the Sacré-Cœur basilica.

Day 4

Morning: Catch the RER suburban train by 8:00 to arrive early at Versailles (before it opens at 9:00). Tour the palace's interior.

Midday: Have lunch in the Gardens at Versailles.

Afternoon: Spend the afternoon touring the Gardens and the Domaine de Marie-Antoinette.

Evening: Have dinner in Versailles town or return to Paris. For dessert, follow this book's "Floodlit Paris Taxi Tour" (in the Entertainment chapter).

Day 5

Morning: Follow this book's Marais Walk and tour the Carnavalet Museum (free). Have lunch on place des Vosges or rue des Rosiers.

Afternoon: Tour the Pompidou Center and the Jewish Art and History Museum.

Evening: Enjoy the Trocadéro scene and a twilight ride up the Eiffel Tower.

Day 6

Morning: Take an Impressionist escape to Giverny or Auvers-sur-Oise.

Afternoon: Follow this book's Left Bank Walk (featuring art galleries, boutiques, historic cafés, and grand boulevards), mix in some shopping (see "Sèvres-Babylone to St. Sulpice" in the Shopping chapter), then relax in Luxembourg Garden or at a nearby café (see "Les Grands Cafés de Paris," page 417).

Evening: Join the parade along the Champs-Elysées (which offers a different scene at night than the daytime walk you enjoyed on Day 2). If you haven't hiked to the top of the Arc de Triomphe yet, consider doing it by twilight.

Day 7
Choose from:
More shopping and cafés
Bus #69 tour followed by Père Lachaise Cemetery
Montmartre and Sacré-Cœur (by day)
Marmottan or Jacquemart-André museum
Day trip to Chartres
Day trip to Reims
Day trip to Vaux-le-Vicomte and Fontainebleau
Day trip to Disneyland Paris
Evening: Night bus or boat tour (whichever you have yet to do).

Overview

Tourist Information

Paris tourist offices (abbreviated as "TI" in this book) have long lines, offer little information, and may charge for maps. But all you really need are this book and one of the freebie maps available at any hotel (or in the front of this book). Paris' TIs share a single phone number: 08 92 68 30 00 (from the US, dial 011 33 8 92 68 30 00).

If you must visit a TI, you can do so at several locations, including **Pyramides** (daily 9:00–19:00, at Pyramides Métro stop between the Louvre and Opéra), **Gares de Lyon** and **Nord** (both Mon–Sat 8:00–18:00, closed Sun), and **Montmartre** (two branches: one on place du Tertre, daily 10:00–19:00, and the other above the Anvers Métro stop, daily 10:00–18:00). The official website for Paris' TIs is www.parisinfo.com. Both **airports** have handy information offices (called ADP) with long hours and short lines (see Connections chapter).

Pariscope: The weekly €0.40 *Pariscope* magazine (or one of its clones, available at any newsstand) lists museum hours, art exhibits, concerts, festivals, plays, movies, and nightclubs. Smart sightseers rely on this for the latest listings (see page 445).

Other Publications: Look for the *Paris Times*, which provides helpful English information and fresh insights into living in Paris (available at English-language bookstores, French-American establishments, the American Church, and online at www.theparistimes.com). *L'Officiel des Spectacles* (€0.35), which is similar to *Pariscope,* also lists goings-on around town (in French). The *Paris Voice*, with snappy reviews of concerts, plays, and current events, is available only online at www.parisvoice.com. For a schedule of museum hours and English museum tours, get the free *Musées, Monuments Historiques, et Expositions* booklet at any museum.

American Church and Franco-American Center: This interdenominational church—in the rue Cler neighborhood, facing the river between the Eiffel Tower and Orsay Museum—is a nerve center for the American émigré community. Worship services are at 9:00 and 11:00 on Sunday; the coffee hour after church and the free Sunday concerts (generally Sept–June at 17:00—but not every week) are a good way to get a taste of émigré life in Paris (reception open Mon–Sat 9:00–12:00 & 13:00–22:00, Sun 14:30–19:00, 65 quai d'Orsay, Mo: Invalides, tel. 01 40 62 05 00, www .acparis.org). It's also a handy place to pick up free copies of *Paris Times* (described above) and *France-USA Contacts* (an advertisement paper with info on housing and employment for the 30,000 Americans living in Paris, www.fusac.fr).

Arrival in Paris

For a comprehensive rundown of Paris' train stations and airports, see the Connections chapter.

Helpful Hints

Theft Alert: Troublesome thieves thrive near famous monuments and on Métro and RER lines that serve high-profile tourist sights. Wear a money belt, put your wallet in your front pocket, loop your day bag over your shoulders, and keep a tight grip on your purse or shopping bag. Muggings are rare, but they do occur. If you're out late, avoid the dark riverfront embankments and any place where the lighting is dim and pedestrian activity is minimal.

Paris is taking action to combat crime by stationing an abundance of police at monuments, on streets, and on the Métro, as well as security cameras at key sights. You'll go through quick and reassuring airport-like security checks at many major attractions.

Tourist Scams: Be aware of the latest scams, including these current favorites. The "found ring" scam involves an innocent-looking person who picks up a ring off the ground, and asks if you dropped it. When you say no, the person examines the ring more closely, then shows you a mark "proving" that it's pure gold. He offers to sell it to you for a good price—several times more than he paid for it before dropping it on the sidewalk.

In the "friendship bracelet" scam, a vendor approaches you and asks if you'll help him with a demonstration. He proceeds to make a friendship bracelet right on your arm. When finished, he asks you to pay for the bracelet he created just for you. And since you can't easily take it off on the spot, he counts on your feeling obliged to pay up.

Distractions by "salesmen" can also function as a smoke-screen for theft—an accomplice picks your pocket as you try to wriggle away from a pushy vendor.

In popular tourist spots (such as in front of Notre-Dame) young ladies politely ask if you speak English, then pretend to beg for money while actually angling to pick your pocket.

Street Safety: Parisian drivers are notorious for ignoring pedestrians. Look both ways (many streets are one-way) and be careful of seemingly quiet bus/taxi lanes. Don't assume you have the right of way, even in a crosswalk. When crossing a street, keep your pace constant and don't stop suddenly. By law, drivers are allowed to miss pedestrians by up to just one meter—a little more than three feet (1.5 meters in the countryside). Drivers carefully calculate your speed so they won't hit you, provided you don't alter your route or pace.

With Paris' new "Vélib'" bike program (offering short-term rentals to the French) there are more bikes than ever on the roads (see "Bike Freedom for Parisians" on page 36). When crossing streets, beware of this silent transportation.

Museum Strategies: The worthwhile Paris Museum Pass covers most sights in Paris and is sold at TIs, museums, and monuments. For detailed information, see page 42. For other museum strategies, see "Sightseeing" on page 13.

Advance Tickets: FNAC department stores throughout Paris sell tickets to several key sights, allowing you to skip ticket-buying lines. For sights that can otherwise have long waits (such as the Arc de Triomphe, Opéra Garnier, Versailles, and Monet's gardens in Giverny), their 10–20 percent surcharge can be well worth it. (Note that Versailles and the Arc de Triomphe are covered by the Paris Museum Pass—also sold, but without surcharge, at FNAC stores.)

Bookstores: Paris has many English-language bookstores, where you can pick up guidebooks (at nearly double their American prices). Most carry this book. My favorite is the friendly **Red Wheelbarrow Bookstore** in the Marais neighborhood, run by mellow Penelope (Mon 10:00–18:00, Tue-Sat 10:00–19:00, Sun 14:00–18:00, 22 rue St. Paul, Mo: St. Paul, tel. 01 48 04 75 08). Others include **Shakespeare and Company** (some used travel books, daily 12:00–24:00, 37 rue de la Bûcherie, across the river from Notre-Dame, Mo: St. Michel, tel. 01 43 26 96 50; see page 97 in Historic Paris Walk), **W. H. Smith** (Mon–Sat 9:00–19:30, Sun 13:00–19:30, 248 rue de Rivoli, Mo: Concorde, tel. 01 44 77 88 99), **Brentanos** (Mon–Sat 10:00–19:30, closed Sun, 37 avenue de l'Opéra, Mo: Opéra, tel. 01 42 61 52 50), and **Village Voice** (Mon 14:00–19:30, Tue–Sat 10:00–19:30, Sun 12:00–18:30, near St. Sulpice Church at 6 rue Princesse, tel. 01 46 33 36 47).

Public WCs: Public toilets are free (though it's polite to leave a small tip if there's an attendant). Modern, sanitary street-booth toilets provide both relief and a memory (don't leave small children inside unattended). The restrooms in museums are free and the best you'll find. Or walk into any sidewalk café like you own the place, and find the toilet in the back. Keep toilet paper or tissues with you, as some WCs are poorly supplied.

Parking: Most of the time, drivers must pay to park curbside (buy a parking card at *tabac* shops), but not at night (19:00–9:00), all day Sunday, or anytime in August, when many Parisians are on vacation. There are parking garages under Ecole Militaire, St. Sulpice Church, Les Invalides, the Bastille, and the Panthéon; all charge about €27–34 per day (it gets cheaper per hour the longer you stay). Some hotels offer parking for less—ask. See also "Parking in Paris" on page 484 in the Connections chapter.

Tobacco Stands *(Tabacs):* These little kiosks—usually just a counter inside a café—sell cards for parking meters, some public-transit tickets, postage stamps, and...oh yeah, cigarettes. For more on this slice of Parisian life, see page 184 in the Rue Cler Walk. To find one anywhere in Paris, just look for a *Tabac* sign and the red cylinder-shaped symbol above certain cafés.

Getting Around Paris

Paris is easy to navigate. Your basic choices are Métro (in-city subway), RER (suburban rail tied into the Métro system), public bus, and taxi. (Also consider the hop-on, hop-off bus and boat tours, described under "Tours," later in this chapter.) You can buy tickets and passes at many *tabacs* (tobacco stands) and at Métro stations. And though most Métro stations have staffed ticket windows, some smaller stations have only ticket-vending machines, for which you'll need coins (some take bills).

Public-Transit Tickets: The Métro, RER, and buses all work on the same tickets. (You can transfer between the Métro and RER on a single ticket, but combining a Métro or RER trip with a bus ride takes two tickets.) A **single ticket** costs €1.70. To save money, buy a *carnet* (kar-nay) of 10 tickets for €11.70 (that's €1.17 per ticket—€0.53 cheaper than a single ticket). *Carnets* (not single tickets) are less expensive for kids (ages 4–10 pay €5.70 for a *carnet*). *Carnets* can be shared among travelers.

Passes: The transit system has introduced a chip-card, called the **Passe Navigo,** but for most tourists *carnets* are still the better deal. The new Passe costs €22.50 (including a one-time €5 card fee), covers Monday–Sunday (expires on Sun, even if you buy it on Fri), and requires a photo, which means it's not shareable. In contrast, two 10-packs of *carnets*—enough for most travelers staying a week—cost €23.40, are shareable, and don't expire until they're used. One big advantage of the Passe Navigo is that it's good on buses and trains (Métro and RER). *Carnet* users need separate tickets to transfer between bus and train.

If you do want the pass, ask for the *"Passe Navigo hebdomadaire"* (pahs nah-vee-go day-koo-vairt ehb-doh-mah-dair) and supply a small postage-stamp-size photo of yourself (bring your own, or use the €4 photo booths in major Métro stations). You buy a chip-embedded card (€5 one-time cost), then "load" a weekly value onto it (€17.50, ticket machines do not take American credit cards); this gives you free run of the bus and Métro system. At the Métro/bus turnstile, you scan your Passe to enter, and you're on your way.

A month-long version costs about €56—request a Passe Navigo *mensuelle* (mahn-soo-ehl, good from the first day of the month to the last, also requires photo). The pass covers only central Paris. You can pay more for passes covering regional destinations (such as Versailles), but for most visitors, this is a bad value. Instead, buy individual tickets for longer-distance destinations.

A one-day bus/Métro pass (called **Mobilis**) is available for €5.40 and is handy for busy sightseers. The overpriced **Paris Visite** passes were designed for tourists and offer minor reductions at minor sights (1 day/€9, 2 days/€15, 3 days/€20, 5 days/€28).

By Métro

In Paris, you're never more than a 10-minute walk from a Métro station. Europe's best subway allows you to hop from sight to sight quickly and cheaply (runs daily 5:30–24:30 in the morning). Learn to use it. Begin by studying the color Métro map at the beginning of this book, free at Métro stations, and included on freebie Paris maps at your hotel.

How the Métro Works: To get to your destination, determine the closest "Mo" stop and which line or lines will get you there. The lines have numbers, but they're best known by their end-of-the-line stops. (For example, the La Défense/Château de Vincennes line, also known as line 1, runs between La Défense in the west and Vincennes in the east.) Once in the Métro station, you'll see blue-and-white signs directing you to the train going in your direction (e.g., *direction: La Défense*). Insert your ticket in the automatic turnstile, pass through, reclaim your ticket, and keep it until you exit the system (some stations require you to pass your ticket through a turnstile to exit). *Fare inspectors regularly check for cheaters and accept absolutely no excuses, so keep that ticket or pay a minimum fine of €25!*

Transfers are free and can be made wherever lines cross, provided you do so within 1.5 hours. When you transfer, look for the orange *correspondance* (connection) signs as you exit your first train, then follow the proper direction sign.

Métro Basics

- The same tickets are good on the Métro, RER (within the city), and city buses (but not to transfer between Métro/ RER and bus).
- Save money by buying a *carnet* of tickets or a Passe Navigo.
- Find your train by its end-of-the-line stops.
- Insert your ticket into the turnstile, retrieve it, and keep it until the end of your journey.
- Beware of pickpockets, and don't buy tickets from men roaming the stations.
- Transfers *(correspondances)* within the Métro or RER system are free.
- At the end of your trip, choose the right exit *(sortie)* to avoid extra walking.
- Dispose of used tickets after you complete your ride and leave the station (not before), to avoid confusing them with fresh ones.
- On some trains you must activate the door by pushing a button (but most open automatically).

Key Words for the Métro and RER

French	Pronounced	English
direction	dee-rek-see-ohn	direction
ligne	leen-yuh	line
correspondance	kor-res-pohn-dahns	transfer

Even though the Métro whisks you quickly from one point to another, be prepared to walk significant distances within stations to reach your platform (most noticeable when you transfer). Escalators are common, but they're sometimes out of order. To limit excessive walking, avoid transferring at these sprawling stations: Montparnasse-Bienvenüe, Châtelet-Les Halles, Charles de Gaulle-Etoile, Gare du Nord, and Bastille.

Before leaving the Métro through the *sortie* (exit), check the helpful *plan du quartier* (map of the neighborhood) to get your bearings, locate your destination, and decide which *sortie* you want. At stops with several *sorties*, you can save lots of walking by choosing the best exit.

After you exit the system, toss or tear your used ticket so you don't confuse it with unused tickets—they look almost identical.

sortie	sor-tee	exit
carnet	kar-nay	cheap set of 10 tickets
Pardon, madame/ monsieur.	par-dohn, mah-dahm/ mes-yur	Excuse me, ma`am/ sir.
Je descends.	juh day-sahn	I'm getting off.
Donnez-moi mon porte-monnaie!	duh-nay-mwah mohn port-moh-nay	Give me back my wallet!

Etiquette

- When waiting at the platform, get out of the way of those exiting the train. Only board after everyone is off.
- Avoid using the hinged seats near the doors of some trains when the car is jammed; they take up valuable standing space.
- In a crowded train, try not to block the exit. If you're blocking the door when the train stops, step out of the car and to the side, let others off, then get back on.
- Talk softly in the cars. Listen to how quietly Parisians communicate and follow their lead.
- On escalators, stand on the right and pass on the left.
- When leaving a station, hold the door for the person behind you.

Beware of Pickpockets: Thieves dig the Métro and RER. Be on guard. For example, if your pocket is picked as you pass through a turnstile, you end up stuck on the wrong side (after the turnstile bar has closed behind you) while the thief gets away. Stand away from Métro doors to avoid being a target for a theft-and-run just before the doors close. Any jostling or commotion—especially when boarding or leaving trains—is likely the sign of a thief or a team of thieves in action. Make any fare inspector show proof of identity (ask locals for help if you're not certain). Never show anyone your wallet.

By RER

The RER (Réseau Express Régionale; air-ay-air) is the suburban arm of the Métro, serving outlying destinations (such as Versailles, Disneyland Paris, and the airports). These routes are indicated by thick lines on your subway map and identified by the letters A, B, C, and so on. Some routes, called Transilien, are operated by France's railroad (SNCF)—they function the same way and use the same tickets as the RER. For all of these trains, you need to

Key Buses for Tourists

Of Paris' many bus routes, these are some of the most scenic. They provide a great, cheap, and convenient introduction to the city.

Bus #69 runs east–west between the Eiffel Tower and Père Lachaise Cemetery by way of rue Cler (recommended hotels), quai d'Orsay, the Louvre, and the Marais (recommended hotels). For a self-guided tour, see Bus #69 Sightseeing Tour chapter.

Bus #87 also links the Marais and rue Cler areas, but stays mostly on the Left Bank, connecting the Eiffel Tower, St. Sulpice, Luxembourg Garden (more recommended hotels and restau-

Key Bus Routes

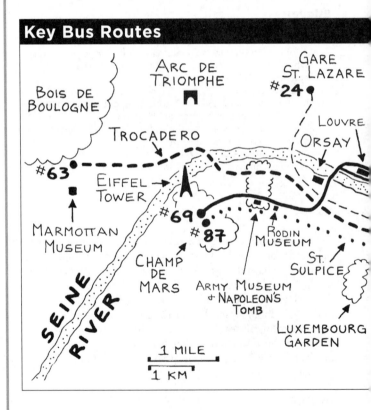

rants), St. Germain-des-Prés, the Latin Quarter, the Bastille, and Gare de Lyon.

Bus #24 runs east–west along the Seine riverbank from Gare St. Lazare to Madeleine, place de la Concorde, Orsay Museum, the Louvre, St. Michel, Notre-Dame, and Jardin des Plantes, all the way to trendy Bercy Village (cafés and shops).

Bus #63 is another good east–west route, connecting the Marmottan Museum, Trocadéro (Eiffel Tower), pont de l'Alma, Orsay Museum, St. Sulpice, Luxembourg Garden, Latin Quarter/Panthéon, and Gare de Lyon.

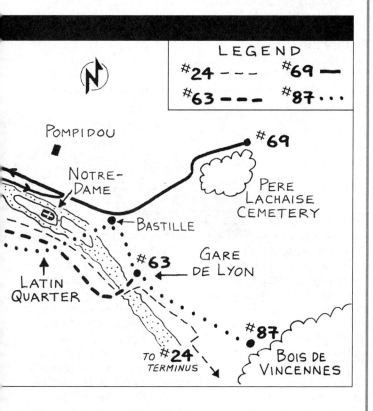

insert your ticket in a turnstile to exit the system.

Within the city center, the RER works like the Métro, but can be speedier (if it serves your destination directly) because it makes fewer stops. Métro tickets and the Passe Navigo card are good on the RER when traveling in the city center. (You can transfer between the Métro and RER systems with the same ticket.) But to travel outside the city (to Versailles or the airport, for example), you'll need to buy a separate, more expensive ticket at the station window (or, to save time, at a ticket-vending machine) before boarding. Also, unlike the Métro, not every train stops at every station along the way; check the sign over the platform to see if your destination is listed as a stop (*"toutes les gares"* means it makes all stops along the way), or confirm with a local before you board.

By City Bus

Paris' excellent bus system is worth figuring out. Buses don't seem as romantic as the famous Métro and are subject to traffic jams, but savvy travelers know that buses can have you swinging through the city like Tarzan in an urban jungle. And one clear advantage of the bus over the Métro is that you can see Paris unfold as you travel. Anywhere you are, you can generally spot a bus stop, and every stop  comes complete with all the information you need: a good city bus map, route maps showing exactly where each bus that uses this stop goes, a frequency chart and schedule, a *plan du quartier* map of the immediate neighborhood, and a *soirées* map explaining night service, if available. Stops are announced; follow along with the on-board route diagrams, which list all of the stops. While the Métro shuts down about 24:30 in the morning, some buses continue much later (called *Noctilien* lines, www.noctilien.fr).

Remember that buses use the same tickets as the Métro and RER, but you can't transfer between the systems on a single ticket—though you can transfer from one bus to another (within 1.5 hours, though this doesn't work with tickets bought on board—go figure). For Métro- or *tabac*-bought tickets that do allow transfers, you must punch your ticket for each bus you board when transferring. One ticket buys you a bus ride anywhere in central Paris—but if you leave the city center (shown as zone 1 on the diagram aboard the bus), you need to validate a second ticket.

You must enter standard buses through the front door

(though on the long, articulated buses, you can go in through any door). Punch your ticket in the machine behind the driver, scan your Passe Navigo, or pay the higher cash fare to get your ticket from the driver. (Remember: Tickets purchased from drivers do

not allow transfers between buses.) When you reach your destination, push the red button to signal you want a stop, then exit through the rear door. Even if you're not certain you've figured out the system, do some joyriding (outside of rush hour: Mon–Fri 8:00–9:30 & 17:30–19:30). Be warned: Not all city buses are air-conditioned, so they can become rolling greenhouses on summer days. For information on some of Paris' most scenic and convenient routes, see "Key Buses for Tourists" on page 32. Handy bus-system maps *(plan des autobus)* are available in any Métro station (and in the €6 *Paris Pratique* map book sold at newsstands). Major stops are displayed on the side of each bus. I've also listed the handiest bus routes for each recommended hotel neighborhood (see Sleeping chapter).

By Taxi

Parisian taxis are reasonable, especially for couples and families. The meters are tamper-proof. Fares and supplements (described in English on the rear windows) are straightforward and tightly regulated.

A taxi can fit three people comfortably, and cabbies are legally required to accept four passengers at a time (you'll be charged €3 extra for the fourth person). Groups of up to five can use a *grand taxi*, which must be booked in advance—ask your hotelier to call. For a sample taxi tour of the city at night, see page 452.

Rates: All Parisian taxis charge a €5.20 minimum. A 10-minute ride (e.g., Bastille to Eiffel Tower) costs about €12 (versus €1.17 per person to get anywhere in town using a *carnet* ticket on the Métro or bus). Drivers charge higher rates at rush hour and at night (17:00–10:00), all day Sunday, and to any of the airports. Your first bag is free; additional pieces of luggage are €1 each. To tip, round up to the next euro (at least €0.50).

How to Catch *un Taxi:* You can try waving down a taxi, but it's often easier to ask someone for the nearest taxi stand (*"Où est une station de taxi?"*; oo ay ewn stah-see-ohn duh "taxi"). Taxi stands are indicated by a circled "T" on good city maps, and on many maps in this book. When you summon a taxi by phone, the

Bike Freedom for Parisians

Those high-tech bike racks you see all over town are part of the city's innovative Vélib' program (from *vélo* + *liberté* or *libre* = "bike freedom" or "free bike"), which gives locals with a Vélib' card access to more than 20,000 bikes around the city. Parisians pay €30 per year for the card, which they swipe to unlock the nearest Vélib' bike. (Tourists can pay to ride one, but only American Express cards work in the machines.) The first half-hour of each ride is free; after that, riders are billed more the longer they have the bike checked out. The system is well-designed—stations show not only the location of other nearby racks, but how many bikes are available there. (There are about 1,450 stations spaced just 300 or so yards apart.) At night, bikes are redistributed by truck so that busy locations always have enough available. Roving repairmen fix broken bikes (when the seat is turned backward, it means the bike is faulty). The program is quite comprehensive, involving aggressive citywide development of bike paths. Copenhagen tried a similar program, providing intentionally ugly and clumsy bikes to lower the risk of theft. Vélib's bikes, however, are great.

meter starts running as soon as the call is received, often adding €5 or more to the bill.

Taxis are tough to find during rush hour, when it's raining, and on Friday and Saturday nights, especially after the Métro closes (around 24:30 in the morning). If you need to catch a train or flight early in the morning, book a taxi the day before. Dial 3607 for a taxi, or ask your hotelier for help.

By Bike

Paris is surprisingly good by bicycle. Riders enjoy more than 275 miles of bike lanes, and the extensive parks have bike-friendly paths that enable anyone on two wheels to get around easily. I biked along the river from Notre-Dame to the Eiffel Tower in 15 minutes. The tourist board has a fine "Paris à Vélo" map showing all the dedicated bike paths.

Fat Tire Bike Tours (listed under "Tours," next) rents bikes *sans* tour for independent types (€2.50/hr, €15/24 hrs, includes helmets and locks, credit-card imprint required for deposit, €4 discount with book for daily rental, daily 9:00–18:00, ask for their map of suggested routes, 24 rue Edgar Faure, Mo: Dupleix, tel. 01 56 58 10 54, www.fattirebiketoursparis.com).

Tours

By Bus

Bus Tours—**Paris Vision** offers bus tours of Paris, day and night (advertised in hotel lobbies). I'd consider a Paris Vision tour only for their nighttime Illumination tour (see page 451) or for tricky-to-reach day trips (such as Vaux-le-Vicomte). During the day, the hop-on, hop-off bus tours (listed immediately below) and the Batobus (see "By Boat," next page) are a better value, providing both transportation between sights as well as commentary.

Hop-on, Hop-off Bus Tours—Double-decker buses connect Paris' main sights, allowing you to hop on and off along the way. You get a disposable set of ear plugs to listen to a basic running commentary (dial English for the so-so narration). You can get off at any stop, tour a sight, then catch a later bus. These are best in good weather, when you can sit up top. There are two companies: L'Open Tours and Les Cars Rouges (pick up their brochures showing routes and stops from any TI or on their buses). You can start either tour at just about any of the major sights, such as the Eiffel Tower (both companies stop on avenue Joseph Bouvard).

L'Open Tours uses bright yellow buses and provides more extensive coverage (and slightly better commentary) on four different routes, rolling by most of the important sights in Paris. Their Paris Grand Tour (the green route) offers the best introduction. The same ticket gets you on any of their routes within the validity period. Buy your tickets from the driver (1 day-€29, 2 days-€32, kids 4–11 pay €15 for 1 or 2 days, allow 2 hours per tour). Two to four buses depart hourly from about 10:00 to 18:00; expect to wait 10–15 minutes at each stop (stops can be tricky to find—look for yellow signs; tel. 01 42 66 56 56, www.paris-opentour.com). A combo-ticket covers both the Batobus boats (described in "By

Boat," next page) and L'Open Tours buses (€44, kids under 12 pay €20, valid 3 days).

Les Cars Rouges' bright red buses offer largely the same service, with only one route and just nine stops, for less (recorded narration, adult-€24, kids 4–12 pay €12, good for 2 days, tel. 01 53 95 39 53, www.carsrouges.com).

Do-It-Yourself Bus Tour—Paris' cheapest "bus tour" is simply to hop on city bus #69 and follow my commentary (see Bus #69 Sightseeing Tour chapter).

By Boat

Several companies run one-hour boat cruises on the Seine (by far best at night, see "Dinner Cruises," page 416). Two of the companies—Bateaux-Mouches and Bateaux Parisiens—are convenient to the rue Cler hotels, and both run daily year-round (April–Oct 10:00–22:30, 2–3/hr; Nov–March shorter hours, runs hourly).

Bateaux-Mouches departs from pont de l'Alma's right bank and has the biggest open-top, double-decker boats. But this company often has too many tour groups, causing these boats to get packed (€10, kids 4–12 pay €5, tel. 01 40 76 99 99, www.bateaux -mouches.com).

Bateaux Parisiens has smaller covered boats with handheld audioguides, fewer crowds, and only one deck. It leaves from right in front of the Eiffel Tower (€11, kids 4–11 pay €5, half-price if you have a valid France or France–Switzerland railpass—does not use up a day of a flexipass, tel. 08 25 01 01 01, www.bateaux parisiens.com).

Vedettes du Pont Neuf offers essentially the same one-hour tour as Bateaux Parisiens, but starts and ends at Pont Neuf, closer to recommended hotels in the Marais and Luxembourg Garden neighborhoods. The boats feature a live guide whose delivery (in English and French) is as stiff as a recorded narration—and as hard to understand, given the quality of their sound system (€12, kids 4–12 pay €6, tip requested, nearly 2/hr, daily 10:30–22:30, tel. 01 46 33 98 38).

Hop-on, Hop-Off Boat Tour—**Batobus** allows you to get on and off as often as you like at any of eight popular stops along the Seine: Eiffel Tower, Champs-Elysées, Orsay/place de la Concorde, the Louvre, Notre-Dame, St. Germain-des-Prés, Hôtel de Ville, and Jardin des Plantes. Safe glass enclosures turn the boats into virtual ovens on hot days (1 day-€12, 2 days-€16, boats run June–Aug 10:00–21:30, mid-March–May and Sept–Oct 10:00–19:00, Nov–early-Jan and Feb–mid-March 10:30–16:30, no service last three weeks in Jan, every 15–20 minutes, 45 min one-way, 1.5-hour round-trip, worthless narration). If you use this for getting around—sort of a scenic, floating alternative to the Métro—this can be worthwhile. But if you just want a guided boat tour, Batobus is not as good a value as the regular tour boats described above.

Low-Key Cruise on a Tranquil Canal—**Canauxrama** runs a lazy 2.5-hour cruise on a peaceful canal out of sight of the Seine. Tours start from place de la Bastille and end at Bassin de la Villette (near Mo: Stalingrad). During the first segment of your trip, you'll pass through a long tunnel (built at the order of Napoleon in the early 19th century, when canal boats were vital for industrial transport). Once outside, you glide—not much faster than you can walk—through sleepy Parisian neighborhoods and slowly climb through four double locks as a guide narrates the trip in French and English (€15, departs at 9:45 and 14:30 across from Opéra Bastille, just below boulevard de la Bastille, opposite #50—where the canal meets place de la Bastille, tel. 01 42 39 15 00). The same tour also goes in the opposite direction, from Bassin de la Villette to place de la Bastille (departs at 9:45 and 14:45). It's OK to bring a picnic on board.

On Foot

Paris Walks—This company offers a variety of two-hour walks, led by British and American guides. Tours are thoughtfully prepared and humorous. Don't hesitate to stand close to the guide to hear (€12–15, generally 2/day—morning and afternoon, private tours available, family guides a specialty, recorded English schedule tel. 01 48 09 21 40, www.paris-walks.com). Tours focus on the Marais (4/week), Montmartre (3/week), medieval Latin Quarter (Mon), Ile de la Cité/Notre-Dame (Mon), the "Two Islands" (Ile de la Cité and Ile St. Louis, Wed), the Revolution (Wed), and Hemingway's Paris (Fri). Call a day or two ahead to hear the current schedule and starting point. Most tours don't require reservations, but specialty tours (such as the Louvre or Chocolate tour) require advance reservations and prepayment with credit card (not refundable if you cancel less than two days in advance).

Context Paris—These "intellectual by design" walking tours are led by docents (historians, architects, and academics) and cover both museums and neighborhoods, often with a fascinating theme (explained on their website). Try to book in advance—groups are limited to six participants and can fill up (€35–55/person plus admissions, generally 3 hours long, tel. 06 13 09 67 11, US tel. 888-467-1986, www.contextparis.com). They also offer private tours.

Classic Walks—If you'd prefer a relaxed, low-brow walking tour, consider this outfit, run by Fat Tire Bike Tours (see "By Bike," next page). Their 3.5-hour "Classic Walk" covers most major sights (€20, daily at 10:00, meet at office—see next page). They also do two-hour walks on various themes and neighborhoods: Montmartre, French Revolution, World War II, *Da Vinci Code,* and Latin Quarter (€12, €2 discount on all walks with this book, leaves several times a week—see website for details, 24 rue Edgar Faure, Mo: Dupleix, tel. 01 56 58 10 54, www.classicwalksparis.com).

Local Guides—For many, Paris merits hiring a Parisian as a personal guide. **Arnaud Servignat** is an excellent licensed guide (€155/half-day, €260/day, also does car tours of the countryside around Paris for a little more, tel. 06 68 80 29 05, www.arnaud-servignat .com, arnotour@mac.com). **Thierry Gauduchon** is a terrific guide well worth his fee (€180/half-day, €350/day, tel. 01 56 98 10 82, mobile 06 19 07 30 77, tgauduchon@aol.com. **Elizabeth Van Hest** is another likeable and capable guide (€175/half-day, €260/day, tel. 01 43 41 47 31, elisa.guide@gmail.com). **Sylvie Moreau** is also good, and charges the same as Elizabeth (mobile 06 87 02 80 67, silvmor@gmail.com).

By Bike

Fat Tire Bike Tours—A hardworking gang of young American expats runs an extensive program of bike, Segway, and walking tours, and rents bikes as well.

Their high-energy guides run four-hour bike tours of Paris, by day and by night. Reservations aren't necessary—just show up. On the day tour, you'll pedal with a pack of 10–20 riders, mostly in parks and along bike lanes, with a lunch stop in the Tuileries Gardens (€26, show this book for a €4/person discount, maximum 2 discounts per book, English only, tours leave daily rain or shine at 11:00, April–Oct at 15:00 as well). Night tours are more lively, and include a boat cruise on the Seine (€28, €4 discount with this book, April–Oct daily at 19:00, March daily at 18:00, end of Feb and all of Nov Tue, Thu, and Sat–Sun at 18:00, no night tours Dec–mid-Feb). Both tours meet at the south pillar of the Eiffel Tower, where you'll get a short history lesson, then walk six minutes to the Fat Tire office to pick up bikes (helmets available upon request at no extra charge, office open daily 9:00–19:00, 24 rue Edgar Faure, Mo: Dupleix, tel. 01 56 58 10 54, toll-free from North America 866-614-6218, www.fattirebiketoursparis.com). They also run bike tours to Versailles and Giverny (reservations required, see website for details). Their office has Internet access with English keyboards.

Fat Tire's pricey four-hour **City Segway Tours**—on stand-up motorized scooters—are novel in that you learn to ride a Segway while exploring Paris (you'll get the hang of it after about half an hour). These tours take no more than eight people at a time, so reservations are required (€75, daily at 9:30, April–Oct also at 14:00 and 18:30, March and Nov also at 14:00, www.citysegway tours.com).

Excursions from Paris

Many companies offer bus tours to regional sights, including all of the day trips described in this book. **Paris Vision** runs mass-produced, full-size bus and minivan tours to several popular regional destinations, including the Loire Valley, Champagne region, D-Day beaches, and Mont St. Michel. Minivan tours are more expensive but are more personal and given in English, and most offer convenient pickup at your hotel (€90–190/person). Their full-size bus tours are multilingual and cheaper than the minivan tours—worthwhile for some travelers simply for the ease of transportation to the sights (about €70, destinations include Versailles and Giverny). Paris Vision's full-size buses depart from 214 rue de Rivoli (Mo: Tuileries, tel. 01 42 60 30 01, www.parisvision.com).

SIGHTS IN PARIS

The sights listed in this chapter are arranged by neighborhood for handy sightseeing. When you see a ✪ in a listing, it means the sight is covered in much more depth in one of my walks or self-guided tours. This is why Paris' most important attractions get the least coverage in this chapter—we'll explore them later in the book.

For tips on sightseeing, see page 13 in the Introduction. For advice on saving money, see "Affording Paris' Sights" on page 54. Best tip: Buy a Paris Museum Pass.

Paris Museum Pass

In Paris there are two classes of sightseers—those with a Paris Museum Pass, and those who stand in line. The pass admits you to many of Paris' most popular sights, allowing you to skip ticket-buying lines. Serious sightseers save time and money by getting this pass.

Buying the Pass

The pass pays for itself with four key admissions in two days (for example, the Louvre, Orsay, Sainte-Chapelle, and Versailles), and lets you skip the ticket line at most sights (2 days/€32, 4 days/€48, 6 days/€64, no youth or senior discount). It's sold at participating museums, monuments, FNAC stores, and TIs (even at airports, see Connections chapter). Try to avoid buying the pass at a major museum (such as the Louvre), where the supply can be spotty and lines long. For more info, visit www.parismuseumpass.com or call 01 44 61 96 60.

Tally up what you want to see from the list in the next section ("What the Paris Museum Pass Covers")—and remember, an advantage of the pass is that you skip to the front of most lines, which can save hours of waiting, especially in summer. Note that at a few sights (including the Louvre, Sainte-Chapelle, Notre-Dame's tower, and the Château de Versailles), everyone has to shuffle through the slow-moving baggage-check lines for security—but you still save time by avoiding the ticket line.

Families: The pass isn't worth buying for children and teens, as most museums are free or discounted for those under 18 (teenagers may need to show ID as proof of age). Generally, your kids can also skip the line if you have a Museum Pass, although a few places (such as the Arc de Triomphe and Army Museum) require you to stand in line to collect your child's free ticket. Of the few museums that charge for children, some allow kids in for free if their parents have a Museum Pass, while others charge admission, depending on age (the cutoff age varies from 5 to 18). The free directory that comes with your pass lists the current hours of sights, phone numbers, and the price that kids pay.

What the Paris Museum Pass Covers

Most of the sights listed in this chapter are covered by the pass, but it does not include: the Eiffel Tower, Montparnasse Tower, Marmottan Museum, Opéra Garnier, Notre-Dame Treasury, Jacquemart-André Museum, Grand Palais, La Grande Arche at La Défense, Catacombs, *Paris Story* film, Montmartre Museum, Sacré-Cœur's dome, Dalí Museum, Museum of Erotic Art, and the ladies of Pigalle. The pass also does not cover these recommended sights outside of Paris: Vaux-le-Vicomte, Auvers-sur-Oise, or Giverny (though it does include Fontainebleau and Chantilly).

Here's a list of included sights and their admission prices without the pass:

In Paris

Louvre (€9)	Notre-Dame Tower (€8)
Orsay Museum (€8)	Paris Archaeological Crypt (€4)
Orangerie Museum (€7.50)	Paris Sewer Tour (€4)
Sainte-Chapelle (€8)	Cluny Museum (€8)
Arc de Triomphe (€9)	Pompidou Center (€12)
Rodin Museum (€6)	Jewish Art and History Museum (€7)
Army Museum (€8.50)	National Maritime Museum (€7)
Conciergerie (€7)	Delacroix Museum (€5)
Panthéon (€8)	Quai Branly Museum (€8.50)

Outside Paris

Versailles (€23.50 total—€13.50 for Château, €10 for
    Domaine de Marie-Antoinette)
Château of Chantilly (€11)
Château of Fontainebleau (€8)

Activating and Using the Pass

Think ahead to make the most of your pass. Validate it only when you're ready to tackle the covered sights on consecutive days. Make sure the sights you want to visit will be open (many museums are closed Mondays or Tuesdays). The Paris Museum Pass even covers most of Versailles (your other option for Versailles is the Le Passeport pass; see Versailles Day Trip chapter). Keep in mind that sights such as the Arc de Triomphe and Pompidou Center are open later in the evening, and that the Louvre and Orsay have late hours on selected evenings, allowing you to stretch the day for your Paris Museum Pass. On days that you don't have pass coverage, visit free sights as well as those not covered by the pass.

The pass isn't activated until the first time you use it (write the starting date on the pass).

To use your pass at sights, boldly walk to the front of the ticket line, hold up your pass, and ask the ticket-taker: *"Entrez, pass?"* (ahn-tray pahs). You'll either be allowed to enter at that point or you'll be directed to a special entrance. For major sights, such as the Louvre and Orsay museums, we've identified passholder entrances on the maps in this book.

With the pass you can pop into sights as you're walking by (even for a few minutes) that otherwise might not be worth the expense (e.g., the Conciergerie or Paris Archaeological Crypt).

Sights

Historic Core of Paris: Notre-Dame, Sainte-Chapelle, and More

✪ Many of these sights are covered in detail in the Historic Paris Walk chapter. If a sight is covered in the walk, I've listed only its essentials here.

▲▲▲**Notre-Dame Cathedral (Cathédrale Notre-Dame de Paris)**—This 700-year-old cathedral is packed with history and tourists. With a pair of 200-foot-tall belltowers, a facade studded with ornate statuary, beautiful stained-glass rose windows, famous gargoyles, a picture-perfect Seine-side location, and textbook fly-

ing buttresses, there's a good reason that this cathedral of "Our Lady" *(Notre-Dame)* is France's most famous church.

Check out the facade: Mary with the baby Jesus (in rose window) above the 28 Kings of Judah (statues that were beheaded during the Revolution). Stroll the interior, echoing with history. Then wander around the exterior, through a forest of frilly buttresses, watched over by a fleet of whimsical gargoyles. The long line to the left is to climb the famous tower (see "Tower," below).

Cost, Hours, Location: Free, cathedral open daily 7:45–19:00; Treasury-€3.50, not covered by Museum Pass, daily 9:30–17:30; audioguide-€5, ask about free English tours—normally Wed and Thu at 14:00, Sat at 14:30; Mo: Cité, Hôtel de Ville, or St. Michel. Tel. 01 42 34 56 10, www.cathedraledeparis.com.

For more on Notre-Dame (including information on weekday and Sun Mass, as well as organ performances and viewings of the Crown of Thorns), ✪ see page 85 in the Historic Paris Walk.

Tower: You can climb to the top of the facade between the towers, and then to the top of the south tower, 400 steps total, for a grand view (€8, covered by Museum Pass but no bypass line for passholders, daily April–Sept 10:00–18:30, June–Aug Sat–Sun until 23:00, Oct–March 10:00–17:30, last entry 45 min before closing, arrive before 10:00 or after 17:00 to avoid long lines).

Paris Archaeological Crypt—This is a worthwhile 15-minute stop with your Museum Pass. You'll visit Roman ruins, trace the street plan of the medieval village, and see diagrams of how early Paris grew, all thoughtfully explained in English.

The first few displays put the ruins in historical context. Three models show the growth of Paris—from an uninhabited riverside plot to the Roman town of Lutèce, then to an early-medieval city with a church that preceded Notre-Dame. A fourth model shows the current Notre-Dame surrounded by buildings, along with the old, straight road—rue Neuve de Notre-Dame—that led up to the church, and ran right down what is now the center of the museum. The ruins in the middle of the museum are a confusing mix of foundations from all these time periods, including parts of the old rue Neuve de Notre-Dame.

Press the buttons on the display cases to light up a particular section, such as the oldest (Gallo-Roman) rampart. Along the far side of the museum, you'll see a medieval Foundling's Hospital, a well-preserved Gallo-Roman–paved room, and a Roman building with "hypocaustal" heating (narrow passages pumped full of hot air to heat the room).

Cost, Hours, Location: €4, covered by Museum Pass, Tue–Sun 10:00–18:00, last entry 30 min before closing, closed Mon, enter 100 yards in front of cathedral.

▲**Deportation Memorial (Mémorial de la Déportation)**—Climb down the steps into this memorial dedicated to the 200,000 French victims of the Nazi concentration camps. As Paris disappears above you, this monument draws you into the victims' experience. Once underground you enter a one-way hallway

Paris Sights

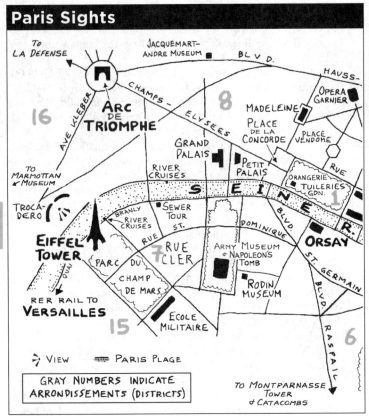

To LA DEFENSE

JACQUEMART-ANDRE MUSEUM

BLVD.

HAUSS-

CHAMPS-ELYSEES

ARC DE TRIOMPHE

AVE KLEBER

16

OPERA GARNIER

MADELEINE

8

PLACE DE LA CONCORDE

PLACE VENDOME

RUE

GRAND PALAIS

To MARMOTTAN MUSEUM

RIVER CRUISES

PETIT PALAIS

ORANGERIE

TUILERIES GDN.

S E I N E   R.

1

TROCA-DERO

BRANLY RIVER CRUISES

SEWER TOUR ST.

BLVD

DOMINIQUE

ORSAY

EIFFEL TOWER

RUE

7 RUE CLER

ARMY MUSEUM & NAPOLEON'S TOMB

ST. GERMAIN

PARC DU

CHAMP DE MARS

RODIN MUSEUM

BLVD

RER RAIL TO VERSAILLES

15

ECOLE MILITAIRE

RASPAIL

6

VIEW   PARIS PLAGE

GRAY NUMBERS INDICATE ARRONDISSEMENTS (DISTRICTS)

To MONTPARNASSE TOWER & CATACOMBS

studded with tiny lights commemorating the dead, leading you to an eternal flame.

Cost, Hours, Location: Free, daily April–Sept 10:00–12:00 & 14:00–19:00, Oct–March 10:00–12:00 & 14:00–17:00. It's at the east tip of the island named Ile de la Cité, behind Notre-Dame and near Ile St. Louis (Mo: Cité, tel. 01 49 74 34 00).

For more on the Deportation Memorial, ✪ see page 94 in the Historic Paris Walk.

Ile St. Louis—The residential island behind Notre-Dame is known for its restaurants (see Eating chapter), great ice cream, and shops (along rue St. Louis-en-l'Ile).

✪ Also see page 94 in the Historic Paris Walk chapter.

Cité Métropolitain Stop and Flower Market—On place Louis Lépine, between the Notre-Dame and Sainte-Chapelle cathedrals, you'll find an early-19th-century subway entrance and a flower market (that chirps with a bird market on Sun).

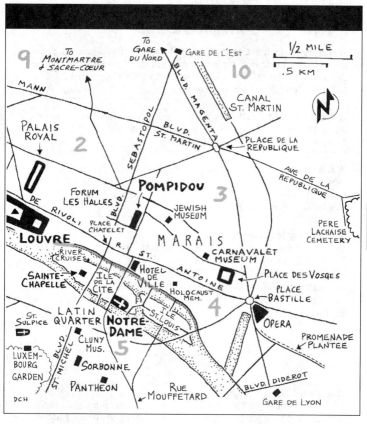

▲▲▲**Sainte-Chapelle**—The interior of this 13th-century chapel is a triumph of Gothic church architecture. Built to house Jesus' Crown of Thorns, Sainte-Chapelle is jam-packed with stained-glass windows, bathed in colorful light, and slippery with the drool of awestruck tourists. Ignore the humdrum exterior and climb the stairs into the sanctuary, where more than 1,100 Bible scenes—from the Creation to the Passion to Judgment Day—are illustrated by light and glass. There are tentative plans for Sainte-Chapelle to have a shared entrance with the Conciergerie (page 50), possibly sometime in 2010.

Cost, Hours, Location: €8, €12.50 combo-ticket includes Conciergerie, under 18 free, covered

Paris at a Glance

▲▲▲**Notre-Dame Cathedral** Paris' most beloved church, with towers and gargoyles. **Hours:** Cathedral daily 7:45–19:00; tower daily April–Sept 10:00–18:30, June–Aug Sat–Sun until 23:00, Oct–March 10:00–17:30; Treasury daily 9:30–17:30. See page 44.

▲▲▲**Sainte-Chapelle** Gothic cathedral with peerless stained glass. **Hours:** Daily March–Oct 9:30–18:00, Nov–Feb 9:00–17:00. See page 47.

▲▲▲**Louvre** Europe's oldest and greatest museum, starring *Mona Lisa* and *Venus de Milo*. **Hours:** Wed–Mon 9:00–18:00, most wings stay open Wed and Fri until 21:45 (except on holidays), closed Tue. See page 51.

▲▲▲**Orsay Museum** Nineteenth-century art, including Europe's greatest Impressionist collection. **Hours:** Tue–Sun 9:30–18:00, Thu until 21:45, closed Mon. See page 53.

▲▲▲**Eiffel Tower** Paris' soaring exclamation point. **Hours:** Daily mid-June–Aug 9:00–24:45 in the morning, Sept–mid-June 9:30–23:45. See page 55.

▲▲▲**Arc de Triomphe** Triumphal arch with viewpoint, marking start of Champs-Elysées. **Hours:** Always viewable; inside daily April–Sept 10:00–23:00, Oct–March 10:00–22:30. See page 67.

▲▲▲**Versailles** The ultimate royal palace (Château), with a Hall of Mirrors, vast gardens, a grand canal, plus a queen's playground (Domaine de Marie-Antoinette). **Hours:** Château Tue–Sun April–Oct 9:00–18:30 (on Sat in summer, King's and Queen's State Apartments may be open 18:30–21:00), Nov–March 9:00–17:30, closed Mon. Domaine Tue–Sun April–Oct 12:00–18:30, Nov–March 12:00–17:30, closed Mon. Gardens generally open daily 9:00 until sunset. See page 80.

▲▲**Orangerie Museum** Monet's water lilies, plus works by Utrillo, Cézanne, Renoir, Matisse, and Picasso, in a lovely setting. **Hours:** Wed–Mon 9:00–18:00, closed Tue. See page 53.

▲▲**Army Museum and Napoleon's Tomb** The emperor's imposing tomb, flanked by army museums. **Hours:** Daily April–Sept 10:00–18:00, Sun until 18:30 and Tue until 21:00, July–Aug tomb stays open until 18:45; daily Oct–March 10:00–17:00, Sun until 17:30. See page 58.

▲▲**Rodin Museum** Works by the greatest sculptor since

Michelangelo, with many sculptures in a peaceful garden. **Hours:** April–Sept Tue–Sun 9:30–17:45, Oct–March Tue–Sun 9:30–16:45, closed Mon. See page 58.

▲▲**Marmottan Museum** Untouristy art museum focusing on Monet. **Hours:** Wed–Sun 11:00–18:00, Tue 11:00–21:00, closed Mon. See page 59.

▲▲**Cluny Museum** Medieval art with unicorn tapestries. **Hours:** Wed–Mon 9:15–17:45, closed Tue. See page 60.

▲▲**Champs-Elysées** Paris' grand boulevard. **Hours:** Always open. See page 67.

▲▲**Jacquemart-André Museum** Art-strewn mansion. **Hours:** Daily 10:00–18:00. See page 72.

▲▲**La Défense and La Grande Arche** The city's own "little Manhattan" business district and its colossal modern arch. **Hours:** Daily April–Sept 10:00–20:00, Oct–March until 19:00. See page 74.

▲▲**Pompidou Center** Modern art in colorful building with city views. **Hours:** Wed–Mon 11:00–21:00, closed Tue. See page 76.

▲▲**Jewish Art and History Museum** Displays history of Judaism in Europe. **Hours:** Mon–Fri 11:00–18:00, Sun 10:00–18:00, closed Sat. See page 76.

▲▲**Carnavalet Museum** Paris' history wrapped up in a 16th-century mansion. **Hours:** Tue–Sun 10:00–18:00, closed Mon. See page 77.

▲▲**Sacré-Cœur** White basilica atop Montmartre with spectacular views. **Hours:** Daily 7:00–23:00. See page 79.

▲**Panthéon** Neoclassical monument celebrating the struggles of the French. **Hours:** Daily 10:00–18:30 in summer, until 18:00 in winter. See page 64.

▲**Opéra Garnier** Grand belle époque theater with a modern ceiling by Chagall. **Hours:** Generally daily 10:00–16:30, July–Aug until 17:30. See page 68.

▲**Père Lachaise Cemetery** Final home of Paris' illustrious dead. **Hours:** Mon–Sat 8:00–18:00, Sun 9:00–18:00. See page 78.

by Museum Pass, daily March–Oct 9:30–18:00, Nov–Feb 9:00–17:00, last entry 30 min before closing, English tours most days at 10:45 and 14:45, 4 boulevard du Palais, Mo: Cité. Tel. 01 53 40 60 80, www.monum.fr.

For a detailed tour of the cathedral's interior, ✪ see page 100 in the Historic Paris Walk.

▲**Conciergerie**—Marie-Antoinette was imprisoned here, as were Louis XVI, Robespierre, Danton, and many others on their way

to the guillotine. Exhibits with good English descriptions trace the history of the building and give some insight into prison life. You can also relive the drama in Marie-Antoinette's cell on the day of her execution—complete with dummies and period furniture.

Cost, Hours, Location: €7, €12.50 combo-ticket includes Sainte-Chapelle, covered by Museum Pass, daily April–Oct 9:30–18:00, Nov–March 9:00–17:00, last entry 30 min before closing, 4 boulevard du Palais, Mo: Cité. Tel. 01 53 40 60 80, www.monum.fr.

✪ Also see page 106 in the Historic Paris Walk chapter.

▲**Paris Plage (Beach)**—The Riviera it's not, but this fanciful faux beach—assembled in summer along a two-mile stretch of the Seine on the Right Bank—is a fun place to stroll, play, and people-watch on a sunny day. Each summer since 2002, the Paris city government has closed the embankment's highway and trucked in potted palm trees, hammocks, lounge chairs, and 2,000 tons of sand to create a colorful urban beach. You'll also find "beach cafés," climbing walls, prefab pools, trampolines, *boules*, a library, beach volleyball, badminton, and Frisbee areas in three zones: sandy, grassy, and wood-tiled. As you take in the playful atmosphere, imagine how much has changed here since the Middle Ages, when this was a grimy fishing community. (Other less-central areas of town, such as Canal St. Martin and Bassin de la Vilette, now take part with their own *plages*.)

Cost, Hours, Location: Free, mid-July–mid-Aug daily 7:00–24:00, no beach off-season; on Right Bank of Seine, just north of Ile de la Cité, between pont des Arts and pont de Sully.

Skaters Gone Wild—Thousands of inline skaters take to the streets Fridays at 22:30 and all day on summer Sundays, when police close off various routes in different parts of downtown (ask at your hotel or a TI for locations). It's serious skaters only on Friday evenings, but anyone can roll with Paris on Sundays (when the expressways along the Right Bank of the Seine are closed for this rolling fun fest).

Major Museums Neighborhood

Paris' grandest park, the Tuileries Garden, was once the private property of kings and queens. Today it links the Louvre, Orangerie, Jeu de Paume, and Orsay museums. And across from the Louvre are the tranquil, historic courtyards of the Palais Royal.

▲▲▲**Louvre (Musée du Louvre)**—This is Europe's oldest, biggest, greatest, and second-most-crowded museum (after the Vatican). Housed in a U-shaped, 16th-century palace (accentuated by a 20th-century glass pyramid), the Louvre is Paris' top museum and one of its key landmarks. It's home to *Mona Lisa*, *Venus de Milo*, and hall after hall of Greek and Roman masterpieces, medieval jewels, Michelangelo statues, and paintings by the greatest artists from the Renaissance to the Romantics (mid-1800s).

Touring the Louvre can be overwhelming, so be selective. Focus on the Denon wing (south, along the river), with Greek sculptures, Italian paintings (by Raphael and da Vinci), and—of course—French paintings (Neoclassical and Romantic). For extra credit, tackle the Richelieu wing (north, away from the river), displaying works from ancient Mesopotamia (today's Iraq), as well as French, Dutch, and Northern art; or the Sully wing (connecting the other two wings), with Egyptian artifacts and more French paintings.

Cost: €9, €6 after 18:00 on Wed and Fri, free on first Sun of month, covered by Museum Pass. Tickets good all day and reentry allowed. Optional additional charges apply for temporary exhibits. English-language guided tours cost €5 and leave twice daily except Sun, normally at 11:00 and 14:00. Audioguides are €6.

Hours: Wed–Mon 9:00–18:00, most wings stay open Wed and Fri until 21:45 (except on holidays), closed Tue. Galleries start closing 30 minutes early. The last entry is 45 minutes before closing. Crowds worst on Sun, Mon, Wed, and mornings.

Location: At Palais Royal–Musée du Louvre Métro stop. (The old Louvre Métro stop, called Louvre-Rivoli, is farther from the entrance.) Tel. 01 40 20 53 17, recorded info tel. 01 40 20 51 51, www.louvre.fr.

○ See the Louvre Tour chapter.

Palais Royal Courtyards—Across from the Louvre are the pleasant courtyards of the stately Palais Royal. Although the palace is closed to the public, the courtyards are open. As you enter, you'll

Major Museums Neighborhood

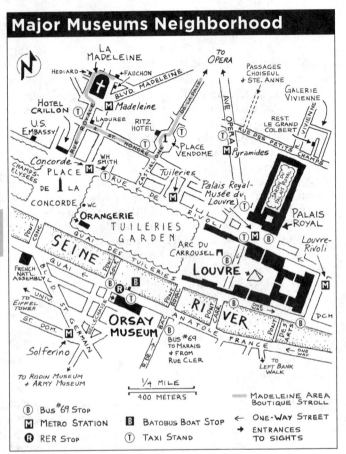

- **B** Bus #69 Stop
- **M** Metro Station
- **R** RER Stop
- **B** Batobus Boat Stop
- **T** Taxi Stand
- ← One-Way Street
- → Entrances to Sights
- Madeleine Area Boutique Stroll

pass through a whimsical courtyard filled with stubby, striped columns and playful fountains (with fun, reflective metal balls) into another, curiously peaceful courtyard. This is where in-the-know Parisians come to take a quiet break, walk their poodles, or enjoy a rendezvous—surrounded by a serene arcade and a handful of historic restaurants.

Though tranquil today, this was once a hotbed of political activism. The palace was built in the 17th century by Louis XIII, and eventually became the headquarters of the powerful Dukes of Orléans. Because the Dukes' digs were off-limits to the police, some shocking free-thinking took

root here. This was the meeting place for the debating clubs—the precursors to modern political parties. During the Revolution, palace resident Duke Phillip (nicknamed Phillip Egalité for his progressive ideas) advocated a constitutional monarchy, and voted in favor of beheading Louis XVI—his own cousin. Phillip hoped his liberal attitudes would spare him from the Revolutionaries, but he, too, was guillotined. His son, Louis-Philippe, grew to become France's first constitutional monarch (r. 1830–1848). The palace's courtyards were backdrops for a riotous social and political scene, filled with lively café culture, revolutionaries, rabble-rousers, scoundrels, and...Madame Tussaud's first wax shop (she used the severed heads of guillotine victims to model her sculptures).

Exiting the courtyard at the side facing away from the Seine brings you to the Galeries Colbert and Vivienne, good examples of shopping arcades from the early 1900s.

Cost, Hours, Location: Courtyards are free and always open. The Palais Royal is directly north of the Louvre on rue de Rivoli (Mo: Palais Royal–Musée du Louvre).

▲▲**Orangerie Museum (Musée de l'Orangerie)**—This Impressionist museum recently reopened after years of renovation. Located in the Tuileries Garden and drenched by natural

light from skylights, the Orangerie (oh-rahn-zheh-ree) is like an Impressionist painting come to life. Start with the museum's claim to fame: Monet's *Water Lilies*. Then head downstairs to enjoy the manageable collection of select works by Utrillo, Cézanne, Renoir, Matisse, and Picasso.

Cost, Hours, Location: €7.50, under 18 free, covered by Museum Pass, audioguide-€5, Wed–Mon 9:00–18:00, closed Tue, located in Tuileries Garden near place de la Concorde, Mo: Concorde. Tel. 01 44 77 80 07, www.musee-orangerie.fr.

✪ See the Orangerie Museum Tour chapter.

▲▲▲**Orsay Museum (Musée d'Orsay)**—The Orsay boasts Europe's greatest collection of Impressionist works. It might be less important than the Louvre—but it's more purely enjoyable.

The Orsay, housed in an atmospheric old train station, picks up where the Louvre leaves off: the second half of the 19th century. This is art from the tumultuous time that began when revolutions swept across Europe in 1848, and ended with the outbreak of World War I in 1914. Begin on the ground floor, which features conservative art of the mid-1800s—careful, idealized Neoclassicism (with a few rebels mixed in). Then glide up the

Affording Paris' Sights

Paris is an expensive city for tourists, with lots of pricey sights, but—fortunately—lots of freebies, too. Smart, budget-minded travelers begin by buying and getting the most out of a **Paris Museum Pass** (see the beginning of this chapter), then considering these frugal sightseeing options.

Free Museums: Some museums are always free (with the possible exception of special exhibits), including the Carnavalet, Petit Palais, Victor Hugo's House, and Fragonard Perfume Museum. Many of Paris' most famous museums offer free entry on the first Sunday of the month, including the Louvre, Orsay, Rodin, Cluny, Pompidou Center, and Delacroix museums. You can also visit the Orsay Museum for free at 17:00 (or Thu at 21:00), an hour before the museum closes. One of the best everyday values is the Rodin Museum's garden, where you'll pay €1 to experience many of Rodin's finest works in a lovely outdoor setting.

Other Freebies: Many worthwhile sights don't charge entry, including the Notre-Dame Cathedral, Père Lachaise Cemetery, Deportation Memorial, Holocaust Memorial, Paris Plage (summers only), St. Sulpice Church (with organ recital), and La Défense (though there is a charge to enter La Grande Arche). And remember that the neighborhood walks described in this book are free unless you enter a sight (Historic Paris, Left Bank, Champs-Elysées, Marais, Rue Cler, and Montmartre).

Paris' glorious, entertaining parks are free, of course. These include Luxembourg Garden, Champ de Mars (under the Eiffel

escalator to the late 1800s, when the likes of Manet, Monet, Degas, and Renoir jolted the art world with their colorful, lively new invention, Impressionism. (Somewhere in there, *Whistler's Mother* sits quietly.) You'll also enjoy the works of their artistic descendents, the post-Impressionists (Van Gogh and Cézanne) and the Primitives (Rousseau, Gauguin, Seurat, and Toulouse-Lautrec). On the mezzanine level, waltz through the Grand Ballroom, Art Nouveau exhibits, and Rodin sculptures.

Cost: €8, €5.50 Fri–Wed after 16:15 and Thu after 18:00, free on first Sun of month and when ticket booth stops selling tickets at 17:00 (Thu at 21:00), covered by Museum Pass. English-language tours usually run daily (except Sun) at 11:30, cost €7.50, and take 1.5 hours. Audioguides are €6. Some tours are occasionally offered at other times (inquire when you arrive).

Tower), Tuileries Garden (between the Louvre and place de la Concorde), Palais Royal Courtyards, Jardin des Plantes, the Promenade Plantée walk, and Versailles' gardens (except on Fountain Spectacle weekends).

Reduced Price: Several museums offer a discount if you enter later in the day, including the Louvre (after 18:00 on Wed and Fri), Orsay (Fri–Wed after 16:15 and Thu after 18:00), Army Museum and Napoleon's Tomb (one hour before closing), and Versailles' Château (after 15:00) and Domaine de Marie-Antoinette (after 16:00).

Free Concerts: Venues offering free or cheap (€6–8) concerts include the American Church, Hôtel des Invalides, Cluny Museum, St. Sulpice Church, La Madeleine Church, and Notre-Dame Cathedral. For a listing of free concerts, check *Pariscope* magazine (under the "Musique" section) and look for events marked *entrée libre*.

Good-Value Tours: At €12–15, Paris Walks' tours are a good value. The €10–12 Seine River cruises, best after dark, are also worthwhile. The Bus #69 Sightseeing Tour, which costs only the price of a transit ticket, could be the best deal of all.

Pricey... but worth it? Certain big-ticket items—primarily the Eiffel Tower, Louvre, and Versailles—are expensive and crowded, but offer once-in-a-lifetime experiences. Think of it as you would a spree in Vegas—budget in a little "gambling" money you expect to lose, then just relax...and enjoy.

Hours: Tue–Sun 9:30–18:00, Thu until 21:45, last entry one hour before closing (45 min before on Thu), closed Mon. Impressionist galleries start closing 45 min early. Crowded on Tue, when Louvre is closed.

Location: Above the RER-C stop called Musée d'Orsay; the nearest Métro stop is Solférino, three blocks southeast of the Orsay. From the Louvre, it's a lovely 15-minute walk through the Tuileries Garden and across the pedestrian bridge to the Orsay. Tel. 01 40 49 48 14, www.musee-orsay.fr.

  See the Orsay Museum Tour chapter.

Eiffel Tower and Nearby

▲▲▲**Eiffel Tower (La Tour Eiffel)**—Built a hundred years after the French Revolution (and in the midst of an industrial one), the tower served no function but to impress. For decades it was the tallest structure the world had ever known, and though it's since been eclipsed, it's still the most visited monument. Ride the elevators to the top of its 1,063 feet for expansive views that stretch 40 miles. Then descend to the two lower levels, where the views are

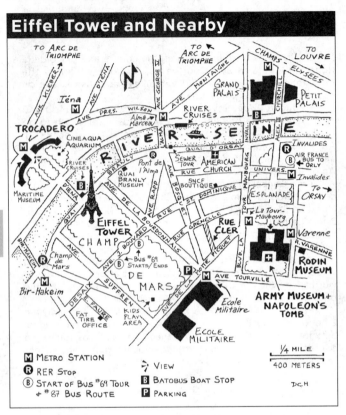

Eiffel Tower and Nearby

Map legend:

- **M** METRO STATION
- **R** RER STOP
- **B** START OF BUS #69 TOUR + #87 BUS ROUTE
- ➹ VIEW
- **B** BATOBUS BOAT STOP
- **P** PARKING

1/4 MILE
400 METERS

DCH

arguably even better, since the monuments are more recognizable. If you're going to Paris, you have to see the tower, so just brave the crowds, pay the money, and go up—if only to say you were there.

Cost: €13 all the way to the top, €8 if you're going only up

to the two lower levels, not covered by Museum Pass. You can skip the elevator line and climb the stairs to the first or second level for €4.50 (or for €3.50 if you're under 25).

Hours: Daily mid-June–Aug 9:00–24:45 in the morning, last ascent to top at 23:30 and to lower levels at 24:00; Sept–mid-June 9:30–23:45, last ascent to top at 22:30 and to lower levels at 23:00 (elevator) or 18:30 (stairs).

Location: Mo: Bir-Hakeim and Trocadéro or Champ de Mars-

Tour Eiffel RER stop (each about a 10-min walk away).

Online Booking: A new online reservation system, which should be operating by the time you visit, will allow you to book a half-hour time slot to begin your ascent—check www.toureiffel.fr (tel. 01 44 11 23 23).

○ See the Eiffel Tower Tour chapter (which also includes tips on avoiding lines).

Quai Branly Museum (Museé du Quai Branly)—This is the best collection I've seen anywhere of so-called Primitive Art from Africa, Polynesia, Asia, and America. It's presented in a wild, organic, and strikingly modern building that's a sightseeing thrill in itself. This museum, opened in 2006, is still big news with locals. Masks, statuettes, musical instruments, clothes, voodoo dolls, and a variety of temporary exhibits and activities are artfully presented and exquisitely lit. It's not, however, accompanied by much printed English information—to really appreciate the exhibit, use the €5 audioguide. It's a 10-minute walk east (upriver) of the Eiffel Tower, along the river.

Cost, Hours, Location: €8.50, more for temporary exhibits, covered by Museum Pass, Tue–Sun 11:00–19:00, Thu–Sat until 21:00, closed Mon, 37 quai Branly, RER: Champ de Mars-Tour Eiffel or Pont de l'Alma. Tel. 01 56 61 70 00, www.quaibranly.fr.

National Maritime Museum (Musée National de la Marine)—This extensive museum houses an amazing collection of ship models, submarines, torpedoes, cannonballs, *beaucoup* bowsprits, and naval you-name-it—including a small boat made for Napoleon. You'll find limited English information on the walls, but kids like the museum anyway (adults-€7, 18 and under free, more during special exhibits, covered by Museum Pass, Wed–Mon 10:00–18:00, closed Tue, on left side of Trocadéro Square with your back to Eiffel Tower, tel. 01 53 65 81 32, www.musee-marine.fr).

▲Paris Sewer Tour (Les Egouts de Paris)—Discover what happens after you flush. This quick, interesting, and slightly stinky visit (a perfumed hanky helps) takes you along a few hundred yards of water tunnels in the world's first underground sewer system. Pick up the helpful English self-guided tour, then drop down into Jean Valjean's world of tunnels, rats, and manhole covers. (Victor Hugo was friends with the sewer inspector when he wrote *Les Misérables*.) You'll pass well-organized displays with helpful English information detailing the evolution of this amazing network. More than 1,500

miles of tunnels carry 317 million gallons of water daily through this underworld. It's the world's longest sewer system—so long, they say, that if it was laid out straight, it would stretch from Paris all the way to Istanbul.

It's enlightening to see how much work goes into something we take for granted. Sewage didn't always disappear so readily. In the Middle Ages, wastewater was tossed from windows to a center street gutter, then washed into the river. In castles, sewage ended up in the moat (enhancing the moat's defensive role). In the 1500s, French Renaissance King François I moved from château to château (he had several) when the moat muck became too much. Don't miss the slide show, fine WCs just beyond the gift shop, and occasional tours in English.

Cost, Hours, Location: €4, covered by Museum Pass, May–Sept Sat–Wed 11:00–17:00, Oct–April Sat–Wed 11:00–16:00, closed Thu–Fri, located where pont de l'Alma greets the Left Bank—on the right side of the bridge as you face the river, Mo: Alma-Marceau, RER: Pont de l'Alma. Tel. 01 53 68 27 81.

▲▲**Army Museum and Napoleon's Tomb (Musée de l'Armée)**—Europe's greatest military museum, in the Hôtel des Invalides, provides interesting coverage of several wars, particularly World Wars I and II. At the center of the complex, the emperor Napoleon lies majestically dead inside several coffins under a grand dome—a goose-bumping pilgrimage for historians. The dome overhead glitters with 26 pounds of thinly pounded gold leaf.

Cost: €8.50, ticket includes Napoleon's Tomb, all museums within Les Invalides complex, and audioguide for tomb. All covered by the Museum Pass except for €1 audioguide. Price drops to €6.50 an hour before closing time; always free for all military personnel in uniform.

Hours: April–Sept daily 10:00–18:00, Sun until 18:30 and Tue until 21:00, July–Aug tomb stays open until 18:45; Oct–March daily 10:00–17:00, Sun until 17:30; last entry 30 min before closing, last entry to tomb 45 min before closing; closed first Mon of every month.

Location: The Hôtel des Invalides is at 129 rue de Grenelle; Mo: La Tour Maubourg, Varenne, or Invalides. Tel. 01 44 42 37 64 or 08 10 11 33 99, www.invalides.org.

❍ See the Army Museum and Napoleon's Tomb Tour chapter.

▲▲**Rodin Museum (Musée Rodin)**—This user-friendly museum is filled with passionate works by the greatest sculptor since Michelangelo. You'll see *The Kiss, The Thinker, The Gates of Hell,* and many more.

Well-displayed in the mansion where the sculptor lived and worked, exhibits trace Rodin's artistic development, explain how his bronze statues were cast, and show some of the studies he created to work up to his masterpiece (the unfinished *Gates of Hell*). Learn about Rodin's tumultuous relationship with his apprentice and lover, Camille Claudel. Mull over what makes his sculptures some of the most evocative since the Renaissance. And stroll the gardens, packed with many of his greatest works (including *The Thinker*). The beautiful gardens are ideal for artistic reflection.

Cost, Hours, Location: €6, under 18 free, free on first Sun of the month, covered by Museum Pass. You'll pay €1 to get into the gardens only—which may be Paris' best deal, as many works are on display there (also covered by Museum Pass). Audioguides are €4, and baggage check is mandatory. Open April–Sept Tue–Sun 9:30–17:45, gardens close at 18:45; Oct–March Tue–Sun 9:30–16:45, gardens close at 17:00, last entry 30 min before closing, closed Mon. It's near the Army Museum and Napoleon's Tomb, 79 rue de Varenne, Mo: Varenne. Tel. 01 44 18 61 10, www.musee-rodin.fr.

○ See the Rodin Museum Tour chapter.

▲▲**Marmottan Museum (Musée Marmottan Monet)**—In this private, intimate and untouristy museum, you'll find the best collection anywhere of works by Impressionist headliner Claude Monet. Follow Monet's life through more than a hundred works, from simple sketches to the *Impression: Sunrise* painting that gave his artistic movement its start—and a name. You'll also enjoy large-scale canvases featuring the water lilies from his garden at Giverny.

Cost, Hours, Location: €9, not covered by Museum Pass, €3 audioguide, Wed–Sun 11:00–18:00, Tue 11:00–21:00, last entry 30 min before closing, closed Mon, 2 rue Louis-Boilly, Mo: La Muette. From the Métro stop, follow the brown museum signs six blocks down chaussée de la Muette through the park; pause to watch kids play on the old-time, crank-powered carousel. Tel. 01 44 96 50 33, www.marmottan.com.

○ See the Marmottan Museum Tour chapter.

Left Bank

○ For more information on these sights, see the Left Bank Walk, the Historic Paris Walk (which dips into the Latin Quarter), and the "Sèvres-Babylone to St. Sulpice" stroll in the Shopping chapter.

▲**Latin Quarter (Quartier Latin)**—This Left Bank neighborhood, just opposite Notre-Dame, was the center of Roman Paris.

But the Latin Quarter's touristy fame relates to its intriguing, artsy, bohemian character. This was perhaps Europe's leading university district in the Middle Ages, when Latin was the language of higher education. The neighborhood's main boulevards (St. Michel and St. Germain) are lined with cafés—once the haunts of great poets and philosophers, now the hangouts of tired tourists. Although still youthful and artsy, much of this area has become a tourist ghetto filled with cheap North African eateries. Exploring a few blocks up or downriver from here gives you a better chance of feeling the pulse of what survives of Paris' classic Left Bank.

○ See the Left Bank Walk chapter.

▲▲**Cluny Museum (Musée National du Moyen Age)**—This treasure trove of Middle Ages (Moyen Age) art fills old Roman

baths, offering close-up looks at stained glass, Notre-Dame carvings, fine goldsmithing and jewelry, and rooms of tapestries. The star here is the exquisite *Lady and the Unicorn* series of six tapestries: A delicate, as-medieval-as-can-be noble lady introduces a delighted unicorn to the senses of taste, hearing, sight, smell, and touch.

Cost, Hours, Location: €8, free on first Sun of month, covered by Museum Pass, Wed–Mon 9:15–17:45, closed Tue, near corner of boulevards St. Michel and St. Germain at 6 place Paul Painlevé; Mo: Cluny-La Sorbonne, St. Michel, or Odéon. Tel. 01 53 73 78 16, www.musee-moyenage.fr.

○ See the Cluny Museum Tour chapter.

St. Germain-des-Prés—A church was first built on this site in A.D. 452. The church you see today was constructed in 1163 and is all that's left of a once sprawling and influential monastery. The colorful interior reminds us that medieval churches were originally painted in bright colors. The surrounding area hops at night with venerable cafés, fire-eaters, mimes, and scads of artists (free, daily 8:00–20:00, Mo: St. Germain-des-Prés).

▲**St. Sulpice Church and Organ Concert**—Since it was featured in *The Da Vinci Code*, this grand church has become a trendy

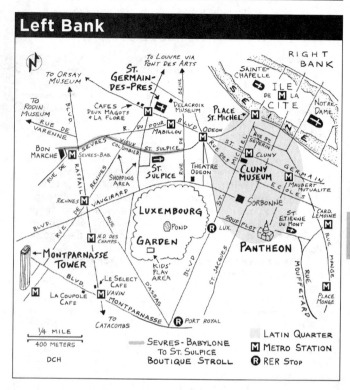

Left Bank

(map) RIGHT BANK — TO LOUVRE VIA PONT DES ARTS — SAINTE-CHAPELLE — ILE DE LA CITE — NOTRE DAME — SEINE — ST. GERMAIN-DES-PRES — TO ORSAY MUSEUM — TO RODIN MUSEUM — RUE DE VARENNE — BLVD. RASPAIL — CAFES DEUX MAGOTS + LA FLORE — DELACROIX MUSEUM — R. DU FOUR — MABILLON — PLACE ST. MICHEL — BLVD. ODEON — RUE ST. SEVERIN — CLUNY — BON MARCHE — SEVRES-BAB. — SEVRES — VIEUX COLOMBIER — ST. SULPICE — RUE DE RENNES — ST. SULPICE — RUE DE SEINE — RUE DES ECOLES — CLUNY MUSEUM — GERMAIN — MAUBERT MUTUALITE — SHOPPING AREA — THEATRE ODEON — RENNES — VAUGIRARD — SORBONNE — CARD. LEMOINE — RUE DE RENNES — RUE DE RENNES — LUXEMBOURG GARDEN — POND — LUX. — SOUFFLOT — ST. ETIENNE DU MONT — PANTHEON — BLVD. — N.D. DES CHAMPS — KIDS' PLAY AREA — RUE ST. JACQUES — RUE MOUFFETARD — RUE MONGE — MONTPARNASSE TOWER — BLVD. — LE SELECT CAFE — VAVIN — DASSAS — PLACE MONGE — LA COUPOLE CAFE — MONTPARNASSE — TO CATACOMBS — PORT ROYAL — ¼ MILE — 400 METERS — DCH — SEVRES-BABYLONE TO ST. SULPICE BOUTIQUE STROLL — LATIN QUARTER — METRO STATION — RER STOP

SIGHTS IN PARIS

stop for the book's many fans. But the real reason to visit is to see and hear its intimately accessible organ. For pipe-organ enthusi-

asts, this is one of Europe's great musical treats. The Grand Orgue at St. Sulpice Church has a rich history, with a succession of 12 world-class organists—including Charles-Marie Widor and Marcel Dupré—that goes back 300 years. Widor started the tradition of opening the loft to visitors after the 10:30 service on Sundays. Daniel Roth (or his understudy) continues to welcome guests in three languages while playing five keyboards. (See www.daniel rothsaintsulpice.org for his exact dates and concert plans.)

The 10:30–11:30 Sunday Mass (come appropriately dressed) is followed by a high-powered 25-minute recital. Then, just after noon, the small, unmarked door is opened (left of entry as you face the rear). Visitors scamper like 16th notes up spiral stairs, past the 19th-century StairMasters that five men once pumped to fill the

The *Da Vinci Code* in Paris

Dan Brown's novel about a Harvard cryptologist on the hunt for the Holy Grail was an international bestseller, a pop-culture craze, and a hot conversation topic. This work of fiction—encrusted with real and invented historical information—has sold millions of copies and been translated into 44 languages, flooding bookstores from Paris to Beijing. The movie version (starring Tom Hanks and Audrey Tautou, a.k.a. Amélie) was filmed in Paris.

Since most of the book (and movie) is set in Paris, *Da Vinci Code* fans flock to the various sights described in the novel. You can even sign up for a special walking tour to satisfy this curiosity (see "Tours on Foot," page 39). And though *The Da Vinci Code* may be a good read, it's not accurate either as history or a good travel guide—there just isn't that much to see. Still, tours do their best to make something of these stops along the Grail trail:

The Louvre's Grand Gallery, near Leonardo's Virgin of the Rocks: "Renowned curator, Jacques Sauniere," the book begins, "staggered through the vaulted archway of the museum's Grand Gallery." He then falls to the parquet floor, smears a cryptic clue in his own blood, and dies. This starts the hunt, as protagonist Robert Langdon and police officer Sophie Neveu follow clues hidden in art, history, and religious lore to solve the murder and, ultimately, find the Holy Grail.

The Louvre's Salle des Etats: Langdon and Neveu find clues in Leonardo's *Mona Lisa*.

The Louvre Pyramid and Arc du Carrousel: Pursued by the police and fearing wrongful arrest, they escape the Louvre and drive off into the night.

The Ritz Hôtel on Place Vendôme: Langdon's address in Paris.

St. Sulpice Church: Home to the astrological clock—a line on the floor that calibrates sunbeams with the calendar—Dan Brown incorrectly calls this the "rose line." (For more on St. Sulpice, see the Left Bank Walk.)

Inverted Pyramid in the Carrousel du Louvre: The final stop on your quest is a shopping mall. You'll find the Holy Grail (says Brown) embedded in modern concrete under an inverted glass pyramid, just next to Virgin Records.

bellows, into a world of 7,000 pipes. You can see the organ and visit with Daniel (or his substitute, who might not speak English). Space is tight; only a few can gather around him at a time, and you need to be quick to allow others a chance to meet him. You'll generally have 20–30 minutes to kill (church views are great and there's a small lounge) before watching the master play during the next Mass; you can leave at any time. If you're late or rushed, show up around 12:30 and wait at the little door. As someone leaves, you can slip in, climb up, and catch the rest of the performance. Tempting boutiques surround the church (see Shopping chapter), and Luxembourg Garden is nearby.

Cost, Hours, Location: Free, church open daily 7:30–19:30, Mo: St. Sulpice or Mabillon.

For more on St. Sulpice, ✪ see page 257 in the Left Bank Walk.

Delacroix Museum (Musée National Eugène Delacroix)— This museum for Eugène Delacroix (1798–1863) was once his home and studio. A friend of bohemian artistic greats—including George Sand and Frédéric Chopin—Delacroix is most famous for the flag-waving painting *Liberty Leading the People*, which is displayed at the Louvre, not here (€5, free on first Sun of the month, covered by Museum Pass, Wed–Mon 9:30–17:00, Sat–Sun until 17:30 in summer, last entry 30 min before closing, closed Tue, 6 rue de Furstenberg, Mo: St. Germain-des-Prés. Tel. 01 44 41 86 50, www.musee-delacroix.fr).

For more on the Delacroix Museum, ✪ see page 254 in the Left Bank Walk.

▲Luxembourg Garden (Jardin du Luxembourg)—This lovely 60-acre garden is an Impressionist painting brought to life. Slip into a green chair and ponder pondside, enjoy the radiant flower-

beds, go jogging, or take in a chess game or puppet show (park open daily dawn until dusk, Mo: Odéon, RER: Luxembourg). Notice any pigeons? The story goes that a very poor Ernest Hemingway used to hand-hunt (read: strangle) them here.

✪ For more on the garden and nearby sights, see page 259 in the Left Bank Walk. Also see the kid-friendly activities in the garden (Paris with Children chapter), cafés listed in "Les Grands Cafés de Paris" (Eating chapter), and the description of the Panthéon mausoleum (below).

If you enjoy Luxembourg Garden and want to see more green spaces, you could visit the more elegant **Parc Monceau**

(Mo: Monceau), the colorful **Jardin des Plantes** (Mo: Jussieu or Gare d'Austerlitz, RER: Gare d'Austerlitz), or the hilly and bigger **Parc des Buttes-Chaumont** (Mo: Buttes-Chaumont).

▲**Panthéon**—This state-capitol-style Neoclassical monument celebrates France's illustrious history and people, balances Foucault's

pendulum, and is the final home of many French VIPs. In 1744, an ailing King Louis XV was miraculously healed by St. Geneviève, the city's patron saint, and he thanked her by replacing her ruined church with a more fitting tribute. By the time the church was completed (1791), however, the secular-minded Revolution was in full swing, and the church was converted into a secular mausoleum honoring the "Champions of French liberty"—Voltaire, Rousseau, Descartes, and others. The Revolutionaries covered up the church's windows (as you can see from outside) to display grand, patriotic murals. On the entrance pediment (inspired by the ancient Pantheon in Rome), they carved the inscription, "To the great men of the Fatherland."

Inside the vast building (360' by 280' by 270') are monuments tracing the celebrated struggles of the French people: a beheaded St. Denis (painting on left wall of nave), St. Geneviève saving the fledgling city from Attila the Hun, and scenes of Joan of Arc (left transept).

Under the dome are four statue groups dedicated to more great Frenchmen: Jean-Jacques Rousseau (1712–1778), the philosopher who championed the idea of an equal Social Contract between government and the people; Diderot (1713–1784), whose Encyclopédie championed secular knowledge; orators and publicists (men in business suits) who served the state; and generals, including Napoleon on horseback.

Foucault's pendulum swings gracefully at the end of a 220-foot cable suspended from the towering dome. It was here in 1851 that the scientist Léon Foucault first demonstrated the rotation of the Earth. Stand a few minutes and watch the pendulum's arc (appear to) shift as you and the earth rotate beneath it.

At the far end of the nave stands an altar dedicated to the political body that opposed the monarchy during the Revolution, inscribed with the familiar motto "Live free or die."

Stairs in the back lead down to the crypt, where a pantheon of greats is buried. Rousseau is along the right wall as you enter, Voltaire faces him across the hall. Also buried here are scientist Marie Curie, Victor Hugo (*Les Misérables*, *The Hunchback of Notre-Dame*), Alexandre Dumas (*The Three Musketeers*, *The Count of Monte Cristo*), and Louis Braille, who invented the script for the blind.

From the main floor you can climb 206 steps to the dome gallery for fine views of the interior as well as the city (accessible only with an escort). Visits leave every hour until 17:30 from the bookshop near the entry—see schedule as you go in.

Cost, Hours, Location: €8, covered by Museum Pass, daily 10:00–18:30 in summer, until 18:00 in winter, last entry 45 min before closing, Mo: Cardinal Lemoine. Ask about occasional English tours or call ahead for schedule. Tel. 01 44 32 18 00, www .monum.fr.

Montparnasse Tower (La Tour Montparnasse)—This 59-story superscraper—cheaper and easier to ascend than the

Eiffel Tower—treats you to one of Paris' best views. (Some say it's the very best, as you can see the Eiffel Tower...and you can't see the Montparnasse Tower.) There may be plenty of dioramas identifying highlights of the star-studded vista, but consider buying the €3 photo-guide, which makes a fun souvenir. As you zip up 56 floors in 38 seconds, watch the altimeter above the door. From the 56th floor, climb to the open terrace on the 59th floor to enjoy the surreal scene of a lonely man in a box, and a helipad surrounded by the window-cleaner track. Here, 690 feet above Paris, you can scan the city with the wind in your hair, noticing the lush courtyards hiding behind grand street fronts. Back inside and downstairs, you'll find a small, overpriced café, fascinating historic black-and-white photos, and a plush little theater playing a worthwhile video that celebrates the big views of this grand city (free, 12 min, shows continuously).

Cost, Hours, Location: €10.50, not covered by Museum Pass, daily April–Sept 9:30–23:30, Oct–March 9:30–22:30, Fri–Sat until 23:00, last entry 30 min before closing, sunset is great but views are disappointing after dark, entrance on rue de l'Arrivée,

Mo: Montparnasse-Bienvenüe—from the Métro stay inside the station and simply follow the signs for *La Tour*. The tower is an efficient stop when combined with a day trip to Chartres, which begins at the Montparnasse train station (see the Chartres Cathedral Day Trip chapter for details). Tel. 01 45 38 52 56, www .tourmontparnasse56.com.

▲**Catacombs**—These underground tunnels (may be closed for renovation—ask your hotelier to call ahead) contain the anonymous bones of six million permanent Parisians. In 1786, the citizens of Paris decided to relieve congestion and improve sanitary conditions by emptying the city cemeteries (which traditionally surrounded churches) into an official ossuary. They found the perfect locale in the many miles of underground tunnels from limestone quarries, which were, at that time,

just outside the city. For decades, priests led ceremonial processions of black-veiled, bone-laden carts into the quarries, where the bones were stacked into piles five feet high and as much as 80 feet deep behind neat walls of skull-studded tibiae. Each transfer was completed by placing a plaque, indicating the church and district where the bones came from and the date that they arrived.

From the entry, a spiral staircase leads 60 feet down. Then you begin a one-mile subterranean walk (allow one full hour). After several blocks of empty passageways, you ignore a sign announcing: "Halt, this is the empire of the dead." Along the way, plaques encourage visitors to reflect on their destiny: "Happy is he who is forever faced with the hour of his death and prepares himself for the end every day." You emerge far from where you entered, with white-limestone-covered toes. Note to wannabe Hamlets: An attendant checks your bag at the exit for stolen souvenirs. A flashlight is handy. Being under 6'2" is helpful.

Cost: €8, not covered by Museum Pass.

Hours: If not closed for renovation, hours are Tue–Sun 10:00–17:00, ticket booth closes at 16:00, closed Mon. Be warned that lines are long (figure an hour wait) and hard to avoid. Arrive no later than 14:30 or risk not getting in.

Location: 1 place Denfert-Rochereau. Take the Métro to Denfert-Rochereau, then find the lion in the big traffic circle; if he looked left rather than right, he'd stare right at the green entrance to the Catacombs. Tel. 01 43 22 47 63.

Photography: Photos without flash are allowed.

Nearby: Rue Daguerre, a pleasing pedestrian street (see the

Shopping chapter) is a block from the Catacombs entrance (cross avenue du Général Leclerc and turn left).

After Your Visit: You'll exit at 36 rue Remy Dumoncel, far from where you started. Turn right out of the exit and walk to avenue du Général Leclerc, where you'll be equidistant from Métro stops Alésia (walk left) and Mouton Duvernet (walk right).

Champs-Elysées and Nearby

▲▲**Champs-Elysées**—This famous boulevard is Paris' backbone, with its greatest concentration of traffic. From the Arc de Triomphe down avenue des Champs-Elysées, all of France seems to converge on place de la Concorde, the city's largest square. And though the Champs-Elysées has become as international as it is local, a walk here is still a must.

To reach the top of the Champs-Elysées, take the Métro to the Arc de Triomphe (Mo: Charles de Gaulle-Etoile) then saunter down the grand boulevard (Métro stops every few blocks, including Charles de Gaulle-Etoile, George V, and Franklin D. Roosevelt).

○ See the Champs-Elysées Walk chapter.

▲▲▲**Arc de Triomphe**—Napoleon had the magnificent Arc de Triomphe commissioned to commemorate his victory at the battle of Austerlitz. The foot of the arch is a stage on which the last two centuries of Parisian history have played out—from the funeral of Napoleon to the goose-stepping arrival of the Nazis to the triumphant return of Charles de Gaulle after the Allied liberation. Examine the carvings on the pillars, featuring a mighty Napoleon and excitable Lady Liberty. Pay your respects at the Tomb of the Unknown Soldier. Then climb the 284 steps to the observation deck up top, with sweeping skyline panoramas and a mesmerizing view down onto the traffic that swirls around the arch.

Cost, Hours, Location: Outside—free, always viewable. Interior—€9, under 18 free, free on first Sun of month Oct–March, covered by Museum Pass, daily April–Sept 10:00–23:00, Oct–March 10:00–22:30, last entry 30 min before closing, place

SIGHTS IN PARIS

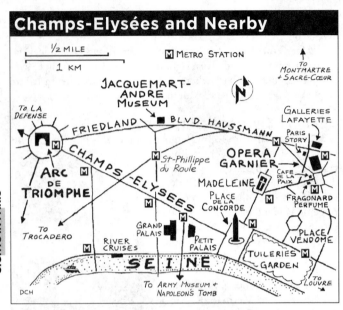

Champs-Elysées and Nearby

Charles de Gaulle, use underpass to reach arch, Mo: Charles de Gaulle-Etoile. Tel. 01 55 37 73 77, www.monum.fr.

○ See the Champs-Elysées Walk chapter.

▲**Opéra Garnier**—This gleaming grand theater of the belle époque was built for Napoleon III and finished in 1875. From avenue de l'Opéra, once lined with

Paris' most fashionable haunts, the recently restored facade suggests "all power to the wealthy." And Apollo, holding his lyre high above the building, seems to declare, "This is a temple of the highest arts." The view of the facade is brilliant from in front of the Opéra Métro stop.

You'll enter around the left side of the building—as you face the front, find the red carpet across from American Express on rue Scribe. The building is huge—though the auditorium itself seats only 2,000. The real show was before and after the performance, when the elite of Paris—out to see and be seen—strutted their elegant stuff in the extravagant lobbies. Think of the grand marble stairway as a theater. As you wander the halls and gawk at the decor, imagine the place filled with the beautiful people of its day. The massive foundations straddle an underground lake (inspiring the mysterious world of the *Phantom of the Opera*). Visitors can

Baron Georges-Eugène Haussmann
(1809–1891)

The elegantly uniform streets that make Paris so Parisian are the work of Baron Haussmann, who oversaw the modernization of the city in the mid-19th century. He cleared out the cramped, higgledy-piggledy, unhygienic medieval cityscape and replaced it with broad, straight boulevards lined with stately buildings and linking modern train stations.

The quintessential view of Haussmann's work is from the pedestrian island immediately in front of the Opéra Garnier. You're surrounded by Paris, circa 1870, when it was the capital of the world. Spin slowly and find the Louvre in one direction, place Vendôme in another, and all the cohesiveness of the uniform buildings. Haussmann's buildings are all five stories tall, with angled, black slate roofs and formal facades. The balconies on the second and fifth floors match up with neighboring buildings to give strong lines of perspective, as the buildings stretch down the boulevard. Haussmann was so intent on putting the architecture at center-stage that he ordered no trees be planted along these streets.

But there was more than aesthetics to the plan. In pre-Haussmann Paris, angry rioters would take to the narrow streets, setting up barricades (as made famous in Hugo's *Les Misérables*) to hold back government forces. With Haussmann's plan government troops could circulate easily and fire cannons down the long, straight boulevards. A whiff of "grapeshot"—chains, nails, and buckshot-type people-busters—could clear out any revolutionaries in a hurry.

The 19th century was a great time to be wealthy, thanks to the city's fancy covered market halls, civilized sidewalks, and even elevators. With the coming of elevators, the wealthy took the higher floors and enjoyed the view.

peek from two boxes into the actual red-velvet performance hall to view Marc Chagall's colorful ceiling (1964) playfully dancing around the eight-ton chandelier (guided tours take you into the performance hall; you can't enter when they're changing out the stage). Note the box seats next to the stage—the most expensive in the house, with an obstructed view of the stage...but just right if you're here only to be seen.

The elitism of this place prompted President François Mitterrand to have a people's opera house built in the 1980s, symbolically on place de la Bastille, where the French Revolution started in 1789. This left the Opéra Garnier home only to ballet and occasional concerts. The library/museum will interest opera buffs, but anyone will enjoy the second-floor grand foyer and Salon du Glacier, iced with decor typical of 1900.

Best Views over the City of Light

Your trip to Paris is played out in the streets, but the brilliance of the City of Light can only be fully appreciated by rising above it all. Invest time to marvel at all the man-made beauty, seen best in the early morning or around sunset. Many of the viewpoints I've listed are free or covered by the Museum Pass; otherwise, expect to pay about €8. Here are some prime locations for soaking in the views:

Eiffel Tower: It's hard to find a grander view of Paris than from the tower's second level. Go around sunset and stay after dark to see the tower illuminated; or go in the early morning to avoid the midday haze and crowds (not covered by Museum Pass, see page 55).

Arc de Triomphe: Without a doubt, this is the perfect place to see the glamorous Champs-Elysées (if you can manage the 284 steps). It's great during the day, but even greater at night, when the boulevard positively glitters (covered by Museum Pass, see page 67).

La Défense and La Grande Arche: This is your best bet for a view of Paris from outside the center. Take the elevator up for a good perspective on the city, its suburbs, and the surrounding forests (not covered by Museum Pass, see page 74). The free view of Paris from the steps of La Grande Arche is decent, too.

Notre-Dame's Tower: This viewpoint is brilliant—you couldn't be more central—but it requires climbing 400 steps and is usually crowded with long lines (try to arrive early). Up high on the tower, you'll get an unobstructed view of gargoyles, the river,

Cost, Hours, Location: €8, not covered by Museum Pass, erratic hours due to performances and rehearsals, but generally daily 10:00–16:30, July–Aug until 17:30, 8 rue Scribe, Mo: Opéra, RER: Auber.

Tours: English tours of the building run during summer and off-season on weekends and Wed, usually at 11:30 and 14:30—call to confirm schedule (€12, includes entry, 1.5 hours, tel. 01 40 01 17 89 or 08 25 05 44 05, press 2 for tours).

Ballet and Concert Tickets: To find out about upcoming performances, ask for a schedule at the information booth, consult *Pariscope* magazine (see page 445), or look on the website (www.opera-de-paris.fr). To buy tickets by phone, call 08 92 89 90 90 (toll call) or from the US dial 011 33 1 72 29 35 35 (office closed Sun). There are usually no performances mid-July–mid-Sept. You can also go directly to the ticket office (open daily 11:00–18:00).

Nearby: The *Paris Story* film and Fragonard Perfume Museum (see below) are on the left side of the Opéra, and the venerable Galeries Lafayette department store (top-floor café with marvelous

the Latin Quarter, and the Ile de la Cité (covered by Museum Pass, see page 44).

Steps of Sacré-Cœur: Join the party on Paris' only hilltop. Walk uphill or take the funicular (if it's running), then hunker down on the Sacré-Cœur's steps to enjoy the sunset and territorial views over Paris. Stay in Montmartre for dinner, then see the view again after dark (free, see page 79).

Galeries Lafayette: Take the elevator to the top floor of this department store for a stunning overlook of the old Opéra district (free, see page 431).

Montparnasse Tower: The top of this solitary skyscraper has some of the best views in Paris, though they're disappointing after dark. Zip up 56 floors on the elevator, then walk to the rooftop (not covered by Museum Pass, see page 65).

Pompidou Center: Take the escalator up and admire the beautiful cityscape along with the exciting modern art. There may be better views over Paris, but this is the best one from a museum (covered by Museum Pass, see page 76).

Trocadéro Square: This is *the* place to see the Eiffel Tower. Come day or night (when the tower is lit up) for a look at Monsieur Eiffel's festive creation. Consider starting or ending your Eiffel Tower visit here (free, see page 188).

Bar at Hôtel Concorde-Lafayette: This otherwise unappealing hotel is noteworthy for its 33rd-floor bar, where you can sip wine and enjoy a stunning Parisian panorama (free elevator but pricey drinks, see page 73).

views, see page 431) is just behind. Across the street, the illustrious Café de la Paix has been a meeting spot for the local glitterati for generations. If you can afford the coffee, this spot offers a delightful break.

Paris Story Film—Simultaneously cheesy, entertaining, and pricey, this film offers a painless overview of the city's turbulent and brilliant past, covering 2,000 years in 45 fast-moving minutes. The theater's wide-screen projection and cushy chairs provide a break from bad weather and sore feet, and the movie usually works for kids. But don't go out of your way to get here.

Cost, Hours, Location: €10, kids-€6, family of four-€26, not covered by Museum Pass, 20 percent discount with this book in 2010, no discount on family rate. The film shows on the hour daily 10:00–18:00. Across from Opéra Garnier at 11 rue Scribe, Mo: Opéra. Tel. 01 42 66 62 06.

Fragonard Perfume Museum—Near Opéra Garnier, this perfume shop masquerades as a museum. Housed in a beautiful 19th-century mansion, it's the best-smelling museum you'll visit in

Paris—and you'll learn a little about how perfume is made too (ask for the English handout, free, daily 9:00–18:00, 9 rue Scribe, tel. 01 47 42 04 56, www.fragonard.com).

▲▲Jacquemart-André Museum (Musée Jacquemart-André)—This thoroughly enjoyable museum (with an elegant café) showcases the lavish home of a wealthy, art-loving, 19th-century Parisian couple. After wandering the grand boulevards, get inside for an intimate look at the lifestyles of the Parisian rich and fabulous. Edouard André and his wife Nélie Jacquemart—who had no children—spent their lives and fortunes designing, building, and then decorating this sumptuous mansion. What makes the visit so rewarding is the excellent audioguide tour (in English, free with admission, plan on spending an hour with the audioguide). The place is strewn with paintings by Rembrandt, Botticelli, Uccello, Mantegna, Bellini, Boucher, and Fragonard—enough to make a painting gallery famous.

Cost, Hours, Location: €10, not covered by Museum Pass, daily 10:00–18:00, 158 boulevard Haussmann, Mo: Miromesnil or Saint-Philippe de Roule, bus #80 makes a convenient connection to Ecole Militaire. Tel. 01 45 62 11 59, www.musee-jacquemart-andre.com.

After Your Visit: Consider a break in the sumptuous museum tearoom, with delicious cakes and tea (daily 11:45–17:30). From here walk north on rue de Courcelles to see Paris' most beautiful park, **Parc Monceau.**

▲Petit Palais (and its Musée des Beaux-Arts)—In this free museum, you'll find a broad collection of paintings and sculpture from the 1600s to the 1900s. It's a museum of second-choice art, but the building itself is impressive, and there are a few 19th-century diamonds in the rough, including pieces by Courbet and Monet.

Enter the museum, ask for a ticket to the permanent collection (free but required), and head toward the left wing. Soak up turn-of-the-century ambience, with Art Nouveau vases and portraits of well-dressed, belle époque–era Parisians. The main hall features Romantics and Realists from the late 19th century. Midway down the main hall, Courbet's soft-porn *The Sleepers* (*Le Sommeil*, 1866) captures two women nestled in post-climactic bliss. His large, dark *Firefighters (Pompiers courant à un incendie)* is a Realist's take on an everyday scene—firefighters rushing to put out a blaze.

Turning the corner, you'll find artwork by Gustave Doré (1832–1883), the 19th century's greatest book illustrator. In the enormous *La Vallée de larmes* (1883), Christ and the cross are the only salvation from this "vale of tears."

At the end of the main hall, enter the smaller room to find Claude Monet's *Sunset on the Seine at Lavacourt* (*Soleil couchant sur la Seine a Lavacourt*, 1880). Painted the winter after his wife died, it looks across the river from Monet's home to two lonely boats in the distance, with the hazy town on the far bank. The sun's reflection is a vertical smudge down the water. Nearby are works by the American painter Mary Cassatt and other Impressionists.

The Palais also has a pleasant garden courtyard and café.

Cost, Hours, Location: Free, Tue–Sun 10:00–18:00, Thu until 20:00 for temporary exhibits, closed Mon, across from Grand Palais on avenue Winston Churchill, a l-o-o-ong block west of place de la Concorde. Tel. 01 53 43 40 00, www.petitpalais.paris.fr.

Grand Palais—This grand exhibition hall, built for the 1900 World's Fair, is used for temporary exhibits. The building's

Industrial Age, erector-set, iron-and-glass exterior is grand, but the steep entry price is only worthwhile if you're interested in any of the several different exhibitions (each with different hours and costs, located in various parts of the building). Many areas are undergoing renovations through 2010. Get details on the current schedule from the TIs, in *Pariscope,* or from the website.

Cost, Hours, Location: Usually €10, not covered by Museum Pass, Thu–Mon 10:00–20:00, Wed 10:00–22:00, last entry 45 min before closing, closed Tue and between exhibitions, avenue Winston Churchill, Mo: Rond Point or Champs-Elysées. Tel. 01 44 13 17 17, www.grandpalais.fr.

View from Hôtel Concorde-Lafayette—For a remarkable Parisian panorama and a suitable location for your next affair, take the Métro to the pedestrian-unfriendly Porte Maillot stop, then follow the *Beauvais Bus* signs. (If you're coming from the rue Cler area, take RER-C from Invalides or Pont de l'Alma toward Pontoise to Porte Maillot). When you pop out of the station, you'll see the glass-and-steel tower of the Hôtel Concorde-Lafayette. (If you're strapped for time, the skies are clear, and the sun's about to set, spring for a taxi.) Ride the free elevators (when entering, head to the rear of the lobby and take the elevators on the right) to the 33rd floor, walk up one flight, and enter a sky-high world of semicircular vinyl make-out booths, glass walls, pricey drinks, and jaw-dropping views that are best before dark and not worthwhile in poor weather (bar open 16:00–1:00 in the morning, 3 place du General Koenig, tel. 01 40 68 50 68, www.concorde-lafayette.com).

▲▲La Défense and La Grande Arche—Though Paris keeps its historic center classic and skyscraper-free, this district, nick-

named "le petit Manhattan," offers an impressive excursion into a side of Paris few tourists see: that of a modern-day economic superpower. La Défense was first conceived more than 60 years ago as a US-style forest of skyscrapers that would accommodate the business needs of the modern world. Today La Défense is a thriving business and shopping center, home to 150,000 employees and 55,000 residents.

For an interesting visit, take the Métro to the La Défense, Grande Arche stop and ride the elevator to the top of La Grande Arche for great city views. Then stroll among the glass buildings to the Esplanade de la Défense Métro station, and return home from there.

La Grande Arche de la Fraternité is the centerpiece of this ambitious complex. Inaugurated in 1989 on the 200th anniver-

sary of the French Revolution, it was, like the Revolution, dedicated to human rights and brotherhood. The place is big—Notre-Dame Cathedral could fit under its arch. The four-sided structure sits on enormous underground pillars and is covered with a veneer of Carrara marble. The arch is a 38-story office building for 30,000 people on more than 200 acres. The left side is government ministries, the right side is corporate offices, and the top is dedicated to human rights. The "cloud"—a huge canvas canopy under the arch—is an attempt to cut down on the wind-tunnel effect this gigantic building creates.

Wander behind the arch to see a cemetery and peek at the Le Corbusier–style planning, separating motor traffic (the freeway and trains that tunnel underneath) from pedestrian traffic (the sky-bridges).

Glass capsule elevators whisk you scenically up to a grand open-air view, a thrilling 20-minute movie (with English subtitles) on the mammoth construction project, and models of the arch. You can also visit an exhibit on computer history, and take advantage of its free Internet access. Don't skip the fascinating set of digital portraits by French artist Dimitri, illustrating *remanence*—"after imagery." After staring at one of these colorful portraits for 30 seconds, close your eyes and see a clear image of the face...behind your eyelids.

Cost, Hours, Location: La Grande Arche elevator and exhibits-€10, kids-€8.50, family deals, not covered by Museum Pass, daily April–Sept 10:00–20:00, Oct–March 10:00–19:00, RER or Mo: La Défense, Grande Arche, follow signs to *La Grande Arche*. Tel. 01 49 07 27 55, www.grandearche.com.

After Your Visit: If you're hungry, head over to glassy Le Dome, where you'll find good sandwiches and salads to go. Have lunch with a view on the steps of La Grande Arche.

The Esplanade: La Défense is much more than its eye-catching arch. Wander from the arch back toward the city center (and to the next Métro stop) along the Esplanade (a.k.a. "le Parvis"), the open area surrounded by skyscrapers. Take in the monumental buildings around you: Les Quatre Temps is a giant shopping mall of 250 stores, and, like malls at home, it's a teenage wasteland when school is out. The Center of New Industries and Technologies (better known as CNIT), built in 1958 and now a congress center, is a feat of modern architecture: It's the largest concrete vault anywhere that rests on only three points. The Nexity Tower (nearest central Paris) looks old compared to the other skyscrapers. Dating from the 1960s, it was one of the first buildings at La Défense.

In France, getting a building permit often comes with a requirement to dedicate two percent of the construction cost to art. Hence the Esplanade is a virtual open-air modern art gallery, sporting pieces by Joan Miró (blue), Alexander Calder (red), and Yaacov Agam (the fountain with colorful stripes and rhythmically dancing spouts), among others. *La Défense de Paris,* the statue that gave the area its name, recalls the 1871 Franco-Prussian war—it's a rare bit of old Paris out here in the 'burbs. Notice how the Wallace Fountain and *boules* courts are designed to integrate tradition into this celebration of modern commerce. Walking toward the Nexity Tower, you'll come to the Esplanade de la Défense Métro station, which zips you out of all this modernity and directly back into town.

Marais Neighborhood and Nearby

○ To connect these sights with a fun, fact-filled stroll leading from place de la Bastille to the Pompidou Center, see the Marais Walk chapter.

Don't waste time looking for the **Bastille,** the prison of Revolution fame. It's Paris' most famous nonsight. The building is long gone and just the square remains, good only for its nightlife and as a jumping-off point for the Marais Walk or Promenade Plantée Park (see page 281).

▲▲**Pompidou Center (Centre Pompidou)**—One of Europe's greatest collections of far-out modern art is housed in the Musée

National d'Art Moderne, on the fourth and fifth floors of this colorful exoskeletal building. Created ahead of its time, the 20th-century art in this collection is still waiting for the world to catch up. After so many Madonnas-and-children, a piano smashed to bits and glued to the wall is refreshing.

The Pompidou Center and the square that fronts it are lively, with lots of people, street theater, and activity inside and out—a perpetual street fair. Kids of any age enjoy the fun, colorful fountain (called *Homage to Stravinsky*) next to the Pompidou Center. Ride the escalator for a great city view from the top (ticket or Museum Pass required), and consider eating at the good mezzanine-level café.

Cost, Hours, Location: €12, free on first Sun of month, Museum Pass covers permanent collection (but not special exhibitions), €3 Panorama Ticket lets you ride to the top for the view (exhibits not included), Wed–Mon 11:00–21:00, ticket counters close at 20:00, closed Tue, Mo: Rambuteau or farther-away Hôtel de Ville. Tel. 01 44 78 12 33, www.centrepompidou.fr.

✪ See the Pompidou Center Tour chapter.

▲▲**Jewish Art and History Museum (Musée d'Art et Histoire du Judaïsme)**—This fine museum, located in a beautifully restored Marais mansion, tells the story of Judaism throughout Europe, from the Roman destruction of Jerusalem to the theft of famous artworks during World War II. Displays illustrate the cultural unity maintained by this continually dispersed population. You'll learn about the history of Jewish traditions from bar mitzvahs to menorahs, and see the exquisite traditional costumes and objects central to daily life. Don't miss the explanation of "the Dreyfus affair," a major event in early 1900s French politics. You'll also see photographs of and paintings by famous Jewish artists, including Marc Chagall, Amedeo Modigliani, and Chaim Soutine. A small but moving section is devoted to the deportation of Jews from Paris during World War II.

Helpful audioguides let you browse at your own pace, and many English explanations make this an enjoyable history lesson.

Cost, Hours, Location: €7, more during special exhibits, includes audioguide, covered by Museum Pass, Mon–Fri 11:00–

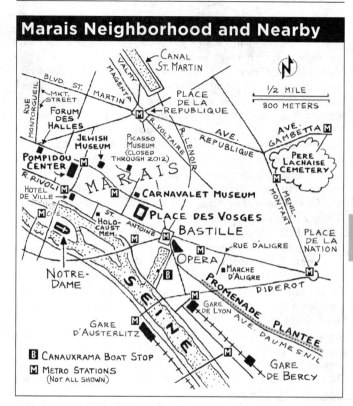

Marais Neighborhood and Nearby

18:00, Sun 10:00–18:00, last entry 45 minutes before closing, closed Sat, 71 rue du Temple, Mo: Rambuteau or Hôtel de Ville a few blocks farther away. Tel. 01 53 01 86 60, www.mahj.org.

▲▲**Picasso Museum (Musée Picasso)**—This museum contains the world's largest collection of Picasso's paintings, sculptures, sketches, and ceramics, along with his small collection of Impressionist art, all displayed in a fine old mansion. The museum is currently closed (as of August 2009) for a major renovation that will last several years.

▲▲**Carnavalet Museum (Musée Carnavalet)**—The tumultuous history of Paris—starring the Revolutionary years—is well portrayed in this converted Marais mansion. Explanations are in French only, but many displays are fairly self-explanatory. You'll see paintings of Parisian scenes, French Revolution paraphernalia, old city store signs, a small guillotine, a model of the 16th-century Ile de la Cité (notice the bridge houses), and rooms full of 17th-century Parisian furniture.

Cost, Hours, Location: Free, occasional fees for (optional) temporary exhibits, Tue–Sun 10:00–18:00, closed Mon; avoid lunchtime (12:00–14:00), when many rooms close; 23 rue de Sévigné, Mo: St. Paul. Tel. 01 44 59 58 58, www.carnavalet.paris.fr.

○ See the Carnavalet Museum Tour chapter.

Victor Hugo's House—France's literary giant lived in this house on place des Vosges from 1832 to 1848. After the phenomenal success of *The Hunchback of Notre Dame*, he moved into this nice address. You'll walk through the elegant and spacious rooms (all 10,000 square feet of them) where he wrote much of *Les Misérables* when he wasn't entertaining Paris' elite. Inside are posters advertising theater productions of his works, paintings of some of his most famous character creations, a few furnished rooms (including his bedroom and study), and fine views onto the square.

Cost, Hours, Location: Free except during special exhibits (€7, not worth paying for), Tue–Sun 10:00–18:00, last entry 20 minutes before closing, closed Mon, 6 place des Vosges. Tel. 01 42 72 10 16, www.musee-hugo.paris.fr.

Holocaust Memorial (Mémorial de la Shoah)—Commemorating the lives of the more than 76,000 Jews deported from France in World War II, this memorial's focal point is underground, where victims' ashes are buried. Displaying original deportation records, the museum takes you through the history of Jews in Europe and France, from medieval pogroms to the Nazi era (free, Sun–Fri 10:00–18:00, Thu until 22:00, closed Sat and certain Jewish holidays, 17 rue Geoffroy l'Asnier, tel. 01 42 77 44 72, www.memorialdelashoah.org). For more on the Memorial, see page 289 in the Marais Walk.

Promenade Plantée Park—This two-mile-long, narrow garden walk on a viaduct was once used for train tracks and is now a great place for a refreshing stroll. Part of the park is elevated. At times you'll walk along the street until you pick up the next segment. The shops below the viaduct's arches (a creative use of once-wasted urban space) make for entertaining window shopping.

Cost, Hours, Location: Free, opens Mon–Fri at 8:00, Sat–Sun at 9:00, closes at sunset (17:30 in winter, 21:30 in summer). It runs from place de la Bastille (Mo: Bastille) along avenue Daumesnil to Saint-Mandé (Mo: Michel Bizot). From place de la Bastille (follow signs for *Sortie Opéra* or *Sortie rue de Lyon* from Bastille Métro station), walk down rue de Lyon with the Opéra immediately on your left. Find the steps up the red brick wall a block after the Opéra.

▲Père Lachaise Cemetery (Cimetière du Père Lachaise)—Littered with the tombstones of many of the city's most illustrious dead, this is your best one-stop look at Paris' fascinating, romantic past residents. More like a small city, the cemetery is confusing, but maps and my self-guided tour will direct you to the graves of Frédéric Chopin, Molière, Edith Piaf, Oscar Wilde, Gertrude

Stein, Jim Morrison, Héloïse and Abélard, and many more. Buy the helpful €2 map at the flower stores located near either entry.

Cost, Hours, Location: Free, Mon–Sat 8:00–18:00, Sun 9:00–18:00, or until dusk if it gets dark before 18:00. It's down avenue du Père Lachaise from Mo: Gambetta (also across the street from the less-convenient Père Lachaise Métro stop and reachable via bus #69—see the Bus #69 Sightseeing Tour chapter). Tel. 01 55 25 82 10.

✪ See the Père Lachaise Cemetery Tour chapter.

Montmartre

✪ Connect these sights with the Montmartre Walk chapter.

▲▲**Sacré-Cœur and Montmartre**—This Byzantine-looking basilica, though only 130 years old, is impressive (church free, daily 7:00–23:00; €5 to climb dome, not covered by Museum Pass, daily June–Sept 9:00–19:00, Oct–May 10:00–18:00). The neighborhood's main square (place du Tertre), one block from the church, was once the haunt of Henri de Toulouse-Lautrec and the original bohemians. Today, it's mobbed with tourists and unoriginal bohemians, but it's still fun (to beat the crowds, go early in the morning).

To get to Montmartre, you have several options. You can take the Métro to the Anvers stop (to avoid the stairs up to Sacré-Cœur, buy one more Métro ticket and ride the funicular, though it's sometimes closed for maintenance). The Abbesses stop is closer but less scenic. Or you can go to place Pigalle, then take the tiny electric Montmartrobus, which drops you right by place du Tertre, near Sacré-Cœur. A taxi to the top of the hill saves time and avoids sweat (about €13, €20 at night).

Dalí Museum (L'Espace Dalí)—The museum offers an entertaining look at some of Dalí's creations (€10, not covered by Museum Pass, daily 10:00–18:30, 11 rue Poulbot, tel. 01 42 64 40 10, www.daliparis.com).

Montmartre Museum (Musée de Montmartre)—This 17th-century home re-creates the traditional cancan and cabaret

Montmartre scene, with paintings, posters, photos, music, and memorabilia (€7, includes audioguide, not covered by Museum Pass, Tue–Sun 11:00–18:00, closed Mon, 12 rue Cortot, tel. 01 49 25 89 39, www.museedemontmartre.fr).

Pigalle—Paris' red light district, the infamous "Pig Alley," is at the foot of Butte Montmartre. *Ooh la la.* It's more racy than dangerous. Walk from place Pigalle to place Blanche, teasing desperate barkers and fast-talking temptresses. In bars, a €150 bottle of cheap champagne comes with a friend. Stick to the bigger streets, hang on to your wallet, and exercise good judgment. Cancan can cost a fortune, as can con artists in topless bars. After dark, countless tour buses line the streets, reminding us that tour guides make big bucks by bringing their groups to touristy nightclubs like the famous Moulin Rouge (Mo: Pigalle or Abbesses).

Museum of Erotic Art (Musée de l'Erotisme)—Paris' sexy museum has five floors of risqué displays—mostly paintings and drawings—ranging from artistic to erotic to disgusting, with a few circa-1920 porn videos and a fascinating history of local brothels tossed in. It's in the center of the Pigalle red light district (€8, €6/person for small groups of four or more, no...it's not covered by Museum Pass, daily 10:00–2:00 in the morning, 72 boulevard de Clichy, Mo: Blanche, tel. 01 42 58 28 73, www.musee-erotisme.com).

Near Paris: Versailles

▲▲▲**Versailles**—Every king's dream, Versailles was the residence of French kings and the cultural heartbeat of Europe for about 100 years—until the Revolution of 1789 ended the notion that God deputized some people to rule for him on earth. Louis XIV spent half a year's income of Europe's  richest country to turn his dad's hunting lodge into a palace fit for a divine monarch. Louis XV and Louis XVI spent much of the 18th century gilding Louis XIV's lily. In 1837, about 50 years after the royal family was evicted, King Louis-Philippe opened the palace as a museum. Today you can visit parts of the huge palace and wander through acres of manicured gardens sprinkled with fountains and studded with statues. Europe's next-best palaces are Versailles wannabes.

Cost: The **Château,** the main palace, costs €13.50 (€10 after 15:00, under 18 free, includes audioguide). It's also covered by the Museum Pass (no audioguide) and Le Passeport Pass (includes audioguide). The **Domaine de Marie-Antoinette,** the queen's estate, costs €10 April–Oct (€6 after 16:00 and Nov–March, under 18 always free, also covered by the Museum Pass and Le Passeport). The gardens are free (but €8 on weekends April–Sept, when the fountains perform; extra charges for tours and audioguides).

Hours: The Château is open Tue–Sun April–Oct 9:00–18:30 (on Sat in summer, King's and Queen's State Apartments may be open 18:30–21:00—ask), Nov–March 9:00–17:30, closed Mon. The Domaine de Marie-Antoinette is open Tue–Sun April–Oct 12:00–18:30, Nov–March 12:00–17:30, closed Mon. The gardens are generally open daily from 9:00 to sunset (17:30–21:30), except on Sat in summer when they close at 18:00 to prepare for evening events. Last entry to all areas is one hour before closing.

Information: Tel. 08 10 81 16 14, www.chateauversailles.fr.
◐ See the Versailles Day Trip on page 486.

HISTORIC PARIS WALK

Ile de la Cité and the Latin Quarter

Paris has been the cultural capital of Europe for centuries. We'll start where it did, on Ile de la Cité, with a foray onto the Left Bank, on a walk that laces together 80 generations of history—from Celtic fishing village to Roman city, bustling medieval capital, birthplace of the Revolution, bohemian haunt of the 1920s café scene, and the working world of modern Paris. Along the way, we'll step into two of Paris' greatest sights—Notre-Dame and Sainte-Chapelle.

Orientation

Length of This Walk: Allow four hours to do justice to this three-mile walk.

Paris Museum Pass: Many sights in this walk that charge admission are covered by the Museum Pass. For many travelers, this is a great money- and time-saver, because it often lets you skip ticket lines (2 days/€32, 4 days/€48, or 6 days/€64, sold at participating sights, see page 42 for details). On the Ile de la Cité you can buy a pass at the Tabac du Palais café (5 boulevard du Palais), across the street from the entrance of Sainte-Chapelle.

Notre-Dame Cathedral: Free, daily 7:45–19:00. Treasury-€3.50, not covered by Museum Pass, daily 9:30–17:30. Audioguides cost €5. Ask about free English tours, normally Wed and Thu at 14:00, Sat at 14:30. The church's "no shorts" dress code is not strictly enforced, but at a minimum, visitors are expected to be quiet and respectful. The cathedral hosts several Masses every morning, plus Vespers at 17:45. The international Mass is on Sun at 11:30, with an organ concert at 16:30. Call or check the website for a full schedule (tel. 01 42 34 56 10,

Historic Paris Walk

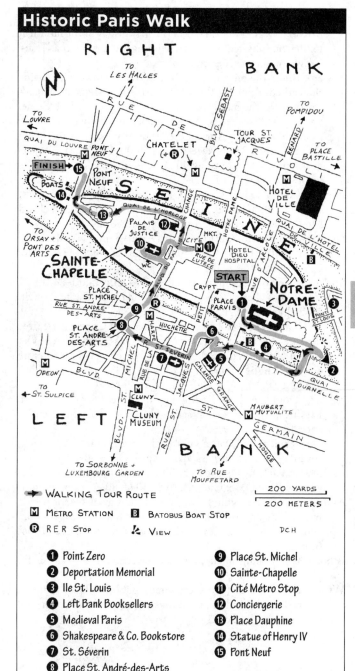

WALKING TOUR ROUTE

M METRO STATION   **B** BATOBUS BOAT STOP

R RER STOP   ⚹ VIEW

DCH

1. Point Zero
2. Deportation Memorial
3. Ile St. Louis
4. Left Bank Booksellers
5. Medieval Paris
6. Shakespeare & Co. Bookstore
7. St. Séverin
8. Place St. André-des-Arts
9. Place St. Michel
10. Sainte-Chapelle
11. Cité Métro Stop
12. Conciergerie
13. Place Dauphine
14. Statue of Henry IV
15. Pont Neuf

www.cathedraledeparis.com, Mo: Cité, Hôtel de Ville, or St. Michel). On Good Friday and the first Friday of the month at 15:00, the (physically underwhelming) relic known as Jesus' Crown of Thorns goes on display.

Tower Climb: The entrance for Notre-Dame's towers is outside the cathedral, along the left side. It's 400 steps up, but it's worth it for the gargoyle's-eye view of the cathedral, Seine, and city (€8, covered by Museum Pass, but no bypass line for passholders; daily April–Sept 10:00–18:30, also June–Aug Sat–Sun until 23:00, Oct–March 10:00–17:30, last entry 45 min before closing; to avoid crowds in peak season, arrive before 10:00 or after 17:00).

Paris Archaeological Crypt: €4, covered by Museum Pass, Tue–Sun 10:00–18:00, last entry 30 min before closing, closed Mon, enter 100 yards in front of the cathedral.

Deportation Memorial: Free, daily April–Sept 10:00–12:00 & 14:00–19:00, Oct–March 10:00–12:00 & 14:00–17:00, Mo: Cité, tel. 01 49 74 34 00.

Shakespeare and Company Bookstore: Daily 12:00–24:00, 37 rue de la Bûcherie, across the river from Notre-Dame, Mo: St. Michel, tel. 01 43 26 96 50.

Sainte-Chapelle: €8, €12.50 combo-ticket with Conciergerie, free if you're under 18, covered by Museum Pass, daily March–Oct 9:30–18:00, Nov–Feb 9:00–17:00, last entry 30 min before closing, English tours most days at 10:45 and 14:45, 4 boulevard du Palais, Mo: Cité, tel. 01 53 40 60 80, www.monum.fr. Avoid the ticket line by buying tickets or the Museum Pass from the *tabac* shop across the street from the security entrance.

Conciergerie: €7, €12.50 combo-ticket with Sainte-Chapelle, covered by Museum Pass, daily April–Oct 9:30–18:00, Nov–March 9:00–17:00, last entry 30 min before closing, 4 boulevard du Palais, Mo: Cité, tel. 01 53 40 60 80, www.monum.fr.

Audio Tour: A free audio tour of this walk is available for people with iPods and other MP3 players at www.ricksteves.com and on iTunes (search for "Rick Steves' tours" in the iTunes Store).

iPhone App: A multimedia, interactive version of this tour is for sale on iTunes.

WCs: There's a free (often crowded) public WC in front of Notre-Dame. Find others at museums (Sainte-Chapelle and Conciergerie) and cafés.

The Walk Begins

• *Start at Notre-Dame Cathedral on the island in the River Seine, the physical and historic bull's-eye of your Paris map. The closest Métro stops are Cité, Hôtel de Ville, and St. Michel, each a short walk away.*

Notre-Dame and Nearby

• *On the square in front of the cathedral, stand far enough back to take in the whole facade. Find the circular window in the center.*

For centuries, the main figure in the Christian "pantheon" has been Mary, the mother of Jesus. Catholics petition her in times

of trouble to gain comfort, and to ask her to convince God to be compassionate with them. The church is dedicated to "Our Lady" *(Notre Dame),* and there she is, cradling God, right in the heart of the facade, surrounded by the halo of the rose window. Though the church is massive and imposing, it has always stood for the grace and compassion of Mary, the "mother of God."

Imagine the faith of the people who built this cathedral. They broke ground in 1163 with the hope that someday their great-great-great-great-great-great grandchildren might attend the dedication Mass two centuries later, in 1345. Look up the 200-foot-tall bell towers and imagine a tiny medieval community mustering the money and energy for construction. Master masons supervised, but the people did much of the grunt work themselves for free—hauling the huge stones from distant quarries, digging a 30-foot-deep trench to lay the foundation, and treading like rats on a wheel designed to lift the stones up, one by one. This kind of backbreaking, arduous manual labor created the real hunchbacks of Notre-Dame.

• *"Walk this way" toward the cathedral, and view it from the bronze plaque on the ground (30 yards from the central doorway) marked...*

❶ Point Zero

You're standing at the center of France, the point from which all distances are measured. It was also the center of Paris 2,300 years ago, when the Parisii tribe fished where the east–west river crossed a north–south

Paris Through History

250 B.C.	Small fishing village of the Parisii, a Celtic tribe.
52 B.C.	Julius Caesar conquers the Parisii capital of Lutetia (near Paris), and the Romans replace it with a new capital on the Left Bank.
A.D. 497	Rome falls to the Germanic Franks. King Clovis (482–511) converts to Christianity and makes Paris his capital.
885–886	Paris gets wasted in a siege by Viking Norsemen = Normans.
1163	Notre-Dame cornerstone laid.
c. 1250	Paris is a bustling commercial city with a university and new construction, such as Sainte-Chapelle and Notre-Dame.
c. 1600	King Henry IV beautifies Paris with buildings, roads, bridges, and squares.
c. 1700	Louis XIV makes Versailles his capital. Parisians grumble.
1789	Paris is the heart of France's Revolution, which condemns thousands to the guillotine.
1804	Napoleon Bonaparte crowns himself emperor in a ceremony at Notre-Dame.
1830 & 1848	Parisians take to the streets again in revolutions, fighting the return of royalty.
c. 1860	Napoleon's nephew, Napoleon III, builds Paris' wide boulevards.
1889	The centennial of the Revolution is celebrated with the Eiffel Tower. Paris enjoys wealth and

road. The Romans conquered the Parisii and built their Temple of Jupiter where Notre-Dame stands today (52 B.C.). Then as now, the center of religious power faced the center of political power (once the Roman military, today the police station, at the far end of the square). When Rome fell, the Germanic Franks sealed their victory by replacing the temple with the Christian church of St. Etienne in the sixth century. See the outlines of the former church in the pavement (in smaller gray stones), showing what were once walls and columns, angling out from Notre-Dame to Point Zero.

The grand equestrian statue (to your right, as you face the church) is of Charlemagne ("Charles the Great," 742–814), King of the Franks, whose reign marked the birth of modern France. He briefly united Europe and was crowned the first Holy Roman

	middle-class prosperity in the belle époque (beautiful age).
1920s	After the draining Great War, Paris is a cheap place to live, attracting expatriates such as Ernest Hemingway.
1940–1944	Occupied Paris spends the war years under gray skies and gray Nazi uniforms.
1968	In May student protests and a general strike bring Paris to a halt.
1981	High-speed rail service (TGV) is inaugurated from Paris to Lyon, putting in motion a trend that would change travel patterns in France (and increase the ability of tourists to easily see more of France).
1981–1995	Under President François Mitterand, Paris' cityscape is enriched by the new Louvre Pyramid, Musée d'Orsay, La Grande Arche de la Défense, and Opéra Bastille.
1998	Playing at its home stadium, France wins the World Cup in soccer. Happy fans bring Paris to a halt.
2005	Lance Armstrong wins his seventh Tour de France.
2008	All bars, cafés, and restaurants in France become smoke-free, officially ending the era of the smoky Parisian café.
2009	Labor unions hold nationwide strikes in March to force the government to protect jobs and salaries.

HISTORIC PARIS WALK

Emperor in 800, but after his death, the kingdom was divided into what would become modern France and Germany.

Before its renovation 150 years ago, this square was much smaller, a characteristic medieval shambles facing a run-down church, surrounded by winding streets and higgledy-piggledy buildings. (Yellowed bricks in the pavement show the medieval street plan and even identify some of the buildings.) The church's huge bell towers rose above this tangle of smaller buildings, inspiring Victor Hugo's story of a deformed bell-ringer who could look down on all of Paris.

Looking two-thirds of the way up Notre-Dame's left tower, those with binoculars or good eyes can find Paris' most photographed gargoyle. Propped on his elbows on the balcony rail, he watches all the tourists in line.

• Much of Paris' history is right under your feet. Some may consider visiting it in the...

Archaeological Crypt

Two thousand years of dirt and debris have raised the city's altitude. In the crypt (entrance 100 yards in front of Notre-Dame's entrance) you can see cellars and foundations from many layers of Paris: a Roman building with central heating; a wall that didn't keep the Franks out; the main medieval road that once led grandly up the square to Notre-Dame; and even (wow) a 19th-century sewer. (For more info, see page 45.)

• Now turn your attention to the...

Notre-Dame Facade

• Look at the left doorway (the Portal of Mary) and, to the left of the door, find the statue with his head in his hands.

St. Denis

When Christianity began making converts in Roman Paris, the bishop of Paris (St. Denis) was beheaded as a warning to those forsaking the Roman gods. But those early Christians were hard to keep down. St. Denis got up, tucked his head under his arm, headed north, paused at a fountain to wash it off, and continued until he found just the right place to meet his maker. The Parisians were convinced by this miracle, Christianity gained

ground, and a church soon replaced the pagan temple.

• Above the central doorway, you'll find scenes from the Last Judgment.

Central Portal

It's the end of the world, and Christ sits on the throne of judgment (just under the arches, holding both hands up). Beneath him an angel and a demon weigh souls in the balance; the demon cheats by pressing down. It's a sculptural depiction of the good, the bad, and the ugly. The good stand to the left, gazing up to heaven. The bad ones to the right are chained up and led off to a six-hour tour of the Louvre

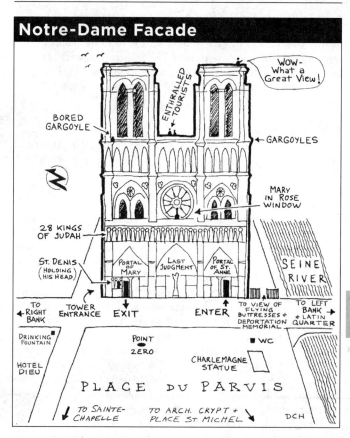

on a hot day. The ugly ones must be the crazy, sculpted demons to the right, at the base of the arch. Find the flaming cauldron with the sinner diving into it headfirst. The lower panel shows Judgment Day, as angels with trumpets remind worshippers that all social classes will be judged—clergy, nobility, army, and peasants. Below that, Jesus stands between the 12 apostles—each barefoot and with his ID symbol (such as Peter with his keys).

• *Take 10 paces back. Above the arches is a row of 28 statues, known as...*

The Kings of Judah

In the days of the French Revolution (1789–1799), these Biblical kings were mistaken for the hated French kings, and Notre-Dame represented the oppressive Catholic hierarchy. The citizens stormed the church, crying, "Off with their heads!" Plop—they lopped off the crowned heads of these kings with glee, creating a row of St. Denises that wasn't repaired for decades.

But the story doesn't end there. A schoolteacher who lived nearby collected the heads and buried them in his backyard for safekeeping. There they slept until 1977, when they were accidentally unearthed. Today, you can stare into the eyes of the original kings in the Cluny Museum, a few blocks away (see page 261).

• *Now let's head into the...*

Notre-Dame Interior

• *Enter the church at the right doorway (the Portal of St. Anne) and find a spot where you can view the long, high central aisle. (Be careful: Pickpockets attend church here religiously.)*

Nave

Remove your metaphorical hat and become a simple bareheaded peasant, entering the dim medieval light of the church. Take a minute to let your pupils dilate, then take in the subtle, mysterious light show that God beams through the stained-glass windows. Follow the slender columns up 10 stories to the praying-hands arches of the ceiling, and contemplate the heavens. Let's say it's dedication day for this great stone wonder. The priest intones the words of the Mass that echo through the hall: *Terribilis est locus iste...*"This place is *terribilis*," meaning awe-inspiring or even terrifying. It's a huge, dark, earthly cavern lit with an unearthly light.

This is Gothic. Taller and filled with light, Notre-Dame was a major improvement over the earlier Romanesque style. Gothic architects needed only a few structural columns, topped by crisscrossing pointed arches, to support the weight of the roof. This let them build higher than ever, freeing up the walls for windows.

Notre-Dame has the typical basilica floor plan shared by so many Catholic churches: a long central nave lined with columns and flanked by side aisles. It's designed in the shape of a cross, with the altar placed where the crossbeam intersects. The church can hold up to 10,000 faithful, and it's probably buzzing with visitors now, just as it was 600 years ago. The quiet, deserted churches we see elsewhere are in stark contrast to the busy, center-of-life places they were in the Middle Ages.

• *Walk up to the main altar.*

Altar

This marks the place where Mass is said and the bread and wine of Communion are blessed and distributed. In olden days, there were no chairs. This was the holy spot for Romans, Christians... and even atheists. When the Revolutionaries stormed the church, they gutted it and turned it into a "Temple of Reason." A woman dressed like the Statue of Liberty held court at the altar as a symbol of the divinity of Man. France today, though nominally Catholic,

Notre-Dame Interior

POINT ZERO •

P L A C E   D U   P A R V I S

1. St. Denis & Portal of Mary (Exit)
2. Last Judgment & Central Portal
3. Portal of St. Anne (Entrance)
4. Glass-Walled Confessional Room
5. Pietà Flanked by Louis XIII & Louis XIV
6. Joan of Arc Statue
7. North Rose Window
8. Thomas Aquinas Painting
9. Scenes of the Resurrected Jesus

remains aloof from Vatican dogmatism. Instead of traditional wooden confessional booths, there's an inviting **glass-walled room** (right aisle), where modern sinners seek counseling as much as forgiveness.

Just past the altar are the walls of the so-called "choir," the area where more intimate services can be held in this spacious building. Looking past the altar to the far end of the choir (under the cross), you'll see a fine **17th-century** *pietà,* flanked by two kneeling kings: Louis XIII (1601–1643, not so famous) and his son Louis XIV (1638–1715, very famous, also known as the Sun King, who ruled gloriously and flamboyantly from Versailles).

Right Transept (and Beyond)

A statue of **Joan of Arc** (Jeanne d'Arc, 1412–1431), dressed in armor and praying, honors the French teenager who rallied her country's soldiers to try to drive English invaders from Paris. The English and their allies burned her at the stake for claiming to hear heavenly voices. Almost immediately, Parisians rallied to condemn Joan's execution, and finally, in 1909, here in Notre-Dame, the former "witch" was beatified.

Join the statue in gazing up to the blue-and-purple, **rose-shaped window** in the opposite transept—with teeny green Mary and baby Jesus in the center—the only one of the three rose windows still with its original medieval glass.

A large painting back down to your right shows portly **Thomas Aquinas** (1225–1274) teaching, while his students drink from the fountain of knowledge. This Italian monk did undergrad and master's work at the multicultural University of Paris, then taught there for several years while writing his theological works. His "scholasticism" used Aristotle's logic to examine the Christian universe, aiming to fuse faith and reason.

• *Continue toward the far end of the church, pausing at the top of the three stair steps.*

Circling the Choir

The back side of the choir walls feature **scenes of the resurrected Jesus** (c. 1350) appearing to his followers, starting with Mary Magdalene. Their starry robes still gleam, thanks to a 19th-century renovation. The niches below these carvings mark the tombs of centuries of archbishops. Just ahead on the right is the Treasury. It contains lavish robes and golden reliquaries, but lacks English explanations and probably isn't worth the €3 entry fee. Surrounding the choir are chapels, each dedicated to a particular saint and funded by a certain guild. One chapel displays models of the church and an exhibit on medieval construction techniques—pulleys, wagons, hamster-wheel cranes, and lots of elbow grease.

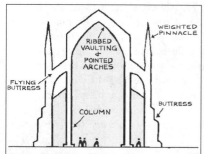

It takes 13 tourists to build a Gothic church: six columns, six buttresses, and one steeple.

The faithful can pause at any of the other chapels to light a candle as an offering, and meditate in the cool light of the stained glass.
• *Amble around the ambulatory, spill back outside, and make a slow U-turn left. Enter the park (recently renamed "Square Jean XXIII") through the iron gates along the riverside.*

Notre-Dame Side View

Alongside the church you'll notice the flying buttresses. These 50-foot stone "beams" that stick out of the church were the key to the complex Gothic architecture. The pointed arches we saw inside cause the weight of the roof to push outward rather than downward. The "flying" buttresses support the roof by pushing back inward. Gothic architects were masters at playing architectural forces against each other to build loftier and loftier

churches, with walls opened up for stained-glass windows.

Picture Quasimodo (the fictional hunchback) limping around along the railed balcony at the base of the roof among the "gar-

goyles." These grotesque beasts sticking out from pillars and buttresses represent souls caught between heaven and earth. They also function as rainspouts (from the same French root as "gargle") when there are no evil spirits to battle.

The Neo-Gothic 300-foot spire is a product of the 1860 reconstruction of the dilapidated old church. Victor Hugo's book *The Hunchback of Notre-Dame* (1831) inspired a young architecture student named Eugène-Emmanuel Viollet-le-Duc to dedicate his career to a major renovation in Gothic style. Find Viollet-le-Duc at the base of the spire among the green apostles and evangelists (visible as you approach the back end of the church). The apostles look outward, blessing the city, while the architect (at top) looks up the spire, marveling at his fine work.

• *Behind Notre-Dame, cross the street and enter through the iron gate into the park at the tip of the island. Look for the stairs and head down to reach the...*

❷ Deportation Memorial (Mémorial de la Déportation)

This memorial to the 200,000 French victims of the Nazi concentration camps (1940–1945) draws you into their experience. France was quickly overrun by Nazi Germany, and Paris spent the war years under Nazi occupation. Jews and dissidents were rounded up and deported—many never returned.

As you descend the steps, the city around you disappears. Surrounded by walls, you have become a prisoner. Your only freedom is your view of the sky and the tiny glimpse of the river below. Enter the dark, single-file chamber up ahead. Inside, the circular plaque in the floor reads, "They went to the end of the earth and did not return."

The hallway stretching in front of you is lined with 200,000 lighted crystals, one for each French citizen who died. Flickering at the far end is the eternal flame of hope. The tomb of the unknown deportee lies at your feet. Above, the inscription reads, "Dedicated

to the living memory of the 200,000 French deportees sleeping in the night and the fog, exterminated in the Nazi concentration camps." The side rooms are filled with triangles—reminiscent of the identification patches inmates were forced to wear—each bearing the name of a concentration camp. Above the exit as you leave is the message you'll find at other Holocaust sites: "Forgive, but never forget."

• *Back on street level, look across the river (north) to the island called...*

❸ Ile St. Louis

If the Ile de la Cité is a tug laden with the history of Paris, it's towing this classy little residential dinghy, laden only with high-rent apartments, boutiques, characteristic restaurants, and famous ice-cream shops.

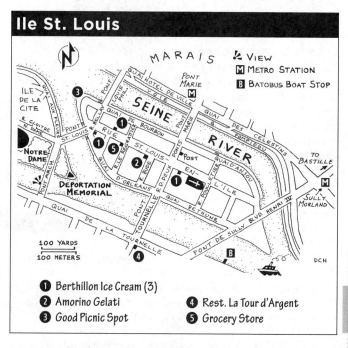

Ile St. Louis

Legend:
- ⚹ VIEW
- Ⓜ METRO STATION
- Ⓑ BATOBUS BOAT STOP

- ❶ Berthillon Ice Cream (3)
- ❷ Amorino Gelati
- ❸ Good Picnic Spot
- ❹ Rest. La Tour d'Argent
- ❺ Grocery Store

This island wasn't developed until much later than the Ile de la Cité (17th century). What was a swampy mess is now harmonious Parisian architecture and one of Paris' most exclusive neighborhoods. Its uppity residents complain that the three local Berthillon ice-cream shops draw crowds until late into the night (one is at 31 rue St. Louis-en-l'Ile, another is across the street, and there's one more around the corner on rue Bellay—see the Ile St. Louis map above). Gelato-lovers head instead to Amorino Gelati (47 rue St. Louis-en-l'Ile).

Now look upstream (east) to the bridge that links the Ile St. Louis with the Left Bank (which is now on your right). Where the bridge meets the Left Bank, you'll find one of Paris' most exclusive restaurants, La Tour d'Argent. Because the top floor has floor-to-ceiling windows, your evening meal comes with glittering views—and a golden price (allow €200 minimum, though you get a free photo of yourself dining elegantly with Notre-Dame floodlit in the background).

• *From the Deportation Memorial, cross the bridge onto the Left Bank and turn right (west). Walk along the river, toward the front end of Notre-Dame. Stairs detour down to the riverbank if you need a place to picnic. This side view of the church from across the river is one of Europe's great sights and is best from river level.*

Left Bank

❹ Left Bank Booksellers

The Rive Gauche, or the Left Bank of the Seine—"left" if you were floating downstream—still has many of the twisting lanes and narrow buildings of medieval times. The Right Bank is more modern and business-oriented, with wide boulevards and stressed Parisians in suits. Here along the riverbank, the "big business" is secondhand books, displayed in the green metal stalls on the parapet. These literary entrepreneurs pride themselves on their easygoing style. With flexible hours and virtually no overhead, they run their businesses as they have since medieval times. For more information, see the *"Les Bouquinistes (Riverside Vendors)"* sidebar on page 435.

• *When you reach the bridge (pont au Double) that crosses over in front of Notre-Dame, veer to the left across the street to a small park (place Viviani; fill your water bottle from fountain on left).*

Angle across the square and pass by Paris' oldest inhabitant—an acacia tree nicknamed Robinier, after the guy who planted it in 1602. Imagine that this same tree might once have shaded the Sun King, Louis XIV. Just beyond the tree you'll find the small rough-stone church of St. Julien-le-Pauvre.

❺ Medieval Paris (1000–1400)

Picture Paris in 1250, when the church of St. Julien-le-Pauvre was still new. Notre-Dame was nearly done (so they thought), Sainte-Chapelle had just opened, the university was expanding human knowledge, and Paris was fast becoming a prosperous industrial and commercial center. The area around the church gives you some of the medieval feel. From the door of the church, you can see half-timbered and whitewashed architecture from that era. Looking along nearby rue Galande, you'll see a few old houses leaning every which way. In medieval days, people were piled on top of each other, building at all angles, as they scrambled for this prime real estate near the main commercial artery of the day—the Seine. The smell of fish competed with the smell of neighbors in this knot of humanity.

Narrow dirt (or mud) streets sloped from here down into the mucky Seine, until the 19th century, when modern quays and embankments cleaned everything up.

• *Return to the river and turn left on rue de la Bûcherie. At #37, drop into the...*

❻ Shakespeare and Company Bookstore

In addition to hosting butchers and fishmongers, the Left Bank has been home to scholars, philosophers, and poets since medieval times. This funky bookstore—a reincarnation of the original shop from the 1920s—has picked up the literary torch. Sylvia Beach, an American with a passion for free thinking, opened Shakespeare and Company for the post-WWI Lost Generation, who came to Paris to find themselves. American writers flocked here for the cheap rent, fleeing the uptight, Prohibition-era United States. Beach's bookstore was famous as a meeting place for Paris' literary expatriate elite. Ernest Hemingway borrowed

books from here regularly. James Joyce struggled to find a publisher for his now-classic novel *Ulysses*—until Sylvia Beach published it. George Bernard Shaw, Gertrude Stein, and Ezra Pound also got their English fix here.

Today, the bookstore carries on that literary tradition. Struggling writers are given free accommodations upstairs in tiny rooms with views of Notre-Dame. Downstairs, travelers enjoy a great selection of used English books.

Notice the green water fountain (1900) in front of the bookstore, one of the many in Paris donated by the English philanthropist Sir Richard Wallace. The hooks below the caryatids once held metal mugs for drinking the water.

• *Continue to rue du Petit-Pont (which becomes rue St. Jacques). This bustling north–south boulevard was the Romans' busiest street 2,000 years ago, with chariots racing in and out of the city. (Roman-iacs can view remains from the third-century baths, along with a fine medieval collection, at the nearby Cluny Museum, located near the corner of boulevards St. Michel and St. Germain; see the Cluny Museum Tour chapter.)*

Walking away from the river for one block up a broad road that has cut straight through Paris since Roman times, turn right at the Gothic church of St. Séverin and walk into the Latin Quarter.

❼ St. Séverin

Don't ask me why, but it took a century longer to build this church than Notre-Dame. This is Flamboyant, or "flame-like," Gothic, and you can see the short, prickly spires meant to make this building flicker in the eyes of the faithful. The church gives us a close-up look at gargoyles, the decorative drain spouts that also functioned to keep evil spirits away.

Inside you can see the final stage of Gothic, on the cusp of the Renaissance. The stained-glass windows favor the greens and reds popular in St. Séverin's heyday. In the apse, admire the lone twisted Flamboyant Gothic column and the fan vaulting. The impressive organ filling the back wall is a reminder that this church is still a popular venue for evening concerts (see gate for information posters, buy tickets at door).

• *At #22 rue St. Séverin, you'll find the skinniest house in Paris, two windows wide. Rue St. Séverin leads right through...*

The Latin Quarter

Although it may look more like the Greek Quarter today (cheap gyros abound), this area is the Latin Quarter, named for the language you'd have heard on these streets if you walked them in the Middle Ages. The University of Paris (founded 1215), one of the leading educational institutions of medieval Europe, was (and still is) nearby.

A thousand years ago, the "crude" or vernacular local languages were sophisticated enough to communicate basic human needs, but if you wanted to get philosophical, the language of choice was Latin. Medieval Europe's class of educated elite transcended nations and borders. From Sicily to Sweden, they spoke and corresponded in Latin. Now the most "Latin" thing about this area is the beat you may hear coming from some of the subterranean jazz clubs.

Walking along rue St. Séverin, you can still see the shadow of the medieval sewer system. The street slopes into a central channel of bricks. In the days before plumbing and toilets, when people still went to the river or neighborhood wells for their water, flushing meant throwing it out the window. At certain times of day, maids on the fourth floor would holler, *"Garde de l'eau!"* ("Watch out for the water!") and heave it into the streets, where it would eventually wash down into the Seine.

As you wander, remember that before Napoleon III commissioned Baron Haussmann to modernize the city with grand boulevards (19th century), Paris was just like this—a medieval tangle. The ethnic feel of this area is nothing new—it's been a

melting pot and university district for almost 800 years.
• *Keep wandering straight, and you'll come to...*

Boulevard St. Michel

Busy boulevard St. Michel (or "boul' Miche") is famous as the main artery for Paris' café and artsy scene, culminating a block away (to the left) at the intersection with boulevard St. Germain. Although nowadays you're more likely to find pantyhose at 30 percent off, there are still many cafés, boutiques, and bohemian haunts nearby.

The Sorbonne—the University of Paris' humanities department—is also nearby, if you want to make a detour, though visitors are not allowed to enter. (Turn left on boulevard St. Michel and walk two blocks south. Gaze at the dome from the place de la Sorbonne courtyard.) Originally founded as a theological school, the Sorbonne began attracting more students and famous professors—such as St. Thomas Aquinas and Peter Abélard—as its prestige grew. By the time the school expanded to include other subjects, it had a reputation for bold new ideas. Nonconformity is a tradition here, and Paris remains a world center for new intellectual trends.
• *Cross boulevard St. Michel. Just ahead is...*

❽ Place St. André-des-Arts

This tree-filled square is lined with cafés. In Paris, most serious thinking goes on in cafés. For centuries these have been social watering holes, where you can get a warm place to sit and stimulating conversation for the price of a cup of coffee. Every great French writer—from Voltaire and Jean-Jacques Rousseau to Jean-Paul Sartre and Jacques Derrida—had a favorite haunt.

Paris honors its writers. If you visit the Panthéon (described on page 64)—a few blocks up boulevard St. Michel and to the left—you will find French writers (Voltaire, Victor Hugo, Emile Zola, and Rousseau), inventors (Louis Braille), and scientists (including Marie and Pierre Curie) buried in a setting usually reserved for warriors and politicians.
• *Adjoining this square toward the river is the triangular place St. Michel, with a Métro stop and a statue of St. Michael killing a devil. Note: If you were to continue west along rue St. André-des-Arts, you'd find more Left Bank action.*

❾ Place St. Michel

You're standing at the traditional core of the Left Bank's artsy, liberal, hippie, bohemian district of poets, philosophers, and winos. Nearby, you'll find international eateries, far-out bookshops, street singers, pale girls in black berets, jazz clubs, and—these days—tourists. Small cinemas show avant-garde films, almost always in the *version originale* (v.o.). For colorful wandering and café-sitting, afternoons and evenings are best. In the morning, it feels sleepy. The Latin Quarter stays up late and sleeps in.

In less commercial times, place St. Michel was a gathering point for the city's malcontents and misfits. In 1830, 1848, and again in 1871, the citizens took the streets from the government troops, set up barricades *Les Miz*–style, and fought against royalist oppression. During World War II, the locals rose up against their Nazi oppressors (read the plaques under the dragons at the foot of the St. Michel fountain).

In the spring of 1968, a time of social upheaval all over the world, young students battled riot batons and tear gas, took over the square, and declared it an independent state. Factory workers followed their call to arms and went on strike, challenging the de Gaulle government and forcing change. Eventually, the students were pacified, the university was reformed, and the Latin Quarter's original cobblestones were replaced with pavement, so future scholars could never again use the streets as weapons. Even today, whenever there's a student demonstration, it starts here.

• *From place St. Michel, look across the river and find the spire of the Sainte-Chapelle church, with its weathervane angel nearby. Cross the river on pont St. Michel and continue north along the boulevard du Palais. On your left, you'll see the doorway to Sainte-Chapelle. You'll need to pass through a metal detector to get into the Sainte-Chapelle complex. This is more than a tourist attraction—you're entering the courtyard of France's Supreme Court (to the right of Sainte-Chapelle). Once you're past the extremely strict security, you'll find restrooms ahead on the left. The line into the church may be long (but you can bypass it with a Museum Pass).*

Enter the humble ground floor (pick up an English info flier and check the concert schedule if you're interested).

Sainte-Chapelle and Nearby

❿ Sainte-Chapelle

This triumph of Gothic church architecture is a cathedral of glass like no other. It was speedily built between 1242 and 1248 for King Louis IX—the only French king who is now a saint—to house the supposed Crown of Thorns (now kept at Notre-Dame and shown only on Good Friday and on the first Friday of the month at 15:00). Its architectural harmony is due to the fact that it was

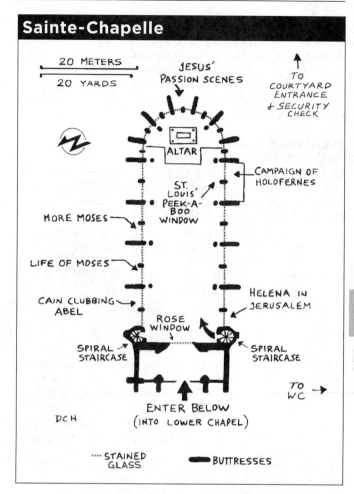

Sainte-Chapelle

20 METERS
20 YARDS

JESUS' PASSION SCENES

TO COURTYARD ENTRANCE & SECURITY CHECK

ALTAR

CAMPAIGN OF HOLOFERNES

ST. LOUIS' PEEK-A-BOO WINDOW

MORE MOSES

LIFE OF MOSES

CAIN CLUBBING ABEL

HELENA IN JERUSALEM

ROSE WINDOW

SPIRAL STAIRCASE

SPIRAL STAIRCASE

TO WC →

DCH

ENTER BELOW (INTO LOWER CHAPEL)

···· STAINED GLASS   ◼◼ BUTTRESSES

completed under the direction of one architect and in only five years—unheard of in Gothic times. Recall that Notre-Dame took over 200 years.

Though the inside is beautiful, the exterior is basically functional. The muscular buttresses hold up the stone roof, so the walls are essentially there to display stained glass. The lacy spire is Neo-Gothic—added in the 19th century. Inside, the layout clearly shows an *ancien régime* approach to worship. The low-ceilinged basement was for staff and other common folks—worshipping under a sky filled with painted fleurs-de-lis, a symbol of the king. Royal Christians worshiped upstairs. The paint job, a 19th-century restoration, helps you imagine how grand this small, painted, jeweled chapel was. (Imagine Notre-Dame painted like this...) Each capital is playfully carved with a different plant's leaves.

• *Climb the spiral staircase to the Chapelle Haute. Leave the rough stone of the earth and step into the light.*

The Stained Glass

Fiat lux. "Let there be light." From the first page of the Bible, it's clear: Light is divine. Light shines through stained glass like God's grace shining down to earth. Gothic architects used their new technology to turn dark stone buildings into lanterns of light. The glory of Gothic shines brighter here than in any other church.

There are 15 separate panels of stained glass (6,500 square feet—two thirds of it 13th-century original), with more than 1,100 different scenes, mostly from the Bible. These cover the entire Christian history of the world, from the Creation in Genesis (first window on the left, as you face the altar), to the coming of Christ (over the altar), to the end of the world (the round "rose"-shaped window at the rear of the church). Each individual scene is interesting, and the whole effect is overwhelming. Allow yourself a few minutes to bask in the glow of the colored light before tackling the window descriptions below, then remember to keep referring to the map to find the windows.

• *Working clockwise from the entrance, look for these worthwhile scenes. (Note: The sun lights up different windows at various times of day. Overcast days give the most even light. On bright, sunny days, some sections are glorious, while others look like a sheet of lead.)*

Genesis—Cain Clubbing Abel (first window on the left, always dark because of a building butted up against it): On the bottom level in the third circle from the left, we see God create the round earth and hold it up. On the next level up, we catch glimpses of naked Adam and Eve. On the third level (far right circle), Cain, in red, clubs his brother Abel, creating murder.

Life of Moses (second window, the bottom row of diamond panels): The first panel shows baby Moses in a basket, placed by his sister in the squiggly brown river. Next he's found by the pharaoh's daughter. Then he grows up. And finally, he's a man, a prince of Egypt on his royal throne.

More Moses (third window, in middle and upper sections):

Stained Glass Supreme

Craftsmen made glass—which is, essentially, melted sand—using this recipe:

- Melt one part sand with two parts wood ash.
- Mix in rusty metals to get different colors—iron makes red; cobalt makes blue; copper, green; manganese, purple; cadmium, yellow.
- Blow glass into a cylinder shape, cut lengthwise, and lay flat.
- Cut into pieces with an iron tool, or by heating and cooling a select spot to make it crack.
- Fit pieces together to form a figure, using strips of lead to hold them in place.
- Place masterpiece so high on a wall that no one can read it.

You'll see various scenes of Moses, the guy with the bright yellow horns—the result of a medieval mistranslation of the Hebrew word for "rays of light," or halo.

Jesus' Passion Scenes (over the altar): These scenes from Jesus' arrest and crucifixion were the backdrop for the Crown of Thorns (originally displayed on the altar), which was placed on Jesus' head when the Romans were torturing and humiliating him before his execution. Stand a few steps back from the altar to look through the canopy and find Jesus in yellow shorts, carrying his cross (fifth frame up from right bottom). A little below that, see Jesus being whipped (left) and—the key scene in this relic chapel—Jesus in purple, being fitted with the painful Crown of Thorns (right). Finally (as high as you can see), Jesus on the cross is speared by a soldier (trust me).

Campaign of Holofernes (window to the right of the altar

wall): On the bottom row are four scenes of colorful knights (refer to map to get oriented). The second circle from the left is a battle scene (the campaign of Holofernes), showing three soldiers with swords slaughtering three men. The background is blue. The men have different-colored clothes—red, blue, green, mauve, and white. Examine some of the details. You can see the folds in the robes, the hair, and facial features. Look at the victim in the center—his head is splotched with blood. Details like the folds in the robes (see the victim in white, lower left) came about either by scratching on the glass or by baking on paint. It was a painstaking process of finding just the right colors, fitting them together to make a scene...and then multiplying by 1,100.

Helena in Jerusalem (first window on the right wall by entrance): This window tells the story of how Christ's Crown of Thorns found its way from Jerusalem to Constantinople to this chapel. Start in the lower-left corner, where the Roman emperor Constantine (in blue, on his throne) waves goodbye to his Christian mom, Helena. She arrives at the gate of Jerusalem (next panel to the right). Her men (in the two-part medallion above Jerusalem) dig through ruins and find Christ's (tiny) cross and other relics. She returns to Constantinople with a stash of holy relics, including the Crown of Thorns. Nine hundred years later, French Crusader knights (the next double medallion above) invade the Holy Land and visit Constantinople. Finally, King Louis IX, dressed in blue (in the panel up one and to the right of the last one), returns to France with the sacred relic.

Rose Window (above entrance): It's Judgment Day, with a tiny Christ in the center of the chaos and miracles. This window, from the Flamboyant period, is 200 years newer than the rest. Facing west and the sunset, it's best late in the day.

If you can't read much into the individual windows, you're not alone. (For some tutoring, a little book with color photos is on sale downstairs with the postcards.)

HISTORIC PARIS WALK

Altar

The altar was raised up high to better display the Crown of Thorns, the relic around which this chapel was built. Notice the staircase: Access was limited to the priest and the king, who wore the keys to the shrine around his neck. Also note that there is no high-profile image of Jesus anywhere—this chapel was all about the Crown.

King Louis IX, convinced he'd found the real McCoy, paid £135,000 for the Crown, £100,000 for the gem-studded shrine to display it in (destroyed in the French Revolution), and a mere £40,000 to build Sainte-Chapelle to house it. Today, the supposed Crown of Thorns is kept by the Notre-Dame Treasury (though it's occasionally brought out for display).

Lay your camera on the ground and shoot the ceiling. Those pure and

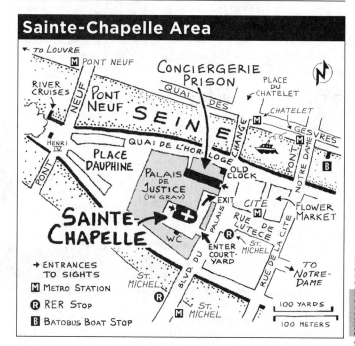

Sainte-Chapelle Area

TO LOUVRE
PONT NEUF
CONCIERGERIE PRISON
PLACE DU CHATELET
RIVER CRUISES
PONT NEUF
QUAI DES
SEINE
CHATELET
GESVRES
HENRI IV
QUAI DE L'HOR-LOGE
CHANGE
PLACE DAUPHINE
PALAIS DE JUSTICE (IN GRAY)
OLD CLOCK
NOTRE DAME
PONT
FLOWER MARKET
SAINTE-CHAPELLE
EXIT
CITE
RUE DE LUTECE
WC
ENTER COURT-YARD
ST. MICHEL
RUE DE LA CITE
TO NOTRE-DAME
→ ENTRANCES TO SIGHTS
Ⓜ METRO STATION
Ⓡ RER STOP
Ⓑ BATOBUS BOAT STOP
ST. MICHEL
BLVD DU PALAIS
ST. MICHEL
100 YARDS
100 METERS

simple ribs growing out of the slender columns are the essence of Gothic structure.

• *Exit Sainte-Chapelle. Back outside, as you walk around the church exterior, look down to see the foundation and take note of how much Paris has risen in the 750 years since Sainte-Chapelle was built.*

Next door to Sainte-Chapelle is the...

Palais de Justice

Sainte-Chapelle sits within a huge complex of buildings that has housed the local government since ancient Roman times. It was the site of the original Gothic palace of the early kings of France. The only surviving medieval parts are Sainte-Chapelle and the Conciergerie prison.

Most of the site is now covered by the giant Palais de Justice,

built in 1776, home of the French Supreme Court. The motto *Liberté, Egalité, Fraternité* over the doors is a reminder that this was also the headquarters of the Revolutionary government. Here they doled out justice, condemning many to imprisonment in the Conciergerie downstairs

or to the guillotine.
• *Now pass through the big iron gate to the noisy boulevard du Palais. Cross the street to the wide, pedestrian-only rue de Lutèce and walk about halfway down.*

⓫ Cité "Metropolitain" Métro Stop

Of the 141 original early-20th-century subway entrances, this is one of only a few survivors—now preserved as a national art treasure. (New York's Museum of Modern Art even exhibits one.) It marks Paris at its peak in 1900—on the cutting edge of Modernism, but with an eye for beauty. The curvy, plantlike ironwork is a textbook example of Art Nouveau, the style that rebelled against the erector-set squareness of the Industrial Age. Other similar Métro stations in Paris are Abbesses and Porte Dauphine.

The flower and plant market on place Louis Lépine is a pleasant detour. On Sundays this square flutters with a busy bird market. And across the way is the Préfecture de Police, where Inspector Clouseau of *Pink Panther* fame used to work, and where the local resistance fighters took the first building from the Nazis in August of 1944, leading to the Allied liberation of Paris a week later.
• *Pause here to admire the view. Sainte-Chapelle is a pearl in an ugly architectural oyster. Double back to the Palais de Justice, turn right onto boulevard du Palais, and enter the...*

⓬ Conciergerie

Though pretty barren inside, this former prison echoes with history (and is free with the Museum Pass—remember that passholders can skip any ticket-buying lines). Positioned next to the courthouse, the Conciergerie was the gloomy prison famous as the last stop for 2,780 victims of the guillotine, including France's last *ancien régime* queen, Marie-Antoinette. Before then, kings had used the building to torture and execute failed assassins. (One of its towers along the river was called "The Babbler," named for the pain-induced sounds that leaked from it.) When the Revolution (1789) toppled the king, the building kept its same function, but without torture. The progressive Revolutionaries proudly unveiled a modern and more humane way to execute people—the guillotine.

Inside, pick up a free map and breeze through. See the spacious, low-ceilinged Hall of Men-at-Arms (Room 1), used as the guards' dining room, with four large fireplaces (look up the chimneys). This big room gives a feel for the grandeur of the Great Hall (upstairs, not open to visitors), where the Revolutionary tribunals grilled scared prisoners on their political correctness. The raised area at the far end of the room (Room 4, today's bookstore) was notorious as the walkway of the executioner, who was known affectionately as "Monsieur de Paris."

Pass through the bookstore to find the Office of the Keeper, or "Concierge" of the place (who monitored torture...and recommended nearby restaurants). Next door is the *Toilette*, where condemned prisoners combed their hair or touched up their lipstick before their final public appearance—waiting for the open-air cart (tumbrel) to pull up outside. The tumbrel would carry them to the guillotine, which was on place de la Concorde.

Upstairs is a memorial room with the names of the 2,780 citizens condemned to death by the guillotine. Here are some of the people you'll find, in alphabetical order: Anne Elisabeth Capet, whose crime was being "sister of the tyrant"; Charlotte Corday *("dite d'Armais"),* a noblewoman who snuck into the bathroom of the revolutionary writer Jean-Paul Marat and stabbed him while he bathed; Georges Danton, a prominent revolutionary who was later condemned for being insufficiently liberal—a nasty crime; Louis XVI (called "Capet: last king of France"), who deserves only a modest mention, as does his wife, Marie-Antoinette (*veuve* means she's widowed); and finally—oh, the irony—Maximilien de Robespierre, the head of the Revolution, the man who sent so many to the guillotine. He was eventually toppled, humiliated, imprisoned here, and beheaded.

Head down the hallway. Along the way, you'll see some reconstructed cells with mannequins that show how the poor slept on straw, whereas the wealthy got a cot.

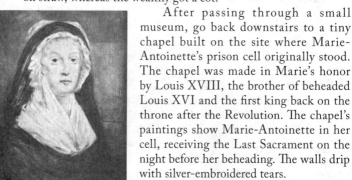

After passing through a small museum, go back downstairs to a tiny chapel built on the site where Marie-Antoinette's prison cell originally stood. The chapel was made in Marie's honor by Louis XVIII, the brother of beheaded Louis XVI and the first king back on the throne after the Revolution. The chapel's paintings show Marie-Antoinette in her cell, receiving the Last Sacrament on the night before her beheading. The walls drip with silver-embroidered tears.

The tour continues outside in the courtyard, where female prisoners were allowed a little fresh air (notice the spikes still guarding from above). In the corner, a door leads to a re-creation of Marie-Antoinette's cell. Imagine the queen spending her last days—separated from her 10-year-old son, and now widowed because the king had already been executed. Mannequins, period furniture, and the real cell wall-paper set the scene. The guard stands modestly behind a screen, while the queen psyches herself up with a crucifix. In the glass display case, see her actual cruci-fix, napkin, and small water pitcher. On October 16, 1793, the queen walked the corridor, stepped onto the cart, and was slowly carried to place de la Concorde, where she had a date with "Monsieur de Paris." Before you leave, check out the video in the next room, which gives a taste of prison life during the Reign of Terror.

• *Back outside, turn left on boulevard du Palais and head toward the river (north). On the corner is the city's oldest public clock. The mechanism of the present clock is from 1334, and even though the case is Baroque, it keeps on ticking.*

Turn left onto quai de l'Horloge and walk west along the river, past the round medieval tower called "The Babbler." The bridge up ahead is the pont Neuf, where we'll end this walk. At the first corner, veer left into a sleepy triangular square called...

⓭ Place Dauphine

It's amazing to find such coziness in the heart of Paris. This city of two million is still a city of neighborhoods, a collection of villages. The French Supreme Court building looms behind like a giant marble gavel. Enjoy the village-Paris feeling in the park. The **Caveau du Palais** restaurant is a nice spot for a drink or light meal. You may see lawyers on their lunch break playing *boules* (see sidebar on page 360).

• *Continue through place Dauphine. As you pop out the other end, you're face to face with a...*

⓮ Statue of Henry IV

Henry IV (1553–1610) is not as famous as his grandson, Louis XIV, but Henry helped make Paris what it is today—a European capital of elegant buildings and quiet squares. He built the place Dauphine (behind you), the pont Neuf (to the right), residences (to the left, down rue Dauphine), the Louvre's long Grand Gallery (down-river on the right), and the tree-filled square Vert-Galant (directly behind the statue, on the tip of the island). The square is one of Paris' make-out spots; its name comes from Henry's nickname, the Green Knight, as Henry was a notorious ladies' man. The park is a great place to relax, dangling your legs over the concrete prow of this boat-shaped island.

• *From the statue, turn right onto the old bridge. Pause at the little nook halfway across.*

⑮ Pont Neuf

This "new bridge" is now Paris' oldest. Built during Henry IV's reign (about 1600), its arches span the widest part of the river. Unlike other bridges, this one never had houses or buildings growing on it. The turrets were originally for vendors and street entertainers. In the days of Henry IV, who promised his peasants "a chicken in every pot every Sunday," this would have been a lively scene. From the bridge, look downstream (west) to see the next bridge, the pedestrian-only pont des Arts. Ahead on the Right Bank is the long Louvre Museum. Beyond that, on the Left Bank, is the Orsay. And what's that tall black tower in the distance?

The Seine

Our walk ends where Paris began—on the Seine River. From Dijon to the English Channel, the Seine meanders 500 miles, cutting through the center of Paris. The river is shallow and slow within the city, but still dangerous enough to require steep stone embankments (built 1910) to prevent occasional floods.

In summer, the roads that run along the river are replaced with acres of sand, as well as beach chairs and tanned locals, creating Paris Plage (see page 50). The success of the Paris Plage event has motivated some city officials to propose the permanent removal of vehicles from those fast lanes—turning them into riverside parks instead.

Any time of year, you'll see tourist boats and the commercial barges that carry 20 percent of Paris' transported goods. And on the banks, sportsmen today cast into the waters once fished by Paris' original Celtic inhabitants.

• *We're done. You can take a boat tour that leaves from near the base of pont Neuf on the island side (Vedettes du Pont Neuf, €12, tip requested, departs hourly on the hour, 2/hr after dark, has live guide with explanations in French and English).*

Or you could take my walking tour of the Left Bank, which begins one bridge downriver (see the Left Bank Walk chapter). You can also catch the Métro to anywhere in Paris (the nearest stop is Pont Neuf, across the bridge on the Right Bank) or hop on the #69 bus (cross pont Neuf, turn left on the quai du Louvre, and find the bus stop; see the Bus #69 Sightseeing Tour chapter). In fact, you can go anywhere—you're standing in the heart of Paris.

LOUVRE TOUR

Musée du Louvre

Paris walks you through world history in three world-class museums—the Louvre (ancient world to 1850), the Orsay (1848–1914, including Impressionism), and the Pompidou (20th century to today). Start your "art-yssey" at the Louvre. With more than 30,000 works of art, the Louvre is a full inventory of Western civilization. To cover it all in one visit is impossible. Let's focus on the Louvre's specialties—Greek sculpture, Italian painting, and French painting.

We'll see "Venuses" through history, from the curvy *Venus de Milo* to the wind-blown *Winged Victory of Samothrace*, from placid medieval Madonnas to the *Mona Lisa* to the symbol of modern democracy. We'll see how each generation defined beauty differently, and gain insight into long-ago civilizations by admiring what they found beautiful.

In addition, those with a little more time can visit some impressive chunks of stone from the "Cradle of Civilization," modern-day Iraq.

Orientation

Cost: €9, €6 after 18:00 on Wed and Fri, free on first Sun of month, covered by Museum Pass. Tickets good all day; reentry allowed. Optional additional charges apply for temporary exhibits.

Hours: Wed–Mon 9:00–18:00, most wings stay open Wed and Fri until 21:45 (except on holidays), closed Tue. Galleries start shutting down 30 minutes early. The last entry is 45 minutes before closing.

When to Go: Crowds are worst on Sun, Mon, Wed, and mornings. Evening visits are peaceful, and the glass pyramid glows after dark.

Getting There: You have a variety of options:

By Métro: The Métro stop Palais Royal–Musée du Louvre is closer to the entrance than the stop called Louvre-Rivoli. From the Palais Royal–Musée du Louvre stop, you can stay underground to enter the museum, or exit above ground if you want to go in through the pyramid (more details below).

By Bus: Handy bus #69 runs every 10–20 minutes. Buses headed west from the Marais drop off passengers next to the Palais Royal–Musée du Louvre Métro stop on rue de Rivoli. Buses headed east from rue Cler drop off along the Seine River (at quai François Mitterand). Note that bus #69 stops running after 21:30 and there is no service on Sundays.

By Taxi: You'll find a taxi stand on rue de Rivoli, next to the Palais Royal–Musée du Louvre Métro station.

Getting In: Enter through the pyramid, or opt for shorter lines elsewhere.

Main Pyramid Entrance: There is no grander entry than through the main entrance at the pyramid in the central courtyard, but metal detectors (not ticket-buyers) can create a long line.

Museum Pass/Group Entrance: Museum Pass–holders can use the group entrance in the pedestrian passageway (labeled *Pavilion Richelieu*) between the pyramid and rue de Rivoli. It's under the arches, a few steps north of the pyramid; find the uniformed guard at the security checkpoint entrance, at the down escalator.

Underground Mall Entrance: You can enter the Louvre from its less crowded underground entrance, accessed through the Carrousel du Louvre shopping mall. Enter the mall at 99 rue de Rivoli (the door with the red awning) or directly from the Métro stop Palais Royal–Musée du Louvre (stepping off the train, exit at the end of the platform, following signs to *Musée du Louvre–Le Carrousel du Louvre*).

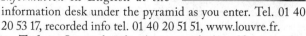

Information: Pick up the free *Plan/ Information* in English at the information desk under the pyramid as you enter. Tel. 01 40 20 53 17, recorded info tel. 01 40 20 51 51, www.louvre.fr.

Buying Tickets: Located under the pyramid, the self-serve ticket machines are faster to use than the ticket windows (machines accept euro notes, coins, and Visa cards). The *tabac* in the underground mall at the Louvre sells tickets to the Louvre,

LOUVRE

Orsay, and Versailles, plus Paris Museum Passes, for no extra charge.

Tours: Ninety-minute English-language **guided tours** leave twice daily except Sun from the *Accueil des Groupes* area, under the pyramid between the Sully and Denon wings (normally at 11:00 and 14:00; €5 plus your entry ticket, tour tel. 01 40 20 52 63). Digital **audioguides** provide eager students with commentary on about 130 masterpieces (€6, available at entries to the three wings, at the top of the escalators). I prefer the self-guided tour described below, which is also available as an **iPhone app,** and as a **free audio tour** for people with iPods and other MP3 players (download from www.ricksteves.com or search for "Rick Steves' tours" in iTunes). You'll also find English explanations throughout the museum.

Length of This Tour: Allow at least two hours.

Baggage Check and WCs: Baggage storage and WCs are located under the escalators to the Denon and Richelieu wings (WCs are scarce once you're in the galleries). Purses and small day bags are okay, but large bags are not allowed. Check these (as well as any small bags to lighten your load) for free. The baggage storage *(Bagagerie)* will not take coats unless they're stuffed into bags. The cloakroom *(Vestiaire)* takes only coats and can have long lines (worst early in the morning and late afternoon). The baggage claim person might ask you in French, "Does your bag contain anything of value?" You can't check cameras, money, passports, or other valuables.

Cuisine Art: The Louvre has several cafés, including **Café Mollien,** located near the end of our tour (€12 for sandwich and drink on terrace overlooking pyramid; see page 130). A reasonably priced self-service lunch **cafeteria** (€9 *plats du jour*) is just up the escalator from the pyramid in the Richelieu wing. But your best bet is in the underground shopping mall, the **Carrousel du Louvre** (daily 8:30–23:00), which has a dizzying assortment of decent-value, multiethnic fast-food eateries, including—*quelle horreur*—a new McDonald's (west of the pyramid and up the escalator near the inverted pyramid). The mall also has glittering boutiques, a post office (after passing security), a La Maison du Chocolat store, and a Métro entrance (Mo: Palais Royal–Musée du Louvre). Stairs at the far end take you right into the Tuileries Garden, a perfect antidote to the stuffy, crowded rooms of the Louvre.

For a fine, elegant lunch near the Louvre, head to the venerable **Café le Nemours** (€11 salads, open daily; leaving the Louvre, cross rue de Rivoli and veer left to 2 place Colette, adjacent to Comédie Française; see Eating chapter, page 420).

LOUVRE

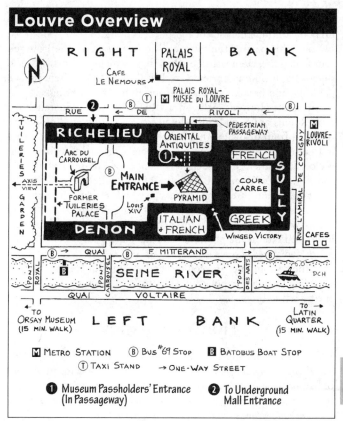

Louvre Overview

RIGHT BANK

PALAIS ROYAL

CAFE LE NEMOURS

PALAIS ROYAL-MUSÉE DU LOUVRE

RUE **2** DE RIVOLI

PEDESTRIAN PASSAGEWAY

RICHELIEU

ORIENTAL ANTIQUITIES **1**

FRENCH

ARC DU CARROUSEL

MAIN **ENTRANCE** ➡ PYRAMID

COUR CARREE

S U L L Y

FORMER TUILERIES PALACE

LOUIS XIV

ITALIAN & FRENCH

GREEK

WINGED VICTORY

DENON

TUILERIES GARDEN

AXIS VIEW

QUAI F. MITTERAND

PONT ROYAL

PONT CARROUSEL

SEINE RIVER

PONT DES ARTS

PCH

QUAI VOLTAIRE

TO ORSAY MUSEUM (15 MIN. WALK)

LEFT BANK

TO LATIN QUARTER (15 MIN. WALK)

RUE DE COLIGNY

RUE L'AMIRAL DE COLIGNY

LOUVRE-RIVOLI

CAFES

- Ⓜ METRO STATION Ⓑ BUS #69 STOP Ⓑ BATOBUS BOAT STOP
- Ⓣ TAXI STAND → ONE-WAY STREET

❶ Museum Passholders' Entrance (In Passageway)   **❷** To Underground Mall Entrance

Photography: Photography without a flash is allowed. (Flash photography damages paintings and distracts viewers.)

Starring: *Venus de Milo*, *Winged Victory*, *Mona Lisa*, Leonardo da Vinci, Raphael, Michelangelo, the French painters, and many of the most iconic images of Western civilization.

Surviving the Louvre

Start by picking up a free map at the information desk and orienting yourself from underneath the glass pyramid.

The Louvre, the largest museum in the Western world, fills three wings of this immense, U-shaped palace. The **Richelieu wing** (north side) houses Oriental antiquities (covered in the second part of this tour), plus French,

Dutch, and Northern art. The **Sully wing** (east side) has extensive French painting and ancient Egypt collections.

For this part of the tour, we'll concentrate on the Louvre's south side: the **Denon and Sully wings,** which hold many of the superstars, including ancient Greek sculpture, Italian Renaissance painting, and French Neoclassical and Romantic painting.

Expect changes—the sprawling Louvre is constantly in flux. Rooms are periodically closed for renovation, and pieces are removed from display if they're being restored or loaned to other museums. In 2010, for example, the pre-Classical Greek section is closed, another Greek section is reopening after renovation, and the *Venus de Milo* may be moved around in the process. Several other collections are temporarily closed while construction continues on an exciting new Islamic art wing due in 2011. To find the artwork you're looking for, ask the nearest guard for its new location. Point to the photo in your book and ask, *"Où est, s'il vous plaît?"* (oo ay see voo play).

The bottom line: You could spend a lifetime here. Concentrate on seeing the biggies quickly, and try to finish the tour with enough energy left to browse.

The Tour Begins

LOUVRE

• *Start at the famous* Venus de Milo *statue (pictured on page 116). You'll find her not far from another famous statue, the* Winged Victory of Samothrace *(pictured on page 118).*

To reach the Venus de Milo *from inside the big glass pyramid, look for signs to the three wings. Head for the Denon wing.*

Escalate up one floor. After showing your ticket, continue up more escalators until you reach the top. Glance at the pyramid out the window, then turn right, heading down a long sculpture hall. When you reach the base of a grand staircase, look up at the Winged Victory of Samothrace. *We'll return to her later.*

To find the Venus de Milo, *walk to the left around the big staircase. You'll soon see* Venus *floating above a sea of worshipping tourists. It's been said that, among the warlike Greeks, this was the first statue to unilaterally disarm.*

Greece (500 B.C–A.D. 1)

The great Greek cultural explosion that changed the course of history unfolded over 50 years (starting around 450 B.C.) in Athens, a Greek town smaller than Muncie, Indiana. Having united the Greeks to repel a Persian invasion, Athens rebuilt, with the Parthenon as the centerpiece of the city. The Greeks dominated the ancient world through brain, not brawn, and their art shows

The Louvre—Greek Statues

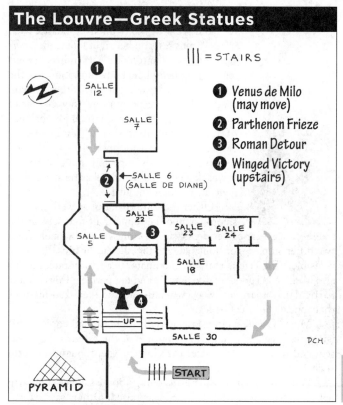

||| = STAIRS

1 Venus de Milo (may move)

2 Parthenon Frieze

3 Roman Detour

4 Winged Victory (upstairs)

SALLE 12

SALLE 7

2 ←SALLE 6 (SALLE DE DIANE)

SALLE 22

SALLE 5

3 SALLE 23 SALLE 24

SALLE 18

4

UP

SALLE 30

START

PYRAMID

DCH

their love of rationality, order, and balance. The ideal Greek was well-rounded—an athlete and a bookworm, a lover and a philosopher, a carpenter who played the piano, a warrior and a poet. In art, the balance between timeless stability and fleeting movement made beauty.

In a sense, we're all Greek: Democracy, mathematics, theater, philosophy, literature, and science were practically invented in ancient Greece. Most of the art that we'll see in the Louvre either came from Greece or was inspired by it.

Venus de Milo (Aphrodite, c. 100 B.C.)

The *Venus de Milo* (or goddess of love, from the Greek island of Melos) created a sensation when it was discovered in 1820. Europe was already in the grip of a classical fad, and this statue seemed to sum up all that ancient Greece stood for. The Greeks pictured their gods in human form (meaning humans are godlike), telling us they had an optimistic view of the human race. Venus' well-proportioned body captures the balance and orderliness of the Greek universe.

Split *Venus* down the middle from nose to toes and see how the two halves balance each other. Venus rests on her right foot (called *contrapposto*, or "counterpoise"), then lifts her left leg, setting her whole body in motion. As the left leg rises, her right shoulder droops down. And as her knee points one way, her head turns the other. *Venus* is a harmonious balance of opposites, orbiting slowly around a vertical axis. The twisting pose gives a balanced S-curve to her body (especially noticeable from the back view) that the Greeks and succeeding generations found beautiful.

Other opposites balance as well, like the smooth skin of her upper half that sets off the rough-cut texture of her dress (size 14). She's actually made from two different pieces of stone plugged together at the hips (the seam is visible). The face is realistic and anatomically accurate, but it's also idealized, a goddess, too generic and too perfect. This isn't any particular woman, but Everywoman—all the idealized features that appealed to the Greeks.

Most "Greek" statues are actually later Roman copies. This is a rare Greek original. This "epitome of the Golden Age" was sculpted three centuries after the Golden Age, though in a retro style.

What were her missing arms doing? Some say her right arm held her dress, while her left arm was raised. Others say she was hugging a male statue or leaning on a column. I say she was picking her navel.

• *Orbit* Venus. *This statue is interesting and different from every angle. Remember the view from the back—we'll see it again later. Now make your reentry to Earth. From* Venus, *browse around this gallery of Greek statues (again, the collection may be in flux in 2010). Head for Salle 6 (also known as Salle de Diane) and locate two carved panels on the wall.*

Parthenon Frieze
(*Les Sculptures du Parthenon*, C. 440 B.C.)

These stone fragments once decorated the exterior of the greatest Athenian temple, the Parthenon, built at the peak of the Greek Golden Age. The right panel shows a centaur sexually harassing a woman. It tells the story of how these rude creatures crashed a party of humans. But the Greeks fought back and threw the brutes out, just as Athens (metaphorically) conquered its barbarian neighbors and became civilized.

The other relief shows the sacred procession of young girls

who marched up the hill every four years with an embroidered veil for the 40-foot-high statue of Athena, the goddess of wisdom. Though headless, the maidens speak volumes about Greek craftsmanship. Carved in only a couple of inches of stone, they're amazingly realistic—more so than anything we saw in the pre-Classical period. They glide along horizontally (their belts and shoulders all in a line), while the folds of their dresses drape down vertically. The man in the center is relaxed, realistic, and *contrapposto*. Notice the veins in his arm. The maidens' pleated dresses make them look as stable as fluted columns, but their arms and legs step out naturally—the human form is emerging from the stone.

• *Head to the nearby Salle 5 and turn left into Salle 22, the Roman Antiquities room (Antiquités Romaines), for a...*

Roman Detour (Salles 22–30)

Stroll among the Caesars and try to see the person behind the public persona. Besides the many faces of the ubiquitous Emperor *Inconnu* ("unknown"), you might spot Augustus (Auguste), the first emperor, and his wily wife, Livia (Livie). Their son Tiberius (Tibère) was the Caesar that Jesus Christ "rendered unto." Caligula was notoriously depraved, curly-haired Domitia murdered her husband, Hadrian popularized the beard, Trajan ruled the Empire at

its peak, and Marcus Aurelius (Marc Aurèle) presided stoically over Rome's slow fall.

The pragmatic Romans (500 B.C.–A.D. 500) were great conquerors but bad artists. One area in which they excelled was realistic portrait busts, especially of their emperors, who were worshipped as gods on earth. Fortunately for us, the Romans also had a huge appetite for Greek statues and made countless copies. They took the Greek style and wrote it in capital letters, adding a veneer of sophistication to their homes, temples, baths, and government buildings.

The Roman rooms take you past several sarcophagi, an impressive mosaic floor that fills a massive courtyard, and beautiful wall-mounted mosaics from the ancient city of Antioch. Weary? Kick back and relax with the statues in the Etruscan Lounge (in Salle 18).

• Continue clockwise through the Roman collection, eventually spilling out at the base of the stairs leading up to the first floor and the dramatic...

Winged Victory of Samothrace
(*Victoire de Samothrace*, c. 190 B.C.)

This woman with wings, poised on the prow of a ship, once stood on a hilltop to commemorate a naval victory. Her clothes are

windblown and sea-sprayed, clinging close enough to her body to win a wet T-shirt contest. (Look at the detail in the folds of her dress around the navel, curving down to her hips.) Originally, her right arm was stretched high, celebrating the victory like a Super Bowl champion, waving a "we're number one" finger.

This is the *Venus de Milo* gone Hellenistic, from the time after the culture of Athens was spread around the Mediterranean by Alexander the Great (c. 325 B.C.). As *Victory* strides forward, the wind blows her and her wings back. Her feet are firmly on the ground, but her wings (and missing arms) stretch upward. She is a pillar of vertical strength, while the clothes curve and whip around her. These opposing forces create a feeling of great energy, making her the lightest two-ton piece of rock in captivity.

The earlier Golden Age Greeks might have considered this statue ugly. Her rippling excitement is a far cry from the dainty Parthenon maidens and the soft-focus beauty of *Venus*. And the statue's off-balance pose, like an unfinished melody, leaves you hanging. But Hellenistic Greeks loved these cliff-hanging scenes of real-life humans struggling to make their mark.

In the glass case nearby is *Victory*'s open right hand with an outstretched finger, found in 1950, a century after the statue itself was unearthed. When the French discovered this was in Turkey, they negotiated with the Turkish government for the rights to it. Considering all the other ancient treasures that France had looted from Turkey in the past, the Turks thought it only appropriate to give the French the finger.

• Enter the octagonal room to the left as you face the Winged Victory, *with Icarus bungee-jumping from the ceiling. Find a friendly window and look out toward the pyramid.*

LOUVRE

View from the Octagonal Room: The Louvre as a Palace

The former royal palace, the Louvre was built in stages over eight centuries. On your right (the eastern Sully wing) was the original medieval fortress. About 500 yards to the west, in the now-open area past the pyramid and the triumphal arch, is where the Tuileries Palace used to stand. Succeeding kings tried to connect these two palaces, each one adding another section onto the long, skinny north and south wings. Finally, in 1852, after three centuries of building, the two palaces were connected, creating a rectangular Louvre. Nineteen years later, the Tuileries Palace burned down during a riot, leaving the U-shaped Louvre we see today.

The glass pyramid was designed by the American architect I. M. Pei (1989). Many Parisians hated the pyramid, just as they hated another new and controversial structure 100 years ago—the Eiffel Tower.

In the octagonal room, a plaque at the base of the dome explains that France's Revolutionary National Assembly (the same people who brought you the guillotine) founded this museum in 1793. What could be more logical? You behead the king, inherit his palace and art collection, open the doors to the masses, and *voilà!* You have Europe's first public museum.

• *From the octagonal room, enter the Apollo Gallery (Galerie d'Apollon).*

Apollo Gallery

This gallery gives us a feel for the Louvre as the glorious home of French kings (before Versailles). Imagine a chandelier-lit party in this room, drenched in stucco and gold leaf, with tapestries of leading Frenchmen and paintings featuring mythological and symbolic themes. The inlaid tables made from marble and semi-precious stones, and many other art objects, show the wealth of France, Europe's number-one power for two centuries.

Stroll past glass cases of royal dinnerware to the far end of the room. In a glass case are the crown jewels. The display varies, but you may see the jewel-studded crown of Louis XV and the 140-carat Regent Diamond, which once graced crowns worn by Louis XV, Louis XVI, and Napoleon.

• *The Italian collection (Peintures Italiennes) is on the other side of* Winged Victory. *Cross back in front of* Winged Victory *to Salle 1, where you'll find...*

Two Botticelli Frescoes

Look at the paintings on the wall to the left. These pure maidens, like colorized versions of the Parthenon Frieze, give us a preview of how ancient Greece would be "reborn" in the Renaissance.

• Continue into large Salle 3.

The Medieval World (1200–1500)

Cimabue—*The Madonna of the Angels* (1280)

During the Age of Faith (1200s), almost every church in Europe had a painting like this one. Mary was a cult figure—even bigger than the 20th-century Madonna—adored and prayed to by the faithful for bringing baby Jesus into the world. After the collapse of the Roman Empire (c. A.D. 500), medieval Europe was a poorer and more violent place, with the Christian Church as the only constant in troubled times.

Altarpieces tended to follow the same formula: somber iconic faces, stiff poses, elegant folds in the robes, and generic angels. Violating 3-D space, the angels at the "back" of Mary's throne are the same size as those holding the front. These holy figures are laid flat on a gold background like cardboard cutouts, existing in a golden never-never land, as though the faithful couldn't imagine them as flesh-and-blood humans inhabiting our dark and sinful earth.

Giotto—*St. Francis of Assisi Receiving the Stigmata* (c. 1290–1295)

Francis of Assisi (c. 1181–1226), a wandering Italian monk of renowned goodness, kneels on a rocky Italian hillside, pondering the pain of Christ's torture and execution. Suddenly, he looks up, startled, to see Christ himself, with six wings, hovering above. Christ shoots lasers from his wounds to burn marks on the hands, feet, and side of the empathetic monk. Francis went on to breathe the spirit of the Renaissance into medieval Europe. His humble love of man and nature inspired artists like Giotto to portray real human beings with real emotions, living in a physical world of beauty.

Like a good filmmaker, Giotto (c. 1266–1337, JOT-toh) doesn't just *tell* us what happened, he *shows* us in the present tense, freezing the scene at its most dramatic moment. Though the perspective is crude—Francis' hut is smaller than he is, and Christ is somehow shooting at Francis while facing us—Giotto creates the illusion of 3-D, with a foreground (Francis), middle ground (his hut), and background (the hillside). Painting a 3-D world on a 2-D surface is tough, and after a millennium of Dark Ages, artists were rusty.

In the *predella* (the panel of paintings below the altarpiece), birds gather at Francis' feet to hear him talk about God. Giotto

catches the late arrivals in mid-flight, an astonishing technical feat for an artist more than a century before the Renaissance. The simple gesture of Francis' companion speaks volumes about his amazement. Breaking the stiff, iconic mold for saints, Francis bends forward at the waist to talk to his fellow creatures. The diversity of the birds—"red and yellow, black and white"—symbolizes how all humankind is equally precious in God's sight. Meanwhile, the tree bends down symmetrically to catch a few words from the beloved hippie of Assisi.

• *The long Grand Gallery displays Italian Renaissance painting, some masterpieces, some not.*

Italian Renaissance

The Grand Gallery

Built in the late 1500s to connect the old palace with the Tuileries Palace, the Grand Gallery displays much of the Louvre's Italian Renaissance art. From the doorway, look to the far end and consider this challenge: I hold the world's record for the Grand Gallery Heel-Toe-Fun-Walk-Tourist-Slalom, going end to end in 1 minute, 58 seconds. Two injured. Time yourself. Along the way, notice some of the...

Features of Italian Renaissance Painting
- **Religious:** Lots of Madonnas, children, martyrs, and saints.
- **Symmetrical:** The Madonnas are flanked by saints—two to the left, two to the right, and so on.
- **Realistic:** Real-life human features are especially obvious in the occasional portrait.

The Louvre—Grand Gallery

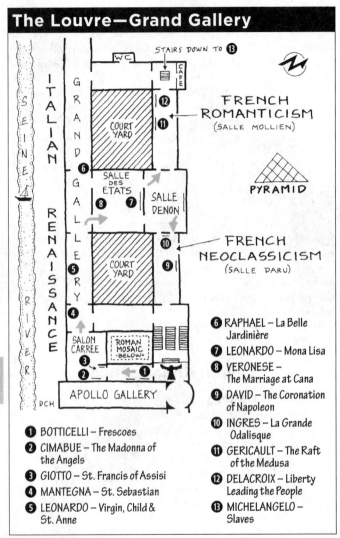

1 BOTTICELLI – Frescoes

2 CIMABUE – The Madonna of the Angels

3 GIOTTO – St. Francis of Assisi

4 MANTEGNA – St. Sebastian

5 LEONARDO – Virgin, Child & St. Anne

6 RAPHAEL – La Belle Jardinière

7 LEONARDO – Mona Lisa

8 VERONESE – The Marriage at Cana

9 DAVID – The Coronation of Napoleon

10 INGRES – La Grande Odalisque

11 GERICAULT – The Raft of the Medusa

12 DELACROIX – Liberty Leading the People

13 MICHELANGELO – Slaves

- **Three-Dimensional:** Every scene gets a spacious setting with a distant horizon.
- **Classical:** You'll see some Greek gods and classical nudes, but even Christian saints pose like Greek statues, and Mary is a *Venus* whose face and gestures embody all that was good in the Christian world.

Andrea Mantegna—*St. Sebastian* (c. 1480)

This isn't the patron saint of acupuncture. St. Sebastian was a

Christian martyr, although here he looks more like a classical Greek statue. Notice the *contrapposto* stance (all of his weight resting on one leg) and the Greek ruins scattered around him. His executioners look like ignorant medieval brutes bewildered by this enlightened Renaissance man. Italian artists were beginning to learn how to create human realism and earthly beauty on the canvas. Let the Renaissance begin.

• *Look for the following masterpieces by Leonardo and Raphael in the Grand Gallery.*

Leonardo da Vinci—*Virgin, Child, and St. Anne* (*La Vierge à l'Enfant Jésus avec Sainte-Anne*, c. 1510)

Three generations—grandmother, mother, and child—are arranged in a pyramid, with Anne's face as the peak and the lamb

as the lower right corner. Within this balanced structure, Leonardo sets the figures in motion. Anne's legs are pointed to our left. (Is Anne *Mona?* Hmm.) Her daughter Mary, sitting on her lap, reaches to the right. Jesus looks at her playfully while turning away. The lamb pulls away from him. But even with all the twisting and turning, this is still a placid scene. It's as orderly as the geometrically perfect universe created by the Renaissance god.

There's a psychological kidney punch in this happy painting. Jesus, the picture of childish joy, is innocently playing with a lamb—the symbol of his inevitable sacrificial death.

The Louvre has the greatest collection of Leonardos in the world—five of them. Look for the neighboring *Virgin of the Rocks* and *John the Baptist.* Leonardo was the consummate Renaissance man. Musician, sculptor, engineer, scientist, and sometimes painter, he combined knowledge from all areas to create beauty. If he were alive today, he'd create a Unified Field Theory in physics—and set it to music.

• *You'll likely find Raphael's art on the right side of the Grand Gallery, just past the statue of Diana the Huntress.*

Raphael—*La Belle Jardinière* (1507)

Raphael (roff-eye-ELL) perfected the style Leonardo pioneered. This configuration of Madonna, Child, and John the Baptist is also a balanced pyramid with hazy grace and beauty. Mary is a mountain of maternal tenderness (the title translates as "The Beautiful

LOUVRE

Italian Renaissance
(1400–1600)

A thousand years after Rome fell, plunging Europe into the Dark Ages, the Greek ideal of beauty was reborn in 15th-century Italy. The Renaissance—or "rebirth" of the culture of

ancient Greece and Rome—was a cultural boom that changed people's thinking about every aspect of life. In politics, it meant democracy. In religion, it meant a move away from Church dominance and toward the assertion of man (humanism) and a more personal faith. Science and secular learning were revived after centuries of superstition and ignorance. In architecture, it was a return to the balanced columns and domes of Greece and Rome.

In painting, the Renaissance meant realism, and for the Italians, realism was spelled "3-D." Artists rediscovered the beauty of nature and the human body. With pictures of beautiful people in harmonious 3-D surroundings, they expressed the optimism and confidence of this new age.

LOUVRE

Gardener"), as she eyes her son with a knowing look and holds his hand in a gesture of union. Jesus looks up innocently, standing *contrapposto* like a chubby Greek statue. Baby John the Baptist

kneels lovingly at Jesus' feet, holding a cross that hints at his playmate's sacrificial death. The interplay of gestures and gazes gives the masterpiece both intimacy and cohesiveness, while Raphael's blended brushstrokes varnish the work with an iridescent smoothness.

With Raphael, the Greek ideal of beauty—reborn in the Renaissance— reached its peak. His work spawned so many imitators who cranked out sickly sweet, generic Madonnas that we often take him for granted. Don't. This is the real thing.

• *The* Mona Lisa (La Joconde) *is near the statue of* Diana, *in Salle 6—the Salle des Etats—midway down the Grand Gallery on the right. After several years and a €5 million renovation,* Mona *is alone behind glass on her own false wall. Six million heavy-breathing people crowd in each year to glimpse the most ogled painting in the world. (You can't miss her. Just follow the signs and the people...it's the only painting you can hear. With all the groveling crowds, you can even smell it.)*

Leonardo da Vinci—*Mona Lisa* (1503–1506)

Leonardo was already an old man when François I invited him to France. Determined to pack light, he took only a few paintings with him. One was a portrait of a Lisa del Giocondo, the wife of a wealthy Florentine merchant. When Leonardo arrived, François immediately fell in love with the painting, making it the centerpiece of the small collection of Italian masterpieces that would, in three centuries, become the Louvre museum. He called it *La Gioconda (La Joconde* in French)—both her last name and a play on the Italian word for "happy woman." We know it as a contraction of the Italian for "my lady Lisa"—*Mona Lisa.*

Mona may disappoint you. She's smaller than you'd expect, darker, engulfed in a huge room, and hidden behind a glaring pane of glass. So, you ask, "Why all the hubbub?" Let's take a closer look. As you would with any lover, you've got to take her for what she is, not what you'd like her to be.

The famous smile attracts you first. Leonardo used a hazy technique called *sfumato,* blurring the edges of her mysterious smile. Try as you might, you can never quite see the corners of her mouth. Is she happy? Sad? Tender? Or is it a cynical supermodel's smirk? All visitors read it differently, projecting their own mood onto her enigmatic face. *Mona* is a Rorschach inkblot...so, how are you feeling?

Now look past the smile and the eyes that really do follow you (most eyes in portraits do) to some of the subtle Renaissance elements that make this painting work. The body is surprisingly massive and statue-like, a perfectly balanced pyramid turned at an angle, so we can see its mass. Her arm is resting lightly on the chair's armrest, almost on the level of the frame itself, as if she's sitting in a window looking out at us. The folds of her sleeves and her gently folded hands are remarkably realistic and relaxed. The typical Leonardo landscape shows distance by getting hazier and hazier.

Though the portrait is most likely of Lisa del Giocondo, the 20-something wife of a Florentine businessman, there are many hypotheses, including the idea that it's Leonardo himself. Or she might be the Mama Lisa. A recent infrared scan revealed that she has a barely visible veil over her dress, which may mean (in the custom of the day) that she had just had a baby.

The overall mood is one of balance and serenity, but there's also an element of mystery. *Mona's* smile and long-distance beauty are subtle and elusive, tempting but always just out of reach, like strands of a street singer's melody drifting through the Métro tunnel. *Mona* doesn't knock your socks off, but she winks at the patient viewer.

• *Before leaving* Mona, *stand back and just observe the paparazzi scene. The huge canvas opposite* Mona *is...*

Paolo Veronese—*The Marriage at Cana* (1562–1563)

Stand 10 steps away from this enormous canvas to where it just fills your field of vision, and suddenly...you're in a party! Help yourself to a glass of wine. This is the Renaissance love of beautiful things gone hog-wild. Venetian artists like Veronese painted the good life of rich, happy-go-lucky Venetian merchants.

In a spacious setting of Renaissance architecture, colorful lords and ladies, decked out in their fanciest duds, feast on a great spread of food and drink, while the musicians fuel the fires of good fun. Servants prepare and serve the food, jesters play, and animals roam. In the upper left, a dog and his master look on. A sturdy linebacker in yellow pours wine out of a jug (right foreground). The man in white samples some wine and thinks, "Hmm, not bad," while nearby a ferocious cat battles a lion. The wedding couple at the far left is almost forgotten.

Believe it or not, this is a religious work showing the wedding celebration in which Jesus turned water into wine. And there's Jesus in the dead center of 130 frolicking figures, wondering if maybe wine coolers might not have been a better choice. With true Renaissance optimism, Venetians pictured Christ as a party animal, someone who loved the created world as much as they did.

Now, let's hear it for the band! On bass—the bad cat with the funny hat—Titian the Venetian! And joining him on viola—Crazy Veronese!

• *Exit behind* Mona *into the Salle Denon. The dramatic Romantic room is to your left, and the grand Neoclassical room is to your right. These two rooms feature the most exciting French canvases in the Louvre. In the Neoclassical room (Salle Daru), kneel before the largest canvas in the Louvre.*

French Neoclassicism (1780–1850)

Jacques-Louis David—*The Coronation of Napoleon* (1806–1807)

Napoleon holds aloft an imperial crown. This common-born son of immigrants is about to be crowned emperor of a "New Rome."

He has just made his wife, Josephine, the empress, and she kneels at his feet. Seated behind Napoleon is the pope, who journeyed from Rome to place the imperial crown on his head. But Napoleon feels that no one is worthy of the task. At the last moment, he shrugs the pope aside, grabs the crown, holds it up for all to see...and crowns himself. The pope looks p.o.'d.

After the French people decapitated their king during the Revolution (1793), their fledgling democracy floundered in chaos. France was united by a charismatic, brilliant, temperamental, upstart general who kept his feet on the ground, his eyes on the horizon, and his hand in his coat—Napoleon Bonaparte. Napoleon quickly conquered most of Europe and insisted on being made emperor (not merely king). The painter David (dah-VEED) recorded the coronation for posterity.

The radiant woman in the gallery in the background center wasn't actually there. Napoleon's mother couldn't make it to see her boy become the most powerful man in Europe, but he had David paint her in anyway. (There's a key on the frame telling who's who in the picture.)

The traditional setting for French coronations was the ultra-Gothic Notre-Dame cathedral. But Napoleon wanted a location that would reflect the glories of Greece and the grandeur of Rome. So, interior decorators erected stage sets of Greek columns and Roman arches to give the cathedral the architectural political correctness you see in this painting. (The *pietà* statue on the right edge of the painting is still in Notre-Dame today.)

David was the new emperor's official painter and propagandist, in charge of color-coordinating the costumes and flags for public ceremonies and spectacles. (Find his self-portrait with curly gray hair in the *Coronation*, way up in the second balcony, peeking around the tassel directly above Napoleon's crown.) His "Neoclassical" style influenced French fashion. Take a look at his *Madame Juliet Récamier* portrait on the opposite wall, showing a modern Parisian woman in ancient garb and Pompeii hairstyle

LOUVRE

reclining on a Roman couch. Nearby paintings, such as *The Oath of the Horatii (Le Serment des Horaces),* are fine examples of Neoclassicism, with Greek subjects, patriotic sentiment, and a clean, simple style.

• *As you double back toward the Romantic room, stop at...*

Jean-Auguste-Dominique Ingres—*La Grande Odalisque* (1819)

Take *Venus de Milo,* turn her around, lay her down, and stick a hash pipe next to her, and you have the *Grande Odalisque.* OK, maybe you'd have to add a vertebra or two.

Using clean, polished, sculptural lines, Ingres (ang-gruh, with a soft "gruh") exaggerates the S-curve of a standing Greek nude. As in the *Venus de Milo,* rough folds of cloth set off her smooth skin. The face, too, has a touch of *Venus'* idealized features (or like Raphael's kindergarten teacher), taking nature and improving on it. Contrast the cool colors of this statue-like nude with Titian's golden girls. Ingres preserves *Venus'* backside for posterior—I mean, posterity.

• *Cross back through the Salle Denon (where you might spot a painting high up titled* The Death of Walter Mondale) *and into a room gushing with...*

French Romanticism (1800–1850)

Théodore Géricault—*The Raft of the Medusa* (*Le Radeau de la Méduse,* 1819)

In the artistic war between hearts and minds, the heart style was known as Romanticism. Stressing motion and emotion, it

was the flip side of cool, balanced Neoclassicism, though they both flourished in the early 1800s.

What better setting for an emotional work than a shipwreck? Clinging to a raft is a tangle of bodies and lunatics sprawled over each other. The scene writhes with agitated, ominous motion—the ripple of muscles, churning clouds, and choppy seas. On the right is a deathly green corpse dangling overboard. The face of the man at left, cradling a dead body, says it all—the despair of spending weeks stranded in the middle of nowhere.

This painting was based on the actual sinking of the ship

Medusa off the coast of Africa in 1816. About 150 people packed onto the raft. After floating in the open seas for 12 days—suffering hardship and hunger, even resorting to cannibalism—only 15 survived. The story was made to order for a painter determined to shock the public and arouse its emotions. That painter was young Géricault (ZHAIR-ee-ko). He interviewed survivors and honed his craft, sketching dead bodies in the morgue and the twisted faces of lunatics in asylums, capturing the moment when all hope is lost.

But wait. There's a stir in the crowd. Someone has spotted something. The bodies rise up in a pyramid of hope, culminating in a flag wave. They signal frantically, trying to catch the attention of the tiny ship on the horizon, their last desperate hope...which did finally save them. Géricault uses rippling movement and powerful colors to catch us up in the excitement. If art controls your heartbeat, this is a masterpiece.

Eugène Delacroix—*Liberty Leading the People* (*La Liberté Guidant le Peuple, 1830*)

The year is 1830. King Charles has just issued the 19th-century equivalent of the "Patriot Act," and his subjects are angry. The Parisians take to the streets once again, *Les Miz*–style, to fight royalist oppressors. The people triumph—replacing the king with Louis-Philippe, who is happy to rule within the constraints of a modern constitution. There's a hard-bitten proletarian with a sword (far left), an intellectual with a top hat and a sawed-off shotgun, and even a little boy brandishing pistols.

Leading them on through the smoke and over the dead and dying is the figure of Liberty, a strong woman waving the French

flag. Does this symbol of victory look familiar? It's the *Winged Victory*, wingless and topless.

To stir our emotions, Delacroix (del-ah-kwah) uses only three major colors—the red, white, and blue of the French flag. France is the symbol of modern democracy, and this painting has long stirred its citizens' passion for liberty. The French weren't the first to adopt democracy (Americans were), nor are they the best working example of it, but they've had to try harder to achieve it than any other country. No sooner would they throw one king or dictator out then they'd get another. They're now working on their fifth republic.

This symbol of freedom is a fitting tribute to the Louvre, the first museum ever opened to the common rabble of humanity. The good things in life don't belong only to a small, wealthy part of society, but to everyone. The motto of France is *Liberté, Egalité, Fraternité*—liberty, equality, and the brotherhood of all.

• *Exit the room at the far end (past a café) and go downstairs, where you'll bump into the bum of a large, twisting male nude looking like he's just waking up after a thousand-year nap.*

More Italian Renaissance

Michelangelo—*Slaves* (1513–1515)

These two statues by earth's greatest sculptor are a fitting end to this museum—works that bridge the ancient and modern worlds. Michelangelo, like his fellow Renaissance artists, learned from the Greeks. The perfect anatomy, twisting poses, and idealized faces appear as if they could have been created 2,000 years earlier.

The so-called *Dying Slave* (also called the *Sleeping Slave*, looking like he should be stretched out on a sofa) twists listlessly against his T-shirt-like bonds, revealing his smooth skin. Compare the polished detail of the rippling, bulging left arm with the sketchy details of the face and neck. With Michelangelo, the body does the talking. This is probably the most sensual nude Michelangelo, the master of the male body, ever created.

The *Rebellious Slave* fights against his bondage. His shoulders rotate one way, his head and leg turn the other. He looks upward, straining to get free. He even seems to be trying to free himself from the rock he's made of. Michelangelo said that his purpose was to carve away the marble to reveal the figures God put inside. This slave shows the agony of that process and the ecstasy of the result.

• *Tour over! These two may be slaves of the museum, but you are free to go. You've seen the essential Louvre. To leave the museum, head for the end of the hall, turn right, and follow signs down the escalators to the* Sortie.

But, of course, there's so much more. After a break (or on a second visit), consider a stroll through a few rooms of the Richelieu wing, which contain some of the Louvre's oldest and biggest pieces. Bible students, amateur archaeologists, and Iraq War vets may find the collection especially interesting.

Richelieu Wing

Oriental Antiquities (Antiquités Orientales)

Saddam Hussein is only the latest iron-fisted, palace-building conqueror to fall in Iraq's long history, which stretches back to the dawn of civilization. Civilization began 6,000 years ago in Iraq, between the Tigris and Euphrates Rivers, in the area called the Fertile Crescent.

In the Richelieu wing, you can quickly sweep through 2,000 years of Iraq's ancient history, enjoying some of the Louvre's biggest and oldest artifacts. See how each new civilization toppled the previous one—pulling down its statues, destroying its palaces, looting its cultural heritage, and replacing it with victory monuments of its own...only to be toppled again by the next wave of history.

• *From under the pyramid, enter the Richelieu wing. Show your ticket, then take the first right. Go up one flight of stairs and one escalator to the ground floor* (rez-de-chaussée), *where you'll find the* Antiquités Orientales. *Walk straight off the escalator, enter Salle 1-a (Mesopotamie Archaïque), and come face-to-face with fragments of the broken...*

Stela of the Vultures
(Stele de victoire d'Eannatum, roi de Lagash, c. 2450 B.C.)

As old as the pyramids, this stela (ceremonial stone pillar) may be the oldest depiction of a historical event—the battle between the city of Lagash (100 miles north of modern Basra) and its archrival, Umma.

Bearded King Eannatum waves the eagle flag of Lagash with one hand, while with the other he clubs a puny enemy soldier trapped in a battle net, making his enemies pledge allegiance to Lagash's gods.

Circle around to the flip side of the stela for the rest of the

story, "reading" from top to bottom. Top level: Behind a wall of shields, a phalanx of helmeted soldiers advances, trampling the enemy underfoot. They pile the corpses (right) and vultures swoop down from above to pluck the remains. Middle level: The king waves to the crowd from his chariot in the victory parade. Bottom

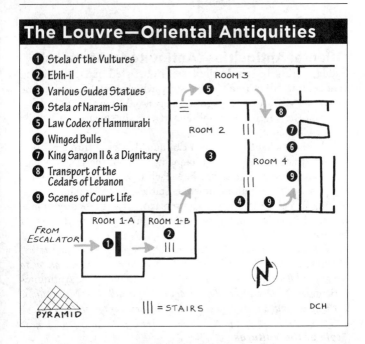

The Louvre—Oriental Antiquities

1. Stela of the Vultures
2. Ebih-il
3. Various Gudea Statues
4. Stela of Naram-Sin
5. Law Codex of Hammurabi
6. Winged Bulls
7. King Sargon II & a Dignitary
8. Transport of the Cedars of Lebanon
9. Scenes of Court Life

ROOM 3

ROOM 2

ROOM 4

FROM ESCALATOR

ROOM 1-A   ROOM 1-B

||| = STAIRS

PYRAMID

DCH

level: They dig a mass grave—1 of 20 for the 36,000 enemy dead—while a priest (top of the fragment) gives thanks to the gods. A tethered ox (see his big head tied to a stake) is about to become a burnt sacrifice.

The inscription on the stela is in cuneiform, the world's first written language, invented by the Sumerians.

• Continue into Salle 1-b, with the blissful statue of...

Ebih-il, The Superintendent of Mari (c. 2400 B.C.)

Bald, bearded, blue-eyed Ebih-il (his name is inscribed on his shoulder) sits in his fleece skirt, folds his hands reverently across his chest, and gazes rapturously into space, dreaming of... Ishtar. Ebih-il was a priest in the goddess Ishtar's temple, and the statue is dedicated to her.

Ishtar was the chief goddess of many Middle Eastern peoples. As goddess of both love and war, she was a favorite of horny soldiers. She was a giver of life (this statue is dedicated "to Ishtar the virile"), yet also miraculously a virgin. She was also a great hunter with bow and arrow, and a great lover ("Her lips are sweet...her figure is beautiful, her eyes are brilliant... women and men adore her," sang the *Hymn to Ishtar*, c. 1600 B.C.).

Ebih-il adores her eternally with his eyes made of seashells and lapis lazuli. The smile on his face reflects the pleasure the goddess has just given him, perhaps through one of the sacred prostitutes who resided in Ishtar's Temple.

• *Go up the five steps behind* Ebih-il, *and turn left into Salle 2, containing a dozen statues, all of a man named...*

Gudea, Prince of Lagash (c. 2125–2110 B.C.)

Gudea (r. 2141–2122 B.C.), in his wool stocking cap, folds his hands and prays to the gods to save his people from invading barbarians. One of Sumeria's last great rulers, the peaceful and pious Gudea (his name means "the destined") rebuilt temples (where these statues once stood) to thank the gods for their help.

• *Behind you, find the rosy-colored...*

Stela of Naram-Sin
(Stele de victoire de Naram-Sin, roi d'Akkad, c. 2230 B.C.)

After a millennium of prosperity, Sumeria was plundered (c. 2250 B.C.) and Akkadia became the new king of the mountain. Here, King Naram-Sin climbs up to the sunny heavens, crowned with the horned helmet of a god. His soldiers look up to admire him as he tramples his enemies. Next to him, a victim tries to remove a spear from his neck, while another pleads to the conqueror for mercy.

• *Exit Salle 2 at the far end and enter Salle 3, with the large black stela of Hammurabi.*

Law Codex of Hammurabi, King of Babylon (c. 1760 B.C.)

Hammurabi (r. c. 1792–1750 B.C.) established the next great civilization, ruling as King of Babylon (50 miles south of modern-day Baghdad). He proclaimed 282 laws, all inscribed on this eight-foot black basalt stela—one of the first formal legal documents, four centuries before the Ten Commandments. Stelas such as this likely dotted Hammurabi's empire, and this one may have stood in Babylon before being moved to Susa, Iran.

At the top of the stela, Hammurabi (standing and wearing Gudea's hat of kingship) receives the scepter of judgment from the god of justice and the sun, who radiates flames from his shoulders. The inscription begins, "When Anu the Sublime...called me, Hammurabi, by name...I did right, and brought about the well-being of the oppressed."

Next come the laws, scratched in cuneiform down the length of the stela, some 3,500 lines reading right to left. The laws cover very specific situations, everything from lying, theft, and trade to marriage and medical malpractice. The legal innovation was the immediate retribution for wrongdoing, often with poetic justice. Here's a sample:

#1: If any man ensnares another falsely, he shall be put to death.

#57: If your sheep graze another man's land, you must repay 20 gur of grain.

#129: If a couple is caught in adultery, they shall both be tied up and thrown in the water.

#137: If you divorce your wife, you must pay alimony and child support.

#218: A surgeon who bungles an operation shall have his hands cut off.

#282: If a slave shall say, "You are not my master," the master can cut off the slave's ear.

The most quoted laws—summing up the spirit of ancient Middle Eastern justice—are #196 ("If a man put out the eye of another man, his eye shall be put out") and #200 ("a tooth for a tooth").

• *Make a U-turn to the right, entering the large Salle 4, dominated by colossal winged bulls with human heads. These sculptures—including five winged bulls and many relief panels along the walls—are from the...*

Palace of Sargon II

Sargon II, the Assyrian king (r. 721–705 B.C.), spared no expense on his palace (see various reconstructions of the palace on plaques around the room). In Assyrian society, the palace of the king—not the temple of the gods—was the focus of life, and each ruler demonstrated his authority with large residences.

Sargon II actually built a whole new city for his palace, just north of the traditional capital of Nineveh (modern-day Mosul).

Just Enough Geography and History for This Tour

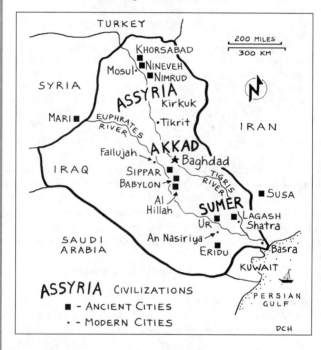

The northern half of Iraq is mountainous, and the southern half is the delta of the Tigris and Euphrates Rivers. Baghdad sits roughly between north and south, along the Tigris. The Sumerians inhabited the south, the Assyrians the north, and the Akkadians and Babylonians the center, around Baghdad.

Here's a brief timeline:

3500–2400 B.C.	Sumerian city-states flourish between the Tigris and Euphrates Rivers. Sumerians invent writing.
2300 B.C.	Akkadians invade Sumer.
1750 B.C.	Hammurabi establishes first Babylonian empire.
710 B.C.	Sargon II rules over a vast Assyrian-controlled empire, encompassing modern Iraq, Israel, Syria, and Egypt.
612 B.C.	Babylonians revolt against the Assyrians and destroy the Assyrian capital of Nineveh (300 miles north of Baghdad), then build their own near Baghdad.

LOUVRE

The Assyrians

This Semitic people from the agriculturally challenged hills of northern Iraq became traders and conquerors, not farmers. They conquered their southern neighbors and dominated the Middle East for 300 years (c. 900–600 B.C.).

Their strength came from a superb army (chariots, mounted cavalry, and siege engines), a policy of terrorism against enemies ("I tied their heads to tree trunks all around the city," reads a royal inscription), ethnic cleansing and mass deportations of the vanquished, and efficient administration (roads and express postal service). They have been called "The Romans of the East."

He called it Dur Sharrukin ("Sargonburg"), and the city's vast dimensions were 4,000 cubits by—oh, excuse me—it covered about 150 football fields pieced together. The whole city was built on a raised, artificial mound, and the 25-acre palace itself sat even higher, surrounded by walls, with courtyards, temples, the king's residence, and a wedding cake–shaped temple (called a ziggurat) dedicated to the god Sin.

• *Start with the two big bulls supporting a (reconstructed) arch.*

Winged Bulls (C. 710 B.C.)

These 30-ton, 14-foot alabaster bulls with human faces once guarded the entrance to the throne room of Sargon II. A visitor to the palace back then could have looked over the bulls' heads and seen a 15-story ziggurat (stepped-pyramid temple) towering overhead. The winged bulls were guardian spirits to ward off demons and intimidate liberals.

Between their legs are cuneiform inscriptions such as: "I, Sargon, King of the Universe, built palaces for my royal residence.... I had winged bulls with human heads carved from great blocks of mountain stone, and I placed them at the doors facing the four winds as powerful divine guardians.... My creation amazed all who gazed upon it."

• *We'll see a few relief panels from the palace, working counterclockwise around the room. Start with the panel just to the left of the two big bulls (as you face them). Find the bearded, earringed man in whose image the bulls were made.*

King Sargon II and a Dignitary
(Le roi Sargon II et un haut dignitaire, c. 710 B.C.)

Sargon II, wearing a fez-like crown with a cone on the top and straps down the back, cradles his scepter and raises his staff to

receive a foreign ambassador who's come to pay tribute. Sargon II controlled a vast empire, consisting of modern-day Iraq and extending westward to the Mediterranean and Egypt.

Before becoming emperor, Sargon II was a conquering general who invaded Israel (2 Kings 17:1–6). After a three-year siege, he took Jerusalem

and deported much of the population, inspiring the legends of the "Lost" Ten Tribes. The prophet Isaiah saw him as God's tool to punish the sinful Israelites, "to seize loot and snatch plunder, and to trample them down like mud in the streets" (Isaiah 10:6).

• *On the wall to the left of Sargon are four panels depicting the...*

Transport of the Cedars of Lebanon
(Transport du bois de cèdre du Liban)

Boats carry the finest quality logs for Sargon II's palace, cross-

ing a wavy sea populated with fish, turtles, crabs, and mermen. The transport process is described in the Bible (1 Kings 5:9): "My men will haul them down from Lebanon to the sea, and I will float them in rafts to the place you specify."

• *Continue counterclockwise around the room—past more big winged animals, past the huge hero Gilgamesh crushing a lion—until you reach more relief panels. These depict...*

Scenes of Court Life

The brown, eroded gypsum panels we see here were originally painted and varnished. Placed side by side, they would have stretched over a mile. The panels read like a comic strip, showing the king's men parading in to serve him.

First, soldiers *(Guerrier en armée)* sheathe their swords and fold their

Ancient Places in Today's Iraq

Lagash, the ancient city of **Prince Gudea** (see page 133), is near modern **Shatra,** in southeast Iraq. In March of 2003, American invasion forces met some of their stiffest resistance in Shatra (before the fall of Baghdad). "Chemical Ali"—Saddam Hussein's cousin and the Ace of Spades in America's deck of most-wanted Iraqis—was thought to be holed up in the city; he eluded capture for a few more months. After shelling Shatra with planes, helicopters, and tanks, US Marines took the town and were met by Iraqis with signs saying *Welcome to Iraq.*

The Stela of the Vultures (on page 131) depicts battles between Lagash and Umma, near modern **An Nasiriyah.** It was there that, in March of 2003, a US soldier named Pfc. Jessica Lynch was injured, captured, hospitalized, and later rescued by US soldiers.

Though discovered in Iran, *Hammurabi's Code* may once have stood in ancient Babylon, 50 miles south of Baghdad in **Al Hillah.** In 2005 and 2007, massive suicide bombs were detonated here, killing hundreds—examples of the new tactic of warfare that emerged in the Iraq War.

Sargon II built his palace outside **Mosul,** now an oil-rich Kurdish center in northern Iraq. After US soldiers drove insurgents from Fallujah in the fall of 2004, many resettled in Mosul. In May of 2008, a US-backed offensive called Operation Lion's Roar was launched against this stronghold of insurgents. In 2009, as US troops prepared to withdraw from urban centers in Iraq, Mosul remained a trouble spot.

LOUVRE

hands reverently. A winged spirit prepares them to enter the king's presence by shaking a pine cone to anoint them with holy perfume. Next, servants (see photo on previous page) hurry to the throne room with the king's dinner, carrying his table, chair, and bowl. Other servants ready the king's horses and chariots.

From Sargon to Saddam

Sargon II's palace remained unfinished and was later burned and buried. Sargon's great Assyrian empire dissolved over the next few generations. When the Babylonians revolted and conquered their northern neighbors (612 B.C.), the whole Middle East applauded. As the Bible put it: "Nineveh is in ruins—who will mourn for her?... Everyone who hears the news claps his hands at your fall, for who has not felt your endless cruelty?" (Nahum 3:7, 19).

The new capital was Babylon (50 miles south of modern Baghdad), ruled by King Nebuchadnezzar, who conquered Judea (586 B.C., the Bible's "Babylonian Captivity") and built a palace with the Hanging Gardens, one of the Seven Wonders of the World.

Over the succeeding centuries, Babylon/Baghdad fell to Persians (539 B.C.), Greeks (Alexander the Great, 331 B.C.), Persians again (second century B.C.), Arab Muslims (A.D. 634), Mongol hordes (Genghis Khan's grandson, 1258), Iranians (1502), Ottoman Turks (1535), British-controlled kings (1921), and military regimes (1958), the most recent headed by Saddam Hussein (1979).

After toppling Saddam Hussein in 2003, George W. Bush declared, "Mission accomplished!" Five thousand years of invasions, violence, and regime change, as well as current events, suggest otherwise.

LOUVRE

ORSAY
MUSEUM TOUR

Musée d'Orsay

The Musée d'Orsay (mew-zay dor-say) houses French art of the 1800s and early 1900s (specifically, 1848–1914), picking up where the Louvre's art collection leaves off. For us, that means Impressionism, the art of sun-dappled fields, bright colors, and crowded Parisian cafés. The Orsay houses the best general collection anywhere of Manet, Monet, Renoir, Degas, Van Gogh, Cézanne, and Gauguin. If you like Impressionism, visit this museum. If you don't like Impressionism, visit this museum. I personally find it a more enjoyable and rewarding place than the Louvre. Sure, ya gotta see the *Mona Lisa* and *Venus de Milo*, but after you get your gottas out of the way, enjoy the Orsay.

Orientation

Cost: €8, €5.50 Fri–Wed after 16:15 and Thu after 18:00, free first Sun of month, covered by Museum Pass. Tickets are good all day.

Hours: Tue–Sun 9:30–18:00, Thu until 21:45 year-round, last entry one hour before closing (45 min before on Thu), closed Mon. The Impressionist galleries begin closing 45 minutes early, frustrating unwary visitors. Tuesdays are particularly crowded, because the Louvre is closed.

Free Entry near Closing Time: Right when the ticket booth stops selling tickets, you're welcome to scoot in free of charge (Tue–Wed and Fri–Sun at 17:00, Thu at 21:00; they won't let you in much after that, however). You'll have 30 minutes of power-touring. Remember that the Impressionist galleries upstairs start shutting down first, so go there right away.

Location: The museum sits above the RER-C stop called Musée d'Orsay. The nearest Métro stop is Solférino, three blocks

Orsay Ground Floor—Overview

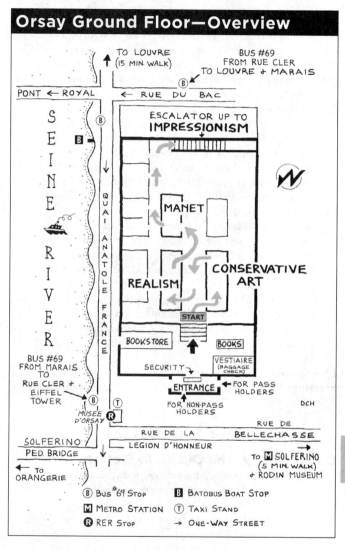

TO LOUVRE (15 MIN. WALK)

BUS #69 FROM RUE CLER TO LOUVRE & MARAIS

PONT ← ROYAL

← RUE DU BAC

S E I N E   R I V E R

QUAI ANATOLE FRANCE

ESCALATOR UP TO **IMPRESSIONISM**

MANET

REALISM

CONSERVATIVE ART

START

BOOKSTORE

BOOKS

SECURITY

VESTIAIRE (BAGGAGE CHECK)

BUS #69 FROM MARAIS TO RUE CLER & EIFFEL TOWER

ENTRANCE

FOR PASS HOLDERS

FOR NON-PASS HOLDERS

DCH

MUSÉE D'ORSAY

RUE DE BELLECHASSE

SOLFERINO PED. BRIDGE

RUE DE LA LEGION D'HONNEUR

← TO ORANGERIE

TO M SOLFERINO (5 MIN. WALK) & RODIN MUSEUM

B Bus #69 Stop

B Batobus Boat Stop

M Metro Station

T Taxi Stand

R RER Stop

→ One-Way Street

ORSAY MUSEUM

southeast of the Orsay. Bus #69 from the Marais neighborhood stops at the museum on the river side (quai Anatole France); from the rue Cler area, it stops behind the museum on the rue du Bac. From the Louvre, catch bus #69 along rue de Rivoli; otherwise, it's a lovely 15-minute walk through the Tuileries Garden and across the river on the pedestrian bridge. The museum is at 1 rue de la Légion d'Honneur. A taxi stand is in front of the entrance on quai Anatole France. The Batobus boat also makes a stop here (see page 38).

Getting In: As you face the front of the museum from rue de la
　　Légion d'Honneur (with the river on your left), passholders
　　enter on the right side of the museum (Entrance C), and ticket
　　purchasers enter closer to the river (Entrance A).

Information: The booth inside the entrance provides free floor
　　plans in English. Tel. 01 40 49 48 14, www.musee-orsay.fr.

Tours: Audioguides cost €6. English guided tours usually run daily
　　(except Sun) at 11:30 (€7.50/90 min). Occasionally, some tours
　　are offered at other times (inquire when you arrive). I recom-
　　mend the self-guided tour described below, which is also
　　available as an iPhone app, and as a free audio tour for people
　　with an iPod or other MP3 player (download from www.rick
　　steves.com or search for "Rick Steves' tours" in iTunes).

Length of This Tour: Allow two hours.

Cloakroom (Vestiaire): Checking bags or coats is free. Day bags
　　(but nothing big) are allowed in the museum. No valuables
　　can be stored in checked bags. The cloakroom clerk might ask
　　you in French not to check cameras, passports, or anything
　　particularly precious.

Cuisine Art: A pricey but *très* elegant restaurant is on the second
　　floor, with affordable tea and coffee served 15:00–17:30 (daily
　　except Thu). A simple fifth-floor café is sandwiched between
　　the Impressionists; above it is an easy self-service place with
　　sandwiches and drinks.

Photography: Photography without a flash is allowed.

Starring: Manet, Monet, Renoir, Degas, Van Gogh, Cézanne,
　　and Gauguin.

The Tour Begins

Gare d'Orsay: The Old Train Station

• *Pick up a free English map upon entering, buy your ticket, and check
your bag. Belly up to the stone balustrade overlooking the main floor,
and orient yourself.*

Trains used to run right under our feet
down the center of the gallery. This former train station, or *gare*, barely escaped
the wrecking ball in the 1970s, when the
French realized it'd be a great place to
house the enormous collections of 19th-
century art scattered throughout the city.

　　The main floor has early 19th-century
art—as usual, Conservative on the right,
Realism on the left. Upstairs (not visible
from here) is the core of the collection—
the Impressionist rooms. If you're pressed

for time, go directly there (see directions following "Opéra Exhibit" on page 149). We'll start with the Conservatives and early rebels on the ground floor, then head upstairs to see how a few visionary young artists bucked the system and revolutionized the art world, paving the way for the 20th century. We'll end the tour with the "other" Orsay on the mezzanine level. Clear as Seine water? *Bien*.

If a painting isn't where I say it is, it's probably on loan (a common occurrence) or being restored—though it's wise to ask a museum guard if it's been moved to another location within the Orsay.

• *Walk down the steps to the main floor, a gallery filled with statues.*

Conservative Art

Main Gallery Statues

No, this isn't ancient Greece. These statues are from the same era as the Theory of Relativity. It's the Conservative art of the French schools that was so popular throughout the 19th century. It was well-liked for its beauty. The balanced poses, perfect anatomy, sweet faces, curving lines, and gleaming white stone—all of this is very appealing. (I'll bad-mouth it later, but for now appreciate the exquisite craftsmanship of this "perfect" art.)

• *Take your first right into the small Room 1, marked* Ingres et l'Ingrisme. *Look for a nude woman with a pitcher of water.*

❶ Jean-Auguste-Dominique Ingres—*The Source* (*La Source,* 1856)

Let's start where the Louvre left off. Ingres (ang-gruh, with a soft "gruh"), who helped cap the Louvre collection, championed a Neoclassical style. *The Source* is virtually a Greek statue on canvas. Like *Venus de Milo*, she's a balance of opposite motions—her hips tilt one way, her breasts the other; one arm goes up, the other down; the water falling from the pitcher matches the fluid curve of her body. Her skin is porcelain-smooth, painted with seamless brushstrokes.

Ingres worked on this painting over the course of 35 years and considered it his "image of perfection." Famous in its day, *The Source* influenced many artists whose classical statues and paintings are in this museum.

In this and the next few rooms, you'll see more of these visions of idealized beauty—nude women in languid poses, Greek myths, and so on. The Romantics, like Eugène Delacroix, added bright colors, movement, and emotion to the classical coolness of Ingres.

ORSAY MUSEUM

The Orsay's "19th Century"
(1848–1914)

Einstein and Geronimo. Abraham Lincoln and Karl Marx. The train, the bicycle, the horse and buggy, the automobile, and the balloon. Freud and Dickens. Darwin's *Origin of Species* and the Church's Immaculate Conception. Louis Pasteur and Billy the Kid. Ty Cobb and V. I. Lenin.

The 19th century was a mix of old and new, side by side. Europe was entering the modern Industrial Age, with cities, factories, rapid transit, instant communication, and global networks. At the same time, it clung to the past with traditional, rural—almost medieval—attitudes and morals.

According to the Orsay, the "19th century" began in 1848 with the socialist and democratic revolutions (Marx's *Communist Manifesto*). It ended in 1914 with the pull of an assassin's trigger, which ignited World War I and ushered in the modern world. The museum shows art that is also both old and new, conservative and revolutionary.

• *Walk uphill (quickly, as this is background stuff) to the last room (Room 3), and find a pastel blue-green painting.*

❷ Alexandre Cabanel—*The Birth of Venus*
(*La Naissance de Vénus,* 1863)

Cabanel lays Ingres' *The Source* on her back. This goddess is a perfect fantasy, an orgasm of beauty. The Love Goddess stretches back

seductively, recently birthed from the ephemeral foam of the wave. This is art of a pre-Freudian society, when sex was dirty and mysterious and had to be exalted into a more pure and divine form. The sex drive was channeled into an acute sense of beauty. French folk would literally swoon in ecstasy before these works of art.

The art world of Cabanel's day was dominated by two conservative institutions: the Academy (the state-funded art school) and the Salon, where works were exhibited to the buying public. The public loved Cabanel's *Venus* (and Napoleon III purchased it).

Get a feel for the ideal beauty and refined emotion of these Greek-style works. (Out in the gallery, you'll find a statue of another swooning Venus.) Go ahead, swoon. If it feels good, enjoy it. Now, take a mental cold shower, and let's cross over to the "wrong side of the tracks," to the art of the early rebels.

• *Exit Room 3 into the main gallery, turn left, and head back toward the entrance, turning right into Room 4, marked* Daumier *(opposite the Ingres room).*

Realism—Early Rebels

❸ Honoré Daumier—*Celebrities of the Happy Medium* (*Célébrités du juste milieu,* 1832–1835)

This is a liberal's look at the stuffy bourgeois establishment that controlled the Academy and the Salon. In these 36 bustlets, Daumier, trained as a political car-toonist, exaggerates each subject's most distinct characteristic to capture with vicious precision the pomposity and self-righteousness of these self-appointed arbiters of taste. The labels next to the busts give the name of the person being caricatured, his title or job (most were members of the French

parliament), and an insulting nickname (like "gross, fat, and satis-fied" or Monsieur "Platehead"). Give a few nicknames yourself. Can you find Reagan, Clinton, Kerry, Pelosi, and Gingrich?

These people hated the art you're about to see. Their prud-ish faces tightened as their fantasy world was shattered by the Realists.

• *Go uphill four steps and through a leafy room to the final room, #6.*

❹ Jean-François Millet—*The Gleaners* (*Les Glaneuses,* 1867)

Millet (mee-yay) shows us three gleaners, the poor women who pick up the meager leftovers after a field has already been harvested

by the wealthy. Millet grew up on a humble farm. He didn't attend the Academy and despised the uppity Paris art scene. Instead of ideal-ized gods, goddesses, nymphs, and winged babies, he painted simple rural scenes. He was strongly affected by the socialist revolution of 1848, with its affirmation of the working class. Here he captures the innate dignity of these stocky, tanned women who bend their backs quietly in a large field for their small reward.

This is "Realism" in two senses. It's painted "realistically," unlike the prettified pastels of Cabanel's *Birth of Venus.* And it's the "real" world—not the fantasy world of Greek myth, but the

Orsay—Conservative Art and Realism

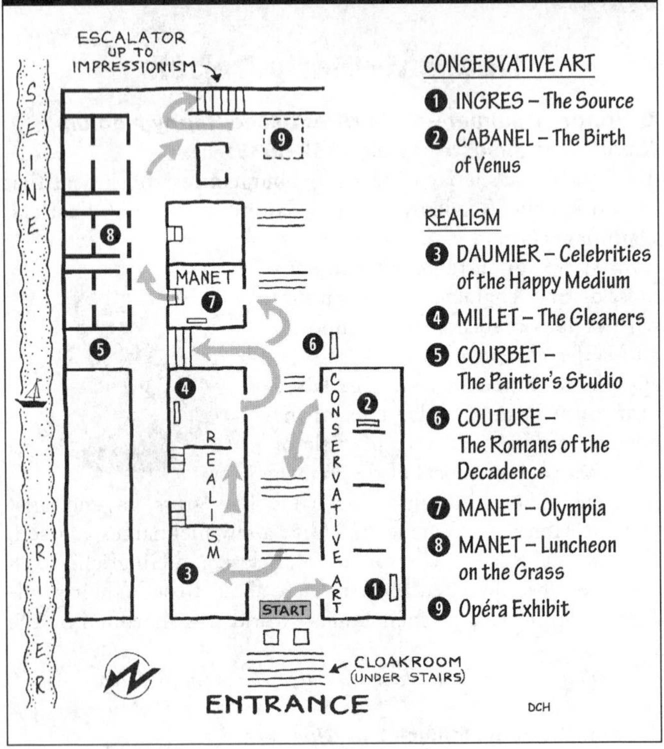

ESCALATOR
UP TO
IMPRESSIONISM

CONSERVATIVE ART

❶ INGRES – The Source

❷ CABANEL – The Birth of Venus

REALISM

❸ DAUMIER – Celebrities of the Happy Medium

❹ MILLET – The Gleaners

❺ COURBET – The Painter's Studio

❻ COUTURE – The Romans of the Decadence

❼ MANET – Olympia

❽ MANET – Luncheon on the Grass

❾ Opéra Exhibit

START

CLOAKROOM (UNDER STAIRS)

ENTRANCE   DCH

(map labels: SEINE RIVER, MANET, REALISM, CONSERVATIVE ART)

---

harsh life of the working poor.

• *Exit Room 6 into the main gallery and make a U-turn to the left, climbing the steps to a large alcove with two huge canvases. On the left is...*

❺ Gustave Courbet—*The Painter's Studio* (*L'Atelier du Peintre,* 1855)

The Salon of 1855 rejected this dark-colored, sprawling, monu-

mental painting of..."What's it about?" In an age when "Realist painter" was equated with "bomb-throwing Socialist," it took courage to buck the system. Dismissed by the so-called experts, Courbet (coor-bay) held his own one-man exhibit. He built a shed in the middle of Paris, defiantly hung

(side tab: ORSAY MUSEUM)

his art out, and basically mooned the shocked public.

Courbet's painting takes us backstage, showing us the gritty reality behind the creation of pretty pictures. We see Courbet himself in his studio, working diligently on a Realistic landscape, oblivious to the confusion around him. Milling around are ordinary citizens, not Greek heroes. The woman who looks on is not a nude Venus but a naked artist's model. And the little boy with an adoring look on his face? Perhaps it's Courbet's inner child, admiring the artist who sticks to his guns, whether it's popular or not.

• *Return to the main gallery. Back across "the tracks," the huge canvas you see is...*

❻ Thomas Couture—*The Romans of the Decadence* (*Les Romains de la Décadence,* 1847)

We see a *fin de siècle* (end-of-century) society that looks like it's packed in a big hot tub. It's stuffed with too much luxury, too much classical beauty, too much pleasure; it's wasted, burned out, and in decay. The old, backward-looking order was about to be slapped in the face.

• *Continue up the gallery, then left into Room 14 (Manet). Find the reclining nude.*

❼ Edouard Manet—*Olympia* (1863)

"This brunette is thoroughly ugly. Her face is stupid, her skin cadaverous. All this clash of colors is stupefying." So wrote a critic when Edouard Manet's nude hung in the Salon. The public hated it, attacking Manet (man-ay) in print and literally attacking the canvas.

Think back on Cabanel's painting, *The Birth of Venus:* an idealized, pastel, Vaseline-on-the-lens beauty. It's basically soft-core pornography, the kind you see selling lingerie and perfume.

Manet's nude doesn't gloss over anything. The pose is clas-

sic, used by Titian, Goya, and countless others. But this is a Realist's take on the classics. The sharp outlines and harsh, contrasting colors are new and shocking. Her hand is a clamp, and her stare is shockingly defiant, with not a hint of the seductive, hey-sailor look of most nudes. This prostitute, ignoring the flowers sent by her last customer, looks out as if to say, "Next." Manet replaced soft-core porn with hard-core art.

Edouard Manet (1832–1883) had an upper-class upbringing and some formal art training, and he had been accepted by the Salon. He could have cranked out pretty nudes and been a successful painter. Instead, he surrounded himself with a group of young artists experimenting with new techniques. Because of his reputation and strong personality, he was their master, though he learned equally from them.

• *Climb the small set of stairs in Room 14. Across the hall (and slightly to the right), you'll find...*

❽ Edouard Manet—*Luncheon on the Grass* (*Le Déjeuner sur l'Herbe*, 1863)

A shocked public looked at this and wondered: What are these scantily clad women doing with these men? Or rather, what will

they be doing after the last baguette is eaten? It isn't the nudity, but the presence of the men in ordinary clothes, that suddenly make the nudes look naked. Once again, the public judged the painting on moral rather than artistic terms.

You can see that a new revolutionary movement was starting to bud—Impressionism. Notice the background: the messy brushwork of trees and leaves, the play of light on the pond, and the light that filters through the trees onto the woman who stoops in the haze. Also note the strong contrast of colors (white skin, black clothes, green grass). This is a true out-of-doors painting, not a studio production. Let the Impressionist revolution begin.

• *Get a sneak peek of that revolution in nearby rooms, with a fine collection of works by Monet. Otherwise, continue to the far end of the gallery, where you'll walk on a glass floor over a model of Paris.*

❾ Opéra Exhibit

Expand to 100 times your size and hover over this scale-model section of the city. In the center sits the 19th-century Opéra Garnier, with its green-domed roof.

Nearby, you'll also see a cross-section model of the Opéra. You'd enter from the right end, buy your ticket in the foyer, then move into the entrance hall with its grand staircase, where you could see and be seen by *tout* Paris. At curtain time, you'd find your seat in the red-and-gold auditorium, topped by a glorious

painted ceiling. (The current ceiling, painted by Marc Chagall, is even more wonderful than the one in the model.) Notice that the stage, with elaborate riggings to raise and lower scenery, is as big as the seating area. Nearby, there are models of set designs from some famous productions. These days, Parisians enjoy their Verdi and Gounod at the modern opera house at place de la Bastille.

• *To the left of the Opéra model, a covered escalator leads up to the often-crowded Impressionist rooms. (To read ahead, consider wandering to the quiet far-left corner of the ground floor, where you'll find a huge painting of a hot-air-balloonist's-eye view of pre–Eiffel Tower Paris, c. 1855).*

Ride the escalator to the top floor. Take your first left for a commanding view of the Orsay. The second left takes you past a bookshop and a giant "backwards" clock (with

great city views) to the art, starting in Room 29. The Impressionist collection is scattered somewhat randomly through the next few rooms. Shadows dance and the displays mingle. You'll find nearly all of the following paintings, but exactly where they're hung is a lot like their brushwork... delightfully sloppy. (If you don't see a described painting, ask a guard or just move on. It's either hanging farther down or it's on vacation.)

ORSAY MUSEUM

Impressionism

Rooms 29–34: Manet, Degas, Monet, Renoir, and More

Light! Color! Vibrations! You don't hang an Impressionist canvas—you tether it. Impressionism features bright colors, easygoing open-air scenes, spontaneity, broad brushstrokes, and the play of light.

The Impressionists made their canvases shimmer by using a simple but revolutionary technique. Let's say you mix red, yellow, and green together—you'll get brown, right? But Impressionists didn't bother to mix them. They'd slap a thick brushstroke of yellow down, then a stroke of green next to it, then red next to

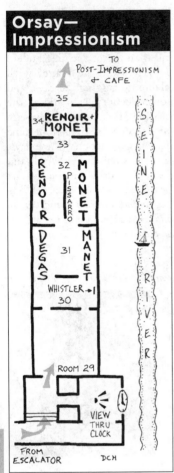

that. Up close, all you see are the three messy strokes, but as you back up...*voilà!* Brown! The colors blend in the eye, at a distance. But while your eye is saying "bland old brown," your subconscious is shouting, "Red! Yellow! Green! Yes!"

There are no lines in nature, yet someone in the classical tradition (Ingres, for example) would draw an outline of his subject, then fill it in with color. Instead the Impressionists built a figure with dabs of paint...a snowman of color.

• *In Room 30, find the non-Impressionist but equally famous...*

James Abbott McNeill Whistler—*Portrait of the Artist's Mother (Portrait de la Mère de l'Auteur, 1871)*

Why's it so famous? I don't know either. Perhaps because it's by an American, and we see in his mother some of the monumental solidity of our own ancestral moms, who were made tough by pioneering the American wilderness.

Or perhaps because it was so starkly different for its day. In a roomful of golden goddesses, it'd stand out like a fish in a tree. The alternate title is *Arrangement in Gray and Black, No. 1,* and the whole point is the subtle variations of dark shades softened by the rosy tint of her cheeks. Nevertheless, the critics kept waiting for it to come out in Colorization.

• *In Room 31, on the left side, is work by...*

Impressionism

The camera threatened to make artists obsolete. Now a machine could capture a better likeness faster than you could say "Etch-a-Sketch."

But true art is more than just painting reality. It gives us reality from the artist's point of view, with the artist's personal impressions of the scene. Impressions are often fleeting, so you have to work quickly.

The Impressionist painters rejected camera-like detail for a quick style more suited to capturing the passing moment. Feeling stifled by the rigid rules and stuffy atmosphere of the Academy, the Impressionists took as their motto, "Out of the studio, into the open air." They grabbed their berets and scarves and went on excursions to the country, where they set up their easels (and newly invented tubes of premixed paint) on riverbanks and hillsides, or they sketched in cafés and dance halls. Gods, goddesses, nymphs, and fantasy scenes were out; common people and rural landscapes were in.

The quick style and everyday subjects were ridiculed and called childish by the "experts." Rejected by the Salon, the Impressionists staged their own exhibition in 1874. They brashly took their name from an insult thrown at them by a critic who laughed at one of Monet's "impressions" of a sunrise. During the next decade, they exhibited their own work independently. The public, opposed at first, was slowly won over by the simplicity, the color, and the vibrancy of Impressionist art.

Edgar Degas—*The Dance Class* (*La Classe de Danse*, c. 1873–1875)

Clearly, Degas loved dance and the theater. (Catch his statue, *Tiny Dancer, 14 Years Old*, in the glass case.) The play of stage lights off

his dancers, especially the halos of ballet skirts, is made to order for an Impressionist. In *The Dance Class*, bored, tired dancers scratch their backs restlessly at the end of a long rehearsal. And look at the bright green bow on the girl with her back to us. In the Impressionist style, Degas slopped green paint onto her dress and didn't even say, *"Excusez-moi."*

Edgar Degas (1834–1917, day-gah) was a rich kid from a family of bankers, and he got the best classical-style art training. Adoring Ingres' pure lines and cool colors, Degas painted in the Academic style. His work was exhibited in the Salon. He gained success and a good reputation, and then...he met the Impressionists.

Degas blends classical lines with Impressionist color, spontaneity, and everyday subjects from urban Paris. Degas loved the unposed "snapshot" effect, catching his models off guard. Dance students, women at work, and café scenes are approached from odd angles that aren't always ideal, but make the scenes seem more real.

Edgar Degas—*In a Café, or The Glass of Absinthe* (*Au Café, dit L'Absinthe,* 1876)

Degas hung out with low-life Impressionists, discussing art, love, and life in the cheap cafés and bars in Montmartre. Here, a weary lady of the evening meets morning with a last, lonely, coffin-nail drink in the glaring light of a four-in-the-morning café. The pale green drink at the center of the composition is the toxic substance absinthe, which fueled many artists and burned out many more.

• *The next few rooms (32–34) feature works by two Impressionist masters at their peak, Monet and Renoir. You're looking at the quintessence of Impressionism. The two were good friends, often working side by side, and their canvases now hang side by side in these rooms.*

Pierre-Auguste Renoir—*Dance at the Moulin de la Galette* (*Bal du Moulin de la Galette,* 1876)

On Sunday afternoons, working-class folk would dress up and head for the fields on butte Montmartre (near Sacré-Cœur basilica)

to dance, drink, and eat little crêpes *(galettes)* till dark. Pierre-Auguste Renoir (1841–1919, ren-wah) liked to go there to paint the common Parisians living and loving in the afternoon sun. The sunlight filtering through the trees creates a kaleidoscope of colors, like the 19th-century equivalent of a mirror ball throwing darts of light onto the dancers.

He captures the dappled light with quick blobs of yellow staining the ground, the men's jackets, and the sun-dappled straw hat (right of center). Smell the powder on the ladies' faces. The painting glows with bright colors. Even the shadows on the ground, which should be gray or black, are colored a warm blue. Like a photographer who uses a slow shutter speed to show motion, Renoir paints a waltzing blur.

Renoir's work is lighthearted, with light colors, almost pastels. He seems to be searching for an ideal, the pure beauty we saw on the ground floor. In later years, he used more and more red tones, as if trying for even more warmth. If you love Renoir, look for more of his work farther along, in Room 39.

Camille Pissarro, Alfred Sisley, and Others

The Orsay features some of the "lesser" pioneers of the Impressionist style. Browse around and discover your own favorites. Pissarro (Room 32) is one of mine. His grainy landscapes are more subtle and subdued than those of the flashy Monet and Renoir—but, as someone said, "He did for the earth what Monet did for the water."

Claude Monet—*The Cathedral of Rouen* (*La Cathédrale de Rouen,* 1893)

Claude Monet (1840–1926, mo-nay) is the father of Impressionism. He fully explored the possibilities of open-air painting and tried to faithfully reproduce nature's colors with bright blobs of paint.

Monet went to Rouen, rented a room across from the cathedral, set up his easel...and waited. He wanted to catch "a series

of differing impressions" of the cathedral facade at various times of day and year. He often had several canvases going at once. In all, he did 30 paintings of the cathedral, and each is unique. The time-lapse series shows the sun passing slowly across the sky, creating different-colored light and shadows. The labels next to the art describe the conditions: in gray weather, in the morning, morning sun, full sunlight, and so on.

ORSAY MUSEUM

As Monet zeroes in on the play of colors and light, the physical subject—the cathedral—is dissolving. It's only a rack upon which to hang the light and color. Later artists would boldly throw away the rack, leaving purely abstract modern art in its place.

Claude Monet—Paintings from Monet's Garden at Giverny

One of Monet's favorite places to paint was the garden he land-scaped at his home in Giverny, west of Paris (and worth a visit, pro-

vided you like Monet more than you hate crowds—see Giverny section of More Day Trips chap-ter). The Japanese bridge and the water lilies floating in the pond were his two favorite subjects. As Monet aged and his eyesight failed, he made bigger canvases of smaller subjects. The final water lilies are monumental smudges of thick paint surrounded by paint-splotched clouds reflected on the surface of the pond.

Monet's most famous water lilies are in full bloom at the Orangerie Museum, across the river in the Tuileries Garden (see Orangerie Museum Tour). You can see more Monet at the Marmottan Museum (see Marmottan Museum Tour).

• *Notice the skylight above you: These Impressionist rooms are appro-priately illuminated by ever-changing natural light. Then carry on to Room 35.*

Post-Impressionism

⑩ Vincent van Gogh

Impressionists have been accused of being "light"-weights. The colorful style lends itself to bright country scenes, gardens, sun-light on the water, and happy crowds of simple people. It took a remarkable genius to add profound emotion to the Impressionist style.

Like Michelangelo, Beethoven, Rembrandt, Wayne Newton, and a select handful of others, Vincent van Gogh (1853–1890, van-go, or van-HOCK by the Dutch and the snooty) put so much of himself into his work that art and life became one. In this room you'll see both Van Gogh's painting style and his life unfold.

Vincent van Gogh—*Peasant Woman near the Hearth* (*Paysanne près de l'Atre,* 1885)

As the son of a Dutch minister, Van Gogh too feels drawn to a religious vocation, and he spreads the gospel among the poorest of the poor—peasants and miners in overcast Holland and Belgium. He paints these hardworking, dignified folks in a crude, dark style reflecting the oppressiveness of their lives...and the loneliness of his own as he roams northern Europe in search of a calling.

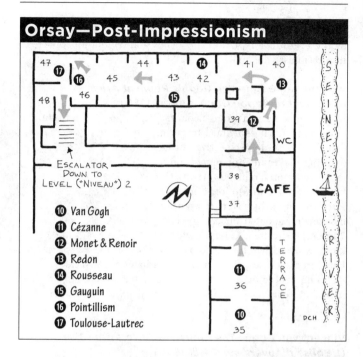

Orsay—Post-Impressionism

- 10 Van Gogh
- 11 Cézanne
- 12 Monet & Renoir
- 13 Redon
- 14 Rousseau
- 15 Gauguin
- 16 Pointillism
- 17 Toulouse-Lautrec

Vincent van Gogh—*Self-Portrait, Paris (Portrait de l'Artiste,* 1887)

Encouraged by his art-dealer brother, Van Gogh moves to Paris, and *voilà!* The color! He meets Monet, drinks with Paul Gauguin and Henri de Toulouse-Lautrec, and soaks up the Impressionist style. (See how he builds a bristling brown beard using thick strokes of red, yellow, and green side by side.)

At first, he paints like the others, but soon he develops his own style. By using thick, swirling brushstrokes, he even infuses life into inanimate objects. Van Gogh's brushstrokes curve and thrash like a garden hose pumped full of wine.

Vincent van Gogh—*Midday* (*La Méridienne,* 1890, based on a painting by Millet)

The social life of Paris becomes too much for the solitary Van Gogh. He moves to the South of France. At first, in the glow of the bright spring sunshine, he has a period of incredible creativity and happiness, as he is overwhelmed by the bright colors, landscape vistas, and common people—an Impressionist's dream.

Vincent van Gogh—*Van Gogh's Room at Arles* (*La Chambre de van Gogh à Arles,* 1889)

But being alone in a strange country begins to wear on him. An ugly man, he finds it hard to get a date. The close-up perspective of this painting makes his tiny rented room look even more cramped. He invites his friend Gauguin to join him, but after two months together arguing passionately about art, nerves get raw. Van Gogh threatens Gauguin with a knife, which drives his friend back to Paris. In crazed despair, Van Gogh mutilates his own ear.

The people of Arles realize they have a madman on their hands and convince Van Gogh to seek help. He enters a mental hospital.

Vincent van Gogh—*The Church at Auvers-sur-Oise* (*L'Eglise d'Auvers-sur-Oise,* 1890)

Van Gogh's paintings done in the peace of the mental hospital are more meditative—fewer bright landscapes, more closed-in scenes with deeper and almost surreal colors. The sky is cobalt blue and the church's windows are also blue, as if we're looking right through the building to an infinite sky. There's a road that leads from us to the church, then splits to go behind it. A choice must be made: which way?

Van Gogh, the preacher's son, saw painting as a calling, and he approached it with a spiritual intensity.

Vincent van Gogh—*Self-Portrait, St. Rémy* (1889)

Van Gogh wavers between happiness and madness. He despairs of ever being sane enough to continue painting.

This self-portrait shows a man engulfed in a confused background of brushstrokes that swirl and rave, setting in motion the waves of the jacket. But in the midst of this rippling sea of mystery floats a still, detached island of a face with probing, questioning, yet wise eyes.

Do his troubled eyes know that only a few months on, he will take a pistol and put a bullet through his chest?

• *Vincent van Gone. Continue to Room 36.*

⑪ Paul Cézanne

Paul Cézanne (1839–1906, say-zahn) brought Impressionism into the 20th century. After the color of Monet, the warmth of Renoir, and Van Gogh's passion, Cézanne's rather impersonal canvases can be difficult to appreciate. Bowls of fruit, landscapes, and a few portraits were Cézanne's passion. Because of his style (not the content), he is often called the first modern painter.

Paul Cézanne—*Self-Portrait* (*Portrait de l'Artiste*, c. 1873–1876)

Cézanne was virtually unknown and unappreciated in his lifetime. He worked alone, lived alone, and died alone, ignored by

all but a few revolutionary young artists who understood his efforts. Cézanne's brush was a blunt instrument. With it, he'd bludgeon reality into submission, drag it across a canvas, and leave it there to dry. But Cézanne, the mediocre painter, was a great innovator. His work spoke for itself—which is good because, as you can see here, he had no mouth.

Paul Cézanne—Landscape (*Rochers près des Grottes au-dessus de Château-Noir,* 1904)

Cézanne used chunks of green, tan, and blue paint as building

blocks to construct this rocky brown cliff. Whereas the Impressionists built a figure out of a mosaic of individual brushstrokes, Cézanne used blocks of paint to give it a more solid, geometrical shape. A block of paint forming part of a rock in the foreground is the same size as one in the background, flattening the scene into a wall of brushstrokes.

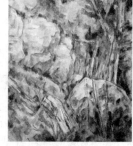

These chunks are like little "cubes." It's no coincidence that his experiments in reducing forms to their geometric basics influenced the...Cubists.

Paul Cézanne—*The Card Players*
(***Les Joueurs de Cartes,*** **c. 1890–1895)**

These aren't people. They're studies in color and pattern. The subject matter—two guys playing cards—is less important than the pleasingly balanced pattern they make on the canvas, two sloping forms framing a cylinder (a bottle) in the center. Later, abstract artists would focus solely on the shapes and colors.

The jacket of the player to the right is a patchwork of tans, greens, and browns. Even the "empty" space between the men—

painted with fragmented chunks of color—is almost as tangible as they are. As one art scholar puts it: "Cézanne confused intermingled forms and colors, achieving an extraordinarily luminous density in which lyricism is controlled by a rigorously constructed rhythm." Just what I said—chunks of color.

• *Exit to the café and consider a well-deserved break. From the café, continue ahead, walking under the large green beam, following signs to* Salles 39–48. *The hallway leads past WCs to Room 39, which often displays* **work by Monet and Renoir (⑫)**, *and may include paintings covered earlier in this tour. Then continue into dark Room 40 in the right corner...*

⑬ Odilon Redon

Flip off the lights and step into Odilon Redon's mysterious *fin de siècle* world. If the Orsay's a zoo, this is the nocturnal house. Prowl around. This is wild, wild stuff. It's intense—imagine Richard Nixon on mushrooms playing sax.

If the Impressionists painted by sunlight, Odilon Redon (1840–1916) painted by moonlight. His pastels (protected by dim lighting) portray dream imagery and mythological archetypes. Classed as Symbolism, Redon's weird work later inspired the Surrealists.

• *Coming out of the darkness, pass into the gallery lined with metal columns, containing the primitive art of Rousseau and Gauguin. Start in the first alcove.*

Primitives

⑭ Henri Rousseau—*War*
(***La Guerre,*** **or *La Chevauchée de la Discorde,*** **1894)**

War, in the form of a woman with a sword, flies on horseback across the battlefield, leaving destruction in her wake: broken bare trees, burning clouds in the background, and heaps of corpses picked at by the birds. Some artists, rejecting the harried, scientific, and rational world, remembered a time before "isms," when works of art weren't scholarly "studies in form and color," but voodoo dolls full of mystery and magic power. They learned from the art of primitive tribes in Africa and the South Seas, trying to re-create a primal Garden of Eden of peace and wholeness. In doing so, they created another "ism": Primitivism.

Henri Rousseau (1844–1910), a man who painted like a child, was an amateur artist who palled around with all the great painters—but they never took his naive style of art seriously. Like a child's drawing of a nightmare, the images are primitive—flat and simple, with unreal colors—but the effect is both beautiful and terrifying.

• *Farther along this columned gallery, you'll find work by...*

⓯ Paul Gauguin—*Arearea,* or *Joyousness* (*Joyeusetés,* 1892)

Paul Gauguin (1848–1903, go-gan) got the travel bug early in childhood and grew up wanting to be a sailor. Instead, he became a stockbroker. In his spare time, he painted, and he was introduced to the Impressionist circle.

He learned their bright clashing colors but diverged from this path about the time Van Gogh waved a knife in his face. At the age of 35, he got fed up with it all, quit his job, abandoned his wife (her stern portrait bust may be nearby) and family, and took refuge in his art. He traveled to the South Seas in search of the exotic, finally settling on Tahiti.

In Tahiti, Gauguin found his Garden of Eden. He simplified his life into a routine of eating, sleeping, and painting. He simplified his painting still more, to flat images with heavy black outlines filled with bright, pure colors. He painted the native girls in their naked innocence (so different from Cabanel's seductive *Venus*). But this simple style had a deep undercurrent of symbolic meaning.

Arearea shows native women and a dog. In the "distance" (there's no attempt at traditional 3-D here), a procession goes by with a large pagan idol. What's the connection between the idol and the foreground figures, who are apparently unaware of it? In primitive societies, religion permeates life. Idols, dogs, and women are holy.

• Farther along, find...

⑯ Pointillist Paintings (Lots of Dots)

Pointillism, as illustrated by many paintings in the next rooms, brings Impressionism to its logical conclusion—little dabs of dif-

ferent colors placed side by side to blend in the viewer's eye. In works such as *The Circus* (*Le Cirque*, 1891), Georges Seurat (1859–1891) uses only red, yellow, blue, and green points of paint to create a mosaic of colors that shimmers at a distance, capturing the wonder of the dawn of electric lights.

• In darkened Room 47 are pastels by...

⑰ Henri de Toulouse-Lautrec—*The Clownesse Cha-U-Kao* (1895)

Henri de Toulouse-Lautrec (1864–1901) was the black sheep of a noble family. At age 15 he broke both legs, which left him dis-

abled. Shunned by his family, a freak to society, he felt more at home in the underworld of other outcasts—prostitutes, drunks, thieves, dancers, and actors. He painted the lowlife in the bars, cafés, dance halls, and brothels he frequented. Toulouse-Lautrec died young of alcoholism.

The Clownesse Cha-U-Kao is one of his fellow freaks, a fat lady clown who made her living by being laughed at. She slumps wearily after a performance, indifferent to the applause, and adjusts her dress to prepare for the curtain call.

Toulouse-Lautrec was a true impression-ist, catching his models in candid poses. He worked spontaneously, never correcting his mistakes, as you can see from the blotches on her dark skirt and the unintentional yellow sash that hangs down. Can you see a bit of Degas here, in the subject matter, snapshot pose, and colors?

Henri de Toulouse-Lautrec—*Jane Avril Dancing* (*Jane Avril dansant,* 1891)

Toulouse-Lautrec hung out at the Moulin Rouge dance hall in Montmartre. One of the most popular dancers was this slim, graceful, elegant, and melancholy woman, who stood out above the rabble of the Moulin Rouge. Her legs keep dancing while her mind is far away. Toulouse-Lautrec, the artistocrat, might have identified with her noble face—sad and weary of the nightlife, but immersed in it.

• You've seen the essential Orsay and are permitted to cut out (the exit is directly below you). But there's an "other" Orsay I think you'll find entertaining.

To reach Level 2 ("niveau 2"), descend three flights (escalator nearby), turn left, and cross to the other side of the gallery.

Along the way, on niveau 2, peek into "Le Restaurant." This was part of the original hotel that adjoined

the station—built in 1900, abandoned after 1939, condemned, and restored to the elegance you see today. The restaurant is pricey, but there's affordable coffee and tea (daily 15:00–17:30 except Thu).

• Now find the palatial Room 51, with mirrors and chandeliers, marked Salle des Fêtes *(Grand Ballroom).*

The "Other" Orsay—Level 2

The beauty of the Orsay is that it combines all the art from 1848 to 1914, both modern and classical, in one building. The classical art, so popular in its own day, has been maligned and was forgotten in the 20th century. It's time for a reassessment. Is it as gaudy and gawd-awful as we've been led to believe? From our 21st-century perspective, let's take a look at the opulent *fin de siècle* French high society and its luxurious art.

ORSAY MUSEUM

⑱ The Grand Ballroom (Salle des Fêtes)

When the Orsay hotel was here, this was one of France's poshest nightspots. You can easily imagine gowned debutantes and white-gloved dandies waltzing the night away to the music of a chamber orchestra. Notice:

• The interior decorating: raspberry marble-ripple ice-cream columns, pastel-colored ceiling painting, gold work, mirrors, and leafy garlands of chandeliers.

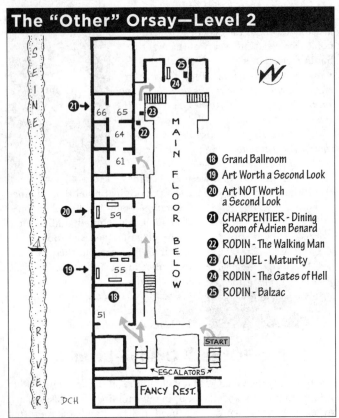

The "Other" Orsay—Level 2

18 Grand Ballroom

19 Art Worth a Second Look

20 Art NOT Worth a Second Look

21 CHARPENTIER - Dining Room of Adrien Benard

22 RODIN - The Walking Man

23 CLAUDEL - Maturity

24 RODIN - The Gates of Hell

25 RODIN - Balzac

- The statue *Bacchante Couchée* sprawled in the middle of the room.
- *La Nature*, a statue of a woman dressed in multicolored marble.
- The statue *Aurore*, with her canopy of hair, hide-and-seek face, and silver-dollar nipples, looking like a shampoo ad.
- The large painting *The Birth of Venus (La Naissance de Vénus)* by William Bouguereau. Van Gogh once said, "If I painted like Bouguereau, I could make money. But the public will never change—they only love sweet things."

    Is this stuff beautiful or merely gaudy? Divine or decadent?

- *Exit the Salles des Fêtes and turn left, then left again onto the mezzanine overlooking the main gallery. Enter the first room on the left (#55), labeled* Naturalism.

⓳ Art Worth a Second Look

We've seen some great art; now let's see some not-so-great art—at least, that's what modern critics tell us. This is realistic art with a subconscious kick.

• *Working clockwise, you'll see...*

Cain

The world's first murderer, with the murder weapon still in his belt, is exiled with his family. Archaeologists had recently discovered a Neanderthal skull, so the artist makes the family part of a prehistoric hunter/gatherer tribe.

The Dream (*Le Rêve*)

Soldiers lie still, asleep without beds, while visions of Gatling guns dance in their heads.

Payday (*La Paye des Moissonneurs*)

Called "the grandson of Courbet and Millet," Leon L'Hermitte depicts peasants getting paid. The subtitle of the work could be, "Is this all there is to life?" (Or, "The Paycheck...After Deductions.")

The Excommunication of Robert le Pieux

The bishops exit after performing the rite. The king and queen are stunned, the scepter dropped. The ritual candle has been snuffed out; it falls, fuming, echoing through the huge hall.... Is this art, or only cheap theatrics?

• *Continue down the mezzanine. Skip the next room, then go left into Room 59.*

⓴ Art Not Worth a Second Look

The Orsay's director once said, "Certainly, we have bad paintings. But we have only the greatest bad paintings." And here they are.

Serenity

An idyll in the woods. Three nymphs with harps waft off to the

right. These people are stoned on something.

The School of Plato (*L'Ecole de Platon*)

Subtitled "The Athens YMCA." A Christ-like Plato surrounded by adoring, half-naked nubile youths gives new meaning to the term "platonic relationship."

Will the pendulum shift so that one day art like *The School of Plato* becomes the new, radical avant-garde style?

• *Return to the mezzanine and continue to the far end. Enter Room 61 (Art Nouveau) and browse through several rooms of curvaceous furniture on your way to the far left corner, Room 66.*

Art Nouveau

㉑ Alexandre Charpentier—*Dining Room of Adrien Benard* (*Boiserie de la Salle à Mangér de la Propriété Benard*)

The Industrial Age brought factories, row houses, machines,

train stations, geometrical precision—and ugliness. At the turn of the 20th century, some artists reacted against the unrelieved geometry of harsh, pragmatic, iron-and-steel Eiffel Tower art with a "new art"—Art Nouveau. (Hmm. I think I had a driver's ed teacher by that name.) This wood-paneled dining room, with its carved vines, leafy garlands, and tree-branch arches, is one of the finest examples of Art Nouveau.

Like nature, which also abhors a straight line, Art Nouveau artists used the curves of flowers and vines as their pattern. They were convinced that "practical" didn't have to mean "ugly" as well. They turned everyday household objects into art. (Another well-known example of Art Nouveau is the curvy, wrought-ironwork of some of Paris' early Métro entrances, commissioned by the same man who ordered this dining room for his home.)

• *Return to the mezzanine and grab a seat in front of the Rodin statue of a man missing everything but his legs.*

㉒ Auguste Rodin—*The Walking Man* (*L'Homme Qui Marche*, c. 1900)

Like this statue, Auguste Rodin (1840–1917) had one foot in the past, while the other was stepping into the future. Rodin combined classical solidity with Impressionist surfaces to become the greatest sculptor since Michelangelo.

This muscular, forcefully striding man could be a symbol of the Renaissance man with his classical power. With no mouth or hands, he speaks with his body. Get close and look at the statue's surface. This rough, "unfinished"

look reflects light like the rough Impressionist brushwork, making the statue come alive, never quite at rest in the viewer's eye.
• *Near the far end of the mezzanine, you'll see a small bronze statue of a couple.*

㉓ Camille Claudel—*Maturity* (*L'Age Mûr,* 1899-1903)

Camille Claudel, Rodin's student and mistress, may have portrayed their doomed love affair here. A young girl desperately reaches out to an older man, who is led away reluctantly by an older woman. The center of the composition is the empty space left when their hands separate. In real life, Rodin refused to leave his wife, and Claudel (see her head sticking up from a block of marble nearby) ended up in an insane asylum.

㉔ Auguste Rodin—*The Gates of Hell* (*La Porte de l'Enfer,* 1880-1917)

Rodin worked for decades on these doors depicting Dante's hell, and they contain some of his greatest hits—small statues that he later executed in full size. Find *The Thinker* squatting above the doorway, contemplating Man's fate. And in the lower left is the same kneeling man eating his children *(Ugolin)* that you'll see in full size nearby. Rodin paid models to run, squat, leap, and spin around his studio however they wanted. When he saw an interesting pose, he'd yell, "freeze" (or "statue maker") and get out his sketch pad. (For more on *The Gates of Hell* and Rodin, see the Rodin Museum Tour.)

㉕ Auguste Rodin—*Honoré de Balzac* (1897)

The great French novelist is given a heroic, monumental ugliness. Wrapped in a long cloak, he thrusts his head out at a defiant angle, showing the strong individualism and egoism of the 19th century Romantic movement. Balzac is proud and snooty—but his body forms a question mark, and underneath the twisted features we can see a touch of personal pain and self-doubt. This is hardly camera-eye realism— Balzac wasn't that grotesque—but it captures a personality that strikes us even if we don't know the man.

From this perch, look over the main floor at all the classical statues between you and the big clock and realize how far we've come—not in years, but in style changes. Many of the statues below—beautiful, smooth, balanced, and idealized—were created at the same time as Rodin's powerful, haunting works. Rodin is a good place to end this tour. With a stable base of 19th-century stone, he launched art into the 20th century.

ORANGERIE MUSEUM TOUR

Musée de l'Orangerie

This Impressionist museum is as lovely as a water lily. Step out of the tree-lined, sun-dappled Impressionist painting that is the Tuileries Garden, and into the Orangerie (oh-rahn-zheh-ree), a little bijou of select works by Monet, Renoir, Matisse, Picasso, and others.

On the main floor you'll find the main attraction, Monet's *Water Lilies (Nymphéas)*, floating dreamily in the oval rooms Monet intended for them. But in the 1960s the museum added a floor above the *Lilies*, cutting them off from the daylight that was, after all, their inspiration and subject matter. In 2006, after a renovation that took six years and $36 million, the upstairs collection was moved underground, and the upper floor was transformed into a tall skylight—drenching the *Lilies* in natural light.

In the Underground Gallery are select works from the personal collection of Paris' trend-spotting art dealer of the 1920s, Paul Guillaume. The museum is small enough to enjoy in a short visit, but complete enough to show the bridge from Impressionism to the Moderns. And it's all beautiful.

Orientation

Cost: €7.50, under 18 free, covered by Museum Pass.

Hours: Wed–Mon 9:00–18:00, closed Tue (galleries shut down 15 minutes before closing time).

Getting There: It's in the Tuileries Garden near place de la Concorde (Mo: Concorde).

Information: Tel. 01 44 77 80 07, www.musee-orangerie.fr.

Audioguide Tours: The €5 audioguide is a bit skimpy on the *Water Lilies*, but it adds good detail about individual canvases in the Walter-Guillaume collection.

Length of This Tour: Allow one hour.
Starring: Claude Monet's water lilies and select works by the pioneers of Modern painting.

The Tour Begins

• *Monet's* Water Lilies *float serenely in two pond-shaped rooms on the main floor. Examine them up close to see Monet's technique; stand back to take in the whole picture.*

Main Floor

Claude Monet (1840–1926)

Hall (Salle) I

Like Beethoven going deaf, a nearly blind Claude Monet wrote his final symphonies on a monumental scale. Even as he struggled with cataracts, he planned a series of huge six-foot-tall canvases of water lilies to hang in special rooms at the Orangerie.

These eight mammoth, curved panels immerse you in Monet's garden. We're looking at the pond in his garden at Giverny—dotted with water lilies, surrounded by foliage, and dappled by the reflections of the sky, clouds, and trees on the surface. The water lilies (*nymphéas* in French) range from plain green lily pads to flowers of red, white, yellow, lavender, and various combos.

The effect is intentionally disorienting; the different canvases feature different parts of the pond from different angles, at different times of day, with no obvious chronological order. Monet mingles the pond's many elements and lets us sort it out.

• *Start with the long wall on your right (as you enter) and work counterclockwise.*

It's *Morning* on the pond at Giverny. The blue pond is the center of the composition, framed by the green, foliage-covered banks at either end. Lilies float in the foreground, and the pond stretches into the distance.

The sheer scale of the Orangerie project was daunting for an artist in his twilight years. This vast painting is made from  four separate canvases stitched together, and spans 6 feet 6 inches by 55 feet—it could cover an entire Paris hotel room. Altogether, Monet painted 1,950 square feet of canvas to complete the *Water Lilies* series. Working at his home in Giverny, Monet built a special studio with skylights and wheeled easels to accommodate the canvases.

The panel at the far end, called *Green Affections*, looks deep into the dark water. Green willow branches are reflected on the water in a vertical pattern; lily pads stretch horizontally.

Along the other long wall *(Clouds)*, green lilies float among lavender clouds reflected in blue water. Staring into Monet's pond, we see the intermingling of the four classical elements—earth (foliage), air (the sky), fire (sunlight), and water—the primordial soup of life.

The true subject of these works is the play of reflected light off the surface of the pond. Monet would work on several canvases at once, each dedicated to a different time of day. He'd move with the sun from one canvas to the next. Pan slowly around this hall. Watch the pond turn from pre-dawn darkness (far end) to clear morning light *(Morning)* to lavender late afternoon *(Clouds)* to glorious sunset.

In *Sunset* (near end), the surface of the pond is stained a bright yellow. Get close and see how Monet worked. Starting from the gray of blank canvas (lower right), he'd lay down big, thick brushstrokes of a single color, weaving them in a (mostly) horizontal and vertical pattern to create a dense mesh of foliage. Over this, he'd add more color for the dramatic highlights, until (in the center of the yellow) he got a dense paste of piled-up paint. Up close, it's a mess—but back up, and the colors begin to resolve into a luminous scene. There are no clearly identifiable objects in this canvas—no lilies, no trees, no clouds—just pure reflected color.

• *Continue into Room II, starting with the long wall on your right and working counterclockwise.*

Hall (Salle) II

In this room, Monet frames the pond with pillar-like tree trunks and overhanging foliage. The compositions are a bit more symmetrical and the color schemes more muted, with blue and lavender and green-brown. Monet is often thought of as a lightweight, but his paintings almost always deal with the foundation of life—

unspoiled nature.

In *Willows on a Clear Morning* (on the long wall to the right), we seem to be standing on the bank of the pond, looking out through overhanging trees at the water. The swirling branches and horizontal ripples on the pond suggest it's windy.

The Two Willows (far end) frame a wide expanse of water dotted with lilies and the reflection of gray-pink clouds.

Stand close in front of *Morning Willows* (long left wall). Notice how a "brown" tree is a tangled Impressionist beard of purple, green, blue, and red. Each leaf is a long brushstroke, each lily pad a dozen smudges.

At the near end, *Reflections of Trees* is a mess of blue-purple paint brightened only by the lone rose lilies in the center. Each lily is made of many Impressionist brushstrokes—each brushstroke is itself a mix of red, white, and pink paints. Monet demonstrates both his mastery of color and his ability to render it with paint, applied generously and deftly. He wanted the vibrant colors to keep firing your synapses.

With this last canvas, darkness descends on the pond. The room's large, moody canvases, painted by an 80-year-old man in the twilight of his life, invite meditation.

For 12 years (1914–1926), Monet worked on these paintings obsessively. A successful eye operation in 1923 gave him new energy. Monet completed all the planned canvases, but never lived to see them installed here. In 1927, the year after Monet's death, these rooms were completed and the canvases were put in place. Some call this the first "art installation"—a space specially designed for the art it displays in order to enhance the experience.

Monet's final work was more "modern" than Impressionist. Each canvas is fully saturated with color, the distant objects as bright as the close ones. Monet's mosaic of brushstrokes forms a colorful design that's beautiful even if you just look "at" the canvas, like wallpaper. He wanted his paintings to be realistic and three-dimensional, but with a pleasant, two-dimensional pattern. As the subjects become fuzzier, the colors and patterns predominate. Monet builds a bridge between Impressionism and modern, abstract art.

To see more of Monet's work, take the Marmottan Museum Tour and day-trip to Giverny, both covered in this book.

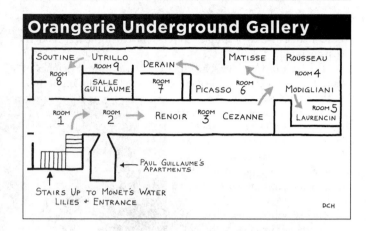

Underground Gallery

Walter-Guillaume Collection

These paintings—Impressionist, Fauvist, and Cubist—were amassed by the art dealer Paul Guillaume. They're a snapshot of what was hot in the world of art, circa 1920. The once-revolutionary Impressionists had become completely old-school, though their paintings—now classics—commanded a fortune. The bohemian Fauvists and Cubists, who invented Modern art atop Butte Montmartre (c. 1900–1915), had suddenly become the darlings of the art world. But they refused to be categorized, and their work in the 1920s branched out in dozens of new directions. Browse through the gallery and watch the various "isms" unfold.

• *Descend the stairs to the lower floor. Turn right and find several Renoir canvases midway down the gallery.*

Pierre-Auguste Renoir (1841–1919)

Renoir loved to paint *les femmes*—women and girls—nude and innocent, taking a bath or practicing the piano, all with rosy red cheeks and a relaxed grace. We get a feel for the happy family life of middle-class Parisians (including Renoir's own family) during the belle époque—the beautiful age of the late 19th century. Renoir's warm, sunny colors (mostly red) are Impressionist, but he adds a classical touch with his clearer lines and, in the later nudes, the voluptuousness of classical statues and paintings.

Paul Cézanne (1839–1906)

These small canvases of simple subjects reinvented the way modern artists painted.

The fruit of Cézanne's still lifes are "built" out of patches of color. There's no traditional shading to create the illusion of 3-D, but these fruit bulge out like cameos from the canvas. The fruit are clearly at eye level, yet they're also clearly placed on a table seen from above. Picasso was fascinated with Cézanne's strange new world that showed multiple perspectives at once.

In his landscapes, Cézanne the Impressionist creates "brown" rocks out of red, orange, and purple; and "green" trees out of green, lime, and purple. Cézanne the proto-Cubist builds the rocks and trees with blocks of thick brushstrokes.

Henri Rousseau (1844–1910)

Rousseau, a simple government official, never traveled outside France, but he created an exotic, dreamlike, completely unique

world. A Parisian wedding is set amid tropical trees. Figures are placed in a 3-D world, but the lines of perspective recede so steeply into the distance that everyone is in danger of sliding down the canvas. The way he put familiar images in bizarre settings influenced the Surrealists. Enjoy France's biggest collection of Rousseaus.

Amedeo Modigliani (1884–1920)

In his short, poverty-stricken, drug-addled life, Modigliani produced timeless-looking portraits of modern people. Born in Italy, Modigliani moved to Paris, where he hung around the fringes of the avant-garde in-crowd in Montmartre. He gained a reputation for his alcoholic excesses and outrageous behavior.

Turning his back on the prevailing Fauvist/Cubist ambience of the times, Modigliani developed a unique style, influenced by primitive tribal masks. His canvases feature stylized heads, almond eyes, long necks, and puckered mouths. *Novo Pilota* (1915) portrays Paul Guillaume as a cool dandy, suavely cradling a cigarette. Modigliani died young, just as his work was gaining recognition.

Paul Guillaume
(1891–1934)

For the first three decades of the 20th century, Paris was the center of the art world, and the center of Paris' art scene was

Paul Guillaume. An art dealer, promoter of "modern" art, and friend of out-there artists, Guillaume rose from humble beginnings to become wealthy and famous.

In his early days, this self-made businessman struggled alongside struggling painters in Montmartre—Picasso, Modigliani, Derain, Laurencin, and many others. When the art market boomed in the 1920s (along with the stock market), he and his fellow bohemians became the toasts of high society. With his flamboyant wife, Domenica (also called Juliette), Guillaume hosted exotic parties featuring what we would now call "performance art" to shock and titillate the buying public.

Many of their artist friends honored Paul and Domenica by painting their portraits. In Modigliani's *Novo Pilota* (pictured above), young Paul strikes a pose as the dapper man-of-the-world he was soon to become. The title of the painting is Italian for "new helmsman," reflecting Paul's growing status as a champion of Modernism. Marie Laurencin's portrait captures the winsome beauty of Domenica, whose charm helped establish the nouveau riche couple in social circles. Andre Derain's and Kees Van Dongen's portraits feature Paul and Domenica when they were older, more confident, and sophisticated.

The Orangerie displays Guillaume's personal collection of favorite paintings. After Paul's death, Domenica married Jean Walter and took her new husband's last name, which is why it's officially called the "Walter-Guillaume" collection.

Marie Laurencin (1883–1956)

As the girlfriend of the poet and art critic Guillaume Apollinaire, Laurencin was right at the heart of the Montmartre circle when Modern art was born. Her work spreads a pastel sheen over this rough time, featuring women and cuddly animals intertwined in pink, blue, and gray tones.

Henri Matisse (1869–1954)

After World War I, Matisse moved to the south of France. He abandoned his fierce Fauvist style, and painted languid women in angular rooms with arabesque wallpaper. These paler tones evoke the sunny luxury of the Riviera. Traditional 3-D perspective is thrown out the occasional hotel window as the women and furnishings in the "foreground" blend with the wallpaper "background" to become part of the decor.

Pablo Picasso (1881–1973)

Picasso is a shopping mall of 20th-century artistic styles. In this room alone, he passes through his "Blue" Period (sad and tragic), "Rose" Period (red-toned nudes with timeless, masklike faces), Cubism (flat planes of interwoven perspectives), and his Classical Period, with massive, sculptural nudes—warm blow-up dolls with substance. If all roads lead to Paris, all art styles flowed through Picasso.

André Derain (1880–1954)

This former wild beast *(fauve)* tamed his colors in the 1920s. He and Picasso rode the rising wave of Classicism that surfaced after the chaos of the war years. With sharp outlines and studied realism, Derain's still lifes portrayed nudes, harlequins, portraits, and landscapes—all in odd, angular poses.

Maurice Utrillo (1883–1955)

This hard-drinking, streetwise bohemian artist is known for his postcard views of Montmartre—whitewashed buildings under perennially cloudy skies.

Chaim Soutine (1893–1943)

When his friend Modigliani died (and Modigliani's widow committed suicide), Soutine went into a tailspin of depression that drove him to paint. The subjects are ordinary—landscapes, portraits, and

a fine selection of your favorite cuts of meat—but the style is deformed and Expressionistic. It shows a warped world in a funhouse mirror, smeared onto the canvas with thick, lurid colors. The never-cheerful Soutine was known to destroy work that did not satisfy him. Stand and ponder why these made the cut.

Did I say that the Orangerie's collection was as beautiful as an Impressionist painting? Well, Soutine's misery is so complete, it's almost a thing of beauty.

RUE CLER WALK

The Art of Parisian Living

Paris is changing quickly, but a stroll down this street introduces you to a thriving, traditional Parisian neighborhood and offers insights into the local culture. Although this is a wealthy district (as reflected in the elegance of its shops), rue Cler retains a certain workaday charm still found in small neighborhoods throughout Paris.

Shopping for groceries is an integral part of everyday life here. Parisians shop almost daily for three good reasons: Refrigerators are small (tiny kitchens), produce must be fresh, and it's an important social event. Shopping is a chance to hear about the butcher's vacation plans, see photos of the florist's new grandchild, relax over *un café,* and kiss the cheeks of friends (the French standard is twice for regular acquaintances, three times for friends you haven't seen in a while).

Rue Cler—traffic-free since 1984—offers plenty of space for tiny stores and their patrons to spill out onto the street. It's an ideal environment for this ritual to survive and for you to explore. The street is lined with the essential shops—wine, cheese, chocolate, bread—as well as a bank and a post office. And the shops of this community are run by people who've found their niche: boys who grew up on quiche, girls who know a good wine. The people in uniform you might see are likely from the Ecole Militaire (military school, Napoleon's alma mater), two blocks away.

For those learning the fine art of living Parisian-style, rue Cler provides an excellent classroom. And if you want to assemble the ultimate French picnic, there's no better place.

The Rue Cler Walk is the only tour in this guidebook you should start while hungry.

Orientation

Length of This Walk: Allow an hour to browse and café-hop along this short walk of two or three blocks.

When to Go: Visit rue Cler when its market is open and lively (Tue–Sat 8:30–13:00 or 15:00–19:30, Sun 8:30–12:00, dead on Mon). Remember that these shops are busy serving regular customers; be careful not to get in the way. Be polite—say *"Bonjour, Madame or Monsieur"* as you enter and *"Au revoir, Madame or Monsieur"* when you leave. If you really want to win a clerk over, follow up your greeting with *"Excusez-moi de vous déranger"* (ek-skew-zay-mwah duh voo day-rahn-zhay)—Pardon me for bothering you—then ask for what you need. Give it a try at least once. And remember, if you're speaking to a woman who looks 30 or under, call her *Mademoiselle.*

Getting There: Start your walk where the pedestrian section of rue Cler begins, at rue de Grenelle (Mo: Ecole Militaire or bus #69 stop).

The Walk Begins

❶ Café Roussillon

This café, a neighborhood fixture, recently dumped its old-fashioned, characteristic look for the latest café style—warm, natural wood tones, easy lighting, and music. To the right of the door, you'll see the *Tarifs des Consommations* sign required by French law, making the pricing clear: Drinks served at the bar *(comptoir)* are cheaper than drinks served at the tables *(salles).* Displayed on the opposite side of the door are various *chèque déjeuner* decals, advertising that this café accepts lunch "checks." In France, an employee lunch subsidy program is an expected perk. Employers—responding to strong tax incentives designed to keep the café culture vital—issue a voucher check (worth about €8) for each day an employee works in a month. Sack lunches are rare, since a good lunch is sacred.

Inside, the bar is always busy. The blackboard lists wines sold by the little (7-centiliter) glass, along with other drinks.

The little **late-night grocery** next door is one of countless corner shops nicknamed *dépanneurs* ("to help you out of difficulty"). Open nightly until midnight, these stores are often run by hardworking North Africans willing to keep crazy hours. Locals happily pay the higher prices for the convenience *dépanneurs* provide.

Rue Cler Walk

• *If you're shopping for designer baby clothes, you'll find them across the street at...*

❷ Petit Bateau

The French spend at least as much on their babies as they do on their dogs—dolling them up with designer jammies. This store is one in a popular chain. Babies-in-the-know just aren't comfortable unless they're making a fashion statement (such as underwear with sailor stripes). In the last generation, an aging and shrinking population has been a serious problem for Europe's wealthier nations. But France now has one of Europe's biggest baby populations—the fertile French average two children per family, compared to 1.6 for the rest of Europe. Babies are trendy today, and the government rewards parents with substantial tax deductions for their first two children—and then doubles the deductions after that. Making babies is good business.

• *Cross rue de Grenelle to find...*

❸ Top Halles Fruits and Vegetables

Each morning, fresh produce is trucked in from farmers' fields to Paris' huge Rungis market—Europe's largest, near Orly Airport—

and then dispatched to merchants with FedEx-like speed and precision. Good luck finding a shopping bag—locals bring their own two-wheeled carts or reusable bags. Also, notice how the earth-friendly French resist excessive packaging.

Parisians—who know they eat best by being tuned in to the seasons—shop with their noses. Try it. Smell the cheap foreign strawberries. One sniff of the torpedo-shaped French ones *(garriguettes)* in June, and you know which is better. Locals call those from Belgium "plastic strawberries"—red on outside, white on inside. Find the herbs in the back. Is today's delivery in? Look at the price of those melons. What's the country of origin? (It must be posted.) If they're out of season, they come from Guadeloupe. Many people buy only local products.

The **Franprix** across the street is a small outpost of a nationwide supermarket chain. Opposite Grand Hôtel Lévêque is Asie Traiteur. Fast Asian food to go is popular in Paris. These shops—about as common as bakeries now—have had an impact on Parisian eating habits.

❹ Le Petit Cler

This small café, until recently a *tabac* (tobacco shop), is a good example of how life is changing on rue Cler. It used to be that only the Brasserie PTT café, at the opposite end of the *rue,* had outdoor tables. Then Café du Marché (described below) joined in. Many locals regret that shops are being lost to trendy café crowds.
• *Just past Grand Hôtel Lévêque is...*

❺ Wine Bacchus

Shoppers often visit the neighborhood wine shop last, after they've assembled their meal and are able to pick the appropriate wine. The wine is classified by region. Most "Parisians" (born elsewhere) have an affinity for the wines of their home region. Check out the great prices. Wines of the month—in the center—sell for as little as €8. You can get a fine bottle for €12. The clerk is a counselor who works with your needs and budget, and he can put a bottle of white in the fridge for you to pick up later (open until 20:00 except Sun).
• *Next door, smell the...*

❻ Fromagerie

A long, narrow, canopied cheese table brings the *fromagerie* into the street. Wedges, cylinders, balls, and miniature hockey pucks are all powdered white, gray, and burnt marshmallow—it's a festival of mold. The street cart and front window feature both cow and goat cheeses. Locals know the shape indicates the region of origin (for example, a pyramid shape indicates a cheese from the Loire). And this is important. Regions create the *terroir* (physical and magical union of sun, soil, and generations of farmer love) that gives the production—whether wine or cheese—its personality. *Ooh la la* means you're impressed. If you like cheese, show greater excitement with more *la*s. *Ooh la la la la.* My local friend once held the stinkiest glob close to her nose, took an orgasmic breath, and exhaled, "Yes, it smells like zee feet of angels." Go ahead...inhale.

Step inside and browse through more than 200 types of French cheese. A cheese shop—lab-coat-serious but friendly, and known as a "BOF" for *beurre, oeuf,* and *fromage*—is where people shop for butter, eggs, and cheese. In the back room, they store *les meules,* the big, 170-pound wheels of cheese (made from 250 gallons of milk). The "hard" cheeses are cut from these. Don't eat the skin of these big ones...they're rolled on the floor. But the skin on most

smaller cheeses—the Brie, the Camembert—is part of the taste. "It completes the package," says my local friend.

At dinner tonight you can take the cheese course just before or instead of dessert. On a good cheese plate you have a hard cheese (like Emmentaler—a.k.a. "Swiss cheese"), a flowery cheese (maybe Brie or Camembert), a bleu cheese, and a goat cheese—ideally from different regions. Because it's strongest, the goat cheese is usually eaten last.

• *Across the street, find the fish shop, known as the...*

❼ Poissonnerie

Fresh fish is brought into Paris daily from ports on the English Channel, 110 miles away. In fact, fish here is likely fresher than in many towns closer to the sea, because Paris is a commerce hub (from here, it's shipped to outlying towns). Anything wiggling? This *poissonnerie*, like all such shops, recently was upgraded to meet the new Europewide hygiene standards.

• *Next door at the Ulysse en Gaule Crêperie (under the awning—get close to see) is a particularly tempting rue Cler storefront.*

❽ No More Horse Meat

The stones and glass set over the doorway advertise horse meat: *Boucherie Chevaline*. While today this store serves souvlaki and crêpes, the classy old storefront survives from the previous occupant. Created in the 1930s and signed by the artist, it's a work of art fit for a museum—but it belongs right here. Notice that the door is decorated with lunch coupon decals for local workers. (Say hi to Stephano, who's happily baking crêpes.)

• *A few steps farther along is a flower shop. (When visiting friends, French people give a gift of flowers. It's classiest to have them delivered before you show up.) Across the street is the...*

❾ Pharmacy and Oldest Building

In France, as in much of Europe, the pharmacist makes the first diagnosis and has the authority to prescribe certain drugs. If it's out of his league, he'll recommend a doctor. Pharmacies are also the only place to get many basic medical items, such as aspirin and simple reading glasses.

Next to the pharmacy is rue Cler's oldest building (with the two garret windows on the roof). It's from the early 1800s, when this street was part of a village near Paris, and was lined with structures like this. Over the years, Paris engulfed these surrounding villages—and now the street is a mishmash of architectural styles.

• *Across the street from this oldest house is...*

⑩ Charcuterie Davoli

Charcuteries sell mouthwatering deli food to go (this one is closed Wed). Because Parisian kitchens are so small, these gourmet delis are handy, even for those who cook. It lets the hosts concentrate on creating the main course, and then buy beautifully prepared side dishes to complete a fine dinner. Each day the charcuteries cook up *plats du jour* (specials of the day), advertised on the board outside. Note the system: Order, take your ticket to the cashier to pay, and return with the receipt to pick up your food.

• *A few doors down is...*

⑪ Café du Marché and More

Café du Marché, on the corner, is *the* place to sit and enjoy the action (described in the Eating chapter). It's rue Cler's living room, where locals gather before heading home, many staying for a relaxed and affordable dinner. The owner priced his menu so that locals could afford to dine out on a regular basis, and it worked—many patrons eat here five days a week. For a reasonable meal, grab a chair and check the chalk menu listing the *plat du jour*. Notice how the new no-smoking-indoors laws have made outdoor seating and propane heaters a huge hit.

The shiny, sterile **Leader Price grocery store** (across the street) is a Parisian Costco, selling bulk items. Because storage space is so limited in most Parisian apartments, bulk purchases are unlikely to become a big deal here. The latest trend is to stock up on nonperishables by shopping online, pick up produce three times a week, and buy fresh bread daily. The awful exterior of this store suggests a sneaky bending of the rules. Normally, any proposed building modification on rue Cler must undergo a rigorous design review in order for the owner to obtain the required permit.

• *From Café du Marché, hook right and side-trip a couple doors down rue du Champ du Mars to visit...*

⑫ L'Epicerie Fine

This fine-foods boutique stands out from the rest because of its gentle owners, Pascal and Joanna. Their mission in life is to explain to travelers, in fluent English, what the French fuss over food is all about. Say *bonjour* to Pascal and company. Let them help you assemble a picnic and tempt you with fine gourmet treats, Berthillon ice cream, and generous tastes of caramel, balsamic vinegar, and French and Italian olive oil (Tue–Fri 9:30–13:00 & 15:00–19:30, Sat 10:00–13:30, Sun 10:00–13:00, closed Mon, tel. 01 47 05 98 18).

• *Return to rue Cler. The neighborhood bakery on the corner is often marked by a line of people waiting to pick up their daily baguette.*

⓭ Boulangerie

Since the French Revolution, the government has regulated the cost of a basic baguette. Locals debate the merits of Paris' many *boulangeries*. It's said that a baker cannot be both good at bread and good at pastry—at cooking school they major in one or the other. Here, the baker makes good bread, and another baker does the tasty little pastries for him.

• *Next door is a strangely out-of-place...*

⓮ Japanese Restaurant

Sushi is for sale everywhere in Paris these days. Locals explain that the phenomenon is the same as when Chinese restaurants were spreading like gastronomic weeds. Real French restaurants found it hard to compete with these inexpensive places, and in some areas, local authorities actually forbid giving business permits to Chinese restaurants.

• *A bit farther along is...*

⓯ La Mère de Famille Gourmand Chocolats Confiseries

This shop has been in the neighborhood for 30 years. The whole-salers wanted the owner to take the new products, but she kept the old traditional candies, too. "The old ladies, they want the same sweets that made them so happy 80 years ago," she says. You can buy "naked bonbons" right out of the jar and chocolate by the piece (about €0.75 each). You're welcome to assemble a small assortment.

Until a few years ago, the chocolate was dipped and decorated right on the premises. As was the tradition in rue Cler shops, the merchants resided and produced in the back and sold in the front.

• *Across the street, you'll find...*

⓰ Oliviers & Co. Olive Oils

This shop, typical of an upscale neighborhood like this, sells fine gourmet goodies from the south of France and olive oil from around the Mediterranean. They are happy to give visitors a taste test. Find the ancient stone mill wheel that was once used to press olives, and try the tapenade. Use their tiny spoons to sample three distinct oils.

• *Walk on to the end of rue Cler (where it hits a busy street).*

⓱ City Info Post

This electronic signpost directs residents to websites for local information—transportation changes, surveys, employment opportunities, community events, and so on. Also notice the big, green recycling stations and see-through green garbage sacks. In the 1990s, Paris suffered a rash of trash-can bombings. Bad guys hid rigged-up camp stove canisters in metal garbage cans, which broke into deadly "shrapnel" when they exploded. Local authorities solved this by replacing the metal cans with these see-through plastic bags.

• *Across the busy street is a* tabac.

⑱ Tabac La Cave a Cigares

Just as the US has liquor stores licensed to sell booze, the only place for people over 16 to buy tobacco legally in France is at a *tabac* (tah-bah) counter. Tobacco counters like this one are a much-appreciated fixture of each neighborhood, offering lots of services (and an insight into the local culture).

Even nonsmokers enjoy perusing the wares at a *tabac*. Notice how European laws require a bold warning sign on cigarettes— about half the size of the package—that says, bluntly, *fumer tue* (smoking kills). Even so, you may not be able to resist the temptation to pick up a *petit Corona*—your chance to buy a fine Cuban cigar for €6 without breaking US law.

Tabacs also serve their neighborhoods as a kind of government cash desk. All sell stamps and some sell public-transit tickets (for the same price you'd pay at Métro stations—but they pocket a five percent profit). Locals pay for parking meters in *tabacs* by buying a card...or pay fines if they don't. Like back home, the LOTO is a big deal—and a lucrative way for the government to tax poor and less-educated people.

• *Rue Cler ends at the post office. The Ecole Militaire Métro stop is just down the street. If you bought a picnic along this walk, head for the nearby benches and gardens: From the post office, avenue de la Motte-Picquet leads to two fine parks—turn left for the Army Museum or right for the Eiffel Tower. Or make a U-turn and dive back into neighborhood Paris.*

EIFFEL TOWER TOUR

La Tour Eiffel

It's crowded, expensive, and there are probably better views in Paris, but this 1,000-foot-tall ornament is worth the trouble. Visitors to Paris may find *Mona Lisa* to be less than expected, but the Eiffel Tower rarely disappoints, even in an era of skyscrapers. This is a once-in-a-lifetime, I've-been-there experience. Making the trip gives you membership in the exclusive society of 245 million other humans who have made the Eiffel Tower the most visited monument in the modern world.

Orientation

Cost: €13 all the way to the top, €8 if you're only going up to the two lower levels, not covered by Museum Pass.

You can skip the elevator line and climb the stairs to the first and second level for €4.50, or for €3.50 if you're under 25. (Elevators and stairs are both free going down.)

Once inside the tower, you can buy your way to the top with no penalty—ticket booths and machines on the first and second levels sell supplements for €5 (€3.50 if you're under 25; walkers need to climb to second level to ride elevator up).

Hours: Daily mid-June–Aug 9:00–24:45 in the morning, last ascent to top at 23:30 and to lower levels at 24:00; Sept–mid-June 9:30–23:45, last ascent to top at 22:30 and to lower levels at 23:00 (elevator) or 18:30 (stairs). During windy weather, the top level may close to tourists.

When to Go: For the best of both worlds, arrive with enough light to see the views, then stay as it gets dark to see the lights (allow an hour in line, more if it's during a school break or key holiday). The views are grand whether you ascend or not. At the top of the hour, a five-minute lighting display features thousands of sparkling lights (best viewed from Trocadéro Square or the grassy park below).

Avoiding Lines: Crowds overwhelm this place much of the year. A new online reservation system should be working by the time you visit, allowing you to book a half-hour time slot for your entry and avoid the one- to two-hour wait in line; check the website for details (www.toureiffel.fr).

If you don't have a reservation, go early (get in line 30 minutes before it opens). Going later is the next best bet (after 19:00 May–Aug, after 17:00 off-season—see "Hours," previous page, for last ascent times). Weekends and holidays are worst, but prepare for ridiculous crowds anytime. Off-season weekdays are not as crowded.

You can bypass the elevator line if you have a reservation at either of the tower's view restaurants (see "Cuisine Art" next page).

There's less of a line for the stairs.

Pickpockets: Tourists in crowded elevators are like fish in a barrel for predatory thieves. *En garde.*

Getting There: The Bir-Hakeim and Trocadéro Métro stops, and the Champ de Mars-Tour Eiffel RER stop, are each about a 10-minute walk away. The Ecole Militaire Métro stop in the rue Cler area is 20 minutes away. Buses #69 and #87 stop nearby on avenue Joseph Bouvard in the Champ de Mars park.

Information: An Eiffel Tower information office is between the north and east pillars. Each level on the tower has displays pointing out the landmarks and monuments visible below. Tel. 01 44 11 23 23, www.toureiffel.fr.

Length of This Tour: Budget three hours to wait in line, get to the top, and sightsee your way back down. With no crowds, figure 90 minutes to the top and back (with time for sightseeing). If you're in line to buy tickets, estimate about 20 minutes for every 100 yards, plus 30 minutes more after you reach the security check near the ticket booths.

Once you've toured the tower and are ready to leave, it's quickest and most memorable to use the stairs to descend the last two levels.

Security Check: Bags larger than 19" × 8" × 12" are not allowed and there is no baggage check. All bags are subject to a secu-

Eiffel Tower Area

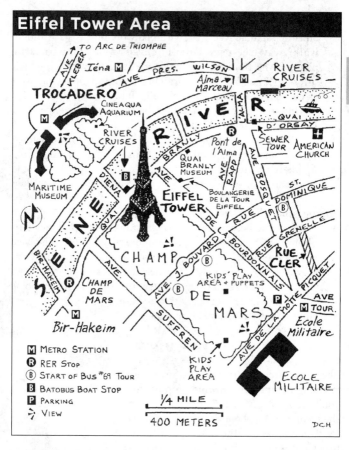

TO ARC DE TRIOMPHE

Iéna M — PRES. WILSON

AVE KLEBER

Alma Marceau M — RIVER CRUISES

TROCADERO

CINEAQUA AQUARIUM

RIVER CRUISES

MARITIME MUSEUM

R I V E R

QUAI D'ORSAY

SEWER TOUR — AMERICAN CHURCH

Pont de l'Alma

QUAI BRANLY MUSEUM

BOULANGERIE DE LA TOUR EIFFEL

EIFFEL TOWER

ST. DOMINIQUE

RUE GRENELLE

RUE CLER

C H A M P

RUE DE LA BOURDONNAIS

KIDS' PLAY AREA + PUPPETS

RUE DE GRENELLE

AVE J. BOUVARD

CHAMP DE MARS

D E   M A R S

Ecole Militaire

AVE DE LA MOTTE PICQUET

P — M TOUR.

Bir-Hakeim

AVE SUFFREN

KIDS' PLAY AREA

ECOLE MILITAIRE

S E I N E

BIR-HAKEIM

QUAI D'IENA

N

M METRO STATION
R RER STOP
B START OF BUS #69 TOUR
B BATOBUS BOAT STOP
P PARKING
VIEW

¼ MILE
400 METERS

DCH

rity search. No knives, glass bottles, or cans are allowed.

Services: There are free WCs at the base of the tower, behind the east pillar. Inside the tower itself, WCs are on all levels, but they're small, with long lines.

Cuisine Art: The first and second levels have small sandwich-and-pizza-type cafés. The tower's two classy restaurants offer great views. On the first level is 58 Tour Eiffel (€45 lunches, €65 dinners, daily 12:00 until late, dinner seatings nightly at about 19:00 and 21:00, reserve a month in advance for view table—less for nonview, toll tel. 08 25 56 66 62, www.restaurants -toureiffel.com). The expensive three-star Michelin Jules Verne Restaurant is on the second level (€85 weekday lunch *menu,* €165–200 weekend lunch *menus,* €200 dinner *menu,* daily 12:15–13:45 & 19:15–21:45, reserve 3 months in advance, tel. 01 45 55 61 44, fax 01 47 05 29 41). Dining at either restaurant lets you skip the long elevator line and ride for free.

At the tower's base, there's not much besides the burger-and-fries stands. Rue Cler, with many options, is a 20-minute walk away (see page 176). The best value among nearby places is the Boulangerie/Pâtisserie de la Tour Eiffel, which offers inexpensive salads, quiche, and sandwiches, as well as cool views of the tower (closed Mon, outdoor and indoor seating, one block southeast of the tower at 21 avenue de la Bourdonnais, tel. 01 47 05 59 81).

Your tastiest option may be to assemble a picnic before-hand from any of several handy shops near Métro stop Ecole Militaire and picnic in the Champ de Mars park (on the side grassy areas or on benches along the central grass; the middle stretch is off-limits).

Photography: All photos and videos are allowed.

Best Views: The best place to view the tower is from Trocadéro Square to the north. It's a 10-minute walk across the river, a happening scene at night, and especially fun for kids. Consider arriving at the Trocadéro Métro stop for the view, then walking toward the tower. Another delightful viewpoint is the Champ de Mars park to the south.

Starring: All of Paris...and beyond.

Overview

There are three observation platforms, at 200, 400, and 900 feet. Although being on the windy top of the Eiffel Tower is a thrill you'll never forget, the view is better from the second level, where you can actually see Paris' monuments. The first level also has nice views and more tourist-oriented sights. All three levels have some displays, WCs (usually with long lines), souvenir stores, and a few other services.

To get to the top, you need to take two different elevators. The first takes you to the second level. (Note: You must bypass the first level on the way up and see it on the way back down.) A separate elevator—with another line—shuttles between the second and third levels.

For the hardy, stairs lead from the ground level up to the first and second levels—and rarely have a long line. It's 360 stairs to the first level and another 360 to the second. The staircase is enclosed with a wire cage, so you can't fall, but those with vertigo issues may still find them dizzying.

If you want to see the entire tower, from top to bottom, then see it...from top to bottom. Ride the elevator to the second level, then immediately line up for the other elevator to the top. Enjoy the views on top, then ride back down to the second level. Frolic there for a while and take in some more views. When you're ready, head to the first level by taking the stairs (no line) or lining up for the elevator. Explore the shops and exhibits on the first level, have a snack, then take the stairs (best) or elevator back to earth.

The Tour Begins

Find the various entrances at the base of the tower's four *piliers* (pillars), named for their compass points: *nord*, *sud*, *est*, and *ouest*.

The various ticket offices can move around from time to time, so make sure you get in the right line. Avoid lines selling tickets only for *groupes*. Follow signs for *individuels* or *visiteurs sans tickets*. If you have a reservation, look for signs indicating *réservations individuelles*. If you want to climb the stairs, pay the fee at the ticket office at the south pillar, next to the Jules Verne Restaurant entrance.

To pass the time in line, read the following background information, or pick up whatever free reading material is available at the ground-level tourist stands. Look up at the tower towering above you, and don't even think about what would happen if someone dropped a coin from the top.

Exterior

Delicate and graceful when seen from afar, the Eiffel Tower is massive—even a bit scary—close up. You don't appreciate its size until you walk toward it; like a mountain, it seems so close but takes forever to reach.

The tower, including its antenna, stands 1,063 feet tall, or slightly higher than the 77-story Chrysler Building in New York. Its four support pillars straddle an area of 3.5 acres. Despite the tower's 7,300 tons of metal and 60 tons of paint, it is so well-engineered that it weighs no more per square inch at its base than a linebacker on tiptoes.

Once the world's tallest structure, it's now eclipsed by a number of towers (e.g., the CN Tower, Toronto, 1,815 feet), radio antennae (KVLY-TV Mast, North Dakota, 2,063 feet), and skyscrapers (the Burj Dubai, UAE, 2,684 feet).

The long green lawn stretching south of the tower is the Champ de Mars, originally the training ground for troops and students of the nearby Military School (Ecole Militaire) and now a park. On the north side, across the Seine, is the curved palace colonnade framing a square called the Trocadéro, site of the 1878 World's Fair.

History

In 1889, the first visitor to Paris' Universal Exposition walked beneath the "arch" formed by the newly built Eiffel Tower and

entered the fair grounds. The World's Fair celebrated both the centennial of the French Revolution and France's position as a global superpower. Bridge-builder Gustave Eiffel (1832–1923) won the contest to build the fair's centerpiece by beating out such rival proposals as a giant guillotine.

Gustave deserved to have the tower named for him. He not only designed it, but he oversaw the entire work, personally financed it, and was legally responsible if the project floundered. His factory produced the iron beams, he designed the cranes and apparatus, his workers built it, and—working on a deadline for the World's Fair—he brought in the project on time and under budget.

The tower was nothing but a showpiece, with no functional purpose except to demonstrate to the world that France had the

wealth, knowledge, and can-do spirit to erect a structure far taller than anything the world had ever seen. The original plan was to dismantle the tower as quickly as it was built after the celebration ended, but it was kept by popular demand.

To a generation hooked on technology, the tower was the marvel of the age, a symbol of progress and human ingenuity. Not all were so impressed, however; many found it a monstrosity. The writer Guy de Maupassant (1850–1893) routinely ate lunch in the tower just so he wouldn't have to look at it.

In subsequent years, the tower has come to serve many functions: as a radio transmitter (1909–present), a cosmic-ray observatory (1910), a billboard (spelling "Citroën" in lights, 1925–1934), a broadcaster of Nazi TV programs (1940–1944), a fireworks launch

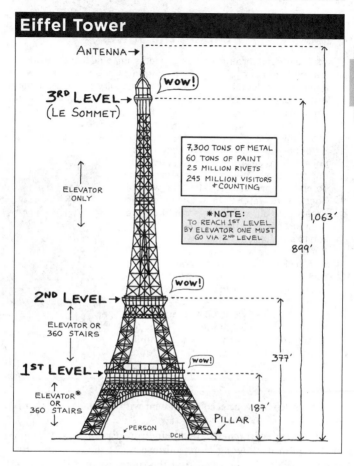

pad (numerous times), and as a framework for dazzling lighting displays, including the current arrangement, designed in 2000 for the millennium celebration.

• *To reach the top, ride the elevator to the second level. From there, get in line for the next elevator and continue to the top. Pop out 900 feet above the ground.*

Third Level (Le Sommet)

The top level, called *le sommet*, is tiny. (It can close temporarily without warning when it reaches capacity.) All you'll find here are wind and grand, sweeping views. The city lies before you, with a panorama guide. On a good day, you can see for 40 miles. Do a 360-degree tour of Paris. (Note that the following compass points are only approximate; in fact, what the tower's displays call "west" is more like southwest, etc.) Feeling proud you made it this high?

Building the Tower

As you ascend through the metal beams, imagine being a worker, perched high above nothing, riveting this thing together. It was a massive project, and it took all the ingenuity of the Industrial Age—including mass production, cutting-edge technology, and capitalist funding.

The foundation was the biggest obstacle. The soil, especially along the river, was too muddy to support big pillars. Gustave Eiffel drew on his bridge-building experience, where support piers needed to be constructed underwater. He sunk heavy compartments (caissons) into the wet soil. These were water-tight and injected with breathable air, so workers could dig out the mud beneath them, allowing the caisson to sink further. When the workers were done, the hole was filled in with cement 20 feet thick and capped with stone. The massive iron pillars were sunk into the ground at an angle, anchored in the subterranean stone.

The tower went up like an 18,000-piece erector set, made of 15-foot iron beams held together with 2.5 million rivets. The pieces were mass-produced

You can celebrate your accomplishment with a €10 glass of champagne.

Looking west *(ouest):* The Seine runs east to west (though at this point it's flowing more southwest). At the far end of the skinny "island" in the river, find the tiny copy of the Statue of Liberty, looking 3,633 miles away to her big sister in New York. Gustave Eiffel, a man of many talents, also designed the internal supports of New York's Statue of Liberty, which was cast in copper by fellow Frenchman Frederic Bartholdi (1886).

The sharp-eyed might spy on the Left Bank a round green patch amid all the buildings—Paris' heliport.

Looking north *(nord):* The vast, forested expanse is the Bois de Bolougne, the three-square-mile park that hosts joggers and *boules* players by day and prostitutes by night. The track with bleachers is Paris' horseracing track, the Hippodrome de Longchamp. At your feet is the curved arcade of the Trocadéro. Beyond, in the far distance, are the skyscrapers of La Défense. Find the Arc de Triomphe, to the right. The lone skyscraper between the Arc and the Trocadéro is the Palais des Congrès, a complex that hosts international conferences and major concerts.

in factories in the suburbs and brought in on wagons. For two years, 300 workers assembled the pieces, the tower rising as they went. First, they used wooden scaffolding to support the lower (angled) sections, until the pillars came together and the tower could support itself. Then the iron beams were lifted up with steam-powered cranes, including cranes on tracks (creeper cranes) that inched up the pillars as the tower progressed. There, daring workers dangled from rope ladders, balanced on beams, and tightroped their way across them as they put the pieces in place. The workers then hammered in red-hot rivets made on-site by blacksmiths. As the rivets cooled, they solidified the structure.

After a mere year and a half of work, the tower already surpassed the previous tallest building in the world—the Washington Monument (555 feet)—which had taken 36 years to build.

The tower was painted a rusty red. Since then, it's sported several colors, including mustard and the current brown-gray. It is repainted every seven years, and will likely be receiving a new coat during your visit (it takes 25 full-time painters 18 months to apply 60 tons of paint by hand—no spraying allowed).

Two years, two months, and five days after construction began, the tower was done. On May 15, 1889, a red, white, and blue beacon was lit on the top, the World's Fair began, and the tower carried its first astounded visitor to the top.

Looking east *(est):* At your feet are the Seine and the pont Alexandre bridge, with its four golden statues. Looking upstream, find the Orsay Museum, the Louvre, and the twin towers and steeple of Notre-Dame.

On the Right Bank (which is to your left), find the Grand Palais, next to the pont Alexandre. Beyond the Grand Palais is the bullet-shaped dome of Sacré-Coeur atop Butte Montmarte.

Looking south *(sud):* In a line, find the Champ de Mars, the Ecole Militaire, the Y-shaped UNESCO building, and the 689-foot Montparnasse Tower skyscraper. To the left is the golden dome of Les Invalides, and beyond that, the state capitol–shaped dome of the Pantheon.

The tippy top: Ascend another short staircase to the open-air top. Look up at all the satellite dishes and communications equipment (and around to find the tiny WC). You'll see the tiny apartment given to the builder of the tower, Gustave Eiffel, now represented by a mannequin (he's the one with the beard).

The mannequins re-create the moment during the 1889 Exhibition when the American Thomas Edison paid a visit to his fellow techie, Gustave (and Gustave's daughter Claire), presenting

them with his new invention, a phonograph. (Then they cranked it up and blasted The Who's "I Can See for Miles.")
• *Catch the elevator down to the...*

Second Level

The second level (400 feet) has the best views because you're closer to the sights, and the monuments are more recognizable. (The best views are up the short stairway, on the platform without the wire-cage barriers.) This level has souvenir shops, public telephones to call home, and a small stand-up café.

The head chef at Jules Verne Restaurant on this level is currently Alain Ducasse, who operates restaurants around the world. One would hope his three-star brand of haute cuisine matches the 400-foot haute of the restaurant.
• *Catch the elevator or take the stairs (5 minutes, 360 steps, free) down to the...*

First Level

The first level (200 feet) has more great views, all well-described by the tower's panorama displays. There are a number of photo exhibits on the tower's history, WCs, a conference hall (closed to tourists), an ATM, and souvenirs. A small café sells pizza and sandwiches (outdoor tables in summer). The 58 Tour Eiffel restaurant has more *accessible* prices than the Jules Verne Restaurant above (both run by Alain Ducasse). In winter, part of the first level is set up for winter activities (most recently as an ice-skating rink).

Videos shown in the small theater (some permanent, some rotating) document the tower's construction, paint job, place in pop culture, and a century of fireworks, capped by the entire millennium blast.

A display on weather shows how the sun warms the metal, causing the top to expand and lean about five inches away from the sun. Nearby, a small model of the tower oscillates slightly, simulating the tower's real-time movement in the wind and sun. Because of its lacy design, even the strongest of winds could never blow the tower down, only cause it to sway back and forth a few inches. In

Up and Down

The tower—which was designed from the start to accommodate hordes of visitors—has always had elevators. Today's elevators are modern replacements. Back in the late 19th  century, elevator technology was so new that this was the one job that Gustave Eiffel subcontracted to other experts (including an American company). They needed a special design to accommodate the angle of the tower's pillars. Today's elevators make about 100 round-trip journeys a day.

There are 1,665 stairs up to the top level, though tourists can only climb 720 of them, up as far as the second level. During a race in 1905, a gentleman climbed from the ground to the second floor—elevation gain 400 feet—in 3 minutes, 12 seconds.

fact, Eiffel designed the tower primarily with wind resistance in mind, wanting a structure seemingly "molded by the action of the wind itself." Many modern skyscrapers follow the mathematics pioneered by Eiffel.

Watch the original hydraulic pump (1889) at work. This once pumped water from this level to the second level to feed the machinery powering the upper elevator. Then look at the big wheels that wind and unwind heavy cables to lift the elevators.

• *Consider a drink or a sandwich while overlooking all of Paris, then take the elevator or stairs (5 minutes, 360 steps, free) to the ground.*

The Tour Ends

Welcome back to earth. Nearby, you can catch the Bateaux Parisiens boat for a Seine cruise (near the base of Eiffel Tower, see page 38 for details). Also nearby are the Quai Branly Museum (page 57), the rue Cler area (page 176), Army Museum and Napoleon's Tomb (page 58), and the Rodin Museum (page 59).

After you've climbed the tower, you come to appreciate it even more from a distance. For a final look, stroll across the river to Trocadéro Square or to the end of the Champ de Mars and look back for great views. However impressive it may be by day, the tower is an awesome thing to see at twilight, when it becomes engorged with light, and virile Paris lies back and lets night be on top. When darkness fully envelops the city, the tower seems to climax with a spectacular light show at the top of each hour...for five minutes.

RODIN
MUSEUM TOUR
Musée Rodin

Auguste Rodin (1840–1917) was a modern Michelangelo, sculpting human figures on an epic scale, revealing through the body their deepest thoughts and feelings. Like many of Michelangelo's unfinished works, Rodin's statues rise from the raw stone around them, driven by the life force. With missing limbs and scarred skin, these are prefab classics, making ugliness noble. Rodin's people are always moving restlessly. Even the famous *Thinker* is moving. While he's plopped down solidly, his mind is a million miles away. The museum presents a full range of Rodin's work, housed in a historic mansion where he once lived and worked.

Orientation

Cost: €6, free on the first Sun of the month, free for kids under 18, €1 for garden only, both museum and garden covered by Museum Pass, temporary exhibits in the entrance hall cost extra (not covered by Museum Pass). Passholders can bypass lines for ticket-buyers and temporary exhibits to get into the permanent collection quickly.

Hours: April–Sept Tue–Sun 9:30–17:45, gardens close at 18:45; Oct–March Tue–Sun 9:30–16:45, gardens close at 17:00; last entry 30 minutes before closing, closed Mon.

Getting There: It's at 79 rue de Varenne, near the Army Museum and Napoleon's Tomb (Mo: Varenne). Bus #69 stops at Grenelle-Bellechasse.

Information: Pick up the museum map. Tel. 01 44 18 61 10, www.musee-rodin.fr.

Audioguide Tours: €4, covering the museum and gardens.

Length of This Tour: Allow one hour.

Baggage Check: Even a fairly small bag must be checked, unless you tuck it under your arm like a purse.

Cuisine Art: There's a peaceful but pricey café in the gardens behind the museum. For better options, leave the museum, cross the esplanade des Invalides, and find many recommended cafés and restaurants in the rue Cler area (a 10-min walk, see page 398).

Photography: Photography without a flash is allowed.

The Tour Begins

Enter and buy tickets in the modern entrance hall. There's a bookstore, a gallery for temporary exhibits, and WCs. Pick up the museum map for the most current info on what's showing. The permanent collection is located outside this hall, in the mansion and the gardens.

• *Exit the entrance hall, walk across the courtyard, and enter the mansion. Turn left (baggage check here) and walk to the first room to start a circular tour of the ground floor.*

Room 1

Rodin's early works match the belle époque style of the time—noble busts of bourgeois citizens, pretty portraits of their daughters, and classical themes. Born of working-class roots, Rodin taught himself art by sketching statues at the Louvre and then sculpting copies.

The Man with the Broken Nose (*L'Homme au nez cassé*, 1865)—a deliberately ugly work—was 23-year-old

Rodin's first break from the norm. He meticulously sculpted this deformed man (one of the few models the struggling sculptor could afford), but then the clay statue froze in his unheated studio, and the back of the head fell off. Rodin loved it! Art critics hated it. Rodin persevered. (Note: The museum rotates the display of two different versions—the broken-headed one and another, repaired version Rodin made later that critics accepted.)

See the painting of Rodin's future wife, Rose Beuret *(Portrait de Madame Rodin)*, who suffered with him through obscurity and celebrity.

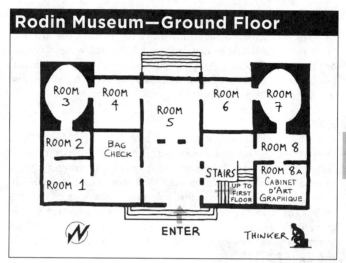

Rodin Museum—Ground Floor

ROOM 3
ROOM 4
ROOM 5
ROOM 6
ROOM 7
ROOM 2
BAG CHECK
ROOM 8
ROOM 1
STAIRS
UP TO FIRST FLOOR
ROOM 8A
CABINET D'ART GRAPHIQUE
ENTER
THINKER

RODIN MUSEUM

Room 2

To feed his new family, Rodin cranked out small-scale works with his boss' name on them—portraits, ornamental vases, nymphs,

and knickknacks to decorate buildings. Still, the series of mother-and-childs (Rose and baby Auguste?) allowed him to experiment on a small scale with the intertwined twosomes he'd do later.

His job gave him enough money to visit Italy, where he was inspired by Michelangelo's boldness, monumental scale, restless figures, and "unfinished" look. Rapidly approaching middle age, Rodin was ready to rock.

Room 3

Rodin moved to Brussels, where his first major work, *The Bronze Age* (*L'âge d'airain*, 1877), brought controversy and the fame that surrounds it. This nude youth, perhaps inspired by Michelangelo's *Dying Slave* (in the Louvre—see page 130), awakens to a new world. It was so lifelike that Rodin was accused of not sculpting it himself, but simply casting it directly from a live body. The boy's left hand looks like he should be leaning on a spear, but it's just that missing

element that makes the pose more tenuous and interesting.

The art establishment still snubbed Rodin as an outsider, and no wonder. Look at his ultra-intense take on the winged symbol of France *(La Défense)*—this Marseillaise screams, "Off with their heads!" at the top of her lungs. Rodin was a slave to his muses, and some of them inspired monsters.

Room 4

Like the hand of a sculptor, *The Hand of God* (*La Main de Dieu*, 1896) shapes Adam and Eve from the mud of the earth to which they will return. Rodin himself worked in "mud," using his hands to model clay figures, which were then reproduced in marble or bronze, usually by his assistants. Spin this masterpiece on its turn-table. (I'm serious, give it a turn.) Rodin wants you to see it from every angle. He first worked from the front view, then checked the

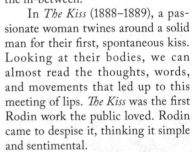

back and side profiles, then filled in the in-between.

In *The Kiss* (1888–1889), a passionate woman twines around a solid man for their first, spontaneous kiss. Looking at their bodies, we can almost read the thoughts, words, and movements that led up to this meeting of lips. *The Kiss* was the first Rodin work the public loved. Rodin came to despise it, thinking it simple and sentimental.

Other works in this room show embracing couples who seem to emerge from the stone just long enough to love. Rodin left many works "unfinished," reminding us that all creation is a difficult process of dragging a form out of chaos.

Room 5

The two hands that form the arch of *The Cathedral* (*La Cathédrale*, 1908) are actually two right hands (a man's and a woman's?).

In the room's center, a bronze man strides forward, as bold as the often-controversial Rodin. The armless and headless *The Walking Man* (*L'Homme Qui Marche*, 1900–1907) plants his back foot forcefully, as though he's about to step, while his front foot already has stepped. Rodin—who had one foot in the classical past, one in the modernist future—captures two poses at once.

Rodin worked with many materials—he chiseled marble (though not often), modeled clay, cast bronze, worked plaster, painted, and sketched. He often created different versions of the same subject in different media.

Room 6

This room displays works by Camille Claudel, mostly in the style of her master. The 44-year-old Rodin took 18-year-old Claudel as his pupil, muse, colleague, and lover. We can follow the arc of their relationship:

Rodin was inspired by young Camille's beauty and spirit, and he often used her as a model. (See several versions of her head.)

As his student, "Mademoiselle C" learned from Rodin, doing portrait busts in his lumpy, molded-clay style. Her bronze bust of Rodin (which might not be on display) shows the steely-eyed sculptor with strong front and side profiles, barely emerging from the materials they both worked with.

Soon they were lovers. *The Waltz* (*La Valse*, 1892) captures the spinning exuberance the two must have felt as they embarked together on a new life. The couple twirls—hands so close but not touching—in a delicate balance.

But Rodin was devoted as well to his lifelong companion, Rose (see her face emerging from a block of marble). Claudel's *Maturity* (*L'Age Mûr*, 1895–1907, also in Orsay Museum) shows

the breakup. A young woman on her knees begs the man not to leave her, as he's led away reluctantly by an older woman. The statue may literally depict a scene from real life, in which a naked, fragile Claudel begged Rodin not to return to his wife. In the larger sense, it may also be a metaphor for the cruel passage of time, as Youth tries to save Maturity from the clutches of Old Age.

Rodin did leave Claudel. Talented in her own right but tormented by grief and jealousy, she became increasingly unstable and spent her final years in an institution. Claudel's *The Wave* (*La Vague*, 1900), carved in green onyx in a very un-Rodin style, shows tiny, helpless women huddling together as a tsunami is about to engulf them.

Room 7 and Room 8

What did Rodin think of women? Here are many different images from which you can draw your own conclusions.

Eve (1881) buries her head in shame, hiding her nakedness. But she can't hide the consequences—she's pregnant.

Rodin became famous, wealthy, and respected, and society ladies all wanted him to do their portraits. In Room 8, you'll see a sculpture of his last mistress *(La Duchesse de Choiseul)*, an American who lived with him here in this mansion. Rodin purposely left in the metal base points (used in the sculpting process), placed suggestively.

Room 8A

This room houses temporary exhibits, often displaying Rodin's works-in-progress—preparatory sketches or plaster casts. The first flash of inspiration for a huge statue might be a single line sketched on notepaper. Rodin wanted nude models in his studio at all times—walking, dancing, and squatting—in case they struck some new and interesting pose. Rodin thought of sculpture as simply "drawing in all dimensions."

• *Upstairs, you'll find a glass display case on the mezzanine that tries hard to explain...*

The Bronze Casting Process

Rodin made his bronze statues not by hammering sheets of metal, but by using the classic "lost wax" technique. He'd start by shaping the figure out of wet plaster. This figure becomes a model that's covered with a form-fitting mold. Pour molten bronze into the narrow space between the model and the mold around it, let it cool, remove the mold, and—*voilà!*— you have a hollow bronze statue ready to be polished and varnished. With a mold, you could produce other copies, which is

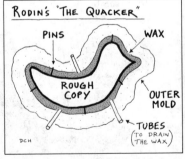

why there are many authorized bronze versions of Rodin's masterpieces all over the world.

As the display case teaches, there are actually a number of additional steps involving two models and two molds. Rodin used the original plaster model to make a first mold, which was used to make a heat-resistant clay copy of the original plaster model. He sanded down the clay copy, coated it with a wax skin, and then touched up the wax to add surface details. He used this

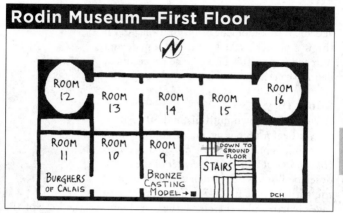

Rodin Museum—First Floor

ROOM 12
ROOM 13
ROOM 14
ROOM 15
ROOM 16

ROOM 11
ROOM 10
ROOM 9
DOWN TO GROUND FLOOR
STAIRS

BURGHERS OF CALAIS

BRONZE CASTING MODEL →■

DCH

RODIN MUSEUM

touched-up copy to make the more detailed final mold. He fitted the mold with ventilation tubes and started pouring in the molten bronze. The wax melted away—the "lost wax" technique—and the bronze cooled and hardened in its place, thus forming the final bronze statue.

Room 9

The Thinker was to have been the centerpiece of a massive project

that Rodin wrestled with for decades—a doorway encrusted with characters from Dante's *Inferno*. These *Gates of Hell* were never completed (we'll later see the partly finished piece in the garden), but the studies for it (scattered throughout this room and in a display cabinet) are some of Rodin's masterpieces.

These figures struggle to come into existence. Rodin was fascinated by the theory of evolution—not Darwin's version of the survival of the fittest, but the Frenchman Jean-Baptiste Lamarck's. His figures survive not by the good fortune of random mutation (Darwin), but by their own striving (Lamarck and Henri-Louis Bergson). They are driven by the life force, a restless energy that animates and shapes dead matter. Rodin must have felt that force even as a child, when he first squeezed soft clay and saw a worm emerge.

Room 10

Rodin's feverish attempts to capture a portrait of the novelist Balzac ranged from a pot-bellied Bacchus to a headless nude cradling an erection (the display changes, showing various versions). In a moment of inspiration, Rodin threw a plaster-soaked robe over a nude and watched it dry. This became the proud, final, definitive version.

Room 11

A virtual unknown until his mid-30s, Rodin slowly began receiving major commissions for public monuments. *The Burghers of Calais* (*Bourgeois de Calais*, in the center of the room, described below in garden section) depicts the actual event in 1347, when, in order to save their people, the city fathers surrendered the keys of the city—and their lives—to the king of England. Rodin portrays them not in some glorious pose drenched in pomp and allegory, but as a simple example of men sacrificing their lives together. As they head to the gallows, with ropes already around their necks, each body shows a distinct emotion, ranging from courage to despair. Compare the small plaster model in this room with the final, life-size bronze group outside the window in the garden (near the street).

• *Double back past the bronze-casting display, to the rooms overlooking the gardens in the back.*

Room 14

Here you'll see studies of the female body in its different forms—crouching, soaring, dying, open, closed, wrinkled, intertwined. Newsreel footage of Rodin is often on display in this room or nearby.

Room 15

Legendary lovers kiss, embrace, and intertwine in yin-yang bliss. In a display case, dancers stretch, pose, and leap.

Room 16

For the 1900 World's Fair, Paris considered building a huge monument honoring common workers, who were powering the Industrial Revolution (and demanding bathroom breaks and overtime pay). Rodin submitted this model of a Tower of Labor *(La Tour du Travail)*. A column wrapped in a corkscrew symbolizes the march of progress. At the base, statues of Day and Night remind everyone that factories operated 24/7. Reliefs spiraling up the column honored workers: workers at the base doing manual labor, then climbing the career ladder to desk jobs and the arts. Crowning the monument are the fruits of man's labor—

RODIN MUSEUM

the spinning angels of Love and Joy. Rodin's model was much admired but never built.

• *Backtrack through Room 14 to reach...*

Room 13

See Rodin's portrait busts of celebrities and some paintings by (yawn, are we through yet?) Vincent van Gogh, Claude Monet, and Pierre-Auguste Renoir. Rodin enjoyed discussions with Monet and other artists and incorporated their ideas into his work. Rodin is often considered an Impressionist because he captured spontaneous "impressions" of figures and created rough surfaces that catch reflected light.

Room 12

Get a sense of Rodin's working process by comparing the small plaster "sketches" (in the glass case) with the final large-scale marble versions that line the walls. Rodin employed and mentored many artists who executed these designs. By the end of his long, productive life, Rodin was more famous than his works.

The Gardens

Rodin lived and worked in this mansion, renting rooms alongside Henri Matisse, the poet Rainer Maria Rilke (Rodin's secretary), and the dancer Isadora Duncan. He loved placing his creations in the overgrown gardens. These are his greatest works, Rodin at his most expansive. The epic human figures are enhanced, not dwarfed, by nature.

• *Leaving the house, you've got five more stops: two on the left and three on the right. Beyond these stops is a big, breezy garden ornamented with statues, a cafeteria, and a WC.*

The Thinker (Le Penseur, 1906)

Leaning slightly forward, tense and compact, every muscle working toward producing that one great thought, Man contemplates his fate. No constipation jokes, please.

This is not an intellectual, but a linebacker who's realizing there's more to life than frat parties. It's the first man evolving beyond his animal nature to think the first thought. It's anyone who's ever worked hard to reinvent himself or to make something new or better. Said Rodin: "It is a statue of myself."

Rodin Museum Gardens

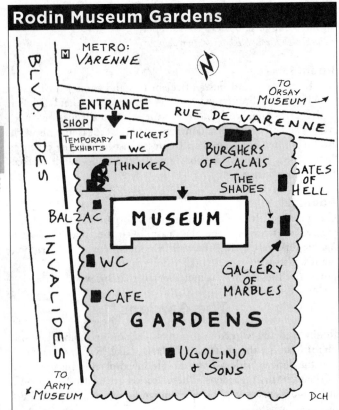

There are 29 other authorized copies of this statue, one of the most famous in the world.
• *To the left of The Thinker, you'll find...*

Balzac (1898)
The iconoclastic novelist turns his nose up at the notion he should be honored with a statue. This final version also stands in the Musée d'Orsay, and on a street median in Montparnasse. When the statue was unveiled, the crowd booed, a fitting tribute to both the defiant novelist and the bold man who sculpted him.
• *Along the street opposite the ticket booth are...*

The Burghers of Calais (1889)
The six city fathers trudge to their execution, and we can read in their faces and poses what their last thoughts are. They mill about, dazed, as each one deals with the decision he's made to sacrifice himself for his city.

• *Circling counterclockwise...*

The man carrying the key to the city tightens his lips in determination. The bearded man is weighed down with grief. Another buries his head in his hands. One turns, seeking reassurance from his friend, who turns away and gestures helplessly. The final key-bearer (in back) raises his hand to his head.

Each is alone in his thoughts, but they're united by their mutual sacrifice, by the base they stand on, and by their weighty robes—gravity is already dragging them down to their graves.

Pity the poor souls; view the statue from various angles (you can't ever see all the faces at once); then thank King Edward III, who, at the last second, pardoned them.

• *Follow* The Thinker's *gaze across the gardens. Standing before a tall, white backdrop is a big, dark door...*

The Gates of Hell (La Porte de l'Enfer, 1880–1917)

These doors (never meant to actually open) were never finished for a museum that was never built. But the vision of Dante's trip into hell gave Rodin a chance to explore the dark side of human experience. "Abandon all hope ye who enter here," was hell's motto. The three Shades at the top of the door point down—that's where we're going. Beneath the Shades, pondering the whole scene from above, is Dante as the Thinker. Below him, the figures emerge from the darkness just long enough to tell their sad tale of depravity. There are Paolo and Francesca (in the center of the right door), who were driven into an illicit love affair that brought them here.

Ugolino (left door, just below center) crouches in prison over his kids. This poor soul was so driven by hunger that he ate the corpses of his own children. On all fours like an animal, he is the dark side of natural selection. Finally, find what some say is Rodin himself (at the very bottom, inside the right doorjamb, where it just starts to jut out), crouching humbly.

You'll find some of these figures writ large in the garden. *The Thinker* is behind you, *The Shades* (c. 1889) are 30 yards to the right (see photo next page), and *Ugolino* (1901–1904) dines in the fountain at the far end.

It's appropriate that the *Gates*—Rodin's "cathedral"—remained unfinished. He was always a restless artist for whom the process of discovery was as important as the finished product.

• *To the right of* The Gates of Hell *is a glassed-in building, the...*

Gallery of Marbles

Unfinished, these statues show human features emerging from the rough stone. Imagine Rodin in his studio, working to give them life.

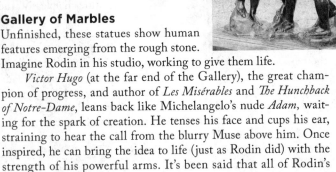

Victor Hugo (at the far end of the Gallery), the great champion of progress, and author of *Les Misérables* and *The Hunchback of Notre-Dame*, leans back like Michelangelo's nude *Adam*, waiting for the spark of creation. He tenses his face and cups his ear, straining to hear the call from the blurry Muse above him. Once inspired, he can bring the idea to life (just as Rodin did) with the strength of his powerful arms. It's been said that all of Rodin's work shows the struggle of mind over matter, of brute creatures emerging from the mud and evolving into a species of thinkers.

ARMY MUSEUM AND NAPOLEON'S TOMB TOUR

Musée de l'Armée

If you've ever considered being absolute dictator of a united Europe, come here first. Hitler did, but still went out and made the same mistakes as his role model. (Hint: Don't invade Russia.) Napoleon's tomb rests beneath the golden dome of Les Invalides church.

In addition to the tomb, the complex of Les Invalides—a former veterans' hospital built by Louis XIV—has various military museums, collectively called the Army Museum. Visiting the different sections, you can watch the art of war unfold from stone axes to Axis powers. See medieval armor, Napoleon's horse stuffed and mounted, Louis XIV-era uniforms and weapons, and much more. The best part is the section dedicated to the two World Wars, especially World War II.

The Army Museum's section on French military history ("Arms and Uniforms") has reopened after years of renovation. Some rooms may still be closed when you visit, but they're scheduled to reopen by 2010...*in théorie.*

Orientation

Cost: €8.50 (or €6.50 within an hour of closing time), ticket covers Napoleon's Tomb and all museums within Les Invalides complex, includes audioguide for tomb. If you have a Museum Pass, note that it covers the admission but not the audioguide (costs €1 with pass), and if you bring kids, you'll need to line up for the free children's tickets. The site is free for all military personnel in uniform.

Hours: Daily April–Sept 10:00–18:00, Sun until 18:30 and Tue until 21:00, July–Aug tomb stays open until 18:45; Oct–March 10:00–17:00, Sun until 17:30, last entry 30 min before closing, last entry to tomb 45 min before closing, closed first Mon of every month.

Getting There: The museum and tomb are at Hôtel des Invalides, with its hard-to-miss golden dome (129 rue de Grenelle, near Rodin Museum; Mo: La Tour Maubourg, Varenne, or Invalides). Bus #69 from the Marais and rue Cler area is also handy. The museum is a 10-minute walk from rue Cler. There are two entrances: one from the grand esplanade des Invalides (river side), the other from behind the gold dome on avenue de Tourville.

Information: A slim English map/guide is available at the ticket office. Pick up the included audioguide when you enter the tomb. Tel. 01 44 42 37 64 or 08 10 11 33 99, www.invalides.org.

Photography: Allowed without flash.

Length of This Tour: Women—two hours, men—three hours.

Cuisine Art: A reasonable cafeteria is next to the ticket office, the rear gardens are picnic-perfect, and rue Cler is a 10-minute walk away (see page 398).

Nearby: You'll likely see the French playing *boules* on the esplanade (as you face Les Invalides, look for the dirt area to the upper right; for the rules of *boules*, see page 360).

The Tour Begins

• *Start at Napoleon's Tomb, underneath the golden dome. The entrance is from the back end (farthest from the Seine) of this vast complex of churches and museums.*

Napoleon's Tomb

Enter the church, gaze up at the dome, then lean over the railing and bow to the emperor lying inside the scrolled, red porphyry tomb (see photo on previous page). If the lid were opened, you'd

find an oak coffin inside, holding another ebony coffin, housing two lead ones, then mahogany, then tinplate... until finally, you'd find Napoleon himself, staring up, with his head closest to the door. When his body was exhumed from the original grave and transported here (1840), it was still perfectly preserved, even after 19 years in the ground.

Born of humble Italian heritage on the French-owned isle of Corsica, Napoleon Bonaparte (1769–1821)

ARMY MUSEUM

Army Museum and Napoleon's Tomb

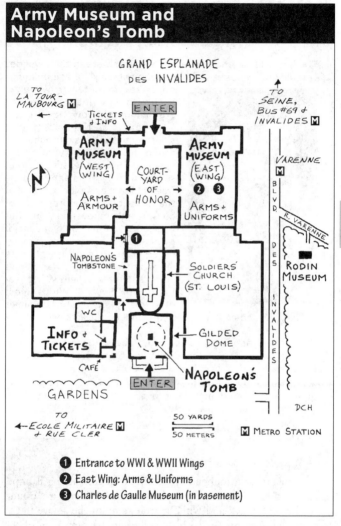

GRAND ESPLANADE
DES INVALIDES

TO
LA TOUR-
MAUBOURG Ⓜ

TO
SEINE,
BUS #69 &
INVALIDES Ⓜ

Tickets & Info

ENTER

ARMY MUSEUM (WEST WING)

ARMS & ARMOUR

COURTYARD OF HONOR

ARMY MUSEUM (EAST WING)

VARENNE Ⓜ

❷ ❸

ARMS & UNIFORMS

B L V D.

R. VARENNE

❶

NAPOLEON'S TOMBSTONE

SOLDIERS' CHURCH (ST. LOUIS)

D E S

RODIN MUSEUM

WC

I N V A L I D E S

INFO & TICKETS

GILDED DOME

CAFÉ

NAPOLEON'S TOMB

GARDENS

ENTER

DCH

TO
ECOLE MILITAIRE Ⓜ
& RUE CLER

50 YARDS
50 METERS

Ⓜ METRO STATION

❶ Entrance to WWI & WWII Wings
❷ East Wing: Arms & Uniforms
❸ Charles de Gaulle Museum (in basement)

ARMY MUSEUM

went to school at Paris' Ecole Militaire, quickly rising through the ranks amid the chaos of the Revolution. The charismatic "Little Corporal" won fans by fighting for democracy at home and abroad. In 1799, he assumed power and, within five short years, conquered most of Europe. The great champion of the Revolution had become a dictator, declaring himself emperor of a new Rome.

Napoleon's red tomb on its green base stands 15 feet high in the center of a marble floor. It's exalted by the dome above, where dead Frenchmen cavort with saints and angels, forming a golden

Overview of the Army Museum and Napoleon's Tomb

The Army Museum and Napoleon's Tomb are in the Invalides complex (or should I say "Napoleon complex"?). The buildings

house several noteworthy sights, each with different entrances. All are included in your ticket price. The tomb is on the back (south) side, and the various museums surround the main courtyard on the north side. For their exact locations, see the map in this chapter and the free English map/guide available at the ticket office. Be prepared for considerable renovation work—this museum is in the middle of a major overhaul.

Pick your favorite war. With limited time, visit only Napoleon's Tomb and the excellent World War I and World War II Wings. Most other displays consist of dummies

in uniforms and endless glass cases full of muskets without historical context.

Of the various sights scattered about, these are the best, rated in order of importance (the first four are described more fully in self-guided tours in this chapter):

▲▲▲Napoleon's Tomb—The emperor's final resting place, under the golden dome of Les Invalides church (at the back of the complex, farthest from the river).

halo over Napoleon.

Napoleon is surrounded by family. After conquering Europe, he installed his big brother, Joseph, as king of Spain (turn around to see Joseph's black-and-white marble tomb in the alcove to the left of the door); his little brother, Jerome, became king of the German kingdom of Westphalia (tucked into the chapel to the right of the door); and his baby boy, Napoleon II (downstairs), sat in diapers on the throne of Rome.

In other alcoves, you'll find more dead war heroes, including Marshal Ferdinand Foch, the commander in chief of the multinational Allied forces in World War I, his tomb lit with otherworldly blue light. These heroes, plus many painted saints, make this the French Valhalla in the Versailles of churches.

• *The stairs behind the altar (with the corkscrew columns) take you down to crypt level for a closer look at the tomb.*

▲▲▲**World War II Wing**—Interesting coverage of this critical war (entrance at southwest corner of courtyard).

▲▲**World War I Wing**—A manageable-sized series of rooms setting the stage for World War II (same entrance as World War II Wing, at southwest corner of courtyard).

▲**Arms and Uniforms** (East Wing)—French military history (c. 1670–1870), with a focus on Napoleon (entrance on east side of courtyard). After an extensive renovation, this wing has now reopened, though some rooms may still be closed when you visit.

Charles de Gaulle Museum—New museum (in the basement of the East Wing) with 25-minute film plus high-tech display of photos tracing the life of France's towering 20th-century figure. An audioguide leads you through his youth in the era of the hot-air balloon, two world wars, his rebuilding of France as president, and the social unrest of the 1960s that toppled him. The museum helps bring France's history of war into the modern age.

Arms and Armour (West Wing)—Weapons from the 13th–17th centuries (entrance on west side of courtyard). Connoisseurs of cannons, swords, suits of armor, crossbows, and early guns will love it; others can browse a few rooms and move on.

The Rest—Your ticket is good for all the exhibits in the complex (consult your free museum map), including the St. Louis Church, the Museum of the Order of Liberation (honoring heroes of the WWII Resistance), and the Musée des Plans Reliefs (on the top floor of the East Wing), which exhibits the 18th-century models (1:1,600 scale) of France's cities that strategists used to thwart enemy attacks. Survey Antibes and ponder which hillside you'd use to launch an attack.

ARMY MUSEUM

The Crypt

Wandering clockwise, read the names of Napoleon's battles on the floor around the base of the tomb. Rivoli marks the battle where the rookie 26-year-old general took a ragtag band of "citizens" and thrashed the professional Austrian troops in Italy, returning to Paris a celebrity. In Egypt *(Pyramides)*, he fought Turks and tribesmen to a standstill. The exotic expedition caught the public eye and he returned home a legend.

Napoleon's huge victory over Austria at Austerlitz on the first anniversary of his coronation made him Europe's top dog. At the head of the million-man Great Army *(La Grande Armée)*, he made a three-month blitz attack through Germany and Austria. As a general, he was daring, relying on top-notch generals and a mobile force of independent armies. His personal charisma on the battlefield was said to be worth 10,000 additional men.

Napoleon Bonaparte
(1769–1821)

Born to Italian parents on the French-ruled isle of Corsica, Napoleon attended French schools, although he spoke the language with an Italian accent to the end of his days. After graduating from Paris' Ecole Militaire (trained in the latest high-tech artillery), his military career took an unexpected turn when the Revolution erupted (1789) and he chose to return to Corsica to fight royalist oppression.

In 1793, as commander of artillery, he besieged Toulon, forcing the royalists to surrender, and earning his first great victory. He later defended the Revolutionary government from royalist mobs in Paris by firing a "whiff of grapeshot" into the crowd (1795). Such daring military exploits and personal charisma earned him promotions and the nickname "The Little Corporal"—not for his height (he was an average 5'6") but as a term of endearment from the rank and file. When he married the classy socialite Josephine Beauharnais, Napoleon became a true celebrity. In 1798, having conquered Italy, Austria, and Egypt, Napoleon returned to Paris, where the weak government declared him First Consul—ostensibly as the champion of democracy, but, in fact, a virtual dictator of much of Europe. He was 29 years old.

During the next 15 years, he solidified his reign with military victories over Europe's kings—now allied against France. Under his rule, France sold the Louisiana Purchase to America, and legal scholars drew up the Code of Napoleon, a system of laws still used by many European governments today. In 1804, his power peaked when he crowned himself emperor in a ceremony in Notre-Dame blessed by the pope. The Revolutionary general was now, paradoxically, part of Europe's royalty. Needing an heir to the throne, he divorced barren Josephine and married an Austrian duchess, Marie Louise, who bore him the boy known to historians as "The King of Rome."

In 1812, Napoleon decided to invade Russia, and the horrendous losses from that failed venture drained his power. It was time to pig-pile on France, and Europe's nations toppled Napoleon, sending him to exile on the isle of Elba (1814). Napoleon escaped long enough to raise an army for a final hundred-day campaign before finally being defeated by British and Prussian forces at the Battle of Waterloo (1815). Guilty of war crimes, he was sentenced to exile on the remote South Atlantic island of St. Helena, where he talked to his dog, studied a little English, penned his memoirs, spoke his final word—"Josephine"—and died.

Pause in the battles to gaze at the grand statue of Napoleon the emperor in the alcove at the head of the tomb—royal scepter and orb of Earth in his hands. By 1804, all of Europe was at his feet. He held an elaborate ceremony in Notre-Dame, where he

 proclaimed his wife, Josephine, an empress, and himself—the 35-year-old son of humble immigrants—as emperor. The laurel wreath, the robes, and the Roman eagles proclaim him the equal of the Caesars. The floor at the statue's feet marks the grave of his son, Napoleon II (*Roi de Rome*, 1811–1832).

Around the crypt are relief panels showing Napoleon's constructive side. Dressed in toga and laurel leaves, he dispenses justice, charity, and pork-barrel projects to an awed populace.

• *In the first panel to the right of the statue...*

He establishes an Imperial University to educate naked boys throughout "*tout l'empire.*" The roll of great scholars links modern France with those of the past: Plutarch, Homer, Plato, and Aristotle. Three panels later, his various building projects (canals, roads, and so on) are celebrated with a list and his quotation "Everywhere I passed, I left durable benefit" *("Partout où mon regne à passé...").*

Hail Napoleon. Then, at his peak, came his fatal mistake.

• *Turn around and look down to* Moscowa *(the Battle of Moscow).*

Napoleon invaded Russia with 600,000 men and returned to Paris with 60,000 frostbitten survivors. Two years later, the Russians marched into Paris, and Napoleon's days were numbered. After a brief exile on the isle of Elba, he skipped parole, sailed to France, bared his breast, and said, "Strike me down or follow me!" For 100 days, they followed him, finally into Belgium, where the British hammered the French at the Battle of Waterloo (conspicuously absent on the floor's decor). Exiled again by a war tribunal, he spent his last years in a crude shack on the small South Atlantic island of St. Helena.

• *To get to the Courtyard of Honor and the various military museums, exit the same way you entered, make a U-turn right, and march past the cafeteria and ticket hall. Pause halfway down the long hallway. On the right, through the glass, you'll see...*

Napoleon's Tombstone (Pierre Tombale)

This bare stone slab, surrounded by shrubs and weeping willows, once rested atop Napoleon's grave on the island of St. Helena. The epitaph was never finished because the French and British wrangled over what to call the hero/tyrant. The stone simply reads, "Here lies…"

• *Continuing to the end of the hallway, you'll find the entrance to the World War I and World War II Wings (in the southwest corner of the main courtyard). Go upstairs, following blue-banner signs reading* Les Deux Guerres Mondiales, 1871–1945. *The museum is laid out so that you first see the coverage of World War I, though some may choose to skip ahead to the more substantial WWII section.*

World War I Wing

World War I (1914–1918) introduced modern technology to the age-old business of war. Tanks, chemical weapons, monstrous cannons, rapid communication, and airplanes made their debut, conspiring to kill nearly 10 million people. In addition, the war ultimately seemed senseless: It started with little provocation, raged on with few decisive battles, and ended with nothing resolved, a situation that sowed the seeds of World War II.

This 20-room museum leads you chronologically through the background, causes, battles, and outcome. There's good English information, but the displays themselves are lackluster and low-tech; move quickly and don't burn out before World War II. Even a quick walk-through gives you the essential background for the next World War. (For a better understanding of World War I, take the fast TGV train from Paris' Gare de l'Est station to Verdun and spend a day touring the battlefields where 700,000 soldiers died.)

Room 1: "Honour to the Unfortunate Bravery"

Paintings of dead and wounded soldiers from the Franco-Prussian War make it clear that World War I actually "began" in 1871, when Germany thrashed France. Suddenly, a recently united Germany was the new bully in Europe.

Rooms 2–3: France Rebounds

Snapping back from its loss, France began rearming itself, with spiffy new **uniforms** and weapons like the American-invented **Gatling gun** (early machine gun).

The French replaced the humiliation of defeat with a proud and extreme nationalism. A **video** shows how fanatic patriots hounded a (Jewish) officer named Alfred Dreyfus on trumped-up treason charges (1890s). They convicted and imprisoned him (after ceremonially breaking his sword in the Invalides courtyard), before he was finally acquitted.

Rooms 4–6: Tensions Rise

France, Germany, and the rest of Europe were in a race for wealth and power, jostling to acquire lucrative colonies in Africa and Asia (**map, video, exotic uniforms**). In a cli-

mate of mutual distrust, nations allied with their neighbors, vowing to protect each other if war ever erupted. In Room 6, a **map of Europe in 1914** shows France, Britain, and Russia (the Allies) teaming up against Germany, Austria-Hungary, and Italy (the Central Powers). Meanwhile, the Ottoman Empire (Turkey and the Balkans) was breaking apart, creating a tense and unstable Western world. Europe was ready to explode, but the spark that would set it off had nothing to do with Germany or France.

Room 7: Assassination, War Begins

Bang. On June 28, 1914, an Austrian archduke was shot to death (see **video** of the political mood, assassination, and mobilization). It happened in Serbia—a region not all central, but very politically charged. One by one, Europe's nations were dragged into the regional dispute by their webs of alliances. All of Europe mobilized its troops. The **1914** stone on the floor is the first of the museum's year-stones. The Great War had begun.

Room 8: The Battle of the Marne

In September, German forces swarmed into France, hoping for a quick knockout blow. Germany brought its big guns (photo and model of **Big Bertha**). The **projection map** shows how the armies tried to outflank each other along a 200-mile battle-front. As the Germans (brown arrows) zeroed in on Paris, the

French (blue arrows) scrambled to send 6,000 crucial reinforcements, shuttled to the front lines in 670 Parisian **taxis.** The German tide was stemmed, and the two sides faced off, expecting to duke it out and get this war over quick. It didn't work out that way.

• *The war continues upstairs.*

Rooms 9–10: The War in the Trenches

By 1915, they'd reached a stalemate, and the two sides settled in to a long war of attrition—French and Britons on one side, Germans

on the other. The battle line, known as the Western Front, snaked 450 miles across Europe from the North Sea to the Alps. For protection against flying bullets, the soldiers dug **trenches,** which soon became home—24 hours a day, 7 days a week—for millions of men.

La guerre des tranchées

Life in the trenches was awful—cold, rainy, muddy, disease-ridden—and, most of all, boring. Every so often, generals waved their swords

and ordered their men "over the top" and into "no man's land." Armed with rifles and bayonets, they advanced into a hail of machine gun fire. In a number of battles, France lost 70,000 men in a single day. The "victorious" side often won only a few hundred yards of meaningless territory that was lost the next day after still more deaths.

The war pitted 19th-century values of honor, bravery, and chivalry against 20th-century **weapons:** grenades, machine guns, tanks, and gas masks. To shoot over the tops of trenches while staying hidden, they even invented **crooked and periscope-style guns.**

Rooms 11–13: "World" War

Besides the Western Front, the War extended elsewhere, including the colonies, where many natives joined the armies of their mother countries. On the Eastern Front, Russia and Germany wore each other down. (Finally, the Russians had enough; they killed their czar, brought the troops home, and fomented a revolution that put Communists in power.)

• *Down a short hallway, enter...*

Room 14: The Allies

By 1917, the Allied forces were beginning to outstrip the Central Powers, thanks to help from around the world. Britain drew heavily from its Commonwealth nations, like Canada and Australia.

And when Uncle Sam said **"I Want You,"** five million Americans answered the call to go "Over There" (in the words of a popular song) and fight the Germans. Though the US

I WANT YOU
FOR U.S. ARMY
NEAREST RECRUITING STATION

ARMY MUSEUM

didn't enter the War until April 1917 (and was never an enormous military factor), its very presence was one more indication that the Allies seemed destined to prevail.

Room 15: Armistice
Under the command of the French Marshal Ferdinand Foch, the Allies undertook a series of offensives that, by **1918,** would prove decisive. At the eleventh hour of the eleventh day of the eleventh month (November 11, 1918), the guns fell silent. Europeans celebrated with **victory parades.**

Room 16: A Costly Victory
Weary soldiers returned home to be honored (painting of **Arc de Triomphe** parade). After four years of battle, the war had left 9.5 million dead and 21 million wounded (see plaster casts of **disfigured faces**). Three out of every four French soldiers had been either killed or wounded. A generation was lost.

Rooms 17–19: From 1918 to 1938
The Treaty of Versailles (1919), signed in the Hall of Mirrors, officially ended the war. A **map** shows how it radically redrew Europe's borders. Germany was punished severely, leaving it crushed, humiliated, stripped of crucial land, and saddled with demoralizing war debts. Marshal Foch said of the Treaty: "This is not a peace. It is an armistice for 20 years."

France, one of the "victors," was drained, trying to hang on to its prosperity and its **colonial empire.**

But by the 1930s—swamped by the Great Depression and a stagnant military (**dummy on horseback**)—France was reeling, unprepared for the onslaught of a retooled Germany seeking revenge.

• *World War II is covered directly across the hall, in the rooms marked* 1939–1942.

World War II Wing

World War II was the most destructive of Earth's struggles. In this exhibit, the war unfolds in photos, displays, and newsreels, with special emphasis on the French contribution. You may never have realized that it was Charles de Gaulle who won the war for us.

The free museum map is helpful for locating the displays we'll see. Climb to the top floor and work back down, from Germany's quick domination (third floor), to the Allies turning the tide (second floor), to the final surrender (first floor).

There are fine English descriptions throughout. Be ready—rooms come in rapid succession—and treat the following text simply as an overview.

Third Floor—Axis Aggression (1939–1941)

Room 1: The Phony War (La Drôle de Guerre)

On September 1, 1939, Germany, under Adolf Hitler, invaded Poland, starting World War II. But in a sense the war had really begun in 1918, when the "war to end all wars" ground to a halt, leaving 9.5 million dead, Germany defeated, and France devastated (if victorious). For the next two decades, Hitler fed off German resentment over the Treaty of Versailles, which humiliated and ruined Germany.

After Hitler's move into Poland, France and Britain mobilized. For the next six months, the two sides faced off, with neither actually doing battle—a tense time known to historians as the "phony" war.

Room 2: The Defeat of 1940 (La Défaite de 1940)

Then, in spring 1940, came the Blitzkrieg ("lightning war"), and Germany's better-trained and better-equipped soldiers and tanks (see **turret**) swept west through Belgium. France was immediately overwhelmed, and British troops barely escaped across the English Channel from Dunkirk. Within a month, Nazis were goose-stepping down the Champs-Elysées, and Hitler was on his way to Napoleon's tomb. Hitler made a three-hour blitz tour of the city, after which he said, "It was the dream of my life to be permitted to see Paris. I cannot say how happy I am to have that dream fulfilled today."

Room 3: The Appeal of June 18, 1940

Just like that, virtually all of Europe was dominated by Fascists. During those darkest days, as France fell and Nazism spread across the Continent, one Frenchman—an obscure military man named **Charles de Gaulle**—refused to admit defeat. He escaped to London, made inspiring speeches over the radio, and slowly convinced a small audience of French expatriates that victory was still possible.

• *Through the small door to your right is...*

Room 4: Charles de Gaulle (1890–1970)

This 20th-century John of Arc had an unshakable belief in his mission to save France. He was born into a literate, upper-class

Our War Album.—44. France's Voice in London

family, raised in military academies, and became a WWI hero and POW. (After the war, he helped administer the occupied Rhineland.) When World War II broke out, he was only a minor officer (the title of "Brigadier General" was hastily acquired during the invasion). He had limited political experience, and was virtually unknown to the French public. But he rallied France, became the focus of French patriotism, and later guided the country in the postwar years.

ARMY MUSEUM

Rooms 5–6: France After the Armistice

After France's surrender, Germany ruled northern France, including Paris—see the **photo** of Hitler as tourist at the Eiffel Tower. The Nazis allowed the French to administer the south and the colonies (North Africa). This puppet government, centered in the city of Vichy, was right-wing and traditional, bowing to Hitler's demands as he looted France's raw materials and manpower for the war machine. (The movie *Casablanca,* set in Vichy-controlled Morocco, shows French officials following Nazi orders while French citizens defiantly sing "The Marseillaise.")

Room 7: The Battle of Britain—June 1940–June 1941

Facing a "New Dark Age" in Europe, British Prime Minister Winston Churchill pledged, "We will fight on the beaches....We will fight in the hills. We will never surrender."

In June 1940, Germany mobilized to invade Britain across the Channel. From June to September, they paved the way, sending bombers—up to 1,500 planes a day—to destroy military and industrial sites. When Britain wouldn't budge, Hitler concentrated on London and civilian targets. This was "The Blitz" of the winter of 1940, which killed 30,000 and left London in ruins. But Britain hung on, armed with newfangled radar, speedy Spitfires, and an iron will.

They also had the Germans' secret "Enigma" code. The **Enigma machine** (in display case), with its set of revolving drums, allowed German commanders to scramble orders in a complex code that could be

broadcast safely to their troops. The British (with crucial help from Poland) captured a machine, broke the code (in a project called "Ultra"), then monitored German airwaves. For the rest of the war, they had advance knowledge of many top-secret plans. (Occasionally, Britain even let Germany's plans succeed—sacrificing its own people—to avoid suspicion.)

By spring 1941, Hitler had given up any hope of invading the Isle of Britain. Churchill said of his people: "This was their finest hour."

Room 10: Germany Invades the Soviet Union— June 1941

Perhaps hoping to one-up Napoleon, Hitler sent his state-of-the-art tanks speeding toward Moscow (betraying his former ally

Joseph Stalin). By winter, the advance had stalled at the gates of Moscow and was bogged down by bad weather and Soviet stubbornness. The Third Reich had reached its peak. From now on, Hitler would have to fight a two-front war. The French Renault **tank** (displayed) was downright puny compared to the big, fast, high-caliber German Panzers. This war was often a battle of factories, to see who could produce the latest technology fastest and in the greatest numbers. And what nation might that be...?

Room 12: The United States Joins the War

"On December 7, 1941, a date which will live in infamy" (as FDR put it), Japanese planes made a sneak attack on the US base at Pearl Harbor, Hawaii, and destroyed the pride of the Pacific fleet in two hours.

The US quickly entered the fray against Japan and her ally, Germany. In two short years, America had gone from isolationist observer to supplier of Britain's arms to full-blown war ally against fascism. The US now faced a two-front war—in Europe against Hitler, and in Asia against Japan's imperialist conquest of China, Southeast Asia, and the South Pacific.

America's first victory came when Japan tried a sneak attack on the US base at Midway Island (June 3, 1942). This time—thanks to the Allies who had cracked the Enigma code—America had the aircraft carrier **USS *Enterprise*** (see model) and two of her buddies lying in wait. In five minutes, three of Japan's carriers (with valuable planes) were fatally wounded, their major attack force was sunk, and Japan and the US were dead even, settling in for a long war of attrition.

Though slow to start, America eventually had an army of 16 million strong, 80,000 planes, the latest technology, $250 million a day, unlimited raw materials, and a population of Rosie the Riveters fighting for freedom to a boogie-woogie beat.

• *Continue downstairs to the second floor.*

Second Floor—The Tide Turns (1942–1944)

In 1942, the Continent was black with fascism, and Japan was secure on a distant island. The Allies had to chip away on the fringes.

Room 13: Battle of the Atlantic

German U-boats (short for *Unterseeboot*, see model) and battleships such as the *Bismarck* patrolled Europe's perimeter, where they laid spiky mines and kept America from aiding Britain. (Until long-range transport planes were invented near war's end, virtually all military transport was by ship.) The Allies traveled in convoys with air cover, used sonar and radar, and dropped depth charges, but for years they endured the loss of up to 60 ships per month.

• *Don't bypass Room 14, tucked in the corner.*

Room 14: The War Turns—El-Alamein, Stalingrad, and Guadalcanal

Three crucial battles in autumn of 1942 put the first chink in the Fascist armor. Off the east coast of Australia, 10,000 US Marines (see kneeling soldier in glass case 14D) took an airstrip on Guadalcanal, while 30,000 Japanese held the rest of the tiny, isolated island. For the next six months, the two armies were marooned together, duking it out in thick jungles and malaria-infested swamps while their countries struggled to reinforce or rescue them. By February 1943, America had won and gained a crucial launch pad for bombing raids.

A world away, German tanks under General Erwin Rommel rolled across the vast deserts of North Africa. In October 1942, a well-equipped, well-planned offensive by British General Bernard ("Monty") Montgomery attacked at El-Alamein, Egypt, with 300 tanks. (See **British tank soldier** with headphones.) Monty drove "the Desert Fox" west into Tunisia for the first real Allied victory against the Nazi *Wehrmacht* war machine.

Then came Stalingrad. (See kneeling **Soviet soldier** in heavy coat.) In August 1942, Germany attacked the Soviet city, an industrial center and gateway to the Caucasus oil fields. By October, the Germans had battled their way into the city center and were fighting house-to-house, but their supplies were running low, the Soviets wouldn't give up, and winter was coming. The snow fell, their tanks had no fuel, and relief efforts failed. Hitler ordered them to fight on through the bitter cold. On the worst days, 50,000 men died. (America lost a total of 58,000 in Vietnam.) Finally, on January 31, 1943, the Germans surrendered, against Hitler's orders. The six-month totals? Eight hundred thousand German and other Axis soldiers dead, 1.1 million Soviets dead. The Russian campaign put hard miles on the German war machine.

Also in 1942, the Allies began long-range bombing of German-held territory, including saturation bombing of civilians. It was global war and total war.

Room 15: The Allies Land in North Africa

Winston Churchill and US President **Franklin D. Roosevelt** (see photo with de Gaulle), two of the 20th century's most dynamic

and strong-willed states-men, decided to attack Hitler indirectly by invading Vichy-controlled Morocco and Algeria. On November 8, 1942, 100,000 Americans and British—under the joint command of an unknown, low-key problem-solver named General Dwight ("Ike") Eisenhower—landed on three separate beaches (including Casablanca). More than 120,000 Vichy French soldiers, ordered by their superiors to defend the Fascist cause, confronted the Allies and...gave up. (See display of some standard-issue **weapons:** Springfield rifle, Colt 45, Thompson machine gun, hand grenade.)

The Allies moved east, but bad weather, inexperience, and the powerful Afrika Korps under Rommel stopped them in Tunisia. But with flamboyant General George S. ("Old Blood-and-Guts") Patton punching from the west, and Monty pushing from the south, they captured the port town of Tunis on May 7, 1943. The Allies now had a base from which to retake Europe.

Room 17: The French Resistance
(also see displays in Room 20)

Inside occupied France, other ordinary heroes fought the Nazis—the "underground," or Resistance. Bakers hid radios within loaves

ARMY MUSEUM

of bread to secretly contact London. Barmaids passed along tips from tipsy Nazis. Communists in black berets cut telephone lines. Farmers hid downed airmen in haystacks. Housewives spread news from the front with their gossip. Printers countered Nazi propaganda with pamphlets.

Jean Moulin (see photo in museum), de Gaulle's assistant, secretly parachuted into France and organized these scattered heroes into a unified effort. In May 1943, Moulin was elected chairman of the National Council of the Resistance. A month later, he was arrested by the Gestapo (Nazi secret police), imprisoned, tortured, and sent to Germany, where he died in transit. Still, Free France now had a (secret) government again, rallied around de Gaulle, and was ready to take over when liberation came.

Room 18: The Red Army

Monty, Patton, and Ike certainly were heroes, but the war was won on the Eastern Front by Soviet grunts, who slowly bled Germany dry. Maps show the shifting border of the Eastern Front.

Rooms 21–22: The Italian Campaign

On July 10, 1943, the assault on Hitler's European fortress began. More than 150,000 Americans and British sailed from Tunis and landed on the south shore of Sicily. (See **maps** and **video clips** of the campaigns.) Speedy Patton and methodical Monty began a "horse race" to take the city of Messina (the US won the friendly competition by a few hours). They met little resistance from 300,000 Italian soldiers, and were actually cheered as liberators by the Sicilian people. Their real enemies were the 50,000 German troops sent by Hitler to bolster his ally Benito Mussolini. By September, the island was captured. On the mainland, Mussolini was arrested by his own people and Italy surrendered to the Allies. Hitler quickly poured troops into Italy (and reinstalled Mussolini) to hold off the Allied onslaught.

In early September, the Allies launched a two-pronged landing onto the beaches of southern Italy. Finally, after four long years of war, free men set foot on the European continent. Lieutenant General Mark Clark, leading the slow, bloody push north to liberate Rome, must have been reminded of the French trenches he'd fought in during World War I. As in that bloody war, the fighting in Italy was a war of attrition, fought on the ground by foot soldiers and costing many lives for just a few miles.

In January 1944, the Germans dug in between Rome and Naples at Monte Cassino, a rocky hill topped by the monastery of St. Benedict. Thousands died as the Allies tried inching up the hillside. In frustration, the Allies air-bombed the historic **monastery** to smithereens (see photo), killing many noncombatants...but no

Germans, who dug in deeper. Finally, after four months of vicious, sometimes hand-to-hand combat by the Allies (Americans, Brits, Free French, Poles, Italian partisans, Indians, etc.), a band of Poles stormed the monastery, and the German back was broken.

Meanwhile, 50,000 Allies had landed on Anzio (a beach near Rome) and held the narrow beachhead for months against massive German attacks. When reinforcements arrived, Allied troops broke out and joined the two-pronged assault on the capital. Without a single bomb threatening its historic treasures, Rome fell on June 4, 1944.

• *Room 23 (with chairs) shows a film on...*

Room 23: D-Day—June 6, 1944, "Operation Overlord"

Three million Allies and six million tons of material were massed in England in preparation for the biggest fleet-led invasion in history—across the Channel to France, then eastward to Berlin. The Germans, hunkered down in northern France, knew an invasion was imminent, but the Allies kept the details top secret. On the night of June 5, 150,000 soldiers boarded ships and planes without knowing where they were headed until they were under way. Each one carried a note from General Eisenhower: "The tide has turned. The free men of the world are marching together to victory."

At 6:30 a.m. on June 6, 1944, Americans spilled out of troop transports into the cold waters off a beach in Normandy, code-named Omaha. The weather was bad, seas were rough, and the prep bombing had failed. The soldiers, many seeing their first action, were dazed and confused. Nazi machine guns pinned them against the sea. Slowly, they crawled up the beach on their stomachs. A thousand died. They held on until the next wave of transports arrived.

All day long, Allied confusion did battle with German indecision; the Nazis never really counterattacked, thinking D-Day was just a ruse, instead of the main invasion. By day's end, the Allies had taken several beaches along the Normandy coast and began building artificial harbors, providing a tiny port-of-entry for the reconquest of Europe. The stage was set for a quick and easy end to the war. Right.

• *Go downstairs to the...*

First Floor—The War Ends...Very Slowly (June 1944–August 1945)

Rooms 24–25: Battle of Normandy and Landing in Provence, August 1944

For a month, the Allies (mostly Americans) secured Normandy by taking bigger ports (Cherbourg and Caen) and amassing troops and supplies for the assault on Germany. In July they broke out and sped eastward across France, with Patton's tanks covering up to 40 miles a day. They had "Jerry" on the run.

On France's Mediterranean coast, American troops under General Alexander Patch landed near Cannes (see **parachute** photo), took Marseilles, and headed north to meet with Patton.

Room 26: "Les Maquis"
French Resistance guerrilla fighters helped reconquer France from behind the lines. (Don't miss the **folding motorcycle** in its parachute case.) The liberation of Paris was started by a Resistance attack on a German garrison.

Room 27: Liberation of Paris
As the Allies marched on Paris, Hitler ordered his officers to torch the city—but they sanely disobeyed and prepared to surrender. On August 26, 1944, General Charles de Gaulle walked ramrod-straight down the Champs-Elysées, followed by Free French troops and US GIs passing out chocolate and Camels. Two million Parisians went ape.

Room 28: Toward Berlin—Offensive from the West
The quick advance through France, Belgium, and Luxembourg bogged down at the German border in autumn of 1944. Patton outstripped supply lines, a parachute invasion of Holland (the Battle of Arnhem) was disastrous, and bad weather grounded planes and slowed tanks.

On December 16, the Allies met a deadly surprise. An enormous, well-equipped, energetic German army appeared from nowhere, punched a "bulge" deep into Allied lines, and demanded surrender. General Anthony McAuliffe sent a one-word response—"Nuts!"—and the momentum shifted. The Battle of the Bulge was Germany's last great offensive.

The Germans retreated across the Rhine River, blowing up bridges behind them. The last bridge, at Remagen, was captured by the Allies just long enough for them to cross and establish themselves on German soil. Soon US tanks were speeding down the autobahns and Patton could wire the good news back to Ike: "General, I have just pissed in the Rhine."

Soviet soldiers did the dirty work of taking fortified Berlin by launching a final offensive in January 1945, and surrounding the city in April. German citizens fled west to surrender to the more-benevolent Americans and Brits. Hitler, defiant to the end, hunkered in his underground bunker. (See photo of **ruined Berlin.**)

On April 28, 1945, Mussolini and his girlfriend were killed and hung by their heels in Milan. Two days later, Adolf Hitler and his new bride, Eva Braun, avoided similar humiliation by committing suicide (pistol in mouth), and having their bodies burned beyond recognition. Germany formally surrendered on May 8, 1945.

In Corridor to the Left of Room 28: Concentration Camps

Lest anyone mourn Hitler or doubt this war's purpose, gaze at photos from Germany's concentration camps. Some camps held political enemies and prisoners of war, including two million French. Others were expressly built to exterminate peoples considered "genetically inferior" to the "Aryan master race"—particularly Jews, Gypsies, homosexuals, and the mentally ill. The criminals who perpetrated these acts were tried and sentenced in an international court—the first of its kind—held in Nuremburg, Germany.

Room 29: War of the Pacific

Often treated as an afterthought, the final campaign against Japan was a massive American effort, costing many lives, but saving millions of others from Japanese domination.

Japan was an island bunker surrounded by a vast ring of fortified Pacific islands. America's strategy was to take one island at a time, "island-hopping" until close enough for B-29 Superfortress bombers to attack Japan itself. The war spread across thousands of miles. In a new form of warfare, ships carrying planes led the attack and prepared tiny islands for troops to land and build an airbase. While General Douglas MacArthur island-hopped south to retake the Philippines ("I have returned!"), others pushed north toward Japan.

In February 1945, marines landed on Iwo Jima, a city-size island-volcano close enough to Japan (800 miles) to launch air raids. Twenty thousand Japanese had dug in on the volcano's top and were picking off the advancing Americans. On February 23, several US soldiers raised the Stars and Stripes on the mountain (that famous photo), which inspired their mates to victory at a cost of nearly 7,000 men.

Japan Surrenders

On March 9, Tokyo was firebombed, and 90,000 were killed. Japan was losing, but a land invasion would cost hundreds of thousands of lives. The Japanese had a reputation for choosing death over the shame of surrender—they even sent bomb-laden "kamikaze" planes on suicide missions.

America unleashed its secret weapon, an atomic bomb (originally suggested by German-turned-American Albert Einstein). On August 6, a B-29 dropped one (named **"Little Boy,"** see the

ARMY MUSEUM

replica dangling overhead) on the city of Hiroshima and instantly vaporized 100,000 people and four square miles. Three days later, a second bomb fell on Nagasaki. The next day, Emperor Hirohito unofficially surrendered. The long war was over, and US

sailors returned home to kiss their girlfriends in public places.

The Closing Chapter

The death toll for World War II (September 1939–August 1945) totaled 80 million soldiers and civilians. The Soviet Union lost 26 million, China 13 million, France 580,000, and the US 340,000.

ARMY MUSEUM

World War II changed the world, with America emerging as the dominant political, military, and economic superpower. Europe was split in two. The western half recovered, with American aid. The eastern half remained under Soviet occupation. For 45 years, the US and the Soviet Union would compete—without ever actually doing battle—in a "Cold War" of espionage, propaganda, and weapons production that stretched from Korea to Cuba, from Vietnam to the moon.

• *Return to the large Courtyard of Honor, where Napoleon honored his troops, Dreyfus had his sword broken, and de Gaulle once kissed Churchill. Two Army Museums—one in the East Wing and one in the West Wing—flank the courtyard. The West Wing contains "Arms and Armour" (see page 213 for a short description). The East Wing houses the recently refurbished "Arms and Uniforms."*

Arms and Uniforms

Louis XIV To Napoleon III (1643-1870)

• *The museum is located in the East Wing of the courtyard. Entering on the ground floor, first browse quickly through the halls to the left (history of the museum) and right (history of the Invalides). Then go upstairs to the main collection on the second floor.*

The museum traces uniforms and weapons through France's glory days, with the emphasis on Napoleon Bonaparte. As you circle the second floor, you'll see it unfold chronologically: the Ancien Régime (Louis XIV, XV, and XVI), the Revolution, the First Empire (Napoleon), and the post-Waterloo world, as a fading France tried to revive its former glory under Napoleon III.

The newly renovated wing (though parts of it may still be closed during your visit) is fitted with interactive computer terminals, sound effects to accompany some displays, and an expanded layout. All of the exhibits have an English translation.

The following is not a room-by-room tour—this is more a museum for browsing. Instead, I've simply highlighted a handful of the (many) exhibits you might see. Explore, and let the museum surprise you.

Hall 1: Ancien Régime (Louis XIV, XV, and XVI)

Louis XIV unified the army as he unified the country, creating the first modern nation-state with a military force. You'll see how gunpowder was quickly turning swords, pikes, and lances to pistols, muskets, and bayonets. Uniforms became more uniform, and everyone got a standard-issue flintlock.

Hall 2: Révolution

With the Revolution, the king's Royal Army became the people's National Guard, protecting their fledgling democracy from Europe's monarchies, while spreading revolutionary ideas by conquest. A young, relatively obscure officer distinguished himself on the battlefield and quickly rose through the ranks—Napoleon Bonaparte. At the Battle of Lodi (1796), the French and Austrians faced off on opposites sides of a northern Italian river, trying to capture a crucial bridge and using cannons to clear the way for a cavalry charge. Brash Bonaparte personally sighted the French cannons on the enemy—normally the job of a lesser officer—which turned the tide of battle and earned him a reputation and a nickname, "The Little Corporal."

Hall 3: Première République— The Reign of Napoleon

While pledging allegiance to Revolutionary ideals of democracy, Napoleon ruled France as a virtual dictator and Emperor. The museum displays General Bonaparte's hat, sword, and medals. His tent is fitted with his bivouac equipment: a bed with mosquito netting, a director's chair, and a table that you can imagine his generals hunched over as they made battle plans.

The museum even has Napoleon's beloved white dog (stuffed, in a glass case) and his Arabian horse, Le Vizir, who weathered many a campaign and grew old with him in exile (also stuffed).

A famous portrait of Napoleon as Emperor (by Jean-Auguste-Dominique Ingres) shows him at the peak of his power, stretching his right arm to supernatural lengths. You'll see memorabilia of

Napoleon's son, the "King of Rome" *(Roi de Rome)*. When he grew up, he looked a lot like his dad—a fact that kept French Royalists wary until his death. Junior's mother was Marie Louise, whom Napoleon married after divorcing barren Josephine.

In 1814—after the disastrous losses in the invasion of Russia—Napoleon was forced to abdicate. Though he returned for one last hurrah, he was finally defeated at the Battle of Waterloo and sent into exile on St. Helena. His reconstructed room from exile lets you imagine a lonely man suffering from ulcers, passing his days in his nightcap and slippers, playing chess, not war. Finally, the museum displays Napoleon's death mask.

BUS #69 SIGHTSEEING TOUR

From the Eiffel Tower to Père Lachaise Cemetery

Why pay €25 for a tour company to give you an overview of Paris, when city bus #69 can do it for the cost of a Metro ticket? Get on the bus and settle in for a ride through some of the city's most interesting neighborhoods. Or hop on and off using this tour as a fun way to lace together many of Paris' most important sightseeing districts (your ticket gives you 90 minutes). On this ride from the Eiffel Tower to Père Lachaise Cemetery, you'll learn how great the city's bus system is—and you'll wonder why you've been tunneling by Métro under this gorgeous city. And if you're staying in the Marais or rue Cler neighborhoods, line #69 is a useful route for just getting around town—except on Sunday, when it doesn't run.

You'll find that the bus goes faster than you can read. It's best to look through this chapter ahead of time, then ride with an eye out for the various sights described here.

Orientation

Cost: €1.70 (one Métro ticket) per one-way ride.

When to Go: You can hop on Monday through Saturday, but avoid Sunday (no service), weekday rush hours (8:00–9:30 & 17:30–19:30), and hot days (no air-conditioning). Evening bus rides are magical in months when it gets dark early enough to see the floodlit monuments before the bus stops running (last trip at 21:15).

Getting There: Eastbound line #69 leaves from the Eiffel Tower on avenue Joseph Bouvard (the street that becomes rue St. Dominique as it crosses the Champ de Mars). The first stop is at the southwestern end of the avenue, across from the Eiffel Tower (with the tower at your back, walk through the grassy park; avenue Joseph Bouvard is the second street you'll cross).

You may want to start on the eastern end of avenue Joseph Bouvard (second stop, just before avenue de la Bourdonnais). Stops are located about every three blocks along the route shown on the map in this chapter. At whatever stop you plan to catch the bus, check if "#69" is posted at the stop to make sure you're on the right route.

Bus Tips: Use a ticket from your *carnet*. Métro tickets work on buses and give you 1.5 hours to complete your one-way trip, jumping on and off buses as often as you like. (Note that you can't use the same ticket to transfer between the bus and Métro.) Board through the front door, then validate your ticket in the machine behind the driver. To let the driver know you'd like to get off at the next stop, push a red button. Exit through the rear door. Buses run every 10–15 minutes (7:30–21:15).

Length of This Tour: Allow one hour.

Overview

Handy line #69 crosses the city east–west, running between the Eiffel Tower and Père Lachaise, and passing these great monuments and neighborhoods: Eiffel Tower, Ecole Militaire, rue Cler, Les Invalides (Army Museum and Napoleon's Tomb), Louvre Museum, Ile de la Cité, Ile St. Louis, Hôtel de Ville, Pompidou Center, Marais, Bastille, and Père Lachaise. You don't have to do the whole enchilada; get on and off wherever you like.

This tour is best done in the direction it's written (east from the Eiffel Tower to Père Lachaise Cemetery), because one-way streets change the route in the other direction. Grab a window seat—right side is best. If you get on at one of the first stops, you're most likely to secure a good seat.

Many find the Bastille a good ending point (where you can begin my walking tour of the Marais; see the Marais Walk chapter). This ride also ties in well after a visit to the Eiffel Tower or on your way to visiting Père Lachaise Cemetery. Think of this as an overview. The sights you'll survey are written up in more depth elsewhere in the book. OK—let's roll.

The Tour Begins

Champ de Mars and the Eiffel Tower

Your tour begins below this 1,000-foot, reddish-brown hood ornament. While you're waiting for the bus, read up on the Eiffel Tower (see the Eiffel Tower Tour chapter). The park surrounding you is called Champ de Mars (named for the god of war). It served as a parade ground for the military school, Ecole Militaire, that seals the park at the right end. Napoleon

Bus #69 Tour

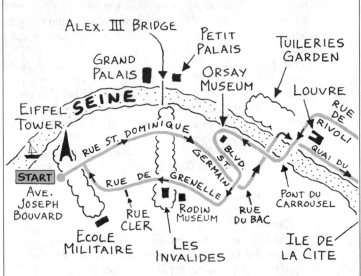

Note 1: Not to scale; from the Eiffel Tower to Père Lachaise is about 4.2 miles (7 km) as the poodle trots.

Note 2: Stops are located about every 3 blocks along the route.

Note 3: There is no service on Sunday nor after 21:15 any night.

Bonaparte is the school's most famous graduate.

In 1889, the Champ de Mars was covered with a massive temporary structure to house exhibitions of all sorts; it was a celebration of the Centennial World's Fair, the same event for which the Eiffel Tower was built. The apartments surrounding the park are among the most exclusive in Paris.

The grass that runs down the center of the park is strictly off-limits—so you can't walk on the grass, except on the side sections. Evening picnics are a delight (where allowed), and warm evenings are grand social affairs. Dogs romp as soccer balls fly past, all within the glow of the Eiffel Tower.

• *Leaving the Champ de Mars, the bus slices through the 7th arrondissement along its primary shopping street. As you head onto rue St. Dominique, notice how well your driver navigates past delivery trucks and illegally parked cars.*

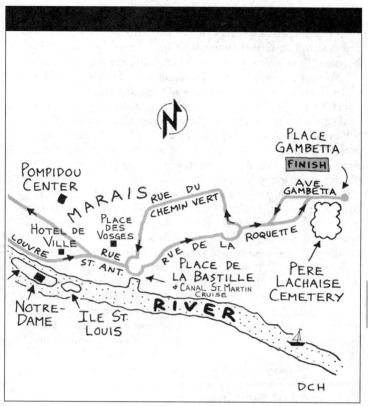

Rue St. Dominique

Paris functions as a city of hundreds of small neighborhoods. This area, which was once the village of Grenelle (before it was consumed by Paris), is a case in point. Shops and cafés line the streets, topped by several floors of apartments, giving the district a liveliness not found in less-vibrant commercial districts. You can shop for anything you need on rue St. Dominique (but not at any hour). Many locals never leave the area, and neighbors trust each other. The dry cleaner knows that if his customer forgets her wallet, she'll return to pay him another time. If the plumber can only come during work hours, locals can leave their apartment keys with the nearest shop owner, who will make sure the plumber gets them.

This area has long been popular with Americans—the American Church (two blocks to the left), American Library, American University, and lots of my readers (in recommended hotels) call this area home.

• *After crossing boulevard de la Tour Maubourg, you'll enter the open world of esplanade des Invalides.*

Esplanade des Invalides

This sprawling esplanade links the **river** (to the left) and Europe's first veteran's hospital, **Les Invalides** (right), built by Louis XIV. Napoleon lies powerfully dead under the brilliant golden dome.

Afternoon *boules* (lawn bowling), near the Invalides building under the trees on the far right, is an engaging spectator sport. I spend more time watching the players' mannerisms than the game itself (see sidebar on page 360). In summer, American football games are played on the grassy esplanade with teams composed of Franco-American friends. They even have a league and drink beer after the games. The Rodin Museum lies just beyond the esplanade, left of Les Invalides.

Look left and see the **pont d'Alexandre III (Alexander III Bridge)** crossing the Seine. Spiked with golden statues and iron-work lamps, the bridge was built to celebrate a turn-of-the-20th-century treaty between France and Russia. Just across the bridge are the glass-and-steel-domed **Grand and Petit Palais** exhibition halls, built for the 1900 World's Fair. Like the bridge, they are fine examples of belle époque architecture. Impressive temporary exhibits fill the huge Grand Palais, and the smaller Petit Palais houses a permanent collection of 19th-century paintings, starring works by Courbet and Monet (among others). The **Air France building** (just this side of the river) is an Orly airport shuttle stop (4/hr).

• *Leaving Les Invalides, you'll reenter narrow streets lined with...*

Government Buildings

Many of France's most important ministries occupy the golden-hued buildings (look for police guarding doorways, heavily barred windows, and people in suits speaking in hushed tones). Opposite the frilly **Gothic church** (on right) sprawls the **Ministry of Defense,** originally the mansion of Napoleon's mother.

• *You'll emerge from the government ghetto onto the stylish and leafy...*

Boulevard St. Germain

Along this stretch, colorful furniture stores tempt the neighborhood's upper-crust residents. Notice the fine Haussmann architecture. Several blocks farther down are the boulevard's famous cafés, once frequented by existentialists Albert Camus and Jean-Paul Sartre. But we turn left onto **rue du Bac,** and cross streets (to the right) filled with antiques, art galleries, and smart hotels. The Orsay Museum is a few blocks to the left (if you need an art break, the best stop for this museum is at Pont Royal, just before the river; ✪ see Orsay Museum Tour).

• *Next, you'll cross the river (see the Orsay Museum behind on the left) and enter the Right Bank.*

Tuileries Garden and Louvre Museum

The Tuileries Garden (Jardin des Tuileries) lies straight ahead as you cross the Seine. This was the royal garden of the Louvre

palace—come here after touring the Louvre to clear your mind. Several cafés are scattered among these pretty gardens, ponds with toy boats for rent, and trampolines for jumping. After turning right along the river, you'll follow the immense Grand Gallery of the **Louvre,** dominating the left side of the street, and **café-boats** on the right. (There are about 2,000 barges docked on the Seine in Paris.)

The U-shaped Louvre, once the biggest building in the world, now houses 12 miles of galleries wallpapered with thousands of the world's greatest paintings. Various kings added new wings, marking their contributions with their initials and medallions carved into the decor. The statues put on a stony toga fashion show as you roll by.

Just before the end of the Louvre building on the right is the view-perfect pedestrian bridge **pont des Arts** (described at the beginning of the ✪ Left Bank Walk). That curved **building with a dome** on the other side is where the Académie Française has met since the 1600s to defend the French language from corrupting influences (like English), and to compose the official French dictionary.

• *Next on the right is the island where Paris was founded. Get ready for quick right-left-right head movements.*

Ile de la Cité

The river splits around this island where Paris began over 2,000 years ago. The first bridge you see dates from about 1600. While it's called **pont Neuf,** meaning "new bridge," it's Paris' oldest. Pont Neuf leads to an equestrian statue of King Henry IV, who doesn't face a tiny and romantic tip-of-the-island park from which Seine tour boats depart (see listing for Vedettes du Pont Neuf on page 38).

On your left is Paris' primary **department-store shopping district.** Next along this street are sidewalk **pet stalls**—a hit with local children, who dream of taking home a turtle, canary, or rabbit. Back across the river, find the squat and round medieval towers (wearing pointy black cone hats) of the **Conciergerie,** named for the concierge (or caretaker) who ran these offices when the king moved to the Louvre. The towers guard the Ile de la Cité's law courts, the Palais de Justice, the prison famous as the last stop for those about to be guillotined. That intricate needle—the **spire of Sainte-Chapelle**—marks the most beautiful Gothic interior in Paris. You'll see the substantial twin towers and thin spire of **Notre-Dame Cathedral** soon after the Conciergerie. Back to the left, the grand **Hôtel de Ville** (Paris' city hall) stands proudly behind playful fountains. Each of the 20 arrondissements (governmental areas) in Paris has its own city hall, and this one is the big daddy of them all. In the summer, the square in front of Hôtel de Ville hosts sand volleyball courts and, at Christmastime, a big ice-skating rink. It's beautifully lit after dark all year. Take a quick look through the trees back across the river to see the gray steel **modern pedestrian bridge** that connects Paris' two islands.

• *The bus leaves the river after city hall and angles through the Marais.*

Le Marais

This is jumbled, medieval Paris at its finest. It's been a swamp, an aristocratic district, and a bohemian hangout. Today, classy stone mansions sit alongside trendy bars, keeping the antiques shops and fashion-conscious boutiques company. The Picasso Museum (currently closed for renovation), Carnavalet Museum, Victor Hugo's House, Jewish Art and History Museum, and Pompidou Center all have Marais addresses. On your left, a couple of blocks past city hall, you'll see the **oldest houses** in Paris—tall, skinny, and half-timbered—clustered around #13.

The narrow street soon merges into **rue St. Antoine,** the main street through the Marais and the main street of Paris in medieval times. The small-but-grand **Church of St. Paul and St. Louis** (on the right, with classical columns) is the only Jesuit church in Paris. It was the neighborhood church of Victor Hugo.

• *Rue St. Antoine leads straight into the place de la Bastille, marked with a giant pillar in the center. If your trip ends here, get off 30 yards before entering place de la Bastille. Options if you get off: Marais Walk (see the Marais Walk chapter), Canauxrama canal boat tour (page 38), Promenade Plantée Park (page 78), and Marais eateries (see the Eating chapter).*

Place de la Bastille

The namesake of this square, a fortress-turned-prison that symbolized royal tyranny, is long gone. But for centuries, the fortress that stood here was used to defend the city, mostly from its own people. On July 14, 1789, angry Parisians swarmed the Bastille, released its prisoners, and kicked off the French Revolution. Since then, the French celebrate their Independence Day on July 14 (a.k.a. Bastille Day) as enthusiastically as Americans commemorate July 4.

In the middle of the square, you'll actually cross over **Canal**

St. Martin (look to the right), which runs from the Seine underneath the tree-lined boulevard Richard Lenoir (on the left) to northern Paris. You'll curve in front of the reflecting-glass **Opéra Bastille.**

• *Leaving place de la Bastille, you'll angle left up rue de la Roquette all the way to Père Lachaise.*

Rue de la Roquette

This street begins at the Bastille in a hip, less touristy neighborhood. Here you'll find a fun mix of galleries, seedy bars, and trendy, cheap eateries. The first street to the right is **rue de Lappe** (described on page 451). One of the wildest nightspots in Paris and popular with gay men, rue de Lappe is filled with a dizzying array of wacky bistros, bars, and dance halls.

• *The bus eventually turns left onto boulevard de Ménilmontant (which locals happily associate with a famous Maurice Chevalier tune) and rumbles past the Père Lachaise Cemetery. Although the bus stops at the front gate of the vast cemetery, I'd recommend staying on to place Gambetta, where bus #69 ends its trip through the heart of Paris. Place Gambetta's centerpiece is another grandiose City Hall (this one for the 20th arrondissement). You'll also see some inviting cafés and avenue du Père Lachaise (opposite City Hall). Follow this street 100 yards, past flower shops selling cyclamen, heather, and chrysanthemums—the standard flowers for funerals and memorials—to the gate of the cemetery. Take a short stroll through the evocative home of so many permanent Parisians (Mo: Gambetta or Père Lachaise).*

Père Lachaise Cemetery

Navigating the labyrinthine rows is a challenge, but maps and my walking tour (◐ see Père Lachaise Cemetery Tour) will help you find the graves of greats such as Frédéric Chopin, Oscar Wilde, Gertrude Stein, and Jim Morrison. The tour is over. What better place for your final stop?

MARMOTTAN MUSEUM TOUR

Musée Marmottan Monet

The Marmottan has the best collection of works by the master Impressionist, Claude Monet. In this mansion on the fringe of urban Paris, you can walk through Monet's life, from black-and-white sketches to colorful open-air paintings to the canvas that gave Impressionism its name. The museum's highlights are scenes of his garden at Giverny, including larger-than-life water lilies. In addition, the Marmottan features a world-class collection of works by Berthe Morisot.

Paul Marmottan (1856–1932) lived here amid his collection of exquisite 19th-century furniture and paintings. He donated his home and possessions to a private trust (which is why your Museum Pass isn't valid here). After Marmottan's death, the more daring art of Monet and others were added.

Because the layout of the museum changes often, this chapter is not designed as a room-by-room tour of the museum, but, rather, as a general background on Monet and some of the paintings you're likely to encounter. Read it before you go, then let the museum surprise you.

Orientation

Cost: €9, not covered by Museum Pass.

Hours: Tue 11:00–21:00, Wed–Sun 11:00–18:00, last entry 30 min before closing, closed Mon.

Getting There: It's in southwest Paris at 2 rue Louis-Boilly. The Métro, RER, and buses all will get you there:

Take the Métro to La Muette, then walk six blocks (10 min), following the brown signs down chaussée de la Muette through the delightful park with its old-time kiddy carousel, to the museum.

From the rue Cler area, take the RER-C from Invalides or Pont de l'Alma (catch any train called NORA or GOTA), get off at the Boulainvilliers stop, and follow signs to *sortie Singer*. Turn left on rue Singer, turn right up rue Boulainvilliers, then turn left down chaussée de la Muette to reach the museum.

Bus #63 is handy from rue Cler and St. Sulpice; bus #32 travels along the classy rue de Passy with stops at Trocadéro and Champs-Elysées; buses #22 and #52 also serve the museum.

Post-Museum Stroll: Wander one of Paris' most pleasant (and upscale) shopping streets, rue de Passy (2 blocks up chaussée de la Muette, opposite direction from La Muette Métro stop). After rue de Passy ends, you can continue straight— on boulevard Delessert—all the way to the Eiffel Tower. It takes one full hour of walking, without stops, to get from the Marmottan Museum to the Eiffel Tower.

Information: Tel. 01 44 96 50 33, www.marmottan.com.

Audioguide: The €3 concise, informative audioguide lets you dial up individual paintings (can be shared by two if you crank the volume).

Length of This Tour: Allow one hour.

Photography: Not allowed.

Cuisine Art: A café may open in 2010 on the first floor.

Starring: Claude Monet, including *Impression: Sunrise* (shown at the top of this chapter); paintings of Rouen Cathedral, Gare St. Lazare, and Houses of Parliament; scenes from Giverny; and water lilies.

Overview

The museum traces Monet's life chronologically, but in a way that's as rough and fragmented as a Monet canvas. The collection is reorganized periodically and some paintings go on road shows, so have patience and hold on to the big picture.

The ground floor generally displays Paul Marmottan's eclectic collection of non-Monet objects—period furnishings, a beautifully displayed series of illuminated manuscript drawings, and non-Monet paintings created in the seamless-brushstroke style that Monet rebelled against.

The permanent collection (mainly Monet) is in the basement and on the first floor. Generally, the basement displays Monet's large-scale works from his gardens at Giverny, whereas the first floor hosts special exhibits and paintings by Impressionist colleagues Pierre-Auguste Renoir, Camille Pissarro, Berthe Morisot, and more.

Now, explore.

The Tour Begins

Claude Monet (1840–1926)

Claude Monet was the leading light of the Impressionist movement that revolutionized painting in the 1870s. Fiercely independent and dedicated to his craft, Monet gave courage to Renoir and others in the face of harsh criticism.

The museum often displays a timeline, where you can survey Monet's long life:

Born in Paris in 1840, Monet began his art career sketching **caricatures** of local townspeople. Baby **Jean** was born to Monet and his partner **Camille** in 1867, the year his work was rejected by the Salon. They moved to the countryside of **Argenteuil,** where he developed his open-air, Impressionist style. *Impression: Sunrise* was his landmark work at the breakthrough 1874 Impressionist Exhibition. He went on to paint several series of scenes, such as *Gare Saint-Lazare,* at different times of day.

After the birth of **Michel,** Camille's health declined, and she later died. Monet traveled a lot, painting landscapes **(Bordighera),** people **(Portrait de Poly),** and more series, including the famous **Cathedral of Rouen.** In 1890, he settled down at his farmhouse in **Giverny** and married **Alice Hoschede.** He traveled less, but visited London to paint the **Halls of Parliament.** Mostly, he painted his own **water lilies** and **flowers** in an increasingly messy style. He died in 1926 a famous man.

Nearby, you may find some Monet memorabilia: letters, an actual palette, or portraits and photos of Monet and his family.

Growing Up in Le Havre—Caricature Drawings (1840–1860)

Teenage Monet's first works—black and white, meticulously

drawn, humorous sketches of small-town celebrities—are as different as can be from the colorful, messy oils that would make him famous. Still, they show his gift for quickly capturing an overall impression with a few simple strokes.

The son of a grocer, Monet defied his family, insisted he was an artist, and sketched the world around him— beaches, boats, and small-town life.

Fellow artist Eugène Boudin encouraged Monet to don a scarf, set up his easel outdoors, and paint the scene exactly as he saw it. Today, we say, "Well, duh!" But "open-air" painting was unorthodox for artists trained to study their subjects thoroughly in the perfect lighting of a controlled studio setting.

At 19, Monet went to Paris but refused to enroll in the official art schools. Letters in the glass case (unless they're out on loan) from Monet asking for survival money from his friends show the price he paid for his early bohemian lifestyle.

The 1870s: Pure Impressionism

Monet teamed up with Renoir and Alfred Sisley, leading them on open-air painting safaris to the countryside. Inspired by the realism of Edouard Manet, they painted everyday things—landscapes, seascapes, street scenes, ladies with parasols, family picnics—in bright, basic colors.

In 1870, Monet married his girlfriend, Camille (the dark-haired woman in many of his paintings), and moved just outside Paris to the resort town of Argenteuil. Playing host to Renoir, Manet, and others, he perfected the Impressionist style—painting nature as a mosaic of short brushstrokes of different colors placed side by side, suggesting shimmering light.

First, he simplified. In *On the Beach at Trouville* (*Sur la Plage à Trouville*, 1870–1871), a lady's dress is a few thick strokes of paint.

Monet gradually broke things down into smaller dots of different shades. If you back up from a Monet canvas, the pigments blend into one (for example, red plus green plus yellow equals a brown boat). Still, they never fully resolve, creating the effect of shimmering light. Monet limited his palette to a few bright basics—cobalt blue, white, yellow, two shades of red, and emerald green abound. But no black—even shadows are a combination of bright colors.

Monet's constant quest was to faithfully reproduce nature in blobs of paint. His eye was a camera lens set at a very slow shutter speed to admit maximum light. Then he "developed" the impression made on his retina with an oil-based solution. Even as the heartbroken Monet watched Camille die of tuberculosis in

MARMOTTAN MUSEUM

1879, he was (he admitted later) intrigued by the changing colors in her dying face.

Impression: *Sunrise (Impression Soleil Levant,* 1873)

Here's the painting that started the revolution—a simple, serene view of boats bobbing under an orange sun (see the photo that opens this chapter). At the first public showing by Monet, Renoir, Degas, and others in Paris in 1874, critics howled at this work and ridiculed the title. "Wallpaper," one called it. The sloppy brushstrokes and ordinary subject looked like a study, not a finished work. The style was dubbed "Impressionist"—an accurate name.

The misty harbor scene obviously made an "impression" on Monet, who faithfully rendered the fleeting moment in quick strokes of paint. The waves are simple horizontal brushstrokes. The sun's reflection on the water is a few thick, bold strokes of orange tipped with white. They zigzag down the canvas, the way a reflection shifts on moving water.

Monet the Traveler

In search of new light and new scenes, Monet traveled throughout France and Europe. As you enjoy landscapes painted in all kinds of weather, picture Monet at work—hiking to a remote spot; carrying an easel, several canvases, brushes (large-size), a palette, tubes of paint (an invention that made open-air painting practical), food and drink, a folding chair, and an umbrella; and wearing his trademark hat, with a cigarette on his lip. He weathered the elements, occasionally putting himself in danger by clambering on cliffs to get the shot.

The key was to work fast, before the weather changed and the light shifted, completely changing the colors. Monet worked "wet-in-wet," applying new paint before the first layer dried, mixing colors on the canvas, and piling them up into a thick paste.

The 1890s: Series

Monet often painted the same subject several times under different light (such as one of Paris' train stations, the Gare St. Lazare, 1870s). In the 1890s, he conceived of a series of paintings to be shown as a group, giving a time-lapse view of a single subject.

He rented several rooms offering different angles overlooking the Rouen Cathedral and worked on up to 14 different canvases at a time, shuffling the right one onto the easel as the sun moved across the sky. The cathedral is made of brown stone, but at sunset it becomes gold and pink with blue shadows, softened by thick smudges of paint. The true subject is not the cathedral, but the full spectrum of light that bounces off it.

Monet's Family

You'll likely see portraits of Monet's wife and children. Monet's first wife, Camille, died in 1879, leaving Monet to raise 12-year-old Jean and babe-in-arms Michel. (Michel would grow up to inherit the family home and many of the paintings that ended up here.) But Monet was also involved with Alice Hoschede, who had recently been abandoned by her husband. Alice moved in with her six kids and took care of the dying Camille, and the two families made a Brady Bunch merger. Baby Michel became bosom buddies with Alice's baby, Jean-Pierre, while teenage Jean Monet and stepsister Blanche fell in love and later married.

These series—of the cathedral, haystacks, poplars, and mornings on the Seine—were very popular. Monet, poverty-stricken until his mid-40s, was slowly becoming famous, first in America, then London, and finally in France.

The 1900s: London

Turning a hotel room into a studio, Monet—working on nearly a hundred different canvases simultaneously—painted the changing

light on the River Thames. The *London Houses of Parliament, Reflected in the Thames* (*Londres, Le Parlement, Reflets sur la Tamise*, 1905) stretch and bend with the tide. *Charing Cross Bridge* is only a few smudgy lines enveloped in fog.

London's fog epitomized Monet's favorite subject—the atmosphere that distorts distant objects. That filtering haze gives even different-colored objects a similar tone, resulting in a more harmonious picture. When the light was just right and the atmosphere glowed, the moment of "instantaneity" had arrived, and Monet worked like a madman.

In truth, Monet started many of his canvases in the open air, and then painstakingly perfected them later in the studio. He composed his scenes with great care—clear horizon lines give a strong horizontal axis, while diagonal lines (of trees or shorelines) create solid triangles. And he wasn't above airbrushing out details that might spoil the composition—such as Cleopatra's Needle near Charing Cross.

Berthe Morisot
(1841–1895)

The Marmottan's large collection of Morisot's work cements her reputation as one of Impressionism's Founding Mothers. Born into a cultured, supportive family, she found early success painting landscapes (in the open air) in the proto-Impressionist style of her mentor, Camille Corot. Still in her twenties, Morisot exhibited to good reviews at the official Salon for seven straight years.

Meanwhile, she'd met Edouard Manet, married his brother, and experimented with the Impressionist style. She threw away her black paint and replaced it with a brighter palette. In 1874, she joined the Impressionist gang, exhibiting her work at the same "Salon des Refusés" where Monet's *Impression: Sunrise* caused a minor revolution.

Her paintings focus mainly on women, either in gardens or in peaceful, domestic situations. Her subjects were landscapes, friends (such as Manet), and family (her daughter, Julie). She had a keen eye for ladies' fashions (*At the Ball*, 1875). Like Manet, Morisot's brand of Impressionism was always naturalistic and understated. She avoided the gritty urban scenes of Degas and the pointillistic color theory of Monet and others. The tranquil Marmottan mansion is the perfect setting for the peaceful world of Morisot.

MARMOTTAN MUSEUM

Paintings of Giverny (1883–1926)
Rose Trellises (L'Allée des Rosiers, several versions) and the *Japanese Bridge (Le Pont Japonais)*

In 1883, Monet's brood settled into a farmhouse in Giverny (50 miles west of Paris, see page 555). Financially stable and domestically blissful, he turned Giverny into a garden paradise and painted nature without the long commute.

In 1890, Monet started work on his Japanese garden, inspired by tranquil scenes from the Japanese prints he collected. He diverted

a river to form a pond, planted willows and bamboo on the shores, filled the pond with water lilies, then crossed it with this wooden footbridge. As years passed, the bridge became overgrown with wisteria. Compare several different versions. He painted the bridge at different times of day and year, exploring different color schemes.

Monet uses the bridge as the symmetrical center of simple, pleasing designs. The water is drawn with horizontal brushstrokes that get shorter as you move up the canvas (farther away), creating the illusion of distance. The horizontal water contrasts with the vertical willows, while the bridge "bridges" the sides of the square canvas and laces the scene together.

In 1912, Monet began to go blind. Cataracts distorted his perception of depth and color, and sent him into a tailspin of despair. The (angry?) red paintings date from this period.

Early Water Lilies (*Nymphéas,* several versions)

As his vision slowly failed, Monet concentrated on painting close-ups of the surface of the pond and its water lilies—red, white, yellow, and lavender. Some lilies are just a few broad strokes on a bare canvas (a study); others are piles of paint formed with overlapping colors.

But more than the lilies, the paintings focus on the changing reflections on the surface of the pond. Pan slowly around the room and watch the pond go from predawn to bright sunlight to twilight.

Early lily paintings (c. 1900) show the shoreline as a reference point. But increasingly, Monet cropped the scene ever closer, until there was no shoreline, no horizon, no sense of what's up or down. Stepping back from the canvas, you see the lilies just hang there on the museum wall, suspended in space. The surface of the pond and the surface of the canvas are one. Modern abstract art—a colored design on a flat surface—is just around the corner.

Nymphéas and Large-Scale Canvases

Big Weeping Willow (*Le Saule Pleureur,* 1918–1919)

Get close—Monet did—and analyze the trunk. Rough "brown" bark is made of thick strokes (an inch wide and four inches long) of pink, purple, orange, and green. Impressionism lives. But to get these colors to resolve in your eye, you'd have to back up all the way to Giverny.

Later Water Lilies (*Nymphéas,* 1915–1926)

In the midst of the chaos of World War I, Monet began a series of large-scale paintings of water lilies. They were installed at the Orangerie (✪ see the Orangerie Museum Tour chapter). Here at the Marmottan are smaller-scale studies for that series.

Some lilies are patches of thick paint circled by a squiggly "caricature" of a lily pad. Monet simplifies in a way that Henri Matisse and Pablo Picasso would envy. But getting close, you can see that the simple smudge of paint that composes the flower is actually a complex mix of different colors. The sheer size of these

studies (and his Orangerie canvases) is impressive.

When Monet died in 1926, he was a celebrity. Starting with meticulous line drawings, he had evolved into an open-air realist, then Impressionist color analyst, then serial painter, and finally master of reflections. In the latter half of his life, Monet's world shrank—from the broad vistas of the world traveler to the tranquility of his home, family, and garden. But his artistic vision expanded as he painted smaller details on bigger canvases and helped invent modern abstract art.

LEFT BANK WALK

From the Seine to Luxembourg Garden

The Left Bank is as much an attitude as it is an actual neighborhood. But this walk, which is a little over a mile—from the Seine to St. Germain-des-Prés to Luxembourg Garden—captures some of the artistic, intellectual, and countercultural spirit long associated with the south side of the river. We'll pass through an upscale area of art galleries, home-furnishing boutiques, antiques dealers, bookstores, small restaurants, classic cafés, evening hot spots, and the former homes of writers, painters, and composers. Though trendy now, the area still has the offbeat funkiness that has always defined the Rive Gauche. (*Gauche*, or left-handed, has come to imply social incorrectness, like giving a handshake with the wrong—left—hand.)

Use this walk as a series of historical markers as you explore

the Left Bank of today. The walk dovetails perfectly with a shopping stroll (see "Sèvres-Babylone to St. Sulpice" in the Shopping chapter). It also works well after a visit to the Louvre or after the Historic Paris Walk, and it's ideal for connoisseurs of contemporary art galleries.

Orientation

Length of This Walk: Allow two hours.

Delacroix Museum: €5, covered by Museum Pass, free first Sun of month, Wed–Mon 9:30–17:00, until 17:30 on summer weekends, last entry 30 min before closing, closed Tue, tel. 01 44 41 86 50, www.musee-delacroix.fr.

St. Germain-des-Prés: Free, daily 8:00–20:00.
St. Sulpice Church and Organ Concert: Free, daily 7:30–19:30,
Sun morning organ concerts (see page 60).
Luxembourg Garden: Free, daily dawn until dusk.

The Walk Begins

• *Start on the pedestrian-only bridge across the Seine, the pont des Arts (next to Louvre, Mo: Pont Neuf or Louvre-Rivoli).*

❶ Pont des Arts

Before dozens of bridges crossed the Seine, the two riverbanks were like different cities—royalty on the right, commoners on the left. This bridge has always been
a pedestrian bridge...and long a
popular meeting point for lovers.

Under the dome of the
Institut de France (the building the pont des Arts leads to),
40 linguists meet periodically to
decide whether it's acceptable to
call mail *"le mail"* (as the French
commonly do), or whether it
should be the French word *cour-
riel* (which linguists prefer). The Académie Française, dedicated to
halting the erosion of French culture, is wary of new French terms
with strangely foreign sounds—like *le week-end*, *le marketing*, *le
fast-food*, and *c'est cool.*

Besides the Académie Française, the Institut houses several
other Académies, such as the Académie des Beaux-Arts, which is
dedicated to subjects appropriate for the Left Bank, such as music
and painting.
• *Circle around the right side of the Institut de France building to the
head of rue de Seine. You're immediately met by a statue in a street-
corner garden.*

❷ Statue of Voltaire

"Jesus committed suicide." The mischievous philosopher Voltaire
could scandalize a party with a wicked comment like that, delivered with an enigmatic smile and a twinkle in his eye (meaning
if Christ is truly God, he could have prevented his crucifixion).
Voltaire—a commoner more sophisticated than the royalty who
lived across the river—introduces us to the Left Bank.

Born François-Marie Arouet (1694–1778), he took up Voltaire
as his one-word pen name. Although Voltaire mingled with aristocrats, he was constantly in trouble for questioning the ruling class

Left Bank Walk

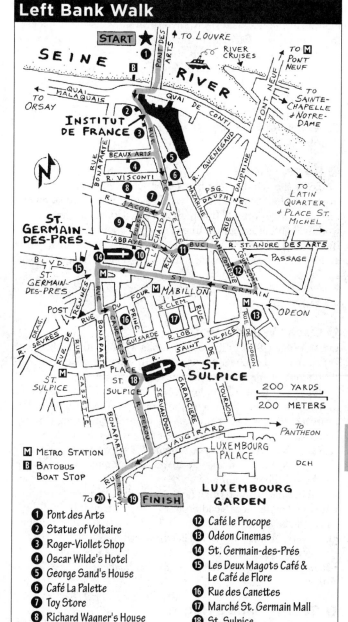

START ★

SEINE RIVER

TO LOUVRE
RIVER CRUISES
TO PONT NEUF
TO SAINTE-CHAPELLE & NOTRE-DAME

QUAI MALAQUAIS
TO ORSAY
QUAI DE CONTI

INSTITUT DE FRANCE

RUE DE NEVERS
RUE GUENEGAUD
RUE DAUPHINE
RUE MAZARINE
PSG. DAUPHINE

RUE BONAPARTE
BEAUX ARTS
R. VISCONTI
R. JACOB
L'ABBAYE

TO LATIN QUARTER & PLACE ST. MICHEL

ST. GERMAIN-DES-PRES

R. DE SEINE
R. L'ECHAUDE
RUE DE BUCI
R. ST. ANDRE DES ARTS
PASSAGE

BLVD. ST. GERMAIN-DES-PRES

RUE DE RENNES

ST. GERMAIN
RUE DE L'ANCIENNE COMEDIE
RUE DU FOUR
MABILLON
R. CLEM.
R. LOB.

ODEON

POST
DRAG.
R. SEVRES
RUE DE RENNES
RUE BONAPARTE
DU PRINC.
GUISARDE
RUE DES CANETTES
SAINT SULPICE
RUE DE
RUE DE L'ODEON

ST. SULPICE

PLACE ST. SULPICE

ST. SULPICE

R. CASSETTE
R. SERVANDONI
R. FEROU
GARANCIERE
TOURNON

200 YARDS
200 METERS

RUE BONAPARTE
VAUGIRARD

TO PANTHEON

LUXEMBOURG PALACE

DCH

RUE DE RENNES
TO ⑳ ↓ ⑲ **FINISH**

LUXEMBOURG GARDEN

Ⓜ METRO STATION
Ⓑ BATOBUS BOAT STOP

LEFT BANK WALK

① Pont des Arts
② Statue of Voltaire
③ Roger-Viollet Shop
④ Oscar Wilde's Hotel
⑤ George Sand's House
⑥ Café La Palette
⑦ Toy Store
⑧ Richard Wagner's House
⑨ Delacroix Museum
⑩ Abbey Mansion
⑪ Heart of the Left Bank

⑫ Café le Procope
⑬ Odéon Cinemas
⑭ St. Germain-des-Prés
⑮ Les Deux Magots Café & Le Café de Flore
⑯ Rue des Canettes
⑰ Marché St. Germain Mall
⑱ St. Sulpice
⑲ Luxembourg Garden
⑳ To Rue Vavin (Cafés La Coupole & Le Select)

and for fueling ideas that would soon spark a revolution. He did 11 months in the Bastille prison, then spent 40 years in virtual exile from his beloved Paris. Returning as an old man, he got a hero's welcome so surprising it killed him.

The rue de Seine and adjoining streets are lined with art galleries and upscale shops selling lamps, sconces, vases, bowls, and statues for people who turn their living rooms into art.

• *From here we'll head south down rue de Seine to boulevard St. Germain, making a few detours along the way. The first stop is at 6 rue de Seine...*

❸ Roger-Viollet

Look in the windows at black-and-white photos from Paris' history—a half-built Eiffel Tower, Hitler in Paris, and so on (the display changes often). This humble shop is the funky origin of a worldwide press agency dealing in historic photographs. The family of photographer Henri Roger expanded his photographs into an archive of millions of photos, chronicling Paris' changes through the years.

• *At the first intersection, a half-block detour to the right leads to 13 rue des Beaux-Arts and...*

❹ Oscar Wilde's Hotel

Oscar Wilde (1854–1900), the Irish playwright with the flamboyant clothes and outrageous wit, died in this hotel on November 30, 1900 (don't blame the current owners).

Just five years before, he'd been at his peak. He had several plays running simultaneously in London's West End and had returned to London triumphant from a lecture tour through America. Then, news of his love affair with a lord leaked out, causing a scandal, and he was sentenced to two years in prison for "gross indecency." Wilde's wife abandoned him, refusing to let him see their children again.

After his prison term, a poor and broken Wilde was exiled to Paris, where he succumbed to an ear infection and died here in a (then) shabby hotel room. Among his last words in the rundown place were: "Either this wallpaper goes, or I do."

Wilde is buried in Paris (see Père Lachaise Cemetery Tour).

• *Return to rue de Seine and continue south. A plaque at 31 rue de Seine marks...*

❺ George Sand's House

George Sand (1804–1876) divorced her abusive husband, left her children behind, and moved into this apartment, determined to become a writer. In the year she lived here (1831), she wrote articles for *Le Figaro* while turning her real-life experiences with men into a sensational novel, *Indiana*. It made her a celebrity and allowed her to afford a better apartment.

George Sand is known for her novels, her cross-dressing (men's suits, slicked-down hair, and cigars), and for her complex love affair with a sensitive pianist from Poland, Frédéric Chopin.

• *At 43 rue de Seine is...*

❻ Café la Palette

Though less famous than more historic cafés, this is a "real" one, where a *café crème,* beer, or glass of wine at an outdoor table costs less than €5. Inside, the 100-year-old, tobacco-stained wood paneling and faded Art Nouveau decor exude Left Bank chic. Toulouse-Lautrec would have liked it here. Have something to drink at the bar, and examine your surroundings—notice the artist palettes above the bar. Nothing seems to have changed since it was built in 1903, except the modern espresso machine (open daily, tel. 01 43 26 68 15).

• *At the fork, you could follow rue de Seine straight down to boulevard St. Germain. But we'll branch off, veering right down small rue de l'Echaudé. Four doors up, at 6 rue de l'Echaudé, is a...*

❼ Toy Store

French and American kids share many of the same toys and story-book characters: Babar the Elephant, Maisy Mouse, Tintin, the Smurfs, Madeline, and the Little Prince.

In *The Little Prince* (1943), written by Antoine de Saint-Exupéry, a pilot crashes in the Sahara, where a mysterious little prince takes him to various planets, teaching him about life from a child's wise perspective.

"Saint-Ex" (1900–1944) was himself a daring aviator who had survived wrecks in the Sahara. After France fell to the Nazis, he fled to America, where he wrote and published *The Little Prince*. A year later, he returned to Europe, then disappeared while flying a spy mission for the Allies. Lost for six decades, his plane was recently found off the coast of Marseille. Then, in 2008, a Luftwaffe pilot—a childhood fan of Saint-Ex—said he believed himself responsible shooting down the plane. However, archival sources dispute this, and the cause of the crash remains a mystery, part of a legend as enduring in France as Amelia Earhart's in the US.

• *A half-block detour to the right down rue Jacob (to #14) leads to...*

❽ Richard Wagner's House

Having survived a storm at sea on the way here, the young German composer (1813–1883) spent the gray winter of 1841–1842 in Paris in this building writing *The Flying Dutchman*, an opera about a ghost ship. It was the restless young man's lowest point of poverty. Six months later, a German company staged his first opera *(Rienzi)*, plucking him from obscurity and leading to a production of *The Flying Dutchman* that launched his career.

Now the premises are occupied by a hip-looking bar.

• *Backtrack along rue Jacob, then turn right and continue south on rue de Furstemberg to #6, the...*

❾ Delacroix Museum

The painter Eugène Delacroix (1798–1863) lived here on this tiny, quiet square. Today, his home is a museum with paintings and memorabilia. It's delightful for his fans, skippable for most, and free with the Museum Pass.

You start in an anteroom with a chronology of his life. An ambassador's son, Delacroix moved to Paris and studied at the Beaux-Arts. By his early 20s, he had exhibited at the Salon. His *Liberty Leading the People* (1831, see page 129) was an instant classic, a symbol of French democracy. Trips to North Africa added exotic Muslim elements to his palette. He hobnobbed with aristocrats and bohemians like George Sand and Frédéric Chopin (whom he painted). He painted large-scale murals for the Louvre, Hôtel de Ville, and Luxembourg Palace.

In 1857, his health failing, Delacroix moved here, seeking a quiet home/studio where he could concentrate on his final great works for the Church of St. Sulpice (which we'll see later).

Next comes the living room, decorated with a few pieces of original furniture, along with portraits and memorabilia. To the left is the bedroom (with fireplace) where Delacroix died in 1863, nursed by his long-time servant, Lucile-Virginie "Jenny" Le Guillou (her portrait is on display). You'll also see a haunting painting of Mary Magdalene and Delacroix's painting table (where he kept his paints). Backtracking, you pass through the library, then go outside and down some stairs to his studio *(atelier)* in the pleasant backyard.

Delacroix built the studio to his own specifications, with high ceilings, big windows, and a skylight, ideal for an artist working prior to electric lights. See his easel and some more paintings, including a small-scale study for *The Death of Sardanapalus,* which hangs in the Louvre. Some of Delacroix's most popular works were book illustrations (lithographs for Goethe's *Faust,* Revolutionary history, and Shakespeare). Admire Delacroix's artistic range—from messy, colorful oils to meticulously detailed lithographs. This room has frequent temporary exhibits.

Finally, in the peaceful backyard, soak up the meditative atmosphere that inspired Delacroix's religious paintings in St. Sulpice.

• *Rue de Furstemberg runs directly into the Abbey Mansion* ❿. *This building (1586) was the administrative center for the vast complex of monks gathered around the nearby church of St. Germain-des-Prés.*

Facing the mansion, turn left on rue de l'Abbaye and work your way two blocks east to the intersection of rue de Seine and rue de Buci. This intersection is, arguably, the...

⓫ Heart of the Left Bank

Explore. The rue de Buci hosts *pâtisseries* and a produce market by day, and bars by night. Mixing earthiness and elegance, your Left Bank is here. A right on rue de Buci leads to boulevard St. Germain. A left on rue de Buci leads to place St. Michel and the Latin Quarter.

• *Wherever you wander, we'll meet up a block south of here on boulevard St. Germain. But first, I'm making a several-block detour to find Voltaire's favorite café. Head east (left) on rue de Buci, which becomes rue St. André-des-Arts in a few blocks. Turn right onto rue de l'Ancienne Comédie and find #13 on the left side of the street.*

⓬ Café le Procope

Le Procope (at 13 rue de l'Ancienne Comédie) is just one of many eating options in this pleasant restaurant mall. Founded in 1686, Le Procope is one of the world's oldest continuously operating restaurants, and was one of Europe's first places to sample an exotic new stimulant—coffee—recently imported from the Muslim culture.

In the 1700s, Le Procope caffeinated the Revolution. Voltaire reportedly drank 30 cups a day, fueling his intellectual passion (his favorite table bears his carved initials). Benjamin Franklin recounted old war stories about America's Revolution. Robespierre, Danton, and Marat plotted coups over cups of double-short-two-percent-frappuccinos. And a young lieutenant named Napoleon Bonaparte ran up a tab he never paid.

Located midway between university students, royalty, and the counterculture Comédie Française, Le Procope attracted literary types who loved the free newspapers, writing paper, and quill pens. Today, the coffeehouse is an appealing restaurant (affordable if mediocre *menus*, open daily). If you're discreet, you can wander the ground floor, with its memorabilia-plastered walls.

• *Exit through Café le Procope's back door to the pedestrian-only passageway called the cour du Commerce. Follow it to the right as it spills out onto boulevard St. Germain at an intersection (and Métro stop) called...*

⓭ Odéon Cinemas

Paris' many lovers of film converge here for the latest releases at several multiplexes in the area. Looking south up rue de l'Odéon, you can see the classical columns of the front of the Théâtre de l'Odéon, the descendant of the original Comédie Française (now housed in the Palais Royal).

• *Walk to the right (west) along busy boulevard St. Germain for six blocks, passing Café Vagenande (famous for its plush Art Nouveau interior) and other fashionable, noisy cafés with outdoor terraces. You'll reach the large stone church and square of...*

⓮ St. Germain-des-Prés

Paris' oldest church, dating from the 11th century (the square bell tower is original), stands on a site where a Christian church has stood since the fall of Rome. (The first church was destroyed by Vikings in the 885–886 siege.)

The restored interior is still painted in the medieval manner, as were Notre-Dame and others. The church is in the Romanesque style, with round—not pointed—arches over the aisles of the nave.

The square outside is one of Paris' great gathering spots on warm evenings. Musicians, mimes, and fire-eaters entertain café patrons. The church is often lit up and open late. This is where the rich come to see and be seen, and the poor come for a night of free spectacle.

• *Note that Métro stop St. Germain-des-Prés is here, and the Mabillon stop is just a couple blocks east. On place St. Germain-des-Prés, you'll find...*

⓯ Les Deux Magots Café and Le Café de Flore

Since opening in 1885, "The Two Chinamen Café" (wooden statues inside) has taken over from Le Procope as the café of ideas. From Oscar Wilde's Aestheticism (1900) to Picasso's Cubism (1910s) to Hemingway's spare prose ('20s) to Sartre's Existentialism (with Simone de Beauvoir and Albert Camus, 1930s and '40s) to rock singer Jim Morrison ('60s), worldwide movements have been born in the simple atmosphere of these two cafés. Le Café de Flore, once frequented by Picasso, is more hip, but Deux Magots, next door, is more inviting for just coffee. Across the street is Brasserie Lipp, a classic brasserie where Hemingway wrote much of *A Farewell to Arms*. (See also "Les Grands Cafés de Paris," at the end of the Eating chapter.)

• *From place St. Germain-des-Prés, cross boulevard St. Germain and*

The Da Vinci Code in St. Sulpice

In Dan Brown's popular novel, this church is supposedly where a secret society, the Priory of Sion, held mysterious rituals. In fact, there's a stained-glass window (above the door in the north transept) with the letters P and S intertwined, but the church has posted a bilingual sign (by the gnomon) refuting the claims of "a recently written novel." In the novel, Silas the murderous monk seeks the "keystone" under a pavement stone in St. Sulpice's astrological clock (which Brown embellishes into a mysterious "rose line"). Sister Sandrine watches from the church's interior balcony, and later has a nasty encounter here with Silas.

---

head south toward the Montparnasse Tower skyscraper (in the distance) on rue Bonaparte (not rue de Rennes). Turn left on busy rue du Four, then right on...

⑯ Rue des Canettes

Small, midpriced restaurants, boutique shops, and comfortable brewpubs make this neighborhood a pleasant nightspot. It's easy to find a *plat du jour* or a two-course *formule* for under €20. Chez Georges (at #11, and recommended in the Eating chapter) is the last outpost of funkiness (and how!) in an increasingly gentrified neighborhood.

• *A one-block detour left down rue Guisarde leads to more restaurants, shops, and pubs, and the ⑰ Marché St. Germain shopping mall, a former farmers' market where fish and produce have been replaced by the Gap and other chain stores.*

Continue south on rue des Canettes to the church of...

⑱ St. Sulpice

The impressive Neoclassical arcaded facade, with two round, half-finished towers, is modeled on St. Paul's in London. It has a remarkable organ and offers Sunday-morning concerts. The lone café on the square in front (Café de la Mairie) is always lively and perfectly located for a break.

Inside, circle the church counterclockwise, making a few stops. In the first chapel on the right, find **Delacroix's three murals** (on the chapel's ceiling and walls) of fighting angels, completed during his final years, while fighting illness. They sum up his long career, from Renaissance/Baroque roots to furious Romanticism to proto-Impressionism.

The most famous is the agitated *Jacob Wrestling the Angel.* The two grapple in a leafy wood that echoes the wrestlers' rippling energy. Jacob fights the angel to a standstill, bringing him a well-earned blessing for his ordeal. The shepherd Laban and his daughter Rachel (Jacob's future wife) hover in the background. Get close and notice the thick brushwork that influenced the next generation of Impressionists—each leaf is a single brushstroke, often smudging two different colors in a single stroke. The "black" pile of clothes in the foreground is built from rough strokes of purple, green, and white. (Too much glare? Take a couple of steps to the right to view it. Also, there are three light buttons nearby.)

On the opposite wall, *Heliodorus Chased from the Temple* has the smooth, seamless brushwork of Delacroix's prime. The Syrian Heliodorus has killed the king, launched a coup, and has now entered the sacred Jewish Temple in Jerusalem trying to steal the treasure. Angry angels launch themselves at him, sending him sprawling. The vibrant, clashing colors, swirling composition, and over-the-top subject are trademark Delacroix Romanticism. On the ceiling, *The Archangel Michael* drives demons from heaven.

Notice the **unmarked door** at the foot of the three steps leading to Delacroix's chapel. On Sundays, just after noon, this door opens, and you can go upstairs to the organ loft to hear music played for the Mass.

Walking up the right side of the church, pause at the **fourth chapel,** with a statue of Joan of Arc and wall plaques listing hundreds upon hundreds of names. These are France's WWI dead—from this congregation alone. In the chapel at the far end of the church, ponder the cryptic symbolism of Mary and Child lit by a sunburst, standing on an orb, and trampling a snake, while a stone cloud tumbles down to a sacrificial lamb.

Continue clockwise around the church. On the wall of the north transept is an Egyptian-style obelisk used as a **gnomon,** or part of a sundial. At Christmas Mass, the sun shines into the church through a tiny hole—it's opposite the obelisk, high up on the south wall (in the upper-right window pane). The sunbeam strikes a mark on the obelisk that indicates the winter solstice. Then, week by week, the sunbeam moves down the obelisk and across the bronze rod in the floor, until, at midsummer, the sun lights up the area near the altar.

In the final chapel before the exit, you may

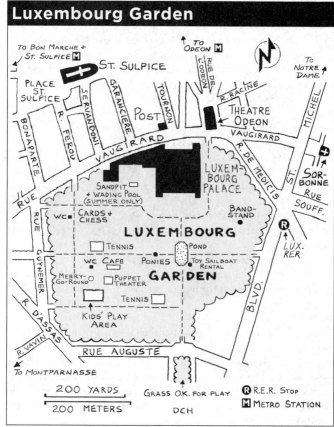

see a display on the **Shroud of Turin.** This burial cloth (which is in Turin, Italy) is purported to have wrapped the body of Christ, who left it with a mysterious, holy stain in his image.

• *Turning left out of the church, continue south on rue Férou, which leads directly to the fenced-in Luxembourg Garden. Enter the garden through the gate ahead of you (or, if it's closed, turn right on busy rue de Vaugirard, then left on rue Guynemer, where you'll find another entrance gate).*

⑲ Luxembourg Garden

Paris' most beautiful, interesting, and enjoyable garden/park/recreational area, le Jardin du Luxembourg, is a great place to watch Parisians at rest and play. These 60-acre gardens, dotted with fountains and statues, are the property of the French Senate, which meets here in the Luxembourg Palace.

The palace was created in 1615 by Marie de Médici. Recently

widowed (by Henry IV) and homesick for Florence, she built the palace as a re-creation of her girlhood home, the Pitti Palace. When her son grew to be Louis XIII, he drove his mother from the palace, exiling her to Germany.

Luxembourg Garden has special rules governing its use (for example, where cards can be played, where dogs can be walked,

where joggers can run, and when and where music can be played). The brilliant flower beds are completely changed three times a year, and the boxed trees are brought out of the orangery in May. Children enjoy the rentable toy sailboats, pony rides, and marionette shows (Les Guignols, or Punch and Judy; described more fully in the Paris with Children chapter).

Challenge the card and chess players to a game (near the tennis courts), or find a free chair near the main pond and take a well-deserved break, here at the end of our Left Bank Walk.

Nearby

The grand Neoclassical-domed Panthéon, now a mausoleum housing the tombs of great Frenchmen, is three blocks away and worth touring (see page 64). The historic cafés of Montparnasse—❷ La Coupole and Le Select—are a few blocks from the southwest-corner exit of the park (down rue Vavin, listed in "Les Grands Cafés de Paris," at the end of the Eating chapter; for the locations, see the map on page 61).

• *Getting home: The Luxembourg Garden is ringed with Métro stops (all a 10-min walk away). North of the garden, the two closest Métro stops are St. Sulpice and Odéon. A convenient RER stop (Luxembourg) is at the park's east entry.*

CLUNY MUSEUM TOUR

Musée National du Moyen Age

The National Museum of the Middle Ages doesn't sound quite so boring as I sink deeper into middle age myself. Aside from the solemn religious art, there is some lively stuff here.

Paris emerged on the world stage in the Middle Ages, the time between ancient Rome and the Renaissance. Europe was awakening from a thousand-year slumber. Trade was booming, people actually owned chairs, and the Renaissance was moving in like a warm front from Italy.

Orientation

Cost: €8, free on first Sun of the month, covered by Museum Pass.

Hours: Wed–Mon 9:15–17:45, closed Tue.

Getting There: The museum, a five-minute walk from the Ile de la Cité, is a block above the intersection of boulevards St. Germain and St. Michel at 6 place Paul Painlevé (Mo: Cluny-La Sorbonne, St. Michel, or Odéon; bus #63 from rue Cler or #86 from the Marais).

Information: The helpful audioguide is included with admission, though Museum Pass–holders must pay €1. Pick up the free and handy museum map. Tel. 01 53 73 78 16, www.musee -moyenage.fr.

Length of This Tour: Allow one hour, though you could spend far more time here. Although this self-guided tour covers the museum's greatest hits, there's much more to the under-rated Cluny (such as medieval altarpieces, weaponry, eighth-century Visigothic crowns, a wonderful chapel with an elaborate stone ceiling, and a medieval garden). The audioguide lets you key in more exhibits.

Baggage Check: Required for bags larger than a purse, and free.
Photography: OK without flash.
Cuisine Art: Just a few blocks away, the charming place de la Sorbonne has several good cafés (see page 413; walk up boulevard St. Michel toward the Panthéon).

The Tour Begins

• *Our official tour begins in Room 6, with medieval stained glass. But enjoy the first two rooms, which are usually reserved for temporary exhibits related to the theme of medieval life.*

Rooms 2 and 3: Temporary Exhibits

The first art you're likely to see is not some grim, gray crucifixion, but a celebration of life. You might see elegant tapestries, golden altarpieces, and statues with a budding realism (exhibits rotate often). Colorful woven fabrics were brought back to France by Crusaders, who went off to conquer barbarian infidels but returned with tales of enlightened peoples on the fringes of Europe.

Not every work of art in the later medieval period was centered on religious themes. Having survived their Y1K crisis, these people realized the world wasn't about to end, and they turned their attention to the beauty of their surroundings.

• *After the first two rooms, you'll enter a small hall. Turn right into a small, dark room full of luminous stained glass.*

Room 6: Stained Glass

Enter the Dark Ages, when life was harsh and violent, angels and demons made regular appearances, and the Church was your only refuge. This room offers a rare close-up look at stained glass, which gave poor people a glimpse of the glories of heaven. These pan-

els (many from the basilica of light, Sainte-Chapelle) give us a window into the magical, supernatural, miraculous—and often violent—medieval mind.

Read clockwise around the room, all at eye level (the bottom): 1) The angel Gabriel blasts his horn on Resurrection morning, rousting the grateful dead from their coffins.

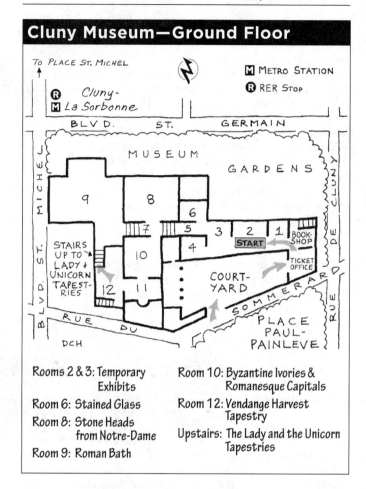

Cluny Museum—Ground Floor

To PLACE ST. MICHEL

Ⓡ Ⓜ Cluny-La Sorbonne

Ⓜ METRO STATION
Ⓡ RER STOP

BLVD. ST. GERMAIN

MUSEUM GARDENS

9 8 6

7 5 3 2 1 BOOK-SHOP
START

STAIRS UP TO LADY & UNICORN TAPESTRIES

10 4 TICKET OFFICE

12 11 COURT-YARD

RUE DU SOMMERARD

PLACE PAUL-PAINLEVE

DCH

Rooms 2 & 3: Temporary Exhibits

Room 6: Stained Glass

Room 8: Stone Heads from Notre-Dame

Room 9: Roman Bath

Room 10: Byzantine Ivories & Romanesque Capitals

Room 12: Vendange Harvest Tapestry

Upstairs: The Lady and the Unicorn Tapestries

Notice that Gabriel's royal robe is made up of several different pieces of glass—purples, whites, blues—held together with lead. 2) Naked Christ is baptized in the squiggly River Jordan. 3) A red-

faced, horned, horny demon, accompanied by an equally lascivious wolf and henchman, carries off a frightened girl in red on a date from hell. 4) Blond, pious Joseph is sold into slavery to camel merchants by his plotting brothers.

Next wall: 5) Samson is about to pull down the temple.... 6) Then he has his eyes gouged out by Philistines. 7) Slaughter on the battlefield. Men with bloodstained hands and faces hack at each other with golden swords. 8) Aaron, disobeying God and Moses, worships a golden calf. 9) A king on a throne closes his eyes to all this wickedness.

Next wall (with some panels from the first Gothic church, St. Denis): 10) Two monks with prayer books gaze up, as one of their brothers disappears into heaven. The Latin inscription *"hec est via"* means "This is the way." 11) Seated Jesus, in a royal purple robe, is consoled by two angels. 12) Theophilus ("Lover of God") has struck a Faustian deal—shaking hands with the red-faced devil, yet feeling buyer's remorse. 13) Sleeping St. Martin is visited by a heavenly vision. 14) Angels in Rock-and-Roll Heaven.

Last wall: Four apostles—John (Ioannes), James (with his scallop shell), Paul, and Peter (Petrus, with key).

Before leaving, turn around and take in all the narrative medieval glass.

Room 8: Stone Heads from Notre-Dame

This room has occasional exhibits, as well as the permanent displays, so be prepared to search for the objects described.

The 21 stone heads (sculpted 1220–1230) of the Biblical kings of Judah once decorated the front of Notre-Dame. In 1793, an angry mob of Revolutionaries mistook the kings of Judah for the kings of France and abused and decapitated the statues. (Today's heads on the

Notre-Dame statues are reconstructions.) Someone gathered up the heads and buried them in his backyard near the present-day Opéra Garnier. There they slept for two centuries, unknown and noseless, until 1977, when some diggers accidentally unearthed them and brought them to an astounded world. Their stoic expressions accept what fate, time, and liberals have done to them.

The statue of Adam (nearby) is also from Notre-Dame. He's scrawny and flaccid by Renaissance standards. And it will be another 200 years before naked Adam can step out from behind that bush.

Room 9: Roman Bath

This echoing cavern was a Roman *frigidarium*. Pretty cool. The museum is located on the site of a Roman bathhouse, which was in the center of town during the Roman years. After hot baths and exercise in adjoining rooms, ordinary Romans would take a cold dip in the sunken pool (in the alcove), then relax cheek to cheek with such notables as Emperor Julian the Apostate (see his statue), who lived next door. As the empire decayed in the fourth century, Julian avoided the corrupt city of Rome and made Paris a northern power base.

The 40-foot-high ceiling is the largest Roman vault in France, and it took the French another 1,000 years to improve on that criss-cross-arch technology. The sheer size of this room—constructed in A.D. 200, when Rome was at its peak—gives an idea of the epic scale on which the Romans built, and it inspired Europeans to greatness during the less civilized Middle Ages.

The four square column fragments *(Le Pilier des Nautes)* are the oldest man-made objects you'll see from Paris. These pillars once fit together to support a 20-foot-high altar to the king of the gods in the Temple of Jupiter, where Notre-Dame now stands. The fragment labeled *Pierre de la dedicace* is inscribed "TIB. CAESARE," announcing that the altar was built in the time of the Emperor Tiberius (A.D. 14–37), and was paid for by the Parisian boatmen's union (see them holding their shields). On the column labeled *Pierre aux quatre divinites*, find the horned Celtic god Cernunnos, who is also known as the Stag Lord and god of the hunt. The eclectic Romans allowed this local "druid" god to support the shrine of Jupiter, in league with their own Vulcan, who hammers, and Castor and Pollux, who pet their horses.

Room 10: Byzantine Ivories and Romanesque Capitals

Rome lived on after the fall of the empire. The finely carved Byzantine ivories (first glass case) show how pagan gods, emper-

ors, and griffins became Christian saints, gargoyles, and icons. Constantinople—the eastern half of the empire that survived the fall—preserved Roman tastes and imagery. In painting, Byzantine gold-background icons inspired medieval altarpieces. Study the exquisite detail. (Adam and Eve, in the tiny double panel, are not really "sword fighting.")

Rome also lived on in the "Roman"-esque grandeur of Christian churches such as St. Germain-des-Prés (see the 12 column capitals). In the central capital, Christ sits in robes on a throne, ruling the world like a Roman emperor. These capitals were originally painted, much like the painted wooden statues across the room.

Don't leave this room before eyeing the tusk of a narwhal (on the wall), which must have convinced superstitious folk to believe in unicorns.

Room 12: Vendange Harvest Tapestry

The large tapestry shows grape-stomping peasants during the *vendange*, the annual autumn harvest and wine celebration. A peasant man treads grapes in a vat, while his wife collects the juice. A wealthy man gives orders. Above that, a peasant with a big wart turns a newfangled mechanical press. On the right, you'll see the joy of picking—pawns, knights, and queens all working side by side.

• *Go upstairs to...*

Room 13 (upstairs): The Lady and the Unicorn Tapestries

As Europeans emerged from the Dark Ages, they rediscovered the beauty of the world around them.

These six mysterious tapestries were designed by an unknown (but probably French) artist before A.D. 1500 and were woven in

Belgium out of wool and silk. Loaded with symbols—some serious, some playful—they have been interpreted many ways, but, in short, the series deals with each of the five senses (handheld English explanations that you can pick up from slots hanging on the wall add more detail).

In medieval lore, unicorns were enigmatic, solitary creatures that could only be tamed by a virgin. In secular society, they symbolized how a feral man was drawn to his lady love. Religiously, the unicorn was a symbol of Christ—radiant, pure, and somewhat remote—who is made accessible to humankind by the Virgin Mary. These tapestries likely draw inspiration from all these traditions.

• *Moving clockwise around the room...*

Taste: A blonde lady takes candy from a servant's dish to feed it to her parakeet. A unicorn and a lion look on. At the lady's feet, a monkey also tastes something, while the little white dog behind her wishes he had some. This was the dawn of the Age of Discovery, when overseas explorers spiced up Europe's bland gruel with new fruits, herbs, and spices.

CLUNY MUSEUM

The lion (symbol of knighthood?) and unicorn (symbol of "bourgeois nobility," purity, or fertility?) wave flags with the coat of arms of the family that commissioned the tapestries—three silver crescents in a band of blue.

Hearing: Wearing a stunning dress, the lady plays sweet music on an organ, which soothes the savage beasts around her. The pattern and folds of the tablecloth are lovely. Humans and their fellow creatures live in harmony in an enchanted blue garden filled with flowers, all set in a red background.

Sight: The unicorn cuddles up and looks at himself in the lady's mirror, pleased with what he sees. The lion turns away and snickers. As the Renaissance dawns, vanity is a less-than-deadly sin.

Admire the great artistic skill in some of the detail work, such as the necklace and the patterns in her dress. This tapestry had quality control in all its stages: the drawing of the scene, its enlargement and transfer to a cartoon, and the weaving. Still, the design itself is crude by Renaissance 3-D standards. The fox and rabbits, supposedly in the distance, simply float overhead, as big as the animals at the lady's feet.

Smell: The lady picks flowers and weaves them into a sweet-smelling wreath. On a bench behind, the monkey apes her. The flowers, trees, and animals are exotic and varied. Each detail is exquisite alone, but step back, and they blend together into pleasing patterns.

Touch: This is the most basic and dangerous of the senses. The lady "strokes the unicorn's horn," if you know what I mean, and the lion gets the double entendre. Unicorns, a species extinct since the Age of Reason, were so wild that only the purest virgins could entice and tame them. Medieval Europeans were exploring the wonders of love and the pleasures of sex.

Tapestry #6: The most talked-about tapestry gets its name from the words on our lady's tent: *A Mon Seul Désir* (To My Sole Desire). What *is* her only desire? Is it jewelry, as she grabs a necklace from the jewel box? Or is she putting the necklace away and renouncing material things in order to follow her only desire?

Our lady has tried all things sensual and is now prepared to follow the one true impulse. Is it God? Love? Her friends the unicorn and lion open the tent doors. Flickering flames cover the tent. Perhaps she's stepping out from the tent. Or is she going in to meet the object of her desire? Human sensuality is awakening, an old dark age is ending, and the Renaissance is emerging.

CHAMPS-ELYSEES WALK

*From the Arc de Triomphe to
the Place de la Concorde*

Don't leave Paris without a stroll along avenue des Champs-Elysées (shahnz ay-lee-zay). This is Paris at its most Parisian: monumental sidewalks, stylish shops, elegant cafés, glimmering showrooms, and proud Parisians on parade. It's a great walk day or night, making you feel a part of an increasingly global scene.

Orientation

Length of This Walk: This two-mile walk takes three hours, including a one-hour visit to the Arc de Triomphe. Métro stops are located every few blocks along the Champs-Elysées.

Arc de Triomphe: Outside—free and always open. Interior—€9, free for kids under 18, free the first Sun of month Oct–March, covered by Museum Pass. Daily April–Sept 10:00–23:00, Oct–March 10:00–22:30, last entry 30 min before closing. It's at place Charles de Gaulle. The arch's elevator, only for people with disabilities, runs to the museum level, but not to the top (which requires a 40-step climb).

Getting There: To reach the Arc de Triomphe, take the Métro to Charles de Gaulle-Etoile. Then follow the *Sortie #1, Champs-Elysées/Arc de Triomphe* signs.

Services: There are WCs underground, south of the Arc de Triomphe, across the Champs-Elysées from the start of this walk. A small WC is inside the Arc de Triomphe, near the top, but it's often crowded.

Cuisine Art: See "Eating near the Champs-Elysées" (page 271).

Starring: Grand boulevards, grander shops, and grandiose monuments.

The Walk Begins

Start at the Arc de Triomphe at the top of the Champs-Elysées (on the right side as you look at the Arc). Take the underground

pedestrian walkway in front of you to the arch. (Don't try to cross in the traffic—there are no crosswalks on the round-about.) It's worthwhile to get to the base of the arch even if you don't climb it; there's no charge to wander around.

• *Cross through the tunnel, take the first left up a few steps, and buy your ticket. Skip the ticket line if you have a Museum Pass or aren't ascending. (If you have both a Museum Pass and kids, however, you'll still need to line up to get free children's tickets.) Then walk up to the arch—stroll around left toward the Champs-Elysées, turn around, and face the arch.*

The Arc de Triomphe
Exterior

Construction of the 165-foot-high arch began in 1809 to honor Napoleon's soldiers, who, in spite of being vastly outnumbered by the Austrians, scored a remarkable victory at the Battle of Austerlitz. Patterned after the ceremonial arches of ancient Roman conquerors (but more than twice the size), it celebrates Napoleon as emperor of a "New Rome." On the arch's massive left pillar, a relief sculpture shows a toga-clad Napoleon posing confidently, while an awestruck Paris—crowned by her city walls—kneels at his imperial feet. Napoleon died prior to the Arc's completion, but it was finished in time for his 1840 funeral procession to pass underneath, carrying his remains (19 years dead) from exile in St. Helena to Paris.

On the right pillar is the Arc's most famous relief, *La Marseillaise* (*Le Départ des Volontaires de 1792*, by François Rude). Lady Liberty—looking like an ugly reincarnation of Joan of Arc—screams, "Freedom is this way!" and points the direction with a sword. The soldiers below her are tired, naked, and stumbling, but she rallies them to carry on the fight against oppression.

Today, the Arc de Triomphe is dedicated to the glory of all French armies. Walk to its center and stand directly beneath it on the faded

Champs-Elysées Walk

400 YARDS
400 METERS

TO LOUVRE
TO ORSAY

W.H. SMITH BOOKS

TUILERIES GARDEN

Orangerie

SEINE

QUAI TUILERIES

FAUCHON

RUE ROYALE

ST. FLOR

CONCORDE

R. ROYALE

MADELEINE

R. ST. HONORE

R. BOISSY

NAT'L. ASSEMBLY

PLACE DE LA
CONCORDE

⑬ END

⑯ PONT CONC.

⑭

⑮

PETIT PALAIS

To ARMY MUSEUM

PALAIS DE L'ELYSEE

MARIGNY

ELYSEES

CHURCHILL

⑫

PONT ALEX. III

COURS DE LA REINE

RIVER

MATIGNON

ROND-POINT

AVE. FRANKLIN

GRAND PALAIS

MONTAIGNE

ROOSEVELT

COLISEE

F.D.R.

IGN

R. BOETIE

⑪

⑨

⑧

Ⓑ

R. DE BERRI

⑩

AVE. DES CHAMPS

⑦

R. WASH

#92

⑥

GEO. V

④

M

GEORGE V

⑤

FRIEDLAND

BALZAC

ARSENE

③

HOCHE

②

MARCEAU

Ⓐ

D'IENA

•WC

RUE DE PRESBOURG

START
METRO: CHARLES DE GAULLE ETOILE

WAGRAM

PED. UNDER-PASS

M

①

KLEBER → TO EIFFEL TOWER

Ⓒ

MACMAHON

RUE DE TILSITT

ARC DE TRIOMPHE

AVE. DE LA GRANDE ARMEE

To LA DEFENSE

DCH

① Arc de Triomphe

② Qatar Embassy & Pedestrian Underpass

③ McDonald's & Peugeot

④ Mercedes-Benz & Lido

⑤ Louis Vuitton

⑥ Fouquet's Café-Rest.

⑦ Ladurée Tea Salon

⑧ Thomas Jefferson Plaque

⑨ Arcades des Champs-Elysées, Sephora, Guerlain & Pharmacy

⑩ Renault

⑪ International Shopping

⑫ De Gaulle Statue; Grand & Petit Palais

⑬ Obelisk of Luxor

⑭ Hôtel Crillon

⑮ US Embassy & Consulate

⑯ Pont de la Concorde

Eateries

Ⓐ Comptoir de L'Arc Rest.

Ⓑ Boulangerie Paul & La Brioche Dorée

Ⓒ Monte Carlo Cafeteria

M METRO STATION   **Ⓣ** TAXI STAND

Ⓑ BATOBUS BOAT STOP   ⤳ VIEW

Eating near the Champs-Elysées

Good eating options on the Champs-Elysées are slim. Most sit-down restaurants have lazy service, mediocre food, and inflated prices. For a better value, try one of these places:

Comptoir de L'Arc, a block from the Arc toward the Eiffel Tower, is a bustling place dishing out good €12 salads and plats du jour to locals just beyond the tourist flow (Mon–Fri 7:00–24:00, closed Sat–Sun, 73 avenue Marceau, tel. 01 47 20 72 04).

Monte Carlo Cafeteria has a surprisingly nice ambience, with reasonably priced daily specials, salads, desserts, and menu combos for about €10 (open daily 11:00–23:00, 9 avenue de Wagram, tel. 01 43 80 02 20).

Boulangerie Paul and **La Brioche Dorée** sit side by side smack on the Champs-Elysées, each offering Champs-side tables and good sandwiches and salads for €5-9 (halfway along this walk at #82).

eagle. You're surrounded by the lists of French victories since the Revolution—19th century on the arch, 20th century in the pave-

ment. On the columns you'll see lists of generals (with a line under the names of those who died in battle). Find the nearby Tomb of the Unknown Soldier (from World War I). Every day at 18:30 since just after World War I, the flame has been rekindled and new flowers set in place.

Like its Roman ancestors, this arch has served as a parade gateway for triumphal armies (French or foe) and important ceremonies. From 1940 to 1944, a large swastika flew from here as Nazis goose-stepped down the Champs-Elysées. In August 1944 Charles de Gaulle led Allied troops under this arch as they celebrated liberation. Today, national parades start and end here with one minute of silence.

Interior and View from the Top

Ascend the Arc de Triomphe via the 284 steps inside the north pillar (the one closest to the ticket office). Catch your breath two-thirds of the way up in the small exhibition area (WC also on this mezzanine level). It hosts rotating exhibits about the arch and its founder, Napoleon.

From the top you have an eye-popping view of *tout Paris*. You're gazing at the home of 11 million people, all crammed into

an area the size of an average city in the US (the city center has 2,170,000 residents and covers 40 square miles). Paris has the highest density of any city in Europe, about 20 times greater than that of New York City.

Looking East: Look down the Champs-Elysées to the Tuileries Garden and the Louvre. Scan the cityscape of downtown Paris. That lonely hill to the left is Montmartre, topped by the white dome of Sacré-Cœur; until 1860, this hill town was a separate city. To the right, find the blue top of the modern Pompidou Center, then the distant twin towers of Notre-Dame, the "state-capitol-dome" of the Panthéon, a block of small skyscrapers on a hill (the Quartier d'Italie), the golden dome of Les Invalides, and the lonely-looking Montparnasse Tower, standing like the box the Eiffel Tower came in. It served as a wake-up call in the early 1970s to preserve the building height restrictions and strengthen urban design standards. Aside from the Montparnasse Tower, notice the symmetry. Each corner building surrounding the arch is part of an elegant grand scheme. The beauty of Paris—basically a flat basin with a river running through it—is man-made. There's a harmonious relationship between the width of its grand boulevards and the standard height and design of the buildings.

Looking West: Cross the arch and look to the west. In the distance, the huge, white, rectangular Grande Arche de la Défense, standing amid skyscrapers, is the final piece of a grand city axis—from the Louvre, up the Champs-Elysées to the Arc de Triomphe, continuing on to a forest of skyscrapers at La Défense, three miles away. Former French president François Mitterrand had the Grande Arche built as a centerpiece of this mini-Manhattan. Notice the contrast between the skyscrapers of La Défense and the more uniform heights of the buildings closer to the Arc de Triomphe. Below you, the wide boulevard lined with grass and trees angling to your left is avenue Foch (named after the WWI hero), which ends at the huge Bois de Boulogne park. Avenue Foch is the best address to have in Paris. Nicknamed the "Avenue of Millionaires," it was home to the Shah of Iran and Aristotle Onassis. Today many fabulously rich Arabs call it home. And though Parisians pride themselves on being discreet, not-so-discreet Homes-of-the-Stars-type tours are offered here.

The Etoile: Gaze down at what appears to be a chaotic traffic mess. The 12 boulevards that radiate from the Arc de Triomphe (forming an *étoile*, or star) were part of Baron Haussmann's master plan for Paris: the creation of a series of major boulevards intersecting at diagonals, with monuments (such as the Arc de Triomphe) as centerpieces of those intersections (see sidebar on page 69). Haussmann's plan did not anticipate the automobile—obvious when you watch the traffic scene below. But see how smoothly it functions. Cars entering the circle have the right of way (the only roundabout in France with this rule); those in the circle must yield. Still, there are plenty of accidents, often caused by tourists oblivious to the rules. Tired of disputes, insurance companies split the fault and damages of any Arc de Triomphe accident 50/50. The trick is to make a parabola—get to the center ASAP, and then begin working your way out two avenues before you want to exit.

• *We'll start our stroll down the Champs-Elysées at the Charles de Gaulle-Etoile Métro stop, on the north (sunnier) side of the street where the tunnel deposits you. Look straight down the Champs-Elysées to the Tuileries Garden at the far end.*

The Champs-Elysées

You're at the top of one of the world's grandest and most celebrated streets, home to big business, celebrity cafés, glitzy nightclubs, high-fashion shopping, and international people-watching. People gather here to celebrate Bastille Day (July 14), World Cup triumphs, the finale of the Tour de France, and the ends of wars.

In 1667, Louis XIV opened the first section of the street as a short extension of the Tuileries Garden. This year is considered the birth of Paris as a grand city. The Champs-Elysées soon became *the* place to cruise in your carriage. (It still is today; traffic can be gridlocked even at midnight.) One hundred years later, the café scene arrived. From the 1920s until the 1960s, this boulevard was pure elegance. Parisians actually dressed up to come here. It was mainly residences, rich hotels, and cafés. Then, in 1963, the government pumped up the neighborhood's commercial metabolism by bringing in the RER (commuter train). Suburbanites had easy access, and *pfft*—there went the neighborhood.

• *Start your descent, pausing at the first tiny street you cross, rue de Tilsitt. This street is part of a shadow ring road—an option for drivers who'd like to avoid the chaos of the Arc—complete with stoplights.*

Half a block down rue de Tilsitt is a building now housing the **Qatar Embassy.** It's one of the few survivors of a dozen uniformly

U-shaped buildings from Haussmann's original 1853 grand design. Peek into the foyer for a glimpse of 19th-century Champs-Elysées classiness.

Back on the main drag, look across to the other side of the Champs-Elysées at the big, gray, concrete-and-glass "Publicis" building. Ugh. In the 1960s, venerable old buildings (similar to the Qatar Embassy building) were leveled to make way for new commercial operations like Publicis. Then, in 1985, a law prohibited the demolition of the old building fronts that gave the boulevard a uniform grace. Today, many modern businesses hide behind pre-served facades. Consider dashing to the center of the Champs for a great Arc view (from a crosswalk, of course), then come back.

The arrival of **McDonald's**—a hundred yards farther down on the left at #140—was a shock to the boulevard. At first it was allowed to have only white arches painted on the window. Today, it spills out legally onto the sidewalk—provided it offers café-quality chairs and flower boxes—and dining at *chez MacDo* has become typically Parisian. A €4 Big Mac here buys an hour of people-watching. (There's a WC inside with quarter-pounder lines.) Notice how many of the happy clients are French. The popularity of *le fast food* in Paris is a sign that life is changing, and that the era of three-hour lunches is over. The French must now compete in a global world, and if that means adopting a more American lifestyle, *c'est la vie.*

The *nouveau* Champs-Elysées, revitalized in 1994, has new benches and lamps, broader sidewalks, all-underground parking, and a fleet of green-suited workers who drive motorized street cleaners. Blink away the modern elements, and it's not hard to imagine the boulevard pre-1963, with only the finest structures lining both sides all the way to the palace gardens.

Glitz

Fancy car dealerships include **Peugeot,** at #136 (showing off its futuristic concept cars, often alongside the classic models), and **Mercedes-Benz,** a block down at #118, where you can pick up a Mercedes watch to go with your new car. In the 19th century this was an area for horse stables; today, it's the district of garages, limo companies, and car dealerships. If you're serious about selling cars in France, you must have a showroom on the Champs-Elysées.

Next to Mercedes is the famous **Lido,** Paris' largest cabaret (and a multiplex cinema). You can walk all the way inside, if you ask nicely, until 18:00. Paris still offers the kind of burlesque-type spectacles combining music, comedy, and scantily clad women that have been performed here since the 19th century. Moviegoing on the Champs-Elysées provides another kind of fun, with theaters showing the very latest releases. Check to see if there are films you recognize, then look for the showings *(séances)*. A "v.o." *(version originale)* next to the time indicates the film will be shown in its original language.

• *Now cross the boulevard. Look up at the Arc de Triomphe, its roof-top bristling with tourists. Notice the variety of architecture along this street—old and elegant, new, and new-behind-old-facades. The white spire you see down avenue Georges V is the American Cathedral. Continue to #101.*

Louis Vuitton

The flagship store of this famous producer of leather bags may be the largest single-brand luxury store in the world. Step inside. The store insists on providing enough salespeople to treat each customer royally—if there's a line, it means shoppers have overwhelmed the place. The vintage suitcase/trunks hanging all around (there are 101 of them, since the address is 101 Champs-Elysées) were Vuitton's claim to fame back in 1854. That's when he came up with this flat, hard-sided, stackable alternative to the standard, rounded trunks of that earlier age.

• *Across the street is a Paris institution.*

Café Culture

Fouquet's café-restaurant (#99), under the red awning, is a popu-lar spot among French celebrities, serving the most expensive shot of espresso I've found in downtown Paris (€8). Opened in 1899 as a coachman's bistro, Fouquet's gained fame as the hangout of France's WWI biplane fighter pilots—those who weren't shot down by Germany's infamous "Red Baron." It also served as James Joyce's dining room.

Since the early 1900s, Fouquet's has been a favorite of French actors and actresses. The golden plaques at the entrance honor winners of France's Oscar-like film awards, the Césars (one is cut into the ground at the end of the red carpet). There are plaques for Gérard Depardieu, Catherine Deneuve, Roman Polanski, Juliette Binoche, and many famous Americans (but not Jerry Lewis). Recent winners are shown on the floor just inside.

The hushed interior is at once classy and intimidating—and also a grand experience...if you dare (to say "I'm just looking" in French, say *"Je regard"*—zhuh ruh-gard). The outdoor setting is more relaxed. Fouquet's was recently saved from foreign purchase and eventual destruction when the government declared it a historic monument. For his election-night victory party in 2007, the flamboyant President Sarkozy celebrated at Fouquet's, along with France's glitterati—including the "French Elvis," Johnny Hallyday.

Ladurée (two blocks downhill at #75, with green-and-purple awning) is a classic 19th-century tea salon/restaurant/*pâtisserie*. Its interior is right out of the 1860s. Non-patrons can discreetly wander in through the door farthest downhill and peek into the cozy rooms upstairs (no photos). A coffee here is *très élégant* (only €3.50). The bakery sells traditional macaroons, cute little cakes, and gift-wrapped finger sandwiches to go (your choice of four mini-macaroons for €7.50).

• *Cross back to the lively (north) side of the street.*

At #92 (next to Triomphe cinema), a wall plaque marks the place **Thomas Jefferson** lived (with his 14-year-old slave, Sally Hemings) while serving as minister to France (1785–1789). He replaced the popular Benjamin Franklin but quickly made his own mark, extolling the virtues of America's Revolution to a country approaching its own.

You'll soon pass two good-value lunch options, **Boulangerie Paul** and **La Brioche Dorée** (see the sidebar near the beginning of this chapter).

French Shopping

Stroll into the **Arcades des Champs-Elysées** mall at #76 (not the unappealing Galerie des Champs). With its fancy lamps, mosaic floors, glass skylight, and classical columns (try to ignore the Starbucks), it captures faint echoes of the *années folles*—the "crazy years," as the roaring '20s were called in France. Architecture buffs can observe how flowery Art Nouveau became simpler, more geometric Art Deco. Down the street at #74, the Galerie du Claridge building sports an old facade. Its ironwork awning, balconies, *putti*, and sculpted fantasy faces disguise an otherwise new building. The current tenant is FNAC, a large French chain that sells electronics, CDs, and concert tickets. They also sell tickets to key sights in and around Paris (including the Arc de Triomphe, Opéra Garnier, Versailles, and the gardens in Giverny)—the time saved is worth their surcharge (10–20 percent).

Take your nose sightseeing at #72 and glide down **Sephora's** ramp into a vast hall of cosmetics and perfumes. Grab a disposable white strip from a lovely clerk, spritz it with a sample, and sniff. The

store is thoughtfully laid out: The entry hall is lined with new products and attractive sales clerks. In the main showroom, women's perfumes line the right wall and men's line the left—organized alphabetically by company, from Armani to Versace. The mesmerizing music, carefully chosen just for Sephora, makes you crave cosmetics. Here you can have your face made over and your nails fixed like new. You can also get the advice of a "skin consultant."

While Sephora seems to be going all out to attract the general public, the venerable **Guerlain** perfume shop next door is more elegant and retains a bit of the Champs-Elysées' old gold-leaf elegance. Notice the 1914 details. Climb upstairs. It's *très* French.

At the intersection with rue la Boëtie, the English-speaking **pharmacy** is open until midnight. Map-lovers can detour one block down this street to shop at **Espace IGN,** France's version of the National Geographic Society (Institut Géographique National).

Car buffs and *Star Trek* fans should detour across the Champs and park themselves at the space-age bar in the **Renault** store (open until midnight, cheap espresso). The car exhibits change regularly, but the high-backed leather chairs looking down onto the Champs-Elysées are permanent.

International Shopping

Back on earth, a half block farther down on the north side, the **Virgin Megastore** (#52–60)—the biggest music store in Paris— sells a world of music. Nearby, the Disney, Gap, Quiksilver, and Adidas stores are reminders of global economics: The French may live in a world of their own, but they love these places as much as Americans do.

Rond-Point and Beyond

At the Rond-Point des Champs-Elysées, the shopping ends and the park begins. This round, leafy traffic circle is always colorful, lined with flowers or seasonal decorations (thousands of pumpkins at Halloween, hundreds of decorated trees at Christmas). Avenue Montaigne, cutting off to the right, is lined by the most exclusive shops in town—the kinds of places where you need to make an appointment to buy a dress.

A long block past the Rond-Point, at avenue de Marigny, look to the other side of the Champs-Elysées to find a statue of **Charles de Gaulle**—ramrod-straight and striding out as he did the day Paris was liberated in 1944.

Grand and Petit Palais

From the statue of de Gaulle, a grand boulevard (avenue Winston Churchill) passes through the site of the 1900 World's Fair, leading between the glass-and-steel-domed Grand and Petit Palais exhibition halls, and across the river over the ornate bridge called pont Alexander III. Imagine pavilions like the two you see today lining this street all the way to the golden dome of Les Invalides— examples of the "can-do" spirit that ran rampant in Europe at the dawn of the 20th century.

Today, the huge Grand Palais (on the right side and pricey) houses impressive temporary exhibits (described on page 73). Classical columns and giant, colorful mosaics running the length of the Palais' facade wowed fairgoers. The Petit Palais (left side and free) houses a permanent collection of lesser paintings by Courbet, Claude Monet, Pissarro and other 19th-century masters, and, more importantly, fine WCs with no lines. It's a breathtaking building with a peaceful café and worth a quick detour (see page 72).

The exquisite pont Alexander III, spiked with golden statues and ironwork lamps, was built to celebrate a turn-of-the-20th-century treaty between France and Russia. Les Invalides was built by Louis XIV as a veterans' hospital for his battle-weary troops (covered in the Army Museum and Napoleon's Tomb Tour). The esplanade leading up to Les Invalides—possibly the largest patch of accessible grass in Paris—gives soccer balls and Frisbees a rare-in-Paris welcome.

• Return to the Champs-Elysées. From here it's a straight shot to the finish line. The plane trees that you'll see are a kind of sycamore, with peeling bark that does well in big-city pollution. They're reminiscent of the big push made by Napoleon III—who ruled as president/emperor from 1849 to 1870—when he had 600,000 trees planted to green up the city. The Elysée Palace, France's version of the White House, sits largely ignored a block to the left at 55 rue St. Honoré. Funny how no one seems to pay much attention to it. You'd think a sexy first lady would have brought some interest.... Finally, you reach the 21-acre place de la Concorde. View it from the obelisk in the center.

Place de la Concorde

During the Revolution, this was the place de la Révolution. The guillotine sat on this square, and many of the 2,780 beheaded during the Revolution lost their bodies here during the Reign of Terror. A bronze plaque in the ground in front of the obelisk memorializes the place where Louis XVI, Marie-Antoinette, Georges Danton, Charlotte Corday, and Maximilien de Robespierre, among about 1,200 others, were made "a foot shorter on top." Three people worked the guillotine: One managed the blade, one held the blood bucket, and one caught the head, raising it high to the roaring crowd. (In 1981, France abolished the death penalty—one of many preconditions for membership in today's European Union.)

The 3,300-year-old, 72-foot, 220-ton, red granite, hieroglyph-inscribed **obelisk of Luxor** now forms the centerpiece of place de la Concorde. Here—on the spot where Louis XVI was beheaded—his brother (Charles X) honored the executed with this obelisk. (Charles became king when the monarchy was restored after Napoleon.) The obelisk was carted here from Egypt in the 1830s.

The gold pictures on the pedestal tell the story of the obelisk's incredible two-year journey: pulled down from the entrance to Ramses II's Temple of Amon in Luxor; encased in wood; loaded onto a boat built to navigate both shallow rivers and open seas; floated down the Nile, across the Mediterranean, along the Atlantic coast, and up the Seine; and unloaded here, where it was re-erected in 1836. Its glittering gold-leaf cap is a recent addition (1998), replacing the original, which was stolen 2,500 years ago.

The obelisk also forms a center point along a line that locals call the "royal perspective." You can hang a lot of history along this straight line (Louvre–obelisk–Arc de Triomphe–Grande Arche de la Défense). The Louvre symbolizes the old regime (divine right rule by kings and queens). The obelisk and place de la Concorde symbolize the people's revolution (cutting off the king's head). The Arc de Triomphe calls to mind the triumph of nationalism (victorious armies carrying national flags under the arch). And the huge modern arch in the distance, surrounded by the headquarters of multinational corporations, heralds a future in which business entities are more powerful than nations.

Near the Place de la Concorde

Your guided walk is over. From here the closest Métro stop is Concorde (entrance on the Tuileries Gardens side of the square, away from the river). But, of course, Paris offers so much more.

The beautiful Tuileries Gardens (with a public WC just inside on the right) are through the iron gates. Pull up a chair next to a pond or at one of the cafés in the gardens. From these gardens you can access the Orangerie Museum and, at the other end, the Louvre (this book includes tours of both museums).

On the north side of place de la Concorde is **Hôtel Crillon,** Paris' most exclusive hotel. Of the twin buildings that guard the entrance to rue Royale (which leads to the Greek-style Church of the Madeleine), it's the one on the left. This hotel is so fancy that one of its belle époque rooms is displayed in New York's Metropolitan Museum of Art. For a memorable splurge, consider high tea at the Crillon (see page 419).

Eleven years before Louis XVI lost his head on this square, he met with Benjamin Franklin in this hotel to sign a treaty recognizing the US as an independent country. (Today's low-profile, heavily fortified **American Embassy** is located next door.)

North of place de la Concorde, you can go to a fancy shopping area near place de la Madeleine (see the Shopping chapter).

South of the place de la Concorde (across the river) stands the building where the French National Assembly (similar to the US Congress) meets. If you walk toward it, you'll cross a bridge, the **pont de la Concorde,** over a freeway underpass. This stretch of road is similar to the one at the pont de l'Alma, three bridges downstream, where Princess Diana lost her life in a 1997 car accident. The pont de la Concorde, built of stones from the Bastille prison (which was demolished by the Revolution in 1789), symbolizes that, with good government, *concorde* (harmony) can come from chaos.

Stand midbridge and gaze upriver (east). Using an imaginary clock as a compass, the Orangerie hides behind the trees at 10 o'clock, and the tall building with the skinny chimneys at 11 o'clock is the architectural caboose of the sprawling Louvre palace. The thin spire of Sainte-Chapelle is dead center at 12 o'clock, with the twin towers of Notre-Dame to its right. The Orsay Museum is closer on the right, connected with the Tuileries Garden by a sleek pedestrian bridge (the next bridge upriver). Paris awaits.

MARAIS WALK

*From Place Bastille to
the Pompidou Center*

This walk takes you through one of Paris' most characteristic quarters, the Marais, and finishes in the artsy Beaubourg district. Naturally, when in Paris you want to see the big sights—but to experience the city, you also need to visit a vital neighborhood. To better appreciate the vitality of this neighborhood, take a look at the Marais section of the Shopping chapter and plan a return trip (ideally on a Sunday afternoon).

The Marais, containing more pre-Revolutionary lanes and buildings than anywhere else in town, is more atmospheric than touristy. It's medieval Paris, and the haunt of the old nobility. After the aristocrats left, the Marais became a dumpy bohemian quarter so sordid it was nearly slated for destruction. But today this thriving, trendy, real community is a joy to explore. It looks the way much of the city did until the mid-1800s, when Napoleon III had Baron Georges-Eugène Haussmann blast out the narrow streets to construct broad boulevards (wide enough for the guns and ranks of the army, too wide for revolutionary barricades), thus creating modern Paris. A big Haussmann-type boulevard was planned to slice efficiently through the Marais, but World War I got in the way.

Orientation

Length of This Walk: Allow about two hours for this two-mile walk. Figure on an additional hour for each museum you visit along the way (listed below).

Victor Hugo's House: Free, €7 during special exhibits—not worth it, Tue–Sun 10:00–18:00, last entry 17:40, closed Mon, 6 place des Vosges.

Carnavalet Museum: Free, fee for temporary exhibits, Tue–Sun 10:00–18:00, closed Mon. Avoid lunchtime (12:00–14:00), when many rooms close. It's at 23 rue de Sévigné. ✪ See the Carnavalet Museum Tour chapter.

Holocaust Memorial: Free, Sun–Fri 10:00–18:00, Thu until 22:00, closed Sat and certain Jewish holidays, 17 rue Geoffroy l'Asnier.

Jewish Art and History Museum: €7, more during special exhibits, includes audioguide, covered by Museum Pass, Mon–Fri 11:00–18:00, Sun 10:00–18:00, last entry 45 min before closing, closed Sat, 71 rue du Temple (described on page 76 of Sights chapter).

Pompidou Center: €12, Museum Pass covers permanent collection (but not special exhibitions), €3 Panorama Ticket just to ride to the top for the view (exhibits not included), free on first Sun of month, Wed–Mon 11:00–21:00, ticket counters close at 20:00, closed Tue. ✪ See the Pompidou Center Tour chapter.

Private Tours: Paris Walks offers guided tours of this area (4/week, see page 39).

Starring: The grand place des Vosges, the Jewish Quarter, several museums, and the boutiques and trendy lifestyle of today's Marais.

The Walk Begins

• *Start at the west end of place de la Bastille. From the Bastille Métro, exit following signs to rue St. Antoine (not the signs to rue du Faubourg St. Antoine). Ascend onto a noisy traffic circle dominated by the bronze Colonne de Juillet (July Column). The bronze god on the top is, like you, headed west. Lean against the black railing in front of the Banque de France.*

❶ Place de la Bastille

There are more Revolutionary images in the Métro station murals than on the square. And though place de la Bastille is famous for its part in the French Revolution of 1789, little from that time remains. The Bastille itself, a royal-fortress-turned-prison that once symbolized old-regime tyranny and now symbolizes the Parisian emancipation, is long gone. Only an outline of the fortress' round turrets survives on the road (under the traffic where rue St. Antoine hits the square), though the story of the Bastille is indelibly etched into the city's psyche.

For centuries the Bastille was used to defend the city (mostly from its own people). On July 14, 1789, the people of Paris stormed the prison, releasing its seven prisoners and hoping to find arms.

Bastille Day in France

Bastille Day—July 14, the symbolic kickoff date of the French Revolution—became the French national holiday in 1880. Traditionally, Parisians celebrate at place de la Bastille starting at 20:00 on July 13, but the best parties are on the numerous smaller squares, where firefighter units sponsor dances. At 10:00 on the morning of the 14th, a grand military parade fills the Champs-Elysées. Then, at 22:30, there's a fireworks display at the Eiffel Tower (arrive by 20:30 to get a seat on the grass). *Vive la France!*

They demolished the stone fortress and decorated their pikes with the heads of a few bigwigs. By shedding blood, the leaders of the gang made sure it would be tough to turn back the tides of revolution. Ever since, the French have celebrated July 14 as their independence day—Bastille Day.

The monument on the square—with its gilded statue of liberty—is a symbol of France's long struggle to establish democracy, commemorating the revolutions of 1830 and 1848. In 1830, the conservative king Charles X—who forgot all about the Revolution of the previous generation—needed to be tossed out. In 1848, a time of social unrest throughout Europe, the streets of Paris were barricaded by the working class, as dramatized in Les Misérables. Today, winged Mercury carries the torch of freedom into the future.

The southeast corner of the traffic circle is dominated (some say overwhelmed) by the flashy, curved, glassy gray facade of the

controversial Opéra Bastille. In a symbolic attempt to bring high culture to the masses, former French president François Mitterrand chose this location for the building that would become Paris' main opera venue, edging out Paris' earlier "palace of the rich," the Garnier-designed opera house (see page 68). Designed by the Canadian architect Carlos Ott, this grand Parisian project was opened with fanfare by Mitterrand on the 200th Bastille Day, July 14, 1989. Tickets are heavily subsidized to encourage the unwashed masses to attend, though how much high culture they have actually enjoyed here is a subject of debate. (For opera ticket information, see page 448.)

You'll now turn your back on this Haussmann-style grandeur

MARAIS WALK

Marais Walk

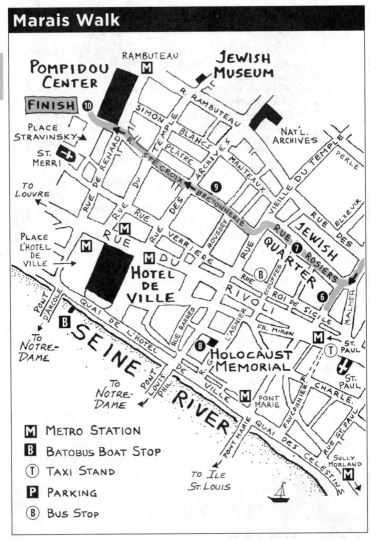

M METRO STATION

B BATOBUS BOAT STOP

T TAXI STAND

P PARKING

B BUS STOP

and walk down what was—before the Revolution—one of the grandest streets in Paris: rue St. Antoine. In 1350, there was a gate to the city here, Porte St. Antoine, defended by a drawbridge and fortress—a *bastille*.

• *Passing the Banque de France, head west down rue St. Antoine about four blocks into the Marais. Notice the minimalist curbside gas station and ponder how much space most gas stations take up in the US. This station is part of a full-service garage with parking (€34/day) and "lavage*

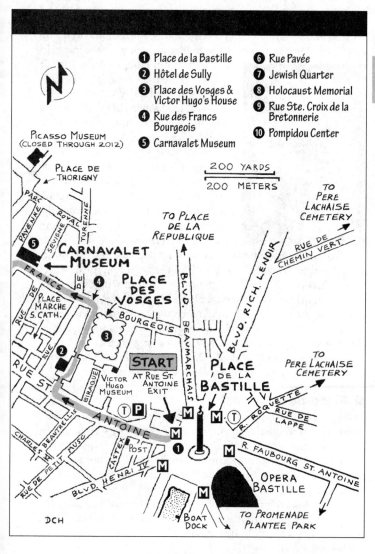

1. Place de la Bastille
2. Hôtel de Sully
3. Place des Vosges & Victor Hugo's House
4. Rue des Francs Bourgeois
5. Carnavalet Museum
6. Rue Pavée
7. Jewish Quarter
8. Holocaust Memorial
9. Rue Ste. Croix de la Bretonnerie
10. Pompidou Center

PICASSO MUSEUM (CLOSED THROUGH 2012)

PLACE DE THORIGNY

PARC ROYAL

PAYENNE

SEVIGNE

TURENNE

200 YARDS
200 METERS

TO PLACE DE LA REPUBLIQUE

TO PERE LACHAISE CEMETERY

RUE DE CHEMIN VERT

BLVD. RICH. LENOIR

5 CARNAVALET MUSEUM

FRANCS

DE

4 PLACE DES VOSGES

BOURGEOIS

BLVD. BEAUMARCHAIS

RUE DE

PLACE MARCHE S. CATH.

RUE DE

3

2

BIRAGUE

VICTOR HUGO MUSEUM

START At Rue St. Antoine Exit

PLACE DE LA BASTILLE

TO PERE LACHAISE CEMETERY

RUE ST.

ANTOINE

T P

M

M

M

R. ROQUETTE

RUE DE LAPPE

T

CHARLES V

BEAUTRELLIS

MUSC

CASTEX

Post

1

R. FAUBOURG ST. ANTOINE

RUE DE PETIT MUSC

BLVD. HENRI IV

M

M

BOAT DOCK

OPERA BASTILLE

TO PROMENADE PLANTEE PARK

DCH

traditionnel à la main" (car wash by hand). At the intersection with rue de Birague, old hippies may wish to make a 100-yard detour to the left, down rue Beautrellis to #17, the nondescript apartment where rock star Jim Morrison died. (For more on Morrison, see page 328.) Otherwise, continue down rue St. Antoine. Continue to 62 rue St. Antoine and enter the grand courtyard of Hôtel de Sully (daily 10:00–19:00, fine bookstore inside). If the building is closed, you'll need to backtrack one block to rue de Birague to reach the next stop, place des Vosges.

❷ Hôtel de Sully

During the reign of Henry IV, this area—originally a swamp (marais)—became the hometown of the French aristocracy. In

the 17th century, big shots built their private mansions (hôtels), like this one, close to Henry's stylish place des Vosges. Hôtels that survived the Revolution now house museums, libraries, and national institutions.

The first of two courtyards is carriage-friendly and elegant, separating the mansion from the noisy and very public street. Look up at statues of Autumn (carrying grapes from the harvest), Winter (a feeble old man), and the four elements.

Continue into a passageway with a bookstore with skillfully carved and painted ceilings. Exit into the back courtyard, where noisy Paris disappears. Use the bit of Gothic window tracery (on the right) for a fun framed photo of your travel partner as a Madonna. At the far end, the French doors are part of a former *orangerie*, or greenhouse, for homegrown fruits and vegetables throughout winter; these days it warms office workers.

• *Continue through the small door at the far right corner of the second courtyard, and pop out into one of Paris' finest squares.*

❸ Place des Vosges

Walk to the center, where Louis XIII on horseback gestures, "Look at this wonderful square my dad built." He's surrounded by locals enjoying their community park. You'll see children frolicking in the sandbox, lovers warming benches, and pigeons guarding their fountains while trees shade this escape from the glare of the big city.

Study the architecture: nine pavilions (houses) per side. The two highest—at the front and back—were for the king and queen (but were never used). Warm red brick-

work—some real, some fake—is topped with sloped slate roofs, chimneys, and another quaint relic of a bygone era: TV antennas. Beneath the arcades are cafés, art galleries, and restaurants—it's a romantic place for dinner (see page 404 in Eating).

Henry IV (r. 1589–1610) built this centerpiece of the Marais in 1605 and called it "place Royal." As he'd hoped, it turned the Marais into Paris' most exclusive neighborhood. Just like Versailles 80 years later, this was a magnet for the rich and powerful of France. With the Revolution, the aristocratic splendor of this quarter passed. To encourage the country to pay its taxes, Napoleon promised naming rights to the district that paid first—the Vosges region (near Germany).

In the 19th century the Marais became a working-class quarter, filled with gritty shops, artisans, immigrants, and a Jewish community. The insightful writer Victor Hugo lived at #6—at the southeast corner of the square—from 1832 to 1848. This was when he wrote much of his most important work, including his biggest hit, *Les Misérables*. Inside you'll wander through eight plush rooms and enjoy a fine view of the square (marked by the French flag in the corner closest to the Bastille; see page 78).

• *Sample the upscale art galleries ringing the square (the best ones are behind Louis), then exit the square at the northwest (far left) corner. Head west on...*

➍ Rue des Francs Bourgeois

From the Marais of yesteryear, immediately enter the lively neighborhood of today. Stroll down a block of cafés and clothing boutiques with the latest fashions. A few doorways (including #8 and #13) lead into courtyards with more shops.

• *Continue west one block along rue des Francs Bourgeois, and turn right on rue Sévigné to reach the entrance (at #23) of the...*

➎ Carnavalet Museum

Housed inside a Marais mansion, this museum features the history of Paris, particularly the Revolution years. Since this is the best possible look at the elegance of the neighborhood back when place des Vosges was place Royal—and the museum is free—I'd interrupt this walk and splice in a trip to the Carnavalet. ➋ See the Carnavalet Museum Tour chapter.

• *From the Carnavalet continue west one block down rue des Francs Bourgeois to the post office. (Modern-art fans: Note that it's not worth seeking out the nearby Picasso Museum, because it's closed for several years for renovation.) Turn left onto...*

➏ Rue Pavée

At #24 you'll pass the 16th-century Paris Historical Library (Bibliothèque Historique de la Ville de Paris). Step into the courtyard of this rare Renaissance mansion to see the clear windows, clean classical motifs, and settling stones. Because the neighborhood is built upon a swamp (marais means "swamp"), many buildings in this area have foundation problems.

Farther down the street, on your right, a funky bookstore at #17 bis has more inside than meets the eye (it's called Mona Lisait, which means "Mona was reading").

Continue along rue Pavée to #10 and find the Agoudas Hakehilos synagogue with its fine (and filthy) Art Nouveau facade (c. 1913, closed to public). It was designed by Hector Guimard, the same architect who designed Paris' Art Nouveau Métro stations.

• *Backtrack a few steps and turn left onto rue des Rosiers (named for the roses that once lined the city wall), which runs straight for three blocks through Paris' Jewish Quarter—lively every day except Saturday.*

❼ Jewish Quarter

Once the largest in Western Europe, Paris' Jewish Quarter is much smaller today but is still colorful. Notice the sign above #4, which

says *Hamam* (Turkish bath). Although still bearing the sign of an old public bath, it now showcases steamy women's clothing. Next door, at #4 bis, the Ecole de Travail (trade school) has a plaque on the wall remembering the headmaster, staff, and students arrested here during World War II and killed at Auschwitz.

The size of the Jewish population here has fluctuated. It expanded in the 19th century when Jews arrived from Eastern Europe, escaping pogroms (surprise attacks on villages). The numbers swelled during the 1930s as Jews fled Nazi Germany. Then, during World War II, 75 percent of the Jews here were taken to concentration camps (for more information, visit the Holocaust Memorial, described later in this tour). And, most recently, Algerian exiles, both Jewish and Muslim, have settled in—living together peacefully here in Paris. (Nevertheless, much of the street has granite blocks on the sidewalk—an attempt to keep out any terrorists' cars.) Currently the district's traditional population is being squeezed out by the trendy boutiques of modern Paris.

The intersection of rue des Rosiers and rue des Ecouffes marks the heart of the small neighborhood that Jews call the Pletzl ("little place"). Lively rue des Ecouffes, named for a bird of prey, is a derogatory nod to the moneychangers' shops that once lined this lane. Rue des Rosiers features kosher *(cascher)* restaurants and fast-food places selling falafel, *shawarma, kefta,* and other Mediterranean dishes. Bakeries specialize in braided challah, bagels, and strudels. Delis offer gefilte fish, piroshkis, and blintzes. Art galleries exhibit Jewish-themed works, and store windows post flyers for community events. Need a menorah? This is a great place to buy one. You may see Jewish men in yarmulkes, a few bearded Orthodox Jews, and Hasidic Jews with black coat and hat, beard, and earlocks.

Lunch: This is a good place for a break. You'll be tempted by kosher pizza and plenty of cheap fast-food joints selling falafel "to go" *(emporter)*. The falafel at L'As du Falafel, with its bustling New York deli atmosphere, is terrific (at #34, sit-down or to go). The Sacha Finkelsztajn Yiddish bakery at #27 is also good (Polish and Russian cuisine, pop in for a tempting treat, sit for the same price as take-away). Across the lane, Chez Marianne cooks up traditional Jewish meals and serves excellent falafel to go (at corner of rue des Rosiers and rue des Hospitalières-St.-Gervais; see page 409 in Eating).

• *Rue des Rosiers dead-ends at rue Vieille du Temple. Here you have two choices: you can continue the walk, or detour to the Holocaust Memorial.*

To continue the walk: Turn left on rue Vieille du Temple from rue des Rosiers, then take your first right onto rue Ste. Croix de la Bretonnerie (and skip down to ❾*, next page).*

Possible detour: To detour to the Holocaust Memorial (and better understand the Jewish suffering during World War II), take this 10-block round-trip detour. From rue des Rosiers, turn left on rue Vieille du Temple and continue straight, crossing rue de Rivoli. Make your second left after rue de Rivoli onto the cobbled passageway, Allée des Justes. You'll see the names of the righteous engraved in a bronze plaque on the right. These are people who were known to have saved Jewish lives during World War II. Next is the entrance to the stark...

❽ Holocaust Memorial (Mémorial de la Shoah)

Opened in 2005, the Holocaust Memorial serves several functions: a WWII deportation memorial, a museum on the Holocaust, and a Jewish resource center. Pass through airport-like security. The entry courtyard contains a cylinder evoking concentration camp smokestacks. Large stone walls are engraved with the names of the 76,000 French Jews deported during the war. Enter the building (with an information desk, bookstore, café, and exhibits) and pick up a brochure. Go downstairs one floor to the crypt, which has a large Star of David in black marble. Ashes from some of the six million victims of Nazi brutality are buried underneath the star, in soil brought from Israel. Behind you is a small corridor containing the original French police files from the arrest, internment, and deportation of Paris' Jews. (Since 1995, the French—thanks to President Chirac's leadership—have acknowledged the Vichy government's complicity in the Nazis' local ethnic cleansing.)

Go downstairs another floor to the permanent exhibition. Photos and videos (most with English explanations) present an introduction to Judaism and the history of Jews in Europe (including pogroms) and in France (including the notorious Dreyfus affair, described on page 76). The displays trace the rise of Nazism, the deportations (including 12,884 Parisians rounded up in a single day), the death camps, and the liberation at the end of the war. The moving finale is a brightly lit collage of children lost to the terror of the Holocaust.

• *Head back the way you came. After crossing rue de Rivoli, take your second left onto...*

❾ Rue Ste. Croix de la Bretonnerie

Gay Paree's openly gay main drag is lined with cafés, lively shops, and crowded bars at night. Check the posters at #7, Le Point Virgule theater (means "The Semicolon") to see what form of edgy musical comedy is showing tonight (most productions are in French). At #38, peruse real-estate prices in the area—€400,000 for a one-bedroom flat?!

At rue du Temple, some may wish to detour half a block to the right to The Studio (41 rue du Temple), a dance school wonderfully located in a 17th-century courtyard. At the restaurant in the courtyard, you can sip a *café crème*—or have a Tex-Mex meal—surrounded by ballet, tap dance, and tango.

A block beyond the dance school is the Jewish Art and History Museum (see page 76).

• *Continue west on rue Ste. Croix (which changes its name to rue St. Merri). Up ahead you'll see the colorful pipes of the...*

❿ Pompidou Center

Survey this popular spot from the top of the sloping square. Tubular escalators lead to a great view and the modern art museum. ✪ See the Pompidou Center Tour chapter.

The Pompidou Center subscribes with gusto to the 20th-century architectural axiom "form follows function." To get a more spacious and functional interior, the guts of this exoskeletal building are draped on the outside and color-coded: vibrant red for people lifts, cool blue for air ducts, eco-green for plumbing, don't-touch-it yellow for

electrical stuff, and white for the structure's bones. (Compare the Pompidou Center to another exoskeletal building, Notre-Dame.)

Enjoy the adjacent *Homage to Stravinsky* fountains. Jean Tinguely and Niki de Saint-Phalle designed these as a tribute to the composer: Every fountain represents one of his hard-to-hum scores. For low-stress meals or an atmospheric spot for a drink, try the lighthearted Dame Tartine, which overlooks the fountains and serves good, inexpensive food, or walk up to the bustling rue Montorgueil market street (below).

Beyond the Marais

From the Pompidou, continue west along the cobbled pedestrian mall, crossing the busy boulevard de Sébastopol to the ivy-covered pavilions of Les Halles. Paris' down-and-dirty central produce market of 800 years was replaced by a glitzy but soulless shopping center in the late 1970s. The mall's most endearing layer is its grassy rooftop park. (The Gothic St. Eustache Church overlooking this contemporary scene has a famous 8,000-pipe organ.)

For a more soulful shopping experience, find your way behind St. Eustache Church and cross rue Montmartre onto the delightfully traffic-free rue Montorgueil (mohn-tor-go-ee). This happy pedestrian street is the site of a flourishing market (open daily throughout the week except Sun afternoon, Mon, and lunchtime—13:00–15:00). If you've walked here all the way from place de la Bastille, you deserve a break at one of the street's lively cafés.

POMPIDOU CENTER TOUR

Centre Pompidou

Some people hate Modern art. But the Pompidou Center contains what is possibly Europe's best collection of 20th-century art. After the super-serious Louvre and Orsay, finish things off with this artistic kick in the pants. You won't find classical beauty here—no dreamy Madonnas-and-children—just a stimulating, offbeat, and, if you like, instructive walk through nearly every art style of the wild-and-crazy last century.

The Pompidou's "permanent" collection...isn't. It changes so often that a painting-by-painting tour is impossible. So, this chapter is more a general overview of the major trends of 20th-century art, with emphasis on artists you're likely to find in the Pompidou. Read this chapter ahead of time for background, or take it with you to the museum to look up specific painters as you stumble across their work.

Orientation

Cost: A €12 combo-ticket gets you into all of the building's various exhibits—both the permanent collection (which we'll cover) and the temporary exhibits that make this place so edgy. The Museum Pass only gets you into the permanent collection, known as the *Musée National d'Art Moderne: Collection Permanente*. A €3 Panorama Ticket lets you ride to the top of the building for the view, but it doesn't include any exhibits. Buy tickets on the ground floor. If lines are long, use the red ticket machines (credit cards only). The museum is free on the first Sunday of the month.

Hours: Wed–Mon 11:00–21:00, ticket counters close at 20:00, closed Tue. During special exhibits it's open Thu until 23:00.

Getting There: Métro stop Rambuteau or, a few blocks farther away, Hôtel de Ville. Bus #69 from the Marais and rue Cler also stops a few blocks away at Hôtel de Ville. The wild, color-coded exterior makes it about as hard to locate as the Eiffel Tower.

Information: Most rooms have informative English explanations. Audioguides can include temporary exhibits (depends on exhibit).

Note that Parisians call the complex the "Centre Beaubourg" (sahn-truh boh-boor), but official publications call it the "Centre Pompidou." Tel. 01 44 78 12 33, www.centrepompidou.fr.

Length of This Tour: Allow one hour.

Cloakroom: Ground floor, free, and required for bags bigger than a large purse.

Shopping: There's a terrific museum store with zany gift ideas on the mezzanine overlooking the main floor.

Cuisine Art: You'll find a sparse, sandwich-and-coffee café on the mezzanine and a pricey view restaurant on Level 6. Outside the museum, the neighborhood abounds with cheap, hip bistros and crêpe stands. My favorite places are to the right of the museum, lining the playful fountain, *Homage to Stravinsky*. Dame Tartine and Crêperie Beaubourg both have reasonable prices.

View Art: The sixth floor (where the pricey restaurant is) has stunning views of the Paris cityscape.

Starring: Matisse, Picasso, Chagall, Dalí, Warhol, and contemporary art.

The Tour Begins

That slight tremor you may feel comes from Italy, where Michelangelo has been spinning in his grave ever since 1977,

when the Pompidou Center first revolted Paris. Still, it's an appropriate modern temple for the controversial art it houses.

The building itself is "exoskeletal" (like Notre-Dame or a crab), with its functional parts—the pipes, heating ducts, and escalator—on the outside, and the meaty art inside. It's the epitome of Modern architecture, where "form follows function."

The *Musée National d'Art Moderne: Collection Permanente* (what we'll see) is on the fourth and fifth floors. But there's plenty more art scattered all over the building. Ask at the ground-floor

information booth, or just wander.
• *Buy your ticket on the ground floor, then ride up the escalator (or run up the down escalator to get in the proper mood). When you see the view, your opinion of the Pompidou's exterior should improve a good 15 percent. Find the permanent collection—the entrance is either on the fourth or fifth floor (it varies).*

Enter, show your ticket, and get the current floor plan (plan du musée). *Generally, art from 1905 to 1960 is on the fifth floor, and the fourth floor contains more recent art. But 20th-century art resents being put in chronological order, and the Pompidou's collection is rarely in any neat-and-tidy arrangement. Use the museum's map to find select artists, and don't hesitate to ask, "Où est Kandinsky?"*

Remember, the following text is not a "tour" of the museum—it's a chronological overview of Modern art.

Modern Art 1905–1960

A.D. 1900: A new century dawns. War is a thing of the past. Science will wipe out poverty and disease. Rational Man is poised at a new era of peace and prosperity....

Right. This cozy Victorian dream was soon shattered by two world wars and rapid technological change. Nietzsche murdered God. Freud washed ashore on the beach of a vast new continent inside each of us. Einstein made everything merely "relative." Even the fundamental building blocks of the universe, atoms, were behaving erratically.

The 20th century—accelerated by technology and fragmented by war—was exciting and chaotic, and the art reflects the turbulence of that century of change.

Cubism: Reality Shattered (1907–1912)

I throw a rock at a glass statue, shatter it, pick up the pieces, and glue them onto a canvas. I'm a Cubist.

Pablo Picasso (1881–1973) and Georges Braque (1882–1963)

Born in Spain, Picasso moved to Paris as a young man, settling into a studio (the Bateau-Lavoir) in Montmartre (see page 346). He worked with next-door neighbor Georges Braque in poverty so dire they often didn't know where their next bottle of wine was coming from. They corrected each other's paintings (it's hard to tell whose is whose without the titles), and they shared ideas, meals, and girlfriends while inventing a whole new way to look at the world.

They show the world through a kaleidoscope of brown and gray. The subjects are somewhat recognizable (with the help of the

titles), but they are broken into geometric shards (let's call them "cubes,"
though there are many different
shapes), then pieced back together.

Cubism gives us several different
angles of the subject at once—say, a
woman seen from the front and side
angles simultaneously, resulting in two
eyes on the same side of the nose. This
involves showing three dimensions,
plus Einstein's new fourth dimension,
the time it takes to walk around the
subject to see other angles. Newfangled
motion pictures could capture this moving 4-D world, but how to
do it on a 2-D canvas? The Cubist "solution" is a kind of Mercator
projection, where the round world is sliced up like an orange peel
and then laid as flat as possible.

Notice how the "cubes" often overlap. A single cube might
contain both an arm (in the foreground) and the window behind
(in the background), both painted the same color. The foreground
and the background are woven together, so that the subject dis-
solves into a pattern.

Picasso: Synthetic Cubism (1912–1915) and Beyond

If the Cubists were as smart as Einstein, why couldn't they draw
a picture to save their lives? Picasso was one Modern artist who
could draw exceptionally well (see his partly finished *Harlequin*).
But he constantly explored and adapted his style to new trends,
and so became the most famous painter of the century. Scattered
throughout the museum are works from the many periods of
Picasso's life.

Picasso soon began to use more colorful "cubes" (1912–1915).
Eventually, he used curved shapes to build the subject, rather than
the straight-line shards of early Cubism.

Picasso married and had children. Works from this period
(the 1920s) are more realistic, with full-bodied (and big-nosed)
women and children. He tries to capture the solidity, serenity, and
volume of classical statues.

As his relationships with women deteriorated, he vented his
sexual demons by twisting the female body into grotesque balloon-
animal shapes (1925–1931).

All through his life, Picasso explored new materials. He made
collages, tried his hand at making "statues" out of wood, wire, or
whatever, and even made statues out of everyday household objects.
These multimedia works, so revolutionary at the time, have become
stock-in-trade today.

Marc Chagall (1887–1985)

At age 22, Marc Chagall arrived in Paris with the wide-eyed wonder of a country boy. Lovers are weightless with bliss. Animals

smile and wink at us. Musicians, poets, peasants, and dreamers ignore gravity, tumbling in slow-motion circles high above the rooftops. The colors are deep, dark, and earthy—a pool of mystery with figures bleeding through below the surface. (Chagall claimed his early poverty forced him to paint over used canvases, inspiring the overlapping images.)

Chagall's very personal style fuses many influences. He was raised in a small Belarus village, which explains his "naïve" outlook and fiddler-on-the-roof motifs. His simple figures are like Russian Orthodox icons, and his Jewish roots produced Old Testament themes. Stylistically, he's thoroughly Modern—Cubist shards, bright Fauve colors, and Primitive simplification. This otherworldly style was a natural for religious works, and so his murals and stained glass, which feature both Jewish and Christian motifs, decorate buildings around the world—including the ceiling of Paris' Opéra Garnier (Mo: Opéra).

Georges Rouault (1871–1958)

Young Georges Rouault was apprenticed to a stained-glass-window-maker. Enough said?

The paintings have the same thick, glowing colors, heavy black outlines, simple subjects, and (mostly) religious themes. The style is Modern, but the mood is medieval, solemn, and melancholy. Rouault captures the tragic spirit of those people—clowns, prostitutes, and sons of God—who have been made outcasts by society.

Henri Matisse (1869–1954)

Matisse's colorful "wallpaper" works are not realistic. A man is a few black lines and blocks of paint. The colors are unnaturally bright. There's no illusion of the distance and 3-D that were so important to Renaissance Italians. The "distant" landscape is as bright any close-up, and the slanted lines meant to suggest depth are crudely done.

Traditionally, the canvas was like a window you looked "through" to see a slice of the real world stretching off into the distance. Now, a camera could do that better. With Matisse, you look "at" the canvas, like wallpaper. Voilà! What was a crudely drawn scene now becomes a sophisticated and decorative pattern of colors and shapes.

Though fully "Modern," Matisse built on 19th-century art—the bright colors of Vincent van Gogh, the primitive figures of Paul Gauguin, the colorful designs of Japanese prints, and the Impressionist patches of paint that blend together only at a distance.

Primitive Masks and Statues

Matisse was one of the Fauves ("wild beasts") who, inspired by African and Oceanic masks and voodoo dolls, tried to inject a bit of the jungle into bored French society. The result? Modern art that looked primitive: long, masklike faces with almond eyes; bright, clashing colors; simple figures; and "flat," two-dimensional scenes.

Abstract Art

Abstract art simplifies. A man becomes a stick figure. A squiggle is a wave. A streak of red expresses anger. Arches make you want a cheeseburger. These are universal symbols that everyone from a caveman to a banker understands. Abstract artists capture the essence of reality in a few lines and colors, and they capture things even a camera can't—emotions, abstract concepts, musical rhythms, and spiritual states of mind. Again, with abstract art, you don't look *through* the canvas to see the visual world, but *at* it to read the symbolism of lines, shapes, and colors.

Wassily Kandinsky (1866–1944)

The bright colors, bent lines, and lack of symmetry tell us that

Kandinsky's world was passionate and intense.

Notice titles like *Improvisation* and *Composition*. Kandinsky was inspired by music, an art form that's also "abstract," though it still packs a punch. Like a jazz musician improvising a new pattern of notes from a set scale, Kandinsky plays with new patterns of related colors as he looks for just the right combination. Using lines and color, Kandinsky translates the unseen reality into a new medium...like lightning crackling over the radio. Go, man, go.

Piet Mondrian (1872–1944)

Like blueprints for Modernism, Mondrian's T-square style boils painting down to its basic building blocks (black lines, white can-

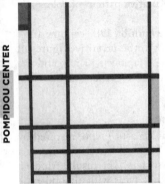

vas) and the three primary colors (red, yellow, and blue), all arranged in orderly patterns.

(When you come right down to it, that's all painting ever has been. A schematic drawing of, say, the *Mona Lisa* shows that it's less about a woman than about the triangles and rectangles of which she's composed.)

Mondrian started out painting realistic landscapes of the orderly fields in his native Netherlands.

Increasingly, he simplified them into horizontal and vertical patterns. For Mondrian, who was heavy into Eastern mysticism, "up vs. down" and "left vs. right" were the perfect metaphors for life's dualities: "good vs. evil," "body vs. spirit," "man vs. woman." The canvas is a bird's-eye view of Mondrian's personal landscape.

Constantin Brancusi (1876–1957)

Brancusi's curved, shiny statues reduce objects to their essence. A bird is a single stylized wing, the one feature that sets it apart from other animals. He rounds off to the closest geometrical form, so a woman's head becomes a perfect oval on a cubic pedestal.

Humans love symmetry (maybe because our own bodies are roughly symmetrical) and find geometric shapes restful, even worthy of meditation. Brancusi follows the instinct for order that has driven art from earliest times, from circular Stonehenge and Egyptian pyramids, to Greek columns and Roman arches, to Renaissance symmetry and the Native American "medicine wheel."

Paul Klee (1879–1940)

Paul Klee's small and playful canvases are deceptively simple, containing shapes so basic they can be read as universal symbols. Klee thought a wavy line, for example, would always suggest motion, whereas a stick figure would always mean a human—like the psychiatrist Carl Jung's universal dream symbols, part of our "collective unconscious."

Klee saw these universals in the art of children, who express themselves without censoring or cluttering things up with learning. His art has a childlike playfulness and features simple figures painted in an uninhibited frame of mind.

Klee also turned to nature. The same forces that cause the wave to draw a line of foam on the beach can cause a meditative artist to draw a squiggly line of paint on a canvas. The result is a universal shape. The true artist doesn't just paint nature, he becomes Nature.

Design: Chairs by Gerrit Rietveld and Alvar Aalto

Hey, if you can't handle Modern art, sit on it! (Actually, please don't.) The applied arts—chairs, tables, lamps, and vases—are as much a part of the art world as the fine arts. (Some say the first art object was the pot.) As machines became as talented as humans, artists embraced new technology and mass production to bring beauty to the masses.

Fernand Léger (1881–1955)

Fernand Léger's style has been called "Tubism"—breaking the world down into cylinders, rather than cubes. (He supposedly got his inspiration during World War I from the gleaming barrel of a cannon.) Léger captures the feel of the encroaching Age of Machines, with all the world looking like an internal-combustion engine.

Robert Delaunay (1885–1941) and Sonia Delaunay (1885–1979)

This husband and wife both painted colorful, fragmented canvases (including a psychedelic Eiffel Tower) that prove the Modern style doesn't have to be ugly or puzzling.

World War I: The Death of Values

Ankle-deep in mud, a soldier shivers in a trench, waiting to be ordered "over the top." He'll have to run through barbed wire, over fallen comrades, and into a hail of machine-gun fire, only to capture a few hundred yards of meaningless territory that will be lost the next day. This soldier was not thinking about art.

World War I left nine million dead. (During the war, France sometimes lost more men in a single month than America lost in the entire Vietnam War.) The war also killed the optimism and faith in mankind that had guided Europe since the Renaissance. Now, rationality just meant schemes, technology meant machines of death, and morality meant giving your life for an empty cause.

Expressionism: Ernst Ludwig Kirchner, Max Beckmann, George Grosz, Chaïm Soutine, Otto Dix, and Oskar Kokoschka

Cynicism and decadence settled over postwar Europe. Artists "expressed" their disgust by showing a distorted reality that emphasized the ugly. Using the lurid colors and simplified figures of the Fauves, they slapped paint on in thick brushstrokes and depicted a hypocritical, hard-edged, dog-eat-dog world that had lost its bearings. The people have a haunted look in their eyes, the fixed stare of corpses and those who have to bury them.

Dada: Marcel Duchamp's Urinal (1917)

When people could grieve no longer, they turned to grief's giddy twin: laughter. The war made all old values, including art, a joke. The Dada movement, choosing a purposely childish name, made art that was intentionally outrageous: a moustache on the *Mona Lisa,* a shovel hung on a wall, or a modern version of a Renaissance "fountain"—a urinal (by either Marcel Duchamp or I. P. Freeley, 1917). It was a dig at all the pompous prewar artistic theories based on the noble intellect of Rational Women and Men. While the experts ranted on, Dadaists sat in the back of the class and made cultural fart noises.

Hey, I love this stuff. My mind says it's sophomoric, but my heart belongs to Dada.

Surrealism: Salvador Dalí, Max Ernst, and René Magritte (1920–1940)

Greek statues with sunglasses, a man as a spinning top, shoes becoming feet, and black ants as musical notes...Surrealism. The world was moving fast, and Surrealists caught the jumble of images. The artist scatters seemingly unrelated items on the canvas, which leaves us to trace the links in a kind of connect-the-dots without numbers. If it comes together, the synergy of unrelated things can be pretty startling. But even if the juxtaposed images don't ultimately connect, the artist has made you think, rerouting your thoughts through new neural paths. If you don't "get" it...you got it.

Complicating the modern world was Freud's discovery of the "unconscious" mind that thinks dirty thoughts while we sleep. Many a Surrealist canvas is an uncensored, stream-of-consciousness "landscape" of these deep urges, revealed in the bizarre images of dreams.

In dreams, sometimes one object can be two things at once: "I dreamt that you walked in with a cat...no, wait, maybe you *were* the cat...no...." Surrealists paint opposites like these and let them speak for themselves.

Salvador Dalí (1904–1989)

Salvador Dalí could draw exceptionally well. He painted "unreal" scenes with photographic realism, thus making us believe they could really happen. Seeing familiar objects in an unfamiliar setting—like a grand piano adorned with disembodied heads of Lenin—creates an air of mystery, the feeling that anything can happen. That's both exciting and unsettling. Dalí's images—crucifixes, political  and religious figures, naked bodies—pack an emotional punch. Take one mixed bag of reality, jumble in a blender, and serve on a canvas...Surrealism.

Abstract Surrealists: Joan Miró, Alexander Calder, and Jean Arp

Abstract artists described their subconscious urges using color and shapes alone, like Rorschach inkblots in reverse.

The thin-line scrawl of Joan Miró's work is like the doodling of a three-year-old. You'll recognize crudely drawn birds,

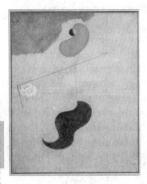

stars, animals, and strange cell-like creatures with whiskers ("Biological Cubism"). Miró was trying to express the most basic of human emotions using the most basic of techniques.

Alexander Calder's mobiles hang like Mirós in the sky, waiting for a gust of wind to bring them to life.

And talk about a primal image! Jean Arp builds human beings out of amoeba-like shapes.

Decorative Art: Pierre Bonnard, Balthus, and Later Picasso and Braque

Most 20th-century paintings are a mix of the real world ("representation") and the colorful patterns of "abstract" art. Artists purposely distort camera-eye reality to make the resulting canvas more decorative. So, Picasso flattens a woman into a pattern of colored shapes, Bonnard makes a man from a shimmer of golden paint, and Balthus turns a boudoir scene into colorful wallpaper.

Patterns and Textures: Jean Dubuffet, Lucio Fontana, and Karel Appel

Increasingly, you'll have to focus your eyes to look *at* the canvases, not *through* them.

Enjoy the lines and colors, but also a new element: texture. Some works have very thick paint piled on—you can see the brushstroke clearly. Some have substances besides paint applied to the canvas, such as Dubuffet's brown, earthy rectangles of real dirt and organic waste. Fontana punctures the canvas so that the fabric itself (and the hole) becomes the subject. Artists show their skill by mastering new materials. The canvas is a tray, serving up a delightful array of different substances with interesting colors, patterns, shapes, and textures.

Alberto Giacometti (1901–1966)

Giacometti's skinny statues have the emaciated, haunted, and faceless look of concentration camp survivors. The simplicity of the figures may be "primitive," but these aren't stately, sturdy, Easter Island heads. Here, man is weak in the face of technology and the winds of history.

Abstract Expressionism

America emerged from World War II as the globe's superpower. With Europe in ruins, New York replaced Paris as the art capital of the world. The trend was toward bigger canvases, abstract designs, and experimentation with new materials and techniques. It was called "Abstract Expressionism"—expressing emotions and ideas using color and form alone.

Jackson Pollock (1912–1956)

"Jack the Dripper" attacks convention with a can of paint, dripping and splashing a dense web onto the canvas. Picture Pollock in his studio, as he jives to the hi-fi, bounces off the walls, and throws

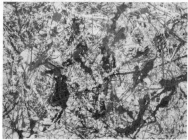

paint in a moment of enlightenment. Of course, the artist loses some control this way—control over the paint flying in midair and over himself, now in an ecstatic trance. Painting becomes a whole-body activity, a "dance" between the artist and his materials.

The act of creating is what's important, not the final product. The canvas is only a record of that moment of ecstasy.

Big, Empty Canvases: Barnett Newman and Robert Rauschenberg

All those big, empty canvases with just a few lines or colors—what reality are they trying to show?

In the modern world, we find ourselves insignificant specks in a vast and indifferent universe. Every morning each of us must confront that big, blank, existentialist canvas and decide how we're going to make our mark on it. Like, wow.

Another influence was the simplicity of Japanese landscape painting. A Zen master studies and meditates for years to achieve the state of mind in which he can draw one pure line. These canvases, again, are only a record of that state of enlightenment. (What is the sound of one brush painting?)

On more familiar ground, postwar painters were following in the footsteps of artists such as Mondrian, Klee, and Kandinsky (whose work they must have considered "busy"). The geometrical forms here reflect the same search for order, but these artists painted to the 5/4 asymmetry of Dave Brubeck's "Take Five" jazz classic.

• *If you're on the fifth floor, descend to the fourth floor, where you'll usually find "contemporary" art, from the last 50 years.*

The Contemporary Collection 1960–Present

Pop Art: Andy Warhol (1928–1987)

America's postwar wealth made the consumer king. Pop art is created from the "pop"-ular objects of that throwaway society—a soup can, a car fender, mannequins, tacky plastic statues, movie icons, advertising posters. Take something out of Sears and hang it in a museum, and you have to think about it in a wholly different way.

Is this art? Are all these mass-produced objects beautiful? Or crap? If they're not art, why do we work so hard to acquire them? Pop art, like Dada, questions our society's values.

Andy Warhol (who coined the idea of everyone having "15 minutes of fame" and became a pop star) concentrated on another mass-produced phenomenon: celebrities. He took publicity photos of famous people and repeated them. The repetition—like the constant bombardment we get from repeated images on television—cheapens even the most beautiful things.

New Media for a New Century

The "modern" world is history. Picasso and his ilk are now gathering dust and boring art students everywhere. Minimalist painting and abstract sculpture are old-school. Enter the "postmodern" world, as seen through the eyes of current artists.

You'll see fewer traditional canvases or sculptures. Artists have traded paintbrushes for blowtorches (Miró said he was out to "murder" painting), and blowtorches for computer mice. Mixed-media work is the norm, combining painting, sculpture, photography, welding, photography and video, computer programming, new resins, plastics, industrial techniques, and lighting and sound systems.

Here are some of the trends:

Installations: An entire room is given to an artist to prepare. Like entering an art funhouse, you walk in without quite knowing what to expect. (I'm always thinking, "Is this safe?") Using the latest technology, the artist engages all your senses by controlling the lights, sounds, and sometimes even smells.

Assemblages: Artists raid Dumpsters, recycling junk into the building blocks for larger "assemblages." Each piece is intended to be interesting and tell its own story, and so is the whole sculpture.

Weird, useless, Rube Goldberg machines make fun of technology.

Natural Objects: A rock in an urban setting is inherently interesting.

The Occasional Canvas: This comes as a familiar relief. Artists of the New Realism labor over painstaking, hyper-realistic canvases to re-create the glossy look of a photo or video image.

Interaction: Some exhibits require your participation, whether you push a button to get the contraption going, touch something, or just walk around the room. In some cases the viewer "does" art, rather than just staring at it. If art is really meant to change, it has to move you, literally.

Deconstruction: Late-20th-century artists critiqued (or "deconstructed") society by examining our underlying assumptions. One way to do it is to take a familiar object (say, a crucifix) out of its normal context (a church), and place it in a new setting (a jar of urine). Video and film can deconstruct something by playing it over and over, ad nauseam. Ad copy painted on canvas deconstructs itself.

Conceptual Art: The *concept* of which object to pair with another to produce maximum effect is the key. (Crucifix + urine = million-dollar masterpiece.)

Performance Art: This is a kind of mixed media of live performance. Many artists—who in another day would have painted canvases—have turned to music, dance, theater, and performance art. This art form is often interactive, by dropping the illusion of a performance and encouraging audience participation. When you finish with the Pompidou Center, go outside for some of the street theater.

Playful Art: Children love the art being produced today. If it doesn't put a smile on your face, well, then you must be a jaded grump like me, who's seen the same repetitive s#%t passed off as "daring" since Warhol stole it from Duchamp. I mean, it's *so* 20th-century.

CARNAVALET MUSEUM TOUR

Musée Carnavalet

At the Carnavalet Museum, French history unfolds in a series of stills—like a Ken Burns documentary, except you have to walk. The Revolution is the highlight, but you get a good overview of everything—from Louis XIV–period rooms to Napoleon to the belle époque.

Orientation

Cost: Free entry, but there can be a fee for some temporary exhibits.

Hours: Tue–Sun 10:00–18:00, closed Mon. Avoid lunchtime (12:00–14:00), when many rooms are closed.

Getting There: It's in the heart of the Marais district at 23 rue de Sévigné (Mo: St. Paul), and on the Marais Walk (page 281). There is a second, larger entrance on rue des Francs Bourgeois, but this tour begins from the courtyard on rue de Sévigné.

Information: Get the free (necessary) map at the information desk *(accueil)*. Tel. 01 44 59 58 58, www.carnavalet.paris.fr.

Length of This Tour: Allow two hours. You could do the Revolution in an hour.

Starring: François I, Louis XIV, Louis XV, Louis XVI, the Bastille, Robespierre, the guillotine, Napoleon, Napoleon III, the Paris Commune, and the belle époque.

Overview

The museum is housed in two Marais mansions connected by a corridor. The first half of the museum (pre-Revolution) is difficult to follow—rooms are numbered out of order, there's no English descriptions, and sections can be closed due to understaffing. See this part quickly, so you can concentrate your energy on the

Revolution and beyond. If you get lost or frustrated, we'll meet up again in Room 45 (on the first floor), where the Revolution begins.

To do this whole tour is a major course in French history. Consider limiting your visit to just the Revolution, located on the second floor (accessed from Room 45 on the first floor). The Revolution section starts on page 310.

The Tour Begins
Main Building—1500-1789

• Begin outside in the...

Courtyard

You're surrounded by the in-your-face richness of the *ancien régime*—back when people generally accepted the notion that some were born to rule, and most were born to be ruled. And the embodiment of that age stands atop the statue in the center: Louis XIV, the ultimate divine monarch.

Notice the date: July 14, 1689, exactly 100 years before the French Revolution ended all that. This statue is a rare surviving pre-Revolutionary bronze. In 1792, nearly all bronzes were melted down to make weapons, as Revolutionary France took on the rest of Europe in an all-out war. Notice the relief below—a great piece of counter-Reformation propaganda. France (the angel with the royal shield) and heaven (portrayed by the angel protecting the Communion Host) are literally stomping the snakes and reformers of Protestantism (Hus, Calvin, Wycliffe, and Luther). Subtle.

• Now find Room 7 on the ground floor. It's not obvious where it is—grab a free map and ask a guard, "Où est salle sept?" (oo ay sahl set). Remember, if you get lost or rooms are closed, we'll meet up again in Room 45, on the first floor (next page).

1500s—Renaissance and Reformation
Room 7

A **model of Ile de la Cité** (made by a monk around 1900) shows the medieval city in about 1520 before France became a world power—crowded, narrow-laned, and steeple-dotted, with houses piled even on top of bridges. There's Notre-Dame on the east end, and Sainte-Chapelle, with its royal palace and gardens, on the west. The only straight road in town was the old Roman road that splits the island north–south and is still used today.

King François I (1494–1547, r. 1515–1547, pictured on next page) brought Paris into the modern world. Handsome, athletic François—a writer of poems, leader of knights, and lover of women—embodied the optimism of the Italian Renaissance. *"Le grand roi François"* (it rhymes) centralized the government around his charismatic self and made a rebuilt Louvre his home. He affirmed his absolute right to rule every time he ordered something done: "For such is our pleasure!"

Rooms 8 and 9

Renaissance open-mindedness brought religious debate, leading to open warfare between Catholics and Protestants (called Huguenots in France). You'll find paintings here of the Catholic **King Charles IX** (1550–1574, r. 1560–1574) and his mother, **Catherine de Médicis,** who plotted to assassinate several prominent Protestants. Their plan quickly snowballed into the slaughter of thousands of Parisian Huguenots on St. Bartholomew's Day in 1572. Paintings in both of these rooms show events organized by the **Catholic League:** parades, Bible studies, and the occasional Protestant barbecue to keep the faithful in good spirits.

Room 10

King Henry IV (1553–1610, r. 1589–1610, Louis XIV's grandfather) was perhaps France's most popular king. His **bust** depicts him with a faint smile and smile lines around the eyes, capturing his reputation as a witty conversationalist and friend of commoners. Henry helped reconcile Catholics and Protestants and rebuilt Paris. Still, that didn't stop a Revolutionary mob from tearing his equestrian statue to pieces *(Fragment du monument).* See **engravings** of Henry's second wife, Marie de Médicis, and of some of Henry's building projects. The grotesque **stone faces** are four of the 300 that adorn Henry's greatest creation, the pont Neuf.

• *Head upstairs to the first floor.*

First Floor

The Luxury of Louis XIV, XV, and XVI

Browse around the furnished rooms, getting a feel for the luxurious life of France's kings and nobles before the Revolution. In fact, several rooms are straight out of the mansions lining the nearby place des Vosges. Use the following material as background.

• *See you in Room 45, located in the far right corner. If you get lost, ask a guard, "Où est la Révolution?," and they'll direct you to the right place.*

Louis XIV (1638–1715, r. 1643–1715)

The flowery walls, Greek-myth ceiling paintings, and powdered-wig portraits offer a tiny glimpse of the opulence of Louis XIV and his greatest monument, the palace at Versailles. You'll see luxurious wallpaper, tables, chairs, parquet floors, clocks, gaming tables, statues, paintings, and even a doghouse that costs more than a peasant hut. Versailles was the physical symbol of Louis' absolute power over the largest, most populous, and richest nation in Europe.

Louis XIV Style: Baroque. In rooms from this period, ceilings are decorated with curved ornamental frames (cartouches) that hold paintings of Greek myths, and furnishings are gilded. The heavy tables and chairs have thick, curved legs, animal feet, and bronze corner-protectors.

Louis XV (1710-1774, r. 1715-1774)

Louis XV ascended the throne of Europe's most powerful nation when his great-grandfather, the Sun King, died after reigning for 72 years. Only five years old at the time, he was for many years a figurehead, while the government was run by his mentors: a regent during his childhood, his teacher during his youth, one of his many mistresses (Madame de Pompadour) during his middle age, and bureaucrats by the end. Louis was intelligent and educated, and he personally embraced the budding democratic ideals of the Enlightenment, but he spent his time at Versailles, where he gamed and consorted with Europe's most cultured and beautiful people. Meanwhile, France's money was spent on costly wars with Austria and England (including the American "French and Indian War"). Louis, basking in the lap of luxury and the glow of the Enlightenment, looked to the horizon and uttered his prophetic phrase: *"Après moi—le déluge!"* ("After me—the flood!").

Louis XV Style: Rococo. The rooms are decorated in pastel colors, with lighter decoration and exotic landscapes. The chairs are made of highly polished, rare woods, with delicate curved legs and padded seats and backs. Note the Chinese decor and objects such as the Ming vase.

Louis XVI (1754-1793, r. 1774-1792)

With a flood watch in effect, the next Louis stubbornly clung to the rules of the *ancien régime* (the traditional chessboard society with king on top, pawns on bottom, and bishops that walk diagonally).

While peasants groaned in the fields, the rich enjoyed their mansions: parties lit by chandeliers glimmering off mirrors, the sound of a string quartet, exotic foods from newly colonized lands, billiards in one room and high-stakes card games in another, a Molière comedy downstairs, dangerous ideas by radicals like Voltaire and Jean-Jacques Rousseau, and dangerous liaisons among social butterflies—male and female—dressed in high heels, makeup, wigs, and perfume.

Louis XVI Style: Neoclassical. Influenced by recently excavated Pompeii, the rooms are simpler—with classical motifs—and the furniture is straighter. The chairs' straight legs taper to a point.

• *From Room 45, walk down three steps, following signs reading* La Révolution, 19e et 20e siècle. *A long corridor of paintings and sketches leads to the next building. Once there, hike up the hardwood stairs to the second floor and* La Révolution Française.

Second Floor

The Revolution: 1789–1799

No period of history is as charged with the full range of human emotions and actions as the French Revolution: bloodshed, martyrdom, daring speeches, murdered priests, emancipated women, backstabbing former friends—all in the name of government "by, for, and of the people." Common people with their everyday concerns were driving the engine of history. Or perhaps they were only foam bubbles swept along in the shifting tides of vast socioeconomic trends.

Room 101: The Estates-General

It's 1789, France is bankrupt from wars and corruption, and the people want change. The large allegorical painting *L'espoir du bonheur* shows King Louis XVI in the boat of France, navigating stormy seas. Lady Truth is trying to light the way, but the winged demon of tyranny keeps nagging at the king. Above shines the fleur-de-lis, whose petals are labeled with the three social groups that held all power in France: clergy, king, and nobles. Now they are laced together by the new power...the people.

In May, the king called each sector of society together at Versailles to solve the financial crisis. But in a bold and unheard-of move, the Third Estate (the people), tired of being outvoted by the clergy and nobility, split and formed their own National Assembly (see *The Oath of the Jeu-de-Paume* on the opposite wall, a preparatory painting by Jacques-Louis David for a huge canvas that was never painted). Amid the chaos of speeches, debate, and deal-making, the people raised their hands, bravely pledging to stick together until a new constitution was written. Vacillating between democratic change and royalist repression, **Louis XVI** (see his pink-faced portrait to the left) ordered the Assembly to dissolve (they refused), sent 25,000 Swiss mercenary soldiers to Paris, and fired his most popular, liberal minister.

Room 102: The Bastille (July 14, 1789)

The Bastille (see the **model**) was a medieval fortress turned prison. With its eight towers and 100-foot-high walls, it dominated the Parisian skyline, a symbol of oppression. (See the series of **paintings** that illustrate some of the following events.)

On the hot, muggy morning of July 14, Paris' citizens waited on edge, listening to reports of attacks on the populace by the

king's Swiss guards. A crowd formed, marched on the Invalides armory, and seized 30,000 rifles... but no gunpowder. Word spread that it was stored across town at the Bastille. The mob grew bigger and angrier as it traveled. By noon they stood at the foot of the walls of the Bastille and demanded gunpowder. They captured the fort's governor, then two citizens managed to scale the wall and cut the chains. The drawbridge crashed down and the mob poured through. Terrified guards opened fire, killing dozens and wounding hundreds. At the battle's peak, French soldiers in red and blue appeared on the horizon...but whose side were they on?

A loud cheer went up as they pointed their cannons at the Bastille and the fort surrendered. The mob trashed the Bastille, opened the dark dungeons, and brought seven prisoners into the light of day. They then stormed City Hall (Hôtel de Ville) and arrested the mayor, who was literally torn apart by the hysterical crowd. His head was stuck on a stick and carried through the city. The Revolution had begun.

Today, the events of July 14 are celebrated every Bastille Day with equally colorful festivities. The Bastille itself was soon dismantled, stone by stone—nothing remains but the open space of place de la Bastille—but the memory became a rallying cry throughout the Revolution: *"Vive le quatorze juillet!"* ("Long live July 14th!")

Room 103: The Celebration
(La Fête de la Fédération, 1790)

Imagine the jubilation! To be able to shout out things formerly whispered in fear—finally.

The large painting of *La Fête de la Fédération* shows the joy and exuberance of the people as they celebrate the first anniversary of Bastille Day (July 14, 1790). Liberty! Equality! Fraternity! Members of every social class (even including, it appears, three women) hugged, kissed, and mingled on the Champ de Mars, where the Eiffel Tower stands today. The crowd built an artificial mound for heroes of the Revolution to ascend while a choir sang. Women

dressed to symbolize Truth, Freedom, Justice, and other capital-letter virtues were worshipped in a new kind of secular religion. Public demonstrations like these must have infuriated the king, queen, bishops, and nobles, who were now quarantined in their palaces, fuming impotently.

The **Declaration ("Tables")** *of the Rights of Man and the Citizen* (see two different versions) made freedom the law. The preamble makes it clear that "*Le Peuple Français*" (the French people)—not the king—were the ultimate authority. "Men are born free and equal," it states, possessing "freedom of the individual, freedom of conscience, freedom of speech."

Room 104: Louis XVI Quietly Responds (De la Monarchie à la République, 1789–1792)

Louis XVI (see the bust)—studious, shy, aloof, and easily dominated—was stunned by the ferocious summer of 1789. The

Bastille's violence spread to the countryside, where uppity peasants tenderized their masters with pitchforks. The Assembly was changing France with lightning speed: abolishing Church privileges, nationalizing nobles' land, and declaring the king irrel-

evant. Louis accepted his role as a rubber-stamp monarch, hoping the furor would pass and trying to appear idealistic and optimistic.

But looming on the horizon was...*Le docteur Joseph-Ignace Guillotin* (see portrait, opposite the window). The progressive Assembly abolished brutal, medieval-style torture and executions. In their place, Dr. Guillotin proposed a kinder, gentler execution device that would make France a model of compassion. The guillotine—also known as "the national razor," or simply "The Machine"—could instantly make someone "a head shorter at the top." (It claimed its last victim in 1977; capital punishment is now abolished in France.)

Room 105: Royalty Loses Its Head (La Famille Royale, 1793)

Louis' wife, **Queen Marie-Antoinette** (several portraits), became the focus of the citizens' disgust. Reports flew that she spent extravagantly and plunged France into debt. More decisive than her husband, she steered him toward repressive measures meant to snuff out the Revolution. Worst of all, she was foreign-born, known simply as "The Austrian," and soon Austria was trying to preserve the monarchy by making war on the French. A rumor spread—one that had been common among the poor in France for over a decade—that when Marie was informed that the Parisians had no bread to eat, she had sneered, "Let them eat cake!" ("Cake" was the term for the burnt crusts peeled off the oven and generally fed only to the cattle.) Historians today find no evidence Marie ever said it.

Enraged and hungry, 6,000 Parisian women (backed by armed men) marched through the rain to Versailles to demand lower bread prices. On the night of October 5, 1789, a small band infiltrated the palace, burst into the Queen's room, killed her bodyguards, and chased her down the hall. The royal family was kidnapped and taken to Paris, where—though still monarchs—they were under house arrest in the Tuileries Palace (which once stood where the Louvre today meets the Tuileries Garden).

Three years later, the royal family became actual prisoners (see the reconstructed and rather cushy **Prison du Temple** in Room 106) after trying to escape to Austria to begin a counterrevolution. One of their servants pretended to be a German baroness, while Louis dressed up as her servant (the irony must have been killing him). When a citizen recognized Louis from his portrait on a franc note, the family was captured, thrown into prison, and soon put on trial as traitors to France. The National Convention (the Assembly's successor) declared the monarchy abolished.

The royal family—Louis, Marie-Antoinette, and their eight-

year-old son—was tearfully split up (see the painting *Les adieux de Louis XVI à sa famille* in Room 105), and Marie-Antoinette was imprisoned in the Conciergerie.

On January 21, 1793 (see **execution painting**), King Louis XVI (excuse me, that's "Citizen Capet") was led to place de la Concorde and laid face down on a slab, and then—*shoop!*—a thousand years of monarchy that dated back before Charlemagne was decapitated. On October 16, 1793 (see **painting**), Marie-Antoinette also met her fate on place de la Concorde. Genteel to the end, she apologized to the executioner for stepping on his foot. The blade fell, the blood gushed, and her head was shown to the crowd on a stick—an exclamation point for the new rallying cry: *Vive la nation!*

Little **Louis XVII** (portrait in corner) died in prison at age 10. Rumors spread that the boy-king had escaped, fueled by Elvis-type sightings and impersonators. But recent DNA evidence confirms that the *dauphin* (heir to the throne) did indeed die in prison in 1795.

Room 108: The Reign of Terror (La Convention— La Terreur, 1793–1794)

Here are **portraits** of key players in the Revolutionary spectacle. Some were moderate reformers, some radical priest-killers. With Europe ganging up on the Revolution, they all lived in fear that any backward step could tip the delicate balance of power back to the *ancien régime.* Enemies of the Revolution were everywhere— even in their own ranks.

By the summer of 1793, the left-of-center Jacobin party took control of France's fledgling democracy. Pug-faced but silver-tongued **Georges Danton** (see portrait of this Newt Gingrich look-alike) drove the Revolution with his personal charisma and bold speeches: "To conquer the enemies of the fatherland, we need daring, more daring, daring now, always daring." He led the Committee of Public Safety to root out and execute those enemies, even moderates opposed to the Jacobins.

More radical still, **Jean-Paul Marat** (the "Friend of the People," portrait next to Danton) dressed and burped like a man of the street, but he wrote eloquently against all forms of authority. Wildly popular with the commoners, he was seen by others as a loose cannon. A beautiful 25-year-old noblewoman named **Charlotte Corday** decided it was her mission in life to save France by silencing him. On July 11, 1793, she entered his home under the pretext of giving him names of counterrevolutionaries. Marat, seated in a bathtub to nurse a skin condition, wrote down the names and said, "Good. I'll have them all guillotined." Corday stood up, whipped a knife out from under her dress, and stabbed him through the heart. Corday was guillotined, and Marat was hailed as a martyr to the cause.

Marat's death was further "proof" that counterrevolutionaries were everywhere. For the next year (summer of 1793 to summer of 1794, see **paintings of guillotine scenes**), the Jacobin government arrested, briefly tried, and then guillotined everyone suspected of being "enemies of the Revolution": nobles, priests, the rich, and many true Revolutionaries who simply belonged to the wrong political party. More than 2,500 Parisians were beheaded, 18,000 were executed by other means, and tens of thousands died in similar violence throughout the country. The violence begun at the **Bastille** in July of 1789 would climax in July of 1794.

Master of the Reign of Terror was **Maximilien de Robespierre** (the portrait next to Danton's), a 35-year-old lawyer who promoted the Revolution with a religious fervor. By July of 1794, the guillotine was slicing 30 necks a day. In Paris' main squares, grim executions alternated with politically correct public spectacles that honored "Liberty," "Truth," and the heroes of France. As the death toll rose, so did public cynicism. Finally, Robespierre even sentenced to death his old friend Danton, who had spoken out against the bloodshed. As Danton knelt under the blade, he joked, "My turn." The people had had enough.

Room 109: Terror Ends (Thermidor— Le Directoire, July 1794)

Engravings show the chaos—riots, assassinations, food shortages, inflation—that fueled Robespierre's meteoric fall from power. Robespierre's own self-righteousness made him an easy target. On July 27, 1794, as Robespierre prepared to name the daily list of victims, his fellow committee members started yelling "Tyrant!" and shouted him down. Stunned by the sudden fall from grace, Robespierre unsuccessfully attempted suicide by shooting himself in the mouth.

The next day he walked the walk he'd ordered thousands to take. Hands tied behind his back, he was carried through the streets on a two-wheeled cart, while citizens jeered and spat on him. At the guillotine, the broken-down demagogue had no last words, thanks to his wounded jaw. When the executioner yanked off the bandage, Robespierre let out a horrible cry, the blade fell, and the Reign of Terror came to an end.

From 1795 to 1799, France caught its breath, ruled by the Directory, a government so intentionally weak and decentralized (two houses of parliament, five executives, and no funding) that it could never create another Robespierre.

Room 110: France vs. Europe (La Guerre)

The blade that dropped on Louis XVI rattled royal teacups throughout Europe. Even as early as 1792, France had to defend its young democracy against Austria and Prussia. France's new army was composed of ordinary citizens from a universal draft and led by daring young citizen-officers, who sang a stirring, blood-thirsty new song, "La Marseillaise." Surprisingly, they quickly defeated the apathetic mercenaries they faced. France vowed to liberate all Europe from tyranny. Europe feared that, by "export-ing Revolution," France would export democracy...plus senseless violence and chaos.

A young Corsican named **Napoleon Bonaparte** (see the bust) rose quickly through the ranks and proved himself by fighting royalists in Italy, Egypt, and on the streets of Paris. In 1799, the 29-year-old general returned to Paris as a conquering hero. Backed by an adoring public, he dis-solved the Directory, established order, and gave himself the Roman-style title of "first consul."

Room 111: The Revolution vs. Religion (Vandalisme et Conservation)

Three-fourths of France's churches were destroyed or vandalized during the Revolution, a backlash against the wealthy and politi-cally repressive Catholic Church. In Notre-Dame, Christ was mothballed, and a woman dressed as "Dame Reason" was wor-shipped on the altar.

Room 113: Souvenirs of Revolution

After the Reign of Terror, *Liberté, Egalité, Fraternité* was just a slogan, remembered fondly on commemorative **plates and knick-knacks.** The Revolution was history.

• *The visit continues down four flights of stairs—or down the elevator—on the ground floor.*

Room 115: Napoleon Conquers Europe (Le Premier Empire, 1799–1815)

Here's **Napoleon I** at the peak of power, master of Western Europe (see **portrait, breastplate, pistols,** and **death mask** in glass case). Dressed in his general's uniform, he's checking the maps to see who's left to conquer. Behind him is a throne with his imperial seal. This Corsican-born commoner (1769–1821, ruled as emperor 1804–1815), educated in Paris' military schools, became a young Revolutionary and a daring general, rising to prominence as a

French National Anthem: "La Marseillaise"

The genteel French have a gory past.

Allons enfants de la Patrie,	Let's go, children of the motherland,
Le jour de gloire est arrivé.	The day of glory has arrived.
Contre nous de la tyrannie	The blood-covered flag of tyranny
L'étendard sanglant est levé.	Is raised against us.
L'étendard sanglant est levé.	Is raised against us.
Entendez-vous dans les campagnes	Do you hear these ferocious soldiers
Mugir ces féroces soldats?	Howling in the countryside?
Qui viennent jusque dans nos bras	They're coming nearly into our grasp
Egorger vos fils et vos compagnes.	To slit the throats of your sons and your women.
Aux armes, citoyens,	Grab your weapons, citizens,
Formez vos bataillons,	Form your battalions,
Marchons, marchons,	We march, we march,
Qu'un sang impur	So that their impure blood
Abreuve nos sillons.	Will fill our trenches.

champion of democracy. Once in power, he preached revolution, but in fact became a dictator and crowned himself emperor (1804).

During the Empire, all things classical became popular. Wealthy socialites such as **Juliette Récamier** (see painting) donned robes and lounged on couches, while Paris was rebuilt with Neoclassical monuments, such as the Arc de Triomphe, to make it the "New Rome."

In 1812, Napoleon foolishly invaded Russia, thus starting a downward spiral that ended in defeat by allied Europe at the Battle of Waterloo in Belgium (1815). Napoleon was exiled. He died in 1821 on the island of St. Helena, off the coast of Africa.

Room 118: The Monarchy Restored (La Restauration, 1815–1830)

After almost 25 years in exile, royalty returned. **Louis XVIII** (see the crowd scene of *Entrée du Louis XVIII à Paris, le 3 mai 1814*) was the younger brother of headless Louis XVI. He returned to Paris with the backing of Europe's royalty and reclaimed the crown as a constitutional monarch.

The next king, **Charles X** (youngest brother of Louis XVI), dressed in glorious coronation robes, revived the fashion and oppression of the *ancien régime* as he plotted to dissolve the people's Assembly. But the French people were not about to turn back the clock.

Room 119: Revolution of 1830 (Juillet 1830)

Parisians again blocked off the narrow streets with barricades to fight the king's red-coated soldiers (see various **street battle paintings**). After "Three Glorious Days" of fighting, order was restored by Louis-Philippe (see **model of Hôtel de Ville**), an unassuming nobleman who appeared on the balcony of the Hôtel de Ville and was cheered by royalists, the middle class, and peasants alike. They made him king.

Room 120: Constitutional Monarchy (La Monarchie de Juillet, 1830–1848)

King Louis-Philippe (1773–1850, r. 1830–1848, see black bust with epaulettes)—a former lieutenant turned banker, with a few drops of royal blood—was a true constitutional monarch, harmlessly presiding over an era of middle-class progress fueled by the Industrial Revolution. Still, liberal reforms came too slowly. New factories brought division between wealthy employers and poor workers, and only 200,000 out of 30 million French citizens (1/150) could vote.

Room 121: Revolution of 1848 (La Deuxième République)

In February of 1848—a time of Europe-wide depression and socialist strikes—Parisians took to the streets again **(battle scenes).** They battled at the Bastille, Palais-Royal, Panthéon, and place de la Concorde, and they toppled the king. After five decades of dictators (including Napoleon), retread Bourbons (the Restoration), and self-proclaimed monarchs (Louis-Philippe), France was back in the hands of the people—the Second Republic.

Room 122: Romanticism (Le Romantisme)

Freedom of expression, the uniqueness of each person, the glories of the human spirit and the natural world—these values from the 1789 Revolution were extolled by artists of the 1800s known as Romantics.

You'll see **caricature busts** of many famous Frenchmen and visitors to Paris, the center of European culture. There's Victor Hugo (author of *Les Misérables* and *The Hunchback of Notre-Dame*), Frédéric Chopin (Polish pianist who charmed Parisian society), Giuseppe Verdi (composer of stirring operas, such as *Aida*), and

Gioacchino Rossini (*William Tell Overture*).

There are also **paintings** of the glamorous pianist Franz Liszt and his mistress, Marie d'Agoult—the ultimate Romantic. She left her husband and children to follow the dynamic Liszt on a journey of self-discovery in Italy and Switzerland—"the years of pilgrimage."

• *Journey upstairs and to the left toward* Paris: Du Second Empire à nos jours—*From the Second Empire to Today.*

Room 128: Napoleon III and the Second Empire (Le Deuxième Empire, 1852–1870)

Louis-Napoleon Bonaparte (1808–1873, ruled as emperor 1852–1871; in the big painting, with red pants and sash, waxed moustache, and goatee) was the nephew of the famous Emperor Napoleon I. He used his well-known name to get elected president by a landslide in 1848, and then combined democracy with monarchy to be voted "Emperor Napoleon III." He suppressed opposition while promoting liberal reforms as well as economic and colonial expansion.

Here he hands an order to **Baron Georges Haussmann** (mutton-chop sideburns) to modernize Paris. Haussmann cut the wide, straight boulevards of today to move goods, open up the crowded city...and prevent barricades in future revolutions. Parks, railroad stations, and the Opéra Garnier made Paris the model for world capitals. (Room 129 shows building projects.)

The **boat-like cradle** (Room 128) is a copy of the famous cradle of Napoleon II (1811–1832, known to history as the King of Rome), the only son of Napoleon I, who died at 21 of tuberculosis before ever ruling anything.

Napoleon III pursued popular wars (the **model** in Room 129 celebrates Crimean War vets, 1855) and unpopular ones (backing Austrian Emperor Maximilian in Mexico). In the summer of 1870, he personally led a jubilant French Army to crush upstart Prussia—"On to Berlin!" Uh-oh.

Room 130: The Franco-Prussian War (Le Siège de Paris, 1870–1871)

Within weeks the overconfident French were surrounded, Napoleon III himself was captured, and he surrendered. Paris was stunned. (See the big **painting of a crowd** hearing the news on the legislature steps.) The Germans quickly put a stranglehold on Paris, and a long, especially cold winter settled in.

Some would not give up. Without an emperor, they proclaimed yet another democratic republic (France's third in a century), and sent minister Léon Gambetta in a newfangled balloon (**painting**) over the Germans' heads to rally the countryside to come save Paris. The Parisians themselves held out bravely (**painting of Tuileries** as army camp), but German efficiency and modern technology simply overwhelmed the French.

Room 131: The Paris Commune
(La Commune, Spring 1871)

The Republic finally agreed to a humiliating surrender. Paris' liberals—enraged at the capitulation after such a brave winter and fearing a return of monarchy—rejected the surrender and proclaimed their own government, the Paris Commune. **Portraits** honor the proud idealists, who barricaded themselves inside Paris' neighborhoods, refusing to bow to the German emperor.

Then, in one "bloody week" in May (**battle scenes**), French troops backing the Republic stormed through Paris, leaving 15,000 dead, 5,000 jailed, and 8,000 deported. The Commune was snuffed out, but the memory was treasured by generations of liberals in popular **souvenirs:** a jar of bread from the hungry winter, a carrier pigeon's feather, a box reading *"Vive la Commune!"*

The church of Sacré-Cœur (see **painting** way up high) was built after the war as a form of national penance for the sins of liberalism.

Rooms 132-142: The Beautiful Age
(La Belle Epoque, 1871-1914)

The Third Republic restored peace to a prosperous middle-class society. The **Eiffel Tower** (Room 132) marked the 1889 centennial of the Revolution, and the **Statue of Liberty** (Room 133) honored America's revolution.

Paris was a capital of world culture in the era known as the belle époque (beautiful age). It was a city of **Impressionist painters** (Room 135) and of writers and actors, including the actress **Sarah Bernhardt** (Room 136), called the world's first international star ("a force of nature, a fiery soul, a marvelous intelligence, a magnificent creature of the highest order," raved one of the smitten).

And it was the city of Art Nouveau (see two delightful **Art Nouveau** rooms, 141-142).

Room 145: World War I (1914-1918)

Three costly wars with Germany—the Franco-Prussian War, World War I, and World War II—drained France's resources. Although **Marshal Foch** (big painting above the elevator) is hailed as the man who coordinated the Allied armies to defeat Germany in World War I, France was hardly a winner. More than 1.5 million Frenchmen died, a generation was lost, and the country would be a pushover when Hitler invaded in 1940. France's long history as a global superpower was over.

Room 147: Remembrance of Things Past (La Vie Littéraire du XXe Siècle)

The last room is filled with portraits of Paris' 20th-century literary greats. By producing such figures as the writer **Marcel Proust** (see his reconstructed bedroom) and the dreamy writer/filmmaker **Jean Cocteau,** France has remained a cultural superpower.

PÈRE LACHAISE CEMETERY TOUR

Cimetière du Père Lachaise

Enclosed by a massive wall and lined with 5,000 trees, the peaceful, car-free lanes and dirt paths of Père Lachaise cemetery encourage parklike meandering. Named for Father *(Père)* La Chaise, whose job was listening to Louis XIV's sins, the cemetery is relatively new, having opened in 1804 to accommodate Paris' expansion. Today, this city of the dead (pop. 70,000) still accepts new residents, but real estate prices are very high.

The 100-acre cemetery is big and confusing, with thousands of graves and tombs crammed every which way, and only a few pedestrian pathways to help you navigate. The maps available from any of the nearby florists help guide your way. But, better still, take my tour and save lots of time as you play grave-hunt with the cemetery's other visitors. This walk takes you on a one-way tour between two convenient Métro/bus stops (Gambetta and Père Lachaise), connecting a handful of graves from some of this necropolis' best-known residents.

Orientation

Cost: Free.

Hours: Mon–Sat 8:00–18:00, Sun 9:00–18:00. If it gets dark before 18:00, the cemetery closes at dusk.

Getting There: Catch bus #69 to the end of the line (see the Bus #69 Sightseeing Tour chapter) or take the Métro to the Gambetta stop. If you're arriving on bus #69, it will stop at place Gambetta on avenue du Père Lachaise, two blocks from the cemetery. If you're taking the Métro, exit at Gambetta Métro (not the Père Lachaise stop, which is less convenient for this tour), take *sortie* #3 (Père Lachaise exit), turn left, and follow signs to Père Lachaise. Either way, it's two short blocks

up avenue du Père Lachaise, which ends at the cemetery.
Along the route, you'll pass flower shops selling €2 maps (not
necessary for this tour, but helpful—especially for finding
additional graves) and a WC just inside the Porte Gambetta
entrance to Père Lachaise.

Information: Tel. 01 55 25 82 10.

Length of This Tour: Allow 1.5 hours for this walk, and another
30 minutes for your own detours. Bring good walking shoes
for the rough, cobbled streets.

Cuisine Art: As you approach the cemetery, there are several
cafés near Métro stop Gambetta and along avenue du Père
Lachaise.

Starring: Oscar Wilde, Edith Piaf, Gertrude Stein, Molière, Jim
Morrison, Frédéric Chopin, Héloïse and Abélard, Colette,
and Rossini.

Overview

From the Porte Gambetta entrance, we'll walk roughly southwest (mostly downhill) through the cemetery. At the end of the

tour, we'll exit Porte Principale
onto boulevard Ménilmontant,
near the Père Lachaise Métro
entrance and another bus #69 stop.
(You can follow the tour heading
the other direction, but it's not
recommended—it's confusing, and
almost completely uphill.)

Remember to keep referring
to the map on the next page (note
that north is not up on the map), and follow street signs posted at
intersections. The layout of the cemetery makes an easy-to-follow
tour impossible. It's a little easier if you buy a more detailed map to
use along with our rather general one. Be patient, make a few discoveries of your own, and ask passersby for graves you can't locate.

The Tour Begins

• *Entering the cemetery at the Porte Gambetta entrance, walk straight
up avenue des Combattants past World War memorials, cross avenue
Transversale No. 3, pass the first building, and look left to the...*

❶ Columbarium/Crematorium

Marked by a dome with a gilded flame and working chimneys on
top, the Columbarium sits in a courtyard surrounded by about
1,300 niches, small cubicles for cremated remains, often decorated
with real or artificial flowers.

Père Lachaise Cemetery Tour

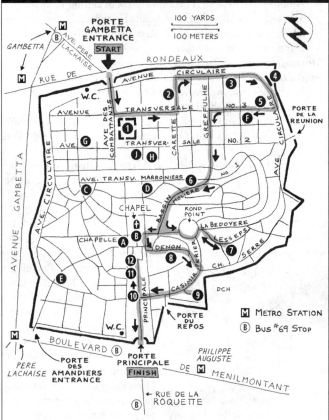

PERE LACHAISE CEMETERY

TOUR

❶ Columbarium/Crématorium
❷ Oscar Wilde
❸ Gertrude Stein
❹ Mur des Fédérés
❺ Edith Piaf
❻ Molière
❼ Jim Morrison
❽ Frédéric Chopin
❾ Héloïse & Abélard
❿ Colette
⓫ Gioacchino Rossini
⓬ Baron Haussmann

OTHER NOTABLE TOMBS

Ⓐ Jacques-Louis David
Ⓑ Théodore Géricault
Ⓒ Eugène Delacroix
Ⓓ J. A. D. Ingres
Ⓔ Georges Seurat
Ⓕ Amadeo Modigliani
Ⓖ Marcel Proust
Ⓗ Sarah Bernhardt
Ⓙ Yves Montand &
   Simone Signoret

Beneath the courtyard (steps leading underground) are about 12,000 smaller niches, including one for Maria Callas (1923–1977), an American-born opera diva known for her versatility, flair for drama, and affair with Aristotle Onassis (niche #16258, down aisle J).

• *Turn around and walk back to the intersection with avenue Transversale No. 3. Turn right, heading southeast on the avenue, turn left on avenue Carette, and walk half a block to the block-of-stone tomb (on the left) with heavy-winged angels trying to fly.*

❷ Oscar Wilde (1854–1900)

The writer and martyr to homosexuality is mourned by "outcast men" (as the inscription says) and by wearers of heavy lipstick, who cover the tomb and the angels' emasculated privates with kisses. Despite Wilde's notoriety, an inscription says "He died fortified by the Sacraments of the Church." There's a short résumé scratched (in English) into the back side of the tomb. For more on Wilde and his death in Paris, see page 252.

"Alas, I am dying beyond my means."

—Oscar Wilde

• *Continue along avenue Carette and turn right (southeast) down avenue Circulaire. A block and a half down, you'll reach Gertrude Stein's unadorned, easy-to-miss grave (on the right just before a yellow stone structure).*

❸ Gertrude Stein (1874–1946)

While traveling through Europe, the twentysomething American dropped out of med school and moved to Paris, her home for the rest of her life. She shared an apartment at 27 rue de Fleurus (a couple of blocks west of Luxembourg Garden) with her brother Leo and, later, with her life partner, Alice B. Toklas (who's also buried here, see gravestone's flipside). Every Saturday night, Paris' brightest artistic lights converged *chez vingt-sept* for dinner and intellectual stimulation. Picasso painted her portrait, Hemingway sought her approval, and Virgil Thompson set her words to music.

America discovered "Gerty" in 1933 when her memoirs, the slyly titled *Autobiography of Alice B. Toklas*, hit the bestseller list. After 30 years away, she returned to the United States for a triumphant lecture tour. Her writing is less well-known than her persona, except for the oft-quoted "A rose is a rose is a rose."

Stein's last words: When asked, "What is the answer?" she replied, "What is the question?"

• *Ponder Stein's tomb again and again and again, and continue southeast on avenue Circulaire to where it curves to the right. Emaciated statues remember victims of the concentration camps and Nazi resistance heroes. Pebbles on the tombstones represent Jewish prayers. At the corner of the cemetery, veer left off the road a few steps, to the wall marked* Aux Morts de la Commune.

❹ Mur des Fédérés

The "Communards' Wall" marks the place where the quixotic Paris Commune came to a violent end.

In 1870, Prussia invaded France, and the country quickly collapsed and surrendered—all except the city of Paris. For six months, through a bitter winter, the Prussians laid siege to the city. Defiant Paris held out, even opposing the French government, which had fled to Versailles and was collaborating with the Germans. Parisians formed an opposition government that was revolutionary and socialist, called the Paris Commune.

The Versailles government sent French soldiers to retake Paris. In May of 1871, they breached the west walls and swept eastward. French soldiers fought French citizens, and tens of thousands died during a bloody week of street fighting (La Semaine Sanglante). The last resisters holed up inside the walls of Père Lachaise and made an Alamo-type last stand before they were finally overcome.

At dawn on May 28, 1871, the 147 Communards were lined up against this wall and shot by French soldiers. They were buried in a mass grave where they fell. With them the Paris Commune died, and the city entered five years of martial law.

• *Return to the road, continue to the next (unmarked) street, avenue Transversale No. 3, and turn right. A half-block uphill, Edith Piaf's grave is on the right. It's one grave off the street, behind a white tombstone with a small gray cross. Edith Gassion-Piaf rests among many graves. Hers is often adorned with photos, fresh flowers, and love notes.*

❺ Edith Piaf (1915–1963)

A child of the Parisian streets, Piaf was raised in her grandma's bordello and her father's traveling circus troupe. The teenager sang in Paris' streets for spare change, where a nightclub owner discovered her. Waif-like and dressed in black, she sang in a warbling voice under the name "La Môme Piaf" (The Little Sparrow). She

became the toast of pre-WWII Paris society.

Her offstage love life was busy and often messy, including a teenage pregnancy (her daughter is buried along with her, in a grave marked *Marcelle Dupont, 1933–1935)*, a murdered husband, and a heartbreaking affair with costar Yves Montand.

With her strong but trembling voice, she buoyed French spirits under the German occupation, and her most famous song, "La Vie en Rose" (The Rosy Life) captured the joy of postwar Paris. Her personal life declined into ill health, alcohol, and painkillers, while onstage she sang, *"Non, je ne regrette rien"* ("No, I don't regret anything").

• *From Edith Piaf's grave, continue up along avenue Transversale No. 3, and turn left on avenue Greffulhe. Follow Greffulhe straight (even when it narrows), until it dead-ends at avenue Transversale des Marronières No. 1. Continue ahead 20 paces on a dirt path, where you reach chemin Molière et La Fontaine. Turn right. Molière lies 30 yards down, on the right side of the street, just beyond the highest point of this lane.*

❻ Molière (1622–1675)

In 1804, the great comic playwright was the first to be reburied in Père Lachaise, a publicity stunt that gave instant prestige to the new cemetery.

Born in Paris, Molière was not of noble blood, but as the son of the king's furniture supervisor, he had connections. The 21-year-old Molière joined a troupe of strolling players, who ranked very low on the social scale, touring the provinces. Twelve long years later, they returned to Paris to perform before Louis XIV. Molière, by now an accomplished comic actor, cracked the king up. He  was instantly famous—writing, directing, and often starring in his own works. He satirized rich nobles, hypocritical priests, and quack doctors, creating enemies in high places.

On February 17, 1675, an aging Molière went on stage in the title role of his latest comedy, *The Imaginary Invalid*. Though ill, he insisted he had to go on, concerned for all the little people. His role was of a hypochondriac who coughs to get sympathy. The deathly ill Molière effectively faked coughing fits...which soon turned to real convulsions. The unaware crowd roared with laughter while his fellow players fretted in the wings.

In the final scene, Molière's character becomes a doctor himself in a mock swearing-in ceremony. The ultimate trouper, Molière finished his final line—"*Juro*" ("I accept")—and collapsed while coughing blood. The audience laughed hysterically. He died shortly after.

Irony upon irony for the master of satire: Molière—a sick man whose doctors thought he was a hypochondriac—dies playing a well man who is a hypochondriac, succumbing onstage while the audience cheers.

Molière lies next to his friend and fellow writer, La Fontaine (1621–1695), who wrote a popular version of Aesop's Fables.

> *"We die only once, and for such a long time."*
>
> —Molière

• *Continue downhill on chemin Molière (which becomes the paved chemin du Bassin), and turn left on avenue de la Chapelle. It leads to the Rond Point roundabout intersection.*

Cross Carrefour Rond Point and continue straight (opposite where you entered, on unmarked chemin de la Bédoyère). Just a few steps along, veer to the right onto chemin Lauriston. Keep to the left on chemin de Lesseps, and look (immediately) for the temple on the right with three wreaths. Jim Morrison lies just behind, often with a personal security guard. You can't miss the commotion.

❼ Jim Morrison (1943–1971)

An American rock star has perhaps the most visited tomb in the cemetery. An iconic, funky bust of the rocker, which was stolen by fans, was replaced with a more toned-down headstone. Even so, Morrison's faithful still gather here at all hours. The headstone's Greek inscription reads: "To the spirit (or demon) within." Graffiti-ing nearby tombs, fans write: "You still Light My Fire" (referring to Jim's biggest hit), "Ring my bell at the Dead Rock Star Hotel," and  "Mister Mojo Risin'" (referring to the legend that Jim faked his death and still lives today).

Jim Morrison—singer for the popular rock band The Doors (named for the "Doors of Perception" they aimed to open)— arrived in Paris in the winter of 1971. He was famous, notorious for his erotic onstage antics, alcoholic, and burned out. Paris was to be his chance to leave celebrity behind, get healthy, and get serious as a writer.

Living under an assumed name in a nondescript sublet apartment near place de la Bastille (head west down rue St. Antoine, and turn left to 17 rue Beautrellis), he spent his days as a carefree artist. He scribbled in notebooks at Le Café de Flore and Les Deux Magots (✪ see the Left Bank Walk chapter), watched the sun set from the steps of Sacré-Cœur, visited Baudelaire's house, and jammed with street musicians. He drank a lot, took other drugs, gained weight, and his health declined.

In the wee hours of July 3, he died in his bathtub at age 27, officially of a heart attack, but likely from an overdose. (Any police investigation was thwarted by Morrison's social circle of heroin users, leading to wild rumors surrounding his death.)

Jim's friends approached Père Lachaise Cemetery about burying the famous rock star there, in accordance with his wishes. The director refused to admit him, until they mentioned that Jim was a writer. "A writer?" he said, and he found a spot.

> *"This is the end, my only friend, the end."*
>
> —Jim Morrison

• *Return to Rond Point, cross it, and retrace your steps—sorry, but there are no straight lines connecting these dead geniuses. Retrace your steps up avenue de la Chapelle. At the intersection with the small park and chapels, turn left onto avenue Laterale du Sud. Walk down two sets of stairs and turn left onto narrow chemin Denon. "Fred" Chopin's grave—usually with flowers and burning candles—is halfway down on the left.*

❽ Frédéric Chopin (1810–1849)

Fresh-cut flowers and geraniums on the gravestone speak of the emotional staying power of Chopin's music, which still connects souls across the centuries. A muse sorrows atop the tomb and a carved relief of Chopin in profile captures the delicate features of this sensitive artist. There may be more flowers and fan worship here than usual this year, as 2010 marks the 200th anniversary of Chopin's birth.

The 21-year-old Polish pianist arrived in Paris, fell in love with the city, and never returned to his homeland (which was occupied by an increasingly oppressive Russia). In Paris, he could finally shake off the "child prodigy" label and performance schedule he'd lived with since age seven. Cursed with stage fright ("I don't like concerts. The crowds scare me, their breath chokes me, I'm paralyzed by their stares..."), and with too light a touch for big venues, Chopin preferred playing at private parties for Paris' elite. They were wowed by his technique; his ability to make a piano sing; and his melodic, soul-stirring compositions. Soon he was recognized as a pianist, composer, and teacher, and even idolized as a brooding genius. He ran in aristocratic circles with fellow artists, such as pianist Franz Liszt, painter Delacroix, novelists Victor Hugo and Balzac, and composer Rossini. (All but Liszt and Hugo lie in Père Lachaise—although Hugo has another memorial in the Panthéon, so he may actually be buried there.)

Chopin composed nearly 200 pieces, almost all for piano, in many different styles—from lively Polish dances to the Bach-like counterpoint of his *Preludes* to the moody, romantic *Nocturnes*.

In 1837, the quiet, refined, dreamy-eyed genius met the scandalous, assertive, stormy novelist George Sand (see the Left Bank Walk chapter). Sand was swept away by Chopin's music and artistic nature. She pursued him, and sparks flew. Though the romance faded quickly, they continued living together for nearly a decade in an increasingly bitter love-hate relationship. When Chopin developed tuberculosis, Sand nursed him for years (Chopin complained she was killing him). Sand finally left, Chopin was devastated, and he died two years later at age 39. At the funeral, they played perhaps Chopin's most famous piece, the *Funeral March* (it's that 11-note dirge that everyone knows). The grave contains Chopin's body, but his heart lies in Warsaw, embedded in a church column.

> *"The earth is suffocating. Swear to make them cut me open, so that I won't be buried alive."*
>
> —Chopin, on his deathbed

• *Continue walking down chemin Denon, as it curves down and to the right. Stay left at the* chemin du Coq *sign and walk down to avenue Casimir Perier. Turn right and walk downhill 30 yards, looking to the left, over the tops of the graves, for a tall monument that looks like a church with a cross perched on top. Under this stone canopy lie...*

❾ Héloïse (c. 1101–1164) and Abélard (1079–1142)

Born nearly a millennium ago, these are the oldest residents in Père Lachaise, and their story is timeless.

In an age of faith and Church domination of all aspects of life,

the independent scholar Peter Abélard dared to say, "By questioning, we learn truth." Brash, combative, and charismatic, Abélard shocked and titillated Paris with his secular knowledge and reasoned critique of Church doctrine. He set up a school on the Left Bank (near today's Sorbonne) that would become the University of Paris. Bright minds from all over Europe converged on Paris, including Héloïse, the brainy niece of the powerful canon of Notre-Dame.

Abélard was hired (c. 1118) to give private instruction to Héloïse. Their intense intellectual intercourse quickly flared into physical passion and a spiritual bond. They fled Paris and married in secret, fearing the damage to Abélard's career. After a year, Héloïse gave birth to a son (named Astrolabe), and the news was out, soon reaching Héloïse's uncle. The canon exploded, sending a volley of thugs to Abélard's bedroom in the middle of the night, where they castrated him.

Disgraced, Abélard retired to a monastery, and Héloïse to a convent, never again to live as man and wife. But for the next

two decades, the two remained intimately connected by the postal service, exchanging letters of love, devotion, and intellectual discourse that survive today. (The dog at Abélard's feet symbolizes their fidelity to each other.) Héloïse went on to become an influential abbess, and Abélard bounced back with some of his most critical writings. (He was forced to burn his *Theologia* in 1121 and was on trial for heresy when he died.) Abélard used logic to analyze Church pronouncements—a practice that would flower into the "scholasticism" accepted by the Church a century later.

When they died, the two were buried together in Héloïse's convent and were later laid to rest here in Père Lachaise. The canopy tomb we see today (1817) is made out of stones from both Héloïse's convent and Abélard's monastery.

> *"Thou, O Lord, brought us together, and when it pleased Thee, Thou hast parted us."*
> —From a prayer of Héloïse and Abélard

PÈRE LACHAISE CEMETERY

Other Notable Residents

Though not along our walking tour, the following folks can be found on our map, as well as the €2 map you get from the florists.

Ⓐ Jacques-Louis David (1748–1825)—Section 56
The Neoclassical painter David chronicled the heroic Revolution and the Napoleonic Era. See his *Coronation of Napoleon* in the Louvre (page 127).

Ⓑ Théodore Géricault (1791–1824)—Section 12
Géricault was the master of painting extreme situations (ship-wrecks, battles) and extreme emotions (noble sacrifice, cour-age, agony, insanity) with Romantic realism. See his *Raft of the Medusa* in the Louvre (page 128).

Ⓒ Eugène Delacroix (1798–1863)—Section 49
For more on this Romantic painter, see his *Liberty Leading the People* in the Louvre (page 129) or visit the Delacroix Museum (see the Left Bank Walk chapter).

Ⓓ Jean-August-Dominique Ingres (1780–1867)—Section 23
Often considered the anti-Delacroix, Ingres was a painter of placid portraits and bathing nudes, using curved outlines and smooth-surfaced paint. Despite his deliberate distortions (see his beautifully deformed *La Grande Odalisque* in the Louvre, page 128), he was hailed as the champion of traditional Neoclassical balance against the furious Romantic style (see his *The Source* in the Orsay, page 143).

Ⓔ Georges Seurat (1859–1891)—Section 66
Georges spent Sunday afternoons in the park with his easel, cap-turing shimmering light using tiny dots of different-colored paint. See his Pointillist canvas *The Circus* in the Orsay (page 160).

Ⓕ Amadeo Modigliani (1884–1920)—Section 96, not far from Edith Piaf
Poor, tubercular, and strung out on drugs and alcohol in Paris, this young Italian painter forged a distinctive style. His portraits and nudes have African mask–like faces, and elongated necks and arms.

• *Continue walking downhill along avenue Casimir Perier, until it crosses avenue Principale, the street at the cemetery's main entrance. Cross Principale to find Colette's grave (third grave from corner on right side).*

❿ Colette (1873–1954)

France's most honored female writer led an unconventional life—thrice married and often linked romantically with other

⑥ Marcel Proust (1871–1922)—Section 85
Some who make it through the seven volumes and 3,000 pages of Proust's autobiographical novel, *Remembrance of Things Past*, close the book and cry, "Brilliant!" Others get lost in the meandering, stream-of-consciousness style, and forget that the whole "Remembrance" began with the taste of a *madeleine* (a type of cookie) that triggered a flashback to Proust's childhood, as relived over the last 10 years of his life, during which he labored alone in his apartment on boulevard Haussmann—midway between the Arc de Triomphe and Gare de l'Est—penning his life story with reflections on Time (as we experience it, not clock time) and Memory...in long sentences.

⑦ Sarah Bernhardt (1844–1923)—Section 44
The greatest actress of her generation, she conquered Paris and the world. Charismatic Sarah made a triumphant tour of America and Europe (1880–1881), starring in *La Dame aux Camélias*. No one could die onstage like Sarah, and in the final scene—when her character succumbs to tuberculosis—she had cowboys and railroad workers sniffling in the audience. Of her hundred-plus stage roles and many silent films, perhaps her most memorable role may have been playing...Hamlet (1899). Offstage, her numerous affairs and passionate, capricious personality set a standard for future divas to aspire to.

**⑧ Yves Montand (1921–1991) and
Simone Signoret (1921–1985)—Section 44**
Yves Montand was a film actor and nightclub singer with blue-collar roots, left-wing politics, and a social conscience. Montand's career was boosted by his lover, Edith Piaf, when they appeared together at the Moulin Rouge during World War II. Yves went on to stardom throughout the world (except in America, thanks partly to a 1960 flop film with Marilyn Monroe, *Let's Make Love*). In 1951, he married actress Simone Signoret, whose on-screen persona was the long-suffering lover. They remain together still, despite rumors of Yves' womanizing. After their deaths, their eternal love was tested in 1998, when Yves' body was exhumed to take a DNA sample for a paternity suit (it wasn't him).

women—and wrote about it in semi-autobiographical novels. Her first fame came from a series of novels about naughty teenage Claudine's misadventures. In her thirties, Colette went on to a career as a music hall performer, scandalizing Paris by pulling a Janet Jackson onstage. Her late novel, *Gigi* (1945)—about a teenage girl groomed to be a professional mistress who blossoms into independence—became a musical film starring Leslie Caron and Maurice Chevalier (1958). Thank heaven for little girls!

"The only misplaced curiosity is trying to find out here, on this side, what lies beyond the grave."

—Colette

• *Retrace your steps to avenue Principale and go uphill a half-block. On the left, find Rossini, with Haussmann a few graves up.*

⓫ Gioacchino Rossini (1792–1868)

Dut. Dutta-dut. Dutta dut dut dut dut dut dut dut, dut dut dut dut dut dut dut....

The composer of the *William Tell Overture* (a.k.a. the *Lone Ranger* theme) was Italian, but he moved to Paris (1823) to bring his popular comic operas to France. Extremely prolific, he could crank out a three-hour opera in weeks, including the highly successful *Barber of Seville* (based on a play by Pierre Beaumarchais, who is also buried in Père Lachaise). When *Guillaume Tell* debuted (1829), Rossini, age 37, was at the peak of his career as an opera composer.

Then he stopped. For the next four decades, he never again wrote an opera and scarcely wrote anything else. He moved to Italy, went through a stretch of bad health, and then returned to Paris, where his health and spirits revived. He even wrote a little music in his old age. Rossini's impressive little sepulchre is empty, as his remains were moved to Florence.

• *Four graves uphill, find...*

⓬ Baron Georges-Eugène Haussmann (1809–1891)

(Look through the green door long enough for your eyes to dilate.) Love him or hate him, Baron Haussmann made the Paris we see today. In the 1860s, Paris was a construction zone, with civil servant Haussmann overseeing the city's modernization. Narrow medieval lanes were widened and straightened into broad, traffic-carrying boulevards. Historic buildings were torn down. Sewers, bridges, and water systems were repaired. Haussmann blew the boulevard St. Michel through the formerly quaint Latin Quarter (as part of Emperor Napoleon III's plan to prevent revolutionaries from barricading narrow streets). The Opéra Garnier, Bois de Boulogne park, and avenues radiating from the Arc de Triomphe were all part of Haussmann's grand scheme, which touched 60 percent of the city. How did he finance it all? That's what the next government wanted to know when they canned him.

Thank God You Can Leave

• *Have you seen enough dead people? To leave the cemetery, return downhill on avenue Principale and exit onto boulevard de Ménilmontant. The*

Père Lachaise Métro stop is one long block to the right. To find the bus #69 stop heading west to downtown, cross boulevard de Ménilmontant and walk down the right side of rue de la Roquette; the stop is four blocks down, on the right-hand side.

MONTMARTRE WALK

From Sacré-Cœur to the Moulin Rouge

Stroll along the hilltop of Butte Montmartre amid traces of the people who've lived here—monks stomping grapes (1200s), farmers grinding grain in windmills (1600s), dust-coated gypsum miners (1700s), Parisian liberals (1800s), Modernist painters (1900s), and all the struggling artists, poets, dreamers, and drunkards who came here for cheap rent, untaxed booze, rustic landscapes, and cabaret nightlife.

Many tourists make the almost obligatory trek to the top of Paris' Butte Montmartre, eat an overpriced crêpe, and marvel at the view—but most miss out on the neighborhood's charm and history. Both are uncovered in this stroll.

We'll start at the radiant Sacré-Cœur church, wander through the hilltop village, browse affordable art, ogle the Moulin Rouge nightclub, and catch echoes of those who once partied to a bohemian rhapsody during the belle époque. We'll end by going through part of a red light district (once adored by American GIs) and finally down a lively neighborhood market street.

Orientation

Length of This Walk: Allow more than two hours for this two-mile uphill/downhill walk.

When to Go: To avoid crowds at Sacré-Cœur, come on a weekday or by 9:30 on a weekend. Sunny weekends are the busiest—especially on Sunday, when Montmartre becomes a pedestrian-only zone and shops stay open. If crowds don't get you down, come for the sunset and stay for dinner. This walk is best under clear skies, when views are sensational. Regardless of when you go, prepare for more seediness than you're accustomed to in Paris.

Getting There: Nearby Métro stops include Anvers, Abbesses, and Pigalle. You have a couple of options to avoid climbing the hill to Sacré-Cœur: The simplest approach is to take the Métro to Anvers, then take the funicular (mentioned in walk, below). Or, from place Pigalle, you can take the tiny electric Montmartrobus, which drops you right by place du Tertre, near Sacré-Cœur (costs one Métro ticket, 4/hr). A taxi from the Seine or the Bastille to Sacré-Cœur costs about €13 (figure on €20 at night).

Sacré-Cœur: Church interior free, open daily 7:00–23:00, €5 to climb dome, not covered by Museum Pass, daily June–Sept 9:00–19:00, Oct–May 10:00–18:00.

Dalí Museum (L'Espace Dalí): €10, not covered by Museum Pass, daily 10:00–18:30, 11 rue Poulbot, tel. 01 42 64 40 10, www.daliparis.com.

Montmartre Museum: €7 (includes audioguide), not covered by Museum Pass, Tue–Sun 11:00–18:00, closed Mon, 12 rue Cortot, tel. 01 49 25 89 39, www.museedemontmartre.fr.

Museum of Erotic Art (Musée de l'Erotisme): €8, €6 per person for groups of four or more, definitely not covered by Museum Pass, daily 10:00–2:00 in the morning, 72 boulevard de Clichy, Mo: Blanche, tel. 01 42 58 28 73, www.musee-erotisme.com.

Cuisine Art: You'll find peaceful, picnic-ready benches all along this walk, and good sandwiches along the rue Norvins (in the heart of Montmartre). See page 416 of the Eating chapter for restaurant recommendations, including L'Eté en Pente Douce.

Starring: Cityscape views, Sacré-Cœur, postcard scenes brought to life, a charming market street, and boring buildings where interesting people once lived.

The Walk Begins

• *To reach Sacré-Cœur by Métro, get off at Métro stop Anvers line 2.*

The **Elysées Montmartre** theater across the street is the oldest cancan dance hall in Paris. Today, it's a rowdy dance club and concert hall, signaling this area's transition. (The famous Chat Noir—or Black Cat—cabaret was half a block down, in the peeling and neglected building with the Trianon sign.) Historically, people have moved to this neighborhood for cheap rents—and though it still feels neglected, urban gentrification is under way, as young professionals restore dilapidated apartments, hotels renovate for a more upscale clientele, and rents increase. A TI kiosk is a few steps to your left (daily 10:00–18:00).

You're standing on boulevard de Rochechouart, where a wall once separated Montmartre from Paris (*boulevard* literally means "road that replaced a wall"). Turn around and notice how better off the other side of the boulevard looks. Let's take a walk on the wild side.

Walk two blocks up rue de Steinkerque (the street to the right of Elysées Montmartre), through an eclectic, low-rent urban bazaar, past bolts of fabric, cheap clothing, and souvenir shops (pick up inexpensive postcards and €3 blue jeans). You'll reach a grassy park way below the white Sacré-Cœur church. The terraced hillside was once dotted with openings to gypsum mines, the source of the white "plaster of Paris" that plastered Paris' buildings for centuries.

• *Hike up to the church, or ride the funicular (station to your left, costs one Métro ticket, closes periodically for maintenance). At the top, find a good viewing spot at the steps of the church.*

❶ Sacré-Cœur Basilica and View

From Paris' highest point (420 feet), the City of Light fans out at your feet. Pan from left to right. The long triangular roof on your left is the Gare du Nord train station. The blue-and-red Pompidou Center is straight ahead, and the skyscrapers in the distance define the southern limit of central Paris. Next is the domed Panthéon, atop Paris' other (and far smaller) butte. Then comes the modern Montparnasse Tower, and, finally (if you're in position to see this far to the right), the golden dome of Les Invalides.

Now face the church. The Sacré-Cœur (Sacred Heart) basilica's exterior, with its onion domes and bleached-bone pallor, looks ancient, but was built only a century ago by Parisians humiliated by German invaders. Otto von Bismarck's Prussian army laid siege to Paris for more than four months in 1870. Things got so bad for residents that urban hunting for dinner (to cook up dogs, cats, and finally rats) became accepted behavior. Convinced they were being punished for the country's liberal sins, France's Catholics raised money to build the church as a "praise the Lord anyway" gesture. Some say the church was also built as a kind of penitence by the French. Many were disgusted that in 1871 their government actually shot their own citizens, the Communards, who held out here on Montmartre after the French leadership surrendered to the Prussians.

The five-domed, Roman-Byzantine–looking basilica took 44 years to build (1875–1919). It stands on a foundation of 83 pillars sunk 130 feet deep, necessary because the ground beneath was honeycombed with gypsum mines. The exterior is laced with gypsum, which whitens with age.

Montmartre Walk

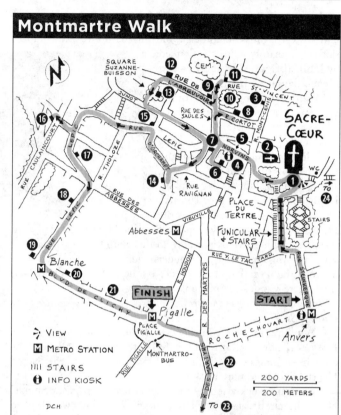

1. Sacré-Cœur Basilica
2. Church of St. Pierre, Bus & Taxi Stop
3. Cabaret de Patachou
4. Place du Tertre
5. Rue Norvins
6. Dalí Museum & Rest. Chez Plumeau
7. Boulangerie & View
8. Montmartre Mus. & Satie's House
9. La Maison Rose Restaurant
10. Clos Montmartre Vineyard
11. Au Lapin Agile Cabaret
12. Renoir's House
13. St. Denis Statue
14. Le Bateau-Lavoir (Picasso's Studio)
15. Moulin de la Galette Rest.
16. Toulouse-Lautrec's House
17. Van Gogh's House
18. Café des Deux Moulins
19. Moulin Rouge
20. Museum of Erotic Art
21. Pig Alley
22. Rue des Martyrs
23. To Notre-Dame-de-Lorette Church & Métro
24. To Rest. L'Eté en Pente Douce

Interior: In the impressive mosaic high above the altar, Christ exposes his sacred heart, burning with love and compassion for humanity. Christ is flanked by biblical figures on the left and French figures on the right. Among the French are Jeanne d'Arc (in her trademark armor, at Jesus' feet), clergymen (who offer a model of this church to the Lord), government leaders (in business suits), and French saints (including St. Bernard, above, with his famous dog, and St. Louis, with the crown of thorns). The centerpiece of the mosaic is the

Holy Trinity: Jesus, a dove representing the Holy Spirit, and God the father high above. Right now, in this church, at least one person is praying for Christ to be understanding of the world's sins—part of a tradition that's been carried out here, day and night, 24/7, since Sacré-Cœur's completion.

• *Find the first pillar to the left (as you face the altar), across from the statue of St. Thérèse.*

A plaque on the pillar (*"L'an 1944..."*) shows where the 13 WWII bombs that hit Paris fell—all in a line, all near the church—killing no one. This fueled local devotion to the Sacred Heart and to this church.

Shuffling clockwise around the ambulatory, find a scale model of the church. Because the church's original windows were broken by the concussion of WWII bombs, all the glass you see is post-1945. Turn around to see colorful mosaics of the Stations of the Cross. Move along and rub St. Peter's bronze foot and look up to the heavens.

Continue your circuit around the church. As you approach the entrance you'll walk straight toward three stained-glass windows dedicated to Joan of Arc (Jeanne d'Arc, 1412–1431). See the teenage girl as she hears the voice of the Archangel Michael (right panel, at bottom), and later (above, on right) as she takes up the Archangel's sword. Next, she kneels to take communion (central panel), then kneels before the bishop to tell him she's been sent by God to rally France's soldiers and save Orléans from English invaders. However, French forces allied with England arrest her, and she's burned at the stake as a heretic (above, on left), dying with her eyes fixed on a crucifix and chanting, "Jesus, Jesus, Jesus...."

• *Exit the church. A public WC is to your left, down 50 steps. To your right is the entrance to the church's...*

Dome and Crypt: For an unobstructed panoramic view of Paris, climb 260 feet up the tight and claustrophobic spiral stairs to the top of the dome (especially worthwhile if you have kids with excess energy). The crypt is just a big, empty basement.

• *Leaving the church, turn right and walk west along the ridge, following tree-lined rue Azaïs. At rue St. Eleuthère, turn right and walk uphill a block to the Church of St. Pierre-de-Montmartre (at top on right).*

The small square in front of the church has a convenient taxi stand and a bus stop for the Montmartrobus to and from place Pigalle (bus costs one Métro ticket).

❷ Church of St. Pierre-de-Montmartre

This church was the center of Montmartre's first claim to fame, a sprawling abbey of Benedictine monks and nuns. The church is one of Paris' oldest (1147), founded by King Louis VI and his wife, Adelaide. (Some say Dante prayed here.) Find Adelaide's tombstone *(pierre tombale)* midway down on the left wall. Older still are the four gray columns—two flank the entrance, and two others are behind the altar. These may have stood in a temple of Mercury or Mars in Roman times. The name "Montmartre" comes from the Roman "Mount of Mars," though later generations—thinking of their beheaded patron St. Denis—preferred a less pagan version, "Mount of Martyrs."

Along the right wall, rub St. Peter's toe (again), look up, and ask for *déliverance* from the tourist mobs outside. Now step back outside, where a sign for the *Café and Cabaret la Bohème* reminds visitors that in the late 19th and early 20th centuries, this was the world capital of bohemian life. The artist-filled place du Tertre awaits.

• *Before entering the square, a short detour to the right leads to 13 rue du Mont-Cenis, the former...*

❸ Cabaret de Patachou

This building, now a pleasant art gallery, is where singer Edith Piaf (1915–1963) once trilled "La Vie en Rose." Piaf—a destitute teenager who sang for pocket change in the streets of pre-WWII Paris—was discovered by a nightclub owner and became a star. Her singing inspired the people of Nazi-occupied Paris. In the heady days after the war, she sang about the joyous, rosy life in the city. For more on this warbling-voiced singer, see page 326.

• *Head back to the always-lively square, and stand on its cusp for the best perspective of...*

❹ Place du Tertre—Bohemian Montmartre

Lined with cafés, shaded by acacia trees, and filled with artists, hucksters, and tourists, the scene mixes charm and kitsch in ever-changing proportions. The place du Tertre has been the town

Maurice Utrillo
(1883–1955)

Born to a free-spirited single mom and raised by his grandmother, Utrillo had his first detox treatment at age 18. Encouraged by his mother and doctors, he started painting as occupational therapy. That, plus guidance from his mother (and, later, from his wife), allowed him to live productively into his seventies, becoming wealthy and famous, despite occasional relapses into drinking and mental problems.

Utrillo grew up on Montmartre's streets. He fought, broke street lamps, and haunted the cafés and bars, buying drinks with masterpieces. A very free spirit, he's said to have exposed himself to strangers on the street, yelling, "I paint with this!"

His simple scenes of streets, squares, and cafés in a vaguely Impressionist style became popular with commoners and scholars alike. He honed his style during his "white period" (c. 1909–1914), painting a thick paste of predominantly white tints—perfect for capturing Sacré-Cœur. In later years, after he moved out of Montmartre, he still painted the world he knew in his youth, using postcards and photographs as models.

Utrillo's mom, Suzanne Valadon, was a former trapeze performer and artist's model who posed for Toulouse-Lautrec, slept with Renoir, studied under Degas, and went on to become a notable painter in her own right.

square of the small village of Montmartre since medieval times. (*Tertre* means "stepped lanes" in French.)

In 1800, a wall separated Paris from this hilltop village. To enter Paris you had to pass tollbooths that taxed anything for sale. Montmartre was a mining community where the wine flowed cheap (tax-free) and easy. Life here was a working-class festival of cafés, bistros, and dance halls. Painters came here for the ruddy charm, the light, and the low rents. In 1860, Montmartre was annexed into the growing city of Paris. The "bohemian" ambience survived, and it attracted sophisticated Parisians ready to get down and dirty in the belle époque of cancan. The Restaurant Mère Catherine is often called the first bistro—this is where Russian soldiers first coined the word by saying, "I'm thirsty, bring my drink *bistro!*" (meaning "right away").

The square's artists, who at times outnumber the tourists, are the great-

great-grandkids of the Renoirs, Van Goghs, and Picassos who once roamed here—poor, carefree, seeking inspiration, and occasionally cursing a world too selfish to bankroll their dreams.

• *Plunge headfirst into the square. The tourist office (Syndicat d'Initiative) across the square sells good maps (daily 10:00–19:00). Just south of the square is the quiet, tiny place du Calvaire, with the recommended café Chez Plumeau (closed Wed). But for now continue west along the main drag, called...*

❺ Rue Norvins

Montmartre's oldest and main street is still the primary commercial artery, serving the current trade—tourism.

• *If you're a devotee of Dalí, take a detour left on rue Poulbot, leading to the...*

❻ Dalí Museum (L'Espace Dalí)

This beautifully lit black gallery (well-described in English) offers a walk through statues, etchings, and paintings by the master of Surrealism. The Spaniard found fame in Paris in the 1920s and '30s, hanging with the Surrealist crowd in Montparnasse, and shocking the world with his dreamscape paintings and experimental films. Don't miss the printed interview on the exit stairs.

• *Return to rue Norvins and continue west a dozen steps to the intersection with rue des Saules, where you'll find a...*

❼ Boulangerie with a View

The venerable *boulangerie* (bakery) on the left, dating from 1900, is one of the last surviving bits of the old-time community, made

famous in a painting by the artist Maurice Utrillo (see sidebar).

From the *boulangerie*, look back up rue Norvins, then back-pedal a few steps to catch the classic view of the dome of Sacré-Cœur rising above the rooftops.

• *Let's lose the tourists. Follow rue des Saules downhill (north) onto the back side of Montmartre. A block downhill, turn right on rue Cortot to the...*

❽ Montmartre Museum and Satie's House

In what is now the museum (at 12 rue Cortot), Pierre-Auguste Renoir once lived here while painting his best-known work, *Bal du Moulin de la Galette* (pictured on page 152). Every day he'd lug the four-foot-by-six-foot canvas from here to the other side of the butte to paint in the open air *(en plein air)* the famous windmill ballroom, which we'll see later.

A few years later, Utrillo lived and painted here with his mom, Suzanne Valadon. In 1893, she carried on a torrid six-month relationship with the lonely, eccentric man who lived two doors up at #6—composer Erik Satie, who wrote *Trois Gymnopédies* and who was eking out a living playing piano in Montmartre nightclubs.

The Montmartre Museum fills several floors in this creaky 17th-century manor house with paintings, posters, old photos, music, and memorabilia to re-create the traditional cancan and cabaret Montmartre scene. An audioguide is free with admission. Highlights include several original Toulouse-Lautrec posters for the Moulin Rouge, a few paintings by Utrillo and Valadon, the original *Lapin Agile* sign, and displays on Montmartre's history, from gypsum mining to the Paris Commune to the Chat Noir cabaret.

• *Return to rue des Saules and walk downhill to...*

❾ La Maison Rose Restaurant

The restaurant, made famous by a Utrillo painting, was once frequented by Utrillo, Pablo Picasso, and Gertrude Stein. Today it serves lousy food to nostalgic tourists.

• *Just downhill from the restaurant is Paris' last remaining vineyard.*

❿ Clos Montmartre Vineyard

What originally drew artists to Montmartre was country charm like this. Ever since the 12th century, the monks and nuns of the large abbey have produced wine here. With vineyards, wheat fields, windmills, animals, and a village tempo of life, it was the perfect escape from grimy Paris. In 1576, puritanical laws taxed wine in Paris, bringing budget-minded drinkers to Montmartre. Today's vineyard is off-limits to tourists except during the annual grape-harvest fest (first Sat in Oct), when a thousand costumed locals bring back the boisterous old days. The vineyard's annual production of 300 liters is auctioned off at the fest to support local charities.

• *Continue downhill to the intersection with rue St. Vincent.*

⓫ Au Lapin Agile Cabaret

The poster above the door gives the place its name. A rabbit *(lapin)* makes an agile leap out of the pot while balancing the bottle of wine that he can now drink—rather than be cooked in. This was the village's hot spot. Picasso and other artists and writers (Renoir,

Utrillo, Paul Verlaine, Aristide Bruant, Amedeo Modigliani, etc.) would gather for "performances" that ranged from serious poetry, dirty limericks, sing-alongs, and parodies of the famous to anarchist manifestos. Once, to play a practical joke on the avant-garde art community, patrons tied a paintbrush to the tail of the owner's donkey and entered the "abstract painting" that resulted in the Salon. Called *Sunset over the Adriatic*, it won critical acclaim and sold for a nice price.

The old Parisian personality of this cabaret survives. Every night except Monday a series of performers take a small, French-speaking audience on a wistful musical journey back to the good old days (for details, see the Entertainment chapter).

• *Before heading back uphill on rue des Saules to the* boulangerie *(at the intersection with rue Norvins), some may wish to make a detour (an extra 15 min) to see a more residential part of Montmartre. If you're pooped, we'll meet you back at the* boulangerie.

Detour to ⑫ Renoir's House and ⑬ St. Denis Statue

• *Walk up rue des Saules and turn right at La Maison Rose, heading west one block on rue de l'Abreuvoir. At the busty bust of singer/actress Dalida (1933–1987, who popularized disco in France), continue straight (west) along the small walkway called allée des Brouillards. You'll pass another of* **Renoir's homes** *(at #6). Walk down the steps at the walkway's end, then stroll up through the small, fenced, multilevel park called Square Suzanne Buisson.*

In the park, find the stone statue of headless **St. Denis.** This

early Christian bishop was sentenced to death by the Romans for spreading Christianity. As they marched him up to the top of Montmartre to be executed, the Roman soldiers got tired and just beheaded him near here. But Denis popped right up, picked up his head, and carried on another three miles north before he finally died. The statue of Denis cradles his head in his hands, looks over a regulation-size *boules* court... and gets ready to play ball.

• *At the top of the park, turn left onto avenue Junot, which turns into rue Norvins. (Wish you could just walk right through these hills? You'll pass a statue that looks like it could do it.) The* boulangerie *is at the top of rue Norvins.*

Once reunited at the boulangerie, *we all go downhill (south). Don't curve right on car-filled rue Lepic; instead, go straight, down the pedestrian-only place J. B. Clement, hugging the buildings on the left. Turn right on rue Ravignan and follow it down to the leafy little square with the TIM Hôtel. Next to the hotel, at 13 place Emile Goudeau, is...*

⑭ Le Bateau Lavoir (Picasso's Studio)

A humble facade marks the place where Modern art was born.

Here, in a lowly artists' abode (destroyed by fire in 1970, rebuilt a few years later), as many as 10 artists lived and worked. This former piano factory, converted to cheap housing, was nicknamed the "Laundry Boat" for its sprawling layout and crude facilities (sharing one water tap). It was "a weird, squalid place," wrote one resident, "filled with every kind of noise: arguing, singing, bedpans clattering, slamming doors, and suggestive moans coming from studio doors."

In 1904, a poor, unknown Spanish émigré named Pablo Picasso (1881–1973) moved in. He met dark-haired Fernande Olivier, his first real girlfriend, in the square outside. She soon moved in, lifting him out of his melancholy Blue Period into the rosy Rose Period. *La belle Fernande* posed nude for him, inspiring a freer treatment of the female form.

In 1907, Picasso started on a major canvas. For nine months he produced hundreds of preparatory sketches, working long into the night. When he unveiled the work, even his friends were shocked. *Les Demoiselles d'Avignon* showed five nude women in a brothel (Fernande claimed they were all her), with primitive mask-like faces and fragmented bodies. Picasso had invented Cubism.

For the next two years, he and his neighbors Georges Braque and Juan Gris revolutionized the art world. Sharing paints, ideas, and girlfriends, they made Montmartre "The Cubist Acropolis," attracting free-thinking "Moderns" from all over the world to visit their studios—the artists Modigliani and Henri Rousseau, the poet Guillaume Apollinaire, and the American expatriate writer Gertrude Stein. By the time Picasso moved to better quarters (and dumped Fernande), he was famous. Still, Picasso would later say, "I know one day we'll return to Bateau-Lavoir. It was there that we were really happy—where they thought of us as painters, not strange animals."

• *Walk back half a block uphill and turn left on rue d'Orchampt. (Notice the windows of another studio on your left.) Walk the length of this short street and into a tiny alley, which spits you out the other end at the intersection with rue Lepic, where you're face-to-face with a wooden windmill.*

⓯ Moulin de la Galette

Only two windmills *(moulins)* remain on a hill that was once dotted with 30 of them. Originally, they pressed monks' grapes and farmers' grain, and crushed gypsum rocks into powdery plaster of Paris. When the gypsum mines closed (c. 1850) and the vineyards sprouted apartments, this windmill turned into the ceremonial centerpiece of a popular outdoor dance hall. Renoir's *Bal du Moulin de*

la Galette (in the Orsay, see page 152) shows it in its heyday—a sunny Sunday afternoon in the acacia-shaded gardens with working-class people dancing, laughing, drinking, and eating the house crêpes, called *galettes*. Some call Renoir's version the quintessential Impressionist work and the painting that best captures—on a large canvas in bright colors—the joy of the Montmartre lifestyle. The Moulin de la Galette restaurant offers good meals and a few historic black-and-white photos of the windmill and old Montmartre (recommended in the Eating chapter).

• *Follow rue Lepic as it winds down the hill. The green-latticed building on the right side was also part of the Moulin de la Galette (the second surviving windmill is just above, through the trees). Rounding the bend, look to the right when you reach rue Tourlaque. The building one block down rue Tourlaque was...*

⓰ Henri de Toulouse-Lautrec's House

Find the building on the southwest corner with the tall, brick-framed art-studio windows under the heavy mansard roof. Every night Toulouse-Lautrec (1864–1901, see page 160)—a nobleman turned painter, whose legs were deformed in a horse-riding accident during his teenage years—would dress up here and then journey down rue Lepic to the Moulin Rouge. One of Henri's occasional drinking buddies and fellow artists lived nearby.

• *Continue down rue Lepic and, at #54, find...*

⓱ Vincent van Gogh's House

Vincent van Gogh lived here with his brother, enjoying a grand city view from his top-floor window from 1886 to 1888. In those two short years, Van Gogh transformed from a gloomy Dutch painter of brown and gray peasant scenes into an inspired visionary with wild ideas and Impressionist colors.

• *Follow rue Lepic downhill as it makes a hard right at #36 and becomes a lively market street. Enjoy the small shops and neighborhood ambience. Two blocks down, on the corner to your right (at #15), you'll find the pink...*

⓲ Café des Deux Moulins

This café has become a pilgrimage site for movie buffs worldwide, since it was featured in the quirky film *Amélie*. Today it's just another funky place with unassuming ambience, frequented by another generation of real-life Amélies who ignore the movie poster on the back wall (daily 7:00–24:00, 15 rue Lepic, tel. 01 42 54 90 50).

• *Now continue downhill on rue Lepic to place Blanche. On busy place Blanche is the...*

⓳ Moulin Rouge

Ooh la la. The new Eiffel Tower at the 1889 World's Fair was

nothing compared to the sight of pretty cancan girls kicking their legs at the newly opened "Red Windmill." The nightclub seemed to sum up the belle époque— the age of elegance, opulence, sophistication, and worldliness. The big draw was amateur night, when working-class girls in risqué dresses danced "Le Quadrille" (dubbed "cancan" by a Brit). Wealthy Parisians slummed it by coming here.

On most nights you'd see a small man in a sleek black coat, checked pants, a green scarf, and a bowler hat peering through his pince-nez glasses at the dancers and making sketches of them— Henri de Toulouse-Lautrec. Perhaps he'd order an absinthe, the dense green liqueur (evil ancestor of today's pastis) that was the toxic muse for so many great (and so many forgotten) artists. Toulouse-Lautrec's sketches of dancer Jane Avril and comic La Goulue hang in the Orsay (see reproductions in the entryway).

After its initial splash, the Moulin Rouge survived as a venue for all kinds of entertainment. In 1906, the novelist Colette kissed her female lover onstage, and the authorities closed the "Dream of Egypt" down. Yves Montand opened for Edith Piaf (1944), and the two fell in love offstage. It has hosted such diverse acts as Ginger Rogers, Dalida, and the Village People—together on one bill (1979). Mikhail Baryshnikov leaped across its stage (1986). And the club celebrated its centennial (1989) with Ray Charles, Tony Curtis, Ella Fitzgerald, and...a French favorite, Jerry Lewis.

Tonight they're showing...well, find out yourself: Walk into the open-air entryway or step into the lobby to mull over the photos, show options, and prices.

• *Turn left out of the Moulin Rouge. The Blanche Métro stop is here in place Blanche, a good place to end if you are tired. (Plaster of Paris from the gypsum found on this mount was loaded sloppily at place Blanche... the white square.) Others may want to sully themselves by continuing east along boulevard de Clichy to the...*

⑳ Museum of Erotic Art (Musée de l'Erotisme)

Basically a sexy art gallery, this museum has five floors of displays— mostly paintings and drawings—ranging from artistic to erotic to disgusting. They also toss in a few circa-1920 porn videos and a fascinating history of local brothels (see page 80).

• *Walk to the center of the boulevard, crossing a bike lane. Paris has fallen in love with bikes, and this separated bike path is part of a 275-mile network of lanes available to cyclists. Continue east down the boulevard and you'll find...*

㉑ Pig Alley

The stretch of the boulevard de Clichy from place Blanche eastward (toward Sacré-Cœur) to place Pigalle is the den mother of all iniquities. Remember, this was once the border between Montmartre and Paris. Today, sex shops, peep shows, live sex shows, chatty pitchmen, and hot dog stands line the busy boulevard. Dildos abound.

It's raunchy now, but the area has always been the place where bistros had tax-free status, wine was cheap, and prostitutes roamed freely. In World War II, GIs nicknamed Pigalle "Pig Alley." Though the government is cracking down on prostitution, and the ladies of the night are being driven deeper into their red-velvet bars as the area is being gentrified, very few think of the great French sculptor Pigalle when they hear the district's name.

Bars lining the streets downhill from place Pigalle (especially rue Pigalle) are lively with working girls eager to share a drink with anyone passing by. Escape home via the fine Art Nouveau Métro stop, Pigalle. After all that, the Métro system seems cleaner.

• *Although you can pop into the Métro from here, the next (optional) leg of this walk starts a block away and takes you downhill six blocks through a lively market street to another Métro station. Continue walking down boulevard de Clichy to the next street, where you turn right on...*

MONTMARTRE WALK

㉒ Rue des Martyrs

As they race from big museum to big museum, it's easy for visitors to miss the market streets and village-like charm that give Paris a warm and human vibrancy. Rue

Cler remains my favorite market street (see the Rue Cler Walk chapter), but many of its down-and-dirty shops are being replaced by trendy restaurants with crowds of tourists. For a real market street serving village Paris, stroll down rue des Martyrs (note that market streets are generally quiet on Sun from 12:00 on, all day Mon, and the rest of the week from 12:00 to 15:00, when shops close for a break).

Entering rue des Martyrs, you pass into a finer neighborhood with broader streets, richer buildings...and signs of the reality of raising a family in an urban setting. Security can be a concern. The school immediately on your right has barriers to keep possible car bombs at a distance. (Since terrorist attacks rocked Paris decades ago, there's been no parking in front of schools or near buildings that serve a predominantly Jewish clientele.) Several side streets are "*voie privée*"—private lanes or high-rise, gated communities.

Slalom past people strolling dogs and babies. Goods spill out onto the sidewalk. People know their butcher and baker as if they lived in a village. Locals willingly pay more in a shop that's not part of a chain. At #58, the traditional charcuterie still sells various meats, but it's morphed with the times into a trendy "*traiteur*" with more variety, food to eat in as well as to go, and prepared dishes sold by weight.

Across the street you'll see one of the countless late-night groceries. These are generally run by North African immigrants who are willing to work the night shift for the convenience of others. Pay attention: Produce with rip-off prices is often priced by the half-kilo.

At #50, a favorite cheesemonger has been serving the neigh-

borhood ever since it actually had goats and cows grazing out back. Notice the marble shelves, old milk jugs, and small artisanal cheeses.

The baker at #39 proudly displays his "best baguette in Paris" award from 2007. Across the street, at #46, the Rose Bakery serves a young, affluent, and health-conscious crowd with top-quality organic and vegetarian breakfasts and lunches.

If you're homesick and looking for barbecued chicken or a banana split, walk a few steps up rue Clauzel for the first African American restaurant in Paris—established by Leroy Haynes in 1939 (€14 *plats*, Tue–Sat 19:00–24:00, closed Sun–Mon, tel. 01 48 78 40 63).

Continuing your stroll, take a look at the traditional butcher at #21. You know he's good because the ceiling hooks—where butchers once hung sides of beef—now display a red medallion that certifies the slaughtered cow's quality.

The *pâtisserie* at #22 is worth popping in to see the typically

French works of art. Bakers often make special treats in sync with the season: Easter, Christmas, First Communion, and so on.

Nearby, the tobacco shop/café at #20 is coping well with the recent smoking ban by putting out heaters (in cool weather) and as many tables as will fit on the sidewalk. Shops like this—once run by rural people from what was then France's poorest region, Auvergne—are now generally managed by Chinese immigrants.

At #10, Eat Sushi delivers its food like a pizzeria—notice the motorbikes parked outside. A step above fast food, places like these are trendy, serving modern professionals who don't want to cook after a long day of work.

Just before rue des Martyrs ends at the neighborhood church—the ㉓ Neoclassical Notre-Dame-de-Lorette (circa 1836)—it reaches a commercial climax.

• *Our walk is over. The Métro station Notre-Dame-de-Lorette awaits (on the opposite side of the church that seals the bottom of rue des Martyrs).*

MONTMARTRE WALK

SLEEPING IN PARIS

I've focused most of my recommendations in three safe, handy, and colorful neighborhoods: the village-like rue Cler (near the Eiffel Tower), the artsy and trendy Marais (near place de la Bastille), and the lively and Latin yet classy Luxembourg (on the Left Bank).

For each neighborhood I list good hotels, helpful hints, and a selection of restaurants (see Eating chapter). Before choosing a hotel, read the descriptions of the neighborhoods closely. Each offers different pros and cons, and your neighborhood is as important as your hotel for the success of your trip. Less expensive and less central accommodations are also listed in chapters on Versailles, Chartres, Reims, and More Day Trips (Vaux-le-Vicomte, Fontainebleau, Giverny, Auvers-sur-Oise, and Disneyland Paris). For accommodations near the two major airports, see the Connections chapter.

Reserve ahead for Paris—the sooner, the better. In August and at other times when business is slower, some hotels offer lower rates to fill their rooms. Check their websites for the best deals. For advice on booking rooms, see "Making Reservations" later in this chapter.

Paris is a good hotel city. A comfortable hotel in Paris costs less than a comparable hotel in London, Amsterdam, or Rome. I like places that are clean, small, central, traditional, friendly, and a good value. Most places I list have at least four of these six virtues.

In this book the price for a double room will normally range from €50 (very simple; toilet and shower down the hall) to €450 (grand lobbies, maximum plumbing, and the works), with most clustering around €100–150.

As you look over the listings, you'll notice that some hotels promise special prices to my readers who book direct (without using a room-finding service or hotel-booking website, which take a commission). To get these rates, mention this book when you reserve (for online reservations, you may be asked to enter a special code listed with the hotel description), then show the book upon arrival. Discounts may not apply towards promotional rates.

Types of Accommodations

Hotels

The French have a simple hotel rating system based on amenities (zero through four stars, indicated in this book by * through ****). One star is modest, two has most of the comforts, and three is generally just a two-star with a fancier lobby and more elaborately designed rooms. Four stars offer more luxury than you have time to appreciate. Two- and three-star hotels are required to have an English-speaking staff, though virtually all hotels I recommend have someone who speaks English (unless I note otherwise in the listing).

Generally, the number of stars does not reflect room size or guarantee quality. Some two-star hotels are better than many three-star hotels. One- and two-star hotels are inexpensive, but some three-star (and even a few four-star hotels) offer good value, justifying the extra cost. Unclassified hotels (no stars) can be bargains or depressing dumps.

Old, characteristic, budget Parisian hotels have always been cramped. Retrofitted with toilets, private showers, and elevators (as most are today), they are even more cramped.

Most hotels have lots of doubles and a few singles, triples, and quads. Traveling alone can be expensive, as singles (except for the rare closet-type rooms that fit only one twin bed) are simply doubles used by one person—so they cost about the same as a double. Room prices vary within each hotel depending on size and whether the room has a bath or shower, and twin beds or a double bed (tubs and twins cost more than showers and double beds). A triple and a double are often the same room, with a double or queen-size bed plus a sliver-sized single. Quad rooms usually have two double beds. Hotels cannot legally allow more in the room than what's shown on their price list. Modern hotels generally have a few family-friendly rooms that open up to each other (*chambres communiquantes*).

If you're on a budget, ask for a cheaper room or a discount (mention this book). Ask if staying for three or more nights will reduce the price. People traveling off-season can show up without reservations and find substantial discounts.

French hotels must charge a daily room tax *(taxe du séjour)* of about €1–2 per person per day. Some hotels include it in the price list, but most add it to your bill.

Types of Rooms

Study the price list on the hotel's website or posted at the desk, so you know your options. Receptionists often don't mention the cheaper rooms—they assume you want a private bathroom or a bigger room. Here are the types of rooms and beds:

une chambre sans douche et WC	room without a private shower or toilet (uncommon these days)
une chambre avec cabinet de toilette	room with a toilet but no shower (some hotels charge for down-the-hall showers)
une chambre avec bain et WC	room with private bathtub and toilet
une chambre avec douche et WC	room with private shower and toilet
chambres communiquantes	connecting rooms (ideal for families)
un grand lit	double bed (55 inches wide)
deux petits lits	twin beds (30–36 inches wide)
un lit single	a true single room
un lit de cent-soixante	queen-size bed (literally 160 centimeters, or 63 inches wide)
le king size	king-size bed (usually two twins pushed together)
un lit pliant	folding bed
un berceau	baby crib
un lit d'enfant	child's bed

You can save as much as €25 by finding the rare room without a private shower or toilet. A room with a bathtub costs €10–15 more than a room with a shower and is generally larger. Hotels often have more rooms with tubs than showers and are inclined to give you a room with a tub (which the French prefer).

A double bed is usually cheaper than twins, though rooms with twin beds tend to be larger, and French double beds are smaller than American double beds. Many hotels have queen-size beds (a bed that's 63 inches wide—most doubles are 55). To learn if a hotel has queen-size beds, ask, *"Avez-vous des lits de cent-soixante?"* (ah-vay-voo day lee duh sahn-swah-sahnt). Some hotels push two twins together under king-size sheets and blankets to make *le king size*.

If you prefer a double bed (instead of twins) and a shower (instead of a tub), you need to ask for it—and you'll save up to €30

Sleep Code

(€1 = about $1.40, country code: 33)

To help you easily sort through these listings, I've divided the rooms into three categories based on the price for a standard double room with bath:

$$$ Higher Priced: Most rooms €150 or more.
$$ Moderately Priced: Most rooms €100–150.
$ Lower Priced: Most rooms €100 or less.

To give maximum information in a minimum of space, I use the following code to describe the accommodations. Prices listed are per room, not per person. When a price range is given for a type of room (such as "Db-€140–180"), it means the price fluctuates with the season, size of room, or length of stay.

S = Single room (or price for one person in a double).
D = Double or twin room.
T = Triple (generally a double bed with a single).
Q = Quad (usually two double beds).
b = Private bathroom with toilet and shower or tub.
s = Private shower or tub only (the toilet is down the hall).
* = French hotel rating system, ranging from zero to four stars.

According to this code, a couple staying at a "Db-€140" hotel would pay a total of €140 per night (about $200) for a double room with a private bathroom. You can assume a hotel takes credit cards unless you see "cash only" in the listing. Unless otherwise noted, hotel staff speak basic English and breakfast is not included (but is usually optional).

All hotels in these listings have elevators, air-conditioning, Internet access (usually a computer available to guests), and Wi-Fi for travelers with laptops, unless otherwise noted. "Wi-Fi only" means there's no public computer available (but you can get online if you have your own laptop).

at more expensive hotels. If you'll take either twins or a double, ask generically for *une chambre pour deux* (room for two) to avoid being needlessly turned away.

Hotels lobbies, halls, and breakfast rooms are off-limits to smokers, though smokers can light up in their rooms. Still, I rarely smell any smoke in my rooms. Some hotels have nonsmoking rooms or floors—ask about them if this is important to you.

Keep Cool

If you're planning to visit Paris in the summer, the extra expense of an air-conditioned room can be money well spent. Most hotel rooms with air-conditioners come with a control stick (like a TV remote) that generally has the same symbols and features: fan icon (click to toggle through wind power, from light to gale); louver icon (choose steady airflow or waves); snowflake and sunshine icons (cold air or heat, depending on season); clock ("O" setting: run X hours before turning off; "I" setting: wait X hours to start); and the temperature control (20 or 21 degrees Celsius is comfortable; also see thermometer diagram on page 594).

Most hotels offer some kind of breakfast (see the Eating chapter for details). Only a few hotels include it the room rates (I've indicated this in the listings)—pay attention when comparing rates between hotels. Hotels hope you'll buy their breakfast, but it's optional unless otherwise noted; to save money, head to a bakery or café instead.

Rooms are safe. Still, keep cameras and money out of sight. Towels aren't routinely replaced every day; drip-dry and conserve. Extra pillows (and extra blankets) are sometimes in the closet or available on request. To get a pillow, ask for *"Un oreiller, s'il vous plait"* (uhn oh-ray-yay, see voo play).

To turn your TV on, press the channel-up or channel-down button on the remote. If it still doesn't work, see if there's a power button on the TV itself, then press the up or down button again.

Get advice from your hotel for safe parking. Consider long-term parking at either airport—Orly is closer and easier for drivers to navigate than Charles de Gaulle. Garages are plentiful (€20–30/day, with special rates through some hotels). Curb parking is free at night (19:00–9:00), all day Sunday, and throughout the month of August. (For more information, see "Parking in Paris" at the end of the Connections chapter.)

Your hotelier, a good source of advice, can direct you to the nearest Internet café (*café internet*, kah-fay an-ter-net) and self-service launderette (*laverie automatique*, lah-vay-ree oh-to-mah-teek). To avoid the time-wasting line at the reception desk in the morning, ask if you can settle your bill the evening before you leave.

Hostels

Parisian hostels charge about €23–34 per bed. Travelers of any age are welcome if they don't mind dorm-style accommodations and meeting other travelers. Cheap meals are sometimes available, and kitchen facilities may be available for do-it-yourselfers. Hostelling International hostels (also known as official hostels) require a hostel membership and charge a few extra euros for nonmembers. If you'll be staying for several days in an official hostel, consider buying a membership card before you go (www.hihostels.com). Hostels that have no such requirements are called independent hostels.

Apartments

It's easy, though not necessarily cheaper, to rent a furnished apartment in Paris. Consider this option if you're either traveling with a family or staying two weeks or longer. For listings, see "For Longer Stays" at the end of this chapter.

Practicalities

Phoning

To call France, you'll need to know its country code: 33. To call France from the US or Canada, dial 011-33-local number (without the initial 0). If calling France from another European country, dial 00-33-local number (without the initial 0). For more information on telephoning, see page 576.

Making Reservations

Given the quality of the accommodations I've found for this book, I recommend that you reserve your rooms in advance, particularly if you'll be traveling during peak season. Book several months ahead, or as soon as you've pinned down your travel dates. Conventions clog Paris in September (worst), October, May, and June (very tough). Note that some national holidays merit your making reservations far in advance (see "Major Holidays and Weekends" on page 4). Just like at home, holidays that fall on a Monday, Thursday, or Friday can turn the weekend into a long one, so book the entire weekend well in advance.

Requesting a Reservation: To reserve, contact hotels directly by email, phone, or fax. Email is the clearest and most economical way to make a reservation. Or you can go straight to the hotel website; many have secure online reservation forms and can instantly inform you of availability and any special deals. But be sure you use the hotel's official site and not a booking agency's site—otherwise you may pay higher rates than you should. If you're phoning from the US, be mindful of time zones (see page 7). Most hotels listed are accustomed to guests who speak only English.

The hotelier will want to know these key pieces of information (also included in the sample request form on page 596 and at www .ricksteves.com/reservation):

- number and type of rooms
- number of nights
- date of arrival
- date of departure
- any special needs (e.g., bathroom in the room or down the hall, twin beds vs. double bed, air-conditioning, quiet, view, ground floor, etc.)

When you request a room, use the European style for writing dates: day/month/year. For example, for a two-night stay in July, I would request: "1 double room for 2 nights, arrive 16/07/10, depart 18/07/10." (Consider carefully how long you'll stay; don't just assume you can extend your reservation for extra days once you arrive.)

If you don't get a reply to your email or fax, it usually means the hotel is already fully booked (but you can try sending the message again, or call to follow up).

Confirming a Reservation: If the hotel's response tells you its room availability and rates, it's not a confirmation. You must tell them that you want that room at the given rate. The hotelier will sometimes request your credit-card number for a one-night deposit to hold the room. Though you can email your credit-card information (I do), it's safer to share that personal info by phone, fax, or a secure online reservation form (if the hotel has one on its website).

Canceling a Reservation: If you must cancel your reservation, it's courteous to do so with as much advance notice as possible—at least three days. Simply make a quick phone call or send an email. Family-run hotels and *chambres d'hôte* lose money if they turn away customers while holding a room for someone who doesn't show up. Understandably, many hotels bill no-shows for one night.

Hotels in larger cities like Paris sometimes have strict cancellation policies. Some hotels require seven days' notice, while most want three days; otherwise, you might lose a deposit. Or you might be billed for the entire visit if you leave early. Ask about cancellation policies before you book.

If canceling by email, request confirmation that your cancellation was received to avoid being accidentally billed.

Reconfirm Your Reservation: Always call to reconfirm your room reservation a day or two in advance from the road. Smaller hotels and *chambres d'hôte* appreciate knowing your time of arrival. At any hotel, let them know if you'll be arriving after 17:00. On the small chance that a hotel loses track of your reservation, bring along a hard copy of their emailed or faxed confirmation.

Reserving Rooms as You Travel: If you're traveling beyond Paris and enjoy having a flexible itinerary, you can make reservations as you travel, calling hotels or *chambres d'hôte* a few days to a week before your visit. If you prefer the freedom of traveling without any reservations at all, you'll have greater success snaring rooms if you arrive at your destination early in the day. When you anticipate crowds (weekends are worst), call hotels at about 9:00 on the day you plan to arrive, when the hotel clerk knows who'll be checking out and just which rooms will be available. If you encounter a language barrier, ask the fluent receptionist at your current hotel to call for you.

In the Rue Cler Neighborhood

(7th arrondissement, Mo: Ecole Militaire, La Tour Maubourg, or Invalides)
Rue Cler, lined with open-air produce stands six days a week, is a safe, tidy, village-like pedestrian street. It's so French that when I step out of my hotel in the morning, I feel like I must have been a poodle in a previous life. How such coziness lodged itself between the high-powered government district and the wealthy Eiffel Tower and Les Invalides areas, I'll never know. This is a neighborhood of wide, tree-lined boulevards, stately apartment buildings, and lots of Americans. The American Church, American Library, American University, and many of my readers call this area home. Hotels here are relatively spacious and a good value, considering the elegance of the neighborhood and the higher prices of the more cramped hotels in other central areas. And for sightseeing, you're within walking distance of the Eiffel Tower, Army Museum, Seine River, Champs-Elysées, and Orsay and Rodin museums.

Become a local at a rue Cler café for breakfast, or join the afternoon crowd for *une bière pression* (a draft beer). On rue Cler you can eat and browse your way through a street full of cafés, pastry shops, delis, cheese shops, and colorful outdoor produce stalls. Afternoon *boules* (outdoor bowling) on the esplanade des Invalides is a relaxing spectator sport (look for the dirt area to the upper right as you face the front of Les Invalides; see "The Rules of *Boules*" sidebar on the next page). The manicured gardens behind the golden dome of the Army Museum are free, peaceful, and filled with flowers (at southwest corner of grounds, closes at about 19:00).

Although hardly a happening nightlife spot, rue Cler offers many low-impact after-dark activities. Take an evening stroll above the river through the parkway between pont de l'Alma and pont des Invalides. For an after-dinner cruise on the Seine, it's a 15-minute walk to the river and the Bateaux-Mouches (see page 38 in Orientation chapter). For a post-dinner cruise on foot, saunter into Champ de Mars park to admire the glowing Eiffel Tower. For more ideas on Paris after hours, see the Entertainment chapter.

The American Church and Franco-American Center is the

The Rules of *Boules*

Throughout Paris—and particularly on Les Invalides' big "front lawn" near the rue Cler neighborhood—you'll see citizens playing *boules*.

Each player starts with three iron balls, with the object of getting them close to the target, a small wooden ball called a *cochonnet*. The first player tosses the *cochonnet* about 30 feet, then throws the first of his iron balls near the target. The next player takes a turn. As soon as a player's ball is closest, it's the other guy's turn. Once all balls have been lobbed, the score is tallied—the player with the closest ball gets one point for each ball closer to the target than his opponent's. The loser gets zero. Games are generally to 15 points.

A regulation *boules* field is 10 feet by 43 feet, but the game is played everywhere—just scratch a throwing circle in the sand, toss the *cochonnet,* and you're off. Strategists can try to knock the opponent's balls out of position, knock the *cochonnet* itself out of position, or guard their best ball with the other two.

community center for Americans living in Paris. It hosts inter-denominational worship services (every Sun at 9:00 and 11:00) and occasional concerts (most Sun at 17:00 Sept–June—but not every week), and distribute the useful *France-USA Contacts* (reception open Mon–Sat 9:00–12:00 & 13:00–22:00, Sun 14:30–19:00, 65 quai d'Orsay, Mo: Invalides, tel. 01 40 62 05 00, www .acparis.org).

Services: There's a large **post office** at the end of rue Cler on avenue de la Motte-Picquet, and a handy **SNCF Boutique** at 80 rue St. Dominique (Mon–Sat 8:30–19:30, closed Sun, get there when it opens to avoid a long wait). At both of these offices, take a number and wait your turn. A smaller post office is closer to the Eiffel Tower on avenue Rapp, one block past rue St. Dominique toward the river.

Markets: Cross Champ de Mars park to mix it up with bargain-hunters at the twice-weekly open-air market, **Marché Boulevard de Grenelle,** under the Métro, a few blocks south-west of Champ de Mars park (Wed and Sun until 12:30, between Mo: Dupleix and Mo: La Motte-Picquet–Grenelle). Two grocery stores, both on rue de Grenelle, are open until midnight: **Epicerie de la Tour** (at #197) and **Alimentation** (at corner with rue Cler). **Rue St. Dominique** is the area's boutique-browsing street.

Internet Access: Two Internet cafés compete in this neigh-borhood: **Com Avenue** is best (about €5/hr, shareable and multi-use accounts, Mon–Sat 10:00–20:00, closed Sun, 24 rue du

Champ de Mars, tel. 01 45 55 00 07); **Cyber World Café** is more expensive but open later (about €7/hr, Mon–Sat 12:00–22:00, Sun 12:00–20:00, 20 rue de l'Exposition, tel. 01 53 59 96 54).

Laundry: Launderettes are omnipresent; ask your hotel for the nearest. Here are three handy locations: on rue Augereau (between rue St. Dominique and rue de Grenelle), on rue Amélie (between rue St. Dominique and rue de Grenelle), and at the southeast corner of rue Valadon and rue de Grenelle.

Métro Connections: Key Métro stops are Ecole Militaire, La Tour Maubourg, and Invalides. The useful RER-C line runs from the pont de l'Alma and Invalides stations, serving Versailles to the southwest; the Marmottan Museum and Auvers-sur-Oise to the northwest; and the Orsay Museum, Latin Quarter (St. Michel stop), and Austerlitz train station to the east.

Bus Routes: Smart travelers take advantage of these helpful bus routes (see map on the next page for stop locations): Line #69 runs east–west along rue St. Dominique and serves Les Invalides, Orsay, Louvre, Marais, and Père Lachaise Cemetery (Mon–Sat only—no Sun service; see Bus #69 Sightseeing Tour chapter). Line #63 runs along the river (the quai d'Orsay), serving the Latin Quarter along boulevard St. Germain to the east (ending at Gare de Lyon), and Trocadéro and the Marmottan Museum to the west. Line #92 runs along avenue Bosquet, north to the Champs-Elysées and Arc de Triomphe (far better than the Métro) and south to the Montparnasse Tower and Gare Montparnasse. Line #87 runs from avenue Joseph Bouvard in the Champ de Mars park up avenue de la Bourdonnais and serves St. Sulpice, Luxembourg Garden, the Sèvres-Babylone shopping area, the Bastille, and Gare de Lyon (also more convenient than Métro for these destinations). Line #80 runs on avenue Bosquet, crosses the Champs-Elysées, and serves Gare St. Lazare. Line #28 runs on boulevard de la Tour Maubourg and serves Gare St. Lazare.

In the Heart of Rue Cler

Many of my readers stay in the rue Cler neighborhood. If you want to disappear into Paris, choose a hotel elsewhere. The first six hotels listed below are within Camembert-smelling distance of rue Cler; the others are within a five- to ten-minute stroll.

$$$ Hôtel Relais Bosquet*** is an excellent value with generous public spaces and comfortable rooms that are large by local standards and feature effective darkness blinds. The staff are politely formal and offer free breakfast (good buffet, including eggs and sausage) to anyone booking direct with this book in 2010 (standard Db-€185, bigger Db-€210, check website for special discounts, extra bed-€30, 19 rue du Champ de Mars, tel. 01 47 05 25 45, fax 01 45 55 08 24, www.relaisbosquet.com, hotel@relaisbosquet.com).

Rue Cler Hotels

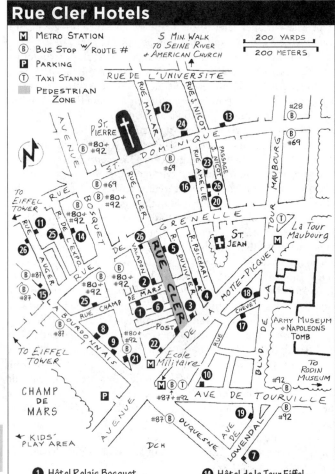

- Ⓜ Metro Station
- Ⓑ Bus Stop w/Route #
- Ⓟ Parking
- Ⓣ Taxi Stand
- ▨ Pedestrian Zone

5 Min. Walk to Seine River & American Church

200 Yards
200 Meters

❶ Hôtel Relais Bosquet
❷ Hôtel du Cadran
❸ Hôtel de la Motte Picquet
❹ Hôtel Beaugency
❺ Grand Hôtel Lévêque
❻ Hôtel du Champ de Mars
❼ Hôtel Duquesne Eiffel
❽ Hôtel La Bourdonnais
❾ Hôtel Eber Mars
❿ Hôtel de Turenne
⓫ Hôtel de Londres Eiffel
⓬ Hôtel de la Tulipe
⓭ Hôtel St. Dominique

⓮ Hôtel de la Tour Eiffel
⓯ Hôtel Kensington
⓰ Hôtel Les Jardins d'Eiffel
⓱ Hôtel Muguet
⓲ Hôtel de l'Empereur
⓳ Hôtel de France
⓴ Best Western Eiffel Park
㉑ Hôtel Prince
㉒ Hôtel Royal Phare
㉓ Paris Home Studios
㉔ SNCF Boutique
㉕ Internet Cafés (2)
㉖ Launderettes (3)

Rue Cler Musts for Temporary Residents

- Watch *boules* action in the afternoon on the Esplanade des Invalides (see "The Rules of *Boules*" sidebar earlier in this chapter).
- Relax in the flowery park at the southwest corner of Les Invalides, where avenue de Tourville meets boulevard de la Tour Maubourg.
- See the Eiffel Tower at night, from the park below and from across the river on Trocadéro Square (dinner picnics are best).
- Linger at a rue Cler café and observe daily life.
- Take a Bateaux-Mouches cruise after dark (see page 38).
- Stroll the paths along the river between the d'Alma and Invalides bridges and see the Invalides dome glow after dark.

$$$ Hôtel du Cadran*, perfectly located a *boule* toss from rue Cler, is daringly modern—with a chocolate shop in the lobby, efficient staff, and stylish rooms featuring cool colors, mood lighting, and every comfort (Db-€210–240, 10 percent discount and free (big) breakfast by entering the code "RickSteves" when you book by email or through their website, discount not valid for promotional rates on website; 10 rue du Champ de Mars, tel. 01 40 62 67 00, fax 01 40 62 67 13, www.hotelducadran.com, info @cadranhotel.com).

$$$ Hôtel de la Motte Picquet*, at the corner of rue Cler and avenue de la Motte-Picquet, is an intimate little place with plush rooms at fair prices (Sb-€150, standard Db-€160, bigger Db-€200, 30 avenue de la Motte-Picquet, tel. 01 47 05 09 57, fax 01 47 05 74 36, www.hotelmottepicquetparis.com, book@hotel mottepicquetparis.com).

$$ Hôtel Beaugency*, a good value on a quieter street a short block off rue Cler, has 30 small rooms with standard furnishings and a lobby you can stretch out in (Sb-€107–117, Db-€117–157, occasional discounts for Rick Steves readers—ask when you book, 21 rue Duvivier, tel. 01 47 05 01 63, fax 01 45 51 04 96, www.hotel -beaugency.com, infos@hotel-beaugency.com).

Warning: The next two hotels are super values, but very busy with my readers (reserve long in advance).

$$ Grand Hôtel Lévêque** faces rue Cler with red and gray tones, a singing maid, and a sliver-sized slow-dance elevator. This busy hotel has a convivial breakfast room but no real lobby. Half the rooms have been renovated and cost more; those on rue Cler come with some noise (S-€75–80, Db-€105–115, Tb-€145–150, 29 rue Cler, tel. 01 47 05 49 15, fax 01 45 50 49 36, www.hotel-leveque.com, info@hotel-leveque.com, helpful staff).

$ Hôtel du Champ de Mars**, with adorable rooms and serious owners Françoise and Stephane, is a cozy rue Cler option. This plush little hotel has a small-town feel from top to bottom. The rooms are snug but lovingly kept, and single rooms can work as tiny doubles. It's an excellent value despite the lack of air-conditioning. This place gets mixed reviews from readers, who wish the management was more professionally good-natured at all times (Sb-€95, Db-€100, 30 yards off rue Cler at 7 rue du Champ de Mars, tel. 01 45 51 52 30, fax 01 45 51 64 36, www.hotelduchampdemars.com, reservation@hotelduchampdemars.com).

Near Rue Cler, Close to Ecole Militaire Métro Stop

The following listings are a five-minute walk from rue Cler, near Métro stop Ecole Militaire or RER: Pont de l'Alma.

$$$ Hôtel Duquesne Eiffel***, a few blocks farther from the action, is calm, hospitable, and expertly run. It features handsome rooms (some with terrific Eiffel Tower views), a welcoming lobby, and a big, hot breakfast for €13 (Db-€180–230, price grows with room size, Tb-€250, 23 avenue Duquesne, tel. 01 44 42 09 09, fax 01 44 42 09 08, www.hde.fr, hotel@hde.fr).

$$$ Hôtel La Bourdonnais*** is *très* Parisian, mixing an Old World feel with creaky, comfortable rooms and generous public spaces. Its mostly spacious rooms are traditionally decorated (Sb-€140, Db-€175, Tb-€195, Qb-€220, Sophie promises a 10 percent discount with this book through 2010, 111 avenue de la Bourdonnais, tel. 01 47 05 45 42, fax 01 45 55 75 54, www.hotel

labourdonnais.fr, hlb@hotellabourdonnais.fr).

$$ Hôtel Eber Mars** has larger-than-most rooms with weathered furnishings, oak-paneled public spaces, and a beam-me-up-Jacques coffin-sized elevator. Half the rooms are newly renovated, air-conditioned, and pricey; the higher rates listed are for those rooms (Db-€130–190, 20 percent cheaper Nov–March and July–Aug, first breakfast free with this book in 2010, 117 avenue de la Bourdonnais, tel. 01 47 05 42 30, fax 01 47 05 45 91, www.hotelebermars.com, reservation@hotelebermars.com, manager Mr. Eber—who looks like Antonio Banderas—is a wealth of information for travelers).

$ Hôtel de Turenne** is modest, with the cheapest air-conditioned rooms I've found and a lobby with windows on the world. Rooms are simple but comfortable, and the price is right. There are five true singles and several connecting rooms good for families (Sb-€70, Db-€84–98, Tb-€120, Wi-Fi only, 20 avenue de Tourville, tel. 01 47 05 99 92, fax 01 45 56 06 04, hotel.turenne .paris7@wanadoo.fr).

Near Rue Cler, Closer to Rue St. Dominique (and the Seine)

$$$ Hôtel de Londres Eiffel*** is my closest listing to the Eiffel Tower and Champ de Mars park. Here you get immaculate, warmly decorated rooms (several are connecting for families), cozy public spaces, and a service-oriented staff. Some rooms are tight—request a bigger room. Show them this book in 2010 for a free Seine cruise (inquire upon arrival). It's less convenient to the Métro (10-min walk) but handy to buses #69 and #87 and to RER-C: Pont de l'Alma (Sb-€165, Db-€185, Db with Eiffel Tower view-€195–215, Tb-€245, 1 rue Augereau, tel. 01 45 51 63 02, fax 01 47 05 28 96, www.londres-eiffel.com, info@londres-eiffel.com). The owners have a good two-star hotel with similar comfort in the cheaper Montparnasse area, Hôtel Apollon Montparnasse (Db-€110–132, 91 rue de l'Ouest, Mo: Pernety, tel. & fax 01 43 95 62 00, www.paris-hotel-paris.net, apollonm@wanadoo.fr).

$$$ Hôtel de la Tulipe***, three blocks from rue Cler toward the river, is a bit pricey but unique. The 20 small but artistically decorated rooms—each one different—come with stylish little bathrooms and surround a seductive, wood-beamed lounge and a peaceful, leafy courtyard (Db-€160, Tb-€180, two-room suite for up to five people-€280, friendly staff, no air-con, no elevator, pay Wi-Fi, 33 rue Malar, tel. 01 45 51 67 21, fax 01 47 53 96 37, www .paris-hotel-tulipe.com, hoteldelatulipe@wanadoo.fr).

$$ Hôtel St. Dominique**, well-located in the thick of rue St. Dominique, has fair rates, formal service, an inviting lobby, a small courtyard, and traditionally decorated rooms—most with minibars (Db-€140–160, extra bed-€20, no air-con, no elevator, Wi-Fi only, 62 rue St. Dominique, tel. 01 47 05 51 44, fax 01 47 05 81 28, www.hotelstdominique.com, saint-dominique .reservations@wanadoo.fr).

$ Hôtel de la Tour Eiffel** is a terrific two-star value on a quiet street near several of my favorite restaurants. The rooms are well-designed, spotless, and comfortable (snug Db-€79, bigger Db-€105–115, no air-con, Wi-Fi only, 17 rue de l'Exposition, tel. 01 47 05 14 75, fax 01 47 53 99 46, www.hotel-toureiffel.com, hte7 @wanadoo.fr).

$ Hôtel Kensington** is a good budget value close to the Eiffel Tower and run by elegant Daniele. It's an unpretentious place with mostly small, simple, but well-kept rooms (Sb-€62, Db-€79, big Db on back side-€94, Eiffel Tower views for those who ask, no air-con, no Internet access, 79 avenue de la Bourdonnais, tel. 01 47 05 74 00, fax 01 47 05 25 81, www.hotel-kensington.com, hk @hotel-kensington.com).

Near La Tour Maubourg Métro Stop

The next four listings are within three blocks of the intersection of avenue de la Motte-Picquet and boulevard de la Tour Maubourg.

$$$ Hôtel Les Jardins d'Eiffel***, on a quiet street, feels like the modern motel it is, with professional service, its own parking garage (€24/day), and a spacious lobby (Sb/Db-€170–230; 15 percent Rick Steves discount when you book direct through 2010, or check website for special discounts; 8 rue Amélie, tel. 01 47 05 46 21, fax 01 45 55 28 08, www.hoteljardinseiffel.com, paris@hotel jardinseiffel.com).

$$ Hôtel Muguet***, a peaceful, stylish, immaculate refuge, gives you three-star comfort for a two-star price. This delightful spot offers 43 tasteful rooms, a greenhouse lounge, and a small garden courtyard. The hands-on owner, Catherine, gives her guests a restful and secure home in Paris (Sb-€110, Db-€145–155, Db with view-€170–190, Tb-€190, 11 rue Chevert, tel. 01 47 05 05 93, fax 01 45 50 25 37, www.hotelmuguet.com, muguet@wanadoo.fr, gentle Jacqueline runs reception).

$$ Hôtel de l'Empereur** lacks intimacy or a personal touch but is a good value with 38 pleasant rooms featuring real wood furniture. Fifth-floor rooms have small balconies with Napoleonic views (Db-€112, Tb-€145, Qb-€165, 2 rue Chevert, tel. 01 45 55 88 02, fax 01 45 51 88 54, www.hotelempereur.com, contact@hotel empereur.com).

$$ Hôtel de France** is a good midrange option away from most other hotels I list. It's well-run by a brother-sister team (Alain and Marie-Héléne) with a small bar/lounge and 60 fairly priced and well-maintained rooms, some with knockout views of the golden dome of Invalides. Rooms on the courtyard are very quiet (Sb-€95, standard Db-€115, bigger Db-€155, Tb-€165, connecting rooms possible for families, no air-con, 102 boulevard de La Tour Maubourg, tel. 01 47 05 40 49, fax 01 45 56 96 78, www .hoteldefrance.com, hoteldefrance@wanadoo.fr).

Lesser Values in the Rue Cler Area

Given how fine this area is, these are acceptable last choices.

$$$ Best Western Eiffel Park*** is a dead-quiet concrete business hotel with all the comforts, a comfy lobby, 36 pleasant if unexceptional rooms, and a rooftop terrace (Db-€240, bigger "luxe" Db-€260, check online for promotional rates, 17 bis rue Amélie, tel. 01 45 55 10 01, fax 01 47 05 28 68, www.eiffelpark.com, reservation@eiffelpark.com).

$$ Hôtel Prince**, across from the Ecole Militaire Métro stop, has a spartan lobby, drab halls, and plain-but-acceptable rooms for the price (Sb-€90, Db with shower-€115, Db with tub-€130, Tb-€150, no Internet access, 66 avenue Bosquet, tel. 01 47 05 40 90, fax 01 47 53 06 62, www.hotelparisprince.com, paris @hotel-prince.com).

$ Hôtel Royal Phare**, facing the busy Ecole Militaire Métro stop, is a humble place. The 34 basic, pastel rooms are unimaginative but sleepable. Rooms on the courtyard are quietest, with peek-a-boo views of the Eiffel Tower from the fifth floor up (Sb-€80, Db with shower-€88–100, Db with tub-€120, Tb-€120, fridges in rooms, no air-con, no Wi-Fi, 40 avenue de la Motte-Picquet, tel. 01 47 05 57 30, fax 01 45 51 64 41, www.hotel-royalphare-paris .com, hotel-royalphare@wanadoo.fr, friendly manager Hocin).

In the Marais Neighborhood

(4th arrondissement, Mo: Bastille, St. Paul, and Hôtel de Ville)
Those interested in a more SoHo/Greenwich Village–type locale should make the Marais their Parisian home. Once a forgotten Parisian backwater, the Marais is now one of Paris' most popular residential, tourist, and shopping areas. This is jumbled, medieval Paris at its finest, where classy stone mansions sit alongside trendy bars, antiques shops, and fashion-conscious boutiques. The streets are a fascinating parade of artists, students, tourists, immigrants, and baguette-munching babies in strollers. The Marais is also known as a hub of the Parisian gay and lesbian scene. This area is *sans doute* livelier (and louder) than the rue Cler area.

In the Marais you have these major sights close at hand: the Carnavalet Museum, Victor Hugo's House, the Jewish Art and History Museum, the Pompidou Center, and the Picasso Museum (closed for a multiyear renovation). You're also a manageable walk from Paris' two islands (Ile St. Louis and Ile de la Cité), home to Notre-Dame and Sainte-Chapelle. The Opéra Bastille, Promenade Plantée park, place des Vosges (Paris' oldest square), Jewish Quarter (rue des Rosiers), and nightlife-packed rue de Lappe are also walkable. (For Marais sight descriptions, see page 75; for the Opéra, see the Marais Walk chapter.)

Most of my recommended hotels are located a few blocks north of the Marais' main east–west drag, rue St. Antoine/rue de Rivoli.

Tourist Information: The nearest TI is in Gare de Lyon (Mon–Sat 8:00–18:00, closed Sun, all-Paris TI tel. 08 92 68 30 00).

Services: Most banks and other services are on the main street, rue de Rivoli, which becomes rue St. Antoine. Marais **post offices** are on rue Castex and at the corner of rue Pavée and rue des Francs Bourgeois. There's a busy **SNCF Boutique** where you can take care of all train needs on rue St. Antoine at rue de Turenne (Mon–Sat 8:30–20:30, closed Sun). A quieter SNCF Boutique is nearer Gare de Lyon at 5 rue de Lyon (Mon–Sat 8:30–18:00, closed Sun).

Markets: The Marais has two good open-air markets: the sprawling **Marché de la Bastille,** around place de la Bastille (Thu and Sun until 12:30); and the more intimate, untouristy **Marché de la place d'Aligre** (Tue–Sun 9:00–14:00, closed Mon, cross place de la Bastille and walk about 10 blocks down rue du Faubourg St. Antoine, turn right at rue de Cotte to place d'Aligre; or, take Métro line 8 from Bastille in the direction of Créteil-Préfecture, get off at the Ledru-Rollin stop, and walk a few blocks southeast). A small **grocery shop** is open until 23:00 on rue St. Antoine (near intersection with rue Castex). To shop at a Parisian Sears, find the **BHV** next to Hôtel de Ville.

Bookstore: The Marais is home to the friendliest English-language bookstore in Paris, **Red Wheelbarrow.** Penelope sells most of my guidebooks at good prices, and carries a great collection of other books about Paris and France for both adults and children (Mon 10:00–18:00, Tue–Sat 10:00–19:00, Sun 14:00–18:00, 22 rue St. Paul, Mo: St. Paul, tel. 01 48 04 75 08).

Internet Access: Try **Paris CY** (Mon–Sat 8:00–20:00, Sun 13:00–20:00, 8 rue de Jouy, Mo: St. Paul, tel. 01 42 71 37 37).

Laundry: There are many launderettes; ask your hotelier for the nearest. Here are three you can count on: on impasse Guéménée (north of rue St. Antoine), on rue Ste. Croix de la Bretonnerie (just east of rue du Temple), and on rue du Petit Musc (south of rue St. Antoine).

Métro Connections: Key Métro stops in the Marais are, from east to west: Bastille, St. Paul, and Hôtel de Ville (Sully-Morland, Pont Marie, and Rambuteau stops are also handy). Métro connections are excellent, with direct service to the Louvre, Champs-Elysées, Arc de Triomphe, and La Défense (all on line 1); the rue Cler area and Opéra Garnier (line 8 from Bastille stop); and four major train stations: Gare de Lyon, Gare du Nord, Gare de l'Est, and Gare d'Austerlitz (all accessible from Bastille stop).

Bus Routes: Line #69 on rue St. Antoine takes you eastbound to Père Lachaise Cemetery and westbound to the Louvre, Orsay, and Rodin museums, plus the Army Museum, ending at the Eiffel Tower (Mon–Sat only—no Sun service; see Bus #69 Sightseeing Tour chapter). Line #86 runs down boulevard Henri IV, crossing Ile St. Louis and serving the Latin Quarter along boulevard St. Germain. Line #87 follows a similar route, but also serves Gare de

Marais Musts for Temporary Residents

- Have dinner or a drink on place du Marché Ste. Catherine.
- Dine or enjoy a drink on place des Vosges.
- Take a late-night art gallery stroll around place des Vosges.
- Stroll the Promenade Plantée elevated park (see page 78).
- Mix it up with local shoppers one morning at the Marché de la place d'Aligre.
- Walk the Ile St. Louis after dark and enjoy the floodlit view of Notre-Dame (see page 450).
- Follow the Marais Boutique Stroll described in the Shopping chapter (best on Sunday afternoon).

Lyon to the east and the Eiffel Tower and rue Cler neighborhood to the west. Line #96 runs on rues Turenne and François Miron and serves the Louvre and boulevard St. Germain (near Luxembourg Garden), ending at Gare Montparnasse. Line #65 runs from Gare de Lyon up rue de Lyon, around place de la Bastille, and then up boulevard Beaumarchais to Gare de l'Est and Gare du Nord.

Taxis: You'll find taxi stands on place de la Bastille (where boulevard Richard Lenoir meets the square), on the south side of rue St. Antoine (in front of St. Paul Church), behind the Hôtel de Ville on rue du Lobau (where it meets rue de Rivoli), and a quieter one on the north side of rue St. Antoine (where it meets rue Castex).

Near Place des Vosges

$$$ **Hôtel Castex***, a well-managed place with tile floors and dark wood accents, lies on a quiet street near place de la Bastille. A clever system of connecting rooms allows families total privacy between two rooms, each with its own bathroom. The 30 rooms are narrow but tasteful; it's a good value year-round. Your fourth night is free in August and from November through February, except around New Year's (Sb-€125, Db-€155, Tb-€220, 5 percent discount and free buffet breakfast with this book through 2010, just off place de la Bastille and rue St. Antoine at 5 rue Castex, Mo: Bastille, tel. 01 42 72 31 52, fax 01 42 72 57 91, www.castexhotel.com, info@castexhotel.com).

$$$ **Hôtel Bastille Spéria***, a short block off place de la Bastille, offers business-type service in a great location. The 42 well-configured rooms are modern and comfortable, with big beds (Sb-€140, Db-€160–180, child's bed-€20, good buffet breakfast-€13, 1 rue de la Bastille, Mo: Bastille, tel. 01 42 72 04 01, fax 01 42 72 56 38, www.hotelsperia.com, info@hotelsperia.com).

Marais Hotels

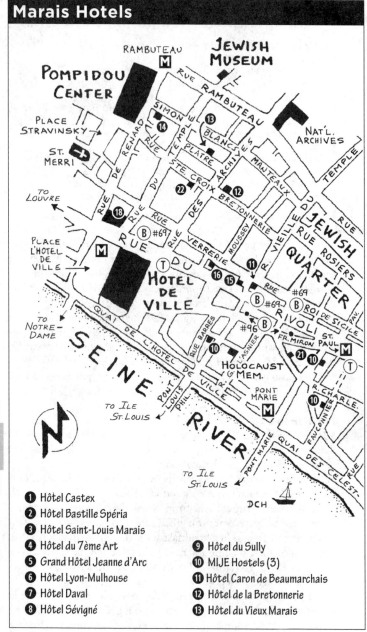

SLEEPING IN PARIS

1 Hôtel Castex
2 Hôtel Bastille Spéria
3 Hôtel Saint-Louis Marais
4 Hôtel du 7ème Art
5 Grand Hôtel Jeanne d'Arc
6 Hôtel Lyon-Mulhouse
7 Hôtel Daval
8 Hôtel Sévigné

9 Hôtel du Sully
10 MIJE Hostels (3)
11 Hôtel Caron de Beaumarchais
12 Hôtel de la Bretonnerie
13 Hôtel du Vieux Marais

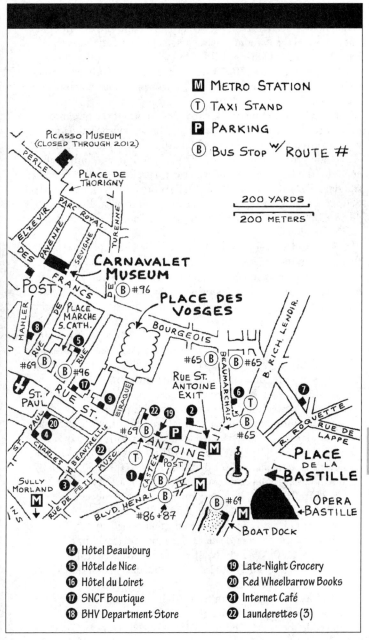

M METRO STATION

T TAXI STAND

P PARKING

B BUS STOP w/ ROUTE #

200 YARDS
200 METERS

PICASSO MUSEUM
(CLOSED THROUGH 2012)

PERLE

PLACE DE THORIGNY

ELZEVIR

PARC ROYAL

PAYENNE

TURENNE

DES

SEVIGNE

CARNAVALET MUSEUM

DE

POST

FRANCS

B #96

PLACE DES VOSGES

MAHLER

RUE

PLACE MARCHE S. CATH.

B

#69

B #96

RUE

BOURGEOIS

BEAUMARCHAIS

B. RICH. LENOIR.

#65 B

B #65

RUE ST. ANTOINE EXIT

B 6

T

ST. PAUL

RUE ST.

BRAQUE

B #65

7

R. ROQUETTE

RUE DE LAPPE

ST. PAUL

CHARLES

BEAUTRELLIS

RED WHEELBARROW

#69 B

P

ANTOINE

M

PLACE DE LA BASTILLE

SULLY MORLAND

M

RUE DE PETIT MUSC

CASTEX

POST

IV

T

BLVD. HENRI

B

#86 + 87

M

B #69

M

OPERA BASTILLE

BOAT DOCK

SLEEPING IN PARIS

14 Hôtel Beaubourg
15 Hôtel de Nice
16 Hôtel du Loiret
17 SNCF Boutique
18 BHV Department Store

19 Late-Night Grocery
20 Red Wheelbarrow Books
21 Internet Café
22 Launderettes (3)

$$ Hôtel Saint-Louis Marais** is a little hotel tucked away on a quiet residential street between the river and rue St. Antoine. The lobby and the 19 rooms have character but need attention (small Db-€115, standard Db-€140, Tb-€160, no air-con, no elevator, pay Wi-Fi only, parking-€20, 1 rue Charles V, Mo: Sully Morland, tel. 01 48 87 87 04, fax 01 48 87 33 26, www.saintlouismarais.com, marais@saintlouishotels.com).

$$ Hôtel du 7ème Art**, two blocks south of rue St. Antoine toward the river, is a young, carefree, Hollywood-nostalgia place with a full-service café-bar and Charlie Chaplin murals. Its 23 good-value rooms have brown 1970s decor, but are comfortable enough. The large rooms are American-spacious (small Db-€93, standard Db-€105, large Db-€120–150, Tb-€140–170, extra bed-€20, no elevator, pay Wi-Fi, 20 rue St. Paul, Mo: St. Paul, tel. 01 44 54 85 00, fax 01 42 77 69 10, www.paris-hotel-7art.com, hotel 7art@wanadoo.fr).

$ Grand Hôtel Jeanne d'Arc**, a lovely little hotel with thoughtfully appointed rooms, is ideally located for (and very popular with) connoisseurs of the Marais. It's a fine value and worth booking way ahead (three months in advance, if possible). Sixth-floor rooms have views, and corner rooms are wonderfully bright in the City of Light. Rooms on the street can be noisy until the bars close (Sb-€62–89, Db-€89, larger twin Db-€116, Tb-€146, good Qb-€160, no air-con, no Internet access, 3 rue de Jarente, Mo: St. Paul, tel. 01 48 87 62 11, fax 01 48 87 37 31, information @hoteljeannedarc.com, www.hoteljeannedarc.com).

$ Hôtel Lyon-Mulhouse**, well-managed by gregarious Nathalia, is located on a busy street barely off place de la Bastille. Though less intimate than some, it is a solid deal, with pleasant, relatively large rooms—five are true singles with partial Eiffel Tower views (Sb-€74, Db-€100, Tb-€130, Qb-€150, pay Wi-Fi, 8 boulevard Beaumarchais, Mo: Bastille, tel. 01 47 00 91 50, fax 01 47 00 06 31, www.1-hotel-paris.com, hotelyonmulhouse@wanadoo.fr).

$ Hôtel Daval**, an unassuming place on the *wild side* of place de la Bastille, is ideal for night owls. Rooms are tiny, halls are narrow, but rates are good and it's air-conditioned. Ask for a quieter room on the courtyard side if sleep matters (Sb-€76, Db-€88, Tb-115, Qb-€130, Wi-Fi only, 21 rue Daval, Mo: Bastille, tel. 01 47 00 51 23, fax 01 40 21 80 26, www.hoteldaval.com, hoteldaval @wanadoo.fr, Didier).

$ Hôtel Sévigné**, run by straight-faced owner Monsieur Mercier, is a snappy little hotel with lavender halls and 30 tidy, comfortable rooms at good prices (Sb-€70, Db-€84–95, Tb-€98–115; one-night, no-refund policy for any cancellation; Wi-Fi only, 2 rue Malher, Mo: St. Paul, tel. 01 42 72 76 17, fax 01 42 78 68 26, www.le-sevigne.com, contact@le-sevigne.com).

SLEEPING IN PARIS

$ Hôtel du Sully, sitting right on rue St. Antoine, is basic, cheap, and central. The entry is narrow, and the rooms are frumpy and dimly lit but sleepable. It's a fair deal and run by friendly Monsieur Zeroual (Db-€65, Tb-€80, Qb-€90, no elevator, no air-con, Wi-Fi only, 48 rue St. Antoine, Mo: St. Paul, tel. 01 42 78 49 32, fax 01 44 61 76 50, www.sullyhotelparis.com, sullyhotel @orange.fr).

$ *MIJE Youth Hostels:* The Maison Internationale de la Jeunesse et des Etudiants (MIJE) runs three classy old residences, ideal for budget travelers. Each is well-maintained, with simple, clean, single-sex (unless your group takes a whole room), one- to four-bed rooms for travelers of any age. The hostels are **MIJE Fourcy** (biggest and loudest, €11 dinners available with a membership card, 6 rue de Fourcy, just south of rue de Rivoli), **MIJE Fauconnier** (no elevator, 11 rue du Fauconnier), and **MIJE Maubisson** (smallest and quietest, no outdoor terrace, 12 rue des Barres). None has double beds or air-conditioning; all have private showers in every room (all prices per person: Sb-€50, Db-€37, Tb-€33, Qb-€31, credit cards accepted, includes breakfast but not towels, required membership card-€2.50 extra/person, 7-day maximum stay, rooms locked 12:00–15:00, curfew at 1:00 in the morning). They all share the same contact information (tel. 01 42 74 23 45, fax 01 40 27 81 64, www.mije.com, info @mije.com) and Métro stop (St. Paul). Reservations are accepted (six weeks ahead online, 10 days ahead by phone)—though you must show up by noon, or call the morning of arrival to confirm a later arrival time.

Near the Pompidou Center

These hotels are farther west, closer to the Pompidou Center than to place de la Bastille. The Hôtel de Ville Métro stop works well for all of these hotels, unless a closer stop is noted.

$$$ Hôtel Caron de Beaumarchais*** on a busy corner, feels like a fluffy folk museum, with 20 lovingly cared-for and character-filled rooms. Its small lobby is cluttered with bits from an elegant 18th-century Marais house (small Db in back-€152, larger Db facing the front-€170, Wi-Fi only, 12 rue Vieille du Temple, tel. 01 42 72 34 12, fax 01 42 72 34 63, www.carondebeaumarchais.com, hotel@carondebeaumarchais.com).

$$ Hôtel de la Bretonnerie***, three blocks from the Hôtel de Ville, makes a fine Marais home. It has a warm, welcoming lobby and 29 tastefully appointed, good-value rooms with an antique, open-beam warmth (perfectly good standard "classic" Db-€135, bigger "charming" Db-€165, Db suite-€195, Tb/Qb-€200, Tb/Qb suite-€220, no air-con, between rue Vieille du Temple and rue des Archives at 22 rue Ste. Croix de la Bretonnerie, tel. 01 48 87 77 63, fax 01 42 77 26 78, www.bretonnerie.com, hotel@bretonnerie.com).

\$\$ Hôtel du Vieux Marais**, with a quirky owner and modern rooms that should all be renovated by the time you get here, lies on a quiet street two blocks east of the Pompidou Center. Say *bonjour* to friendly bulldog Leelou, who runs the small lobby (Sb-€110–125, Db-€130–165, Wi-Fi only, just off rue des Archives at 8 rue du Plâtre, Mo: Rambuteau or Hôtel de Ville, tel. 01 42 78 47 22, fax 01 42 78 34 32, www.vieuxmarais.com, hotel@vieuxmarais .com).

\$\$ Hôtel Beaubourg*** is a solid three-star value on a small street in the shadow of the Pompidou Center. The lounge is inviting, and the 28 rooms are comfy, well-appointed, and quiet (standard Db-€140, bigger twin Db-€160, rates vary wildly by season, 11 rue Simon Le Franc, Mo: Rambuteau, tel. 01 42 74 34 24, fax 01 42 78 68 11, www.hotelbeaubourg.com, reservation@hotel beaubourg.com).

\$\$ Hôtel de Nice**, on the Marais' busy main drag, features a turquoise-and-fuchsia "Marie-Antoinette-does-tie-dye" decor. Its narrow halls are littered with paintings and layered with carpets, and its 23 Old-World rooms have thoughtful touches and tight bathrooms. Twin rooms, which cost the same as doubles, are larger and on the street side—but have effective double-paned windows (Sb-€90, Db-€120, Tb-€145, extra bed-€25, Wi-Fi only, reception on second floor, 42 bis rue de Rivoli, tel. 01 42 78 55 29, fax 01 42 78 36 07, www.hoteldenice.com, contact@hoteldenice.com, laissez-faire management).

\$ Hôtel du Loiret* is a centrally located (some noise) and rare Marais budget hotel. If you can get past the lobby, you'll be surprised at how much better the rooms are (S with WC across hall-€50, Db-€70–90, Tb-€100, no air-con, pay Internet access, no Wi-Fi, 8 rue des Mauvais Garçons, tel. 01 48 87 77 00, fax 01 48 04 96 56, www.hotel-loiret.fr, hotelduloiret@hotmail.com).

In the Historic Core, on Ile St. Louis

The peaceful, residential character of this river-wrapped island, its brilliant location, and its homemade ice cream have drawn Americans for decades, allowing hotels to charge dearly. There are no budget values here, but the island's village ambience and proximity to the Marais, Notre-Dame, and the Latin Quarter help compensate for higher rates. All of the following hotels are on the island's main drag, rue St. Louis-en-l'Ile, where I list several restaurants (see page 410 in the Eating chapter). Use Mo: Pont Marie or Sully-Morland.

\$\$\$ Hôtel du Jeu de Paume****, occupying a 17th-century tennis center, is the most expensive hotel I list in Paris. When you

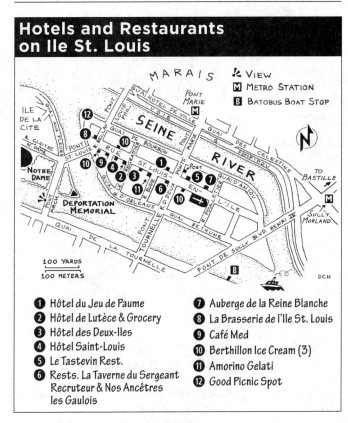

Hotels and Restaurants on Ile St. Louis

View
M Metro Station
B Batobus Boat Stop

- ❶ Hôtel du Jeu de Paume
- ❷ Hôtel de Lutèce & Grocery
- ❸ Hôtel des Deux-Iles
- ❹ Hôtel Saint-Louis
- ❺ Le Tastevin Rest.
- ❻ Rests. La Taverne du Sergeant Recruteur & Nos Ancêtres les Gaulois
- ❼ Auberge de la Reine Blanche
- ❽ La Brasserie de l'Ile St. Louis
- ❾ Café Med
- ❿ Berthillon Ice Cream (3)
- ⓫ Amorino Gelati
- ⓬ Good Picnic Spot

enter its magnificent lobby, you'll understand why. Greet Scoop, *le chien*, then take a spin in the glass elevator for a half-timbered-tree-house experience. The 30 quite comfortable rooms are carefully designed and *très* tasteful, though small for the price (you're paying for the location and public spaces—check for deals on their website). Most rooms face a small garden; all are pin-drop peaceful (Sb-€190–290, standard Db-€285, larger Db-€370, deluxe Db-€450, €18 breakfast, 54 rue St. Louis-en-l'Ile, tel. 01 43 26 14 18, fax 01 40 46 02 76, www.jeudepaumehotel.com, info@jeude paumehotel.com).

$$$ Hôtel de Lutèce*** charges top euro for its island address but comes with a sit-awhile wood-paneled lobby, a real fireplace, and warmly designed rooms. Twin rooms are larger and the same price as double rooms (Db-€200, Tb-€235, 65 rue St. Louis-en-l'Ile, tel. 01 43 26 23 52, fax 01 43 29 60 25, www.hoteldelutece .com, info@hoteldelutece.com).

$$$ Hôtel des Deux-Iles*** is bright and colorful, with marginally smaller rooms than other hotels on this street (Db-€200,

Wi-Fi only, 59 rue St. Louis-en-l'Ile, tel. 01 43 26 13 35, fax 01 43 29 60 25, www.2iles.com, hotel.2iles@free.fr).

$$$ Hôtel Saint-Louis*** has less personality but good enough rooms with parquet floors and comparatively good rates (Db-€150–165, extra bed-€50, Wi-Fi only, 75 rue St. Louis-en-l'Ile, tel. 01 46 34 04 80, fax 01 46 34 02 13, www.hotelsaintlouis .com, slouis@noos.fr).

In the Historic Core, on Ile de la Cité

$$ Hôtel Dieu Hospitel Paris is the only Paris hotel with an Ile de la Cité address. It's located in the oldest city hospital of Paris, on the square in front of Notre-Dame (find the hospital on the map on page 83). Originally intended to receive families of patients, it now offers rooms for tourists as well. To get a spot in this prime location, you'll need to book well in advance (only offers 14 rooms). You'll be surprised by the modern, comfortable decor and may even forget you're in a hospital (Sb-€120, Db-€135, some rooms have peek-a-boo views of Notre-Dame, 1 place du Parvis, tel. 01 44 32 01 00, www.hotel-hospitel.com, hospitelhoteldieu @wanadoo.fr). Enter the hotel's main entrance, turn right, follow signs to wing B2, and take the elevator to the sixth floor.

Luxembourg Garden Area (St. Sulpice to Pantheon)

(5th and 6th arrondissements, Mo: St. Sulpice, Mabillon, Odéon, and Cluny–La Sorbonne; RER: Luxembourg)

This neighborhood revolves around Paris' loveliest park and offers quick access to the city's best shopping streets and grandest café-hopping. Sleeping in the Luxembourg area offers a true Left Bank experience without a hint of the low-end commotion of the nearby Latin Quarter tourist ghetto. The Luxembourg Garden, boulevard St. Germain, Cluny Museum, and Latin Quarter are all at your doorstep. Here you get the best of both worlds: youthful Left Bank energy and the classic trappings that surround the monumental Panthéon and St. Sulpice Church.

Hotels in this central area are more expensive than in other neighborhoods I list.

Having the Luxembourg Garden at your back door allows strolls through meticulously cared-for flowers, a great kids' play area (see Paris with Children chapter), and a purifying escape from city traffic. Place St. Sulpice offers an elegant, pedestrian-friendly square and quick access to some of Paris' best boutiques (see Shopping chapter). Sleeping in the Luxembourg area also puts several movie theaters at your fingertips (at Métro stop: Odéon), as well as lively cafés on boulevard St. Germain, rue de Buci, rue des

Canettes, place de la Sorbonne, and place de la Contrescarpe, all of which buzz with action until late.

While it takes only 15 minutes to walk from one end of this neighborhood to the other, I've located the hotels by the key monument they are close to (St. Sulpice Church, the Odéon Theater, and the Panthéon). Most hotels are within a five-minute walk of the Luxembourg Garden (and none is more than 15 minutes away).

Services: The nearest **TI** is across the river in Gare de Lyon (Mon–Sat 8:00–18:00, closed Sun, all-Paris TI tel. 08 92 68 30 00). There are two useful **SNCF Boutiques** for easy train reservations and ticket purchase: at 79 rue de Rennes and at 54 boulevard Saint-Michel (Mon–Sat 8:30–18:00, closed Sun).

Markets: The colorful street market at the south end of rue Mouffetard is a worthwhile 10- to 15-minute walk from these hotels (Tue–Sat 8:00–12:00 & 15:30–19:00, Sun 8:00–12:00, closed Mon, five blocks south of place de la Contrescarpe, Mo: Place Monge).

Bookstore: The **Village Voice** bookstore carries a full selection of English-language books (including mine), and is near St. Sulpice. Say hello to Michael but don't ask his opinion of *The Da Vinci Code* (Mon 14:00–19:30, Tue–Sat 10:00–19:30, Sun 12:00–18:30, 6 rue Princesse, tel. 01 46 33 36 47, www.villagevoice bookshop.com).

Internet Access: You'll find it at **Le Milk** (always open, between the Luxembourg Garden and Panthéon at 17 rue Soufflot).

Métro Connections: Métro lines 10 and 4 serve this area (10 connects to the Austerlitz train station, and 4 runs to the Montparnasse, Est, and Nord train stations). Neighborhood stops are Cluny-La Sorbonne, Mabillon, Odéon, and St. Sulpice. RER-B (Luxembourg station is handiest) provides direct service to Charles de Gaulle airport and Gare du Nord trains, and access to Orly airport via the Orlybus (transfer at Denfert-Rochereau).

Bus Routes: Buses #63, #86, and #87 run eastbound through this area on boulevard St. Germain, and westbound along rue des Ecoles, stopping on place St. Sulpice. Lines #63 and #87 provide direct connections west to the rue Cler area. Line #63 also serves the Orsay, Army, Rodin, and Marmottan museums to the west and Gare de Lyon to the east. Lines #86 and #87 run east to the Marais, and #87 continues to Gare de Lyon.

Hotels near St. Sulpice Church

These hotels are all within a block of St. Sulpice Church and two blocks from famous boulevard St. Germain. This is nirvana for boutique-minded shoppers—and you'll pay extra for the location. Métro stops St. Sulpice and Mabillon are equally close.

Hotels and Restaurants near St. Sulpice and the Odéon Theater

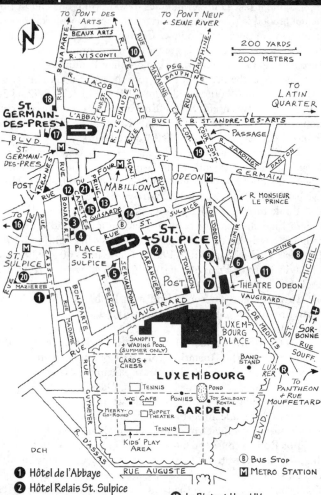

Ⓑ Bus Stop Ⓜ Metro Station

1. Hôtel de l'Abbaye
2. Hôtel Relais St. Sulpice
3. Hôtel la Perle
4. Hôtel Bonaparte
5. Hôtel le Récamier
6. Hôtel Relais Médicis
7. Hôtel Michelet Odéon
8. Brasserie Bouillon Racine
9. La Méditerranée Rest.
10. Le Bistrot Mazarin
11. Restaurant Polidor
12. La Crêpe Rit du Clown
13. Le Bistrot Henri IV
14. Lou Pescadou-Chez Julien
15. Chez Georges
16. To La Cigale Récamier & Au Sauvignon Café
17. Les Deux Magots & Le Café de Flore
18. Café Bonaparte
19. Café le Procope
20. SNCF Boutique
21. Village Voice Books

$$$ Hôtel de l'Abbaye**** is a lovely refuge just west of Luxembourg Garden; it's a find for well-heeled connoisseurs of this area. The hotel's four-star luxury includes refined lounges inside and out, with 44 sumptuous rooms and every amenity at surprisingly reasonable rates (Db-€240–270, bigger Db-€350–390, suites and apartments available for €550, includes breakfast, 10 rue Cassette, tel. 01 45 44 38 11, fax 01 45 48 07 86, www.hotel-abbaye .com, hotel.abbaye@wanadoo.fr).

$$$ Hôtel Relais St. Sulpice***, on the small street just behind St. Sulpice Church, is a dark little boutique hotel with a cozy lounge and 26 pricey and stylish rooms, most surrounding a leafy glass atrium. Top-floor rooms get more light and are worth requesting (Db-€185–220 depending on size, includes breakfast, sauna free for guests, Wi-Fi only, 3 rue Garancière, tel. 01 46 33 99 00, fax 01 46 33 00 10, www.relais-saint-sulpice.com, relais stsulpice@wanadoo.fr).

$$$ Hôtel la Perle*** is a spendy pearl in the thick of the lively rue des Canettes, a block off place St. Sulpice. At this snappy, modern, business-class hotel, sliding glass doors open onto the traffic-free street, and you're greeted by a fun lobby built around a central bar and atrium (standard Db-€195, bigger Db-€215, luxury Db-€250, check website or call for last-minute deals within five days of your stay, includes breakfast, 14 rue des Canettes, tel. 01 43 29 10 10, fax 01 46 34 51 04, www.hotellaperle.com, booking @hotellaperle.com).

$$ Hôtel Bonaparte**, an unpretentious place wedged between boutiques, is a few steps from place St. Sulpice. Although the 29 Old World rooms don't live up to the handsome entry, they're plenty comfortable and spacious by Paris standards, with big bathrooms, traditional decor, and molded ceilings (Sb-€103–127, Db-€136–158, big Db-€170, Tb-€175, includes breakfast, 61 rue Bonaparte, tel. 01 43 26 97 37, fax 01 46 33 57 67, www.hotel bonaparte.fr, reservation@hotelbonaparte.fr; helpful Fréderic, Sabine, and Eric at reception).

$$–$$$ Hôtel le Récamier**, romantically tucked in the corner of place St. Sulpice, was closed for renovation on my last visit. But the location is exceptional and the work should be completed by your visit (new rates will include breakfast, 3 bis place St. Sulpice, tel. 01 43 26 04 89, fax 01 46 33 27 73, hotelrecamier @wanadoo.fr).

Near the Odéon Theater

These two hotels are between the Odéon Métro stop and Luxembourg Garden (five blocks east of St. Sulpice), and may have rooms when others don't. In addition to the Odéon Métro stop, the RER-B Luxembourg stop is a short walk away.

Luxembourg Musts for Temporary Residents

- Pass oodles of time at Luxembourg Garden, sitting in a green chair with your feet propped up on the pond's edge.
- Observe Daniel Roth's Sunday organ mastery up close at St. Sulpice Church (see page 60).
- Join the locals at the only café on place St. Sulpice for a morning coffee or afternoon drink.
- Stroll rue Mouffetard day or night, and stop for a drink on place de la Contrescarpe.
- Window-shop the boutiques between Sèvres-Babylone and St. Sulpice (described on page 434).
- Spend too much for a coffee at a grand café and watch the world go by (see "Les Grands Cafés de Paris," page 417).
- Wander the rue de Buci and find Voltaire's favorite café (see Left Bank Walk chapter).
- Ponder the history of France in the Panthéon (see page 64).

$$$ Hôtel Relais Médicis* is perfect in every way—if you've always wanted to live in a Monet painting and can afford it. Its 16 rooms surround a fragrant little garden courtyard and fountain, giving you a countryside break fit for a Medici in the heart of Paris. This delightful refuge is tastefully decorated with floral Old-World charm, and is permeated with thoughtfulness (Sb-€172, Db-€208–228, deluxe Db-€258, Tb-€298, €30 cheaper mid-July–Aug and Nov–March, includes extravagant continental breakfast, faces the Odéon Theater at 23 rue Racine, tel. 01 43 26 00 60, fax 01 40 46 83 39, www.relaismedicis.com, reservation @relaismedicis.com).

$$ Hôtel Michelet Odéon sits in a corner of place de l'Odéon with big windows on the square. Though it lacks personality, it's a fair value in this pricey area, with 24 simple rooms with modern decor and views of the square (Db-€115–135, Tb-€170, Qb-€190, no air-con, pay Wi-Fi, 6 place de l'Odéon, tel. 01 53 10 05 60, fax 01 46 34 55 35, www.hotelmicheletodeon.com, hotel @micheletodeon.com).

Near the Panthéon and Rue Mouffetard

The last two listings in this section are cheap dives, but in a great area.

$$ Hôtel des Grandes Ecoles* is idyllic. A private cobbled lane leads to three buildings that protect a flower-filled garden

Hotels and Restaurants near the Panthéon

M METRO STATION
R R.E.R. STOP

1. Hôtel des Grandes Ecoles
2. Hôtel des 3 Collèges & Hôtel Cujas Panthéon
3. Hôtel Cluny Sorbonne
4. Hôtel Central
5. Young & Happy Hostel
6. Hôtel de France
7. Port-Royal-Hôtel
8. Hôtel de L'Espérance
9. Hôtel des Mines
10. Restaurant Perraudin
11. Le Soufflot Café
12. Place de la Sorbonne Eateries
13. Café Delmas
14. Le Mouffetard Café
15. Les Papillons Restaurant
16. Cave de Bourgogne
17. To Café de la Mosque
18. Internet Café
19. SNCF Boutique

courtyard, preserving a sense of tranquility rare in this city. Its 51 rooms are French-countryside-pretty, spotless, and reasonably spacious, but have no air-conditioning. This romantic spot is deservedly popular, so book ahead, though reservations are not accepted more than four months in advance (Db-€118–143 depending on size, extra bed-€20, parking garage-€30, Wi-Fi only, 75 rue du Cardinal Lemoine, Mo: Cardinal Lemoine, tel. 01 43 26 79 23, fax 01 43 25 28 15, www.hotel-grandes-ecoles.com, hotel.grandes.ecoles @wanadoo.fr, mellow Marie speaks English, Mama does not).

$$ Hôtel des 3 Collèges** greets clients with a bright lobby, narrow hallways, and unimaginative rooms with low ceilings...but fair rates (Sb-€84–110, Db-€110–155, Tb-€155–175, pay Wi-Fi only, 16 rue Cujas, tel. 01 43 54 67 30, fax 01 46 34 02 99, www.3colleges .com, hotel@3colleges.com).

$$ Hôtel Cujas Panthéon** gives traditional two-star comfort sans air-conditioning at fair prices (Db-€104, Tb-€140, Wi-Fi only, 18 rue Cujas, tel. 01 43 54 58 10, fax 01 43 25 88 02, www .hotelcujaspantheon.com, hotel-cujas-pantheon@wanadoo.fr.)

$ Hôtel Cluny Sorbonne** is a modest place warmly run by Monsieur and Madame Berber. It's located in the thick of things across from the famous university and below the Panthéon. Rooms are well-worn but clean and comfortable, with wood furnishings (standard Db-€95, really big Db-€160, check website for deals, no air-con, Wi-Fi only, 8 rue Victor Cousin, tel. 01 43 54 66 66, fax 01 43 29 68 07, www.hotel-cluny.fr, cluny@club-internet.fr).

$ Hôtel Central*, wedged between two cafés, has a smoky, dingy reception, a steep, slippery stairway, dumpy beds, and mildewed rooms. Bottom line: It's youth-hostel cheap, but with a charm only romantic hobos will appreciate. All rooms have showers, but toilets are down the hall (Ss-€33–38, Ds-€46–51, cash only, no elevator, no air-con, no Internet access, no mucho, 6 rue Descartes, Mo: Cardinal Lemoine, tel. 01 46 33 57 93). Do your best to get a smile out of Madame Pilar, who doesn't speak English.

$ Young & Happy Hostel is easygoing, well-run, and English-speaking, with Internet access, kitchen facilities, and acceptable hostel conditions. It sits dead-center in the rue Mouffetard bar, café, and people action...which can be good or bad (all rates per person: bunk in 4- to 10-bed dorms-€26, in 3- to 5-bed dorms-€28, in double rooms-€30, includes breakfast, sheets-€2.50, credit cards accepted, no air-con, no lockers but safety box at reception, rooms closed 11:00–16:00 but reception stays open, no curfew, 80 rue Mouffetard, Mo: Place Monge, tel. 01 47 07 47 07, fax 01 47 07 22 24, www.youngandhappy.fr, smile@youngandhappy.fr).

Farther Away from the Seine, at the Bottom of Rue Mouffetard

These hotels, away from the Seine and other tourists in an appealing workaday area, offer more room for your euro. They require a longer walk or Métro ride to sights, but often have rooms when others don't. Rue Mouffetard is the bohemian soul of this area, running south from its heart—place de la Contrescarpe—to rue de Bazeilles. Two thousand years ago it was the principal Roman road south to Italy. Today, this small, meandering street has a split personality. The lower half thrives in the daytime as a pedestrian shopping street. The upper half sleeps during the day but comes alive after dark, teeming with bars, restaurants, and nightlife. Use Métro stop Censier-Daubenton or Les Gobelins.

$$ Hôtel de France, on a busy street, offers modern, comfortable rooms. The best and quietest are *sur la cour* (on the courtyard), though streetside rooms are acceptable (Db-€135–155, Tb-€150–175, 108 rue Monge, Mo: Censier-Daubenton, tel. 01 47 07 19 04, fax 01 43 36 62 34, www.hotelfrancequartierlatin.com, hotel.de.fce@wanadoo.fr).

$ Port-Royal-Hôtel* has only one star, but don't let that fool you. Its 46 rooms are polished top to bottom and have been well-run by the same proud family for 68 years. You could eat off the floors of its spotless, comfy rooms...but you won't find air-conditioning, Internet access, or Wi-Fi. Ask for a room away from the street (S-€42–56, D-€56, Db-€80–90 depending on size, big shower down the hall-€3, cash only, nonrefundable cash deposit required, on busy boulevard de Port-Royal at #8, Mo: Les Gobelins, tel. 01 43 31 70 06, fax 01 43 31 33 67, www.hotelportroyal.fr, portroyal hotel@wanadoo.fr).

$ Hôtel de L'Espérance** is a terrific two-star value. It's quiet, pink, and cushy, with feminine rooms and canopy beds (Sb-€75–80, Db-€80–90, Tb-€107, 15 rue Pascal, Mo: Censier-Daubenton, tel. 01 47 07 10 99, fax 01 43 37 56 19, www.hoteldelesperance.fr, hotel.esperance@wanadoo.fr).

On the South Side of Luxembourg Garden

$$$ Hôtel des Mines** is less central but worth the walk. Its 50 well-maintained rooms are a fair value and come with updated bathrooms and a welcoming lobby (Db-€150, Tb-€180, Qb-€210, frequent Web deals, between Luxembourg and Port-Royal stations on the RER-B line, a 10-min walk from Panthéon, one block past Luxembourg Garden at 125 boulevard St. Michel, tel. 01 43 54 32 78, fax 01 46 33 72 52, www.hoteldesminesparis.com, hotel @hoteldesminesparis.com).

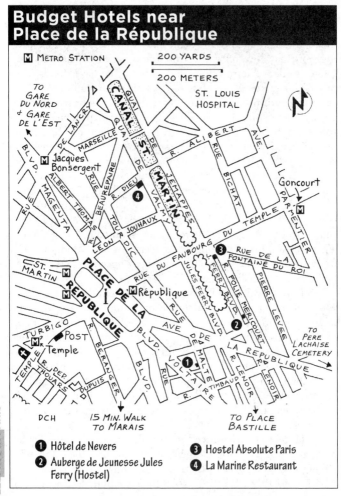

Budget Hotels near Place de la République

M METRO STATION

200 YARDS
200 METERS

ST. LOUIS HOSPITAL

TO GARE DU NORD & GARE DE L'EST

CANAL ST. MARTIN

QUAI DE VALMY

QUAI DE JEMMAPES

Jacques Bonsergent

Goncourt

BLVD. MAGENTA

RUE ALBERT THOMAS

RUE BEAUREPAIRE

R. DIEU

R. ALIBERT

RUE BICHAT

AVE. PARMENTIER

RUE DE LANCRY

RUE MARSEILLE

R. LEON JOUHAUX

TOUR DIC

RUE DU FAUBOURG DU TEMPLE

RUE DE LA FONTAINE DU ROI

ST. MARTIN

PLACE DE LA RÉPUBLIQUE

République

RUE DU FAUBOURG

JULES FERRY BLVD.

R. FOLIE MÉRICOURT

PIERRE LEVÉE

TURBIGO

POST

R. RÉPUBLIQUE

RUE BÉRANGER

BLVD.

AVE. DE LA RÉPUBLIQUE

TO PÈRE LACHAISE CEMETERY

Temple

TEMPLE

R. DUPUIS

R. DEP THOUARS

BLVD. VOLTAIRE

RUE DE MALTE

R. RIMBAUD

R. LENOIR

DCH

15 MIN. WALK TO MARAIS

TO PLACE BASTILLE

❶ Hôtel de Nevers
❷ Auberge de Jeunesse Jules Ferry (Hostel)
❸ Hostel Absolute Paris
❹ La Marine Restaurant

Near Place de la République

(10th and 11th arrondissements, Mo: République, Oberkampf)
The three budget accommodations below are in the neighborhood north of the Marais, between place de la République and Canal St. Martin. This area is untouristy, young, and *très* international (read "melting pot"). It's definitely unpolished (and edgy to some) and more remote—but if you can put up with some rough edges and don't mind using the Métro and buses for all your sightseeing, you'll find some good deals here.

$ Hôtel de Nevers* is a cheap one-star hotel with a historic elevator and pretty good rooms for the price, despite the dim room lighting (D-€46 with free shower down the hall, Ds-€57, Db-€68, Tb-€85, Qb-€97, Internet access but no Wi-Fi, 53 rue de Malte, tel. 01 47 00 56 18, fax 01 43 57 77 39, www.hoteldenevers.com, reservation@hoteldenevers.com).

$ Auberge de Jeunesse Jules Ferry is a relaxed youth hostel right on the parkway that runs above Canal St. Martin. Arrive before 10:00 or book online to be assured a room (€23 per bunk in pleasant, sink-equipped 2-, 4-, or 6-bed rooms, higher rates for nonmembers; small lockers available, rooms closed 10:30–14:00, 8 boulevard Jules Ferry, tel. 01 43 57 55 60, fax 01 43 14 82 09, www .hihostels.com, paris.julesferry@fuaj.org).

$ Hostel Absolute Paris is part two-star hotel, part four-beds-per-room hostel. It faces the canal and is filled with backpackers. The rooms are industrial-strength clean and adequate—but only worth considering if you don't mind dorm-style accommodations (€25 each in 4-bed room with private bathroom, Db-€85, Tb-€100, includes breakfast, 1 rue de la Fontaine du Roi, tel. 01 47 00 47 00, fax 01 47 00 47 02, www.absolute-paris.com, bonjour @absolute-paris.com).

For Longer Stays

Staying a week or longer? Consider the advantages that come with renting a furnished apartment. Complete with a small, equipped kitchen and living room, this option is also great for families on shorter visits. Among the many English-speaking organizations ready to help, the following have proven most reliable. Their websites are generally excellent, and essential to understanding your options. Read the rental conditions very carefully.

Most of the agencies listed below are middlemen, offering an ever-changing selection of private apartments for rent on a weekly basis (or longer). If staying a month or longer, save money by renting directly from the apartment owners. Check the housing section in the ad-filled paper *France-USA Contacts* (available at the American Church and elsewhere in Paris), or check out www .fusac.fr. Some readers have reported good success using Craig's List (www.craigslist.org). Remember that Paris apartments, like hotel rooms, are small by US standards.

Paris Perfect is a French-owned, London-based business that seeks the "perfect apartment" for its clients, and is selective about what they offer. Their apartments (which run about €300/night, 10-percent discount for Rick Steves readers) are named for wines, and their service gets rave reviews. Most come with air-conditioning and washers and dryers (to reach their British tel. & fax from the US, call 011-44-20-7938-2939, fax 011-44-20-7937-2115, www .parisperfect.com).

Paris Appartements Services rents studios (€100–170/night) and one-bedroom apartments (€140–230/night) in central neighborhoods (20 rue Bachaumont, tel. 01 40 28 01 28, fax 01 40 28 92 01, www.paris-apts.com).

France Homestyle is run by Claudette, a service-oriented French woman who now lives in Seattle and has hand-picked every apartment she lists (US tel. 206/325-0132, www.francehomestyle .com, info@francehomestyle.com).

Home Rental Service has been in business for 14 years and offers a big selection of apartments throughout Paris with no agency fees (120 Champs-Elysées, tel. 01 42 25 65 40, fax 01 42 25 65 45, www.homerental.fr).

Locaflat offers accommodations ranging from studios to five-room apartments, with occasional specials online (63 avenue de la Motte-Picquet, tel. 01 43 06 78 79, fax 01 40 56 99 69, www .locaflat.com).

Immo Marais has over 100 apartments in all sizes in the Marais (60 rue Roi de Sicile, tel. 01 42 74 06 17, www.immomarais .net).

Paris Home is a small outfit with only two small studios, but both are located on rue Amélie in the heart of the rue Cler area (see map page 362). Each has modern furnishings and laundry facilities. Friendly Slim, the owner, is the best part (€500/week, one-week minimum, special rates for longer stays, credit cards accepted, free Internet access and US or France telephone calls, free maid service, tel. 06 19 03 17 55, http://parishome2000.free.fr, parishome2000@yahoo.fr).

Paris For Rent is a San Francisco–based group that has been renting top-end apartments in Paris for more than a decade (US tel. 415/642-1111, www.parisforrent.com).

EATING IN PARIS

The Parisian eating scene is kept at a rolling boil. Entire books (and lives) are dedicated to the subject. Paris is France's wine-and-cuisine melting pot. Though it lacks a style of its own (only French onion soup is truly Parisian), it draws from the best of France. Paris could hold a gourmet Olympics and import nothing.

Parisians eat long and well. Relaxed lunches, three-hour dinners, and endless hours of sitting in outdoor cafés are the norm. Local cafés, cuisine, and wines become a highlight of any Parisian adventure—sightseeing for your palate. Even if the rest of you is sleeping in a cheap hotel, let your taste buds travel first-class in Paris. (They can go coach in London.)

You can eat well without going broke, but choose carefully—you're just as likely to blow a small fortune on a mediocre meal as you are to dine wonderfully for €20. Follow the suggestions offered in this chapter, and you'll have a better dining experience.

The no-smoking revolution hit France in 2008, when a new law mandated that all café and restaurant interiors be smoke-free. Today the only smokers you'll find are at outside tables which—unfortunately—may be exactly where you want to be.

Waiters probably won't overwhelm you with friendliness (their tip is included in the bill, so there's less schmoozing than we're used to at home). Notice how hard they work. They almost never stop. Cozying up to clients (French or foreign) is probably the last thing on their minds. To get a waiter's attention, say, "*S'il vous plaît*" (see voo play)—"please." To get the most out of your Parisian restaurant—slow down. Allow enough time for the meal, engage the waiter, show you're serious about food, and enjoy the experience as much as the food itself.

Breakfast

You'll almost always have the option of breakfast at your hotel, which is pleasant and convenient. *Petit déjeuner* (puh-tee day-zhuh-nay) starts with café au lait, hot chocolate, or tea; a roll with butter and marmalade; and a croissant. Some hotels offer only this classic continental breakfast for about €8–15, while others put out a buffet breakfast for a few euros more (cereal, yogurt, fruit, cheese, croissants, juice, and the occasional hard-boiled egg)—which I usually spring for.

If all you want is coffee or tea and a croissant, the corner café is cheaper (though you get more coffee at your hotel). Go local at the café and ask for *une tartine* (oon tart-een; baguette slathered with butter or jam) with your café au lait. To keep it really cheap, pick up some fruit at a grocery store and pastries at your favorite *boulangerie* and have a picnic breakfast, then savor your coffee at the bar (*comptoir*) while standing (like locals do). For a less atmospheric alternative, some fast-food places offer very cheap breakfasts.

Picnics and Snacks

Great for lunch or dinner, Parisian picnics can be first-class affairs and adventures in high cuisine. Be daring. Try the smelly cheeses, ugly pâtés, sissy quiches, and minuscule yogurts. Local shopkeepers are accustomed to selling small quantities of produce. Try the tasty salads-to-go, and ask for a plastic fork *(une fourchette en plastique)*. A small container is *une barquette*.

Gather supplies early for a picnic lunch; you'll probably visit several small stores to assemble a complete meal, and many close at noon for their lunch break. Look for a *boulangerie*, a *crémerie* or *fromagerie* (for cheeses), a *charcuterie* or *traiteur* (for deli items, prepared salads, meats, and pâtés), an *épicerie* or *magasin d'alimentation* (small grocery store with veggies, drinks, and so on), and a *pâtisserie* (for delicious pastries). For fine picnic shopping, check out the street market recommendations in the Shopping chapter. Wine may be taboo in public places in the US, but it's *pas de problème* in France.

Supermarchés offer less color and cost, more efficiency, and adequate quality. Department stores often have supermarkets in the basement, along with top-floor cafeterias offering not-really-cheap but low-risk, low-stress, what-you-see-is-what-you-get meals. For a quick meal to go, look for bakeries selling take-out sandwiches and drinks, or sidewalk stands selling crêpes or other foods. For an affordable sit-down meal, try a *crêperie* or café.

In stores, unrefrigerated soft drinks and beer are half the price of cold drinks. Milk and boxes of fruit juice are the most inexpensive. Avoid buying drinks to go at streetside stands; you'll find them far cheaper in a shop. Try to keep a water bottle with you. Water quenches your thirst better and cheaper than anything you'll find in a store or café. I drink tap water in Paris and use that to refill my bottle. You'll pass many fountains on Paris streets with good water (but if it says *non potable*, it's not drinkable).

For good lunch picnic sites, consider these suggestions: The Palais Royal (across place du Palais Royal from the Louvre) is a good spot for a peaceful, royal picnic, as is the little triangular Henry IV park on the west tip of Ile de la Cité. The pedestrian pont des Arts bridge, across from the Louvre, has great views and plentiful benches, as does the Champ de Mars park below the Eiffel Tower (picnic off to the sides of the central area, which is off-limits). For great people-watching, try the Pompidou Center (by the *Homage to Stravinsky* fountains), the elegant place des Vosges (closes at dusk), the gardens behind Les Invalides, and the Tuileries and Luxembourg gardens (parks close at dusk).

Sandwiches, Quiche, and Pizza

Across Paris you'll find bakeries and small stands selling baguette sandwiches, quiche, and pizza-like items to go for €4–6. Usually filling and tasty, they also streamline the picnic process. (If you don't want your sandwich drenched in mayonnaise, ask for it *sans mayonnaise;* sahn my-oh-nehz.) Here are some sandwiches you'll see:

Anything *à la provençal* (ah lah proh-vehn-sahl): A sandwich with marinated peppers, tomatoes, and eggplant.

Fromage (froh-mahzh): Cheese (white on beige).

Jambon beurre (zhahn-bohn bur): Ham and butter (boring for most).

Jambon crudités (zhahn-bohn krew-dee-tay): Ham with tomatoes, lettuce, cucumbers, and mayonnaise.

Poulet crudités (poo-lay krew-dee-tay): Chicken with tomatoes, lettuce, maybe cucumbers, and always mayonnaise.

Saucisson beurre (saw-see-sohn burr): Thinly sliced sausage and butter.

Thon crudités (tohn krew-dee-tay): Tuna with tomatoes, lettuce, and maybe cucumbers, but definitely mayonnaise.

Look also for grilled *panini* sandwiches *à la italienne.*

Café Culture

French cafés and brasseries provide budget-friendly meals and a relief from museum and church overload. At either, feel free to order only a bowl of soup and a salad or *plat* (main course) for lunch or dinner. Cafés and brasseries generally open by 7:00, but closing hours vary.

Unlike restaurants, which open only for lunch and dinner,

some cafés and all brasseries serve food throughout the day (though with a more limited menu than at restaurants)—making them the best option for a late lunch or an early dinner.

If you're a novice, it's easier to sit and feel comfortable when you know the system. Check the price list first, which by law must be posted prominently. You'll see two sets of prices; you'll pay more for the same drink if you're seated at a table *(salle)* than if you're seated at the bar or counter *(comptoir)*. At large cafés, outdoor tables are most expensive, and prices can rise after 22:00. For tips on beverages, see the next page.

Standard Menu Items: *Croque monsieur* (grilled ham and cheese sandwich) and *croque madame* (*monsieur* with a fried egg on top) are generally served day and night. Sandwiches are least expensive, but plain—and much better—at the *boulangerie* (bakery). To get more than a piece of ham *(jambon)* on a baguette, order a sandwich *jambon crudité*, which means garnished with veggies. Omelets come lonely on a plate with a basket of bread. The daily special—*plat du jour* (plah dew zhoor), or just *plat*—is your fast, hearty, and garnished hot plate for €13–18. At

most cafés, feel free to order only *entrées* (which in French means the starter course); many find these lighter and more interesting than a main course. A vegetarian can enjoy a tasty, filling meal by ordering two *entrées*. Regardless of what you order, bread is free; to get more, just hold up your bread basket and ask, "*Encore, s'il vous plâit?*"

Salads: They're typically large—one is perfect for lunch or a light dinner. To get salad dressing on the side, order *la sauce à côté* (lah sohs ah co-tay). The classic salads include:

Salade niçoise (nee-swahz), a specialty from Nice, usually features green salad topped with green beans, boiled potatoes, tomatoes, anchovies, olives, hard-boiled eggs, and lots of tuna.

Salade au chèvre chaud is a mixed green salad topped with warm goat cheese on toasted croutons.

Salade composée is "composed" of any number of ingredients, such as *lardons* (bacon), *comté* (a Swiss-style cheese), *roquefort* (blue cheese), *œuf* (egg), *noix* (walnuts), and *jambon* (ham,

Coffee and Tea Lingo

By law, the waiter must give you a glass of tap water with your coffee or tea if you request it; ask for *"un verre d'eau, s'il vous plaît"* (uhn vayr doh, see voo play).

Coffee

French	Pronounced	English
un express	uh nex-press	shot of espresso
une noisette	oon nwah-zeht	espresso with a shot of milk
café au lait	kah-fay oh lay	coffee with lots of steamed milk (closest to an American latte)
un grand crème	uhn grahn krehm	big café au lait
un petit crème	uhn puh-tee krehm	small café au lait
un café allongé (a.k.a. *café longue*)	uhn kah-fay ah-lohn-zhay (kah-fay lohn)	closest to an American cup of coffee
un décaffiné	uhn day-kah-fee-nay	decaf—available for any of the above drinks

Tea

French	Pronounced	English
un thé nature	uhn tay nah-tour	plain tea
un thé au lait	uhn tay oh lay	tea with milk
un thé citron	uhn tay see-trohn	tea with lemon
une infusion	oon an-few-see-yohn	herbal tea

generally thinly sliced).

Salade paysanne usually comes with potatoes *(pommes de terre)*, walnuts *(noix)*, tomatoes, ham, and egg.

Salade aux gesiers has chicken gizzards (and often slices of duck).

Wine and Beer: House wine at the bar is cheap (about €3 per glass, cheapest by the pitcher—*pichet*, pee-shay), and the local beer is cheaper on tap *(une pression;* oon pres-yohn) than in the bottle *(bouteille;* boo-teh-ee). France's best beer is Alsatian; try Kronenbourg or the heavier Pelfort (even heavier is the Belgian beer Leffe). *Une panaché* (oon pan-a-shay) is a refreshing French shandy (7-Up and beer).

Soft Drinks: For a fun, bright, nonalcoholic drink of 7-Up with mint syrup, order *un diabolo menthe* (uhn dee-ah-boh-loh mahnt); for 7-Up with fruit syrup, order *un diabolo grenadine* (think

French Specialties by Region

Alsace

The German influence is obvious: sausages, potatoes, onions, and sauerkraut. Look for *choucroute garnie* (sauerkraut and sausage—although it seems a shame to eat it in a fancy restaurant), the more traditionally Alsatian *Baeckeoffe* (potato, meat, and onion stew), *Rösti* (an oven-baked potato-and-cheese dish), fresh trout, foie gras, and *flammekueche* (a paper-thin pizza topped with bacon, onions, and sour cream).

Burgundy

Considered by many to be France's best, Burgundian cuisine is peasant cooking elevated to an art. This wine region excels in *coq au vin* (chicken with wine sauce), *bœuf bourguignon* (beef stew cooked with wine, bacon, onions, and mushrooms), *œufs en meurette* (eggs poached in red wine), escargots (snails), and *jambon persillé* (ham with garlic and parsley).

Basque

Mixing influences from the mountains, sea, Spain, and France, it's dominated by seafood, tomatoes, and red peppers. Look for anything *basquaise* (cooked with tomatoes, eggplant, red peppers, and garlic), such as *thon* (tuna) or *poulet* (chicken). Try *piperade,* a dish combining peppers, tomatoes, garlic, and eggs (ham optional), and *ttoro,* a seafood stew that is the Basque answer to bouillabaisse.

Languedoc and Périgord

The cuisine of these regions is referred to in Paris as "Southwest cuisine" *(cuisine du sudouest).* This hearty peasant cooking uses full-bodied red wines and lots of duck. Try the hearty cassoulet

---

Shirley Temple). Kids love the local orange drink (*orange pressé;* oh-rhan-juh preh-say, you'll need to add sugar) and the flavored syrups mixed with bottled water (*sirops à l'eau;* see-roh ah loh). In France *limonade* (lee-moan-ahd) is Sprite or 7-Up. The ice cubes melted after the last Yankee tour group left.

Tipping

All cafés and restaurants include a service charge in the bill (12–15 percent, referred to as *service compris* or *prix net*), but it's polite to round up for a drink or meal well-served. This bonus tip is usually about five percent of the bill (e.g., if your bill is €19, leave €20). If you want the waiter to keep the change when you pay, say, "*C'est bon*" (say bohn), meaning, "It's good." Tipping is not necessary if you order food at a counter.

(white bean, duck, and sausage stew), *canard* (duck), *pâté de foie gras* (goose-liver pâté), *pommes sarladaise* (potatoes fried in duck fat), *truffes* (truffles, earthy mushrooms), and anything with *noix* (walnuts).

Normandy and Brittany

Normandy specializes in cream sauces, sea salt, organ meats (sweetbreads, tripe, and kidneys—the "gizzard salads" are great), and seafood *(fruits de mer)*. Dairy products are big here. Try the *moules* (mussels) and *escalope normande* (veal in cream sauce). Brittany is famous for its oysters and crêpes. Both regions use lots of *cidre* (hard apple cider) in their cuisine.

Provence

The almost extravagant use of garlic, olive oil, herbs, and tomatoes makes Provence's cuisine France's liveliest. To sample it, order anything *à la provençale*. Among the area's spicy specialties are ratatouille (a thick mixture of vegetables in an herb-flavored tomato sauce), *brandade* (a salt cod, garlic, and cream mousse), aioli (a garlicky mayonnaise often served atop fresh vegetables), tapenade (a paste of puréed olives, capers, anchovies, herbs, and sometimes tuna), *soupe au pistou* (vegetable soup with basil, garlic, and cheese), and *soupe à l'ail* (garlic soup).

Riviera

The Côte d'Azur gives Provence's cuisine a Mediterranean flair. Local specialties are bouillabaisse (the spicy seafood stew/soup that seems worth the cost only for those with a seafood fetish), *bourride* (a creamy fish soup thickened with aioli garlic sauce), and *salade niçoise* (nee-swahz; a tasty tomato, potato, olive, anchovy, and tuna salad).

Restaurants

Choose restaurants filled with locals. Consider my suggestions and your hotelier's opinion, but trust your instincts. If a restaurant doesn't post its prices outside, move along. Refer to my restaurant recommendations to get a sense of what a reasonable meal should cost.

Restaurants open for dinner around 19:00, and small local favorites get crowded after 21:00. To minimize crowds, go early (around 19:30). Many restaurants close Sunday and Monday.

If a restaurant serves lunch, it generally begins at 11:30 and goes until 14:00, with last orders taken at about 13:30. If you're hungry when restaurants are closed (late afternoon), go to a brasserie; for more information, see "Café Culture," earlier in this chapter.

If you ask for the *menu* (muh-noo) at a restaurant, you won't get a list of dishes; you'll get a fixed-price meal. *Menus*, which usually include three or four courses, are generally a good value if you're hungry: You get your choice of soup, appetizer, or salad; your choice of three or four main courses with vegetables; plus a cheese course and/or a choice of desserts. Service is included (*service compris* or *prix net*), but wine and other drinks are generally extra. Restaurants that offer a *menu* for lunch often charge about €5 more for the same *menu* at dinner.

Many restaurants offer cheaper versions of their *menu*, with a choice of two courses, rather than three or four. These pared-down *menus* are commonly called *formules* and feature an *entrée et plat* (first course and main dish), or *plat et dessert* (main dish and dessert). Most restaurants offer a reasonable *menu-enfant* (kids' menu).

Ask for *la carte* (lah kart) if you want to see a menu and order à la carte, as the locals do. Request the waiter's help in deciphering the French. Consider his or her recommendations and anything *de la maison* (of the house), as long as it's not an organ meat *(tripes, rognons,* or *andouillette).* Galloping gourmets should bring a menu translator; the *Marling Menu-Master* is good. The *Rick Steves' French Phrase Book*, with a Menu Decoder, works well for most travelers. The wines are often listed in a separate *carte des vins.*

Remember that in France an *entrée* is the appetizer, and *le plat* or *le plat du jour* (plate of the day) is the main course with vegetables (usually €13–20). If all you want is a salad or soup, find a café instead.

Parisians are willing to pay for bottled water with their meal (*eau minérale;* oh mee-nay-rahl) because they prefer the taste over tap water. If you prefer a free pitcher of tap water, ask for *une carafe d'eau* (oon kah-rahf doh). Otherwise, you may unwittingly buy bottled water. To get inexpensive wine at a restaurant, order table wine in a pitcher (*un pichet;* uhn pee-shay), rather than a bottle (though finer restaurants usually offer only bottles of wine). If all you want is a glass of wine, ask for *un verre de vin* (uhn vehr duh van). A half carafe of wine is *un demi-pichet* (uhn duh-mee pee-shay), a quarter carafe (ideal for one) is *un quart* (uhn kar).

Parisian Cuisine

There is no "Parisian cuisine" to speak of. The fun part of dining in Paris is that you can sample fine cuisine from throughout France. Many restaurants specialize in a particular region's cuisine (I list restaurants specializing in food from Provence, Burgundy, Alsace, Normandy, Dordogne, Languedoc, and the Basque region). So be a galloping gourmet and try a few of these regional restaurants (see "French Specialties by Region," on the previous page).

The French eat dinner in courses, rather than all on one plate. For general, classic, anywhere-in-France dishes, consider these suggestions:

First Course *(Entrée)*

Crudités: A mix of raw and lightly cooked fresh vegetables, usually including grated carrots, celery root, tomatoes, and beets, often with a hefty dose of vinaigrette dressing. If you want the dressing on the side, say, *"La sauce à côté, s'il vous plaît"* (lah sohs ah koh-tay, see voo play).

Escargots: Snails cooked in parsley-garlic butter. You don't even have to like the snail itself. Just dipping your bread in garlic butter is more than satisfying. Prepared a variety of ways, the classic is *à la bourguignon* (served in their shells).

Foie gras: Rich and buttery in consistency, this pâté is made from the swollen livers of force-fed geese (or ducks, in *foie de canard*). Spread it on bread with your knife, and do not add mustard to this pâté dish.

Huîtres: Oysters served raw any month and delivered fresh from nearby Brittany. This food is particularly popular at Christmas and New Year's, when every café seems to have overflowing baskets lining the storefront.

Pâtés and Terrines: Slowly cooked ground meat (usually pork, though chicken and rabbit are also common) that is highly seasoned and served in slices with mustard and *cornichons* (little pickles). Pâtés are smoother than the similarly prepared but chunkier *terrines*.

Salade au chèvre chaud: A mixed green salad topped with warmed goat cheese and croutons.

Salade niçoise: Famous as a specialty from Nice (in southern France), this classic salad is served throughout the country. There are many versions, though most include a base of green salad topped with green beans, boiled potatoes (sometimes rice), tomatoes (sometimes corn), anchovies, lots of tuna, and hard-boiled eggs.

Soupe à l'oignon: Hot, salty, and filling, French onion soup is a beef broth served with a baked cheese-and-bread crust over the top. This soup is not easy to find in Paris, as locals prefer other types of soup.

Main Course *(Plat Principal)*

Bœuf bourguignon: Another Burgundian specialty, this classy beef stew is cooked slowly in red wine, then served with onions, potatoes, and mushrooms.

Confit de canard: This Southwest favorite is duck that has been preserved in its own fat, then cooked in its fat, and often served with potatoes cooked in the same fat. Not for dieters.

Coq au vin: This Burgundian dish is rooster marinated ever so slowly in red wine, then cooked until it melts in your mouth. It's served (often family-style) with vegetables.

Escalope normande: A specialty of Normandy, this is turkey or veal in a cream sauce.

Gigot d'agneau: Leg of lamb served in many styles, often with white beans. The best lamb is *pré salé*, which means the lamb has been raised in salt-marsh lands (like at Mont St. Michel).

Poulet roti: Roasted chicken on the bone—French comfort food.

Saumon: You'll see salmon dishes served in various styles. The salmon usually comes from the North Sea and is always served with sauce, most commonly a sorrel *(oseille)* sauce.

Steak: Referred to as *pavé* (thick hunk of prime steak*)*, *bavette* (skirt steak*)*, *faux filet* (sirloin), or *entrecôte (*rib steak*)*, French steak is usually thinner than American steak and is always served with sauces (*au poivre* is a pepper sauce, *une sauce roquefort* is a cheese sauce). You will also see *steak haché*, which is a lean, gourmet hamburger patty served *sans* bun. By American standards, the French undercook meats: rare, or *saignant* (seh-nyahn), is close to raw; medium, or *à point* (ah pwan), is rare; and well-done, or *bien cuit* (bee-yehn kwee), is medium.

Steak tartare: This wonderfully French dish is for adventurous types only. It's very lean, raw hamburger served with spices (usually Tabasco, capers, raw onions, salt, and pepper on the side) and topped with a raw egg. This is not hamburger as we know it, but freshly ground beef.

Cheese Course *(Le Fromage)*

In France the cheese course is served just before (or instead of) dessert. It not only helps with digestion, it gives you a great opportunity to sample the tasty regional cheeses. There are more than 400 different French cheeses to try. Some restaurants will offer a cheese platter, from which you select a few different cheeses. A good cheese plate has four types: hard cheese (like Emmentaler—a.k.a. Swiss cheese), a flowery cheese (like Brie or Camembert), a bleu or Roquefort cheese, and a goat cheese.

Cheeses most commonly served in Paris are *brie de Meaux* (mild and creamy, from just outside Paris), Camembert (semi-creamy and pungent, from Normandy), *chèvre* (goat cheese with a sharp taste, usually from the Loire), and Roquefort (strong and blue-veined, from south-central France).

If you'd like a little of several types of cheese from the cheese plate, say, *"Un assortiment, s'il vous plaît"* (uhn ah-sor-tee-mahn, see voo play). If you serve yourself from the cheese plate, observe

French etiquette and keep the shape of the cheese. It's best to politely shave off a slice from the side or cut small wedges.

Dessert (Le Dessert)

If you order espresso, it will always come after dessert. To have coffee with dessert, ask for *"café avec le dessert"* (kah-fay ah-vehk luh day-sayr). See the list of coffee terms earlier in this chapter.

Here are the types of treats you'll see:

Baba au rhum: Pound cake drenched in rum, served with whipped cream.

Café gourmand: An assortment of small desserts selected by the restaurant—a great way to sample several desserts and learn your favorite.

Crème brûlée: A rich, creamy, dense, caramelized custard.

Crème caramel: Flan in a caramel sauce.

Fondant au chocolat or *Moelleux au chocolat:* A molten chocolate cake with a runny (not totally cooked) center.

Fromage blanc: A light dessert similar to plain yogurt (yet different), served with sugar or herbs.

Ile flottante: A light dessert consisting of islands of meringue floating on a pond of custard sauce.

Mousse au chocolat: Chocolate mousse.

Profiteroles: Cream puffs filled with vanilla ice cream, smothered in warm chocolate sauce.

Riz au lait: Rice pudding.

Sorbets: Light, flavorful, and fruity ices (known to us as sherbets), sometimes laced with brandy.

Tartes: Narrow strips of fresh fruit, baked in a crust and served in thin slices (without ice cream).

Tarte tatin: Apple pie like grandma never made, with caramelized apples, cooked upside down, but served upright.

Restaurants

My recommendations are centered on the same great neighborhoods listed in the Sleeping chapter; you can come home exhausted after a busy day of sightseeing and find a good selection of restaurants right around the corner. And evening is a fine time to explore any of these delightful neighborhoods, even if you're sleeping elsewhere.

To save piles of euros, review the budget eating tips above and restaurant recommendations below. Remember that service is always included (so little or no tipping is required—although it's nice to round up for good service), and consider dinner picnics (great take-out dishes available at charcuteries). Watch out: Smokers love outdoor tables.

In the Rue Cler Neighborhood

The rue Cler neighborhood caters to its residents. Its eateries, while not destination places, have an intimate charm. I've provided a full range of choices from cozy ma-and-pa diners to small and trendy boutique restaurants to classic big, boisterous bistros. You'll generally find great dinner *menus* for €20–36, *plats du jour* for around €14–18, and meal-sized salads for €10–12. Eat early with tourists or late with locals. For all restaurants listed in this area, use the Ecole Militaire Métro stop (unless another station is listed).

Close to Ecole Militaire, Between Rue de la Motte-Picquet and Rue de Grenelle

$$$ Le Florimond is good for a special occasion. The setting, while spacious and quiet, is also intimate and welcoming. Locals come for classic French cuisine with elegant indoor or breezy streetside seating. Friendly English-speaking Laurent—whose playful ties change daily—serves one small room of tables gracefully and loves to give suggestions. Try the explosively tasty stuffed cabbage (€36 *menu*, closed Sun, reservations smart, good house wine by the carafe, affordable wine selection, 19 avenue de la Motte-Picquet, tel. 01 45 55 40 38).

$$ Restaurant Pasco, perched elegantly overlooking Les Invalides, is semidressy, with a special enthusiasm for fish. The hard-working owner, Pasco Vignes, attracts a loyal following with his modern Mediterranean cuisine, generously endowed with olive oil. Though there's some outdoor seating, I'd come here for the cozy redbrick interior (€20 *plats*, €22–36 *menus*, daily, reservations smart, 74 boulevard de la Tour Maubourg, Mo: La Tour Maubourg, tel. 01 44 18 33 26).

$$ Café le Bosquet is a modern, chic Parisian brasserie with dressy waiters and your choice of a mod-elegant interior or sidewalk tables on a busy street. Come here for a bowl of French onion soup or a full three-course *menu* with good fish and meat choices. Say *bonsoir* to lanky owner Jean-François, who likes to be called Jeff. Escargots are great here; the house red wine is plenty good, too (€15 *plats*, closed Sun, reservations smart Fri–Sat, fun menu includes vegetarian options, corner of rue du Champ de Mars and avenue Bosquet, 46 avenue Bosquet, tel. 01 45 51 38 13).

$$ La Terrasse du 7ème is a sprawling, happening café with grand outdoor seating and a living room–like interior with comfy love seats. Located on a corner, it overlooks a busy intersection with

Restaurant Price Code

To help you choose among these listings, I've divided the restaurants into three categories, based on the price for a typical
meal without wine.

$$$ **Higher Priced**—Most meals €35 or more.
 $$ **Moderately Priced**—Most meals €20-35.
  $ **Lower Priced**—Most meals €20 or less.

---

a constant parade of people. Chairs are set up facing the street, as a
meal here is like dinner theater—and the show is slice-of-life Paris
(€16 daily *plats*, no fixed-price *menu*, good €14 *salade niçoise*, daily
until at least 24:00 and sometimes until 2:00 in the morning, at
Ecole Militaire Métro stop, tel. 01 45 55 00 02).

$ **Café du Marché** boasts the best seats, coffee, and prices on
rue Cler. The owner's philosophy: Brasserie on speed—crank out
good food at great prices to trendy locals and savvy tourists. It's
high-energy, with young waiters who barely have time to smile...
très Parisian. This place is ideal if you want to eat an inexpensive
one-course meal among a commotion of people and are willing
to go with the small menu. The chalkboard lists your choices:
good, hearty €11 salads or more filling €12 *plats du jour* (Mon–Sat
11:00–23:00, Sun 11:00–17:00, arrive before 19:30 for dinner—it's
packed at 21:00, and service can be slow; free water served without
a grimace, at the corner of rue Cler and rue du Champ de Mars, at
38 rue Cler, tel. 01 47 05 51 27).

$ **Tribeca Italian Restaurant,** next door to Café du Marché,
is run by the same people with essentially the same formula. They
offer similar (if not even better) value and more space, a calmer
ambience, and more patient service. This family-friendly eatery
offers €12 pizzas and €13 Italian *plats*.

$ **Le Petit Cler** is a popular, tiny café with long leather booths,
a traditional interior, and a handful of outdoor tables serving fine,
inexpensive dishes (€9 omelets, €7 soup of the moment, €12 salads,
great *crème au chocolat* or *au vanille*, closed Mon, next to Grand
Hôtel Lévêque at 29 rue Cler, tel. 01 45 50 17 50).

$ **Crêperie Ulysée en Gaule** offers the best cheap seats on
rue Cler. Their crêpes are €3–10 to go, with no extra charge to sit
for readers of this book if you buy a drink. The Ulysée family—
Stephanos, Chrysa, and Marcos—seem to make friends with all
who drop by for a bite. The family loves to serve Greek dishes, and
their excellent crêpes are your least expensive rue Cler hot meal (28
rue Cler, tel. 01 47 05 61 82).

Rue Cler Restaurants

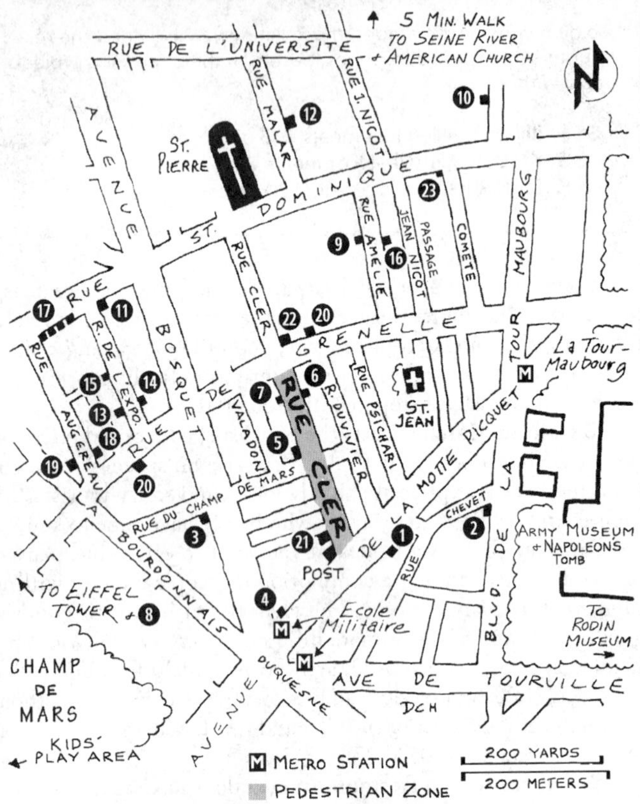

M METRO STATION

▨ PEDESTRIAN ZONE

200 YARDS

200 METERS

❶ Le Florimond

❷ Restaurant Pasco

❸ Café le Bosquet

❹ La Terrasse du 7ème

❺ Café du Marché & Tribeca Italian Rest.

❻ Le Petit Cler

❼ Crêperie Ulysée en Gaule

❽ To 58 Tour Eiffel & Jules Verne Restaurants

❾ Le Petit Niçois

❿ Au Petit Tonneau

⓫ La Fontaine de Mars

⓬ L'Ami Jean

⓭ Le P'tit Troquet

⓮ Billebaude Bistro

⓯ La Casa Campana

⓰ Chez Pierrot

⓱ "The Constant Line-Up"

⓲ La Varangue

⓳ La Gourmandise Pizzeria

⓴ Late-Night Groceries (2)

㉑ Petite Brasserie PTT

㉒ Café la Roussillon

㉓ O'Brien's Pub

Between Rue de Grenelle and the River

$$$ 58 Tour Eiffel is in the Eiffel Tower, 95 meters—about 300 feet—above the ground. It's the latest creation of famed French chef Alain Ducasse, who also owns the even-pricier Jules Verne restaurant on the next level and is making a habit of turning troubled restaurants around. Reserve a month in advance for a view table (€45 lunches, €65 dinners, daily 12:00-late, dinner seatings nightly at about 19:00 and 21:00; before you ascend to dine, drop by the booth between the north/nord and east/est pillars to buy your Eiffel Tower ticket and pick up a pass that enables you to skip the line; Mo: Bir-Hakeim or Trocadéro, RER: Champ de Mars-Tour Eiffel, toll tel. 08 25 56 66 62, www.restaurants-toureiffel.com).

$$$ Le Petit Niçois is all about fish. Come here for everything from bouillabaisse to bass to paella to mussels and enjoy the area's top seafood at fair prices. The marmite du pêcheur is a cheap and delicious version of *bouillabaisse,* the puréed potatoes are sinful, and the café gourmand dessert just about did me in. The atmosphere is warm, the welcome is genuine, and the cuisine is excellent (€29 two-course menu, €32 three-course menu, daily, 10 rue Amèlie, Mo: La Tour Maubourg, tel. 01 45 51 83 65).

$$$ Au Petit Tonneau is a souvenir of old Paris. Fun-loving owner-chef Madame Boyer prepares everything herself, wearing her tall chef's hat like a crown as she rules from her family-style kitchen. The small, plain dining room doesn't look like it's changed in the 27 years she's been in charge. Her steaks and lamb are excellent (€10 starters, €18–22 *plats*, daily, 20 rue Surcouf, Mo: La Tour Maubourg, tel. 01 47 05 09 01).

$$$ La Fontaine de Mars is a longtime favorite for locals (and for US President Barack Obama and his family in June of 2009), charmingly situated on a classic, tiny Parisian street and jumbled square. It's a pricey, happening scene, with tables jammed together for the serious business of good eating. Reserve in advance for a table on the ground floor (or in summer on the square). The upstairs room lacks panache—skip it (€20–30 *plats du jour*, superb foie gras, superb-er desserts, open nightly, where rue de l'Exposition and rue St. Dominique meet, 129 rue St. Dominique, tel. 01 47 05 46 44).

$$$ L'Ami Jean offers excellent Basque specialties at fair prices. The chef has made his reputation on the quality of his cuisine. Arrive by 19:30 or call ahead (€35 *menu*, closed Sun–Mon, 27 rue Malar, Mo: La Tour Maubourg, tel. 01 47 05 86 89).

$$ Le P'tit Troquet, a petite eatery taking you back to the Paris of the 1920s, is gracefully and earnestly run by Dominique. The fragile elegance here makes you want to hug a flapper. Dominique is particularly proud of her foie gras and lamb, and of her daughter's breads and pastries. The delicious three-course €32 *menu* comes with traditional choices. Its delicate charm and gourmet flair make this restaurant a favorite of connoisseurs (opens at 18:00, closed Sun, reservations smart, 28 rue de l'Exposition, tel. 01 47 05 80 39).

$$ Billebaude, run by patient Pascal, is an authentic Parisian bistro where the focus is on what's fresh and meats from the hunt (€31 *menu*, closed Sun–Mon, 29 rue de l'Exposition, tel. 01 45 55 20 96).

$$ La Casa Campana, almost across the street from Billebaude, is worth a visit if you're sleeping in the rue Cler area and crave Italian food. The gentle owners recently moved to Paris from southern Italy, bringing their tasty and unspoiled cuisine with them. The handmade ravioli are bellisimo (*menus* from €20, daily, 20 rue de l'Exposition, tel. 01 45 51 37 71).

$$ Chez Pierrot is a warm, welcoming bistro with 12 tables. On a quiet street, it offers large portions of traditional fare—try the beef stew (€18 *plats*, €12 big salads, 9 rue Amélie, Mo: La Tour Maubourg, tel. 01 45 51 50 08).

$–$$$ The Constant Lineup: Ever since leaving the venerable Hôtel le Crillon, famed chef Christian Constant has based his career on making gourmet cuisine less pricey and less snooty—accessible to people like us. Today you'll find four of his restaurants strung along one block of rue St. Dominique between rue Augereau and rue de l'Exposition, each offering a different experience and price range. The restaurants go from the lively **Café Constant** (my favorite, described below), to the refined **Le Violon d'Ingres** (where Christian won his first Michelin star and reservations are required), to **Les Cocottes** (a trendy, bar-stool-only place serving simple dishes in small iron pots), to **Les Fables de la Fontaine** (a tiny, classy place serving fish only). For more details check out www.leviolondingres.com.

$ Café Constant is a tiny, cool, two-level place that feels more like a small bistro–wine bar than a café. Delicious and affordably priced dishes are served in a fun setting to a well-established clientele. Arrive early to get a table (downstairs seating is better); the friendly staff speaks English (€11 entrées, €15 *plats*, €7 desserts, closed Sun–Mon, no reservations, corner of rue Augereau and rue St. Dominique, next to recommended Hôtel Londres Eiffel, tel. 01 47 53 73 34).

$ La Varangue is an entertaining one-man show featuring English-speaking Philippe, who ran a French catering shop in Pennsylvania for three years. He lives upstairs, and has found his niche serving a mostly American clientele, who are all on a first-name basis. The food is cheap and basic, the tables are few, and he opens early (at 17:30). Norman Rockwell would dig his tiny dining room—with the traditional kitchen sizzling just over the counter. Philippe is so fun and accessible that you are welcome to join him in the kitchen and help cook your meal. Try his snails and chocolate cake...but not together (€12 *plats*, €18 *menu*, always a vegetarian option, closed Sun, 27 rue Augereau, tel. 01 47 05 51 22).

$ La Gourmandise is a tiny, friendly pizzeria across the street from La Varangue. Its good, cheap pizza is ideal for kids (closed Sun, eat in or take out, 28 rue Augereau, tel. 01 45 55 45 16).

Picnicking in Rue Cler

Rue Cler is a moveable feast that gives "fast food" a good name. The entire street is clogged with connoisseurs of good eating. Only the health-food store goes unnoticed. A festival of food, the street is lined with people whose lives seem to be devoted to their specialty: polished produce, rotisserie chicken, crêpes, or cheese.

○ For a self-guided tour of all the temptations, see the Rue Cler Walk chapter.

For a magical picnic dinner at the Eiffel Tower, assemble it in no fewer than five shops on rue Cler. Then lounge on the best grass in Paris, with the dogs, Frisbees, a floodlit tower, and a cool breeze in the Champ de Mars park (picnics are allowed off to the sides of the central area, which is off-limits).

Asian delis (generically called *Traiteur Asie*) provide tasty, low-stress, low-price take-out treats (€8 dinner plates, the one on rue Cler near rue du Champ de Mars has tables). **Crêperie Ulysée en Gaule,** the Greek restaurant on rue Cler across from Grand Hôtel Lévêque, sells take-away crêpes (described above). There's a small **late-night grocery** at 197 rue de Grenelle (open daily until midnight), and another where rues Cler and Grenelle cross.

Breakfast in Rue Cler

Hotel breakfasts, though convenient, are generally not a good value. For a great rue Cler start to your day, drop by the **Petite Brasserie PTT,** where Alexi promises Rick Steves readers a *deux pour douze* breakfast special (2 "American" breakfasts—juice, a big coffee, croissant, bread, ham, and eggs—for €12; closed Sun, 2-min walk from most area hotels, opposite 53 rue Cler).

Nightlife in Rue Cler

This sleepy neighborhood is not ideal for night owls, but there are a few notable exceptions. **Café du Marché** and **La Terrasse du 7ème** (both listed above) are busy with a Franco-American crowd until at least midnight, as is the younger **Café la Roussillon** (occasional happy hours from 18:00–20:00—but every hour seems happy, €11 salads, €14 *plats*, fine for a French pub atmosphere, corner of rue de Grenelle and rue Cler). **O'Brien's Pub** is a relaxed Parisian rendition of an Irish pub, full of Anglophones (77 avenue St. Dominique, Mo: La Tour Maubourg).

In the Marais Neighborhood

The trendy Marais is filled with locals enjoying good food in colorful and atmospheric eateries. The scene is competitive and changes all the time. I've listed an assortment of eateries—all handy to recommended hotels—that offer good food at decent prices, plus a memorable experience.

On Romantic Place des Vosges

This square offers Old-World Marais elegance and a handful of eateries (use Bastille or St. Paul Métro stops). Strolling around the arcade after dark is more important than dining here—fun art galleries alternate with enticing restaurants. Choose a restaurant that best fits your mood and budget; most have arcade seating and provide big space heaters to make outdoor dining during colder months an option. Also consider a drink or dessert on the square at Café Hugo or Nectarine after eating elsewhere.

$$$ Ma Bourgogne is a classic old eatery where you'll sit under warm arcades in a whirlpool of Frenchness, as bow-tied and black-aproned waiters serve you traditional French specialties: blood-red steak, lots of French fries, escargot, and good red wine. Although service comes with few smiles, the staff of this venerable Marais fixture enjoys the work and cares about your experience. Monsieur Cougoureux (koo-gah-roo), who's run this place since de Gaulle was sniveling at Americans, offers anyone with this book a free *amuse-bouche* ("amusement for your mouth") of *steak tartare*. This is your ideal chance to try this "raw spiced hamburger" delicacy without dedicating an entire meal to it...and the quality here is famous (€36 *menu*, daily, dinner reservations smart, cash only, at northwest corner at #19, tel. 01 42 78 44 64).

$$ At Les Bonnes Soeurs, barely off the square, you'll mix it up with a loyal, thirty-something clientele. Welcoming owner Cécile blends modern and traditional fare with light-hearted and contemporary ambience. Portions are big and inventive. The delicious *pressé de chèvre* starter (a hunk of goat cheese topped with tapenade and tomatoes) should be split among several diners. The French hamburger would feed a soccer team and comes with a salad, and Cécile serves the best fries I've tasted in Paris (*plats* from €16, no *menu*, daily, 8 rue du pas de la Mule, tel. 01 42 74 55 80).

$ Nectarine is small and demure—with a wicker, pastel, and feminine atmosphere. This peaceful teahouse serves healthy €11 salads, quiches, and €13 *plats du jour* day and night. Its *menu* lets you mix and match omelets and crêpes, and the huge desserts are splittable (daily, at #16, tel. 01 42 77 23 78).

$ Café Hugo, named for the square's most famous resident, is best for drinks only, as the cuisine does not live up to its setting (daily, at #22, tel. 01 42 72 64 04).

Near the Bastille

To reach these restaurants, use the Bastille Métro stop.

$$ Brasserie Bofinger, an institution for over a century, is famous for fish and traditional cuisine with Alsatian flair. You're surrounded by brisk, black-and-white-attired waiters. The sprawling interior features elaborately decorated rooms reminiscent of the Roaring Twenties. Eating under the grand 1919 *coupole* is a memorable treat (as is using the "historic" 1919 WC downstairs). Check out the boys shucking and stacking seafood platters out front before you enter. Their €25 two-course and €32 three-course *menus,* while not top cuisine, are a good value. If you've always wanted one of those picturesque seafood platters, this is a good place—you can take the standard platter or create one à la carte (open daily and nightly, fun kids' menu, reasonably priced wines, 5 rue de la Bastille, don't be confused by the lesser "Petite" Bofinger across the street, tel. 01 42 72 87 82).

$$ Chez Janou, a Provençal bistro, tumbles out of its corner building and fills its broad sidewalk with happy eaters. At first glance, you know this is a find. Don't let the trendy and youthful crowd intimidate you—it's relaxed and charming, with helpful and patient service. The curbside tables are inviting, but I'd sit inside (with very tight seating) to immerse myself in the happy commotion. The style is French Mediterranean, with an emphasis on vegetables (€16–19 *plats du jour* that change with the season, daily from 19:45, 2 blocks beyond place des Vosges at 2 rue Roger Verlomme, tel. 01 42 72 28 41). They're proud of their 81 different varieties of *pastis* (licorice-flavored liqueur, €3.50 each, browse the list above the bar).

$$ Vins des Pyrénées ("Wines of the Pyrenees") is a fun-loving bistro that attracts a young, lively clientele with its convivial setting. Its varying *menus* have piles of choices that feature cuisine from the southwest of France. Hardworking, English-speaking owner Olivier manages the place with panache and offers fair-priced wines. Don't come here for a romantic dinner (€10 starters, €20 *plats,* daily, 25 rue Beautreillis, tel. 01 42 72 64 94).

$ Au Temps des Cerises is a *très* local wine bar, with a woody 1950s atmosphere, tight seating, and wads of character. Although they serve three-course, €15 lunch *menus,* I'd come here for wine and heavy munchies pre- or post-dinner—or even for dinner. "Dinner" is limited to bread, dry sausage, cheese, and wine served by goateed Yves, Michele, or Sara. Full plates of cold cuts run around €13, a small mixed plate of cheese (€5), meat (€5), and a carafe of good wine (€4–8) surrounded by the intimate Old World atmosphere can make a good light meal (Mon–Sat until about 22:00, closed Sun, at rue du Petit-Musc and rue de la Cerisaie).

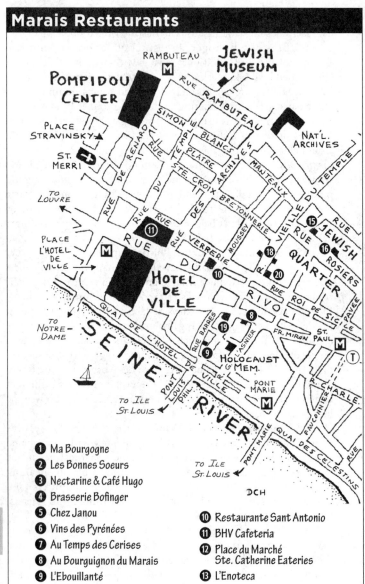

Marais Restaurants

- ① Ma Bourgogne
- ② Les Bonnes Soeurs
- ③ Nectarine & Café Hugo
- ④ Brasserie Bofinger
- ⑤ Chez Janou
- ⑥ Vins des Pyrénées
- ⑦ Au Temps des Cerises
- ⑧ Au Bourguignon du Marais
- ⑨ L'Ebouillanté
- ⑩ Restaurante Sant Antonio
- ⑪ BHV Cafeteria
- ⑫ Place du Marché Ste. Catherine Eateries
- ⑬ L'Enoteca

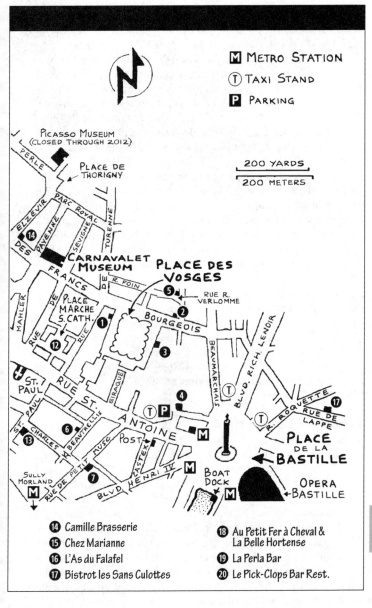

M METRO STATION

T TAXI STAND

P PARKING

Picasso Museum
(CLOSED THROUGH 2012)

PLACE DE
THORIGNY

200 YARDS
200 METERS

CARNAVALET
MUSEUM

PLACE DES
VOSGES

RUE R.
VERLOMME

PLACE
MARCHÉ
S. CATH.

BOURGEOIS

ST.
PAUL

RUE ST.

ANTOINE

POST

PLACE
DE LA
BASTILLE

SULLY
MORLAND

BOAT
DOCK

OPERA
BASTILLE

⑭ Camille Brasserie

⑮ Chez Marianne

⑯ L'As du Falafel

⑰ Bistrot les Sans Culottes

⑱ Au Petit Fer à Cheval &
   La Belle Hortense

⑲ La Perla Bar

⑳ Le Pick-Clops Bar Rest.

Closer to Hôtel de Ville

These eateries, near the Pompidou Center, appear on the map on page 406. To reach them, use the Hôtel de Ville Métro stop.

$$$ Au Bourguignon du Marais is a handsome wine-bar/bistro for Burgundy-lovers, where excellent wines (Burgundian only, available by the glass) blend with a good selection of well-designed dishes and efficient service (Philippe is clearly in charge). The *œufs en meurette* were the best I've ever had, and the *bœuf bourguignon* could feed two (€10–14 starters, €18–22 *plats*, closed Sun–Mon, indoor and outdoor seating, 52 rue Francois Miron, tel. 01 48 87 15 40).

$ L'Ebouillanté is a breezy crêperie-café, romantically situated near the river on a broad, cobbled lane behind a church. With great outdoor seating and an artsy, cozy interior, it's ideal for an inexpensive and relaxing tea, snack, or lunch—or for dinner on a warm evening. Try a *brick*, the light-hearted chef's specialty (think beefy crêpe). The salads and desserts are also good (€13 *plats*, Tue–Sun 12:00–21:30, closed Mon, 6 rue des Barres, tel. 01 42 71 09 69).

$ Restaurante Sant Antonio is bustling and cheap, serving up €11 pizzas and salads on a fun Marais square (daily, barely off rue de Rivoli on place du Bourg Tibourg).

$ BHV Department Store's fifth-floor cafeteria provides nice views, an escape from the busy streets below, and no-brainer, point-and-shoot cafeteria cuisine (Mon–Sat 11:30–18:00, closed Sun, at intersection of rue du Temple and rue de la Verrerie, one block from Hôtel de Ville).

In the Heart of the Marais

These are closest to the St. Paul Métro stop.

$$ *On place du Marché Ste. Catherine:* This small, romantic square, just off rue St. Antoine, is an international food festival cloaked in extremely Parisian, leafy-square ambience. On a balmy evening, this is clearly a neighborhood favorite, with a handful of restaurants offering €20–30 meals. Study the square and you'll find two popular French bistros (**Le Marché** and **Au Bistrot de la Place,** each with €23 three-course *menus*, tight seating on flimsy chairs indoors and out, both open daily) and other inviting eateries serving a variety of international food—Russian, Korean, Italian, and so on. You'll eat under the trees, surrounded by a futuristic-in-1800 planned residential quarter.

$$ L'Enoteca is a high-spirited, half-timbered spot serving affordable Italian cuisine (no pizza) with a tempting *antipasti* bar. It's a fun, open setting with busy, blue-aproned waiters serving two floors of local eaters (€17 pastas, €30 three-course *menu*, good-value wines, daily, across from L'Excuse at rue St. Paul and rue

Charles V, 25 rue Charles V, tel. 01 42 78 91 44).

$$ Camille, a traditional corner brasserie, is a neighborhood favorite with a lively interior and minimal sidewalk seating. Its waiters serve €13 salads and very French *plats du jour* (€22) from the chalkboard list to a down-to-earth but sophisticated clientele (daily, 24 rue des Francs Bourgeois at corner of rue Elzévir, tel. 01 42 72 20 50).

$ Several hardworking **Asian fast-food eateries,** great for a €8 meal, line rue St. Antoine.

On Rue des Rosiers in the Jewish Quarter

To reach the Jewish Quarter, use the St. Paul Métro stop.

$ Chez Marianne, a neighborhood fixture, offers classic Jewish meals and Parisian atmosphere. Choose from several indoor zones with a cluttered wine shop/deli feeling, or sit outside. You'll select from two dozen "Zakouski" elements to assemble your €15 plate (great vegetarian options, eat cheap with a €8 falafel sandwich—only €6 if you order it to go), long hours daily, corner of rue des Rosiers and rue des Hospitalières-St.-Gervais, tel. 01 42 72 18 86). For takeout, pay inside first and get a ticket before you order outside.

$ L'As du Falafel rules the falafel scene in the Jewish quarter. Monsieur Isaac, the "Ace of Falafel" here since 1979, brags he's got "the biggest pita on the street...and he fills it up." (Apparently it's Lenny Kravitz's favorite, too.) Your inexpensive meal comes on plastic plates, in a bustling setting that seems to prove he's earned his success. The €7 "special falafel" is the big hit, but many Americans enjoy his lighter chicken version *(poulet grillé)* or the tasty and filling *assiette de falafel.* Their take-out service draws a constant crowd; the interior is air-conditioned (day and night until late, closed Sat, 34 rue des Rosiers, tel. 01 48 87 63 60).

Picnicking in the Marais

Picnic at peaceful place des Vosges (closes at dusk) or on the Ile St. Louis *quais* (see below). Stretch your euros at the basement supermarket of the **Monoprix** department store (closed Sun, near place des Vosges on rue St. Antoine). You'll find small **groceries** open until 23:00 at 48 rue St. Antoine and on the Ile St. Louis.

Nightlife in the Marais

The best scene for hard-core night owls is the dizzying array of wacky eateries, bars, and dance halls on **rue de Lappe.** This street is what the Latin Quarter aspires to be. Just east of the stately place de la Bastille, it's one of the wildest nightspots in Paris and not for everyone. Sitting amid the chaos like a Van Gogh painting is the popular, old-time **Bistrot les Sans Culottes.**

Trendy cafés and bars—popular with gay men—also cluster on rue Vieille du Temple, rue des Archives, and rue Ste. Croix de la Bretonnerie (closing at about 2:00 in the morning). You'll find a line of bars and cafés providing front-row seats for the buff parade on rue Vieille du Temple, a block north of rue de Rivoli (the horseshoe-shaped **Au Petit Fer à Cheval** bar-restaurant and the atmospheric **La Belle Hortense** bookstore/wine bar are the focal points of the action). Nearby, rue des Rosiers bustles with youthful energy, but there are no cafés to observe from. **Vins des Pyrénées** (described earlier) is young and fun—find the small bar in the back. **La Perla** is full of Parisian yuppies in search of the perfect margarita (26 rue François Miron).

$ Le Pick-Clops bar-restaurant is a happy peanuts-and-lots-of-cocktails diner with bright neon, loud colors, and a garish local crowd. It's perfect for immersing yourself in today's Marais world—a little boisterous, a little edgy, a little gay, fun-loving, easygoing...and no tourists. Sit inside on old-fashioned diner stools, or streetside to watch the constant Marais parade. The name means "Steal the Cigarettes"—but you'll pay €11 for your big salad (daily 7:00–24:00, 16 rue Vieille du Temple, tel. 01 40 29 02 18).

The most enjoyable peaceful evening may be simply donning your floppy "three musketeers" hat and slowly strolling place des Vosges, window-shopping the art galleries.

On Ile St. Louis

Ile St. Louis is a romantic and peaceful neighborhood where you can amble around for plenty of promising dinner possibilities. Surprisingly, this upscale island is home to several inexpensive and good restaurants. Cruise the island's main street for a variety of options, from cozy *crêperies* to Italian eateries (intimate pizzerias and upscale) to typical brasseries (a few with fine outdoor seating facing the bridge to Ile de la Cité). After dinner sample Paris' best ice cream (described under "Ice-Cream Dessert," later in the chapter) and stroll across to the Ile de la Cité to see Notre-Dame illuminated, or enjoy a scenic drink on the deck of a floating café moored under Notre-Dame's right transept. All these listings line the island's main drag, rue St. Louis-en-l'Ile (see map on page 375; to get here use the Pont Marie Métro stop).

$$$ Le Tastevin is an intimate mother-and-son-run restaurant serving top-notch traditional French cuisine with white-tablecloth, candlelit, gourmet elegance under heavy wooden beams. The romantic setting (and the elegantly romantic local couples enjoying the place) naturally makes you whisper. The three-course *menus* start at about €39 and offer a handful of classic choices that change with the season to ensure freshness (daily, reserve for late-evening dining, good wine list, 46 rue St. Louis-en-l'Ile, tel.

01 43 54 17 31, owner Madame Puisieux and her gentle son speak just enough English).

$$$ *Medieval Theme Restaurants:* La Taverne du Sergeant Recruteur, famous for its rowdy, medieval-cellar atmosphere, is ideal for hungry warriors and their wenches who like to swill hearty wine. For as long as anyone can remember, they've served up a rustic all-you-can-eat buffet with straw baskets of raw veggies and bundles of sausage (cut whatever you like with your dagger), massive plates of pâté, a meat course, and all the wine you can stomach for €41. The food is just food; burping is encouraged. If you want to eat a lot, drink a lot of wine, be surrounded with tourists (mostly French), and holler at your friends while receiving smart-aleck buccaneer service, this food fest can be fun. And it comes with an historic twist: The "Sergeant Recruiter" used to get young Parisians drunk and stuffed here, then sign them into the army (daily from 19:00, #37 rue St. Louis-en-l'Ile, tel. 01 43 54 75 42). Next door, **Nos Ancêtres les Gaulois** is a bit goofier and grittier, and serves the same basic formula. As the name implies ("Our Ancestors the Gauls"), this place makes barbarians feel right at home (tel. 01 46 33 66 07). You might swing by both and choose the..."ambience" is not quite the right word...that fits your mood.

$$ Auberge de la Reine Blanche's friendly owner Michel welcomes diners willing to rub elbows with their neighbors in a cozy setting while enjoying delicious cuisine at unbeatable prices (€20 two-course *menu*, €25 three-course *menu*, daily, 30 rue St. Louis-en-l'Ile, tel. 01 46 33 07 87).

$$ La Brasserie de l'Ile St. Louis is situated at the prow of the island's ship as it faces Ile de la Cité, offering purely Alsatian cuisine (try the *choucroute garni* for €18), served in a Franco-Germanic setting with no-nonsense brasserie service. This is a good balmy-evening perch for watching the Ile St. Louis promenade—or, if it's chilly, the interior is plenty characteristic for a memorable night out (closed Wed, no reservations, 55 quai de Bourbon, tel. 01 43 54 02 59).

$ Café Med, near the pedestrian bridge to Notre-Dame at #77, has inexpensive salads, crêpes, and a €13–20 *menu* served in a tight but cheery setting (open daily, limited wine list, tel. 01 43 29 73 17). Two similar *crêperies* are just across the street.

Riverside Picnic for Impoverished Romantics

On sunny lunchtimes and balmy evenings, the *quai* on the Left Bank side of Ile St. Louis is lined with locals who have more class than money, spreading out tablecloths and even lighting candles for elegant picnics. And tourists can enjoy the same budget meal. There's the handy grocery store at #67 on the main drag (Wed–Mon until 22:00, closed Tue) that has tabouli and other simple, cheap take-away dishes for your picnicking pleasure.

Ice-Cream Dessert

Half the people strolling Ile St. Louis are licking an ice-cream cone, because this is the home of *les glaces Berthillon*. The original **Berthillon** shop, at 31 rue St. Louis-en-l'Ile, is marked by the line of salivating customers (closed Mon–Tue). Another Berthillon shop is across the street, and there's one more around the corner on rue Bellay (all are located on map on page 375). The three shops are so popular that the wealthy people who can afford to live on this fancy island complain about the congestion they cause. For a less famous but at least as tasty treat, the home-made Italian gelato a block away at **Amorino Gelati** is giving Berthillon competition (no line, bigger portions, easier to see what you want, and they offer little tastes—Berthillon doesn't need to, 47 rue St. Louis-en-l'Ile, tel. 01 44 07 48 08). Having some of each is not a bad thing.

In the Luxembourg Garden Area

Sleeping in the Luxembourg neighborhood puts you near many appealing dining and after-hours options. Because my hotels in this area cluster around the Panthéon and St. Sulpice Church (see Sleeping chapter), I've organized restaurant listings the same way. Restaurants near the Panthéon tend to be calm, those around St. Sulpice more boisterous; it's a short walk from one area to the other. Anyone sleeping in this area is close to the inexpensive eateries that line the always-bustling rue Mouffetard. You're also within a 15-minute walk of the *grands cafés* of St. Germain and Montparnasse (with Paris' first café and famous artist haunts; see "Les Grands Cafés de Paris," later in this chapter).

Near the Panthéon

For locations, see the map on page 381. These eateries are served by the Cluny-La Sorbonne Métro stop and the RER-B Luxembourg station.

$$ Restaurant Perraudin is a welcoming, family-run, red-checkered-tablecloth eatery understandably popular with tourists. Friendly Monsieur Correy serves classic *cuisine bourgeoise* with an emphasis on Burgundian dishes in air-conditioned comfort. The decor is vintage turn-of-the-20th-century, with big mirrors and old wood paneling (€20 lunch *menus*, €30 dinner *menus*, daily, *bœuf bourguignon* is a specialty here, between the Panthéon and Luxembourg Garden at 157 rue St. Jacques, tel. 01 46 33 15 75).

$ Le Soufflot Café, between the Panthéon and Luxembourg Garden, is well-positioned for afternoon sun and soft light in the evening. It has a nifty library-like interior, lots of outdoor tables, point-blank views of the Panthéon, and happy waiters (Frédéric and Serge are owners). The cuisine is café-classic, day or night:

good €10 salads, omelets, and *plats du jour* (daily, a block below the Panthéon on the right side of rue Soufflot as you walk toward Luxembourg Garden, tel. 01 43 26 57 56).

$ Place de la Sorbonne: This cobbled and green square, with a small fountain facing the Sorbonne University just a block from the Cluny Museum, offers several opportunities for a quick outdoor lunch or light dinner. At amiable Carole's tiny **Baker's Dozen,** you'll pay take-away prices for light fare you can sit down to eat (€5 salads and sandwiches, Mon–Fri until 15:30, closed Sun). **Café de l'Ecritoire** is a typical, lively brasserie with happy diners enjoying €11 salads, €13 *plats*, and fine square seating (daily, tel. 01 43 54 60 02). **Patios,** with appealing decor inside and out, seems more popular. It serves inexpensive Italian fare, including pizza (daily until late, tel. 01 45 38 71 19).

Near the Odéon Theater

To reach these, use the Odéon Métro stop. In this same neighborhood is Café le Procope, listed under "Les Grands Cafés de Paris," later in this chapter.

$$ Brasserie Bouillon Racine takes you back to 1906 with an Art Nouveau carnival of carved wood, stained glass, and old-time lights reflected in beveled mirrors. The over-the-top decor, energetic waiters, and affordable menu combine to give it an inviting conviviality. Check upstairs before choosing a table. Their roast suckling pig (€18) is a house favorite. There's good beer on tap and a fascinating history on the menu (€18 *plats*, €29 *menu*, traditional French with lots of fish and meat, daily 12:00–14:00 & 19:00–23:00, 3 rue Racine, tel. 01 44 32 15 60, Phillipe).

$$ La Méditerranée is all about having fish in a pastel and dressy setting...with similar clientele. The scene and the menu are sophisticated yet accessible, and the view of the Odéon is *formidable*. The sky-blue tablecloths and the lovingly presented dishes add to the romance (€27 two-course *menus*, €32 three-course *menus*, daily, smart to book ahead, facing the Odéon at 2 place de l'Odéon, tel. 01 43 26 02 30).

$$ Le Bistrot Mazarin is perfectly Parisian, tucked behind the Institut de France building on a quiet corner in the St. Germain neighborhood. Locals are wild about this place (arrive early). Choose from the warm interior or the pleasant sidewalk scene. Try the good wines *en carafe* and a great *magret de canard*— duck breast (€20 *plats*, daily; from Odéon Métro stop walk up rue de l'Ancienne Comédie, continue past Café le Procope as the street turns into rue Mazarine, 42 rue Mazarine; tel. 01 43 29 99 01).

$ Restaurant Polidor, a bare-bones neighborhood fixture since the 19th century, is much-loved for its unpretentious quality cooking, fun old-Paris atmosphere, and fair value. Stepping inside, you know this is a winner—noisy, happy diners sit tightly at shared tables as waiters chop and serve fresh bread. The selection features classic bourgeois *plats* from every corner of France; their *menu fraîcheur* is designed for lighter summer eating (€12–15 *plats*, €20–30 three-course *menus*, daily 12:00–14:30 & 19:00–23:00, cash only, no reservations, 41 rue Monsieur-le-Prince, tel. 01 43 26 95 34).

On Rue Mouffetard

Lying several blocks behind the Panthéon, rue Mouffetard is a conveyer belt of comparison-shopping eaters with wall-to-wall budget options (fondue, crêpes, Italian, falafel, and Greek). Come here to sift through the crowds and eat a less expensive meal (you get what you pay for). This street stays up late and likes to party (particularly around place de la Contrescarpe). The gauntlet begins on top, at thriving place de la Contrescarpe, and ends below where rue Mouffetard stops at St. Médard Church. Both ends offer fun cafés where you can eat, drink, and watch the action. The upper stretch is pedestrian and touristic; the bottom stretch is purely Parisian. Anywhere between is no-man's land for consistent quality. Still, strolling with so many fun-seekers is enjoyable, whether you eat or not. To get here, use the Censier-Daubenton Métro stop.

$ **Café Delmas,** at the top of rue Mouffetard on picturesque place de la Contrescarpe, is *the* place to see and be seen. Come here for a before- or after-dinner drink on the broad outdoor terrace, or for typical but pricey café cuisine (€15 salads, €20 *plats*, great chocolate ice cream, daily).

$ **Le Mouffetard,** a traditional café with a lively location in the heart of rue Mouffetard, is good for an inexpensive lunch or dinner (€13 lunches, €16 two-course *menus*, closed Sun evening and all day Mon, 116 rue Mouffetard, tel. 01 43 31 42 50).

$ Bar-restaurant **Les Papillons** is a down-and-dirty local diner where a few outdoor tables tangle with pedestrians and no one seems to care (€12 *plats*, closed Sun–Mon, 129 rue Mouffetard, tel. 01 43 31 66 50).

$ **Cave de Bourgogne** is *très* local and serves reasonably priced café fare at the bottom of rue Mouffetard. Outside has picture-perfect tables on a raised terrace; inside is warm and cozy (€13–16 *plats*, specials listed on chalkboards, daily, 144 rue Mouffetard).

Near St. Sulpice Church: Rue des Canettes and Rue Guisarde

For an entirely different experience, roam the streets between the St. Sulpice Church and boulevard St. Germain, abounding with restaurants, *crêperies*, wine bars, and jazz haunts (use Mo: St. Sulpice). Find rue des Canettes and rue Guisarde, and window-shop the many French and Italian eateries—most with similar

prices, but each with a slightly different feel. For tasty crêpes, try
$ La Crêpe Rit du Clown (Mon–Sat 12:00–23:00, closed Sun,
6 rue des Canettes, tel. 01 46 34 01 02). For comfortable atmosphere and above-average bistro fare in a zone where every res-
taurant looks the same, consider **$$ Le Bistrot Henri IV** (daily,
only indoor seating, 6 rue Princesse, tel. 01 46 33 51 12) or **$$ Lou
Pescadou-Chez Julien** (daily, some outdoor seating, 16 rue
Mabillon, tel. 01 43 54 56 08).

And for a bohemian pub lined with black-and-white photos
of the artsy and revolutionary French '60s, have a drink at **Chez
Georges.** Sit in a cool little streetside table nook, or venture downstairs to find a hazy, drippy-candle, traditionally French world in
the Edith Piaf–style dance cellar (cheap drinks from old-fashioned
menu, Tue–Sat 14:00–2:00 in the morning, closed Sun–Mon and
in Aug, 11 rue des Canettes, tel. 01 43 26 79 15).

Near Sèvres-Babylone
$$$ La Cigale Récamier is a classy place for a quiet meal with
appealing indoor and outdoor seating. It's on a short pedestrian
alley a block off rue de Sèvres (€20 *plats*, à la carte only, closed
Sun, 4 rue Récamier, Mo: Sèvres-Babylone, tel. 01 46 48 86 58).

Elsewhere in Paris
In the Galerie Vivienne, Behind the Palais Royal
$$$ Le Grand Colbert, appropriately located in the elegant
Galerie Vivienne (see the Shopping chapter), gives its clients the
feel of a luxury restaurant at relatively moderate prices. It's a stylish, grand brasserie with hurried waiters, leather booths, and brass
lamps, serving all the classic dishes from steak *frites* to escargots
(*menus* from €42, daily, 4 rue Vivienne, Mo: Palais Royal/Musée
du Louvre or Pyramides, tel. 01 42 86 82 38).

Along Canal St. Martin, North of République
Escape the crowded tourist areas and enjoy a breezy canalside
experience. Take the Métro to place de la République and walk
down rue Beaurepaire to Canal St. Martin. There you'll find a few
worthwhile cafés with similarly reasonable prices. **$ La Marine**
is a good choice (daily, 55 bis quai de Valmy, tel. 01 42 39 69 81).
In summertime most bars and cafés offer beer and wine to go *(à
emporter)*, so you can take it to the canal's edge and picnic there
with the young locals.

Near Opéra Garnier
$ Bouillon Chartier is a noisy, old, classic eatery. It's named for
the bouillon it served the neighborhood's poor workers back in
1896, when its calling was to provide an affordable warm meal for

those folks. Workers used to eat *à la gamelle* (from a tin lunchbox). That same spirit—complete with surly waiters and a cheap menu—survives today. Among more than 300 simple seats and 15 frantic waiters, you can still see the restaurant's napkin drawers for its early regulars (€4 starters, €12 *plats*, daily 11:30–15:00 & 18:00–22:00, east of the Opéra Garnier near boulevard Poissonniere, 7 rue de Faubourg-Montmartre, Mo: Grands Boulevards, tel. 01 47 70 86 29).

Montmartre

Montmartre is extremely touristy, with many mindless mobs following guides to cancan shows. But the ambience is undeniably fun, and an evening up here overlooking Paris is a quintessential experience in the City of Light. The steps in front of Sacré-Cœur are perfect for a picnic with a view, though the spot comes with lots of company. Along the touristy main drag (near place du Tertre and just off it), several fun piano bars serve crêpes along with great people-watching. To reach this area, use the Anvers Métro stop. More eateries are mentioned in the Montmartre Walk chapter.

$$ Restaurant Chez Plumeau, just off jam-packed place du Tertre, is touristy yet moderately priced, with formal service but great seating on a tiny, characteristic square (elaborate €17 salads, €18–22 *plats,* closed Wed, place du Calvaire, tel. 01 46 06 26 29).

$$ Moulin de la Galette lets you dine with Renoir under the historic windmill in a comfortable setting with good prices. Find the old photos scattered about the place (€17 two-course *menu*, €25 three-course *menu*, daily, 83 rue Lepic, Mo: Abbesses, tel. 01 46 06 84 77).

$ L'Eté en Pente Douce is a good Montmartre choice, hiding under the generous branches of street trees. Just downhill from the crowds on a classic neighborhood corner, it features cheery indoor and outdoor seating, €10 *plats du jour* and salads, vegetarian options, and good wines (daily, many steps below Sacré-Cœur to the left as you leave, down the stairs below the WC, 23 rue Muller, tel. 01 42 64 02 67).

Dinner Cruises

The following companies all offer dinner cruises (reservations required). Bateaux Mouches and Bateaux Parisiens have the best reputations and the highest prices. They offer multicourse meals and music in aircraft carrier–size dining rooms with glass tops and good views. For both, proper dress is required—no denim, shorts, or sport shoes; Bateaux Mouches requires a jacket and tie for men. The main difference between these companies is the music:

Bateaux Mouches offers violin and piano to entertain your romantic evening, whereas Bateaux Parisiens boasts a lively atmosphere with a singer, band, and dance floor.

Bateaux Mouches, started in 1949, is hands-down the most famous. You can't miss its sparkling port on the north side of the river at Pont de l'Alma. The boats usually board 19:30–20:15, depart at 20:30, and return at 22:45 (€95–130/person, RER: Pont de l'Alma, tel. 01 42 25 96 10, www.bateauxmouches.com).

Bateaux Parisiens leaves from Port de la Bourdonnais, just east of the bridge under the Eiffel Tower. Begin boarding at 19:45, leave at 20:30, and return at 23:00 (€100–145/person, 3 price tiers, depends on seating, tel. 08 25 62 75 13, www.bateauxparisiens .com). The middle level is best. Pay the few extra euros to get seats next to the windows—it's more romantic and private, with sensational views.

Le Capitaine Fracasse offers the budget option (€50/person, €70 with wine and coffee; tables are first-come, first-serve, so get there early; boarding times vary by season and day of week, closed Mon, walk down stairs in the middle of Bir Hakeim bridge near the Eiffel Tower to Iles aux Cygne, Mo: Bir-Hakeim or RER: Champ de Mars-Tour Eiffel, tel. 01 46 21 48 15, www.croisiere -paris.com).

Les Grands Cafés de Paris

Here's a short list of grand Parisian cafés, worth the detour only if you're not in a hurry or on a tight budget (some ask outrageous prices for a shot of espresso). Think of these cafés as monuments to another time and learn why they matter as much today as they did yesterday (see sidebar). For tips on enjoying Parisian cafés, review "Café Culture," near the beginning of this chapter.

St. Germain-des-Prés

For locations, see the map on page 378. Use the St. Germain-des-Prés Métro stop.

Where the boulevard St. Germain meets rue Bonaparte you'll find two famous cafés (both open daily). **Les Deux Magots** offers prime outdoor seating and a warm interior. Once a favorite of Ernest Hemingway (in *The Sun Also Rises*, Jake met Brett here) and Jean-Paul Sartre (he and Simone de Beauvoir met here), today the café is filled with international tourists. **Le Café de Flore,** next door, feels much more literary—wear your black turtleneck. Pablo Picasso was a regular at the time he painted *Guernica.*

For scenic outdoor seating and the same delightful view for less just a block away, set up for coffee or a light lunch at **$ Café**

History of Cafés in Paris

The first café in the Western world was in Paris—established in 1686 at Le Procope (still a restaurant today; see below). The French had just discovered coffee, and their robust economy was growing a population of pleasure-seekers and thinkers looking for places to be seen, to exchange ideas, and to plot revolutions—both political and philosophical. And with the advent of theaters such as La Comédie-Française, the necessary artsy, coffee-sipping crowds were birthed. By 1700, more than 300 cafés had opened their doors; at the time of the Revolution (1789), there were more than 1,800 cafés in Paris. Revolutionaries from Jean-Paul Marat and Napoleon to Salvador Dalí enjoyed the spirit of free-thinking that the cafés engendered.

Café society took off in the early 1900s. Life was changing rapidly, with new technology and wars on a global scale. Many retreated to Parisian cafés to try to make sense of the confusion. Vladimir Lenin, Leon Trotsky, Igor Stravinsky, Ernest Hemingway, F. Scott Fitzgerald, James Joyce, Albert Einstein, Jean-Paul Sartre, Gene Openshaw, and Albert Camus were among the devoted café society. Some practically lived at their favorite café, where they kept their business calendars, entertained friends, and ate every meal. Parisian apartments were small, walls were thin (still often the case), and heating (particularly during war times) was minimal, making the warmth of cafés all the harder to leave.

There are more than 12,000 cafés in Paris today, though their numbers are shrinking. They're still used for business meetings, encounter sessions, political discussions, and romantic interludes. Most Parisians are loyal to their favorites and know their waiter's children's names. The 2008 smoking ban could draw an ever-more health conscious French population back to its café roots.

Bonaparte (on the sunny side of the street, from Les Deux Magots, one block up rue Bonaparte toward river, tel. 01 43 26 42 81).

Paris' first and most famous, **$ Café le Procope** (1686), lies an enchanting five-minute stroll away. This was a *café célèbre*, drawing notables such as Voltaire, Rousseau, Honoré de Balzac, Emile Zola, Maximilien de Robespierre, Victor Hugo, and two Americans, Benjamin Franklin and Thomas Jefferson (beautiful restaurant and café but average cuisine, daily 10:00–24:00, 13 rue de l'Ancienne Comédie, tel. 01 40 46 79 00). To reach it from Café Bonaparte, walk down rue de l'Abbaye, then continue onto rue de Bourbon-le-Château. Veer left on the picturesque rue de Buci (more cafés), and turn right on rue de l'Ancienne Comédie.

Boulevard du Montparnasse

An eclectic assortment of historic cafés gathers along the busy boulevard du Montparnasse near its intersection with boulevard Raspail (Mo: Vavin). Combine these historic cafés with a visit to the Luxembourg Garden, which lies just a few blocks away, down rue Vavin (next to Le Select).

$$ La Coupole, built in the 1920s, was decorated by aspiring artists (Fernand Léger, Constantin Brancusi, and Marc Chagall, among others) in return for free meals. It still supports artists with regular showings on its vast walls. This cavernous café feels like a classy train station, with acres of seating, brass decor, and tuxedoed waiters by the dozen. Bring your friends and make noise. The food is fine; the service can be impersonal, but that's not the reason you came (€24 two-course *menu*, €31 three-course *menu*, daily, food served from 12:00 until the wee hours, come early to get better service, 102 boulevard du Montparnasse, tel. 01 43 20 14 20).

$$ Le Select, more easygoing and traditional, was once popular with the more rebellious types—Leon Trotsky, Jean Cocteau, and Pablo Picasso loved it. It feels rather conformist today, with good outdoor seating and pleasant tables just inside the door— though the locals hang out at the bar farther inside (€11–14 salads, €17 *plats*, daily, 99 boulevard du Montparnasse, across from La Coupole, tel. 01 45 48 38 24).

Avenue des Champs-Elysées

To reach these two cafés, use the George V Métro stop. These are also described in more detail in the Champs-Elysées Walk chapter.

$$$ Fouquet's, which opened in 1899, has played host to coachmen, biplane fighter pilots, artists, today's celebrities...and tourists. Though the intimidating interior is impressive, the outdoor setting is Champs-Elysées great, with pay-for-view €6 espresso (daily, 99 avenue des Champs-Elysées, tel. 01 47 23 70 60).

$$ Ladurée, two blocks downhill, is a classic on Paris' grandest boulevard (Mon–Sat 7:30–24:00, Sun 8:30–24:00, a block below avenue George V at #75, tel. 01 40 75 08 75).

On Place de la Concorde

$$$ Hôtel Crillon's four-star elegance can be yours for an afternoon. Considered the most exclusive (and expensive) hotel in Paris (and the last of the great hotels to be French-owned), it gives you a taste of royal life. Wear the best clothes you packed, arrive after 15:00, let the bellhop spin the door, and settle into the royal chairs in the *salon du thé*. You'll be surrounded by famous people you won't recognize (€10 for a pot of tea or double *café au lait*, about €34 for high tea served daily, €48 if you toss in a glass of champagne, 15:30–18:00, 10 place de la Concorde, Mo: Concorde).

Near the Louvre

$ Café le Nemours, a staunchly Parisian fixture serving pricey but good light lunches, is tucked into the corner of the Palais Royal adjacent to the Comédie Française. With elegant brass and Art Deco style, and outdoor tables under an arcade two minutes from the pyramid, it's a great post-Louvre retreat (fun and filling €12 salads, open daily; leaving the Louvre, cross rue de Rivoli and veer left to 2 place Colette—see Louvre map on page 113; Mo: Palais Royal, tel. 01 42 61 34 14).

At Gare de Lyon

$$$ Le Train Bleu is a grandiose restaurant with a low-slung, leather-couch café-bar area built right into the train station for

the Paris Exhibition of 1900 (which also saw the construction of the pont Alexandre III and the Grand and Petit Palais). It's simply a grand-scale-everything experience, with over-the-top belle époque decor that speaks of another age, when going to dinner was an event—a chance to see and be seen—and intimate dining was out. Forty-one massive paintings of scenes along the old rail lines tempt diners to consider a getaway. Many films have featured this restaurant. Reserve ahead for dinner, or drop in for a drink before your train leaves (€50 *menu*, €7 beer, €5 espresso, daily, up the stairs opposite track L, tel. 01 43 43 09 06, www.le-train-bleu.com). If you're in a rush (a pity), you can have the €50 *menu TGV*—two gourmet courses served in less than 45 minutes, with coffee.

Honorable Mention

$ Café de la Mosque, behind the Jardins des Plantes and attached to Paris' largest mosque (see map on page 381), beams you straight to Morocco, with outdoor courtyards and an interior room, all in North African tearoom decor with a full menu to match (€14–18 couscous, daily 10:00–24:00, 39 rue Geoffroy St. Hilaire, Mo: Place Monge, tel. 01 43 31 38 20). Consider an afternoon tea-and-pastry stop (€2 pastries, to eat in or take out).

$ Café la Palette, on *le* Left Bank, is across the river and a few blocks from the Louvre. Over 100 years old, this café feels real and unaffected by the passage of time (reasonably priced drinks, 43 rue de Seine, Mo: Mabillon). For more on this café, see page 253 in the Left Bank Walk.

$ Au Sauvignon Café, the smallest of the cafés described in this section, is perfectly positioned for people-watching near Sèvres-Babylone boutiques (see map page 378). The interior is vintage Paris with wall-to-ceiling décor and a fine zinc bar (€4.50–6 glasses of wine, daily, 10 rue de Sèvres, Mo: Sèvres-Babylone, tel. 01 45 48 49 02).

PARIS WITH CHILDREN

Paris works surprisingly well with children—smart adults enjoy the "fine art" of simply being in Paris' great neighborhoods, parks, and monuments while watching their kids uncover the City of Light. After enjoying so many family-friendly sights, your children may want to return to Paris before you do. Consider these tips:

- Hotel selection is critical. Stay in a kid-friendly area near a park. The rue Cler and Luxembourg neighborhoods are both good. If you're staying a week or more, rent an apartment (see "For Longer Stays," page 385).
- Before you go, get your kids into the Parisian spirit by reading (see "Kids' Reading List," next page). Bring along plenty of kids' books; they're harder to find and expensive in Paris. If you run out, visit one of the English-language bookstores listed on page 27.
- If traveling with infants, pack a light stroller and a child backpack. Strollers are tough in the Métro (piles of stairs) and not allowed at some sights, but are ideal for neighborhood walks. Backpacks are easier on the Métro and buses, but prohibited at many museums (in which case strollers are generally allowed and sometimes even provided).
- Don't overdo it. Tackle one key sight each day (Louvre, Orsay, Versailles), and mix it with a healthy dose of fun activities. To minimize unnecessary travel, try to match kid activities with areas where you'll be sightseeing (e.g., the Louvre is near the kid-friendly Palais Royal's courtyards and Tuileries Garden). Kids prefer the Louvre after dark, when it's very quiet (Wed and Fri only).
- The double-decker bus tours (see page 37) are a good way to start your visit.
- Follow this book's crowd-beating tips to the letter. Kids

despise long lines more than you do.

- Check the Paris TI website for current information on children's activities from shows to museums to park events (www .parisinfo.com).

- Eat dinner early, before the sophisticated local crowd dines (aim for 19:00–19:30 at restaurants, earlier at cafés). Skip romantic places. Look for cafés (or fast-food restaurants) where kids can move around without bothering others. Picnics work well.

- The cheapest toy selection is usually in the large department stores, such as Bon Marché (see Shopping chapter).

- French marionette shows, often called *guignols* (geen-yohl), are fun for everyone. They take place in several locations in Paris, mostly in big parks (usually Wed, Sat, and Sun around 15:00). See *Pariscope* or *L'Officiel des Spectacles* (sold at newsstands), under "Marionettes," for times and places. Even in French, the plots are easy to follow, and the price is right (€2–5). Arrive 20 minutes early for good seats.

- Involve your children in the trip. Let them help choose daily activities, lead you through the Métro, and so on.

- The best thing we did on one trip was buy a set of *boules* (a form of outdoor bowling—for the rules, see the sidebar on page 360). We'd play *boules* before dinner, side by side with real players at the neighborhood park. Buy your *boules de pétanque* at the BHV store in the Marais (next to Hôtel de Ville) or at a sporting-goods store. The *boules* make great (if weighty) souvenirs and are fun to play back at home.

- Some Paris parks host temporary amusement parks. The summer Ferris wheel and rides in the Tuileries Garden are the best—my daughter preferred it to Disneyland Paris (for Disneyland Paris details, see the More Day Trips chapter). Consider visiting an amusement park as an end-of-trip reward.

- Note that Wednesdays can be busy days at children's sights, because school lets out early. This is also when more kid activities are likely to take place in parks (puppet shows, horse rides, toy boat rental, and the like).

- Consider hiring a babysitter for a night or two—check www .babychou.com (click on "Babysitting in Paris Hotels") and www.paris-anglo.com (click on "Classifieds").

Kids' Reading List

Pick up books at the library and rent videos. Watch or read the Madeline stories by Ludwig Bemelmans, *The Hunchback of Notre-Dame* by Victor Hugo, *The Three Musketeers* by Alexandre Dumas, or Dumas' *The Man in the Iron Mask*. *Anni's Diary of France*, by

Anni Axworthy, is a fun, picture-filled book about a young girl's trip; it could inspire your children.

How Would You Survive in the Middle Ages? by Fiona MacDonald is an appealing "guide" for kids. Serious kid historians will devour *The Kingfisher History Encyclopedia. Cathedral* by David Macauley re-creates the building of a French Gothic cathedral in detailed pen-and-ink sketches. If your children are interested in art, get your hands on *The History of Art for Young People* by Anthony Janson and *Discovering Great Artists: Hands-On Art for Children in the Styles of the Great Masters* by MaryAnn Kohl. (Also see "Recommended Books and Movies," including some good choices for teenagers, on page 589 of the appendix.)

Top Sights and Activities

Luxembourg Garden

This is my favorite place to mix kid business with pleasure. This perfectly Parisian park has it all—from tennis courts to cafés—as

well as an extensive big-toys play area with imaginative slides, swings, jungle gyms, and chess games (see map on page 259). To find the big-toys play area, head to the southwest corner (small fee, entry good all day, many parents watch from chairs outside the play area, open daily, usually 10:00–19:00 in summer, until 16:00 in winter). Kids also like the speedy merry-go-round (small fee), the pony rides (by the tennis courts), and the toy rental sailboats in the main pond (activities open daily in summer, otherwise only Wed and Sat–Sun). Near the main building is a toddler wading pool (summer only) and sand pit (both free). Adults and kids enjoy the terrific puppet shows *(guignols)* held on Wednesday, Saturday, and Sunday afternoons (about 15:00) near the children's play area, also located in the southwest corner of the park (€2–5, times listed in *Pariscope* as "Marionnettes du Luxembourg" under "Enfants" section). The park has big, open areas perfect for kicking a ball. Kids can even play in the grass opposite the palace (Mo: St. Sulpice, Odéon, or Notre-Dame-des-Champs, tel. 01 43 26 46 47).

Eiffel Tower, Champ de Mars Park, and Trocadéro

You could fill an entire kid-fun day here. Come early and ride the elevator up the tower before crowds appear, or ride it above the lights at night (see the ✪ Eiffel Tower Tour chapter). The Champ de Mars park stretches out from the tower's base, with picnic-perfect benches, big toys, sand pits, pony rides, puppet shows, and pedal go-carts. Big toys are located at the non-river end of the park (with your back to the tower, it's to the right). The pony rides, puppet shows, and go-carts are in the center in the park (after 11:00 Wed, Sat–Sun, and on all summer days; after 15:00 otherwise, Mo: Ecole Militaire; RER-C: Champ de Mars-Tour Eiffel; or bus #69).

All ages enjoy the view from Trocadéro across the river to the Eiffel Tower, especially after dark (Mo: Trocadéro). There's a terrific **National Maritime Museum** (Musée National de la Marine) docked at Trocadéro, with all things nautical and many ship models (kids 18 and under free, adults-€7, covered by Museum Pass, Wed–Mon 10:00–18:00, closed Tue, unfortunately very little in English, the museum is to your right as you face the tower from Trocadéro Square). See page 57 for more information. The **Musée de l'Homme**, next door, is an anthropological museum, but has zero information in English. The **Cinéaqua** aquarium in the gardens below the Trocadéro boasts 10,000 fish in more than 40 tanks and offers regular shows (students and kids under 12-€16, adults-€20, daily 10:00–20:00, 2 avenue des Nations Unies, Mo: Trocadéro, tel. 01 40 69 23 23, www.cineaqua.com).

Notre-Dame, Towers, and Crypt

Paris' famous Gothic cathedral doesn't have to be dry and dull. Replay Quasimodo's stunt and climb the tower (go early to avoid long lines). Kids love being on such a lofty perch with a face-to-face look at a gargoyle. The crypt on the square in front of Notre-Dame is quick and interesting (covered by Museum Pass). Kids can push buttons to highlight remains of Roman Paris and leave with a better understanding of how different civilizations build on top of each other. The small but beautiful park along the river outside Notre-Dame's right transept has sandboxes, picnic benches, and space to run (Mo: Cité). My pre-teen son loved the traffic-free lanes of the Latin Quarter across the river.

✪ See the Historic Paris Walk chapter.

Riverboat Rides

A variety of companies offer one-hour Seine cruises on huge glass-domed boats, with departures until 22:30 (best at sunset or after dark). Or hop on a Batobus, a river bus connecting eight stops along the river: Eiffel Tower, Champs-Elysées, Orsay/place de la Concorde, Louvre, Notre-Dame, St. Germain-des-Prés, Hôtel de Ville, and Jardin des Plantes. Longer boat trips ply the tranquil waters of Canal St. Martin between the Bastille and Bassin de la Villette (see "Tours—By Boat," page 38).

Arc de Triomphe and Champs-Elysées

This area is popular with teenagers, day and night. Mine couldn't get enough of it. Watch the crazy traf-
fic rush around the Arc de Triomphe for endless entertainment, then stroll avenue des Champs-Elysées with its car dealerships (particularly Renault's space-age café), Virgin Megastore (music), Disney store, and the river of humanity that flows along its broad sidewalks. Take your teenager to see a movie on the Champs-Elysées ("v.o."
next to the showtime means it's shown in the original language).

○ See the Champs-Elysées Walk chapter.

Tuileries Garden

This central park, located between the Louvre and place de la Concorde, across the river from the Orsay Museum, comes in handy for kid breaks. You'll find the usual children's activities on Wednesdays, Saturdays, and Sundays (toy sailboat rental in pond and pony rides) and a new activity—trampolines—in the northwest corner of the park near the Place de la Concorde Métro stop (same hours as other kid activities). The Tuileries Garden also hosts a summer fair with rides, games, and a huge Ferris wheel.

Versailles

This massive complex of palaces, gardens, fountains, and forest can be brutal—or a good family getaway if well-planned. Avoid Tuesdays and Sundays, when the place is packed from open to close. On other days, arrive around 11:00, and do the gardens first and the interior late, when crowds subside. Rent a bike or (even better) a golf cart to explore the gardens. Driving around the grounds in a golf cart, while pricey (€30/hr), is great fun and extremely easy. (They'll want parents to do the driving for liabil-ity reasons, but once away from the palace, you're on your own.) Or you can row row row a boat on the canal. The Domaine de Marie-Antoinette has trails for scampering on and her Hamlet has barnyard animals up close and personal (keep in mind that the Domaine does not open until noon). Be careful of crowds on summer weekends, when the fountains are flowing.

○ See the Versailles Day Trip chapter.

Jardin des Plantes

These colorful gardens are a must for gardeners and good for kids. Located across the river just east of the Marais, the park is short on grass but long on kid activities, including a small *ménagerie* (zoo) near the river (kids-€5, adults-€7, daily 9:00–18:00), several play areas, and two kid-friendly natural science museums (both closed Tue).

Young kids enjoy the dinosaur exhibit at the **Galerie d'Anatomie Comparée et de Paléontologie;** there are no English explanations, but they're not really needed (kids-€5, adults-€7, Wed–Mon 10:00–17:00, until 18:00 on April–Sept weekends, closed Tue, busiest on weekends, entrance faces river next to McDonald's).

The **Grande Galerie de l'Evolution,** at the non-river end of the park, is a dazzling museum describing the evolution of animals, with huge models and fun exhibits. English explanations are not provided, so you'll need the good guidebook (*Grande Galerie de l'Evolution*, €10) available in English at the museum's bookstore (kids-€7, adults-€9, not covered by Museum Pass, Wed–Mon 10:00–18:00, closed Tue, busiest on weekends, tel. 01 40 79 30 00, www.mnhn.fr/evolution). From the park entrance on place Valhubert, the museums line the left side of the park (Mo: Gare d'Austerlitz or Jussieu).

Outside the park, just behind Grande Galerie de l'Evolution, is the Moroccan-themed Café de la Mosque (see page 420 in the Eating chapter).

Pompidou Center

Teens like the Pompidou Center for its crazy outdoor entertainers, throngs of young people, happening cafés, and fun fountains next door (dead on Tue, when museum is closed). Inside, the temporary exhibits and gift shops on the main floor are visually impressive. The *Star Wars*–esque escalator to the top is fun for all ages, but you need a Museum Pass or Pompidou combo-ticket to escalate (Mo: Rambuteau).

✪ See the Pompidou Center Tour chapter.

Jardin des Enfants aux Halles

This is a terrific place to drop your child for an hour (ages 7–11 only, no adults allowed inside, call at least an hour ahead to reserve, tel. 01 45 08 07 18). It's outdoors, in front of Les Halles shopping center near St. Eustache church. Kids get one supervised hour (that's it) to negotiate a great play area filled with clever activities, including a small toboggan ride, a maze, a volcano, and much more. The staff speaks enough English and is accustomed to non-French-speaking kids (free, Tue and Thu–Fri 9:00–12:00 & 14:00–18:00, Wed and Sat 10:00–18:00, Sun 13:00–18:00, closed Mon and if rainy, 105 rue Rambuteau, Mo: Les Halles).

Aquaboulevard

Paris' best pool/waterslide/miniature golf complex is easy to reach and a timely escape from the museum scene. Indoor and outdoor pools with high-flying slides, waves, geysers, and whirl-pool tubs draw kids of all ages. It's pricey (and steamy inside) but a fun opportunity to see soaked Parisians at play. Ride the Métro to the end of line 8 (Balard stop), walk two blocks under the elevated freeway, veer left across the traffic circle, and find Aquaboulevard in a complex of theaters and shops (kids under 12-€10/6 hrs, adults-€25/6 hrs, much cheaper rates for more than one visit, daily 9:00–23:00, English-speaking staff, keep a €1 coin for lockers, boys and men need Speedo-style swimsuits—€6–10 at the Decathlon sporting-goods store right there, see map on page 432 for location, tel. 01 40 60 10 00).

SHOPPING IN PARIS

Even staunch anti-shoppers may be tempted to partake in chic Paris. Wandering among elegant and outrageous boutiques provides a break from the heavy halls of the Louvre, and, if you approach it right, a little cultural enlightenment.

In this chapter, you'll find information on shopping for souvenirs, clothing, food, and bargains. Most travelers are interested in finding a few souvenirs and maybe an article of clothing. Here's a simple approach that works for most:

- If you need just souvenirs, find a souvenir shop or consult your neighborhood supermarket for that Parisian box of tea, jam, or cookies—perfect for tucking into your suitcase at the last minute.
- For more elaborate purchases, large department stores provide painless one-stop shopping in elegant surroundings.
- Neighborhood boutiques offer the greatest reward at the highest risk. Clerks and prices can be intimidating, but the selection is more original and the experience is purely Parisian.
- Don't leave souvenir shopping for Sunday, when most stores are buttoned up tight.

For information on VAT refunds and customs regulations, see page 12.

Tips on Shopping

Before you enter a Parisian store, remember the following points:

- In small stores, always say, *"Bonjour, Madame* or *Mademoiselle* or *Monsieur"* when entering. For extra credit, apologize for bothering the clerk: *"Excusez-moi de vous déranger."* And remember to say *"Au revoir, Madame* or *Mademoiselle* or *Monsieur"* when leaving.

Key Phrases

English	French	Pronounced
Just looking.	Je regard.	zhuh ruh-gar
Pardon me for bothering you.	Excusez-moi de vous déranger.	ek-skew-zay-mwah duh voo day-rahn-zhay
How much is it?	Combien?	kohm-bee-ehn
Too big/small/ expensive	Trop grand/ petit/cher	troh grahn/ puh-tee/sher
May I try it on?	Je peux l'essayer?	zhuh puh luh-say-yay
Can I see more?	Auriez vous autre chose à me proposer?	oh-ree-ay voo zoh-truh shohz ah muh proh-poh-zay?
I'd like this.	Je voudrais ça.	zhuh voo-dray sah
On sale	Solde	sold
Discounted price	Prix réduit	pree ray-dwee
Big discounts	Prix choc	pree shock

- The customer is not always right. In fact, figure the clerk is doing you a favor by waiting on you.
- Except in department stores, it's not normal for the customer to handle clothing. Ask first before you pick up an item: *"Pourrais-je voir de plus près?"* (poo-ray-zhuh vwahr duh ploo pray; means "May I see this closer?").
- For clothing size comparisons between the US and France, see page 593 of the appendix.
- Forget returns (and don't count on exchanges).
- Saturday afternoons are busiest.
- Observe French shoppers. Then imitate.
- Stores are generally closed on Sunday, except at the Carrousel du Louvre (underground shopping mall at the Louvre), and some shops near Sèvres-Babylone, along the Champs-Elysées, and in the Marais.
- Don't feel obliged to buy. The expression for "window-shopping" in French is *faire du lèche-vitrines* ("window-licking").

Souvenir Shops

Avoid souvenir carts in front of famous monuments. Prices and selection are better in shops and department stores. Look around the Pompidou Center, on the streets of Montmartre, and in department stores (see below). The riverfront stalls near Notre-Dame sell a variety of used books, old posters and postcards, magazines, and some tourist paraphernalia in the most romantic setting; see *"Les Bouquinistes* (Riverside Vendors)" sidebar. You'll find better deals at the souvenir shops that line rue d'Arcole between Notre-Dame and Hôtel de Ville and on rue de Rivoli, alongside the Louvre.

Department Stores (Les Grands Magasins)

Like cafés, department stores were invented here (surprisingly, not in America). The stores may seem overwhelming at first, but they generally work like ours, and those listed here are accustomed to wide-eyed foreign shoppers and have English-speaking staff. These stores are not only beautiful monuments to a more relaxed, elegant era, but also a great lesson in how others live. It's instructive to see what's in style, check out Parisians' current taste in clothes and furniture, and compare the selection with stores back home.

Parisian department stores begin with their showy perfume sections, almost always central on the ground floor, and worth a visit to see how much space is devoted to pricey, smelly water. Helpful information desks are usually near the perfume section (handy floor plans in English). Most stores have a good selection of souvenirs and toys at fair prices, plus reasonable restaurants; some have view terraces. Stores are generally open Monday through Saturday from 10:00 to 19:00. Some are open later on Thursdays, and all are jammed on Saturdays and closed on Sundays.

Galeries Lafayette and Printemps

You'll find both Galeries Lafayette and Printemps (pran-tom) department stores in several Parisian neighborhoods. The most convenient and best sit side by side behind the old Opéra, complementing that monument's similar, classy era (Mo: Chaussée d'Antin-La Fayette, Havre-Caumartin, or Opéra). Both stores sprawl over three buildings and consume entire city blocks. The selection is huge, crowds can be huger (especially on summer Saturdays), and the prices are considered pretty high.

Galeries Lafayette is the must see-store. Don't miss the sensational belle époque dome (enjoy from the railing on the third or fourth floor) or the grand, open-air rooftop view on the seventh floor (free, open daily May–Sept, climb there from the cafeteria on the sixth floor). Fashion shows for the public take place year-round at Galeries Lafayette on Fridays at 15:00 (call 01 42 82 30 25 to confirm time and to reserve—they speak English, in auditorium on seventh floor, www.galerieslafayette.com). Beware the *"mode seduction"* on the third floor. Continue your shopping by walking from this area to place Vendôme (see "Boutique Strolls," later in this chapter).

Shopping in Paris

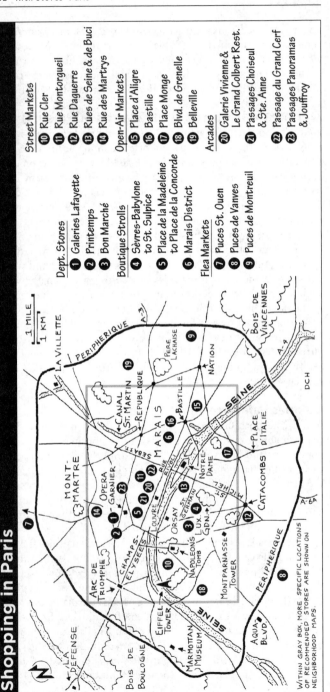

Dept. Stores
1 Galeries Lafayette
2 Printemps
3 Bon Marché

Boutique Strolls
4 Sèvres-Babylone to St. Sulpice
5 Place de la Madeleine to Place de la Concorde
6 Marais District

Flea Markets
7 Puces St. Ouen
8 Puces de Vanves
9 Puces de Montreuil

Street Markets
10 Rue Cler
11 Rue Montorgueil
12 Rue Daguerre
13 Rues de Seine & de Buci
14 Rue des Martrys

Open-Air Markets
15 Place d'Aligre
16 Bastille
17 Place Monge
18 Blvd. de Grenelle
19 Belleville

Arcades
20 Galerie Vivienne & Le Grand Colbert Rest.
21 Passages Choiseul & Ste. Anne
22 Passage du Grand Cerf
23 Passages Panoramas & Jouffroy

WITHIN GRAY BOX, MORE SPECIFIC LOCATIONS OF RECOMMENDED STORES ARE SHOWN ON NEIGHBORHOOD MAPS.

Bon Marché

Combine a visit to Paris' oldest department store with a great neighborhood shopping experience. Take the Métro (or bus #87)

to Sèvres-Babylone and find the Bon Marché behind a small park. The Bon Marché ("inexpensive") opened in 1852, when fascination with iron and steel construction led to larger structures (like train stations, exhibition halls, and Eiffel Towers). The Bon Marché was the first large-scale store to offer fixed prices (no bargaining) and a vast selection of items under one glass roof. This rocked the commercial world and forever changed the future of shopping. High-volume sales allowed low prices and created loyal customers—can you say "Costco"?

Start your tour at the perfume section in the center—check out the fine scarf selection next to this area—then escalate up a few floors for a better perspective. Consider a new couch on the top floor (is it just me, or do the clerks at their desks seem more like loan officers?), then find the trendy restaurants and the good toy selection in the basement. Graze the gourmet groceries in the store's second building (La Grande Epicerie, behind the main building), ideal for food souvenirs such as mustards, teas, and chocolates. I buy a small picnic here for the park in front.

To find my favorite boutique-store streets, walk through the small park and down rue de Sèvres, passing the grand Hôtel Lutetia—which was built for shoppers by the Bon Marché's owners—on your right (see "Sèvres-Babylone to St. Sulpice," next page).

Boutique Strolls

Give yourself a vacation from your sightseeing-focused vacation by sifting through window displays, pausing at corner cafés, and feeling the rhythm of neighborhood life (or have you been playing hooky and doing this already?) Though

smaller shops are more intimate, sales clerks are more formal—so mind your manners. Here are three very different areas to lick some windows.

Sèvres-Babylone to St. Sulpice

This shopping stroll allows you to sample smart clothing boutiques and clever window displays while enjoying one of Paris' more attractive neighborhoods. This leisurely one-hour saunter starts at the Bon Marché department store (described above) and ends at the church of St. Sulpice. It can also easily be extended to the nearby Luxembourg Garden or boulevard St. Germain, tying in well with this book's Left Bank Walk (see map on page 251). Some stores on this walk are open Sunday afternoons, though the walk is better on other days.

After visiting the Bon Marché (Mo: Sèvres-Babylone), walk by the small park and cross boulevard Raspail, with Hôtel Lutetia to your right, and start down rue de Sèvres.

La Maison du Chocolat, next to Hôtel Lutetia (19 rue de Sèvres), makes a good first stop. The shop sells handmade chocolates in exquisitely wrapped boxes and delicious ice-cream cones in season. Parisians commonly offer chocolates when invited over, and no gift box better impresses than this.

Cross the street, walk down a block, and find a seat at the atmospheric **Au Sauvignon Café** (10 rue de Sèvres, open daily), ideal for lunch or a drink, and well-situated for watching the conveyor belt of well-dressed shoppers glide by. Check in for a hot or cold drink, and check out the zinc bar and picture-crazy interior. If your feet hurt, relief is at hand—a **Mephisto** shoe store is almost next door. A block farther down rue de Sèvres, a wicked half-man, half-horse statue (ouch) stands guard.

From here boutique-lined streets fan out like spokes on a wheel (from left to right): rue de Grenelle, rue du Dragon, rue du Cherche Midi, and rue du Vieux Colombier. Each street merits a detour if shopping matters to you. Rue du Cherche Midi (follow the horse's fanny) offers an ever-changing but always chic selection of shoe, purse, and clothing stores. Find Paris' most celebrated bread—beautiful round loaves with designer crust—at the low-key **Poilâne** at #8 and enter for a sample (closed Sun). Notice the care with which each loaf of bread is wrapped. Next door, the small **Cuisine de Bar** café is a *bar à pains* (bread bar) and serves open-faced sandwiches *(tartines)* and salads with Poilâne bread (closed Sun–Mon).

Back at the horse, turn right and continue down rue du Vieux Colombier. You'll pass the **Théâtre du Vieux-Colombier** (1913), one of three key venues for La Comédie-Française, a historic state-run troupe. Enter and find the timeline to the right—any names you recognize? Imagine how two world wars affected business here. At **Longchamps** (#21) you can hunt for a stylish bag in any color. Cross busy rue de Rennes, gasping at the dreadful Montparnasse Tower, and continue down rue du Vieux Colombier. Many stores

Les Bouquinistes (Riverside Vendors)

The used-book sellers *(bouquinistes)* you see along the Seine around Notre-Dame are a Parisian fixture. They've been here since the mid-1500s, when shops and stalls lined most of the bridges in Paris. In 1557, these merchants were tagged as thieves for selling forbidden Protestant pamphlets during the Wars of Religion (Parisians were staunchly Catholic).

The term *bouquinistes* (boo-keen-eest) probably comes from the Dutch word *boeckin*, meaning "small book." First using wheelbarrows to transport and sell their goods, these hardy entrepreneurs eventually fastened trays to the parapets of the bridges with thin leather straps. After the Revolution, business boomed when entire libraries were liberated from nobles or clergymen and wound up for sale cheap on the banks of the Seine. In 1891, *bouquinistes* received permission to permanently attach their boxes to the quaysides. Today, the waiting list to become one of Paris' 250 *bouquinistes* is eight years.

Each *bouquiniste* is given four boxes, all of a specified size, and rent is paid only for the stone on which the boxes rest (less than €100 per year). The most coveted spots are awarded based on seniority. Maintenance costs, including the required *vert* wagon paint (the green color of old train cars), are paid by the *bouquinistes*. With little overhead, prices are usually reasonable. While these days tourists prefer magnets and posters over vintage books, the city "officially" allows no more than one box of souvenirs for every three boxes of books.

Bouquinistes must be open at least four days a week, or they lose their spot. Wednesdays are best (when school is out), and warm, dry days are golden (notice that every item is wrapped in protective plastic). And yes, they do leave everything inside when they lock up at night; metal bars and padlocks keep things safe.

in this area offer just one or two items, but in a variety of colors and patterns. Check out **Vilebrequin** if the man or *petit-garçon* in your life needs a swimsuit.

St. Sulpice Church awaits a block farther down. The **Café de la Mairie** has a privileged location on this lovely square. Here you can visit St. Sulpice (see page 60) and either cross the square to Luxembourg Garden (page 63) or backtrack to rue Bonaparte, turning right to reach boulevard St. Germain (and more shopping and several *grands cafés*, described on page 417). If you need a bookstore, take a detour left on rue Mabillon, another left on rue Guisarde, then find the **Village Voice** at 6 rue Princesse.

For Paris' best pastries—according to local shopkeepers and my wife—continue along rue St. Sulpice, with the church on your right, passing **Café Estrella** (closed Sun, 34 rue St. Sulpice, excellent teas and coffee with *real* French roast, and a friendly owner, Jean-Claude). A few blocks beyond, take a left onto rue de Seine (marked *rue du Tournon* to the right) and find **Gérard Mulot's Pâtisserie/Bakery.** Ogle the window display and try his chocolate macaroons and savory quiches—oh, baby (closed Wed, 76 rue de Seine, tel. 01 43 26 85 77).

From here the closest Métro station is Odéon. To get there, continue on rue de Seine up to boulevard St. Germain and walk a couple of blocks to the right. You can also continue down rue de Seine to the river and follow my Left Bank Walk.

Place de la Madeleine, Rue Royale, Place Vendôme, and Place de la Concorde

The ritzy streets connecting these high-priced squares form a miracle mile of gourmet food shops, glittering jewelry stores, four-star hotels, exclusive clothing boutiques, and people who spend more on clothes in one day than I do all year. This walk highlights the value Parisians place on outrageously priced products. If you include the place Vendôme detour (with brief stops to shop), this walk takes about 90 minutes. For most, the one-hour walk *sans* detour, ending on place de la Concorde, offers a sufficient sample of conspicuous consumption. Skip this walk on Sundays, when all shops are closed.

Place de la Madeleine: Start at place de la Madeleine for a gourmet food fantasy (see map on page 52; Mo: Madeleine). From the Métro, follow *sortie* signs to the back of the Madeleine (sortie 1 to rue de la Madeleine is ideal), and circumnavigate counterclockwise around the square, starting at the black-and-white awnings of...

Fauchon: This bastion of over-the-top food products has faded from its glory days, and today caters to a largely tourist clientele—though it can still make your mouth water and your pocketbook ache. Fauchon outposts were found all over Paris until competitor Le Nôtre snapped them up. Now the only Fauchon that remains is this mothership store—the place where it all began.

Two separate pink-streaked shops are necessary to meet demand. The *Boulangerie-Traiteur* (Mon–Sat 9:00–20:00, closed Sun, tel. 01 70 39 38 96) is like a delicatessen with prepared foods—meats, meals, *pâtisseries* (pastries), breads, and cookies (of course, there are always *madeleines* on this square). Peruse the sumptuous desserts and take-away dinner *plats* that cost more than most restaurant meals. Above the *Traiteur,* you can have a meal or a drink in the *Salon de Thé* (Mon–Sat 8:00–19:00, closed Sun, tel. 01 70 39 38 78).

The **Confiserie et Epicerie** (candies and grocery) is Fauchon's more impressive shop, across the small street (Mon–Sat 9:00–21:00, closed Sun). This razzle-dazzle store makes me feel important when I enter. It's all about style, branding, and packaging. Tourists gobble up anything wrapped in pink and black—provided Fauchon's name is emblazoned on it. Stroll downstairs to find the wine cellar. Look for the €3,500 (that's $4,500) bottles of century-old Cognac on shelves—who buys this stuff? Find the elevator and ride two floors up to see a fashionable restaurant with view tables of La Madeleine.

More Shops on Place de la Madeleine: Turn right out of Fauchon's and find **Marquise de Sévigné** next door, where well-coiffed chocolate consultants are just waiting to match you with the perfect box of chocolate (Mon–Sat 10:00–19:00, closed Sun).

Hédiard lies across the square at #21 (Mon–Sat 9:00–21:00, closed Sun, tel. 01 43 12 88 85). This older, more appealing, and

more accessible gourmet food shop was founded in 1854. It showcases handsomely displayed produce and meats, a nifty atrium wine shop, and a smart café above (take the glass elevator up for a coffee or lunch). The small red containers make good souvenirs, with flavored mustards, jams, coffee, candies, and tea. Anyone can enter the glass doors of the wine cellar, marked *Le Chais,* and be greeted by the sommelier (find the €2,500 bottles of Petrus), but you need special permission to access *Les Vénérables* wines.

Two doors down is **La Maison des Truffe** (19 place de la Madeleine, Mon–Sat 10:00–21:00, closed Sun, tel. 01 42 65 53 22). Go inside this small shop to get a look at and a whiff of the product. Ponder how something so ugly, smelly, and deformed can sell for so much (up to €1,000 a pound). The shop also houses a sharp little restaurant serving a variety of dishes, all with truffles (opens at 12:00). The menu is surprisingly reasonable—a truffle omelet for €23, chocolate cake with truffles for €15. You'll also see every possible food that can be made with truffles—even Armagnac brandy—as well as white truffles from Italy that sell for €2,500 a pound. Small jars of black truffles cost €40.

Next is **Mariage Frères'** fine teas. Walk in to learn how good tea can smell and to see how beautifully it can be displayed (Mon–Sat 10:30–19:00, closed Sun).

At #17, **Caviar Kaspia,** you can add Iranian caviar, eel, and vodka to your truffle collection. Find the price list on the counter: The stronger caviars are cheaper (€110 for a small tin); the "finer" caviars sell for up to €16,000 a kilo (I have a hard time visualizing 2.2 pounds of caviar, and a harder time visualizing paying for it). The restaurant upstairs serves what you see downstairs—at exorbitant prices (Mon–Sat 10:00–24:00, closed Sun). A caviar competitor recently opened next door (Caviar Prunier), so demand must be strong.

Rue Royale: Pass the snazzy Baccarat crystal shop on your right and keep going straight, crossing three crosswalks. The view to your right of a grand boulevard anchored by a monument—the Church of St. Augustin, in this case—is vintage Haussmann (for more on the man who shaped modern-day Paris, see the sidebar on page 69). Now trade expensive food for expensive stuff (I'm not sure how Toto landed a storefront here). Keep left, then round the bend to the right and strut one block down rue Royale (consider a dip into the classy Village Royale mini-mall). At rue du Faubourg St. Honoré, cross rue Royale to your left—pausing in the middle for a great view both ways—and find **Ladurée** at 16 rue Royale, for an out-of-this-world pastry break in an 1800s setting (look for the green awning, Mon–Sat 8:30–19:00, Sun 10:00–19:00).

Place Vendôme: A detour left on rue du Faubourg St. Honoré leads several blocks past clothing boutiques to the *très* elegant square, place Vendôme, home to the Hôtel Ritz (Hemingway liberated the bar in World War II) and upper-crust jewelry stores—Van Cleef & Arpels, Dior, Chanel, Cartier, and others (if you have to ask how much...). Only jewelry stores are allowed on place Vendôme. The square was created by Louis XIV during the 17th century as a setting for a statue of himself. One hundred and fifty years later, Louis XIV was replaced by a statue of Napoleon. The column at the center was raised by Napoleon to commemorate his victory at the Battle of Austerlitz; the encircling bronze reliefs were made from cannons won in this and other battles.

Leave place Vendôme by walking up rue de la Paix—strolling by still more jewelry, high-priced watches, and crystal—and enter place de l'Opéra, where you'll find the *Paris Story* film, the Opéra Garnier (described on page 68), and Galeries Lafayette and Printemps department stores—if you're not shopped out yet (see descriptions earlier in this chapter). Or return to our walk on rue Royale. If you need a drink, the **Café de la Paix** across from the Opéra makes an appropriately elegant place to end this tour (daily, 12 boulevard des Capucines).

Place de la Concorde: If you skip the place Vendôme detour, continue two more blocks down rue Royale to its end at place de la Concorde. Browse the crystal and jewelry shops, then end your stroll at **Hôtel Crillon**'s classy café (see "Les Grands Cafés de Paris," page 419).

The Marais

For more eclectic, avant-garde stores, peruse the artsy shops between the place des Vosges and the Pompidou Center. Follow the route suggested for the Marais Walk (see map on page 284), starting at the place des Vosges and ending where you like. Stick to the west–east axes formed by rue des Francs-Bourgeois, rue des Rosiers, and rue Ste. Croix de la Bretonnerie. This area is rich with jewelry, shoes, and trendy clothing boutiques. On Sunday afternoons, when the rest of Paris naps, the neighborhood comes alive with shoppers and café crowds, and enjoys little car traffic. But it's quiet on Saturdays, when the Jewish community rests.

Start by inspecting the galleries under the arcades of the place des Vosges. Consider a daring new piece for that blank wall at home. Exit via rue des Francs-Bourgeois and enter an intense stretch of trendy shops. **L'Art du Soin** at #8 is all about taking care of your body (and prides itself on its stylish window displays). Turn left on rue de Pavée and find the adorable teddy bear shop at #18 (**l'Ours du Marais**), which seems out of place in this trendy area (Tue–Sat 11:30–19:30, Sun 14:30–19:30, closed Mon).

Rounding the corner to the right onto rue des Rosiers lands you in the epicenter of Marais hipness and fashion. Before plunging in, take a break at **Le Loir dans la Théière** (at #3), which offers baked goods, hot drinks, and a welcoming ambience for tired travelers (daily 12:00–19:00). Next door, the shiny **Adidas** store sells black skirts and high fashion—they've come a long way from sneakers. Walk at a snail's pace through the heart of Paris' Jewish quarter, then turn left onto rue Vieille du Temple and head to #29, where **Tout au Beurre** ("Everything made with butter") awaits. Choose from their assortment of tasty eats to nibble between shops—with a name like that, you just can't go wrong. At #31, **La Belle Hortense** is a bookstore/wine bar oozing with atmosphere (daily 17:00–24:00). Get your *chocolat* fix at **Cacao et Chocolat** (at #36), serving deliciously beautiful chocolates in a place that feels right out of the movie *Chocolat.*

Backpedal down rue Vieille du Temple and turn left onto rue Ste. Croix de la Bretonnerie. Tea enthusiasts should keep an eye out for the luxurious tea extravaganza at **Mariage Frères,** just off rue Ste. Croix de la Bretonnerie at 30 rue du Bourg Tibourg (daily 10:30–19:30, serving tea from 12:00). Don't miss the colorful shopping at **Pylones** (13 rue Ste. Croix de la Bretonnerie). From here you can continue to the Pompidou Center and find more shops. Le Forum des Halles, a few blocks past the Pompidou Center, is a multilevel modern shopping mall. To experience how much the

French love their pets—or to pick up a souvenir for the choosy *chien* in your life—walk a block toward the river and drop into **Un Chien dans le Marais,** where you can peruse the bejeweled doggie collars and clothes (at 35 bis rue du Roi de Sicile, which parallels rue Ste. Croix de la Bretonnerie). And for that item you meant to pack but left behind, stop by the **BHV** (Bazar de l'Hôtel de Ville) department store, which sells just about everything from hardware to lingerie at affordable prices (at 14 rue de Rivoli, where rue de Rivoli meets rue Vieille du Temple).

Puces St. Ouen—The Flea Market at Porte de Clignancourt

Paris' sprawling flea markets (*marché aux puces;* mar-shay oh-poos; *puce* is French for "flea") are oversized garage sales. They started in the Middle Ages, when middlemen sold old, flea-infested clothes and discarded possessions of the wealthy at bargain prices to eager peasants. Buyers were allowed to rummage through piles of aristocratic garbage.

Today **Puces St. Ouen** (poos sahn-wahn), at Porte de Clignancourt, carries on that tradition. This is the mother of all flea markets, with more than 2,000 vendors selling everything from flamingos to faucets, but mostly antiques (Sat 9:00–18:00, Sun 10:00–18:00, Mon 11:00–17:00, closed Tue–Fri, pretty dead the first 2 weeks of Aug, tel. 01 58 61 22 90, www.st-ouen-tourisme .com and www.parispuces.com).

This market shows off Paris' gritty, seamy underbelly and can be intimidating. No event brings together the melting-pot population of Paris better than this carnival-like market. Some find it claustrophobic, over-crowded, and threatening; others find French *diamants*-in-the-rough and return happy. You can bargain a bit (best deals are made with cash at the end of the day), though don't expect swinging deals here.

The St. Ouen "market" is actually a collection of individual markets. Most of these are a covered alley, each with a different name and specializing in a particular angle on antiques, bric-a-brac, and junk. You'll see *marchés* Vernaison, Dauphine, Biron, Serpette (classy antiques), and Paul Bert by walking down rue des Rosiers. Look for a map (at shops or the TI) that tries to explain the general character of each.

Space for this flea market was created in the 1800s, when the city wall was demolished (now a freeway), leaving large tracts of land open. The vacuum eventually was filled by street vendors, then antique dealers. The hodgepodge pattern of markets reflects their unplanned evolution. Strolling the markets can feel more like touring a souk in North Africa, a place of narrow alleys packed with people and too much to see.

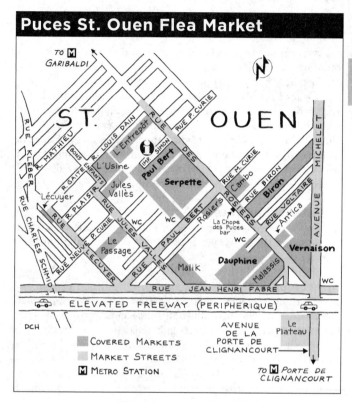

Even if antiques, African objects, and T-shirts aren't your thing, you can still find this market worth the Métro ride. Pretend you just rented a big, empty apartment...and need to furnish it. Come for lunch in one of the many lively and reasonable cafés and receive a reality check, away from the beautiful people and glorious monuments of Paris. You'll get a dose of life in "the 'burbs." **La Chope des Puces bar,** on rue des Rosiers, has live Gypsy music concerts on Saturday and Sunday afternoons, complete with a questionable clientele (open 14:00–19:00, tel. 01 40 11 02 49).

To get to the Puces St. Ouen, take Métro line 4 to the end of the line at Porte de Clignancourt, then carefully follow *Sortie, Marché aux Puces* signs. Walk straight out of the Métro down avenue de la Porte de Clignancourt, passing by leather stores and through blocks of stalls hawking trinkets and cheap clothing. Your destination is just beyond the elevated freeway (white bridge). Cross under the freeway, leaving Paris and entering the suburb of St. Ouen, veering left on the angled street. Turn left onto rue des Rosiers, the spine that links the many markets of St. Ouen. If you're considering buying a large item, note that shipping is very expensive (Camard company has the best reputation, tel. 01 49 46 10 82).

Wear your money belt; pickpockets and scam artists thrive in these wall-to-wall-shopper events. Don't use ATMs here if you can help it, as many are tampered with by con artists.

Other Flea Markets: Puces de Vanves is comparatively tiny and civilized, and preferred by many flea-market connoisseurs who find better deals at less famous markets (Sat–Sun 7:00–17:00, closed Mon–Fri, Mo: Porte de Vanves). The mega–**Puces de Montreuil** is the least organized and most traditional of them all, with chatty sellers and competitive buyers (Sat–Mon 8:00–18:00, closed Tue–Fri, Mo: Porte de Montreuil).

Open-Air Markets

Browse these markets for picnics, or find a corner café from which to appreciate the scene. I've listed Paris' most appealing markets below.

Street Markets

Several traffic-free street markets overflow with flowers, produce, fish vendors, and butchers, illustrating how most Parisians shopped before there were supermarkets and department stores. Markets are open daily except Sunday afternoons, Monday, and lunchtime throughout the week (13:00–15:00).

Rue Cler—a wonderful place to sleep and dine as well as shop—is a refined street market serving an upscale neighborhood near the Eiffel Tower (Mo: Ecole Militaire; for details, see Rue Cler Walk chapter and the Sleeping and Eating chapters).

Rue Montorgueil is a thriving and less touristy market street. Ten blocks from the Louvre and five blocks from the Pompidou Center, rue Montorgueil (mohn-tor-go-ee) is famous as the last vestige of the once-massive Les Halles market (just north of St. Eustache church, Mo: Etienne Marcel; gather a picnic here and take it to the park at Les Halles). Once the home of big warehouses and wholesale places to support the market, these have morphed into retail outlets to survive. Other traffic-free streets cross rue Montorgueil—don't miss the nearby covered arcade, passage du Grand Cerf (down rue Marie Stuart at the Les Halles end of rue Montorgueil).

Rue Daguerre, near the Catacombs and off avenue du Général Leclerc, is the least touristy of the street markets listed here (Mo: Denfert-Rochereau; for Catacombs description, see page 66).

Rue de Seine and rue de Buci combine to make a central and colorful market within easy reach of many sights (Mo: Odéon; see also "Les Grands Cafés de Paris," page 417, and my Left Bank Walk).

Rue des Martyrs near Montmartre makes Paris feel like a village. Consider exploring this lively market scene as part of my Montmartre Walk.

Larger, Morning-Only Markets

Offering cheaper prices and more selection, these markets take over selected boulevards and squares throughout Paris generally 8:00–12:30. Expect a lively combination of flea- and street-market atmosphere and items.

Marché de la place d'Aligre, 10 blocks behind the Opéra Bastille down rue de Faubourg St. Antoine, is an intimate open-air market where you'll see few tourists (daily 9:00–12:00, place d'Aligre, Mo: Ledru-Rollin).

Marché de la Bastille is huge, with a vast selection of products (Thu and Sun, Mo: Bastille); consider combining either of these two markets with a stroll through Promenade Plantée park (see page 78) and my Marais Walk.

Marché place Monge is comparatively minuscule, specializing in high-quality foods (Wed, Fri, and Sun; near rue Mouffetard, Mo: Monge).

Marché boulevard de Grenelle, a few blocks southwest of Champ de Mars park and the rue Cler area, is packed with produce, nonperishable goods, and Parisians in search of a good value (Wed and Sun, between Dupleix and La Motte Picquet-Grenelle Métro stops).

Marché Belleville is big and very untouristy (Tue and Fri, Mo: Belleville).

Arcaded Shopping Streets *(Passages)*

More than 200 of these covered shopping streets once crisscrossed Paris, providing much-needed shelter from the rain. The first were built during the American Revolution, though the ones you'll see date from the 1800s. Today only a handful remain to remind us where shopping malls got their inspiration, although they now sell things you would be more likely to find in flea markets than at JCPenney. Here's a short list to weave into your sightseeing plan. (They're found on the map in this chapter and on the "East Paris" color map at the beginning of this book.)

Galerie Vivienne, behind the Palais Royal off rue des Petits-Champs and a few blocks from the Louvre, is the most refined and accessible of the *passages* for most, though they don't reflect the typical, more funky *passages* (Mo: Pyramides or Palais Royal). Check out Le Grand Colbert, a surprisingly affordable yet elegant restaurant with decent cuisine (2 rue Vivienne, recommended in the Eating chapter).

Passage Choiseul and **Passage Ste. Anne,** four blocks west of

Galerie Colbert and Galerie Vivienne, are fine examples of most Parisian *passages,* selling used books, paper products, trinkets, and snacks (down rue des Petits-Champs toward avenue de l'Opéra, same Métro stops).

Passage du Grand Cerf is a more elegant arcade, easily combined with a visit to the nearby rue Montorgueil street market described earlier (Mo: Etienne Marcel).

Passage Panoramas and **Passage Jouffroy** are long galleries that connect with several other smaller *passages* to give you the best sense of the elaborate network of arcades that once existed (on both sides of boulevard Montmartre, between Métro stops Grands Boulevards/rue Montmartre and Richelieu Drouot).

ENTERTAINMENT IN PARIS

Paris is brilliant after dark. Save energy from your day's sightseeing and experience the City of Light lit. Whether it's a concert at Sainte-Chapelle, a boat ride on the Seine, a walk in Montmartre, a hike up the Arc de Triomphe, or a late-night café, you'll see Paris come alive. Night walks in Paris are wonderful. Any of the self-guided walking tours in the book are fun after dark.

The *Pariscope* magazine (€0.40 at any newsstand, in French) offers a complete weekly listing of music, cinema, theater, opera, and other special events—I decipher this useful periodical for you below. The *Paris Voice* website, in English, has a helpful monthly review of Paris entertainment (www.parisvoice.com).

Paris, a lovely destination any time of year, can be a surprisingly good choice for a winter trip. At the end of this chapter you'll find a round-up of winter-time highlights, activities, and entertainment.

Pariscope

The weekly *Pariscope* (€0.40, comes out on Wed) or *L'Officiel des Spectacles* (€0.35) is essential if you want to know what's going on in Paris. I prefer *Pariscope*. Pick one up at a newsstand and page through it. The order of the contents changes periodically, but the basics described below are always there...somewhere.

The magazine, all in French, begins with a listing of "Théâtre" and what's playing at all key theater venues. "Musique" lists each day's events, from jazz to classical to dance (program, location, time, price), including both opera houses if performances are scheduled. Remember that some concerts are free *(entrée libre)*.

A third of the magazine is devoted to *cinéma*—a Parisian forte. While a code marks films as "Comédie," "Documentaire," "Drame," "Karaté," "Erotisme," and so on, the key mark for non-French-speakers is "v.o.," for *version originale* (original-language version)—this means the movie hasn't been dubbed in French. Films are listed alphabetically, by neighborhood ("Salles Paris") and by genre. To find a showing near your hotel, simply look for a cinema in the same arrondissement. "Salles Périphérie" means the cinema is located out in the suburbs. Many cinemas offer discounts on Monday or Wednesday nights.

"Arts" gives hours and locations for gallery showings ("expositions," big and small), and up-to-date hours at museums in and near Paris (*tlj* = daily, *sf* = except, *Ent* = entry price, *TR* = reduced price—usually for students and children).

The "Enfants" section covers a myriad of possible children's activities from *High School Musical* performances to treasure hunts. "Spectacles" are shows (like magic shows); you'll also see many "Marionettes" (puppet) shows and "Cirques" (circuses). These events usually are offered only in French, but they can be worthwhile even for non-French-speakers.

"Promenades et Loisirs" covers outdoor events and sights, including open-air theater, flea markets, sound-and-light shows *(son et lumières),* key monuments such as the Eiffel Tower and Arc de Triomphe, river cruises, parks, zoos, and aquariums.

For cancan mischief, look under "Paris la Nuit."

Music

Jazz and Blues Clubs

With a lively mix of American, French, and international musicians, Paris has been an internationally acclaimed jazz capital since World War II. You'll pay €12–25 to enter a jazz club (may include one drink; if not, expect to pay €5–10 per drink; beer is cheapest). See *Pariscope* magazine under "Musique" for listings, or, even better, the American Church's *Paris Voice* website for a good monthly review. You can also check each club's website (all have English versions), or drop by the clubs to check out the calendars posted on their front doors. Music starts after 21:00 in most clubs. Some offer dinner concerts from about 20:30 on. Here are several good bets:

Caveau de la Huchette, a characteristic, old jazz/dance club, fills an ancient Latin Quarter cellar with live jazz and frenzied dancing every night (admission about €12 on weekdays, €14 on weekends, €6–8 drinks, Tue–Sun 21:30–2:30 in the morning or later, closed Mon, 5 rue de la Huchette, Mo: St. Michel, recorded info tel. 01 43 26 65 05, www.caveaudelahuchette.fr).

For a spot teeming with late-night activity and jazz, go to the two-block-long rue des Lombards, at boulevard Sébastopol, midway between the river and the Pompidou Center (Mo: Châtelet). **Au Duc des Lombards** is one of the most popular and respected jazz clubs in Paris, with concerts nightly in a great, plush, 110-seat theater-like setting (admission about €20, cheap drinks, shows at 20:00 and 22:00, 42 rue des Lombards, tel. 01 42 33 22 88, www .ducdeslombards.fr). **Le Sunside,** run for 15 years by Stephane Portet, is just a block away. The club offers two little stages (ground floor and downstairs): le Sunset stage is devoted to contemporary world jazz; le Sunside stage features more traditional jazz—Dixieland and big band (concerts range from free to €20, check their website, generally at 21:00, 60 rue des Lombards, tel. 01 40 26 21 25, www.sunset-sunside.com).

For a less pricey—and less central—concert club, try **Utopia**. From the outside it's a hole in the wall, but inside it's filled with devoted fans of rock and folk blues. Though officially a private club (and one that permits smoking), you can pay €3 to join for an evening, then pay a reasonable charge for the concert (usually €10 or under, concerts start about 22:00). It's located in the Montparnasse area (79 rue de l'Ouest, Mo: Pernety, tel. 01 43 22 79 66, www .utopia-cafeconcert.fr).

Cabaret

Old-Time Parisian Cabaret on Montmartre: Au Lapin Agile—This historic cabaret maintains the atmosphere of the heady days when bohemians would gather here to enjoy wine, song, and sexy jokes. For €24 you gather with about 25 French people in a dark room for a drink and as many as 10 different performers—mostly singers with a piano. Performers range from sweet and innocent Amélie types to naughty Maurice Chevalier types. And though tourists are welcome, it's exclusively French, with no accommodation for English speakers (except on their website), so non-French-speakers will be lost. You sit at carved wooden tables in a dimly lit room, taste the traditional drink (brandy with cherries), and are immersed in a true Parisian ambience. The soirée covers traditional French standards, love ballads, sea chanteys, and more. The crowd sings along, as it has here for a century (Tue–Sun 21:00–2:00 in the morning, closed Mon, best to reserve ahead, 22 rue des Saules, tel. 01 46 06 85 87, www.au-lapin-agile.com; described in ✪ Montmartre Walk).

A Modern Cabaret near Canal St. Martin: Chez Raymonde—This club proves that the art of dinner cabaret is still alive in Paris. Your evening begins with a good three-course dinner (including apéritif, wine, a half-bottle of champagne, and coffee) in an intimate dining room, where you get to know your neighbors. Around 22:00 the maître d'hôtel and the chef himself kick off the performance with a waltz together. Then it's feather boas, song, and dance—audience participation is encouraged (€65–100/person based on how elaborate a *menu* you choose, Fri–Sun evenings only,

dinner starts at 20:00 when *le chef* greets you in person, performance usually finishes about 23:00, reservations necessary, 119 avenue Parmentier, Mo: Goncourt, Parmentier, or République, tel. 01 43 55 26 27, www.chez-raymonde.com). On Sunday afternoons, you can also attend a performance over lunch (same prices, starts at 12:30).

Beyond Cabaret in the Latin Quarter: *Rocky Horror Picture Show*—For a splash of cross-cultural cross-dressing, join the local Rocky Horror club for a goofy evening at the Studio Galande theater near the church of St. Julien-le-Pauvre. For 25 years this artsy little theater has hosted *Rocky Horror Picture Show* enthusiasts every weekend (€8, Fri and Sat at 22:00, drop by to get tickets in advance, 42 rue Galande, Mo: St. Michel, www.rocky.fr).

Concerts and Operas

Classical Concerts—For classical music on any night, consult *Pariscope* magazine (check "Concerts Classiques" under "Musique" for listings), and look for posters at tourist-oriented churches.

From March through November, these churches regularly host concerts: St. Sulpice, St. Germain-des-Prés, Ste. Madeleine, St. Eustache, St. Julien-le-Pauvre, and Sainte-Chapelle. It's well worth the €25 entry for the pleasure of hearing Mozart or Vivaldi while surrounded by the stained glass of the tiny Sainte-Chapelle (unheated—bring a sweater). Pick up concert schedules and tickets during the day at the small ticket booth to the left of the chapel entrance. Or call 01 42 77 65 65 to reserve ahead; you can leave your message in English (just speak clearly and spell your name). Seats are unassigned, so arrive 30 minutes early to snare a good view. There are often two concerts per evening, at 19:00 and 20:30; specify which one you want when you buy or reserve your ticket.

The **Salle Pleyel** hosts world-class artists, from string quartets and visiting orchestras to international opera stars. Tickets are usually expensive and hard to come by, so it's best to order online in advance (252 rue du Faubourg Saint-Honoré, Mo: Ternes, tel. 01 42 56 13 13, www.sallepleyel.fr).

Look also for daytime concerts in parks, such as the Luxembourg Garden. Even the Galeries Lafayette department store offers concerts. Many concerts are free *(entrée libre)*, such as the Sunday atelier concert sponsored by the American Church (generally Sept–June at 17:00 but not every week, 65 quai d'Orsay, Mo: Invalides, RER: Pont de l'Alma, tel. 01 40 62 05 00).

Opera—Paris is home to two well-respected opera venues. The **Opéra Bastille** is the massive modern opera house that dominates place de la Bastille. Come here for state-of-the-art special effects and modern interpretations of classic ballets and operas. In the spirit of this everyman's opera, unsold seats are available at a big discount to seniors and students 15 minutes before the show. Standing-room-only tickets for €15 are also sold for some performances (Mo: Bastille). The **Opéra Garnier,** Paris' first opera house, hosts opera and ballet performances. Come here for less expensive tickets and grand belle époque decor (Mo: Opéra). To get tickets for either opera house, call 08 92 89 90 90, or, easier, reserve online at www.operadeparis.fr. You can also go direct to the Opéra Bastille's ticket office (open daily 11:00–18:00).

Art in the Evening

Various **museums** are open late on different evenings, offering the opportunity for more relaxed, less crowded visits: the Louvre (Wed and Fri until 21:45), Orsay (Thu until 21:45), Grand Palais (Wed until 22:00), and Pompidou Center (Wed–Mon until 21:00).

Art gallery openings are a fun way to check out new work by contemporary artists. Opening night receptions *(vernissage)* are classy and free. Check upcoming events listed on the *Paris Voice* website (www.parisvoice.com), or just follow the route of the ✪ Left Bank Walk and see what's happening.

Seine River Cruises

Several companies offer dinner cruises on huge glass-domed boats (or open-air decks in summer) with departures along the Seine, including from the Eiffel Tower; see page 416 in the Eating chapter.

Night Walks

Go for an evening walk to best appreciate the City of Light. Break for ice cream, pause at a café, and enjoy the sidewalk entertainers as you join the post-dinner Parisian parade. Use any of this book's self-guided walking tours as a blueprint, and remember to avoid poorly lit areas and stick to main thoroughfares. Consider the following suggestions; most are partial versions of this book's longer walking tours.

▲▲▲Trocadéro and Eiffel Tower—This is one of Paris' most spectacular views at night. Take the Métro to the Trocadéro stop and join the party on place du Trocadéro for a magnificent view of the glowing Eiffel Tower. It's a festival of gawkers, drummers, street acrobats, and entertainers. Pass the fountains and cross the river to the base of the tower, worth the effort even if you don't go up (tower open daily mid-June–Aug until 24:45, Sept–mid-June until 23:45). See the ✪ Eiffel Tower Tour chapter.

From the Eiffel Tower you can stroll through Champ de Mars park past tourists and romantic couples, and take the Métro home (Ecole Militaire stop, across avenue de la Motte-Picquet from far southeast corner of park). Or there's a handy RER stop (Champ de

Mars-Tour Eiffel) two blocks west of the Eiffel Tower.

▲▲Champs-Elysées and the Arc de Triomphe—The avenue des Champs-Elysées glows after dark (see the ✪ Champs-Elysées Walk chapter). Start at the Arc de Triomphe (observation deck open daily, April–Sept until 23:00, Oct–March until 22:30), then stroll down Paris' lively grand promenade. A right turn on avenue George V leads to the Bateaux-Mouches river cruises. A movie on the Champs-Elysées is a fun experience (weekly listings in *Pariscope* under "Cinéma").

▲Ile St. Louis and Notre-Dame—Take the beautiful ✪ Historic Paris Walk after dinner on Ile St. Louis (see page 82).

To get to Ile St. Louis, take the Métro (line 7) to the Pont Marie stop, then cross pont Marie to Ile St. Louis. Turn right up rue St. Louis-en-l'Ile, stopping for dinner—or at least a Berthillon ice cream at #31 or Amorino Gelati at #47. At the end of Ile St. Louis, cross pont St. Louis to Ile de la Cité, with a great view of Notre-Dame. Wander to the Left Bank on quai de l'Archevêché, and drop down to the river to the right for the best floodlit views. From May through September you'll find several permanently moored barges *(péniches)* that operate as bars. Although I wouldn't eat dinner here, the atmosphere is great for a drink, often including live music on weekends (daily until 2:00 in the morning, closed Oct–April, live music often Thu–Sun from 21:00). End your walk on place du Parvis Notre-Dame in front of Notre-Dame (on Sat–Sun June–Aug, tower open until 23:00), or go back across the river to the Latin Quarter.

Place de la Concorde, Place Vendôme, and Place de l'Opéra—These three squares tie together nicely for an elegant post-dinner walk (see page 436 in the Shopping chapter). Take the Métro to place de la Concorde and splurge for a pricey drink at the most expensive hotel in Paris (Hôtel Crillon, see "Les Grands Cafés de Paris" near the end of the Eating chapter). Get out to the obelisk for a terrific view of the Champs-Elysées and the beautifully lit, Greek-looking National Assembly building (to your left looking up the Champs-Elysées). Then walk up rue Royale toward the Madeleine church, turn right on rue St. Honoré, then left after several blocks on rue Castiglione. The sumptuous place Vendôme makes me wish I were rich. Exit place Vendôme at the opposite end and walk up rue de la Paix to find Opéra Garnier, stunning at night (see page 68; Mo: Opéra is right there to take you home).

Montmartre—Take the Métro to the area near Sacré-Cœur (church open daily until 23:00) and join the party (see the ✪ Montmartre Walk). Follow the walking tour as far as you like, but keep to the top of the hill (avoid place Pigalle and boulevard de Rochechouart). Have a drink on place du Tertre and get your portrait sketched. Montmartre was a nighttime destination for

Parisians in search of a lively evening even before the Impressionists arrived. For some old-time cabaret music, consider Au Lapin Agile (mentioned earlier in this chapter). Sit in front of the Sacré-Cœur church (to leave the rabble, jump the fence for a spot on the grass) and marvel at the glorious city view.

Rue de Lappe—Take a walk on Paris' wild side along the three-block stretch of rue de Lappe behind the Bastille, from boulevard Richard Lenoir to rue de Charonne (Mo: Bastille). Nightclubs, bouncer-staffed bars, and youthful boy-meets-girl energy power this late-night scene.

Marais—This artsy neighborhood is a hotbed for nightlife, full of cafés and tiny bars catering to locals and tourists alike. The action centers around rue Vieille du Temple (Mo: St. Paul), which offers something for every taste and attracts all age groups and sexual persuasions. Look for the Au Petit Fer à Cheval bar and the bookstore/winebar La Belle Hortense (daily 17:00–24:00, 31 rue Vieille du Temple, tel. 01 48 04 71 60).

Place St. Germain-des-Prés and Odéon—These areas are close to each other, worth combining for evening fun. Place St. Germain-des-Prés, along the Left Bank's main east–west route, hosts street theater and musicians that are better than ones you'll hear in the Métro. The church of St. Germain-des-Prés is often lit up and open at night, and Parisians sip drinks at two famous nearby cafés: Les Deux Magots and Le Café de Flore (see page 256; Mo: St. Germain-des-Prés). Nearby, night owls prowl along rues des Canettes and Guisarde (see "Near St. Sulpice Church" on page 414 of the Eating chapter). The Odéon, a few blocks away, is home to several movie theaters and still more lively cafés.

After-Dark Bus Tour

Several companies offer evening tours of Paris. I've described two companies offering the most tours below. These trips are sold through your hotel (brochures in lobby) or directly at the offices listed below. You save no money by buying direct. (For the cost of two after-dark bus tickets, you can more than pay for my private taxi tour of floodlit Paris, described below.)

Paris Illumination Tours, run by Paris Vision, connect all the great illuminated sights of Paris with a 100-minute bus tour in 12 languages. The double-decker buses have huge windows, but the most desirable front seats are sometimes reserved for customers who've bought tickets for the overrated Moulin Rouge. Left-side seats are better. Visibility is fine in the rain.

These tours are not for everyone. You'll stampede on with a United Nations of tourists, get a set of headphones, dial up your language, and listen to a tape-recorded spiel (which is interesting, but includes an annoyingly bright TV screen and a pitch for the other, more expensive excursions). Uninspired as it is, the ride provides an entertaining first-night overview of the city at its floodlit and scenic best. Bring your city map to stay oriented as you go. You're always on the bus, but the driver slows for photos at viewpoints (€27/person, kids under 12 ride free, 1.5 hours, departs at 19:00 Nov–March, at 22:00 April–Oct, reserve one day in advance, arrive 30 min early to wait in line for best seats, departs from Paris Vision office at 214 rue de Rivoli, across the street from Mo: Tuileries, tel. 01 42 60 30 01, www.parisvision.com). Skip their pricier minivan night tours.

L'Open Tour runs a similar night tour on open-top, double-decker buses and with no hawking of other packages (€30, departs at 22:00 from place des Pyramides, Mo: Tuileries, June Fri–Sat only, daily July–Sept, closed Oct–May, must book in advance, tel. 01 42 66 56 56, www.paris-opentour.com). If it's warm out, this is a great option.

▲▲Floodlit Paris Taxi Tour

Seeing the City of Light floodlit is one of Europe's great travel experiences and a great finale to any day in Paris. For less than the cost of two seats on a big bus tour, you can hire your own cab (maximum four passengers) and have a glorious hour of illuminated Paris on your terms and schedule. The downside: You don't have the high vantage point and big windows. The upside: it's cheaper, you go when and where you like, and you can jump out anywhere to get the best views and pictures.

Tour Overview: This is a circular one-hour route—from Notre-Dame to the Eiffel Tower along the Left Bank, then back along the Right Bank. Start at the taxi stand at Notre-Dame or any convenient point along the route (or from your hotel) and make any stops you like. Suggested stops are listed in bold on the list in "Taxi Instructions" (*"petit arrêt"* means "little stop"). To make it more of a party, bring a bottle of red wine and some chocolate to enjoy each time you hop out of the taxi (not in the taxi).

Taxi Logistics: Taxis have a strict meter (€26/hr plus about €1 per kilometer). This suggested loop takes an hour and costs around €40 (a bit more on Sunday). If your cabbie was easy to work with, add a 10 percent tip; if not, tip just five percent. Traffic is sparse and lights are bright between 22:00 and 24:00 every night. Your only timing concern: The Eiffel Tower twinkles for only the first five minutes of each hour after dark. If you start at Notre-Dame at half past the hour, you should be right on time for the sparkles. You might talk the driver into taking four people in a cab, though this is tight for decent sightseeing (with three, everyone gets a window).

Give the driver the instructions printed on page 454. Before you go, photocopy it (ask at your hotel) or rip the page out (but trace the route on another map so that you can follow along). Make sure the driver understands the plan—and enjoys the challenge. Review with the driver exactly where you hope to stop before you start. Ask him to drive as slowly as possible (say *"Conduisez lentement, s'il vous plait"*—cone-dwee-zay lawn-tuh-mohn see voo play) so that you can enjoy the ever-changing scene.

And you're on your way. Roll the windows down, learn your driver's name and use it (no first names, use *Monsieur* or *Madame* _____), and turn the cab light on to read if you like (this is no problem for the driver). Let the cabbie add a few little deviations (which can be great) as long as he understands your general plan. Stop when you want (but remember that the meter runs at about €0.50 per minute when stopped). Some cabbies might speak a little English; if not, learn and use the following key words:

English	French	Pronounced
What is your name?	*Comment vous appelez-vous?*	coh-moh vooz ah-play-voo
Slower, please.	*Lentement, s'il vous plaît.*	lawn-tuh-mohn see voo play
Stop, please.	*Arrêtez, s'il vous plaît.*	ah-ret-tay see voo play
Wait, please.	*Patientez, s'il vous plaît.*	pah-see-yahn-tay see voo play
I love Paris!	*J'aime Paris!*	zhem pah-ree

The Tour Begins: Start at Notre-Dame (taxi stand just in front, on left). Drive over pont d'Arcole to Hôtel de Ville, then turn right along the Seine (the white stripe of light is a modern bridge connecting the two islands).

Cross Ile St. Louis on pont Marie. Stop on the next bridge (pont de la Tournelle) just after the island, get out, and giggle with delight at the city and illuminated Notre-Dame. Then turn right along the Seine on quai de la Tournelle, motoring scenically past Notre-Dame.

Drive west along the entire length of the long Louvre—once the world's biggest building (across the river), then under the Orsay Museum (above you, on left). The National Assembly (on left) faces place de la Concorde (on right). The ornate pont Alexandre comes next (on right).

Turn left down Esplanade des Invalides to the gilded dome of Les Invalides, marking Napoleon's Tomb. As you approach the grand building, watch the illusion of the fancy dome sinking behind the facade. Circle clockwise around Invalides for a close-up

Taxi Instructions

Greetings, Monsieur/Madame. We are tourists and would like a tour of Paris at night. Are you willing to take us on the following route? We expect to be with you for an hour, with a few short stops. We will pay the metered rate. How much do you expect this to cost?

Bonjour, Monsieur/Madame. Nous sommes des tour-istes et nous voulons faire un circuit touristique de Paris illuminé. Est-ce que c'est possible de suivre la route suivante? Nous resterions avec vous une heure, avec quelques petits arrêts. Nous paierons le montant indiqué sur le compteur. Combien cela va t-il coûter approximativement?

1. Notre-Dame
2. Hôtel de Ville
3. Pont Marie
4. **Pont de la Tournelle (arrêt)**
5. Quai de la Tournelle
6. Musée d'Orsay
7. Esplanade des Invalides
8. Invalides
9. **Place Vauban/Eglise du Dome (arrêt)**
10. **Champ de Mars (place Jacques Rueff—arrêt)**
11. Tour Eiffel
12. Pont d'Iena
13. **Place du Trocadéro (arrêt)**
14. Avenue Kléber
15. Arc de Triomphe (2 révolutions)
16. Champs-Elysées
17. **Place de la Concorde (1 ou 2 révolutions)**
18. Quai François Mitterrand
19. **Musée du Louvre/Place du Carrousel/Pyramide (arrêt)**
20. Quai du Louvre
21. Notre-Dame

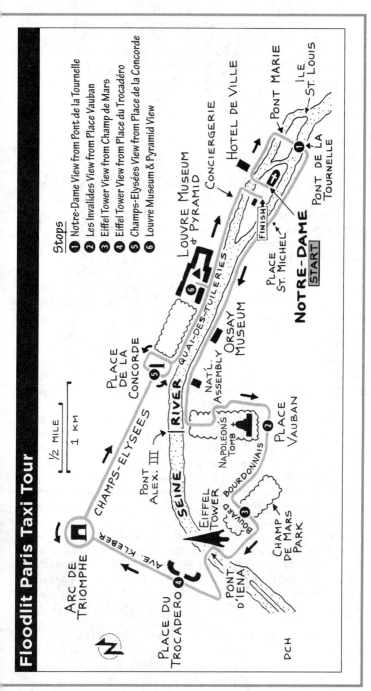

Floodlit Paris Taxi Tour

Stops

1 Notre-Dame View from Pont de la Tournelle
2 Les Invalides View from Place Vauban
3 Eiffel Tower View from Champ de Mars
4 Eiffel Tower View from Place du Trocadéro
5 Champs-Elysées View from Place de la Concorde
6 Louvre Museum & Pyramid View

ÎLE ST. LOUIS
PONT MARIE
HOTEL DE VILLE
CONCIERGERIE
LOUVRE MUSEUM + PYRAMID
QUAI-DES-TUILERIES
ORSAY MUSEUM
NAT'L. ASSEMBLY
PLACE DE LA CONCORDE
PONT ALEX. III
SEINE RIVER
CHAMPS-ELYSEES
ARC DE TRIOMPHE
AVE. KLEBER
PLACE DU TROCADERO
PONT D'IENA
EIFFEL TOWER
CHAMP DE MARS PARK
BOURDONNAIS
NAPOLEON'S TOMB
PLACE VAUBAN
ORSAY MUSEUM
PLACE ST. MICHEL
NOTRE-DAME
START
FINISH
PONT DE LA TOURNELLE

½ MILE
1 KM

N

DCH

view. Get out at place Vauban (behind the dome) and marvel at its symmetry.

Take avenue de Tourville to avenue de la Bourdonnais, which runs alongside the Champ de Mars park (former military training grounds that now serve as the Eiffel Tower's backyard). Turn left onto avenue Joseph Bouvard, leading to a circle made to order for viewing the Eiffel Tower. Get out and gasp.

Pont d'Iéna leads from directly in front of the tower across the Seine to place du Trocadéro for another grand Eiffel view (get out again and walk toward the tower to get the best photos and to enjoy the night scene here).

Avenue Kléber leads through one of Paris' ritziest neighborhoods to the Arc de Triomphe. Battle twice around the eternal flame marking the Tomb of the Unknown Soldier and Paris' craziest traffic circle: Ask for "*Deux révolutions, s'il vous plait*" (duh ray-voh-loo-see-yohn see voo play). Notice the rules of the road: Get to the center ASAP, those entering have the right-of-way, and any accidents are no-fault (insurance companies just split the costs down the middle). As you circle, notice the uniform boulevards reaching out like spokes from this hub. Try to find the huge and modern La Grande Arche in the distance opposite the Champs-Elysées.

When ready to continue, say the rhyme, "Champs-Elysées, *s'il vous plait*" (shahnz ay-lee-zay see voo play). Cruise down Europe's grandest boulevard—past fancy restaurants, car dealerships, and theaters—to the bold white obelisk marking the former site of the guillotine, place de la Concorde.

Circle once (maybe twice) around place de la Concorde, picking out all the famous landmarks near and far. Stop at the center to look up the Champs-Elysées. Then continue east (reminding your cabbie the next stop is "la Pyramide") along the Seine on quai des Tuileries (the two train-station clocks across the river mark the Orsay Museum) and sneak (via a taxi/bus-only lane) into the courtyard of the Louvre for a close look at the magically glowing pyramid. Stop here.

Return to the riverfront along the Right Bank and pass the oldest bridge in Paris, pont Neuf, and the impressive Conciergerie with its floodlit medieval turrets (this is where Marie-Antoinette was imprisoned during the Revolution). Turn right on pont de Notre-Dame and you complete the loop back where you (and Paris) started, at place du Parvis, facing Notre-Dame on the Ile de la Cité.

Montmartre Extra: For an extra €15 you can extend your night drive to Montmartre and end your taxi tour there. You'll pass many more floodlit sights, and you'll experience the night scene on Paris' rollicking hill. The steps in front of Sacré-Cœur are filled with tourists and pickpockets. The café scene on and around place du Tertre is always lively. It's touristy and fun for those with the right mindset. (For more information, see the ✪ Montmartre Walk.) After you finish exploring, you can catch any taxi back to your hotel.

Here's the Montmartre side-trip route: Start at the pyramid at the Louvre and drive through place Vendôme (with Hôtel Ritz on your left) to the Opéra Garnier. Then go up rue de la Chaussée past the Trinity Church; then head up rue Jean Baptiste to rue Pigalle. Drive up rue Pigalle (slowly, to peek into the many bars strewn with prostitutes). At place Pigalle, head left, past the sex shows and Moulin Rouge nightclub (with a mile-long line of tour buses marking the touristy cancan shows), to place Clichy, then drive up, up, up to the top of Montmartre. Say *au revoir* to your cabbie at the steps of the Sacré-Cœur, with the City of Light spreading out before you forever.

Winter in Paris

The City of Light sparkles year-round, but Paris has a special appeal in winter. You'll find inexpensive airfares, fewer crowds, and soft prices for hotel rooms and apartments (rent one for a week or more). Sure, the weather can be cold and rainy (average high in Dec is 44°F), but if you dress in layers, you'll keep warm and easily deal with temperature changes as you go from cold streets to heated museums and cafés.

Paris in winter offers so much to do indoors. Museums, restaurants, and stores stay open as usual; the concert and arts season is in full bloom; and Paris belongs to the Parisians. So go local, save money, and skip the museum lines that confront peak-season travelers. There are worse ways to spend a wintry day than enjoying world-class art, architecture, and shopping during the day and lingering over a fine (smoke-free) dinner at a cozy corner bistro in the evening. As Cole Porter put it: "I love Paris in the winter, when it drizzles."

Slow down and savor your favorite museums and monuments—spending one-on-one time with Mona and Venus is worth the extra clothes you had to pack. Attend a cooking demonstration, take a short course in art or architecture, or dabble in a wine-tasting class (for details, see the appendix). Duck into cafés for a break from sightseeing or shopping, and to warm up. Get on a first-name basis with the waiter at your corner café—just because you can now.

Easter marks the start of the tourist season, when locals find they need to make reservations for their favorite restaurants and can't find seats on the Métro.

This section reviews off-season highlights in Paris, but

remember—your reward for traveling in winter is the joy of feeling part of a city, like you almost belong here. That's what you'll find on a trip to Paris from November to March.

November

From late October well into November, leaves tumble from Paris's trees, revealing magnificent building facades and turning parks into austere yet romantic places with paths and vistas. Winter also brings early sunsets and long evenings, ideal for floodlit neighborhood walks, boat rides, and taxi tours that allow you to view the city of light at a reasonable hour.

Beginning one minute after midnight on the third Thursday of November and running through mid-December, Paris welcomes the arrival of the **Beaujolais Nouveau** with uncharacteristic enthusiasm for such a controlled people. The fresh, fruity wine is rushed from vineyards a bit north of Lyon direct to Paris, where wine bars and most cafés serve it happily and buzz with news of the latest vintage. The first 24 hours is the most fun and raucous, and it's easy to join the party if you don't mind elbowing your way to the *comptoir* for *un verre*. Cafés and bistros continue the celebration for weeks, many offering dishes with a glass of the Beaujolais Nouveau.

And speaking of wine, the annual *Salon des Vignerons Independents* (independent wine-makers' show) is held the last weekend of November at the Porte de Versailles exhibition center (Mo: Porte de Versailles, line 12). Here, anyone can sample fine wines from more than 1,000 different stands for about a €6 entry fee.

December

One of Europe's greatest treats is strolling down the glowing Champs-Elysées in winter. From late November through early January, **holiday lights** adorn city streets, buildings, and monuments, and the Champs-Elysées beams with a dazzling display of lights on the trees that line the long boulevard. The city springs for 1,000 fresh-cut fir trees to put up and decorate around town, 300 of which ring the Rond-Point roundabout at the lower end of the Champs-Elysées. You'll also find cheerful lighting displays on many traffic-free streets, including rues Cler, Montorgueil, and Daguerre.

Parisians live to **window-shop** (*faire du lèche vitrines*—literally "window-licking"). Do some licking of your own along boulevard Haussmann and view the storefront lights and wild window displays at the grand department stores such as Printemps and Galeries Lafayette. Here you can have your picture taken with Père Noël—France's slimmer version of Santa Claus, dressed in red trimmed with white fur. The seasonal displays in neighborhood boutiques around Sèvres-Babylone and in the Marais (among other areas) are more intimate and offer a good contrast to the shows of glitz around the department stores.

Several **ice-skating rinks** open up in festive locations: in front of the Hôtel de Ville (City Hall, look also for a small sled run), at the base of the Montparnasse skyscraper, and, in some winters,

most spectacular of all—200 feet in the air on the first level of the Eiffel Tower. The rinks are free to use (around €5 to rent skates, open Dec–March from noon into the evening), though for the Eiffel Tower rink, you have to pay the tower admission, of course.

For the kids, there are **Christmas carousels** (*Manèges de Noël)* that whirl at various locations, including the biggies at Hôtel de Ville and the Eiffel Tower. As soon as school lets out, the parks are alive with pony rides, puppet shows, and other activities.

The Christmas Season

With the arrival of St. Nicholas on December 6, the Christmas season kicks into gear. (Bear in mind, though, that Paris celebrates Christmas with only about 10 percent of the holiday cheer that you'll find in the States.) In mid-December **Christmas markets** pop up in the *arrondissements*, particularly on the Left Bank (St. Sulpice and St. Germain-des-Prés) and along the Champs-Elysées. At **Notre-Dame** a big Christmas tree goes up, and they may have a living crêche in front. The **Pompidou Center** has started an avant-garde tradition: an exhibit of contemporary artists' takes on the Christmas tree. Locals pick up modest Christmas trees for their homes at flower shops—if you rent an apartment, you could do the same. Be sure to check the *Pariscope* magazine for the popular and often free or inexpensive **Christmas concerts.**

Christmas Eve and Christmas Day

The big event is the Christmas Eve dinner, called **La Réveillon**—"the awakening"—when Parisians stay awake late to celebrate the arrival of Jesus. Traditionally, they attend evening Mass (at Notre-Dame among others), then meet with family and friends for a big feast. The meal begins with (what else?) escargots, smoked salmon or oysters, and then foie gras. The main dish, similar to American's Thanksgiving, is turkey, served with a sort of cranberry sauce, and potatoes *(gratin dauphinois).* This evening is normally celebrated at home and with family, though some Paris restaurants (and other businesses) stay open late to accommodate parties indulging in raw

Seasonal Foods

Winter is the season for the hunt, when you'll find game birds and venison on restaurant menus. Seventy percent of France's oysters are eaten in the month of December, most of them raw and on the half-shell. Look for busy shuckers outside big cafés, where most oysters are consumed. On street corners you'll hear shouts of *"Chaud les marrons!"* from vendors selling chestnuts roasting on coals. Chocolatiers (including La Maison du Chocolat's five stores) and pastry shops everywhere do a bang-up business during the holiday season, serving traditional treats such as Epiphany cakes (flaky marzipan cakes called *roi de galettes*). Bakeries overflow with these popular cakes starting January 6.

If you like gourmet food, take a spin around place de la Madeleine, comparing Fauchon's festive displays with Hédiard's, and spring for a truffle omelet at La Maison des Truffles (after all, winter is truffle season). Just because it's cold doesn't mean that outdoor markets are quiet—au contraire, you'll find markets (e.g., on place d'Aligre, and along rue de Grenelle) alive with shoppers and vendors no matter what the weather.

One of the great pleasures Paris offers is watching the city bustle while you linger at an outdoor table with a *café crème*, a *vin chaud* (hot wine), or, best, a hot chocolate (simply called *chocolat* and très popular in winter). Most cafés fire up the braziers to keep things toasty outside. And with the new smoking laws, café and restaurant interiors are wonderfully free of any trace of smoke.

oysters, cheese, and the Yule Log (*Bûche de Noël*)—a log-shaped sponge cake iced with chocolate "bark." After dinner the kiddies leave their slippers next to the fireplace for Père Noël to fill with treats.

On Christmas Day Paris is very sleepy—make arrangements ahead of time if you've got a plane to catch, and don't plan on visiting the Louvre (which is closed, along with most museums and businesses). Visitors looking for **services in English** will find no shortage of churches to attend—choose between the interdenominational American Church, American Cathedral, Unitarian Church, and St. George's Anglican Church (listed in the appendix). Many of these churches—especially the American Church—also offer Christmas concerts.

January

Start the **New Year** off with a bang at the over-the-top fireworks display at the Eiffel Tower, when thousands of Parisians congregate on the Champ de Mars before midnight. All of Paris parties on New Year's Eve, and a table at a restaurant is next to impossible to land (book early or dine at a café). The holidays aren't over yet—Paris celebrates the arrival of the Three Kings on **Epiphany** (Jan 6) with as much fanfare as Christmas itself. The after-Christmas sales (*soldes*) are an even bigger post-holiday tradition, as locals jam the boutiques and department stores looking for bargains up to 50 percent off. These sales, which last until early February, force stores to keep longer hours.

Parisians celebrate the **Chinese New Year** in a big way (usually falls near the end of January) with parades, decorations, and fanfare. Ask your hotelier or a TI for parade locations.

February and March

These are the quiet months, when Paris is most alone with itself. And though holiday decorations disappear, the City of Light is as beautiful and seductive as ever. Visit Paris in winter and—for a few days—become a Parisian.

CONNECTIONS

This chapter covers Paris' two main airports, one smaller airport, six train stations, and its main bus station. It also includes parking tips for drivers.

When leaving Paris, get to your departure point early to allow time for waiting in lines. Figure on 2–3 hours for an overseas flight; 1–2 hours for flights within Europe (particularly if flying with one of the budget airlines, which tend to have long check-in lines); and 40 minutes for a train trip or long-distance bus ride, if you're doing anything beyond simply boarding (Eurostar trains require you to check in at least 30 minutes early). Whether arriving or departing, always keep your luggage safely near you.

Airports

Charles de Gaulle Airport

The airport has three terminals: T-1, T-2, and T-3 (see map on next page). Most flights from the US use T-1 or T-2. To see which terminal serves your airline, check your ticket, or contact the airport (toll tel. 3950, www.adp.fr). T-1 and T-2 have airport information desks and tourist office desks (where you can buy museum passes).

The RER (Paris suburban train, connecting to Métro) stops at T-2 and T-3; the TGV (high-speed train) station is at T-2. The free CDGVAL automated shuttle train links the three terminals and two parking garages (free, every 10 min, 24/7). Allow 30 minutes total travel time to get between your gates at T-1 and T-2.

Pickpockets prey on jet-lagged tourists on the CDGVAL shuttle trains and on RER trains. Don't take an unauthorized taxi from the men greeting you on arrival; official taxi stands are well-signed.

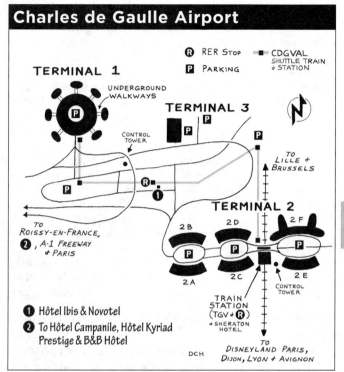

Charles de Gaulle Airport

Terminal 1 (T-1)

This circular terminal has one main entry and three key floors—arrival (*arrivées*, top floor), departure (*départs*, one floor down) and CDGVAL shuttle trains and shops/boutiques (basement level). For information on getting to Paris, see "Transportation Between Charles de Gaulle Airport and Paris," later in this chapter.

Arrival Level (*niveau arrivée*): You'll find a variety of services at the gates listed below. Expect some changes to this lineup.

- Gate 36: Called "Meeting Point" (Point de Rencontre), this gate has an information counter with English-speaking staff, a café, and an ATM.
- Gate 34: Outside are Air France buses to Paris (see "Transportation Between Charles de Gaulle Airport and Paris," below) and Orly Airport (see "Connecting Paris Airports" later in this chapter).
- Gate 30: Outside are Roissy-Buses to Paris (buy tickets from driver) and hotel shuttle buses (*navettes hôtels*).
- Gates 24–30: Car rental desks.
- Gate 10: Taxis outside (this gate is most prone to changes).

Departure Level (*niveau départ*): Flight check-in, access to basement level and CDGVAL shuttle trains, restaurants, a PTT (post office), a pharmacy, boutiques, and a handy grocery store one floor below the ticketing desks (*niveau* 2 on the elevator).

Terminal 2 (T-2)

This long, horseshoe-shaped terminal is dominated by Air France and is divided into six subterminals (or halls), labeled A through F. Free shuttle buses (look for *Navette* signs) circle, connecting the halls with T-2's RER and TGV stations. The RER and TGV stations are below the Sheraton Hotel (and are within walking distance of some of the halls). Stops for Air France buses and Roissy-Buses are all well-marked near each hall (follow *Paris by Bus* signs and see "Transportation Between Charles de Gaulle Airport and Paris," below). Car-rental offices, post offices, pharmacies, and ATMs (*Distributeurs*) are also well-signed. Confused? Orange ADP information desks are located near Gate 6 in each hall (ask where to buy a Paris Museum Pass).

Baggage storage is available (inquire at any information desk), but is pricey (€16) and requires a six-hour minimum. I'd stash my bag at a Paris train station instead (described later in this chapter).

Transportation Between Charles de Gaulle Airport and Paris

Three public-transportation routes, airport vans, and taxis link the airport's terminals with central Paris. If you're traveling with one or two companions, carrying lots of baggage, or are just plain tired, taxis are worth the extra cost (avoid the airport vans going in the airport-to-Paris direction; see why later in this section).

RER-B trains from the airport to Paris stop at T-2 and near T-3 (connections from T-1 via the CDGVAL shuttle train), then stop in central Paris at Gare du Nord, Châtelet-Les Halles, St. Michel, and Luxembourg (€8.60, 4/hr, runs 5:00–24:00, 30 min to Gare du Nord). Follow *Paris by Train* signs, then *RER* signs (the RER station at T-2 mixes with a busy main train station, so pay attention—look for *Paris/Ile de France* ticket windows and expect lines). It's faster to buy tickets from the machines (requires €8.60 in coins, break your bills at an airport shop) as lines can be long at ticket windows. The T-3 RER station is less crowded and just five minutes away by CDGVAL shuttle train.

RER-B trains from Paris to the airport run about every 20–30 minutes. Make sure the sign over the platform shows *Roissy-Charles de Gaulle* as a stop served (the line splits, so not every line B train serves the airport). If you're not clear, ask another rider (*air-o-por sharl duh Gaul?*). Beware of pickpockets on these trains; wear your money belt. The other transportation options described below have far fewer theft problems.

Public Transportation to Recommended Hotels

There are many options for traveling between Charles de Gualle Airport and Paris (described below). These are especially handy for getting to recommended hotels.

Rue Cler area: Take Roissy-Bus to Opéra, then take Métro line 8 (direction: Balard) and get off at the La Tour Maubourg or Ecole Militaire stop. Or take RER-B to the St. Michel stop, transfer to RER-C toward Versailles Rive Gauche, and get off at the Pont de l'Alma stop.

Marais: Take an Air France bus to the Gare de Lyon, go inside the train station to find the Métro, then take a quick trip on Métro line 1, direction: La Défense. Get off at the Bastille, St. Paul, or Hôtel de Ville stop. Or, take RER-B to the Châtelet Les Halles stop and transfer to Métro line 1, direction: Château de Vincennes (long walk in a huge station), and get off at Hôtel de Ville, St. Paul or Bastille.

Luxembourg Garden: RER-B to the Luxembourg stop.

Roissy-Buses run every 15–20 minutes to the Opéra Métro stop (€9, runs 6:30–21:00, 50 min, buy ticket on bus). You'll arrive at a bus stop on rue Scribe on the left side of the Opéra building. To get to the Métro entrance, turn left out of the bus and walk counterclockwise around the Opéra. The Métro station entrance faces the Opéra's front. For rue Cler hotels, take Métro line 8 (direction: Balard) to La Tour Maubourg or Ecole Militaire. For hotels in the Marais neighborhood, take line 8 (direction: Créteil Préfecture) to the Bastille stop. You can also take a taxi (about €12) to any of my listed hotels from behind the Opéra (the stand is in front of Galeries Lafayette department store).

Air France buses serve central Paris on two routes and continue to Orly Airport (€16, at least 2/hr, 5:45–23:00). Allow 45 minutes from the airport to the Arc de Triomphe and Porte Maillot; 45 minutes to the Gare de Lyon train station; and 60 minutes to the Montparnasse Tower/train station. To reach Marais hotels from the Gare de Lyon, take Métro line 1 (direction: La Défense) to the Bastille, St. Paul, or Hôtel de Ville stop; or walk 10 minutes up rue de Lyon to place de la Bastille.

Taxis run about €55 for up to three people (more if traffic is bad). Your hotel can call for a taxi to the airport. Specify that you want a real taxi (*un taxi normal*), and not a limo service that costs €20 more (and gives your hotel a kickback).

Airport vans go straight to and from your hotel, but work better getting you from your hotel to the airport. (They don't work as well going from the airport to your hotel because you have to book a set pick-up time at the airport in advance, even though you don't know exactly when you'll arrive, get your baggage, go through customs, and so on.) The hotel-to-airport service is a particularly good deal for single travelers or families of four or more (which is too many people for a taxi). If your hotel doesn't work with a van service, reserve directly (book at least a day in advance—most hoteliers will make the call for you). Airport vans cost about €35 for one person, €45 for two, and €55 for three. Here are a couple of companies to consider: **Paris Airport Shuttle** (tel. 01 53 39 18 18, www.parisshuttle.com) and **Airport Connection** (tel. 01 43 65 55 55, www.airport-connection.com). **Paris Webservices** rents private minivans and meets you inside the terminal (€155/up to 4 people round-trip, €185/up to 6 people, 10 percent discount for Rick Steves readers—use promo code RSteves07, tel. 01 53 62 02 29, fax 01 53 01 35 84, www.pariswebservices.com, contactpws @pariswebservices.com). **Golden Air** also rents private minivans (tel. 01 43 62 82 75, www.goldenair.net).

A **Disneyland shuttle van** is at each terminal (€17, runs every 20 min daily 8:30–20:00ish, 30 min). TGV trains also run to Disneyland from the airport, but leave less frequently (hourly) and require shuttle buses at each end—take the shuttle van instead.

Sleeping at or near Charles de Gaulle Airport

Hôtel Ibis**, outside the T-3 RER stop, is huge and offers standard airport accommodations (Db-€95–130, tel. 01 49 19 19 19, fax 01 49 19 19 21, www.ibishotel.com, h1404@accor.com). **Novotel***** is nearby and the next step up. Book early for the best rates (Db-€130–180, can rise to €280 for last-minute rooms, tel. 01 49 19 27 27, fax 01 49 19 27 99, www.novotel.com, h1014@accor.com). Both places have restaurants.

The small village of **Roissy en France** (you'll see signs just before the airport as you come from Paris), which gave its name to the airport (Roissy Charles de Gaulle), has better-value chain hotels with free shuttle service to and from the airport and the RER Roissy Rail station (4/hr, 15 min, look for *navettes hôtels* signs). Hotels have reasonably priced restaurants with long hours. Many hotels are listed on www.campanile.fr, including **Hôtel Campanile** (Db-€70–95, tel. 01 34 29 80 40, fax 01 34 29 80 39, wroissy@campanile.fr) and **Hôtel Kyriad Prestige** (Db-€90–150, tel. 01 34 29 00 00, fax 01 34 29 00 11, www.kyriad.fr, roissy @kyriadprestige.fr). The cheapest option is **B&B Hôtel**, where many flight attendants stay (Db-€55, tel. 01 34 38 55 55, www .hotelbb.com). Most hotels list specials on their websites.

To avoid rush-hour traffic, drivers can consider sleeping north of Paris in either **Auvers-sur-Oise** (30 min west of airport, see accommodations on page 564) or in the pleasant medieval town of **Senlis** (15 min north of airport). The **Ibis Senlis Hôtel** is a few minutes from town (Db-€80–100, Wi-Fi, route nationale A1, tel. 03 44 53 70 50, fax 03 44 53 51 93, www.ibishotel.com, h0709 @accor.com). If you don't have a car, sleep elsewhere.

Orly Airport

This airport feels small. It's good for rental-car pickup and drop-off, as it's closer to Paris and far easier to navigate than Charles de Gaulle Airport.

Orly has two terminals: Ouest (west) and Sud (south). Air France flights arrive at Ouest, and all others use Sud. At the Sud terminal you'll exit the baggage claim (near Gate H) and see signs directing you to city transportation, car rental, and so on. Turn left to enter the main terminal area, where you'll find exchange offices with bad rates, an American Express office, an ATM, the ADP counter (*Espace Tourisme*, a quasi-tourist office that offers free city maps and basic sightseeing information, open until 24:00), and an SNCF rail desk (next to ADP, open daily, sells train tickets and even Eurailpasses). Downstairs is a sandwich bar, WCs, a bank (same bad rates), a newsstand (buy a phone card here), and a post office. Car-rental offices are located in the parking lot in front of the terminal opposite Gate C. For flight info on any airline serving Orly, call 3950. For information on either of Paris' airports, visit www.adp.fr.

Transportation Between Orly Airport and Paris

Several efficient public-transportation routes, taxis, and a couple of airport vans link Orly with central Paris. The gate locations listed below apply to Orly Sud, but the same transportation services are available from both terminals.

Air France buses (outside Gate L) run to Montparnasse train station (with many Métro lines) and to the Invalides Métro stop (€12, 4/hr, 40 min to Invalides). These buses are handy for those staying in or near the rue Cler neighborhood (from Invalides bus stop, take the Métro to La Tour Maubourg or Ecole Militaire to reach recommended hotels; see also "RER trains," next page). Remember that to continue on the Métro, you'll need to buy a separate ticket (for ticket types and prices, see page 28).

Jetbus (outside Gate H, €6.50, 4/hr) is the quickest way to the Paris Métro and a good way to the Marais and Luxembourg Garden neighborhoods. First, take the Jetbus to the Villejuif-Louis Aragon Métro stop. To reach the Marais neighborhood, take the Métro to the Sully-Morland stop; for the Luxembourg area, take the same train to the Censier-Daubenton or Place Monge stop. If taking the Jetbus from the Marais to the airport, make sure before you board the Métro that your train is going to Villejuif-Louis

Aragon (not Mairie d'Ivry), as the route splits at the end of the line.

The **Orlybus** (outside Gate H, €6.40, 3/hr) takes you to the Denfert-Rochereau RER-B line and the Métro, offering Métro access to central Paris, including the Luxembourg area and Notre-Dame Cathedral, as well as the Gare du Nord train station.

Shuttle buses to Disneyland depart from Gate H (€17, daily 8:30–19:45, confirm gate and schedule at ADP *Espace Tourisme* office—described earlier).

These two routes provide access to Paris on **RER trains**: an ADP shuttle from Gate F (**Orly Rail bus**) takes you to RER-C (Pont d'Orly stop), with connections to Gare d'Austerlitz, St. Michel/Notre-Dame, Musée d'Orsay, Invalides, and Pont de l'Alma stations, and is handy for some rue Cler hotels (outside Gate G, €6.20, 4/hr). **Orlyval trains** take you from Gate K to the Antony stop on RER-B (serving Luxembourg and many recommended hotels, Châtelet-Les Halles, St. Michel, and Gare du Nord stations in central Paris; €9.70, includes RER ticket).

Taxis are to the far right as you leave the terminal, at Gate M. Allow €38 with bags for a taxi into central Paris.

Airport vans are good for single travelers or families of four or more (too many for a taxi) if going from Paris to the airport (see page 465; from Orly, figure about €23/1 person, €30/2 people, less per person for larger groups and kids).

Sleeping near Orly Airport

Two chain hotels, owned by the same company, are your best option near Orly. **Hôtel Ibis**** is reasonable, basic, and nearby (Db-€80–100, tel. 01 56 70 50 60, fax 01 56 70 50 70, www.ibis hotel.com, h1413@accor.com). **Hôtel Mercure***** provides more comfort for a higher price; check website for special discounts (Db-€130–200, book early for better rate, tel. 01 49 75 15 50, fax 01 49 75 15 51, www.accorhotel.com, h1246@accor.com). Both places have free shuttles to the terminal.

Beauvais Airport

Budget airlines such as Ryanair use this small airport, offering dirt-cheap airfares but leaving you 50 miles north of Paris. Still, this airport has direct buses to Paris (see below), and is ideal for drivers who want to rent a car here and head to Normandy or north to Belgium. The airport is basic (the terminal for departing passengers and baggage claim is under a tent, and waiting areas are crowded and have few services), but it's being improved as it deals with an increasing number of passengers (airport tel. 08 92 68 20 66, www.aeroportbeauvais.com; Ryanair tel. 08 92 68 20 73, www .ryanair.com).

Transportation Between Beauvais Airport and Paris:
Buses depart from the airport about 20 minutes after flights arrive
and take 90 minutes to reach Paris. Buy your ticket at the little
kiosk to the right as you exit the airport (€14) or online at tickets.
aeroportbeauvais.com. Buses wait nearby, depart when they're full
(baggage goes underneath), and arrive at Porte Maillot on the west
edge of Paris, which has a Métro and RER stop. The closest taxi
stand is at Hôtel Concorde-Lafayette.

Transportation Between Paris and Beauvais Airport: Buses
depart Paris for Beauvais Airport about 3.25 hours before scheduled flight departures. Catch the bus at Porte Maillot in the parking lot on boulevard Pershing next to Hôtel Concorde-Lafayette.
Arrive with enough time to purchase your bus ticket before boarding (Beauvais Airport tel. 08 92 68 20 66, www.aeroportbeauvais
.com).

Trains connect Beauvais' city center and Paris' Gare du Nord
(20/day, 80 min).

Taxis run from Beauvais Airport to Beauvais' train station or
city center (€12) or central Paris (allow €120).

Cheap Flights

If you're visiting one or more French cities on a longer European
trip—or linking up far-flung French cities (such as Paris and
Nice)—you might consider intra-European airlines. Although
trains are still the best way to connect places that are close together,
a flight can save both time and money on long journeys. When
comparing a flight versus a train trip, consider the time it takes to
get to the airport and how early you'll need to arrive to check in
before the flight. Most flights make sense only as an alternative to
a train ride five hours or more in length.

A visit to www.skyscanner.net, www.mobissimo.com, www
.kayak.com, or www.wegolo.com sorts out the numerous options
offered by the many discount airlines, enabling you to see the best
schedules for your trip and come up with the best deal.

Well-known cheapo airlines include **easyJet** (www.easyjet
.com), which flies out of Charles de Gaulle and Orly airports, and
RyanAir, which flies out of Beauvais Airport (www.ryanair.com).
Also check Air France for specials. Be aware of the potential draw-
backs of flying on the cheap: nonrefundable and nonchangeable
tickets, rigid baggage restrictions (and fees if you have more than
what's officially allowed), airports far outside town, tight schedules
that can mean more delays, little in the way of customer assistance
if problems arise, and, of course, no frills. To avoid unpleasant surprises, read the small print—especially baggage policies—before
you book. If you're traveling with lots of bags, a cheap flight can
quickly become a bad deal, due to per-piece baggage fees.

Trains

Station Overview

Paris is Europe's rail hub, with six major stations and one minor one, each serving different regions:

- Gare du Nord (northern France and Europe)
- Gare Montparnasse (northwestern France and TGV service to France's southwest)
- Gare de Lyon (southeastern France and Italy)
- Gare de l'Est (northeastern France and eastbound trains)
- Gare St. Lazare (northwestern France)
- Gare d'Austerlitz (southwestern France and Europe)
- Gare de Bercy (smaller station, departure point for most night trains to Italy)

Any train station has schedule information, can make reservations, and can sell tickets for any destination. Buying tickets is handier from an SNCF neighborhood office. See "SNCF Boutiques" on page 480 for a more extensive list.

Schedules change by season, weekday, and weekend. Verify train schedules shown in this book—on the Web, check Germany's excellent all-Europe schedule site, http://bahn.hafas.de/bin/query .exe/en. The French rail website (www.sncf.com) shows ticket prices and sells some tickets online (worth checking if you're traveling on one or two long-distance trains without a railpass, as advance-purchase discounts can be a great deal).

While there's no deadline to buy any train ticket, the fast, reserved TGV trains can fill up. It's wise to book ahead for any TGV you cannot afford to miss. Tickets go on sale 90 days in advance, and the cheapest tickets sell out early. You can buy tickets online at www.raileurope.com (a US company that delivers tickets to your home but doesn't always have the lowest rates), or, better, at www.tgv-europe.com/en/home. If you choose a country other than the US and outside of western Europe, you'll be able to print tickets at home or pick them up in the station (if you choose, say, France, the site will be in French, and if you choose the US, you'll be redirected to www.raileurope.com).

All six main train stations have banks or change offices, ATMs, train information desks, telephones, cafés, newsstands, and clever pickpockets. Because of security concerns, not all have baggage checks, though those with this service are identified below.

Métro and RER trains, as well as buses and taxis, are well-marked at every station. When arriving by Métro, follow signs for *Grandes Lignes-SNCF* to find the main tracks.

Each station offers two types of rail service: long distance to other cities, called *Grandes Lignes* (major lines); and suburban

CONNECTIONS

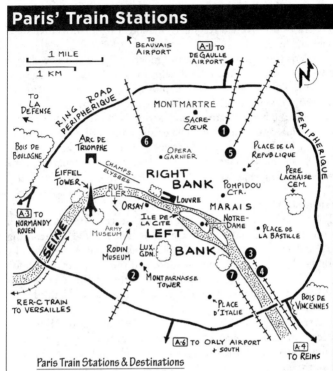

Paris' Train Stations

Paris Train Stations & Destinations

1 Gare du Nord: To London, Brussels, Amsterdam, Copenhagen & N. France (also Chantilly & Auvers-sur-Oise)

2 Gare Montparnasse: To Spain, SW France (Languedoc & Dordogne), Loire Valley, Brittany & Mont St. Michel (also Chartres)

3 Gare de Lyon: To Italy & SE France (Burgundy, Alps, Provence & Riviera; also Fontainebleau & Melun/Vaux-le-Vicomte)

4 Gare de Bercy: Night trains to Italy

5 Gare de l'Est: To NE France (Reims, Champagne & Alsace), Germany, Switzerland & Austria

6 Gare St. Lazare: To Normandy (also Vernon/Giverny)

7 Gare d'Austerlitz: To Spain, SW France & Loire Valley

service to outlying areas, called *Banlieue* or RER. Both *Banlieue* and RER trains serve outlying areas and the airports; the only difference is that *Banlieue* lines are operated by SNCF (France's train system, called Transilien) and RER lines are operated by RATP (Paris' Métro and bus system). You also may see ticket windows identified as *Ile de France*. This is for Transilien (SNCF) trains serving destinations outside Paris in the Ile de France region (usually no more than an hour from Paris). Trains marked TER, or "Transport Express Regional," denote a regional train system operated by SNCF.

Paris train stations can be intimidating, but if you slow down, take a deep breath, and ask for help, you'll find them manageable and efficient. Bring a pad of paper for clear communication at ticket/info windows. All stations have helpful information booths (*accueil*); the bigger stations have roving helpers, usually wearing red or blue vests. They're capable of answering rail questions more quickly than the staff at the information desks or ticket windows. I make a habit of confirming my track number and departure time with these helpers.

Gare du Nord

The granddaddy of Paris' train stations serves cities in northern France and international destinations north of Paris, including Copenhagen, Amsterdam (see "To Brussels and Amsterdam by Thalys Train," later in this chapter), and the Eurostar to London (see "To London by Eurostar Train," later in this chapter), as well as two of the day trips described in this book (Chantilly and Auvers-sur-Oise).

Arrive early to allow time to navigate this station. From the Métro, follow *Grandes Lignes* signs (main lines) and keep going up until you reach the tracks at street level. *Grandes Lignes* depart from tracks 3–21 (tracks 20 and 21 are around the corner), suburban *Banlieue/Transilien* lines from tracks 30–36 (signed *Réseau Ile-de-France*), and RER trains from tracks 37–44 (tracks 41–44 are one floor below). Glass train information booths (*accueil*) are scattered throughout the station, and information-helpers circulate (all rail staff are required to speak English).

The tourist information kiosk is near track 19 (Mon–Sat 8:00–18:00, closed Sun). Information booths for the **Thalys** trains (high-speed trains to Brussels and Amsterdam) are opposite track 8. All non-Eurostar ticket sales are at the windows opposite tracks 4 and 12. Passengers departing on **Eurostar** trains (London via Chunnel) can buy tickets and must check in at least 30 minutes early on the second level, opposite track 6. Check-in is similar to an airline—you'll fill out a "landing card" and go through security. Monet-esque views over the trains and peaceful, air-conditioned cafés hide on the upper level, past the Eurostar ticket windows (find the cool view WCs down the steps in the café). Other WCs are down the stairs across from track 10 (€1). Baggage check and rental cars are at the far end, near track 3 and down the steps. Taxis are at the door past track 3. Steps down to the Métro are opposite tracks 10 and 19.

Key Destinations Served by Gare du Nord *Grandes Lignes*:

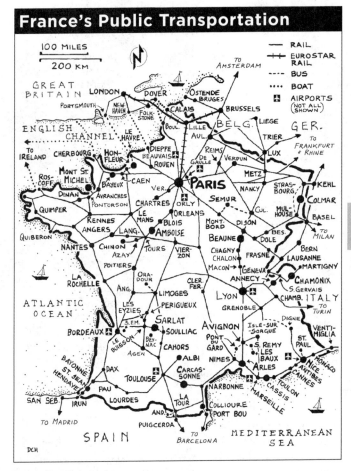

France's Public Transportation

CONNECTIONS

Chantilly-Gouvieux (hourly, fewer on weekends, 25 min, also served by slower RER lines), **Brussels** (about 2/hr, 1.5 hrs, see "To Brussels and Amsterdam by Thalys Train," later in this chapter), **Bruges** (about 2/hr, 2.5 hrs, change in Brussels), **Amsterdam** (nearly hourly, 4–5 hrs, change in Brussels, see "To Brussels and Amsterdam by Thalys Train," later in this chapter), **Berlin** (6/day, 9 hrs, 1–2 changes, better connections from Gare de l'Est), **Copenhagen** (7/day, 14–18 hrs, two night trains), **Koblenz** (9/day, 5 hrs, most change in Köln), and **London** via Eurostar Chunnel train (12–15/day, 2.5 hrs, tel. 08 36 35 35 39, see "To London by Eurostar Train," later in this chapter).

By *Banlieue*/**RER Lines**: **Chantilly-Gouvieux** (3/hr, 45 min), **Charles de Gaulle Airport** (4/hr, 30 min, runs 5:00–24:00, track 4), **Auvers-sur-Oise** (2/hr, 1 hr, transfer at Pontoise or St. Ouen).

Key Transportation Phrases

French	Pronounced	English
accueil	ah-koy	information/ assistance
niveau	nee-voh	level
billets	bee-yay	tickets
réservation	ray-zehr-vah-see-yohn	reservation
départs	day-par	departures
arrivées	ah-ree-vay	arrivals
aller simple	ah-lay sam-pluh	one-way
aller-retour	ah-lay ruh-toor	round-trip
a l'heure	ah loor	on time
fenêtre/couloir	fuh-neh-truh/ kool-wahr	window/aisle seat
fenêtre isolée	fuh-neh-truh ee-zoh-lay	single seat by window (first class only)
voyageurs munis de billets	voh-yah-zhoor moo-nee duh bee-yay	travelers with tickets
navette	nah-veht	shuttle bus
Grandes Lignes	grahnd leen	major domestic and international lines
RER	air ay air	suburban lines

Gare Montparnasse

This big, modern station covers three floors, serves lower Normandy and Brittany, and has TGV service to the Loire Valley and southwestern France, as well as suburban service to Chartres. At street level you'll find a bank, *Banlieue* trains (you can also reach the *Banlieue* trains from the second level), and ticket windows for Ile de France trains in the center, just past the escalators. TER trains to Chartres depart mostly from level 2.

Most services are provided on the second (top) level, where the *Grandes Lignes* arrive and depart. Ticket windows and an information booth are to the far left (with your back to glass exterior). *Banlieue* trains depart from tracks 10–19. The main rail information office (*accueil*) is opposite track 15. WCs and baggage check are on the mezzanine level. Taxis and car rentals are to the far left as you leave the tracks. Air France buses to Orly and Charles de Gaulle Airports stop in front of the station, down the escalators and outside. City buses are outside to the left (#28 connects conveniently to the rue Cler area).

French	Pronounced	English
Transilien	trahn-seel-ee-yehn	suburban lines
RATP	air ah tay pay	Paris' Métro and bus system
SNCF	es en say ef	France's country-wide train system
TGV	tay zhay vay	high-speed lines
banlieue	bahn-lee-yuh	suburban
quai	kay	platform
accès aux quais	ahk-seh oh kay	access to the platforms
voie	vwah	track
retard	ruh-tar	delay
salle d'attente	sahl dah-tahnt	waiting room
consigne (also called *espaces bagages*)	kohn-seen	baggage check
consigne automatique	kohn-seen oh-toh-mah-teek	storage lockers
première classe	pruhm-yair klahs	first class
deuxième classe	duhz-yehm klahs	second class
point d'argent	pwan dar-zhahn	ATM
PTT	pay tay tay	post office

CONNECTIONS

Key Destinations Served by Gare Montparnasse: Chartres (10/day, 1 hr, *Banlieue* lines), **Amboise** (12/day in 1.5 hrs with change in St. Pierre-des-Corps, requires TGV reservation; non-TGV trains leave from Gare d'Austerlitz), **Pontorson/Mont St. Michel** (7/day, 3.5–4 hrs, via Rennes or Dreux, some with bus from Rennes), **Dinan** (6/day, 4 hrs, change in Rennes and Dol), **Bordeaux** (20/day, 3.5 hrs), **Sarlat** (7/day, allow 6 hrs; 3/day with change in Bordeaux-St. Jean or Libourne, then TGV; 4/day to Souillac, then bus), **Toulouse** (13/day, 5–7 hrs, most require change, usually in Bordeaux or Montpellier), **Albi** (6/day, 6–7.5 hrs, change in Toulouse, also night train), **Carcassonne** (14/day, 6.5 hrs, most require changes in Toulouse or Montpellier, direct trains take 8 hrs, night train also available), **Tours** (18/day, 1 hr), **Madrid** (3/day, 13.5 hrs, one overnight via Irun, more night trains from Gare d'Austerlitz), and **Lisbon** (1/day, 21.5 hrs via Irun or Madrid).

Gare de Lyon

This huge, bewildering station offers TGV and regular service to southeastern France, Italy, and other international destinations (for more trains to Italy, see "Gare de Bercy" at the end of this section). Frequent *Banlieue* trains serve Melun (near Vaux-le-Vicomte) and Fontainebleau (some depart from the main *Grandes Lignes* level, more frequent departures are from one level down, follow RER-D signs, and ask at any information booth or ticket window where the next departure leaves from). Don't leave this station without visiting Le Train Bleu Restaurant lounge, up the stairs opposite track G (see page 420).

Grande Ligne trains arrive and depart from street level, but are divided into two areas (tracks A–N in the blue area, and 5–23 in the yellow area). Monitors will show either yellow or blue even before the track is posted, so you know which general area your train leaves from. The two areas are connected by the long platform along tracks A and 5, and by the hallway adjacent to track A and opposite track 9. This hallway has all the services, including ticket windows, ticket information, WCs, banks, and shops (Virgin Records/Books sells some books in English). Transilien ticket windows are just inside the hall adjacent to track A (*billets Ile de France*). *Grandes Lignes* and *Banlieue* lines share the same tracks.

A tourist office (Mon–Sat 8:00–18:00, closed Sun) and a train information office are both opposite track L. From the RER or Métro, follow signs for *Grandes Lignes Arrivées* and take the escalator up to reach the platforms. Train information booths are opposite tracks A and 11 and downstairs. Baggage check (daily 6:15–22:00, €4–10) is down the stairs opposite track 13. Taxi stands are well-signed in front of, and underneath, the station. If you need a quiet waiting area, here are two to choose from: Le Train Bleu's pricey but way-cool bar-lounge opposite track G; or opposite track 13, follow *consigne* (baggage check) signs down one floor and find a seat.

Air France buses to Montparnasse (easy transfer to Orly Airport) and direct to Charles de Gaulle Airport stop outside the station's main entrance (opposite tracks A–L, walk across the parking lot—the stop is opposite the Café Européen on the right; €16, 2/hr, normally at :15 and :45 after the hour).

Key Destinations Served by Gare de Lyon: Vaux-le-Vicomte (train to Melun, 2/hr by train, 30 min; 3/hr by RER, 45 min), **Fontainebleau** (nearly hourly, 45 min), **Disneyland** (RER line A-4 to Marne-la-Vallée-Chessy, at least 3/hr, 45 min), **Beaune** (nearly hourly, 2.5 hrs, most require change in Dijon), **Dijon** (nearly hourly, 1.5 hrs), **Chamonix** (6–8/day, 6–8 hrs, night train possible in summer), **Annecy** (13/day, 4–5 hrs, many with change

Train Tips

- Arrive at the station with plenty of time before your departure to find the right platform, confirm connections, and so on. In small towns your train may depart before the station opens; if so, go directly to the tracks and find the overhead sign that confirms your train stops at that track.
- Larger stations have platforms with monitors showing each car's layout (numbered forward or backward) so you can figure out where your *voiture* will stop on the long platform and where to board each car. Notice the low baggage area placed every two cars—people use it to avoid hoisting their suitcases to the high overhead rack.
- Check schedules in advance if possible. Upon arrival at a station, learn your departure possibilities. Large stations have a separate information window or office; at small stations, the ticket office gives information.
- If you have a rail flexipass, write the date on your pass each day you travel.
- Validate tickets (not passes) and reservations in yellow machines before boarding. If you're traveling with a pass and have a reservation for a certain trip, you must validate the reservation.
- Reservations for all TGV trains are required, and often sell out. You can reserve any train at any station or through SNCF Boutiques (small offices in city centers). A limited number of reservations are allocated for railpass users during peak times—reserve as far ahead as you can for Friday and Sunday afternoons and Saturday mornings.
- Before getting on a train, confirm that it's going where you think it is. For example, if you want to go to Chartres, ask the conductor or any local passenger, *"À Chartres?"* (ah shart-ruh, meaning, "To Chartres?").
- Some longer trains split cars en route. Make sure your train car is continuing to your destination by asking, *"Cette voiture va à Chartres?"* (seht vwah-toor vah ah shart-ruh, meaning, "This car goes to Chartres?").
- If a non-TGV train seat is reserved, it will usually be labeled *réservé*, with the cities to and from which it is reserved.
- Verify with the conductor all of the transfers you must make (*"Correspondance à?"* meaning, "Transfer to where?").
- To guard against theft, keep your bags overhead. If you must store them at the end of the car, make sure you can see them from your seat (they're most vulnerable to theft when the train stops).
- Note your arrival time, so you'll be ready to get off.
- Use the train's free WCs before you get off (but not while the train is stopped).

in Lyon), **Lyon** (at least hourly, 2 hrs), **Avignon** (9/day in 2.5 hrs to Avignon TGV station, 5/day in 3.5 hrs to Avignon Centre-Ville station, more connections with change—3–4 hrs), **Arles** (11/day, 2 direct TGVs in 4 hrs, 9 with change in Avignon in 5 hrs), **Nice** (10/day, 6 hrs, may require change, 11-hr night train possible out of Gare d'Austerlitz), **Venice** (3/day, 4/night, 10–13 hrs with change in Milan; 1 direct overnight, 13 hrs, important to reserve ahead), **Rome** (3/day, 13–16 hrs, plus several overnight options, important to reserve ahead), **Bern** (9/day: 1 direct train in morning and 1 in evening—4.5 hrs, otherwise 5.5 hrs; faster trains from Gare de l'Est), **Interlaken** (nearly hourly, 6.5 hrs, night train possible via Basel from Gare de l'Est), and **Barcelona** (3/day, 9 hrs, 1–2 changes; night train possible from Gare d'Austerlitz).

Gare de Bercy: This smaller station handles some night train service to Italy (Mo: Bercy, one stop east of Gare de Lyon on line 14, exit the Métro station and it's across the street). Facilities are limited—just a WC and a sandwich-fare takeout café.

Gare de l'Est

This two-floor station (with underground Métro) is relatively easy to navigate. All trains depart at street level from tracks 1–30. A train information office is opposite track 17, ticket sales are in the hall opposite track 8. All other services are down the escalator through the hall opposite tracks 12–16 (baggage check, car rental, WC, small grocery store, and Métro access). A Virgin Records store with some books in English is at the top of the escalator, in the hall opposite track 16. Access to taxis and buses is out the front of the station (exit with your back to the tracks).

Key Destinations Served by Gare de l'Est: Colmar (12/day with TGV, 3.5 hrs, change in Strasbourg), **Strasbourg** (hourly with TGV, 2.5 hrs), **Reims** (12/day with TGV, 45 min), **Verdun** (9/day with TGV, 1.5–3 hrs with transfer in Metz or Chalôns-sur-Marne), **Bern** (9/day, 4.5–5 hrs, 1–2 changes), **Interlaken** (night train possible via Basel with changes at 5:00 and 8:00, daytime trains run from Gare de Lyon), **Zürich** (2/day direct, 4 hrs; 7/day with changes, 5–6.5 hrs; night train), **Vienna** (7/day, 12–17 hrs, 1–3 changes, night train), **Prague** (5/day, 12–18 hrs, night train possible via Berlin), **Munich** (4/day, 6–7 hrs, some require changes), and **Berlin** (6/day, 8–9 hrs, 1–2 changes, many via Belgium; 1 direct night train, 11.25 hrs). The Paris-Berlin night train may be combined with the Paris-Munich train in 2010, so that the train divides at Karlsruhe, avoiding Belgium and the need to include Belgium on a railpass.

Gare St. Lazare

This relatively small station serves upper Normandy, including

Coping with Strikes

Going on strike (*en grève*) is a popular pastime in this revolution-happy country. President Sarkozy is pushing unions to their limits, and because bargaining between management and employees is not standard procedure, workers strike to get attention. Trucks and tractors block main roads and autoroutes (in a movement called Opération Escargot: "Operation Snail's Pace"), baggage handlers bring airports to their knees; museum workers make Mona Lisa off-limits to tourists; and Métro and train personnel seem to strike every year—perhaps during your trip. What does the traveler do? You could *jeter l'éponge* (throw in the sponge) and go somewhere less strike-prone (Switzerland's nice), or learn to accept certain events as being out of your control. Strikes in France generally last no longer than a day or two, and if you're aware of them, you can usually plan around them. Your hotelier will know the latest (or can find out). Make a habit of asking your hotel receptionist about strikes.

Rouen and Giverny. All trains arrive and depart one floor above street level. The station is undergoing renovation, so be prepared for the temporary displacement of shops and services.

From the Métro, follow signs to *Grandes Lignes* to reach the tracks (long walk). The ticket office and car rental are near track 27. *Grandes Lignes* depart from tracks 17–27; *banlieue* trains depart from 1–16. Train information offices (*accueil*) are scattered about the station. Taxis, the Métro, and buses are well-signed. This station has no baggage check.

Key Destinations Served by Gare St. Lazare: Giverny (train to Vernon, 6–8/day, 45 min), **Rouen** (hourly, 1–1.5 hrs), **Honfleur** (13/day, 2–3.5 hrs, via Lisieux, then bus), **Bayeux** (9/day, 2.5 hrs, some change in Caen), **Caen** (14/day, 2 hrs), and **Pontorson/Mont St. Michel** (2/day, 4–5.5 hrs, via Caen; more trains from Gare Montparnasse).

Gare d'Austerlitz

This small station provides non-TGV service to the Loire Valley, southwestern France, and Spain. All tracks are at street level. The information booth is opposite track 17, and all ticket sales are in the hall opposite track 10. Baggage check, WCs (with €6 showers that include towel, soap, and the works), and car rental are along the side of the station, opposite track 21. To get to the Métro and RER, you must walk outside and along either side of the station.

Key Destinations Served by Gare d'Austerlitz: Versailles (via RER line C, 4/hr, 30–40 min), **Amboise** (10/day direct in 2 hrs; faster TGV connection from Gare Montparnasse), **Cahors** (5/day, 5 hrs, 1 direct night train; other slower trains from Gare Montparnasse), **Barcelona** (1/night, 12 hrs; day trains from Gare de Lyon), and **Madrid** (2/night, 13 hrs direct, 16 hrs via Irun; day trains from Gare Montparnasse).

SNCF Boutiques

You can save time and stress by buying train tickets or making train reservations at an SNCF Boutique. These small branch offices of the French national rail company are conveniently located throughout Paris, with offices near most of my recommended hotels and museums and at Orly and Charles de Gaulle Airports. Arrive when they open to avoid lines (generally open Mon–Sat 8:30–19:00 or 20:00, closed Sun).

Historic Core
- 18 rue du Pont Neuf, Mo: Pont Neuf

Marais
- 2 rue de Turenne, Mo: St. Paul
- 5 rue de Lyon, Mo: Gare de Lyon

Near Major Museums
- Musée d'Orsay RER station, below Orsay Museum
- Forum des Halles shopping mall, basement sublevel 4, returns office (*Salle d'Echanges*), Mo: Châtelet-Les Halles

Champs Elysées
- 229 rue du Faubourg Saint-Honoré, Mo: Saint-Philippe-du-Roule

Farther North on the Right Bank
- 53 rue Chaussée d'Antin, Mo: Chaussée d'Antin (near Opéra Garnier and Galeries Lafayette)
- 32/34 rue Joubert, Mo: Haussman-St. Lazare (near Gare St. Lazare)
- 71/73 boulevard Magenta, Mo: Gare du Nord (Gare du Nord)
- 82 avenue de la Grande Armée, Mo: Porte Maillot (near Hôtel Concorde-Lafayette and Beauvais Airport bus stop)

Montmartre
- 27 rue Lepic, Mo: Blanche

Eiffel Tower/Rue Cler
- 80 rue Saint Dominique, Mo: La Tour Maubourg
- 19 rue de Passy, Mo: Passy (near Marmottan Museum)
- Invalides Métro/RER station

Latin Quarter/Luxembourg Garden
- 54 boulevard Saint-Michel, Mo: Cluny-Sorbonne
- 79 rue de Rennes, Mo: St. Sulpice

Farther South on the Left Bank
- 17 rue Littré, Mo: Montparnasse-Bienvenüe (near Luxembourg Garden and grand cafés)

- 68 avenue du Maine: Mo. Montparnasse-Bienvenüe (near grand cafés)
- 30 avenue d'Italie, in Centre Commerciale Galaxie, Mo: Place d'Italie

You'll also find quieter SNCF Boutiques in train stations of the towns I suggest for day trips from Paris, such as Versailles, Fontainebleau, Melun (for Vaux-le-Vicomte), Chartres, Chantilly, Vernon (for Giverny), and Pontoise (for Auvers-sur-Oise).

To Brussels and Amsterdam by Thalys Train

The pricey Thalys train has the monopoly on the rail route between Paris and Brussels (for a cheaper option, try the Eurolines bus, described later in this chapter). Without a railpass you'll pay about €80–100 second class for the Paris–Amsterdam train (compared to €45 by bus) or about €60–80 second class for the Paris–Brussels train (compared to €25 by bus). Even with a railpass, you need to pay for train reservations (second class-€14.50; first class-€27, includes a meal). Book at least a day ahead, as seats are limited (www.thalys.com). Or hop on the bus, Gus.

Crossing the Channel

To London by Eurostar Train

The fastest and most convenient way to get from the Eiffel Tower to Big Ben is by rail. Eurostar, a joint service of the Belgian, British, and French railways, is the speedy passenger train that zips you (and up to 800 others in 18 sleek cars) from downtown Paris to downtown London (at least 15/day, 2.5 hrs) faster and more easily than flying. The actual tunnel crossing is a 20-minute, black, silent, 100-mile-per-hour nonevent. Your ears won't even pop. Eurostar's monopoly expires at the beginning of 2010, and Air France has already announced plans to start a competing high-speed rail service between London and Paris in late autumn 2010.

Eurostar Fares

Channel fares are reasonable but complicated. Prices vary depending on how far ahead you reserve, whether you can live with restrictions, and whether you're eligible for any discounts (children, youths, seniors, roundtrip travelers, and railpass holders all qualify).

Fares can change without notice, but typically a **one-way, full-fare ticket** (with no restrictions on refundability) runs about $425 first-class and $300 second-class. **Cheaper seats** come with more restrictions and can sell out quickly (figure $80–160 for second-class, one-way). Those traveling with a railpass that covers France or Britain should look first at the **passholder** fare (about $85–130

for second-class, one-way Eurostar trips). For more details, visit
www.ricksteves.com/rail/eurostar.htm.

Buying Eurostar Tickets

Only the most expensive (full-fare) ticket is fully refundable, so
don't reserve until you're sure of your plans. But if you wait too
long, the cheapest tickets will get bought up.

Once you're confident about
the time and date of your crossing, you can check and book fares
by phone or online in the US,
and pay to have your ticket delivered to you in the US. (Order
online at www.ricksteves.com
/rail/eurostar.htm, prices listed
in dollars; order by phone at US
tel. 800-EUROSTAR). Or you
could order from a French company (French tel. 08 92 35 35 39,
www.eurostar.com, prices listed
in euros) and pick up your ticket
at the train station. In Europe
you can buy your Eurostar ticket
at any major train station in any

country, at neighborhood SNCF offices (see "SNCF Boutiques,"
above), or at any travel agency that handles train tickets (expect
a booking fee). You can purchase passholder discount tickets at
Eurostar departure stations, online, or by phone, but they may be
harder to get at other train stations and travel agencies.

Note that the arrival and departure times printed on your
ticket are local times, and that France's time zone is one hour later
than Britain's. For example, your departure from Paris is listed in
French time, and the arrival in London is British time.

Taking the Eurostar

Check in at Gare du Nord at least 30 minutes in advance for your
Eurostar trip. It's very similar to an airport check-in: You pass
through airport-like security, fill out a customs form, show your
passport to customs officials, and find a TV monitor to locate your
departure gate. The currency-exchange booth here has rates about
the same as you'll find on the other end.

Crossing the Channel by Ferry

Ferries are cheaper than the Eurostar train, but twice as complicated and time-consuming. They're a good idea, however, if you're

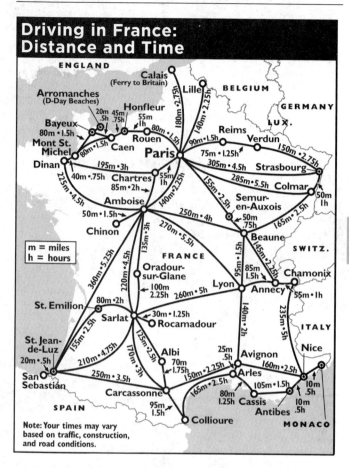

Driving in France: Distance and Time

ENGLAND

Calais (Ferry to Britain)
Lille
BELGIUM
GERMANY

Arromanches (D-Day Beaches)
Honfleur
LUX.
Bayeux
20m .5h 45m .75h 55m 1h
80m 1.5h
Reims
Verdun
150m • 2.75h
Mont St. Michel
Caen
Rouen
90m•1.5h
75m • 1.25h
305m•4.5h Strasbourg
Dinan
80m•1.5h
Paris
285m•5.5h Colmar
195m •3h
50m 1h
40m•.75h
Chartres
55m 1h
155m•2.5h
Semur-en-Auxois
165m•2.5h
225m•4.5h
85m•2h
140m•2.25h
250m • 4h
50m .75h
Amboise
Chinon
50m•1.5h
270m•5.5h
Beaune
SWITZ.
m = miles
h = hours
135m•3h
FRANCE
Oradour-sur-Glane
95m•1.5h
85m 1.5h
145m•2.5h
Chamonix
360m•5.25h
220m•4.5h
100m 2.25h
Lyon
260m • 5h
Annecy
55m•1h
St. Emilion
80m•2h
Sarlat
30m • 1.25h
Rocamadour
140m•2h
235m•5h
ITALY
St. Jean-de-Luz
155m•2.5h
125m•2.5h
Albi
25m .5h
Avignon
Nice
20m•.5h
210m•4.75h
170m•2.5h
70m 1.75h
150m•2.25h
160m•2.5h
San Sebastián
250m • 3.5h
Arles
105m•1.5h
10m .5h
Carcassonne
165m • 2.5h
80m 1.25h Cassis
10m .5h
SPAIN
95m 1.5h
Antibes
MONACO
Note: Your times may vary based on traffic, construction, and road conditions.
Collioure

CONNECTIONS

traveling on the fly and haven't booked a Eurostar ticket in advance. See www.posl.com and www.aferry.to for routes and fares.

Buses

The main bus station is the Gare Routière du Paris-Gallieni (28 avenue du Général de Gaulle, in suburb of Bagnolet, Mo: Gallieni, tel. 01 49 72 51 51). Buses provide cheaper—if less comfortable and more time-consuming—transportation to major European cities. The bus is also the cheapest way to cross the English Channel; book at least two days in advance for the best fares. Eurolines' buses depart from here (tel. 08 36 69 52 52, www.eurolines.com). Look on their website for offices in central Paris.

Driving

Parking in Paris

Street parking is free from 19:00 to 9:00, on Sundays, and in August. To pay for streetside parking, you must go to a *tabac* and buy a parking card (*une carte parking*), sold in €10, €20, and €30 denominations. Insert the card into the meter and punch the desired amount of time (generally €1–2/hour), then take the receipt and put it inside your windshield. Meters limit street parking to a maximum of two hours. For a longer stay, park for less at an airport (about €10/day) and take public transport or a taxi into the city. You'll pay more to park in a downtown lot (about €20–27/day, €55/3 days, and €10/day more after that). Underground lots are numerous in Paris; look online (www.vincipark.com). Otherwise, ask your hotelier for suggestions.

DAY TRIPS FROM PARIS

VERSAILLES DAY TRIP

Château de Versailles

If you've ever wondered why your American passport has French writing in it, you'll find the answer at Versailles (vehr-"sigh")—every king's dream palace. The powerful court of Louis XIV at Versailles set the standard of culture for all of Europe, right up to modern times. Today, if you're planning to visit just one palace in all of Europe, make it Versailles.

Versailles offers three blockbuster sights. The main attraction is the palace itself, called the **Château.** Here you walk through dozens of lavish, chandeliered rooms once inhabited by Louis XIV and his successors. Next come the expansive **Gardens** behind the palace, a landscaped wonderland dotted with statues and fountains. Finally, at the far end of the Gardens, is the **Domaine de Marie-Antoinette,** a pastoral area featuring several small palaces and Marie's Hamlet—perfect for getting away from the mobs at the Château.

Visiting Versailles can seem daunting because of its size and hordes of visitors. But it's manageable. Arm yourself with a pass to skip ticket-buying lines; arrive early or late to avoid the crowds; and use this self-guided tour to focus on the highlights. I've provided all the details in "Orientation," next. First-timers can simply follow my recommended strategy in "Planning Your Time at Versailles" on page 491.

The entire complex has been under renovation for many years (some changes and closures are possible), but the serious work is finally done and all parts of the Château should be open for your visit.

Orientation

Cost: I recommend buying either a Paris Museum Pass or Versailles' "Le Passeport" Pass, both of which give you access to the most important parts of the complex (see "Passes" below).

You can also buy individual tickets for each of the three different sections:

1. The Château, the main palace, costs €13.50 (€10 after 15:00, under 18 always free, includes audioguide). Your Château ticket includes the King's and Queen's State Apartments ("les Grands Appartements"), with the famous Hall of Mirrors, the Royal Chapel, and several lesser rooms.

2. The Domaine de Marie-Antoinette, the estate of the queen, costs €10 April–Oct; €6 after 16:00 and Nov–March; under 18 always free. This ticket gives you access to the far corner of the Gardens and entry into several small palaces: the queen's Hamlet, the Grand and Petit Trianons, and a smattering of nearby buildings.

3. The Gardens are free, except on weekends April–Sept, when the fountains blast and the price is €8 (see "Fountain Spectacles," page 492).

Passes: Smart travelers arrive at Versailles with one of these two passes in hand. Either pass can save you money—and allows you to skip the long ticket-buyer lines (though everyone must endure security checks before entering the palaces).

The **Paris Museum Pass** covers the Château and the Domaine de Marie-Antoinette (a €23.50 value) and is the best solution for most, but doesn't include an audioguide or the Gardens on Fountain Spectacle weekends. For Paris Museum Pass pricing and details, see page 42.

The **Le Passeport** one-day pass is a good deal for serious sightseers who don't have a Paris Museum Pass and must see the whole shebang. Le Passeport covers your entrance to the Château, Domaine de Marie-Antoinette, and Gardens, along with two things not covered by the Paris Museum Pass: an audioguide and the weekend Fountain Spectacles. From April to Oct, Le Passeport costs €20 Mon–Fri, €25 Sat–Sun; from Nov to March it's €16 Tue–Sun. This pass is a poor value on Mon, when only the Gardens are open.

Buying Passes and Tickets: You can buy Le Passeport in Paris at a FNAC store, at Versailles' town TI (no line), at the Château box office (long lines), or online at www.chateauversailles.fr. Individual tickets are sold at the website and Château box office but not at the TI. If you arrive sans ticket and only want to see the Château, save line-time by purchasing your ticket at Café Bleu Roi (on the right side of the parking lot as you approach the Château, daily from 7:00; they also sell Le Passeport but it's more easily purchased at the TI; 7 rue Colbert, tel. 01 39 50 05 79).

Hours: The **Château** is open Tue–Sun April–Oct 9:00–18:30 (on Sat in summer, King's and Queen's State Apartments may be open 18:30–21:00—ask), Nov–March 9:00–17:30, closed Mon. The **Domaine de Marie-Antoinette** is open Tue–Sun April–Oct 12:00–18:30, Nov–March 12:00–17:30, closed Mon. The **Gardens** are generally open daily 9:00 to sunset (17:30–21:30), but close at 18:00 on Sat in summer to prepare for evening events. Last entry to all of these areas is one hour before closing.

Crowd Control: Versailles is a zoo May–Sept 10:00–13:00, and all day Tue and Sun. For fewer crowds, go early or late. If you go early, arrive by 9:00 (when the palace opens), and tour the Château first, then the Gardens. If you arrive later, tour the Gardens first (remembering that the Domaine de Marie-Antoinette opens at noon), then visit the Château after 13:00 when crowds dissipate (except on Tue and Sun, when the place is packed from open to close). The last guided tours of the day generally depart by 15:00.

Skip the ticket-buying line by using a Paris Museum Pass or Le Passeport, buying and printing your own ticket or Le Passeport on the Versailles website, or booking a guided tour (see below). Everyone must wait in security-check lines to enter the Château and the Grand and Petit Trianons.

Pickpockets: Assume pickpockets are working the tourist crowds.

Getting There: The town of Versailles is 30 minutes southwest of Paris. For most the best option is to take the **RER-C train** (4/hr, 30–40 min one-way, €6 round-trip) from any of these Paris RER stops: Gare d'Austerlitz, St. Michel, Musée d'Orsay, Invalides, Pont de l'Alma, and Champ de Mars. Scan the list of departing trains. Any train whose name starts with a V (e.g., "Vick") goes to Versailles; don't board other trains. Get off at the last stop (Versailles R.G., or "Rive Gauche"). Exit through the turnstiles by inserting your ticket. To reach the palace, turn right out of the train station, then left at the first boulevard, and walk 10 minutes. All trains leaving Versailles from the Rive Gauche train station serve all downtown Paris RER stops on the C line. (To visit Versailles and Chartres on the same day using public transportation, see page 519.)

Besides Rive Gauche, Versailles has two other train stations that may be useful to some travelers. Trains run from Paris' Gare St. Lazare to both of these stations: Rive Droite

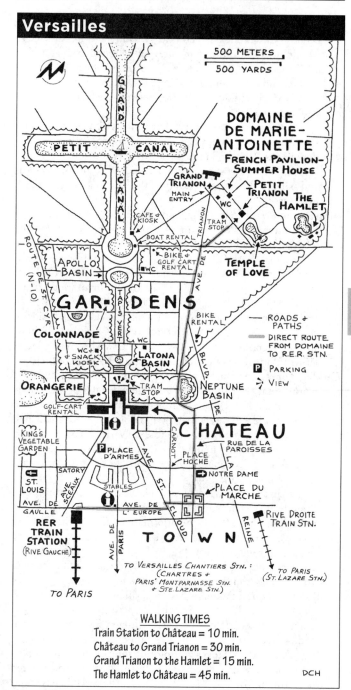

Versailles

500 METERS
500 YARDS

GRAND CANAL

PETIT CANAL

DOMAINE DE MARIE-ANTOINETTE

FRENCH PAVILION-SUMMER HOUSE

GRAND TRIANON

PETIT TRIANON

THE HAMLET

MAIN ENTRY

CAFE & KIOSK

WC

TRAM STOP

BOAT RENTAL

ROUTE DE ST. CYR (N-10)

APOLLO BASIN

BIKE & GOLF CART RENTAL

WC

AV. DE TRIANON

TEMPLE OF LOVE

GAR-DENS

TAPIS VERT

COLONNADE

BIKE RENTAL

AV. DE

BLVD. DE

ROADS & PATHS

DIRECT ROUTE FROM DOMAINE TO R.E.R. STN.

P PARKING

VIEW

WC & SNACK KIOSK

WC

LATONA BASIN

ORANGERIE

TRAM STOP

NEPTUNE BASIN

GOLF-CART RENTAL

KINGS VEGETABLE GARDEN

CHATEAU

RUE DE LA PAROISSES

PLACE D'ARMES

AV. CARNOT

PLACE HOCHE

NOTRE DAME

PLACE DU MARCHE

SATORY

STABLES

AV. ST CLOUD

ST. LOUIS

AV. DE SCEAUX

AVE. DE L'EUROPE

RIVE DROITE TRAIN STN.

AVE. DE GAULLE

RER TRAIN STATION (RIVE GAUCHE)

AVE. DE PARIS

TOWN

REINE

TO PARIS

TO VERSAILLES CHANTIERS STN.: (CHARTRES & PARIS' MONTPARNASSE STN. & STE. LAZARE STN.)

TO PARIS (ST. LAZARE STN.)

WALKING TIMES
Train Station to Château = 10 min.
Château to Grand Trianon = 30 min.
Grand Trianon to the Hamlet = 15 min.
The Hamlet to Château = 45 min.

DCH

and Chantiers (4/hr, 25 min one-way; €5 round-trip). You can also catch trains to Versailles' Chantiers from Paris' Gare Montparnasse (5/hr, 15 min one-way, €4 round-trip) and from Chartres. It's a 20-minute walk to the Château from Rive Droite, and a 25-minute trek from Chantiers.

Taxis for the 30-minute ride between Versailles and Paris cost about €55.

By **car** it's a 30-minute drive to reach Versailles from Paris, if the traffic's not bad. Get on the *périphérique* freeway that circles Paris, and take the toll-free A13 autoroute toward Rouen. Follow signs into Versailles, then look for *château* signs and park in the huge pay lot (€4.80/2 hrs, €8.50/4 hrs, €13/8 hrs, free 19:30–8:30).

Information: Visit Versailles' good website before you go: www.chateauversailles.fr. Versailles has two information offices: the town's official TI (helpful, less crowded), and one at the palace (long waits). Both sell Paris Museum Passes and Le Passeport. You'll pass the town TI on your walk from the main RER station to the palace—it's just past the Pullman Hôtel (daily April–Sept 9:00–19:00, Oct–March 9:00–18:00, tel. 01 39 24 88 88). The Château's information office is on the left side of the Château courtyard (as you face the Château, tel. 08 10 81 16 14). The useful *Versailles Orientation Guide* brochure (free at either information office) explains your sightseeing options.

Guided Tours: For a basic visit, this chapter's self-guided tour works great. But the primary 1.5-hour English guided tour does have a few extras: commentary from trained guides, access to a few extra rooms (the interior of the Royal Chapel, some private apartments—the line-up varies), plus it's a good way to skip ticket-buying lines if you don't have a pass. The guided tours are long, but those with an appetite for palace history enjoy them.

Skip the tours hawked as you leave the train station; book directly at the Château. Reserve your tour upon arrival (tours can sell out by 13:00) at the information office in the Château courtyard (€7.50 plus Château admission or pass, 1.5 hours, departing roughly every 45 min 10:00–15:00). Don't wait in the ticket-buying line—instead, walk to the front of the line, where you'll find the guided tour desk to the right.

Audioguide Tours: Audioguides are available at the entrance to the Château. They're free with Le Passeport or individual Château tickets. With the Paris Museum Pass, the Château audioguide costs €6 (€10 on Fountain Spectacle weekends).

A free **Rick Steves audioguide tour** of the most important rooms of the King's and Queen's State Apartments is available for users of iPods and other MP3 players at

Planning Your Time at Versailles

Here's what I'd do on a first visit to Versailles:

In Paris, buy a Paris Museum Pass, or buy Le Passeport at a FNAC store or online (see "Passes," page 487). You can

also get Le Passeport at the Versailles TI, but doing so will put you at the palace gates a few minutes later.

Leave Paris by 8:00 and arrive at the palace just before it opens at 9:00. Tour the Château following my self-guided tour, which hits the highlights (Royal Chapel, King's and Queen's State Apartments, and the Hall of Mirrors). Consider supplementing the tour in this chapter with an audioguide (free with Le Passeport).

Have lunch in the Gardens, at one of the sandwich kiosks or cafés. Spend the afternoon touring the Gardens and the Domaine de Marie-Antoinette. On spring or summer weekends, catch the Fountain Spectacles in the Gardens. Stay for dinner in Versailles town (see recommended restaurants at the end of this chapter), or head back to Paris.

www.ricksteves.com and an interactive **iPhone app** version of my Versailles tour is for sale on iTunes. You also may want to check out the multimedia section at www.chateauversailles.fr.

Length of This Day Trip: With the usual lines, allow 1.5 hours each for the Château, the Gardens, and the Domaine de Marie-Antoinette. Add another two hours for round-trip transit, plus another hour for lunch...and, at around eight hours, Versailles is a full day trip from Paris.

Baggage Check: Free checkrooms are at the main entrances to the main Château and the two Trianons. Use them to check forbidden items (food, big bags, baby carriages, and so on). Strollers are not allowed inside the Château, so today's a good day for parents to either hire a babysitter (see page 423) or carry the *bébé* in a backpack with a child-seat.

Services: Reminiscent of the days when dukes urinated behind the potted palm trees, WCs at the Château are few and far between, and some come with long lines. Use the public WC just before the palace gates, or find the quieter WC after you enter the Château (skip the lineup at the one in the entry courtyard). You'll also find WCs tucked away in several locations in the Gardens.

Cuisine Art: A cafeteria and WCs are to the right of the Château's golden gate. Sandwich kiosks and cafés are scattered about the Gardens (stop at the first one below the Château, as the others come with long lines). Two restaurants are near the Apollo Basin and canal.

In the **town,** restaurants are on the street to the right of the parking lot (as you face the Château), though the best eateries line the lively market square, place du Marché, in the town center. A handy McDonald's is immediately across from the train station (WC without crowds, Internet café next door). An appealing assortment of reasonable restaurants lines rue de Satory between the station and the palace (see the end of this chapter).

Photography: Allowed indoors without a flash.

Fountain Spectacles: On spring and summer weekends, loud classical music fills the king's backyard, and the Garden's fountains are in full squirt. Louis XIV had his engineers literally reroute a river to fuel these gushers. Even by today's standards, they are impressive.

The fountains run April–Sept Sat–Sun 11:00–12:00 & 15:30–17:00, with the finale 17:20–17:30. On these "spray days," the Gardens cost €8. (Pay at the ticket booth near the golf-cart rental in the Gardens; covered by Le Passeport but not Paris Museum Pass; not included in individual Château ticket.) Pick up the helpful *Les Grandes Eaux Musicales* brochure and ask about the various evening spectacles (Sat in July–Aug).

Starring: Louis XIV, Marie-Antoinette, and the *ancien régime.*

Overview

The main sights to see at Versailles—all covered by this self-guided tour—are the Château (the palace), the landscaped Gardens in the "backyard," and the small palaces of the Domaine de Marie-Antoinette. If your time is limited, stick to the Château and the Gardens just outside. It's a 40-minute walk from the Château through the Gardens to the heart of the Domaine at the far end (longer if you stop along the way).

In the Château, the highlights are the King's and Queen's State Apartments, the Royal Chapel, and the Hall of Mirrors. We'll see all these on our self-guided tour. It's crowded in there, so prepare to shuffle along at a snail's pace.

Versailles Palace Ground Floor and Entrances

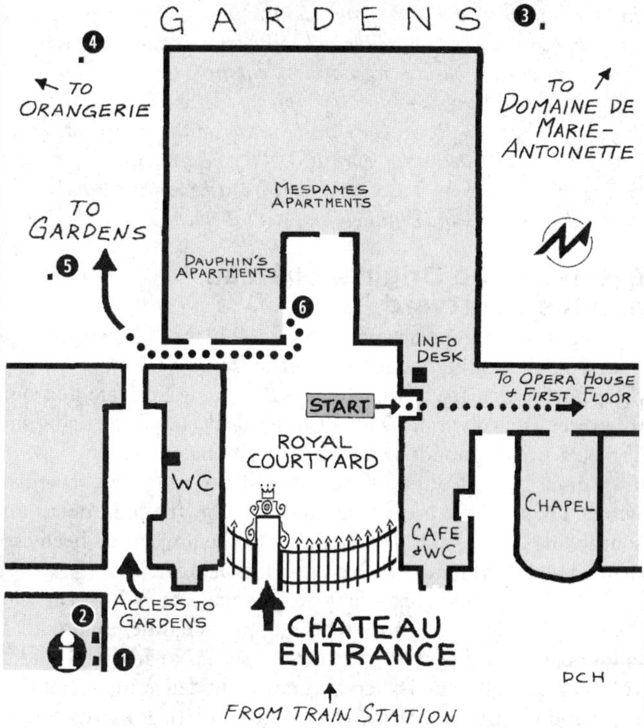

G A R D E N S ❸.

❹

← TO ORANGERIE

TO DOMAINE DE MARIE- ANTOINETTE ↗

TO GARDENS

❺

MESDAMES APARTMENTS

DAUPHIN'S APARTMENTS

❻

INFO DESK

START

To OPERA HOUSE + FIRST FLOOR →

ROYAL COURTYARD

WC

CHAPEL

CAFE +WC

ACCESS TO GARDENS

❷ ❶

CHATEAU ENTRANCE

DCH

↑ FROM TRAIN STATION

VERSAILLES

❶ Chateau Ticket & Pass Sales
❷ Guided Tour Reservations & Departure Point
❸ Tram (Petit Train)
❹ Golf-Cart Rental (Voitures Eléctrique)
❺ Fountain Spectacles Ticket Booth (weekends only)
❻ Exit from State Apartments;
  Entrance to Dauphin's Apartments

••• Self-Guided Tour of State and Private Apartments

The Tour Begins

• *Stand in the courtyard and face the palace. If you need to buy a ticket, find the line to the far left. If you want to book a tour, skip the ticket line—tours are booked just to the right of the ticket office (no lines).*

If you already have a ticket or pass, enter the Château through the modern glass entry ahead on the left (prepare for a security-check line). The original golden Royal Gate in the center of the courtyard, nearly 260 feet long and decorated with 100,000 gold leaves, "disappeared" during the Revolution. This replica (which cost €5 million to build) was installed in 2008—and definitely makes a statement.

Exterior—The Original Château and the Courtyard

The section of the palace with the clock is the original château, once a small hunting lodge where little Louis XIV spent his happiest boyhood years. Naturally, the Sun King's private bedroom (the three arched windows beneath the clock) faced the rising sun. The palace and grounds are laid out on an east–west axis.

Once king, Louis XIV expanded the lodge by attaching wings, creating the present U-shape. Later, the long north and south wings were built. The total cost of the project has been estimated at half of France's entire GNP for one year.

Think how busy this courtyard must have been 300 years ago. As many as 5,000 nobles were here at any one time, each with an entourage. They'd buzz from games to parties to amorous rendezvous in sedan-chair taxis. Servants ran about delivering secret messages and roast legs of lamb. Horse-drawn carriages arrived at the fancy gate with their finely dressed passengers, having driven up the broad boulevard that ran directly from Paris (the horse stables still line the boulevard). Incredible as it seems, both the grounds and most of the palace were public territory, where even the lowliest peasants could come to gawk—provided they passed through a metal detector and followed a dress code. Then, as now, there were hordes of tourists, pickpockets, palace workers, and men selling wind-up children's toys.

• *Enter the Château at door "H" on the right. When inside, go with the flow, following signs for* Les Grands Appartements/State Apartments *(helpful information desk as you enter). The lavish Royal Chapel comes soon on the right.*

Royal Chapel and Drawing Room

Royal Chapel

Every morning at 10:00, the organist and musicians struck up the music, the big golden doors opened, and Louis XIV and his family

Versailles Royal Opera House (Opéra Royale)

Your tour may include a visit to Versailles' recently reopened Royal Opera House. This 700-seat oval-shaped theater is a dizzying mix of pink, green, and blue, dazzling with mirrors and chandeliers, and all laced with gold. The entire structure is made of wood, carved to look like Ionic columns or painted to simulate marble. When Marie-Antoinette married the future Louis XVI in 1770, they had their reception here in this building, which was built specifically for the occasion by architect Ange-Jacques Gabriel. It was used not only as a theater, but could also be converted into a ballroom or audience hall quickly by machinery that raised the auditorium floor to the same level as the stage. If you get inside, look up above the double balconies to the chandeliers: It took thousands of candles to light the place for a single night, so performances were rare and treasured.

walked through to attend Mass. While Louis XIV entered through the upstairs and looked down on the golden altar, the lowly nobles on the ground floor (like us) knelt with their backs to the altar and

looked up—worshipping Louis worshipping God. Important religious ceremonies took place here, including the marriage of young Louis XVI to Marie-Antoinette.

In the vast pagan "temple" that is Versailles—built to glorify one man, Louis XIV—this Royal Chapel is a paltry tip of the hat to that "other" god...the Christian one. It's virtually the first, last, and only hint of Christianity you'll see in the entire complex. Versailles celebrates Man, not God, by raising Louis XIV to almost godlike status, the personification of all good human qualities. In

a way, Versailles is the last great flowering of Renaissance humanism and revival of the classical world.

• *From here you may be directed to the end of a lo-o-ong sculpture-lined hall, where you'll visit the Opera House (which just reopened after a lo-o-ong renovation—see sidebar above).*

More likely, you'll be directed left through a series of rooms that set the stage for what you'll see upstairs—think royal foreplay. You'll pass rooms showing the genealogy of the kings and queens of France, the reign of Louis XIII, the transition to Louis XIV, and much more. Either way you'll end up climbing steps to the next floor, where you'll enter a hall that overlooks the Royal Chapel.

Kings and Queens and Guillotines

• *You could read this on the train ride to Versailles. Relax...the palace is the last stop.*

Come the Revolution, when they line us up and make us stick out our hands, will you have enough calluses to keep them from shooting you? A grim thought, but Versailles raises these kinds of questions. It's the symbol of the *ancien régime*, a time when society was divided into rulers and the ruled, when you were born to be rich or to be poor. To some it's the pinnacle of civilization; to others, the sign of a civilization in decay. Either way, it remains one of Europe's most impressive sights.

Versailles was the residence of the king and the seat of France's government for a hundred years. Louis XIV (r. 1643–1715) moved out of the Louvre in Paris, the previous royal residence, and built an elaborate palace in the forests and swamps of Versailles, 10 miles west. The reasons for the move were partly personal—Louis XIV loved the outdoors and disliked the sniping environs of stuffy Paris—and partly political.

Louis XIV was creating the first modern, centralized state. At Versailles he consolidated Paris' scattered ministries so that he could personally control policy. More importantly, he invited France's nobles to Versailles in order to control them. Living a life of almost enforced idleness, the "domesticated" aristocracy couldn't interfere with the way Louis ran things. With 18 million people united under one king (England had only 5.5 million), a booming economy, and a powerful military, France was Europe's number-one power.

Around 1700, Versailles was the cultural heartbeat of Europe, and French culture was at its zenith. Throughout Europe, when you said "the king," you were referring to the French king—Louis XIV. Every king wanted a palace like Versailles. Everyone learned French. French taste in clothes, hairstyles, table manners, theater, music, art, and kissing spread across the Continent. That cultural dominance continued, to some extent, right up to the 20th century.

Louis XIV
At the center of all this was Europe's greatest king. He was a true Renaissance man, a century after the Renaissance: athletic, good-looking, a musician, dancer, horseman, statesman, art-

After seeing the Royal Chapel from Louis' perspective, take a map flyer by the door on the right, then enter the next room, a large space with a fireplace and a colorful painting on the ceiling.

Hercules Drawing Room
Pleasure ruled. The main suppers, balls, and receptions were held in this room. Picture elegant partygoers in fine silks, wigs, rouge,

lover, lover. For all his grandeur, he was one of history's most polite and approachable kings, a good listener who could put even commoners at ease in his presence.

Louis XIV called himself the Sun King because he gave life and warmth to all he touched. He was also thought of as Apollo, the Greek god of the sun. Versailles became the personal temple of this god on earth, decorated with statues and symbols of Apollo, the sun, and Louis XIV himself. The classical themes throughout underlined the divine right of France's kings and queens to rule without limit.

Louis XIV was a hands-on king who personally ran affairs of state. All decisions were made by him. Nobles, who in other countries were the center of power, became virtual slaves dependent on Louis XIV's generosity. For 70 years he was the perfect embodiment of the absolute monarch. He summed it up best himself with his famous rhyme—*"L'état, c'est moi!"* (lay-tah say-mwah): "The state, that's me!"

Another Louis or Two to Remember

Three kings lived in Versailles during its century of glory. Louis XIV built it and established French dominance. Louis XV, his great-grandson (Louis XIV reigned for 72 years), carried on the tradition and policies, but without the Sun King's flair. During Louis XV's reign (1715–1774), France's power abroad was weakening, and there were rumblings of rebellion from within.

France's monarchy was crumbling, and the time was ripe for a strong leader to reestablish the old feudal order. They didn't get one. Instead, they got Louis XVI (r. 1774–1792), a shy, meek bookworm, the kind of guy who lost sleep over Revolutionary graffiti... because it was misspelled. Louis XVI married a sweet girl from the Austrian royal family, Marie-Antoinette, and together they retreated into the idyllic gardens of Versailles while Revolutionary fires smoldered.

lipstick, and fake moles (and that's just the men), as they dance to the strains of a string quartet.

On the wall opposite the fireplace is an appropriate painting showing Christ in the middle of a Venetian party. The work—by Paolo Veronese, a gift from the Republic of Venice—was one of Louis XIV's favorites, so they decorated the room around it. (Stand by the fireplace for the full effect: The room's columns, arches, and

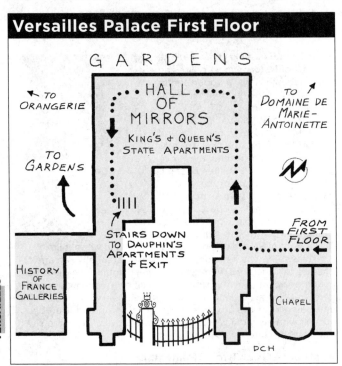

Versailles Palace First Floor

GARDENS

TO ORANGERIE

TO GARDENS

•••HALL•••
OF
MIRRORS

KING'S & QUEEN'S
STATE APARTMENTS

TO
DOMAINE DE
MARIE-
ANTOINETTE

FROM
FIRST
FLOOR

STAIRS DOWN
TO DAUPHIN'S
APARTMENTS
& EXIT

HISTORY
OF
FRANCE
GALLERIES

CHAPEL

VERSAILLES

DCH

frieze match the height and style of Veronese's painted architecture, which makes the painting an extension of the room.)

The ceiling painting of Hercules being crowned a god gives the room its name. Hercules (with his club) hurries up to heaven on a chariot, late for his wedding to the king of the gods' daughter. Louis XIV built the room for his own daughter's wedding reception in the style of

the day—pure Baroque. As you wander, the palace feels bare, but remember that entire industries were created to furnish and decorate the place with carpets, mirrors, furniture, and tapestries.

• *From here on it's a one-way tour—getting lost is not allowed. Follow the crowds into the small green room with a goddess in pink on the ceiling. The names of the rooms generally come from the paintings on the ceilings.*

The King's and Queen's State Apartments

The King's Wing

Salon of Abundance

If the party in the Hercules Room got too intense, you could always step in here for some refreshments. Silver trays were loaded up with liqueurs, exotic stimulants (coffee), juice, chocolates, and, on really special occasions, three-bean salad.

The ceiling painting shows the cornucopia of riches poured down on invited guests. Around the edges of the ceiling are painted versions of the king's actual dinnerware and treasures. The two black chests of drawers are from Louis' furniture collection (most of it was lost in the Revolution). They rest on heavy bases and are heavily ornamented—the so-called Louis XIV style.

Louis himself might be here. He was a gracious host who enjoyed letting his hair down at night. If he took a liking to you, he might sneak you through those doors there (in the middle of the wall) and into his own private study, or "cabinet of curiosities," where he'd show off his collection of dishes, medals, jewels, or... the *Mona Lisa*, which hung on his wall. Louis' favorite show-and-tell items are now in the Louvre.

The paintings on the walls are of Louis XIV's heirs. He reigned for more than 70 years and outlived three of them, finally leaving the crown to his pink-cheeked, five-year-old great-grandson, Louis XV (on the right).

Venus Room

Love ruled at Versailles. In this room, couples would cavort beneath the Greek goddess of love (on the ceiling), who sends

down a canopy of golden garlands to ensnare mortals in delicious *amour*. Notice how a painted garland goes "out" the bottom of the central painting, becomes a golden garland held by a satyr, transforms into a gilded wood garland, and then turns back into a painting again. Baroque artists loved to mix their media to fool the eye. Another illusion is in the paintings at both ends of the room—the painted columns match the room's real ones, and so extend this grand room into mythical courtyards.

Don't let the statue of a confident Louis XIV as a Roman emperor fool you. He started out as a poor little rich kid with a chip on his shoulder. His father died before Louis was old enough to rule, and, during the regency period, the French

Parliament treated little Louis and his mother like trash. They were virtual prisoners, humiliated in their home (at that time, the Royal Palace was the Louvre in Paris) with bland meals, hand-me-down leotards, and pointed shoes. After Louis XIV attained power and wealth, there was one topic you never discussed in his presence: poverty. Maybe Versailles was his way of saying that "Living well is the best revenge."

Diana Room

Here in the billiards room, Louis and his men played on a table that stood in the center of the room, while ladies sat surrounding them on Persian-carpet cushions, and music wafted in from next door. Louis was a good pool player, a sore loser, and a king—thus, he rarely lost.

The famous bust of Louis by Giovanni Lorenzo Bernini (in the center) shows a handsome, dashing, 27-year-old playboy-king. His gaze is steady amid his windblown cloak and hair. Young Louis loved life. He hunted animals by day (notice Diana the Huntress on the ceiling) and chased beautiful women at night.

Games were actually an important part of Louis' political strategy, known as "the domestication of the nobility." By distracting the nobles with the pleasures of courtly life, he was free to run the government his way. Billiards, dancing, and concerts were popular, but the biggest distraction was gambling, usually a card game similar to blackjack. Louis lent money to the losers, making them even more indebted to him. The good life was an addiction, and Louis kept the medicine cabinet well-stocked.

As you move into the next room, notice the fat walls that hid thin servants, who were to be at their master's constant call—but out of sight when not needed.

Mars Room

Also known as the Guard Room (as it was the room for Louis' Swiss bodyguards), this room is decorated with a military flair. On the ceiling there's Mars, the Greek god of war, in a chariot pulled by wolves. The bronze cupids in the corners are escalating from love arrows to heavier artillery. But it's not all war. Louis loved music and playing his guitar, and enjoyed concerts here in the Mars Room nearly every evening.

Out the window are sculpted gardens in the style of a traditional Italian villa—landscaped symmetrically, with trimmed hedges and cone-shaped trees lining walkways that lead to fountains.

Mercury Room

Louis' life was a work of art, and Versailles was the display case. Everything he did was a public event designed to show his subjects how it should be done. This room served as Louis' official

(not actual) bedroom, where the Sun King would ritually rise each morning to warm his subjects.

From a canopied bed (like this 18th-century one), Louis would get up, dress, and take a seat for morning prayer. Meanwhile, the nobles would stand behind a balustrade, in awe of his piety, nobility, and clean socks. At breakfast they murmured with delight as he deftly decapitated his boiled egg with a knife. And when Louis went to bed at night, the dukes and barons would fight over who got to hold the candle while he slipped into his royal jammies. Bedtime, wakeup, and meals were all public rituals.

Apollo Room

This was the grand throne room. Louis held court from a 10-foot-tall, silver-canopied throne on a raised platform placed in the center of the room. (Notice the four small metal rings in the ceiling that once supported the canopy.)

Everything in here reminds us that Louis XIV was not just any ruler, but the Sun King, who lit the whole world with his presence. On the ceiling the sun god Apollo drives his chariot, dragging the sun across the heavens to warm the four corners of the world (counterclockwise from above the exit door): 1) Europe, with a sword; 2) Asia, with a lion; 3) Africa, with an elephant; and 4) good ol' America, an Indian maiden with a crocodile. Notice the ceiling's beautifully gilded frame and *Goldfinger* maidens.

The famous portrait by Hyacinthe Rigaud over the fireplace gives a more human look at Louis XIV. He's shown in a dancer's pose, displaying the legs that made him one of the all-time dancing fools of kingery. At night they often held parties in this room, actually dancing around the throne.

Louis XIV (who was 63 when this was painted) had more than 300 wigs like this one, and he changed them many times a day. This fashion first started when his hairline began to recede, then sprouted all over Europe, and even spread to the American colonies in the time of George Washington.

Louis XIV may have been treated like a god, but he was not an overly arrogant man. His subjects adored him because he was a symbol of everything a man could be, the fullest expression of the Renaissance Man. Compare the portrait of Louis XIV with the one across the room of his last successor, Louis XVI—same arrogant pose, but without the inner confidence to keep his head on his shoulders.

The War Room

"Louis Quatorze was addicted to wars," and France's success made other countries jealous and nervous. At the base of the ceiling (in

semi-circular paintings), we see Germany (with the double eagle), Holland (with its ships), and Spain (with a red flag and roaring lion) ganging up on Louis XIV. But Lady France (center of ceiling), protected by the shield of Louis XIV, hurls thunderbolts down to defeat them. The stucco relief on the wall shows Louis XIV on horseback, triumphing over his fallen enemies.

Versailles was good propaganda. It showed the rest of the world how rich and powerful France was. A visit to the palace and Gardens sent visitors reeling. And Louis XIV's greatest triumph may be the next room, the one that everybody wrote home about.

The Hall of Mirrors

No one had ever seen anything like this hall when it was opened. Mirrors were still a great luxury at the time, and the number and size of these monsters was astounding. The hall is nearly 250 feet long. There are 17 arched mirrors, matched by 17 windows letting in that breathtaking view of the Gardens. Lining the hall are 24 gilded candelabra, eight busts of Roman emperors, and eight classical-style statues (seven of them ancient). The ceiling decoration chronicles Louis' military accomplishments, topped off by

Louis himself in the central panel (with cupids playing cards at his divine feet), doing what he did best—triumphing. Originally, two huge carpets mirrored the action depicted on the ceiling.

Imagine this place lit by the flames of thousands of candles, filled with ambassadors, nobles, and guests dressed in silks and powdered wigs. At the far end of the room sits the king, on the canopied throne moved in temporarily from the Apollo Room. Servants glide by with silver trays of hors d'oeuvres, and an orchestra fuels the festivities. The mirrors reflect an age when beautiful people loved to look at themselves. It was no longer a sin to be proud of good looks and fine clothes, or to enjoy the good things in life: laughing, dancing, eating, drinking, flirting, and watching the sun set into the distant canal.

From the center of the hall you can fully appreciate the epic scale of Versailles. The huge palace (by architect Louis Le Vau), the fantasy interior (by Charles Le Brun), and the endless Gardens (by André Le Nôtre) made Versailles *le* best. In 1871, after the Prussians defeated the French, Otto von Bismarck declared the establishment of the German Empire in this room. And in 1919, Germany and the Allies signed the Treaty of Versailles, ending World War I (and, some say, starting World War II) right here, in the Hall of Mirrors.

• *From the Hall of Mirrors, a short detour takes you to the heart of the palace...*

King's Bedroom and Council Rooms

Pass through a first room to find Louis' bedroom. Look out the window and notice how this small room is at the exact center of the immense horseshoe-shaped building, overlooking the main courtyard and—naturally—facing the rising sun in the east. Imagine the humiliation on that day in 1789 when Louis XVI was forced to stand here and acknowledge the angry crowds that filled the square demanding the end of the divine monarchy. Though this was his bedroom, he also worked here and the rooms on either side were for top council meetings.

• *Return to the Hall of Mirrors. At the far end is the...*

Peace Room

By the end of the Sun King's long life, he was tired of fighting. In this sequel to the War Room, peace is granted to Germany, Holland, and Spain as cupids play with the discarded cannons, armor, and swords. Louis XIV advised his great-grandson to "be a peaceful king."

The oval painting above the fireplace shows 19-year-old Louis XV bestowing an olive branch on Europe. Beside him is his Polish wife, Marie Leszczynska, cradling their baby twin daughters.

The Peace Room marks the beginning of the queen's half of the palace. The Queen's Wing is a mirror image of the King's Wing. The King's Wing was mostly ceremonial and used as a series of reception rooms; the Queen's Wing is more intimate. For instance, on Sundays the queen

held chamber-music concerts in this room for family and friends (notice the gilded music motifs).

• *Enter the first room of the Queen's Wing, with its canopied bed.*

The Queen's Wing

The Queen's Bedchamber

It was here that the queen rendezvoused with her husband. Two queens died here, and this is where 19 princes were born. The chandelier is where two of them were conceived. (Just kidding.) Royal babies were delivered in public to prove their blue-bloodedness.

True, Louis XIV was not the most faithful husband. There was no attempt to hide the fact that the Sun King warmed more than one bed, for he was above the rules of mere mortals. Adultery became acceptable—even fashionable—in court circles. The secret-looking door on the left side of the bed was for Louis' late-night liaisons—it led straight to his rooms.

Some of Louis XIV's mistresses became more famous and powerful than his rather quiet queen, but he was faithful to the show of marriage and had genuine affection for his wife. Louis XIV made a point of sleeping with the queen as often as possible, regardless of whose tiara he tickled earlier in the evening.

This room looks just like it did in the days of the last queen, Marie-Antoinette, who substantially redecorated the entire wing. That's her bust over the fireplace, and the double eagle of her native Austria in the corners. The big chest to the left of the bed held her jewels.

The queen's canopied bed is a reconstruction. The bed, chair, and wall coverings switched with the seasons. This was the cheery summer pattern.

Salon of the Nobles

The wife of Louis XV and her circle of friends met here, seated on the stools, under paintings by Boucher—popular with the queen for their pink-cheeked Rococo exuberance. Discussions ranged from politics to gossip, food to literature, fashion to philosophy. All three of Versailles' rulers considered themselves enlightened monarchs who promoted the arts and new ideas. Louis XIV laughed at the anti-authoritarian plays of Molière, and Louis XV gave free room and board here to the political radical Voltaire. Ironically, these discussions planted the seeds of liberal thought that would grow into the Revolution.

Queen's Antechamber

The royal family dined here publicly, while servants and nobles fluttered around them, admired their table manners, and laughed at the king's jokes like courtly Paul Shaffers. A typical dinner consisted of four different soups, two whole birds stuffed with truffles, mutton, ham slices, fruit, pastries, compotes, and preserves.

The central portrait is of luxury-loving, "let-them-eat-cake" Marie-Antoinette, who became a symbol of decadence to the peasants. The portrait at the far end is a public-relations attempt to soften her image by showing her with three of her children.

Queen's Guard Room

On October 5, 1789, a mob of Revolutionaries—perhaps appalled by their queen's taste in wallpaper—stormed the palace. They were fed up with the ruling class leading a life of luxury in the countryside while they were starving in the grimy streets of Paris.

The king and queen locked themselves in. Some of the Revolutionaries gained access to this upper floor. They burst into this room where Marie-Antoinette was hiding, overcame her bodyguards, and dragged off her and her husband. (Some claim that, as they carried her away, she sang, "Louis, Louis, oh-oh...we gotta go now.")

The enraged peasants then proceeded to ransack the place as revenge for the years of poverty and oppression they'd suffered. (The stripped palace was refurnished a decade later under Napoleon and turned into a national museum.) Marie-Antoinette and Louis XVI were later taken to the place de la Concorde in Paris, where they knelt under the guillotine and were made a foot shorter at the top.

Did the king and queen deserve it? Were the Revolutionaries destroying civilization or clearing the decks for a new and better one? Was Versailles a symbol of progress or decadence?

Coronation Room

No sooner did the French throw out a king than they got an emperor. The Revolution established democracy, but it was shaky in a country that wasn't used to it (hmmm, sounds familiar). In the midst of the confusion, the upstart general Napoleon Bonaparte took control and soon held dictatorial powers. This room captures the glory of the Napoleon years, when he conquered most of Europe. In the huge canvas on the left-hand wall, we see him crowning himself emperor of a new, revived "Roman" Empire. (Though also painted by the master, Jacques-Louis David, this is a lesser-quality version of the famous one hanging in the Louvre.)

Turn and face the windows to see the portrait (between the windows) of a dashing, young, charismatic Napoleon in 1796, when he was just a general in command of the Revolution's army in Italy. Compare this with the adjacent portrait from 10 years later—looking less like a revolutionary and more like a Louis. Above the young Napoleon is a portrait of Josephine, his wife and France's empress. In David's *Distribution of Eagles* (opposite the *Coronation*), the victorious general, in imperial garb, passes out emblems of victory to his loyal troops. In *The Battle of Aboukir* (opposite the window), Joachim Murat, Napoleon's general and brother-in-law, looks bored as he slashes through a tangle of dark-skinned warriors. His horse, though, has a look of, "What are we doing in this mob? Let's get out of here!" Let's.

• *Stairs lead down to the ground floor, where you could tour more rooms (The Dauphin's Apartments) before exiting left to the central courtyard—but I wouldn't. Instead, head to the Gardens (les Jardins), behind the Château and well-signed.*

Now might be a good time to break for lunch (see "Cuisine Art" on page 492). When you're ready for the Gardens, plan your time with the "Getting Around the Gardens" sidebar on page 508.

The Gardens

Controlling Nature

Louis XIV was a divine-right ruler. One way he proved it was by controlling nature like a god. These lavish grounds—elaborately planned, pruned, and decorated—showed everyone that Louis was in total command. Louis loved his Gardens and, until his

last days, presided over their care. He personally led VIPs through them and threw his biggest parties here. With their Greco-Roman themes and incomparable beauty, the Gardens further illustrated his immense power (well-explained in the free *Garden*

All the King's Veggies & Horses: Lesser Sights near the Palace

Two sights located a few minutes' walk from the Château give a different take on life in royal times. For locations, see the map on page 489.

The King's Vegetable Garden (Le Potager du Roi)

When Louis XIV demanded fresh asparagus in the middle of winter, he got it, thanks to his vegetable garden. The 22-acre garden—still productive—is open to visitors. Stroll through symmetrically laid-out plots planted with vegetables both ordinary and exotic, among thousands of fruit trees. The garden is surrounded by walls and sunk below street level to create its own microclimate. Overseeing the central fountain is a statue of the agronomist Jean de la Quintinie, who wowed Louis XIV's court with Versailles-sized produce. Even today, the garden sprouts 20 tons of vegetables and 50 tons of fruit a year, which you can buy in season (weekdays-€4.50, weekends-€6.50, April–Oct Tue–Sun 10:00–18:00, closed Mon and Nov–March, 10 rue du Maréchal Joffre).

The Equestrian Performance Academy (Academie du Spectacle Equestre)

The art of horseback riding has returned to Versailles. On most weekends from May through mid-December, you can watch the basic training sessions (no choreography), or enjoy choreographed performances—including "equestrian fencing"—performed to classical music (training sessions-€12, 60 min, Sat–Sun only at 11:15; musical shows-€25, Sun and some Thu at 15:00 plus Sat at 20:00 May–July and at 18:00 Sept–Dec, maybe also Tue–Sun mid-Feb–mid-March and April, but schedule is sporadic—check website for closure dates and extra performances). The stables (Grandes Ecuries) are across the parking square from the Château, next to the post office. For information, call 01 39 02 07 14. For reservations, call 08 92 68 18 91 or visit www.acadequestre.fr.

VERSAILLES

and Groves flier, available at the TIs and also at the garden entry on Fountain Spectacle weekends).

• *Entering the Gardens, with the palace to your back, go to the far left to reach the stone railing. You'll pass through cookie-cutter patterns of shrubs and green cones. Stand at the railing overlooking the courtyard below and the Louis-made lake in the distance.*

The Orangerie

The warmth from the Sun King was so great that he could even grow orange trees in chilly France. Louis XIV had a thousand of these to amaze his visitors. In winter they were kept in the

Getting Around the Gardens

On Foot: It's a 40-minute walk from the palace, down to the Grand Canal, and past the two Trianon palaces to the Hamlet—the heart of the Domaine de Marie-Antoinette. Allow more time if you stop along the way. After enduring the slow Château shuffle, stretching your legs out here feels pretty good.

By Bike: A rental bike gives you the most freedom to explore the Gardens economically (€6.50/hr, near the Grand Canal, kid-size bikes available). Bikes are not allowed inside the Domaine de Marie-Antoinette.

By *Petit Train:* The fast-looking, slow-moving tram leaves from behind the Château (north side) and serves the Grand Canal and the Domaine. You can hop on and off as you like (€7, 4/hr, three stops).

By Golf Cart: This makes for a fun drive through the Gardens, complete with music and a relaxing commentary. But you can't go wherever you want—the cart shuts off automatically if you diverge from the prescribed route (which does not include the Domaine de Marie-Antoinette). Be warned: To make it out to the Hamlet and back within your allotted hour, you'll need to put the pedal to the metal without stops,  including parking outside the Domaine's grounds and walking there. If you're late you'll pay extra (€30/hr, rent at Orangerie side of palace or down by the canal).

greenhouses (beneath your feet) that surround the courtyard. On sunny days, they were wheeled out in their silver planters and scattered around the grounds.

• *Make an about-face and walk back toward the palace. Sit on the top stairs and look away from the palace.*

View Down the Royal Drive

This, to me, is the most stunning spot in all of Versailles. With the palace behind you, it seems as if the grounds stretch out forever. Versailles was laid out along an eight-mile axis that included the grounds, the palace, and the town of Versailles itself, one of

the first instances of urban planning since Roman times and a model for future capitals, such as Washington, D.C., and Brasilia.

Looking down the Royal Drive (also known as "The Green Carpet"), you see the round Apollo fountain far in the distance. Just beyond that is the Grand Canal. The groves on either side of the Royal Drive were planted with trees from all over, laid out in an elaborate grid, and dotted with statues and fountains. Of the original 1,500 fountains, 300 remain.

Looking back at the palace, you can see the Hall of Mirrors—it's the middle story, with the arched windows.

• *Stroll down the steps to get a good look at the frogs and lizards that fill the round...*

Latona Basin

Everything in the garden has a symbolic meaning. The theme of Versailles is Apollo, the god of the sun, associated with Louis XIV. This round fountain tells the story of the birth of Apollo and his sister, Diana. On top of the fountain are Apollo and Diana as little kids with their mother, Latona (they're facing toward the Apollo fountain). Latona, an unwed mother, was insulted by the local peasants. She called on the king of the gods, Zeus (the children's father), to avenge the insult. Zeus swooped down and turned all the peasants into the frogs and lizards that ring the fountain.

• *As you walk down past the basin toward the Royal Drive, you'll pass by "ancient" statues done by 17th-century French sculptors. The Colonnade is hidden in the woods on the left-hand side of the Royal Drive, about three-fourths of the way to the Apollo Basin (you'll spot it off the main path through an opening).*

The Colonnade

Versailles had no prestigious ancient ruins, so the king built his own. This prefab Roman ruin is a 100-foot circle of 64 marble columns supporting arches. Beneath the arches are small birdbath fountains (imagine them all spouting water). Nobles would picnic in the shade to the tunes of a string quartet and pretend that they were the enlightened citizens of the ancient world.

The Apollo Basin

The fountains of Versailles were its most famous attraction, a marvel of both art and engineering. This one was the centerpiece, showing the sun god—Louis XIV—in his sunny chariot as he starts his journey across the sky. The horses are half-submerged, giving the impression, when the fountains play, of the sun rising out of the mists of dawn. Most of the fountains were only turned on when the king walked by, but this one played constantly for the benefit of those watching from the palace.

All the fountains are gravity-powered. They work on the same principle as blocking a hose with your finger to make it squirt. Underground streams (pumped into Versailles by Seine River pressure) feed into smaller pipes at the fountains, which shoot the water high into the air.

Looking back at the palace from here, realize that the distance you just walked is only a fraction of this vast complex of buildings, gardens, and waterways. Be glad you don't have to mow the lawn.

The Grand Canal

Why visit Venice when you can just build your own? In an era before virtual reality, this was the next best thing to an actual trip. Couples in gondolas would pole along the waters accompanied by barges with orchestras playing "O Sole Mio." The canal is actually cross-shaped; you're looking at the longest part, one mile from end to end. Of course, this, too, is a man-made body of water with no function other than to please. Originally, authentic gondoliers, imported with their boats from Venice, lived in a little settlement next to the canal.

• To enter the Domaine de Marie-Antoinette—the Queen's playground—you'll need to pay a separate €10 entry fee (€6 after 16:00 and Nov–March), unless you have a Paris Museum Pass or Le Passeport. You can enter/exit the Domaine at several spots: near the palace known as the Grand Trianon (where we'll enter), near the Petit Trianon, or near The Hamlet.

You can rent a bike or golf cart, or catch the pokey tourist train, but the walk is half the fun. It's about a 30-minute walk from here to the end of the tour, plus another 40-minute walk back to the palace. You can't take your bike or golf cart into the Domaine de Marie-Antoinette.

To get to our starting point, the Grand Trianon (see the map on page 489), follow the Grand Canal and veer right a bit after the rowboat rental (just past the snack kiosk and restaurant; don't take the hard *right on the bigger street). You'll follow a dirt path with signs to the Grand Trianon.*

Domaine de Marie-Antoinette

The Trianon Area—Retreat from Reality

Versailles began as an escape from the pressures of kingship. But in a short time, the palace became as busy as Paris ever was. Louis XIV needed an escape from his escape and built a smaller palace out in the boonies. Later, his successors retreated still farther into the garden and built a fantasy world of simple pleasures, allowing them to ignore the real world that was crumbling all around them.

Grand Trianon

• *Enter the Grand Trianon, passing through security. In the bookshop, pick up the essential flyer that escorts you clockwise through the rooms. You'll see the king's apartments first, then pass through numerous light and airy rooms that were cheery even when skies were gray. Compare this to the heavy-metal decor in the mother Château.*

This was the king's private residence away from the main palace. Louis XIV usually spent a couple of nights a week here, but the two later Louises spent more and more time retreating. While the main palace of Versailles was a screen separating French reality from the royal utopia, the Trianon palaces were engulfed in the royals' fantasy world, and therefore favored.

• *Exit into the gardens and look back.*

The facade of this one-story building is a charming combination of pink, yellow, and white, a welcome contrast to the imposing Baroque facade of the main palace. The flower gardens were changed daily for the king's pleasure—for new color combinations and new "nasal cocktails."

• *To continue this tour, stay in the gardens and walk clockwise around the palace and keep going. You'll leave the Grand Trianon gardens across a footbridge, and enter the intimate gardens of the French Pavilion.*

French Pavilion—Summer House

This small, white building with four rooms fanning out from the center was one more step away from the modern world. Here Marie-Antoinette spent summer evenings with family and a few friends, listening to music or playing parlor games. She and her friends explored all avenues of *la douceur de vivre,* the sweetness of living. Nearby are the buildings of the menagerie, where her servants kept cows, goats, chickens, and ducks.

• *The next stop lies a short distance away to the left, where you can peek into...*

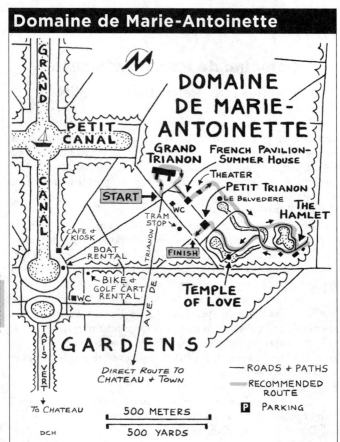

Domaine de Marie-Antoinette

DOMAINE DE MARIE-ANTOINETTE

GRAND CANAL

PETIT CANAL

GRAND TRIANON FRENCH PAVILION-SUMMER HOUSE

THEATER

PETIT TRIANON

LE BELVEDERE

THE HAMLET

START

WC

TRAM STOP

CAFE & KIOSK

BOAT RENTAL

AVE. DE TRIANON

FINISH

BIKE & GOLF CART RENTAL

WC

TEMPLE OF LOVE

VERSAILLES

TAPIS VERT

GARDENS

DIRECT ROUTE TO CHATEAU & TOWN

To CHATEAU

DCH

500 METERS

500 YARDS

ROADS & PATHS

RECOMMENDED ROUTE

P PARKING

Marie-Antoinette's Theater

Marie-Antoinette adored the theater and was an aspiring performer herself. In this intimate playhouse, far from the rude intrusions of the real world, Marie-Antoinette and her friends acted out plays. The soft blue decor and upholstered walls and benches give the theater a dollhouse feel.

• *Continue through the oh-so-bucolic gardens. The bigger building on the right is the Petit Trianon (where we'll eventually exit). For now, wander deeper into Marie's Domaine, tracking a path left along a pond and to the circular le Belvedere pavilion. Veer right after le Belvedere, and continue frolicking along the paths. In the distance you'll see a smattering of half-timbered buildings. Head there to find the Hansel-and-Gretel-like hamlet.*

The Hamlet (Le Hameau)

Marie-Antoinette longed for the simple life of a peasant—not the hard labor of real peasants, who sweated and starved around her—

but the fairytale world of simple country pleasures. She built this complex of 12 buildings as her own private "Normand" village (thatched roofs and all).

This was an actual working farm with a dairy, a water mill, and domestic animals. The harvest was served at Marie-Antoinette's table. Marie-Antoinette didn't do much work herself, but she "supervised," dressed in a plain, white muslin dress and a straw hat. Though the royal family is long gone, kid-pleasing animals still inhabit the farm, and fat fish swim languid circles in the pond.

The main building is the Queen's House—actually two buildings connected by a wooden gallery. It's the only one without a thatched roof. Like any typical peasant farmhouse, it had a billiard room, library, elegant dining hall, and two living rooms.

• *Head back toward the Petit Trianon (veering left from the Hamlet). In about five minutes you'll see the white, round...*

Temple of Love

A circle of 12 marble Corinthian columns supports a dome, decorating a path where lovers could stroll. Underneath there's a statue of Cupid making a bow (to shoot arrows of love) out of the club of Hercules. It's a delightful monument to a society where the rich could afford that ultimate luxury, romantic love. When the Revolution came, I bet they wished they'd kept the club.

• *And, finally, you'll reach the...*

Petit Trianon

Louis XV developed an interest in botany. He wanted to spend more time near the French Gardens, but the Summer House just wasn't big enough. He constructed the Petit Trianon ("Small Trianon") at the urging of his first mistress, Madame de Pompadour, and

it later became home to his next mistress, Madame du Barry.

This gray, cubical building is a masterpiece of Neoclassical architecture, built by the same architect who created the Opera House in the main palace. It has four distinct facades, each a perfect and harmonious combination of Greek-style columns, windows, and railings. Walk around it and find your favorite.

When Louis XVI became king, he gave the building to his new bride, who made this her home base. Despite her bad reputation with the public, Marie-Antoinette was a sweet girl from Vienna who never quite fit in with the fast, sophisticated crowd at Versailles. Here at the Petit Trianon, she could get away and re-create the simple home life she remembered from her childhood. On the lawn outside, she installed a carousel.

You can tour the handsome interior (pick up the helpful flier), though poor crowd management lessens the appeal. English explanations are provided in some rooms, as are interactive screens. The baroque WC was a head of its time.

• *The real world and the main palace are a 40-minute walk to the southeast.*

For a slightly shorter walk back, and a chance to see the Neptune Basin (an impressive miniature lake with fountains), walk straight down from the Petit Trianon and turn left on avenue de la Trianon (see map on page 489). If you stay straight as an arrow, you'll run into the Neptune Basin, where the grand finale takes place on fountain days. Leave Neptune at the far left corner gate and you'll pop out onto rue de la Paroisses, the town's main shopping drag, which takes you into the market square. From here a right on avenue de l'Europe takes you to the Rive Gauche train station and the RER back to Paris.

Sleeping in Versailles

For a less expensive and laid-back alternative to Paris, within easy reach of the big city by RER train (4/hr, 30–40 min), Versailles can be a good overnight stop, especially for drivers. Park in the palace's main lot while looking for a hotel, or leave your car there overnight (€4.50/2 hrs, free 19:30–8:30). Get a map of Versailles at your hotel or at the TI.

$$$ Hôtel de France*,** in an 18th-century townhouse, offers Old World class, with mostly air-conditioned, appropriately royal rooms, a pleasant courtyard, elaborate public spaces, a bar, and a restaurant (Db-€141, Tb-€180, Qb-€240, Wi-Fi, just off parking lot across from Château at 5 rue Colbert, tel. 01 30 83 92 23, fax 01 30 83 92 24, www.hotelfrance-versailles.com, hotel-de-france -versailles@wanadoo.fr).

$$ Hôtel le Cheval Rouge,** built in 1676 as Louis XIV's stables, now houses tourists. It's a block behind the place du Marché in a quaint corner of town on a large, quiet courtyard with free parking and crisp, sufficiently comfortable rooms, many with open beams (Db with shower-€80, Db with tub-€95, Tb-€115,

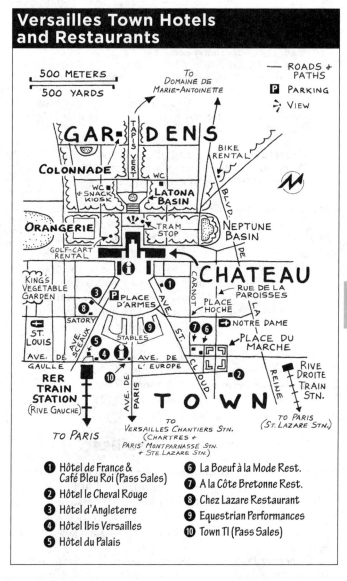

Versailles Town Hotels and Restaurants

500 METERS
500 YARDS

— ROADS & PATHS
P PARKING
✦ VIEW

To DOMAINE DE MARIE-ANTOINETTE

GAR-DENS

COLONNADE

TAPIS VERT

WC

WC & SNACK KIOSK

LATONA BASIN

BIKE RENTAL

BLVD.

ORANGERIE

TRAM STOP

NEPTUNE BASIN

GOLF-CART RENTAL

CHATEAU

KING'S VEGETABLE GARDEN

❸ **P** PLACE D'ARMES

❶

CARNOT

RUE DE LA PAROISSES

❽

SATORY

AVE.

PLACE HOCHE

NOTRE DAME

ST. LOUIS

AVE. DE SCEAUX

STABLES

❺

❾

❹

❼ ❻

LA

PLACE DU MARCHE

AVE. DE GAULLE

RER TRAIN STATION (RIVE GAUCHE)

❿

AVE. DE PARIS

ST. CLOUD

AVE. DE L'EUROPE

❷

REINE

RIVE DROITE TRAIN STN.

T O W N

TO PARIS

TO VERSAILLES CHANTIERS STN. (CHARTRES & PARIS' MONTPARNASSE STN. & STE. LAZARE STN.)

TO PARIS (ST. LAZARE STN.)

❶ Hôtel de France & Café Bleu Roi (Pass Sales)
❷ Hôtel le Cheval Rouge
❸ Hôtel d'Angleterre
❹ Hôtel Ibis Versailles
❺ Hôtel du Palais

❻ La Boeuf à la Mode Rest.
❼ A la Côte Bretonne Rest.
❽ Chez Lazare Restaurant
❾ Equestrian Performances
❿ Town TI (Pass Sales)

VERSAILLES

Qb-€125, 18 rue André Chénier, tel. 01 39 50 03 03, fax 01 39 50 61 27, www.chevalrouge.fr.st, chevalrouge@club-internet.fr).

$$ Hôtel d'Angleterre**, away from the frenzy, is a tranquil, homey place with smiling, Polish-born Madame Kutyla in control. Rooms are modest, comfortable, and spacious. Park in the nearby Château lot (D-€52, Db-€80–90, family Qb-€120, extra bed-€15, Wi-Fi, just below palace to the right as you exit, 2 rue de Fontenay,

Sleep Code

(€1 = about $1.40, country code: 33)
S = Single, **D** = Double/Twin, **T** = Triple, **Q** = Quad, **b** = bathroom,
s = shower only. Everyone speaks English and accepts credit cards.

To help you easily sort through these listings, I've divided the rooms into three categories, based on the price for a standard double room with bath.

$$$ Higher Priced—Most rooms €125 or more.
$$ Moderately Priced—Most rooms between €80–125.
$ Lower Priced—Most rooms €80 or less.

tel. 01 39 51 43 50, fax 01 39 51 45 63, www.hotel-angleterre -versailles.com, hotel.angleterre.versailles@wanadoo.fr).

$ Hôtel Ibis Versailles** offers a good weekend value and modern comfort, with 85 air-conditioned rooms but no character (Db-€78 Fri–Sun, €110 Mon–Thu, extra bed-€10, parking-€10, across from RER station, 4 avenue du Général de Gaulle, tel. 01 39 53 03 30, fax 01 39 50 06 31, www.ibishotel.com, h1409@accor .com).

$ Hôtel du Palais, facing the RER station and next to Starbucks, rents 24 very clean and simple rooms—the cheapest I list in this area. Ask for a quiet room off the street (Db-€62, Tb-€77, piles of stairs, 6 place Lyautey, tel. 01 39 50 39 29, fax 01 39 50 80 41, hotelpalais@ifrance.com).

Eating in Versailles

In the pleasant town center, around place du Marché Notre-Dame, you'll find a thriving open market (Sun, Tue, and Fri mornings until 13:00) and a variety of reasonably priced restaurants, cafés, and a few cobbled lanes (see map on page 515). The square is a 15-minute walk from the Château (veer left when you leave the Château).

On or near Place du Marché Notre-Dame: This square is lined with colorful and inexpensive eateries. Troll the intriguing options or try one of these: **La Bœuf à la Mode,** right on the square, is a bistro with traditional cuisine and a passion for red meat (€18 *plats,* €30 three-course dinner *menu,* open daily, 4 rue au Pain, tel. 01 39 50 31 99). **A la Côte Bretonne** is your best bet for crêpes in a friendly, cozy setting. Yann-Alan and his family have served up the cuisine of their native Brittany region since 1951 (€4–10 crêpes from a fun and creative menu, Tue–Sun 12:00–14:30 &

19:00–22:30, closed Mon, fine indoor and outdoor seating, a few steps off the square on traffic-free rue des Deux Portes at #12, tel. 01 39 51 18 24).

On Rue de Satory: This pedestrian-friendly street is on the south side of the Château, near Hôtel d'Angleterre (10-min walk, angle right out of the Château). The street is lined with a rich variety of restaurants, ranging from cheap ethnic to more pricey and formal French. Friendly **Chez Lazare** is a good value inside or out, with €14–16 *plats* (closed Sun–Mon, 18 rue de Satory, tel. 01 39 50 41 45).

CHARTRES CATHEDRAL DAY TRIP

Some of the children who watched Chartres' old church burn to the ground on June 10, 1194, grew up to build Chartres Cathedral and attend its dedication Mass in 1260. That's astonishing, considering that other Gothic cathedrals, such as Paris' Notre-Dame, took hundreds of years to build. Having been built so quickly, Chartres is arguably Europe's best example of pure Gothic, with a unity of architecture, statues, and stained glass that captures the spirit of the Age of Faith.

Chartres is an easy day trip from Paris and gives travelers a pleasant break in a midsize town. Its welcoming, cobbled old center is overshadowed by its great cathedral. Discover the picnic-friendly park behind the cathedral and wander the quiet alleys and peaceful squares. For accommodations and eateries, see the end of this chapter.

Orientation to Chartres

Cost: Church entry free; climbing the 300-step north tower costs €7 (free on first Sun of the month, and for those under 18). Skip the Chartres Pass sold at the TI.

Hours: Church open daily 8:30–19:30. Tower open May–Aug Mon–Sat 9:30–12:30 & 14:00–18:00, Sun 14:00–18:00; Sept–April closes at 16:30 (entrance inside church after bookstore on left). Mass held Mon–Fri at 11:45 (in the crypt) and 18:15; Sat at 11:45 (in the crypt) and 18:00; Sun at 9:15 (Gregorian) and 11:00.

Restoration: In 2010, the interior will undergo routine restoration work. Visitors may encounter scaffolding, especially around the choir area.

Getting There: Chartres is a one-hour train trip from Paris' Gare

Montparnasse (10/day, about €13 one-way, buy tickets at Ile-de-France ticket windows in center of station, street level). Figure on a round-trip total of three hours from Paris to cathedral doorstep and back.

Upon arrival at the Chartres train station, plan ahead and jot down return times to Paris (last train generally departs Chartres around 21:00). Exiting Chartres Station, you'll see the spires of the cathedral dominating the town, a five-minute walk uphill. On your way to the cathedral, stop at the TI (see "Information," below).

Combining with Versailles: TER trains link Versailles and Chartres frequently (up to 30/day), on the route from Paris to Le Mans. In Versailles this train stops at the Chantiers station (that's "Versailles C.H.")—not the more-convenient Versailles R.G., or Rive Gauche station. The Versailles C.H. train station is a 25-minute walk to the palace (just ask locals, "Château?").

Bring: Binoculars, if you got 'em. You can rent binoculars cheaply at a souvenir shop near the south porch of the church (at 10 cloître Notre-Dame), but you must leave a deposit.

Information: At the **TI**, pick up the good map with basic information on the town and cathedral. The TI has specifics on cathedral tours with Malcolm Miller, and also rents audioguides for the old town—both are described below (open April–Sept Mon–Sat 9:00–19:00, Sun 9:30–17:30; Oct–March Mon–Sat 9:00–18:00, Sun 9:30–17:00; located 100 yards in front of church, tel. 02 37 18 26 26, www.chartres-tourisme.com).

The church has two **bookstores.** One is inside near the entrance; the other—called La Crypte—is outside near the south porch (church tel. 02 37 21 59 08, www.diocese-chartres .com).

Cathedral Tours by Malcolm Miller: This fascinating English scholar, who moved here 50+ years ago when he was 24, has dedicated his life to studying this cathedral—and sharing its wonder through his guided lecture tours. His 75-minute tours are worthwhile, even if you've taken my self-guided tour (below). No reservation is needed; just show up—but there's no tour if he doesn't get at least four takers (€10, offered Mon–Sat at 12:00 and 14:45, no tours last half of Aug and Jan–Feb). Some visitors take two tours on the same day, as every tour is different. Tours begin inside the church at the orange-and-purple *Cathedral Tours* sign by the bookstore. Consult this sign for changes or cancellations. He also offers private tours (private tour info tel. 02 37 28 15 58, fax 02 37 28 33 03, millerchartres@aol.com). For a detailed look at Chartres' windows, sculpture, and history, pick up Malcolm Miller's two guidebooks (sold at cathedral).

Audioguides: You can rent audioguides from the bookstore inside the cathedral near the entrance. Routes include the cathedral (€4.20, 45 min), the choir only (€3.20, 25 min), or both (€6.20, 70 min). The TI offers an audioguide for the often-missed old town (€5.50, €8.50/double set, about 2 hours, available only at the TI, leave passport as a deposit).

Crypt Tours: The crypt (which means "hidden") is the foundation of the previous ninth-century church. Today these foundations can be visited only as part of a very boring guided tour in French (with an English handout). You'll see remnants of the earlier churches, a modern copy of the old wooden Mary-and-baby statue, and hints of the old well and Roman wall (€2.70; April–Oct at 11:00, 14:15, 15:15, and 16:30; June–July also at 17:15, 2/day Nov–March, 30-min tours start in La Crypte bookstore, located outside church near south porch, tel. 02 37 21 75 02).

Length of This Tour: Allow one hour for the cathedral. The additional three hours you'll spend in transit means that Chartres is effectively an all-day excursion from Paris.

The Chartres Generation—the 1200s

• *Kill train time by reading this.*

From king to bishop and knight to pawn, French society was devoted to the Christian faith. It inspired knights to undertake the formidable Crusades, artists to re-create heaven in statues and stained glass, and architects to build skyscraping cathedrals filled with the mystic light of heaven. They aimed for a golden age, blending faith and reason. But misguided faith often outstripped reason, resulting in very un-Christian intolerance and violence.

Timeline

c. 1194   The old cathedral burns down.

1200   The University of Paris is founded, using human reason to analyze Christian faith. Borrowing from the pagan Greek philosopher Aristotle, scholars described the Christian universe as a series of concentric rings spinning around the Earth in geometrical perfection.

1202   The pope calls on all true Christians to rescue the Holy Land from Muslim "infidels" in the Fourth Crusade (1202–1204). This crusade ends disastrously in the sacking of Constantinople, a Christian city.

1206   Chartres' cornerstone is laid. The style is *opus franci-genum* ("French-style work")—which is what the people in Gothic times called Gothic. Chartres is just one of several great cathedrals under construction in Europe.

1207   Francis of Assisi, a rebellious Italian youth, undergoes a conversion to a life of Christian poverty and love. His open spirit inspires many followers, including France's King Louis IX (a generation later).

1209   France's King Philip Augustus, based in Paris, invades southern France and massacres fellow Christians (members of the Cathar sect) as heretics.

1212   Thousands of boys and girls idealistically join the Children's Crusade to save the Holy Land. Most die in transit or are sold into slavery.

1220   The external structure of Chartres Cathedral is nearly finished. Work begins on the statues and stained glass.

1226   Eleven-year-old Louis IX is crowned as *rex et sacerdos,* "King and Priest," beginning a 45-year Golden Age combining church and state. His mother, Blanche of Castile (granddaughter of Eleanor of Aquitaine), is his lifelong mentor.

1230   Most of Chartres' stained glass is completed.

1244   At age 30, Louis IX falls sick and sees a vision while in a coma that changes his life. His personal integrity helps unify the nation. He reforms the judicial system along Christian lines, helping the poor.

1245   The last Albigensian heretics are burned at Montségur, in a crusade ordered by Louis IX and his mother, Blanche.

1248   Louis IX personally leads the Seventh Crusade by walking barefoot from Paris to the port of departure. During the fighting he is captured and ransomed. He later returns home a changed man. Humbled, he adopts the poverty of the Franciscan brotherhood. His devotion earns him the title of St. Louis.

1260   Chartres Cathedral is dedicated. The church is the physical embodiment of the Age of Faith, with architecture as mathematically perfect as God's Creation, sculpture serving as sermons in stone, and stained glass lit by the light of God.

Mary's Church and Mary's Veil ("Notre Dame" = "Our Lady" of Chartres)

The church is (at least) the fourth church on this spot dedicated to Mary, the mother of Jesus, who has been venerated here for some 1,700 years. There's even speculation that the pagan Romans dedicated a temple here to a mother-goddess. In earliest times Mary was honored next to a natural spring of healing waters (not visible today).

In 876, the church acquired the torn, 2,000-year-old veil (or birthing gown) supposedly worn by Mary when she gave birth to Jesus. The veil (now on display—see below) became the focus of worship at the church. By the 11th century, Mary (a.k.a. "Queen of All Saints") was hugely popular. God was obscure and scary, but motherhood was accessible, and Mary provided a handy go-between for Christians and their Creator. Chartres, a small town of 10,000 with a prized relic, found itself in the big time on the pilgrim circuit.

When the fire of 1194 incinerated the old church, the veil was feared lost. Lo and behold, several days later, they found it miraculously unharmed in the crypt (beneath today's choir). The people were so stoked, they worked like madmen to erect this grand cathedral in which to display it. The small town built a big-city church, one of the most impressive structures in all of Europe. Thinkers and scholars gathered here, making it a leading center of learning in the Middle Ages (until the focus shifted to Paris' university).

The Book of Chartres

Historian Malcolm Miller calls Chartres a picture book of statues, stained glass, and symbolic architecture, telling the entire Christian story—from Creation to Christ's birth (the north side of the church), from Christ and his followers up to the present (south entrance), to the end of time when Christ returns as judge (west entrance).

The Christian universe is a complex web of heaven and earth, angels and demons, and prophets and martyrs. Much of the medieval symbolism is obscure today. Expect to be overwhelmed by the thousands of things to see, but appreciate the perfect unity of this Gothic masterpiece.

You don't go to the library to read all the books, and you don't go to the cathedral to read all the windows. Think of it as the world's biggest comic strip, or the best and most intact library of medieval religious iconography in existence.

The Tour Begins

❶ The Main Entrance (West Facade), c. 1150

Chartres' soaring (if mismatched) steeples announce to pilgrims that they've arrived. For centuries pilgrims have come here to see holy relics, to honor "Our Lady," and to feed their souls.

The facade is about the only survivor of the intense, lead-melting fire that incinerated the rest of the church in 1194. The church we see today was rebuilt behind this facade in a single generation (1194–1260).

Towers: The right (south) tower, with a Romanesque stone

Chartres Cathedral

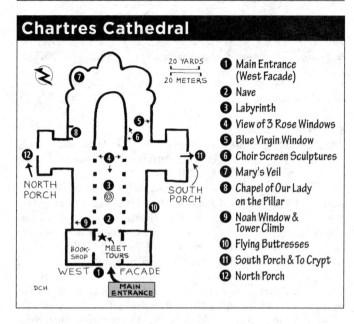

1	Main Entrance (West Facade)
2	Nave
3	Labyrinth
4	View of 3 Rose Windows
5	Blue Virgin Window
6	Choir Screen Sculptures
7	Mary's Veil
8	Chapel of Our Lady on the Pillar
9	Noah Window & Tower Climb
10	Flying Buttresses
11	South Porch & To Crypt
12	North Porch

steeple, survived the fire. The left (north) tower lost its wooden steeple in the 1194 fire. In the 1500s, it was topped by a steeple bigger than the tapered lower half was meant to hold.

The West Doors: The emaciated column-like statues flanking the three doors are pillars of the faith. These kings of Judah, prophets, and Old Testament big shots foretold the coming of Christ. With solemn gestures and faces, they patiently endure the wait.

What they predicted came to pass. History's pivotal event is shown above the **right door,** where Mary (seated) produces baby Jesus from her loins. This Mary-and-baby sculpture is a 12th-century stone version

of an even older wooden statue that burned in 1793. Centuries of pilgrims have visited Chartres to see Mary's statue, gaze at her veil, and ponder the mystery of how God in Heaven became Man on Earth, as He passed through immaculate Mary like sunlight through stained glass.

Over the **central door** is Christ in majesty, surrounded by animals symbolizing Matthew, Mark, Luke, and John. Over the **left door,** Christ ascends into heaven after his death and resurrection.

• *Enter the church (from a side entrance, if the main one is closed) and wait for your pupils to enlarge.*

❷ Nave

The place is huge—the nave is 427 feet long, 20 feet wide, and 120 feet high. Notice the height of the entrance doors compared to the tourists...the doors are 24 feet tall!

The long, tall central nave is lined with 12 pillars. These support pointed, crisscrossed arches on the ceiling, which lace together the heavy stone vaulting. The pillars themselves are supported by flying buttresses on the outside of the church (which we'll see later). This skeleton structure was the miracle of Gothic, making it possible to build tall cathedrals with ribbed walls and lots of stained-glass windows (see the big saints in the upper stories of the nave). Chartres has 28,000 square feet of stained glass. The narrow nave is flanked by raised side aisles. This design was for crowd flow, so pilgrims could circle the church without disturbing worshippers.

Try to picture the church in the Middle Ages—painted in greens, browns, and golds. It was full of pilgrims, a rough cross between a hostel, a soup kitchen, and a flea market. The floor of the nave slopes in to the center, for easy drainage when hosing down dirty pilgrims who camped here. Looking around the church, you'll see stones at the base of the columns smoothed by centuries of tired pilgrim butts. With all the hubbub in the general nave, the choir (screened-off central zone around the high altar) provided a holy place with a more sacred atmosphere.

• *On the floor, midway up the nave, find the...*

❸ Labyrinth

The round maze inlaid in black marble on the floor is a spiritual

journey. Mazes like this were common in medieval churches. Pilgrims enter from the west rim by foot or on their knees and wind inward, meditating, on a metaphorical journey to Jerusalem. About 900 feet later, they hope to meet God in the middle. (The chairs are removed on Fridays. To let your fingers do the walking, you'll

Surviving the Centuries

Chartres contains the world's largest collection of medieval stained glass, with over 150 early 13th-century windows, about 80 percent still the original glass. Through the centuries, much of the rest of France's stained glass was destroyed by various ideologues: Protestant puritans who disapproved of papist imagery, Revolutionaries who turned churches into "temples of reason" (or stables), Baroque artists who preferred clear windows and lots of light, and the bombs of World War II.

Chartres was spared many (but not all) of these ravages. During World War II the citizens removed all the windows and piled sandbags to protect the statues. Today, Chartres survives as Europe's best-preserved medieval cathedral.

find a small model of the maze just outside the gift shop, where the tours begin.)

• *Walk up the nave to where the transept crosses. As you face the altar, north is to the left.*

❹ The Rose Windows— North, South, and West

The three big, round "rose" (flower-shaped) windows over the entrances receive sunlight at different times of day. All three are predominantly blue and red, but each has different "petals," and each tells a different part of the Christian story in a kaleidoscope of fragmented images.

As we've all read, stained glass was a way to teach Bible stories to the illiterate medieval masses...who apparently owned state-of-the-art binoculars. The windows were used many ways: They tell stories, allow parents to teach children simple lessons, help theologians explain complex lessons, enable worshippers to focus on images as they meditate or pray...and, of course, they light a dark church in a colorful and decorative way.

The brilliantly restored **north rose window** charts history from the distant past up to the birth of Jesus. On the outer rim, murky, ancient (barely visible) prophets foretell Christ's coming. Then (circling inward) there's a ring of red squares with kings who are Jesus' direct ancestors. Still closer, a circle of white doves and winged angels zero in on the central event of history—Mary, the heart of the flower, with her newborn baby, Jesus.

This window was donated by King Louis IX, who built Paris' stained-glass masterpiece of a church, Sainte-Chapelle. See his coat of arms (yellow fleur-de-lis on a blue background) just below the rose, alongside his mom's coat of arms, Blanche of Castile (gold castles on a red background).

The **south rose window** tells how the Old Testament prophecies were fulfilled. Christ sits in the center (dressed in blue, with a red background), setting in motion radiating rings of angels, beasts, and instrument-playing apocalyptic elders who labor to bring history to its close. The five lancet windows below show Mary flanked by four Old Testament prophets (Isaiah, Daniel, Jeremiah, and Ezekiel) lifting New Testament writers (Matthew, Mark, Luke, and John) on their shoulders. (In the first window on the left, see white-robed Luke riding piggyback on dark-robed Jeremiah.) These demonstrated how the ancients prepared the way for Christ—and how the New Testament evangelists had a broader perspective from their lofty perches.

In the center of the **west rose window,** a dark Christ rings in history's final Day of Judgment. Around him winged angels blow their trumpets and the dead rise, face judgment, and are sent to hell or raised to eternal bliss. The frilly edge of this glorious "rose" is flecked with tiny clover-shaped dewdrops.

• *Now walk around the altar to the right (south) side and find the window with a big, blue Mary (second one from the right).*

❺ The Blue Virgin Window

Mary, dressed in blue on a rich red background, cradles Jesus, while the dove of the Holy Spirit descends on her. This very old window (from 1150) was the central window behind the altar of the church that burned in 1194. It survived and was reinserted into this frame in the new church around 1230. Mary's glowing dress is an example of the famed "Chartres blue," a sumptuous color made by mixing cobalt oxide into the glass (before cheaper materials were introduced). The Blue Virgin was one of the most popular stops for pilgrims—especially pregnant ones—of the cult of the Virgin-about-to-give-birth. Devotees prayed, carried stones to repair the church, and donated to the church coffers; Mary rewarded them with peace of mind, easy births, and occasional miracles.

Below Mary (bottom panel), see **Christ being tempted** by a red-faced, horned, smirking devil.

The **Zodiac Window** (two windows to the left) shows the 12 signs of the zodiac (in the right half of the window; read from the bottom up—Pisces, Aries, Gemini in the central cloverleaf, Taurus, Cockroach, Leo, Virgo, etc.). On the left side are the corresponding months (February warming himself by a fire, April offering flowers, and so on).

CHARTRES CATHEDRAL

GOD = LIGHT

You can try to examine the details, but a better way to experience the mystery of Chartres is to just sit and stare at these enormous panels as they float in the dark of empty space like holograms or space stations or the Queen of Heaven's crown jewels. Ponder the medieval concept that God is light.

To the Chartres generation, the church was a metaphor for how God brings his creation to life, like the way light animates stained glass. They were heavy into mysticism, feeling a oneness with all creation in a moment of enlightenment. The Gospel of John (as well as a writer known to historians as the Pseudo-Dionysus) was their favorite. Here are select verses from John 1:1–12 (loosely translated):

In the beginning was The Word.
Jesus was the light of the human race.
The light shines in the darkness, and the darkness cannot resist it.
It was the real light coming into the world, the light that enlightens everyone.
He was in the world, but the world did not recognize Him. But to those who did,
He gave the power to become the children of God.

• *Now turn around and look behind you.*

❻ The Choir Screen—Life of Mary

The choir (enclosed area around the altar where church officials sat) is the heart *(coeur)* of the church. A stone screen rings it with **41 statue groups** illustrating Mary's life. Although the Bible says little about the mother of Jesus, legend and lore fleshed out her life. Take some time to learn about the Lady this church is dedicated to.

Scene #1 (south side) shows Mary's dad hearing the news that Mary is on the way. In #4, Mary is born, and maidens bathe the new baby. In #6, Mary marries Joseph (sculpted with the features of King François I). In scene #7, an angel announces to Mary she'll

be the mother of the Messiah, and (#10) she gives birth to Jesus in a manger. In #12, the Three Kings—looking like the three musketeers—arrive. In #14, Herod orders all babies slaughtered but Mary's son survives to begin his mission.

Next come episodes from the life of Jesus. On the other side of the choir screen, in #27, Jesus is crucified and, in #28, lays lifeless in his mother's arms. Scene #34 depicts the Ascension, as Jesus takes off, Cape Canaveral–style, while his awestruck followers look up at the bottoms of his rocketing feet. In #39, Mary has died and is raised by angels into heaven, where (#40) she's crowned Queen of Heaven by the Father, Son, and Holy Ghost.

The **plain windows** surrounding the choir date from the 1770s, when the dark mystery of medieval stained glass was replaced by the open light of the French Enlightenment. The plain windows and the choir are some of the only "new" features. Most of the 13th-century church has remained intact, despite style changes, Revolutionary vandals, and war bombs.

• *Continue around the ambulatory to the very back of the church. In the next chapel you encounter (Chapel of the Sacred Heart of Mary—see map), you'll find a gold frame holding a fragment of Mary's venerated veil. These days it's kept—for its safety and preservation—out of the light and behind bulletproof glass.*

❼ Mary's Veil

This **veil** (or tunic) was supposedly worn by Mary when she gave birth to Jesus. It became the main object of adoration for the cult

of the Virgin. The great King of the Franks, Charlemagne (742/47–814), received the veil as a present from Byzantine Empress Irene. Charlemagne's grandson gave the veil to Chartres in 876. In A.D. 911, with the city surrounded by Vikings, the bishop hoisted the veil like a battle flag and waved it at the invaders. It scared the bejeezus out of them, and the town was saved.

In the frenzy surrounding the fire of 1194, the veil mysteriously disappeared, only to reappear three days later (recalling the Resurrection). This was interpreted by church officials and the townsfolk as a sign from Mary that she wanted a new church, and thus the building began. Recent tests confirm that the material itself and the weaving technique used to make the cloth date to the first century A.D., lending support to claims of the relic's authenticity.

Continue on a few more chapels until you find the one with Mary on ᵗᵍar.

❽ Chapel of Our Lady on the Pillar

A 16th-century **statue of Mary and baby**—draped in cloth, crowned and sceptered—sits on a 13th-century column in a wonderful carved-wood alcove. This is today's pilgrimage center, built to keep visitors from clogging up the altar area. Modern pilgrims (including lots of new moms pushing strollers) honor the Virgin by leaving flowers, lighting candles, and kissing the column.

• *Return to the west end and find the last window on the right (near the tower entrance).*

❾ The Noah Window and Tower Climb

Read Chartres' windows in the medieval style: from bottom to top. In the bottom diamond, God tells Noah he'll destroy the

earth. Next, Noah hefts an axe to build an ark, while his son hauls wood (diamond #2). Two by two, he loads horses (cloverleaf, above left), purple elephants (cloverleaf, right), and other animals. The psychedelic ark sets sail (diamond #3). Waves cover the earth and drown the wicked (two cloverleaves). The ark survives (diamond #4), and

Noah releases a dove. Finally, up near the top (diamond #7), a rainbow (symbolizing God's promise never to bring another flood) arches overhead, God drapes himself over it, and Noah and his family give thanks.

Chartres was a trading center, and its merchant brotherhoods donated money to make 42 of the windows. For 800 years these panes have publicly thanked their sponsors. In the bottom left is a man making a wheel. More workers are to the right. The panels announce that "These windows are brought to you by..." the wheel, axe, and barrel-making guilds.

• *If you'd like to climb the north tower, find the entrance nearby. Then exit the church (through the main entrance or the door in the south transept) to view its south side.*

❿ South Exterior—Flying Buttresses

On the south side, six flying buttresses (the arches that stick out from the upper walls) push against six pillars lining the nave inside, helping to hold up the heavy stone ceiling and sloped, lead-over-wood roof. The ceiling and roof push down onto the pillars, of course, but also outward (north and south) because of the miracle of Gothic: the pointed arch. The flying buttresses push back, channeling the stress outward to the six vertical buttresses, then down to the ground. The result is a tall cathedral held up by

slender pillars buttressed from the outside, allowing the walls to be opened up for stained glass.

The church is built from large blocks of limestone. Peasants trod in hamster-wheel contraptions to raise these blocks into place—a testament to their great faith.

❶ South Porch

The south porch may be covered by scaffolding when you visit (it's being cleaned, a process that could take several years). The three doorways of the south entrance show the world from Christ to the present, as Christianity triumphs over persecution.

Center Door—Christ and Apostles: Standing between the double doors, **Jesus** holds a book and raises his arm in blessing. He's a simple, itinerant, bareheaded, barefoot rabbi, but underneath his feet he tramples symbols of evil: the dragon and lion. Christ's face is among the most noble of all Gothic sculpture.

Christ is surrounded by his **apostles,** who spread the good news to a hostile world. **Peter** (to the left as you face Jesus), with

curly hair and beard, holds the keys to the kingdom of heaven and the slender upside-down cross on which he was crucified. **Paul** (to the right of Jesus) fingers the sword of his martyrdom and contemplates the inevitable loss of his head and the hair upon it. In fact, all of these apostles were killed or persecuted, and their faces are humble, with sad eyes. But their message prevailed, and under their feet they crush the squirming rulers who once persecuted them.

The final triumph comes above the door in the **Last Judgment.** Christ sits in judgment, raising his hands, while Mary and John beg him to take it easy on poor mankind. Beneath Christ the souls are judged—the righteous ▯ur left, and the wicked on the right, who are thrown into the ▯aws of hell. Farther to the right (above the statues of Paul and the apostles), horny demons subject wicked women to an eternity of sexual harassment.

Left Door—Martyrs: Eight martyrs flank the left door. **St. Lawrence** (second from left) cradles the grill (it looks like a book) on which he was barbecued alive. His last brave words to the Romans actually were: "You can turn me over—I'm done on this side." **St. George** (far right) wears the knightly uniform of the 1200s, when Chartres was built and King Louis IX was crusading. Depicted beneath the martyrs are gruesome **methods of torture,** such as George stretched on the wheel. Many of these techniques were actually used in the 1200s against heretics, Muslims, Jews, and Christian Cathars.

• *Reach the north side by circling around the back end of the church (great views) or by cutting through the church.*

⓬ North Porch

In "the Book of Chartres," the north porch is chapter one, from the Creation up to the coming of Christ.

Look between the double doors to see **Baby Mary** (headless), in the arms of her mother Anne, marking the end of the Old Testament world and the start of the New.

History begins in the tiny details in the concentric arches over the doorway. **God creates Adam** (at the peak of the outermost arch) by cradling his head in his lap like a child.

Next look at the statues that flank the doors. **Melchizedek** (farthest to the left of Mary and Anne), with the cap of a king and the cup of communion, is the Biblical model of the *rex et sacerdos* (king-priest), the title bestowed on King Louis IX.

Abraham (second from left) holds his son by the throat and raises a knife to slit him for sacrifice. Just then, he hears something and turns his head up to see God's angel, who stops the bloodshed. The drama of this frozen moment anticipates Renaissance naturalism by 200 years.

John the Baptist (fourth to the right from Mary/Anne), the last Old Testament prophet who prepared the way for Jesus, holds a lamb, the symbol of Christ. John is skinny from his diet of locusts and honey. His body and beard twist and flicker like a flame.

All these prophets, with their beards turning down the corners of their mouths, have the sad, wise look of having been around since the beginning of time and having seen it all—from Creation to Christ to Apocalypse. Over the door is the culmination of all this history: **Christ on his throne,** joined by Mary, the Queen of Heaven. They are some of the last work done on the church, completing the church's stone-and-glass sermon.

Imagine all this painted and covered with gold leaf in preparation for the dedication ceremonies in 1260, when the Chartres generation could finally stand back and watch as their great-grandchildren, carrying candles, entered the cathedral.

Chartres Town

Chartres is worth a quick stroll. You can rent an audioguide or just wander, following the route marked on the free tourist map (audioguide and map at TI—see "Audioguides" in "Orientation," at the top of this chapter). The walk takes you on a one-hour loop from the cathedral down along the river and back.

In medieval times Chartres was actually two towns—the pilgrims' town around the cathedral, and the industrial town along the river, which powered the mills.

You'll start by walking to the right of the cathedral, down rue des Changes. Notice the streets with evocative names, including rue des Changes (pilgrims needed to change money), rue au Lait (milk), and rue aux Herbes (folks smoked hemp). A half-block to the left is place de la Poissonnerie (fish market), today marked by a fine half-timbered building.

Continuing along rue des Changes, you'll pass today's open-air produce market on place Billard. Several blocks later, you'll run into a classic, old, half-timbered house. As the population grew, so did the fire hazard, and the town required half-timbered buildings to be plastered over for safety. Today, the town government—interested in pumping up the touristic charm—pays folks to peel away the plaster and re-expose those timbers. You can see that this building is one of the oldest—note the tilting lintel and the asymmetrical windows.

Turn left at the house and go down the *tertre,* a series of stair-step terraces that link the upper and lower towns. At the bottom turn right, heading past the Church of St. Pierre (great photo-op of flying buttresses). A block past the church, turn left, and you're at the river.

The Eure River is another photogenic spot, with old buildings, humpback bridges, and the cathedral steeples in the distance. The river was once lined with busy mills and warehouses. This was the industrial town. The worst polluters were kept downstream

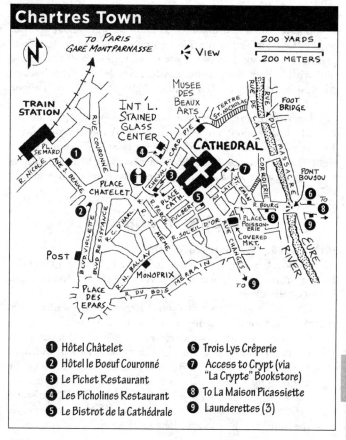

Chartres Town

TO PARIS
GARE MONTPARNASSE

VIEW

200 YARDS
200 METERS

TRAIN STATION

INT'L. STAINED GLASS CENTER

MUSEE DES BEAUX ARTS

TERTRE ST. NICHOLAS

FOOT BRIDGE

CATHEDRAL

PONT BOUJOU

PLACE CHATELET

RUE COURONNE

R. NICOLE

AVE J. BEAUCE

CHEVAL R. CARD. PIE

R. PERCH.

R. C. D'HARL.

PLACE CATH.

R. FULBERT

AU LAIT

R. TENN.

R. BOURG

PLACE POISSON-ERIE

COVERED MKT.

CORROIRERIE

RUE DU MASSACRE

EURE RIVER

POST

BLVD VIOLETTE

BLVD RESISTANCE

R. N. BALLAY

MONOPRIX

R. MEME

R. SOLEIL D'OR

RUE CHANGES

MERRAIN

R. DU BOIS

PLACE DES EPARS

TO

TO

❶ Hôtel Châtelet
❷ Hôtel le Boeuf Couronné
❸ Le Pichet Restaurant
❹ Les Picholines Restaurant
❺ Le Bistrot de la Cathédrale
❻ Trois Lys Crêperie
❼ Access to Crypt (via "La Crypte" Bookstore)
❽ To La Maison Picassiette
❾ Launderettes (3)

(dyeing, tanning, slaughterhouses). Notice the names of the riverside lanes: rue du Massacre, rue de la Tannerie.

When the industry moved out to make room for Chartres' growing population, laundry places replaced the old mills. These were two-story structures—the wash cycle downstairs at the river, then the dry cycle upstairs, where vents allowed the wind to blow through. The last riverside laundry closed in the 1960s.

As you double back to the cathedral along the river, stop at Queen Bertha's Staircase (Escalier de la Reine Berthe), a spiral staircase hugging a half-timbered house on rue des Ecuyers.

Back at the cathedral, consider a stop at the nearby **International Stained Glass Center** to learn the techniques behind the mystery of this fragile but enduring art (Centre International du Vitrail, €4, Mon–Fri 9:30–12:30 & 13:30–18:00, Sat 10:00–12:30 & 14:30–18:00, Sun 14:30–18:00, just 50 yards from cathedral, tel. 02 37 21 65 72, www.centre-vitrail.org).

Near Chartres: La Maison Picassiette

If you have time to burn and enjoy oddities, walk about 20 minutes (or take the bus) to the home created by local artist Raymond Isidore. La Maison Picassiette is covered wall-to-wall (inside and out) with broken-pottery mosaics (€5, April–Nov Wed–Sat and Mon 10:00–11:45 & 14:00–17:45, Sun 14:00–18:00, closed Tue and Dec–March, tel. 02 37 34 10 78).

Getting There: Leave the old town downhill (behind the cathedral, direction: Porte Guillaume). Walk straight on rue Faubourg Guillaume, which becomes rue Ste. Chernon. Take a right on rue du Repos. It's at #22. You can also take bus #4 (direction: La Madeleine, buy ticket from driver, no bus on Sun or holidays).

Sleeping in Chartres

(€1 = about $1.40, country code: 33)
Sleep Code: S = Single, **D** = Double/Twin, **T** = Triple, **Q** = Quad, **b** = bathroom, **s** = shower only. Everyone speaks English and accepts credit cards.

Chartres, a good getaway from Paris, can also be a first or last overnight stop for those flying to or from Orly Airport.

Chartres has three **launderettes.** One is in the lower town (across from recommended Trois Lys Créperie, near pont Boujou, a 15-min walk from cathedral). Another is in the upper town by the market (daily 7:00–21:00, 16a place de la Poissonerie). The third is at 32 rue St. Michel (daily 7:00–20:00, a 5-min walk from cathedral down rue des Changes). For **Internet access,** look for cyber cafés near the train station on avenue Jehan de Beauce, or ask at the TI.

In Chartres

The first hotel is 200 yards straight out of the train station (300 yards below the cathedral). The second hotel is 100 yards closer to the cathedral.

$$ Hôtel Châtelet*,** run by friendly owners, is comfortable, from its welcoming lobby to its spotless, spacious, well-furnished rooms, all of which are nonsmoking. Choose between plush, modern, recently renovated "privilege" rooms with air-conditioning, or the cheaper "standing" rooms with Old World charm (Sb-€94–120, Db-€106–132, extra bed-€22, parking-€8, 6 avenue Jehan de Beauce, tel. 02 37 21 78 00, fax 02 37 36 23 01, www.hotelchatelet .com, reservation@hotelchatelet.com).

$ Hôtel le Boeuf Couronné** is warmly run by Madame Vinsot, with 21 clean but slightly worn rooms and a handy location (S-€33, Sb-€50, D-€39, Db-€60–72, elevator, 15 place

Châtelet, tel. 02 37 18 06 06, fax 02 37 21 72 13, leboeufcouronne @hotmail.fr).

Near Chartres

$ Chambres d'Hôte Brossollet, practical only for drivers, is a pleasant haven of tranquility in Saint-Prest, about four miles from Chartres. This spacious property has an enclosed garden, thatched roofs, two rooms to rent, and kind hosts, Claire and Etienne Brossollet (Db-€55, includes breakfast, tel. 02 37 22 25 31, claire .etienne.brossollet@gmail.com). Leave Chartres to the north and follow signs to Saint-Prest. Once in the village, continue just over a mile straight through on the main road until you see the thatched roof on your left-hand side.

Eating in Chartres

Le Pichet, run by friendly Marie-Sylvie and Xavier, is reasonable and homey, with good daily specials (€12–18 *plats*, €12–15 daily *menu*, closed Tue and Sun evenings and all day Wed, 19 rue du Cheval Blanc, near TI, tel. 02 37 21 08 35).

Les Picholines is a favorite for Mediterranean-inspired cuisine. Come here to get your fix of tapas and olives, or to feast on €11–14 pastas and salads (€16–19 lunch *menu*, €24–29 dinner *menu*, daily except closed for dinner on Sun, rue du Cheval Blanc, tel. 02 37 36 85 84).

Le Bistrot de la Cathédrale is fine for salads and traditional bistro fare, but you'll pay for the view (*menus* from €20, daily, south side of cathedral at 1 cloître Notre-Dame, tel. 02 37 36 59 60).

Trois Lys Crêperie makes good, cheap crêpes just across the river on pont Boujou (€13 two-course meals, closed Sun–Mon, 3 rue de la Porte Guillaume, across from one of the recommended launderettes, tel. 02 37 28 42 02).

REIMS DAY TRIP

With its Roman gate, Gothic cathedral, Champagne caves, and vibrant pedestrian zone, Reims (pronounced "rance," which rhymes with France) feels both historic and youthful. And thanks to the TGV bullet train, it's just a 45-minute ride from Paris.

Reims has a turbulent history: This is where 26 French kings were crowned, where Champagne first bubbled, where WWI devastation met miraculous reconstruction during the Art Deco age (all but 70 buildings were damaged in 1918), and where the Germans officially surrendered in 1945, bringing World War II to a close in Europe. The town's sights give you an entertaining peek at the entire story.

Planning Your Time

You can see Reims' essential sights in an easy day (either as a day trip from Paris or a stop en route to or from Paris). Twelve daily TGV trains make the trip from Paris a breeze. Take a morning train from Paris and explore the cathedral and city center before lunch, then spend your afternoon below ground, in a cool, chalky Champagne cellar. You can be back at your Parisian hotel in time for a rest before dinner.

To best experience contemporary Reims, explore the busy shopping streets between the cathedral and the train station. Rue de Vesle, rue Condorcet, and place Drouet d'Erlon are most interesting.

Orientation to Reims

Reims' hard-to-miss cathedral marks the city center and makes an easy orientation landmark. Most sights of interest are within a 15-minute walk from the Reims-Centre train station. Easy-to-use loop bus routes connect the harder-to-reach Champagne *caves* with the train station and cathedral. The city is ambitiously renovating its downtown, and is converting the square and streets around the cathedral into pedestrian zones.

Tourist Information

At the TI outside the cathedral's left transept, pick up a free map of the town center and a map of the Champagne *caves* (TI open Easter–mid-Oct Mon–Sat 9:00–19:00, Sun 10:00–18:00; mid-Oct–Easter Mon–Sat 9:00–17:00, Sun 11:00–16:00; public WCs across street, tel. 03 26 77 45 00, www.reims-tourisme.com). The TI can book a visit to any *cave* that accepts visitors, and can call a taxi to get you there. Better yet, go by *cyclopolitain* (tricycle taxi) or bus (for more on both, see "Getting Around Reims," next page). The TI also rents pricey audioguide tours covering the cathedral, city center, and Art Deco architecture (single-€5, each additional set-€4).

Arrival in Reims

By Train: From Paris' Gare de l'Est, it's a 45-minute TGV ride (12/day). You'll arrive at the easy-to-navigate Reims-Centre Station (no baggage check). You can reach the cathedral by foot in 15 minutes: Walk straight out of the station, cross the tree-lined boulevards Joffre and Foch, and stroll up the pedestrian place Drouet d'Erlon. Turn left on rue Condorcet, then right on rue de Talleyrand. The time-saving Citadine bus runs from the station (see "Getting Around Reims," next page) to the cathedral and to the Taittinger and Martel *caves* (described in "Champagne Tours and Sights," page 543).

By Car: Follow *Centre-Ville* and *Cathédrale* signs and park on the street approaching the cathedral (rue Libergier) or in the well-signed Parking Cathédrale structure (€1.50/hour).

Helpful Hints

Internet Access: You can surf and snack at **Clique et Croque** (€4/hr, Mon–Sat 10:00–24:00, Sun 14:00–20:00, near the cathedral at 19 rue Chanzy, tel. 03 26 86 93 92).

Laundry: Laverie Chanzy is a few blocks in front of the cathedral (daily 7:00–21:30, 59 rue Chanzy).

Taxi: Call 03 26 47 05 05. A taxi from the train station to the farthest Champagne *cave* will cost about €8.

Car Rental: Avis is at the train station (cours de la Gare, tel. 08 20 05 05 05); **Europcar** is at 76 boulevard Lundy (tel. 08 25 04 52 82); and **Hertz** is at 26 boulevard Joffre (tel. 03 26 47 98 78; all three usually open Mon–Sat 8:00–12:00 & 14:00–19:00, closed Sun).

Local Guide: British expat Jon Catt can show you around the city, its champagne *caves*, and the battlefields near Reims. Jon does not drive, so you must have your own transport if you go beyond Reims (€160/half-day, €240/day, plus expenses, tel. & fax 03 25 73 74 52, mobile 06 17 44 49 67, http://tourguide champagne.blogspot.com, Jon.Catt@wanadoo.fr).

Getting Around Reims

By Citadine Bus: Although most sights are close, two Champagne *caves* (Taittinger and Martel) are a 30-minute walk from the station. Two Citadine bus lines link the historic center with these far-flung cellars, in a circular route starting and ending at the Reims-Centre train station (every 12 min, none on Sun, €1, pay driver). Line #1 does the route clockwise; line #2 does it counterclockwise. To catch the bus, cross the parking lot in front of the train station and look for the yellow Citadine bus stop before crossing the boulevard. From in front of the station, Citadine #1 runs to the cathedral and TI (stop: Cathédrale) in five minutes, and to Taittinger and Martel (stop: St. Niçaise) in 10 minutes. To return, board at the same bus stop where you were dropped off, and continue the loop back to the station. Bus line #K also runs from the station (catch it just across the street from Hertz car rental, direction Béthany), getting you close to the Mumm Champagne *cave* (stop: Justice).

By *Cyclopolitain* Tricycle: These modern lightweight electric tricycles carry one or two passengers and function like taxis, but for shorter trips. The young drivers (called Cyclonautes) speak English and are happy to take you anywhere within the city limits (€2 per person per trip, €20 for 30-min tour; flag one down, have the TI call for you, or call direct at 06 27 95 54 72). If you take a tour, it'd be nice to tip €2–3; otherwise there's no need to tip for simple transport from point to point.

Sights in Reims

▲▲▲Reims Cathedral

The cathedral of Reims, begun in 1211, is a glorious example of Gothic architecture, and one of Europe's greatest churches (free, daily 7:30–19:30). Clovis, the first king of the Franks, was baptized at a church on this site in A.D. 496, establishing France's Christian roots that hold firm today. Since Clovis' baptism, Reims' cathedral has served as *the* place for the coronation of 25 French kings and queens—allowing it to play a more important role in France's political history than Paris' Notre-Dame cathedral. A self-assured Joan of Arc led a less-assured Charles VII to be crowned here in 1429. The French rallied around their new king to push the English

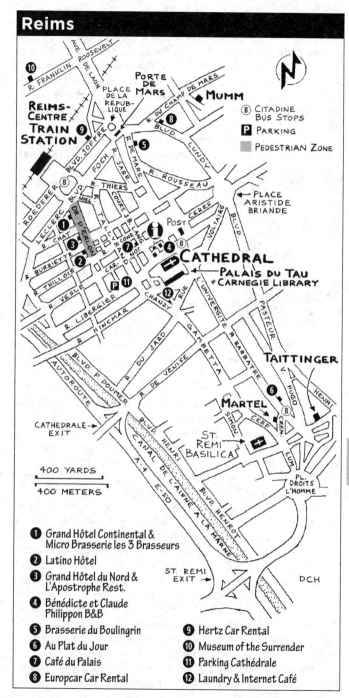

Reims

Legend:
- Ⓑ CITADINE BUS STOPS
- Ⓟ PARKING
- PEDESTRIAN ZONE

Map labels: AVE. ROOSEVELT, R. FRANKLIN, RUE DE LAON, PORTE DE MARS, DE MARS, MUMM, PLACE DE LA REPUBLIQUE, REIMS-CENTRE TRAIN STATION, R. DU CHAMP DE MARS, BLVD, R. DE MARS, BLVD. JOFFRE, FOCH, SARP, R. THIERS, LUNDY, R. ROUSSEAU, PLACE ARISTIDE BRIANDE, ROEDERER, BLVD. LECLERC, DR. D'ERLON, NOEL, CHAT, R. BURRIETTE, COURS J.B. LANGLET, TAL, R. CONBLANC, CERES, POST, VOLTAIRE, BLVD, CATHEDRAL, PALAIS DU TAU & CARNEGIE LIBRARY, R. THILLOIS, CAR, NOEL, R. VESLE, CHANZY, RUE, L'UNIVERSITE, R. BARBATRE, PASTEUR, R. LIBERGIER, R. HINCMAR, R. DU JARD, R. DE VENISE, GAMBETTA, TAITTINGER, AUTOROUTE, BLVD. P. DOUMER, HUGO, HENRI, MARTEL, CERF, GREN, CATHEDRALE EXIT, BLVD. HENRI, CANAL DE L'AISNE A LA MARNE, A-4 E-50, SIMON, ST. REMI BASILICA, LUM, PL. DROITS L'HOMME, BLVD. HENROT, ST. REMI EXIT, DCH

400 YARDS
400 METERS

REIMS

1. Grand Hôtel Continental & Micro Brasserie les 3 Brasseurs
2. Latino Hôtel
3. Grand Hôtel du Nord & L'Apostrophe Rest.
4. Bénédicte et Claude Philippon B&B
5. Brasserie du Boulingrin
6. Au Plat du Jour
7. Café du Palais
8. Europcar Car Rental
9. Hertz Car Rental
10. Museum of the Surrender
11. Parking Cathédrale
12. Laundry & Internet Café

out of France and to finally end the Hundred Years' War. During the French Revolution, the cathedral was converted to a temple of reason (as was Notre-Dame in Paris). After the restoration of the monarchy, the cathedral hosted the crowning of Charles X in 1825—the last coronation in France. During World War I, it was devastated by severe bombing. Then it was completely rebuilt, thanks in large part to John D. Rockefeller...just in time for the start of World War II.

Stand on the square in front of the cathedral and admire perhaps the best west portal anywhere, with more than 2,000 stat

ues festooning its walls inside and out. (Medieval churches face east, toward the Holy Land, so you almost always enter through a church's west portal.) Like the cathedrals in Paris and in Chartres, this church is dedicated to "Our Lady" (Notre Dame). Statues depicting the crowning of the virgin take center stage on the facade. For eight centuries Catholics have prayed to the "Mother of God," kneeling here to ask her to intervene with God on their behalf. In 1429, Joan of Arc received messages from Mary encouraging her to rally French troops against the English at the Siege of Orléans.

Notice the flying buttresses soaring from the sides of the church. These massive "beams" are critical to supporting this structure. The pointed arches inside the church push the weight of the roof outward, rather than downward. The "flying" buttresses support the roof by pushing back inward, creating a delicate balance between the two forces. Gothic architects learned by trial and error—many church roofs caved in as they tested their theories and strove to build ever higher. Work on this cathedral began decades after the Notre-Dame cathedrals in Paris and Chartres, allowing architects to take advantage of what they'd learned from those magnificent earlier structures.

Contemplate the lives of the people who built this huge building, starting in 1211. Construction on a scale like this required a wholesale community effort—all hands on deck. Most townsfolk who participated donated their money or their labor knowing that neither they, nor their children, nor their children's children, would ever see it completed—such was their pride, dedication, and faith. Imagine the effort it took to raise the funds and manage the workforce. Master masons supervised, while the average Jean did much of the sweat work. Labor was something even the poorest medieval peasant could donate generously.

Walk inside. The weight of the roof is supported by a few towering columns that seem to sprout crisscrossing pointed arches. This technique allowed the church to grow higher, and liberated the walls to become window frames. Now, look back at the entry wall, with 120 statues filling the niches. The rose window (high above on this wall) contains the best original stained glass in the church (from 1255, removed during World War I to be spared destruction). Most of the windows are clear and newer: 18th- and 19th-century tastes called for more light, and the original, dark stained glass was replaced.

The south transept windows, destroyed in World War I, were replaced in 1954 by the local Champagne-makers. The windows show the connection of the Champagne industry to this town and its church with scenes portraying the tending of vines (left), the harvest (center), and the time-honored double-fermentation process (right). Notice, around the edges, the churches representing all the grape-producing villages in the area.

The apse (east end, behind the altar) holds a luminous set of Marc Chagall stained-glass windows from 1974. Chagall's

inimitable style lends itself to stained glass, and he enjoyed opportunities to adorn great churches with his windows. The left window shows scenes from the Old Testament, and the center features the resurrection of Christ. On the right the tree of Jesse is extended to symbolically include the royalty of France—both affirming the divine power of the monarchs and stressing the responsibility to rule with wisdom and justice. Helpful English explanations offer historical detail.

Palais du Tau—This former Archbishop's Palace houses artifacts from the cathedral (with scant English information). You'll look into the weathered eyes of original statues from the cathedral's facade (taken in from the acidic open air for their own preservation). A set of precious tapestries, telling stories from the life of Mary, are the originals that warmed the walls of the cathedral's choir in the 16th century. As mentioned earlier, Reims hosted the last French coronation—that of Charles X in 1825. Since the coronation jewels, vestments, and other garb were lost a generation earlier in the French Revolution, what you see here was mostly made especially for this event (€7, May–Aug Tue–Sun 9:30–18:30, Sept–April Tue–Sun 9:30–12:30 & 14:00–17:30, closed Mon, tel. 03 26 47 81 79).

REIMS

More Sights

▲Museum of the Surrender (Musée de la Reddition)—World War II buffs enjoy visiting the historic room where the Germans signed the document of surrender of all German forces in the early morning of May 7, 1945. The news was announced the next day, turning May 8 into Victory in Europe (V-E) Day. Anyone interested in World War II will find the extensive collection of artifacts fascinating (particularly the ticker tape with the happy news, old photos, and a 10-minute video

shown on request). The room of the signing still has the maps with troop positions on the walls and the 13 chairs with name tags, each in their original spots (€3, Wed–Mon 10:00–12:00 & 14:00–18:00, closed Tue, 12 rue Franklin Roosevelt, tel. 03 26 47 84 19).

Porte de Mars—The last vestige of Reims' ancient Roman heritage—an entry gate—is a short walk from the Reims-Centrale train station. The Porte de Mars, built in the second century A.D., was one of four principal entrances into the ancient Gallo-Roman town and the only one still standing. Inspired by triumphal arches that Rome built to herald war victories, this one was constructed to celebrate the Pax Romana (a period of peace and stability—after all of Rome's foes were vanquished). Unlike most of the rest of town, the Porte was undamaged in World War I, but it bears the marks of other eras, such as its integration into the medieval ramparts. Find the ruts under the arcade that guided chariots, and look for the depiction of the legend of Romulus and Remus (extremely faint on ceiling under left arch), complete with suckling she-wolf, from which Reims gets its name (free, always open, place du Boulingrin).

▲Carnegie Library (Bibliotheque Carnegie)—The legacy of the Carnegie Library network, funded generously by the 19th-century American millionaire Andrew Carnegie and his steel fortune (notice the American flag above the main entrance on the

left), extends even to Reims. Built in the flurry of interwar reconstruction, this beautiful Art Deco building still houses the city's public library. Entrance is free and it's just behind the cathedral—it's worth a quick look. Visitors are welcome to admire the mosaics, onyx-laden entrance hall, and Jacque Simon chandelier, but are asked not to enter the reading room (some come here to study). Peek through the reading room door to admire the stained-glass windows of this temple of thinking. The gorgeous wood-paneled card-catalogue room takes older visitors back to their childhoods (notice how each card is tediously typed), or even back to 1928, the year the library was inaugurated (free, Tue–Sat 10:00–13:00 & 14:00–19:00, closed Thu morning and Sun–Mon, place Carnegie).

Art Deco on Place Drouet d'Erlon—Place Drouet d'Erlon is a long street-like square marking the commercial center of town. (From the train station, it's directly across the park-like boulevards.) The square's centerpiece, a fountain with a winged figure of victory at the top, celebrates the major rivers of this district. It hasn't worked as a fountain since WWI bombings—a reminder of the devastation brought on this city. All around you'll see the stylized features—geometric reliefs, motifs in iron work, rounded corners, and simple concrete elegance—of Art Deco. The only hints that this was once a Middle Ages town are the narrow lots that struggle to fit today's buildings. Pop into the Waida Pâtisserie (3 place Drouet d'Erlon) for a pure, typical Art Deco interior. As you stroll about, keep an eye open for "Biscuits Roses"—light, rose-colored egg-and-sugar cookies that date from 1756. They're the locals' favorite munchie to accompany a glass of Champagne (most places that sell the treat offer free samples).

Champagne Tours and Sights
In Reims

▲▲**Champagne Tours**—Reims is the capital of the Champagne region. While the bubbly stuff's birthplace is closer to Epernay, you can tour several interesting Champagne *caves* right in Reims. All charge for tastings and are open daily. Most have a few daily English tours (often booked for groups) and sometimes allow individuals to join these tours. Call in advance for the schedule and to secure a spot on a tour (Martel offers the most personal and best-value tour). Bring a sweater, even in summer, as the *caves* are cool and clammy.

Mumm ("moome") is closest to the train station (15-minute walk) and welcomes the public. Its "traditional visit" (€10, 1 hour) includes a good 10-minute video, a small museum of old Champagne-making contraptions, and a tour of its industrial-size, modern-feeling chalk cellars where 25 million bottles are stored. The video explains the place's history back to 1827 and the Champagne-making process with the enthusiasm of an advertisement ("Cordon Rouge is dedicated to the audacity and passion of exceptional men and women, with a subtle balance between freshness and intensity"). The tour ends with a glass of bubbly Cordon Rouge. You can pay more for the same tour with extra "guided" tastings—€15 for two tastes, or €20 for three (tours depart March–Oct daily 9:00–11:00 & 14:00–17:00, Nov–Feb weekend afternoons and weekdays by reservation, tel. 03 26 49 59 69, www.mumm.com, guides@mumm.com). Mumm is four blocks left out of the train station, on the other side of place de la République at 34 rue du Champ de Mars (also accessible by bus line #K from the train station). Visits begin in the building on the right, #34, at the end of the courtyard. Follow *Visites des Caves* signs.

Taittinger (tay-tan-zhay) is one of the biggest, priciest, and most renowned of Reims' *caves*. They run a few morning and afternoon tours in English through their impressive cellars (call for times and to reserve a spot, about 20–30 people per tour). After seeing their 10-minute promo-movie (hooray for Taittinger!), follow your guide—mine reminded me of an old-time airline hostess—for 45 chilly minutes and 80 steps down to a chalky underworld of *caves*, the deepest of which were dug by ancient Romans. You'll tour part of the three miles of *caves*, pass some of the three million bottles stored here, and learn all you need to know about the Champagne process from your well-informed guide. Popping corks signal when the tour's done and the tasting's begun (€10, includes tasting, 1 hour, tours daily mid-March–mid-Nov 9:30–12:00 & 14:00–16:30, closed weekends off-season, 9 place St. Nicaise, tel. 03 26 85 84 33, www.taittinger.com).

Martel gives a homey contrast to Taittinger's big-business style. It's a small operation with less extensive *caves* and is *sans* doubt the best deal in town. Call to set up a visit and expect a small group that might be yours alone. Friendly Emmanuel runs the place with a relaxed manner. Only 20 percent of their product is exported (mostly to Europe), so you won't find much of their Champagne in the US. Their €9, 45-minute visit focuses on the basics and includes an informative 10-minute film and a tour of their small cellars peppered with rusted, old wine-making tools. It culminates with a tasting of three different Champagnes in a casual living-room atmosphere (daily 10:00–19:00, open through lunch, 17 rue des Créneaux, tel. 03 26 82 70 67, www.champagne martel.com).

Getting to Taittinger and Martel: These two places are a few blocks apart, about 30 minutes by foot southeast of the cathedral. It's easiest and cheap (€1) to get there by Citadine bus (see "Getting Around Reims," page 538). A handy Citadine stop is just

REIMS

behind the cathedral (find the yellow stop a block to the left at the rear of the cathedral and take #1). Get off at stop St. Nicaise (stops are digitally displayed on the bus or ask driver) and you'll see the long walls of Taittinger and the green sign to little Martel. If you take a taxi from the train station, figure on €8 one way (cellars will call a cab for you after the tour). By *cyclopolitain* tricycle, it's €2 per person. If you walk, take rue de l'Université (from behind the cathedral's right transept), then rue du Barbâtre.

Near Reims

Epernay—Champagne purists may want to visit Epernay (16 miles away, well-connected to Paris and Reims), where the grand-daddy of Champagne companies, **Moët et Chandon,** offers tours with three pricey tasting possibilities (€14 for single tasting, €21 for 2 tastes, €26 for 3, no reservation needed, daily mid-March–mid-Nov 9:30–11:30 & 14:00–16:30, closed weekends off-season, tel. 03 26 51 20 20, www.moet.com). From the Epernay train station, walk five minutes straight up rue Gambetta to place de la République, and take a left on avenue de Champagne (how fitting). According to the story, it was near here that in about 1700 the monk Dom Perignon, after much fiddling with double fermentation, stumbled onto this bubbly treat. On that happy day, he ran through the abbey shouting, "Brothers, come quickly...I'm drinking stars!"

Route de la Champagne—Drivers can joyride through the scenic and prestigious vineyards just south of Reims (the TI has maps). Follow D-9 south to Cormontreuil, then Louvois, then Bouzy, to see the chalky soil and vines that produce Champagne's costly wines. Many of the villages have small hotels if you'd like to sleep surrounded by vineyards.

Sleeping in Reims

(€1 = about $1.40, country code: 33)

Sleep Code: S = Single, **D** = Double/Twin, **T** = Triple, **Q** = Quad, **b** = bathroom, **s** = shower only. Everyone speaks English and accepts credit cards.

The first three of my listings are on place Drouet d'Erlon.

$$ Grand Hôtel Continental* is a fine old hotel with well-priced, three-star comfort; stay-awhile public spaces; and helpful Maxeme at the desk (standard Db-€85–109, "junior suite" Db-€159, "superior suite" Db-€165–185, apartments for 3–8 available, 10 percent discount for Rick Steves readers on all but standard rooms, some nonsmoking rooms, air-con, elevator, laundry service, pricey Wi-Fi, parking-€6, 5-min walk from the train station at 93 place

Drouet d'Erlon, tel. 03 26 40 39 35, fax 03 26 47 51 12, www.grand
hotelcontinental.com, grand-hotel-continental@wanadoo.fr).

$ **Latino Hôtel** lives up to its name with spicy music and 11
colorful, funky rooms at fair rates. It's above a bar, so it can be
noisy on weekends. Rooms facing the back are quieter but smaller
and face the adjacent building (Db-€54–74, 33 place Drouet
d'Erlon, tel. 03 26 47 48 89, fax 03 26 86 92 67, www.latinocafe.fr,
latinocafe@latinocafe.fr).

$ **Grand Hôtel du Nord**** delivers basic two-star comfort in
high-ceilinged rooms (Db-€65, 75 place Drouet d'Erlon, tel. 03 26
47 39 03, fax 03 26 40 92 26, www.hotel-nord-reims.com).

$ **Bénédicte et Claude Philippon Chambres d'Hôte** is
Reims' best lodging value. This delightful couple offers two comfortable, homey, and centrally located rooms on place du Chapitre
(#21), 100 yards from the cathedral's left transept. Look for the
yellow *Chambres d'Hôte* sign (S-€45, D-€55, T-€70, shared bathroom, includes French breakfast, fourth floor with elevator, parking on square, tel. 03 26 91 06 22, mobile 06 77 76 20 13, claude
.philippon@sfr.fr).

Eating in Reims

Find good people-watching opportunities—if not high cuisine—
with the scads of restaurants on place Drouet d'Erlon. All of these
recommendations make good lunch or dinner options.

L'Apostrophe, an appealing place with a snazzy-cozy interior,
offers a well-presented, creative cuisine that draws a loyal clientele
(€15 *plats,* €22 and €29 *menus,* look for specials, daily, 59 place
Drouet d'Erlon, tel. 03 26 79 19 89).

Micro Brasserie les 3 Brasseurs is a rollicking, Alsatian-
flavored microbrewery with copper vats and a young, inviting
feel. You'll get good brasserie fare and (rare in France) more beer
than wine (€8 salads, €10–13 *plats,* €16 choucroute, daily, 73 place
Drouet d'Erlon, tel. 03 26 47 86 28).

Brasserie du Boulingrin is the oldest brasserie in town,
gushing with Art Deco. A Reims institution, it serves traditional
French cuisine at blue-collar prices (€15–18 *plats,* €18–25 *menus,*
closed Sun; 10-min walk north of the TI or central train station at
49 rue de Mars, or take the Citadine bus #2, stop Boulingrin; tel.
03 26 40 96 22).

Au Plat du Jour, near the Martel and Taittinger *caves,* makes
a useful pre- or post-Champagne-tasting option. Casually elegant,
with old posters and Champagne labels adorning the walls, this
is a good spot to enjoy hearty, classic French cuisine (€14–19
plats, €16–21 *menus,* daily but closed for dinner Sat–Sun, 219 rue
Barbâtre, tel. 03 26 85 27 60).

Café du Palais is appreciated by older locals who don't mind paying a premium to eat a meal or sip coffee wrapped in 1930s ambience. Reims' most venerable café-bistro stands across from the Grand Theater (€32 *menus*, €20–30 *plats*, daily but closed for dinner Sun–Mon, 14 place Myron Herrick, tel. 03 26 47 52 54).

MORE DAY TRIPS

- *Grand Châteaux near Paris*
- *Impressionist Excursions: Giverny and Auvers-sur-Oise*
- *Disneyland Paris*

Efficient trains bring dozens of day trips within the grasp of temporary Parisians. Châteaux, flowery gardens, riverfront villages, and an amusement park await the traveler looking for a refreshing change from urban Paris.

Grand Châteaux near Paris

The region around Paris (Ile de France) is littered with sumptuous palaces. Paris' booming upper class made it the heartland of European château-building in the 16th and 17th centuries. Most of these châteaux were lavish hunting lodges—getaways from the big city. The only things they defended were noble and royal egos. Try to avoid visiting on weekends, when they are most crowded.

Consider four very different châteaux:

▲▲▲**Versailles**—For its history, grandeur, and accessibility (closed Mon); see the Versailles Day Trip chapter.

▲▲▲**Vaux-le-Vicomte**—For sheer beauty and intimacy (open daily, closed early Nov–mid-March); see next page.

▲▲**Fontainebleau**—For its history, fine interior, and pleasant city (closed Tue); see page 552.

▲**Chantilly**—For its beautiful setting and fine collection of paintings (closed Tue); see page 554.

If you only have time for one château, choose between Vaux-le-Vicomte and Versailles. Except for Versailles, these châteaux are quiet on weekdays. Versailles, Fontainebleau, and Chantilly are covered by the Paris Museum Pass (described at the beginning of the Sights chapter).

Vaux-le-Vicomte

Versailles may be most travelers' first choice for its sheer historic weight, but Vaux-le-Vicomte (voh luh vee-komt) offers an intimate interior and a better sense of 17th-century château life. Located in a huge forest, with magnificent gardens and no urban sprawl in sight, Vaux-le-Vicomte gave me just a twinge of palace envy.

Vaux-le-Vicomte was the architectural inspiration for Versailles and set the standard for European châteaux to come. The proud owner, Nicolas Fouquet (Louis XIV's finance minister), threw a château-warming party. Louis XIV was so jealous that he arrested his host; took his architect (Louis Le Vau), artist (Charles Le Brun), and landscaper (André Le Nôtre); and proceeded with the construction of the bigger and costlier (but not necessarily more splendid) palace of Versailles. Monsieur Fouquet's party, and later arrest, feature prominently in the third Musketeer book by Alexandre Dumas, and at least two versions of *The Man in the Iron Mask* were filmed here.

Vaux-le-Vicomte is more difficult to visit than Versailles (because of transportation), but it's a joy to tour. Most rooms have some English explanations. For more information, rent an audioguide (with a pro-Fouquet perspective) or get a souvenir booklet at the gift shop. Outside the gift shop is a reasonably priced café (limited menu, daily 11:30–18:00, until 24:00 during candlelit visits).

Start your tour with the fine exhibit of carriages *(équipages)* in the old stables. Next, stroll like a wide-eyed peasant across the

stone bridge (any fish down there?) and up the front steps into the château. Turn around to admire the symmetry and elegance of the stables; horses lived well here.

As you wander through Fouquet's dream home, you'll understand Louis XIV's jealousy. Versailles was a simple hunting lodge when this was built. The furniture in Vaux-le-Vicomte is not original—Louis XIV confiscated the real stuff for Versailles. You'll see cozy bedrooms upstairs and grand living rooms downstairs (billiards room, library, card room, and dining room; feel free to fast-forward the 90-min audioguide tour—the first few rooms set the scene). The kitchen and wine cellar are in the basement. Climb the cupola for a great view (worth the wait, check out the build-your-own-dome sketches on the way up). An interesting exhibit on Le Nôtre's

Day Trips from Paris

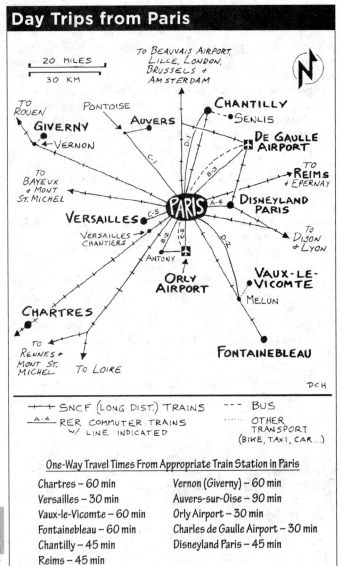

20 MILES
30 KM

TO BEAUVAIS AIRPORT,
LILLE, LONDON,
BRUSSELS +
AMSTERDAM

TO ROUEN

PONTOISE

CHANTILLY
• SENLIS

GIVERNY

AUVERS

← VERNON

DE GAULLE
AIRPORT

D-1

C-1

B-3

TO BAYEUX
+ MONT
ST. MICHEL

TO REIMS
+ EPERNAY

A-4

DISNEYLAND
PARIS

PARIS

VERSAILLES C-5

VERSAILLES →
CHANTIERS

B-4

C-4

D-2

TO DIJON
+ LYON

ANTONY

VAUX-LE-VICOMTE

ORLY
AIRPORT

• MELUN

CHARTRES

FONTAINEBLEAU

TO RENNES +
MONT ST.
MICHEL

TO LOIRE

DCH

+++ SNCF (LONG DIST.) TRAINS   --- BUS

A-4 — RER COMMUTER TRAINS   ..... OTHER
       W/ LINE INDICATED   TRANSPORT
                                      (BIKE, TAXI, CAR...)

One-Way Travel Times From Appropriate Train Station in Paris

Chartres – 60 min	Vernon (Giverny) – 60 min
Versailles – 30 min	Auvers-sur-Oise – 90 min
Vaux-le-Vicomte – 60 min	Orly Airport – 30 min
Fontainebleau – 60 min	Charles de Gaulle Airport – 30 min
Chantilly – 45 min	Disneyland Paris – 45 min
Reims – 45 min	

gardens is in the basement, with little English information.

Survey the garden from the palace's back steps. Landscaper Le Nôtre's first claim to fame, this garden was the cutting edge of sculpted French gardens. He integrated ponds, shrubbery, and trees in a style that would be copied in palaces all over Europe. Take the 30-minute walk (one-way) to the viewpoint atop the grassy hill far in the distance. Rentable golf carts (Club Cars, 45 min-€18, ID and deposit required) make the trip easier.

Cost and Hours: €16 covers château (all floors), gardens, and carriage museum, €14 includes main floor of château only, €8 for gardens only, not covered by Museum Pass, audioguide-€2. Open Thu–Tue 10:00–18:00, gardens until 19:00, closed Wed except July–Aug, closed early Nov–mid-March. Tel. 01 64 14 41 90, www.vaux-le-vicomte.com. From April through Oct, the impressive fountains run 15:00–18:00 on the second Sat and last Sat of each month.

Candlelit Visits: Two thousand candles and piped-in classical music illuminate the palace from early May to early Oct on Sat and holiday nights (€19, 20:00–23:00); call to ask about any upcoming holidays. Note that the gardens are hard to see by candlelight. These *visites aux chandelles* re-create the party thrown in Louis XIV's honor in 1661, but it doesn't get really dark until 22:00 in late May, June, and July, and the last train to Paris leaves Melun at about 22:00. Skip it if you're not driving.

Getting to Vaux-le-Vicomte: To reach Vaux-le-Vicomte by a **train-and-taxi** combination, take the RER-D train to Melun from Paris' Gare de Lyon, Gare du Nord, or Châtelet–Les Halles stations (direction: Montereau, 3/hr, 45 min). Faster SNCF *Banlieue* trains to Melun leave from Gare de Lyon (2/hr, 30 min, about €8 one-way). From Melun's train station, taxis make the 15-minute drive to Vaux-le-Vicomte (€15 one-way Mon–Sat, €18 eves and Sun, taxi tel. 01 64 52 51 50, other numbers posted above taxi stand). Ask a staff person at the château to call a cab for your return, or schedule a pickup time with your driver. In either direction, seek others to split the fare with (regular taxis can take three people maximum, minivan taxis can take four). On peak-season weekends (April–Oct Sat–Sun), a **Veoila shuttle bus** *(navette-châteaubus)* provides limited service between Melun's train station (stop is across the street from the gate) and the château (€7 round-trip, 15 min one-way, call château or check website for schedule, extra trips on Sat eves July–Aug for candlelight visits). With time to kill before your return train, or to make more of your excursion, consider exploring Melun's small medieval center, 10 easy minutes on foot from the station (walk down avenue Gallieni past the ugly concrete buildings, then turn right on rue Thiers and cross the river).

The Paris Vision tour company offers **minibus excursions** to Vaux-le-Vicomte (www.parisvision.com; see page 40). Many travelers find these worthwhile given the tricky train access.

By **car** from Paris, take the A-6 autoroute toward Lyon, then follow signs to Melun. In Melun, follow signs to Meaux (N-36), then Vaux-le-Vicomte.

Adding Fontainebleau: Vaux-le-Vicomte and Fontainebleau can be combined into a full, though manageable, day trip by car, taxi, or train from Paris (except on Tue, when Fontainebleau is closed). Fontainebleau is 12 minutes by train from Melun (allow €40 by taxi).

Sleeping near Vaux-le-Vicomte: Drive 15 minutes to Fontainebleau and sleep at Hôtel de Londres (listed at the end of the next section).

Château of Fontainebleau

Fontainebleau's history rivals that of more modern Versailles. Many French kings have called this glamorous hunting lodge home. Louis XIII was born here, Louis XV married here, and Napoleon was baptized here.

The little emperor also welcomed the pope to this château during his coronation celebration, and it was here that he abdicated his rule when exiled to Elba in 1814. Many years later, General Patton set up headquarters at this château on his way to Berlin.

While Vaux-le-Vicomte and Versailles are French-designed, Fontainebleau was built a century earlier by an Italian. The palace you see today was largely financed by Renaissance King François I. Inspired by his travels through Renaissance Italy, he hired Italian artists to build his palaces. He even encouraged one artist to abandon his native Italy and settle in France for the last three years of his life—Leonardo da Vinci.

Visit the information room to orient yourself using its huge model of the château (first door on your right in the grand courtyard, look for blue "I"). The palace entry/ticket office is 50 yards farther down. Regular entry provides access to the Chinese rooms and the main rooms of the château, called *les grands appartements*. Free audioguides give good room-by-room descriptions (allow one hour), and basic English explanations are posted throughout. Napoleon buffs will enjoy the interesting little museum of Napoleonic history, or a visit to his *petits appartements*. Both can be visited only with a guided tour (most are in French; see "Tours," next page).

MORE DAY TRIPS

In the main château, start downstairs with the small but impressive Chinese collection of Napoleon III's empress, then climb to the main rooms of the palace. Highlights include the stunning Renaissance hall of François I, the opulent dance hall with piped-in music *(salle de bal)*, Napoleon's throne room, and Diana's Gallery (library). The gardens, designed a century later by the landscaper André Le Nôtre, are worth a stroll.

Cost and Hours: €8, includes audioguide, covered by Museum Pass, free first Sun of the month. Open June–Sept Wed–Mon 9:30–18:00, Oct–May closes at 17:00, last entry 45 minutes before closing, closed Tue.

Information: Tel. 01 60 71 50 70, www.musee-chateau-fontainebleau.fr.

Tours: Guided tours of the Napoleon museum and apartments, including one with a Napoleon III Second Empire theme, are usually offered only in French. Call ahead to see if an English visit is possible (price and hours vary, tel. 01 60 71 50 60).

Getting to Fontainebleau: Catch a train at the *Grande Ligne* tracks from Paris' Gare de Lyon in the direction of Montereau (nearly hourly, 45 min, about €8 one-way) to Fontainebleau-Avon Station. Cross under the tracks and catch the bus to the château (every 20 min, 5 min, about €1.60, Paris Metro tickets valid). Check return train times before leaving the station, as there can be big gaps—note that your train might make an unscheduled stop in the middle of the forest to drop off hikers. Taxis to the château cost about €7; to nearby Vaux-le-Vicomte, about €40 (taxi tel. 01 64 22 00 06).

Town of Fontainebleau: Turn right out of the château courtyard and keep right to reach the town center, where cafés and restaurants abound. The helpful **TI** is two blocks across from the château behind Hôtel Londres, has hiking maps and bikes for rent, and posts train/bus schedules (Mon–Sat 10:00–18:00, Sun 10:00–13:00 & 14:00–17:30, Nov–April closed Sun afternoon, 4 rue Royale, tel. 01 60 74 99 99, www.fontainebleau-tourisme.com). When you're ready to catch the Line A bus back to the train station, you'll find bus stops across the street from the TI next to Chez Bernard café, and at the post office in the city center.

English Bookstore: Check out **ReelBooks** at 9 rue de Gerrare, and say hi to Sue and Judy (Tue–Sat 11:00–19:00, closed Sun–Mon, tel. 01 64 22 85 85).

Sleeping and Eating in Fontainebleau

$$ Hôtel de Londres*** is run by gentle Philippe, who has left no stone unturned in his zeal to make everything perfect. The 15 rooms are big, immaculate, and *très* country French. Many have point-blank views of the château, and most have air-conditioning (smaller Db-€120, spacious Db with château view-€160, no elevator, 1 place du Général de Gaulle, tel. 01 64 22 20 21, fax 01 60 72 39 16, www.hoteldelondres.com, hdelondres1850@aol.com).

Fontainebleau's old city has eateries at all price ranges. Here are two of many: **Croquembouche** (*menus* from €26, closed Wed and Sun, 43 rue de France, tel. 01 64 22 01 57) or dine by candlelight under the arches at **Caveau des Ducs** (€24–41 dinner *menus*, daily, 24 rue de Ferrare, tel. 01 64 22 05 05).

Château of Chantilly

Chantilly (shahn-tee-yee), 30 minutes north of Paris, floats serenely on a reflecting pond amid grand gardens. This extrava-

gant hunting palace is the quintessence of a château—filled with great art, surrounded by a luxurious garden and a moat, and accessed by a drawbridge.

Though other châteaux are more interesting to tour for their own sake, Chantilly's claim to fame is its art collection. Because of the social upheaval in France during the Revolution of 1848, the château's owner, Prince de Condé, fled to England. Twenty years later, when blue blood was safe again in France, he returned to his château with a fabulous art collection (800 paintings, including three Raphaels) and book collection. He turned his palace into the museum you see today and willed it to France on the condition that it would be maintained as he left it, and the collections would never be loaned to any other museum.

As most of the château was destroyed during the French Revolution, today's château is largely rebuilt in a fanciful 19th-century style. It's divided into two parts: apartments and art gallery. The plush-but-nothing-really-special private apartments require an included guided tour (20 min, leaving every few minutes, generally in French). The painting gallery and library are impressive, and the free audioguide gives them meaning. Gallery highlights are paintings by Raphael, Titian, Nicolas Poussin, and Eugène Delacroix. Of the 13,000 books in the prince's library, the most exquisite is the 40-page *Book of Hours* by Jean Fouquet (c. 1460).

The gardens immediately behind the château are formal and austere. With your back to the château, follow the signs to the right to *le Hameau*. This little hamlet, with an enchanting garden café, was the prototype for the more famous *hameau* at Versailles. Just beyond is a small kiosk offering boat trips along the canals.

Cost and Hours: Château and park-€11, park only-€6, covered by Museum Pass, Wed–Mon April–Oct 10:00–18:00, Nov–March 10:30–17:00, closed Tue, tel. 02 44 27 31 80.

Live Horse Stables (Les Ecuries Vivant): The Prince de Condé believed he'd be reincarnated as a horse, so he built this opulent horse château for his next go-round (a 5-minute walk from château). The stable museum—with displays on everything from horse medicine to racing to circuses—includes 40 live horses in their stables and daily demonstrations (€10, hours vary but generally Mon and Wed–Fri 14:00–17:00, Sat–Sun 10:30–17:30, last ticket sold one hour before closing, closed Tue; demonstrations usually at 14:30—check schedule online, tel. 03 44 57 40 40, www.museevivantducheval.fr). On the first Sunday of each month there's a grand one-hour show where horses prance to music; call or check the website for times and prices (about €22).

Getting to Chantilly: Leave from Paris' Gare du Nord for Chantilly-Gouvieux (on the Creil line). The RER serves Chantilly, but service is faster on the main lines at the *Grandes Lignes* level. Ask any information desk for the next departure (hourly, fewer on weekends, 25 min, about €8 one-way). Upon arrival in Chantilly, confirm return times (fewer trips on weekends). A free shuttle bus runs from the station to the château (no shuttle on Sun, 10 min, get schedule from TI) or catch the bus heading toward Senlis (hourly). You can also walk 30 minutes to the château (get a map from TI and follow signs, stay on path, turn right before gas station, cross grassy field, "château" in distance is stables, real château is beyond that), or take a taxi (about €7, ask at TI, they extort people with €17 château pickups). The **TI** is across from the train station (Mon–Sat 9:30–12:30 & 14:30–17:30, closed Sun, tel. 03 44 67 37 37).

Impressionist Excursions: Giverny and Auvers-sur-Oise

Giverny

Claude Monet's gardens at Giverny are like his paintings—brightly colored patches that are messy but balanced. Flowers were his brushstrokes, a bit untamed and slapdash, but part of a carefully composed design. Monet spent his last (and most creative) years cultivating his garden and his art at Giverny (zhee-vayr-nee), the Camp David of Impressionism (1883–1926). Visiting the Marmottan and/or the Orangerie museums in Paris before

your visit here, or least reading
the chapters on these museums,
will heighten your appreciation
of these gardens.

In 1883, middle-aged
Claude Monet, his wife Alice,
and their eight children from
two families settled into a
farmhouse here, 50 miles west
of Paris (for more on Monet's family, see sidebar on page 245).
Monet, at that point a famous artist and happiest at home, would
spend 40 years in Giverny, traveling less with each passing year.
He built a pastoral paradise complete with a Japanese garden and a
pond full of floating lilies.

In the last half of his life (beginning in 1912), Monet—the
greatest visionary, literally, of his generation—began to go blind
with cataracts. He used larger canvases and painted fewer details.
The true subject is not really the famous water lilies, but the changing reflections on the pond's surface—the blue sky, white clouds,
and green trees that line the shore.

Getting to Giverny

By Tour: Big tour companies do a Giverny day trip from Paris for
around €70. If you're interested, ask at your hotel—but note that
you can easily do the trip yourself by train and bus for about €30.

By Car: From Paris's Périphérique ring road, follow A-13
toward Rouen, get off at Vernon, follow *Centre Ville* signs, then
signs to Giverny. You can park right at Monet's house or at one of
several nearby lots.

By Train to Vernon: Take the Rouen-bound train from Paris'
Gare St. Lazare station to Vernon, about four miles from Giverny
(normally leaves from tracks 20–25, 45 min one-way, about €24
round-trip, no baggage check). The first train leaves Paris at around
8:15 and is ideal for this trip, with more departures about every two
hours after that (8/day Mon–Sat, 6/day Sun). Before boarding, use
an information desk in Gare St. Lazare to get return times from
Vernon to Paris.

From Vernon's Train Station to Giverny: From the Vernon
train station to Monet's garden (4 miles one-way), you have four
good options: by bus, taxi, bike, or on foot.

The Vernon–Giverny **bus** meets every train from Paris for the
15-minute run to Giverny and connects to every return train to
Paris. If you miss the bus, find others to share a taxi (see below).
To reach the bus stop to Giverny, walk through the station, then
follow the tracks—the stop is across from the L'Arrivée de Giverny
café (don't dally—the bus leaves soon after your train arrives). A

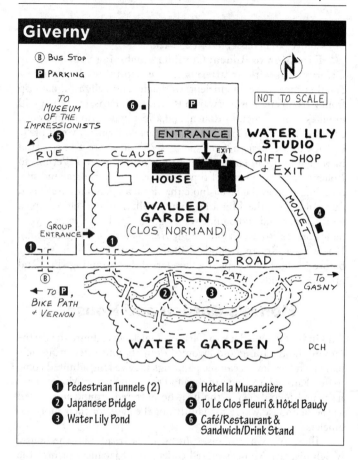

Giverny

Ⓑ BUS STOP
Ⓟ PARKING

NOT TO SCALE

TO MUSEUM OF THE IMPRESSIONISTS ⑤

Ⓟ

⑥ ▪

ENTRANCE

EXIT

RUE CLAUDE

WATER LILY STUDIO
GIFT SHOP & EXIT

HOUSE

WALLED GARDEN (CLOS NORMAND)

MONET

④ ▪

GROUP ENTRANCE

① ①

D-5 ROAD

① Ⓑ
← TO Ⓟ, BIKE PATH & VERNON

PATH

② ③

TO GASNY →

WATER GARDEN

DCH

① Pedestrian Tunnels (2)
② Japanese Bridge
③ Water Lily Pond
④ Hôtel la Musardière
⑤ To Le Clos Fleuri & Hôtel Baudy
⑥ Café/Restaurant & Sandwich/Drink Stand

bus-and-train timetable is posted at the Vernon and Giverny bus stops (note return times). The bus leaves Giverny from the same stop where it drops you off (turn left out of Monet's home and then left on the first street, then right on the footpath that follows the main road, then passes under it); the bus stop is immediately to the right in the parking lot.

If you take a **taxi,** allow €12 for up to three people, €13 for four (tel. 06 77 49 32 90, or 02 32 21 31 31). With buses meeting every train, taxis are unnecessary (unless you miss the bus). Taxis wait in front of the station in Vernon.

You can rent a **bike** at L'Arrivée de Giverny, the café opposite the train station (€12, tel. 02 32 21 16 01), and follow a paved bike path *(piste cyclable)* that runs from near Vernon along an abandoned railroad right-of-way (figure about 30 min to Giverny). Get the easy-to-follow map to Giverny with your bike, and you're in business.

Hikers can go on **foot** to Giverny, following the bike instructions above, and take a bus or taxi back.

Extension to Rouen: Consider combining your morning Giverny visit with an afternoon side trip to nearby Rouen—together they make an efficient, workable, and delightful day trip from Paris. Vernon is halfway to Rouen from Paris; by train it's 40 minutes from Vernon to Rouen, and a 75-minute trip from Rouen back to Paris. If you arrive at Giverny when it opens, you'll likely be back to the Vernon train station by about noon. You can land in Rouen by 13:30 (several lunchtime trains go from Vernon to Rouen), and have plenty of time to see Rouen's cathedral and surrounding medieval quarter (note that Rouen's museums are closed Tue). In Rouen, the TI is a 15-minute walk from the station—pick up their map and audioguide walking tour (or, better yet, get your hands on the Rouen chapter of my *Rick Steves' France* guidebook). If you leave Rouen around 17:30, you'll pull into Paris shortly before 19:00, having spent a wonderful day sampling rural and urban Normandy.

Monet's Garden and House

All kinds of people flock to Giverny. Gardeners admire the earth-moving landscaping and layout, botanists find interesting new plants, and art lovers can see paintings they've long admired come to life. Fans enjoy wandering around the house where Monet spent half his life and seeing the boat he puttered around in, as well as the henhouse where his family got the eggs for their morning omelets.

There are two gardens, split by a busy road, plus the house, which displays Monet's prized collection of Japanese prints. The gardens are always flowering with something; theyre at their most colorful April through July.

Cost and Hours: €6, €4.50 for gardens only, not covered by Paris Museum Pass, April–Oct daily 9:30–18:00, last entry 17:30, closed Nov–March.

Information: Tel. 02 32 51 90 31, www.fondation-monet .com. Audioguides may be available by the time you visit.

Avoiding Crowds: Though lines may be long and tour groups may trample the flowers, true fans still find magic in the gardens. Minimize crowds by arriving a little before 9:30, when it opens (catch the first

An Impressionist's Garden

Impressionism was a revolutionary movement in European art—all the rage in the 1880s. Artists abandoned photo-realism in favor of a wispy style that captured light, glimmers, feelings, and impressions. Impressionists—capturing nature as a mosaic of short brushstrokes of different colors placed side by side, suggesting shimmering light— were committed to conveying the subtleties of nature. And there is no better nature for an Impressionist ready to paint than Monet's delightful mix of weeping willows, luminous clouds, delicate bridges, reflecting ponds...and lush water lilies.

train from Paris), or late, before it closes. Crowds recede briefly during lunch (12:00–13:30), but descend en masse after lunch. The busiest time of year here is May and June.

If you can't arrive early or late, buy your tickets for a bit more at any FNAC store in Paris—allowing you to skip the ticket-buying line here and use the group entrance.

◐ Self-Guided Tour: After you get in, go directly into the Walled Garden (Clos Normand) and work your way around clock-

wise. Smell the pretty scene. Monet cleared this land of pine trees and laid out symmetrical beds, split down the middle by a "grand alley" covered with iron trellises of climbing roses. He did his own landscaping: flowerbeds of lilies, irises, and clematis, and arbors of

climbing roses. The arched trellises leading to the home's entry form a natural tunnel that guides your eye down the path—an effect exploited in his *Rose Trellis* paintings (on display in Paris at the Marmottan Museum). In his careless manner, Monet throws together hollyhocks, daisies, and poppies. But each flowerbed has an overall color scheme that contributes to the look of the whole garden.

In the far corner of the Walled Garden, you'll find a pedestrian tunnel that leads under the road to the Water Garden. Cross under the road and follow the meandering path to the Japanese bridge, under weeping willows, over the pond filled with water lilies, and past countless scenes that leave artists aching for an easel. Find a bench. Monet landscaped like he painted—he built an Impressionist pattern of blocks of color. After he planted the gardens, he painted them, from every angle, at every time of day, in all kinds of weather. Assisted by his favorite step-daughter, Blanche (also a painter, who married Monet's son Jean from an earlier marriage), he worked on several canvases at once, moving with the sun from one to the next. In a series of canvases, you can watch the sunlight sweep over the gardens from early dawn to twilight.

Back on the other side, continue your visit with a wander through Monet's mildly interesting home (pretty furnishings, Japanese prints, old photos, and a room filled with copies of his paintings). The gift shop at the exit is the actual sky-lighted studio where Monet painted his water-lily masterpieces (displayed at the Orangerie Museum in Paris). Many visitors spend more time in this tempting gift shop than in the gardens themselves.

Nearby Sights

All of Giverny's sights and shops string along rue Claude Monet, which runs in front of Monet's house. The bright, modern **Museum of the Impressionists** (Musée des Impressionnismes) houses temporary exhibits of Impressionist art—check its website for current shows—and has picnic-pleasant gardens in front (€5.50, daily May–Oct 10:00–18:00, closed Nov–April; to reach it, turn left after leaving Monet's place and walk 200 yards; tel. 02 32 51 94 00, www.mdig.fr).

If you have time to kill at Vernon's station, take a five-minute walk into **town** and sample untouristy France. Walk between the tracks and the café behind the station, and follow the street as it curves left and becomes rue d'Albuféra. You'll find a smattering of Norman half-timbered homes near Hôtel de Ville (remember, you're in Normandy), and several good cafés and shops—including the killer Boulangerie/Pâtisserie Rose, which has intense quiche and a good selection of sandwiches (74 rue d'Albuféra, tel. 02 32 51 03 98).

Sleeping and Eating in Giverny

(€1 = about $1.40, country code: 33)
$$ Hôtel la Musardière** is nestled in the village of Giverny two blocks from Monet's home (exit right when you leave Monet's). Carole welcomes you with 10 sweet rooms that Claude would have

felt at home in, a reasonable and homey *crêperie*-restaurant (€8–10 crêpes, €26 non-crêpe *menu*), and a lovely yard with outdoor tables (Db-€80–90, Tb-€100–120, Qb-€135, 123 rue Claude Monet, tel. 02 32 21 03 18, fax 02 32 21 60 00, www.lamusardiere.fr, resa @lamusardiere.fr).

$ Le Clos Fleuri is a lovely *chambre d'hôte* in a modern house with three fine rooms and a secluded garden, a 15-minute walk from Monet's place. It's run by charming, English-speaking Danielle, who serves up a generous breakfast (Db-€80, includes breakfast, cash only, 5 rue de la Dîme, tel. 02 32 21 36 51, http: //giverny.org/hotels/fouche).

A flowery **café/restaurant** and a **sandwich/drink stand** sit right next to the parking lot across from Monet's home. Enjoy your lunch in the nearby gardens of the Museum of the Impressionists.

Rose-colored **Hôtel Baudy**, once a hangout for American Impressionists, offers an appropriately pretty setting for lunch or dinner (outdoor tables in front, *menus* from €23, popular with tour groups, closed Mon evening, 5-min walk past Museum of the Impressionists at 81 rue Claude Monet, tel. 02 32 21 10 03). Don't miss a stroll through the artsy gardens behind the restaurant.

Auvers-sur-Oise

There's no better place to get a feel for life during the Impressionist era than on the banks of the lazy Oise River, about a 45-minute drive (or 1.5-hour train ride) north-west of Paris.

Auvers-sur-Oise (oh-vehr soor wahz) is famous as the village where Vincent van Gogh committed suicide after relocating from southern France to be near his sympathetic doctor (Paul Gachet). But many other artists enjoyed this peaceful rural retreat, including Charles-François Daubigny, Jean-Baptiste-Camille Corot, Camille Pissarro, and Paul Cézanne.

Today, this modest little town opens doors to visitors with a few sights, walking trails leading to scenes painted by the artists (some with copies of the paintings posted), and a tranquil break from the big city. Come for the afternoon (some sights are closed

MORE DAY TRIPS

in the morning) and avoid weekends if you can. Auvers has cafés, restaurants, and bakeries with sandwiches. Most sights are closed Mondays and Tuesdays and from November to Easter.

Getting to Auvers-sur-Oise

By Train: Frequent trains to Auvers (with a transfer in Pontoise or St. Ouen) leave from Gare du Nord and Gare St. Lazare, though the easiest trip is via RER-C to Pontoise (2/hr, 1 hr, catch in Paris at St. Michel, Orsay, Invalides, or Pont de l'Alma stops). Pontoise is the end of the line and makes an easier transfer to Auvers than St. Ouen does.

To get from Pontoise to Auvers, a 10-min ride away, take the train in direction: Creil (if it's leaving soon), or hop on bus #9507 (runs more frequently than train, catch it to the right out of the station; look for the posted schedule—you're at "Chemin de la Gare" in Pontoise, and you want the "Marie" stop in Auvers, which is a short walk to the TI). Taxis wait outside the Pontoise station to the left (€10 to Auvers, tel. 01 30 75 95 95; for a bit more money, the same taxi can pick you up in Auvers for the return).

If you arrive in Auvers by train, you can reach the TI by turning left on the main road leaving Auvers' station (look for signs, TI has bus schedules to Pontoise). For a taxi in Auvers, call 06 71 60 50 06 or 06 08 24 54 88.

By Car: Auvers is about 45 minutes northwest of Paris, off Autoroute A-15 (exit #7 to N-184, then follow direction: Beauvais).

Sights in Auvers

Start at the eager-to-help TI, which has good information on all village sights, bus and RER train schedules, a few picnic tables, a rustic WC, and a helpful €0.50 map of Auvers showing the walking routes, with famous art scenes posted (Tue–Sun 9:30–12:30 & 14:00–18:00, Nov–March closes at 17:00, closed Mon, rue de la Sansonne, well-signed, tel. 01 30 36 10 06, www.auvers-sur -oise.com).

The skippable **Musée Daubigny**, one floor up from the TI, houses a small collection of works from artists who came to work with Monsieur Daubigny, an ardent defender of the Impressionists (€4, Wed–Sun 14:00–18:00, Nov–March closes at 17:00, closed Mon–Tue, tel. 01 34 48 03 03).

The best way to spend a few hours in Auvers is to wander the streets between the TI and the château to spot locations where paintings were set, and to visit the dazzling château—the town's most worthwhile sight.

To reach **Château d'Auvers,** follow the *Château* signs along the small road that runs above the TI (15 min on foot). The entire château has been transformed into a re-creation of life during the Impressionist years. Elaborate multimedia displays use an audioguide, video screens, and lasers to guide you along the Impressionist route that led from Montmartre to the sea, giving you a keen appreciation of life's daily struggles and pleasures during this time (€12, family rates, not covered by Paris Museum Pass; April–Sept Tue–Sun 10:30–18:00; Oct–March Tue–Fri 10:30–16:30, Sat–Sun 10:30–17:30; closed Mon; tel. 01 34 48 48 45, www.chateau-auvers.fr).

Van Gogh enthusiasts can visit the home of Dr. Gachet (**Maison du Docteur Gachet**), Vincent's personal physician in Auvers-sur-Oise. The doctor was also a painter, and entertained famous artists such as Cézanne, Monet, Renoir, and Pissarro (€4, May–late Oct Wed–Sun 10:30–18:30, closed Mon–Tue and late Oct–April, 78 rue du Dr. Gachet, tel. 01 30 36 81 27).

You can walk through the same crow-infested wheat fields Vincent did. From the château, return to Auvers along the same road, but veer left when you reach rue Daubigny, then turn right on rue du Montier, and turn right again up a dirt trail. As you stroll through the wheat fields (can be muddy), ponder how amazed the artist would be at his popularity today. You can go as far as the cemetery and visit the tombs of Vincent and his brother Theo (15 min on trail; as you enter cemetery, tombs on left wall halfway down), or take the dirt-trail shortcut a few hundred yards before the cemetery down to the **Church at Auvers** (depicted in van Gogh's painting, now at Paris' Orsay Museum). From here it's a short walk down to the train station and bus stop to Pontoise.

Some van Gogh fans make a pilgrimage to **Auberge Ravoux** (also called "Maison de van Gogh"), where Vincent died after shooting himself. Informative English-information plaques in the free courtyard explain Vincent's tragic life. Wooden steps lead to his small room (€5, March–Oct Wed–Sun 10:00–18:00, closed Mon–Tue and Nov–Feb, includes 12-min slide-show and possible English commentary, otherwise tour on your own). Food connoisseurs can skip the visit and have a tasty lunch in the *auberge*'s perfectly preserved restaurant (€36 *menus*).

Sleeping and Eating in Auvers

(€1 = about $1.40, country code: 33)

Auvers is a handy first or last stop for drivers using Charles de Gaulle Airport.

$$ Hostellerie du Nord*** is small, friendly, and polished—a treat for those who want to sleep in luxury. It has modern, spacious rooms and a seriously good restaurant that requires reservations (Db-€100–130, suites-€190, *menus* from €60, a block from train station at 6 rue du Général de Gaulle, tel. 01 30 36 70 74, fax 01 30 36 72 75, www.hostelleriedunord.fr).

The place to eat in Auvers is **Auberge Ravoux,** unchanged (except for its prices) since 1876, when painters would meet here over a good meal (€28–36 *menus,* closed Mon–Tue, below TI on place de la Mairie, tel. 01 30 36 60 60).

Disneyland Paris

Europe's Disneyland is a remake of California's, with most of the same rides and smiles. The main difference is that Mickey Mouse speaks French, and you can buy wine with your lunch. My kids went ducky.

Disneyland is easy to get to, and may be worth a day, if Paris is handier than Florida or California.

Getting to Disneyland Paris

By Train: The slick 45-minute RER trip is the best way to get to Disneyland from downtown Paris. Take RER line A-4 to Marne-la-Vallée-Chessy; check the signs over the platform to be sure Marne-la-Vallée-Chessy is served, because the line splits near the end. Catch it from Paris' Charles de Gaulle-Etoile, Auber, Châtelet-Les Halles, or Gare de Lyon stations (at least 3/hr, drops you 45 min later right in the park, about €8 each way). The last train back to Paris leaves shortly after midnight. When returning, remember to use your same RER ticket for your Métro connection in Paris.

By Bus and Train from the Airport: Both of Paris' major airports have direct shuttle buses to Disneyland Paris (every 20 min, 30 min, daily 8:30–20:00ish, about €17). Fast TGV trains run from Charles de Gaulle to Disneyland in 10 minutes, but they're less frequent and pricier—the shuttle bus makes more sense.

By Car: Disneyland is about 40 minutes (20 miles) east of Paris on the A-4 autoroute (direction Nancy/Metz, exit #14). Parking is about €10 per day at the park.

Dis-orientation

The Disneyland Paris Resort is a sprawling complex housing two theme parks (Disneyland Paris and Walt Disney Studios), a few entertainment venues, and several hotels. Opened in 1992, it was the second Disney resort built outside the US (Tokyo was first). With upward of 15 million visitors a year, it quickly became Europe's leading single tourist destination. Mickey has arrived.

Disneyland Paris: This park has a corner on the fun market, with the rides and Disney characters you came to see. You'll find familiar favorites wrapped in French packaging, like Space Mountain (a.k.a. *De la Terre à la Lune*) and Pirates of the Caribbean *(Pirates des Caraïbes)*.

Skipping Lines: The free FASTPASS system is a worthwhile timesaver (get FASTPASS card at entry, good for the five most popular rides, at ride insert card in machine to get a window of time to enter—often within 45 min). You'll also save time by buying your tickets ahead (at airport TIs, some Métro stations, or along the Champs-Elysées at the TI, Disney Store, or Virgin Megastore).

Walt Disney Studios: This zone, which opened in 2002 next to the amusement park, has a Hollywood focus geared for an older crowd, with animation, special effects, and movie magic "rides." The Aerosmith Rock 'n' Roller Coaster is nothing special. The highlight is the Stunt Show Spectacular, filling a huge back-lot stadium five times a day for 45 minutes of car chases and thriller filming tips. An actual movie sequence is filmed with stunt drivers, audience bit players, and brash MTV-style hosts.

Cost: Disneyland Paris and Walt Disney Studios charge the same. You can pay separately for each or buy a combined "Hopper" ticket for both. A one-day pass to either park is about €50 for adults and €42 for kids aged 3–11 (check their website for special offers). Kids under 3 are free. In the summer, save 25 percent by going after 17:00.

A one-day Hopper ticket for entry to both parks is about €65 for adults (less for kids). Two- and three-day deals are available. Regular prices are discounted about 25 percent Nov–March and promotions are offered occasionally (check www.disneylandparis.com).

Hours: Disneyland—daily 10:00–19:00, until 23:00 mid-July–Aug, some weekends have longer hours—check website or at ticket office. Walt Disney Studios—summer daily 9:00–18:00; winter Mon–Fri 10:00–18:00, Sat–Sun 9:00–18:00.

Information: Disney brochures are in every Paris hotel. For more info and to make reservations, call 08 25 30 60 30 (€0.15/min) or try www.disneylandparis.com or www.mickey-mouse.com.

Avoiding Crowds: Saturday, Sunday, Wednesday, public holidays, and any day in July and August are the most crowded. After dinner, crowds are gone.

Eating with Mickey: Food is fun and not outrageously priced. (Still, many smuggle in a picnic.)

Sleeping at Disneyland

Most are better off sleeping in reality (Paris), though with direct buses and freeways to both airports, Disneyland makes a convenient first- or last-night stop. Seven different Disney-owned hotels offer accommodations at or near the park in all price ranges. Prices are impossible to pin down, as they vary by season and by the "package deal" you choose (deals that include park entry are usually a better value). The cheapest is **Davy Crockett's Ranch,** but you'll need a car. **Hôtel Santa Fe**** offers the best midrange value, with frequent shuttle service to the park. The most expensive is the **Disneyland Hotel******, right at the park entry, about twice the price of the Santa Fe. The **Dream Castle Hotel****** is another higher-end choice, with its nearly 400 rooms done up to look like a lavish 17th-century palace (40 avenue de la Fosse des Pressoirs, tel. 01 64 17 90 00, www.dreamcastle-hotel.com, info@dreamcastle-hotel.com). To reserve any Disneyland hotel, call 01 60 30 60 30, fax 01 60 30 60 65, or check www.disneylandparis.com. The prices you'll be quoted include entry to the park.

FRENCH HISTORY AND CONTEMPORARY POLITICS

History

Celts and Romans (52 B.C.–A.D. 500)

Julius Caesar conquered the Parisii, turning Paris from a tribal fishing village into a European city. The mix of Latin (southern) and Celtic (northern) cultures, with Paris right in the middle, defined the French character.

Sights
• Cluny Museum (Roman baths)
• Louvre (Roman antiquities)
• Paris Archaeological Crypt (in front of Notre-Dame)

Dark Ages (500–1000)

Roman Paris fell to German pirates ("Franks" = France), and later to the Vikings ("Norsemen" = Normans). During this turbulent time, Paris was just another island state ("Ile de France") in the midst of many warring kingdoms. The lone bright spot was the reign of Charlemagne (A.D. 768–814), who briefly united the Franks, giving a glimpse of the modern nation-state of France.

Sights
• Cluny Museum (artifacts)
• Statue of Charlemagne (near Notre-Dame)

Border Wars with England (1066–1500)

In 1066, the Norman duke William the Conqueror invaded and conquered England. This united England, Normandy, and much of what is today western France; sparked centuries of border wars; and produced many kings of England who spoke French. In 1328

Typical Church Architecture

History comes to life when you visit a medieval church. Knowing a few simple terms will enrich your experience. Note that not every church will have every feature, and a "cathedral" isn't a type of church architecture, but rather a governing center for a local bishop.

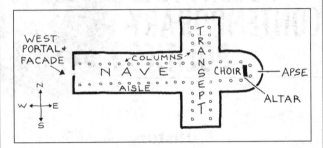

Aisles: The long, generally low-ceilinged arcades that flank the nave.

Altar: The raised area with a ceremonial table (often adorned with candles or a crucifix), where the priest prepares and serves the bread and wine for Communion.

Apse: The space beyond the altar, generally bordered with small chapels.

Choir: A cozy area, often screened off, located within the church nave and near the high altar where services are sung in a more intimate setting.

Cloister: A square-shaped series of hallways surrounding an open-air courtyard, traditionally where monks and nuns got fresh air.

Facade: The outer wall of the church's main (west) entrance, viewable from outside and generally highly decorated.

Groin Vault: An arched ceiling formed where two equal barrel vaults meet at right angles. Less common usage: term for a medieval jock strap.

Narthex: The area (portico or foyer) between the main entry and the nave.

Nave: The long, central section of the church (running west to east, from the entrance to the altar) where the congregation stood through the service.

Transept: The north–south part of the church, which crosses (perpendicularly) the east–west nave. In a traditional Latin cross-shaped floor plan, the transept forms the "arms" of the cross.

West Portal: The main entry to the church (on the west end, opposite the main altar).

King Charles IV died without an heir, and the Norman king of England tried to claim the throne of France, which led to more than 100 years of Franco-Anglo battles, called the Hundred Years' War. Rallied by the teenage visionary Joan of Arc in 1429, the French finally united north and south, and drove the English across the Channel in 1453. Modern France was born, with Paris as its capital.

Sights
- Notre-Dame Cathedral
- Sainte-Chapelle
- Cluny Museum (tapestries)
- Carnavalet Museum
- The Sorbonne
- The Latin Quarter

Renaissance and Religious Wars (1500s)

A strong, centralized France emerged, with French kings setting Europe's standard. François I made Paris a cultural capital, inviting Leonardo and Mona Lisa to visit. Catholics and Protestants fought openly, with 2,000 Parisians slaughtered in the St. Bartholomew's Day Massacre in 1572. The Wars of Religion subsided for a while when the first Bourbon king, Henry IV, took the throne in 1589 after converting to Catholicism. (In 1598, he signed the Edict of Nantes, which instituted freedom of worship.)

Sights
- Louvre (palace and Renaissance art)
- Pont Neuf
- Place des Vosges
- Fontainebleau

Louis XIV, the Absolute Monarch (1600s)

Louis XIV solidified his power, neutered the nobility, revoked the Edict of Nantes, and moved the capital to Versailles, which also became the center of European culture. France's wealth sparked "enlightened" ideas that became the seeds of democracy.

Sights
- Versailles
- Vaux-le-Vicomte
- Hôtel des Invalides
- Paintings by Nicolas Poussin and Claude Lorrain

Decadence and Revolution (1700s)

This was the age of Louis XV, Louis XVI, Marie-Antoinette, Voltaire, Jean-Jacques Rousseau, Maximilien de Robespierre, and Napoleon. A financial crunch from wars and royal excess drove the French people to revolt. On July 14, 1789, they stormed the Bastille. A couple of years later, the First French Republic arrested and then beheaded the king and queen. Thousands lost their heads—guillotined if suspected of hindering progress. A charismatic commoner rose amid the chaos, promising stability—Napoleon Bonaparte.

Sights
• Versailles
• Place de la Concorde
• Place de la Bastille
• Conciergerie
• Paintings by Antoine Watteau, François Boucher, Jean-Honoré Fragonard, and Jacques-Louis David

Elected Emperors and Constitutional Kings (1800s)

Napoleon conquered Europe, crowned himself emperor, invaded Russia, was defeated on the battlefields of Waterloo, and ended up exiled to an island in the Atlantic. The monarchy was restored, but rulers toed the democratic line—or were deposed in the popular uprisings of 1830 and 1848. The latter resulted in the Second French Republic, whose first president was Napoleon's nephew. He rewrote the constitution with himself as Emperor Napoleon III, and presided over a wealthy, middle-class nation with a colonial empire in slow decline. The disastrous Franco-Prussian War in 1870 ended his reign, leading to the Third Republic. France's political clout was fading, even as Paris remained the world's cultural center during the belle époque, or beautiful age.

Sights
• Arc de Triomphe
• Baron Haussmann's wide boulevards
• Eiffel Tower
• Les Invalides and Napoleon's Tomb
• Pont Alexandre III
• Grand Palais
• Petit Palais
• Montmartre
• Opéra Garnier
• Paintings by Jean-Auguste-Dominique Ingres and Eugène Delacroix (Louvre)

• Impressionist and Postimpressionist paintings (Edouard Manet, Claude Monet, Pierre-Auguste Renoir, Edgar Degas, Henri de Toulouse-Lautrec, Paul Cézanne, and so on) at the Orsay, Marmottan, and Orangerie museums

War and Depression (1900–1950)

France began the turn of the 20th century as top dog, but two world wars with Germany (and the earlier Franco-Prussian War) wasted the country. France lost millions of men in World War I, sank into an economic depression, and was easily overrun by Hitler in World War II. Paris, now dirt cheap, attracted foreign writers and artists.

This was the age of Pablo Picasso, Maurice Ravel, Claude Debussy, Erik Satie, Igor Stravinsky, Vaslav Nijinsky, Ernest Hemingway, F. Scott Fitzgerald, Gertrude Stein, Ezra Pound, Jean-Paul Sartre, Edith Piaf, and Maurice Chevalier.

Sights
• Picasso Museum (currently closed for renovation)
• Deportation Memorial
• Holocaust Memorial
• Pompidou Center (art from this period)

Postwar France (1950–Present)

After the war, France reestablished a democracy with the Fourth Republic. But France's colonial empire dissolved after bitter wars in Algeria and Vietnam, which helped mire an already unsteady government. Wartime hero Charles de Gaulle was brought back in 1958 to assist with France's regrowth. He rewrote the constitution, beginning the Fifth (and current) Republic. Immigrants from former colonies flooded Paris. The turbulent '60s, progressive '70s, socialist-turned-conservative '80s, and the middle-of-the-road '90s bring us to the début de siècle, or the beginning of the 21st century.

Sights
• Montparnasse Tower
• La Défense
• Louvre's pyramid
• Pompidou Center (modern art)

Contemporary Politics in France

Today, the key political issues in France (like everywhere) are mainly about the economy. And though France has suffered less than the US (they didn't get involved in risky home loans and are less invested in the stock market), unemployment is high (about 10 percent) and taxes are higher (about 44 percent of the gross domestic product). Other French concerns are the steadily increasing percentage of ethnic minorities (10 percent of France's population is of North African descent), the extent of the European Union's power, and balancing cushy workers' benefits against the need to compete in a global marketplace. The challenge for the French leadership is to address these issues while maintaining the level of social services that the French expect from their government.

France is part of the 27-member European Union (a kind of "United States of Europe") that has successfully dissolved borders and implemented a single currency, the euro. France's governments have been decidedly pro-EU; however, its people are more skeptical. In 2005, the French voted against ratifying an EU constitution that would have increased the EU's political powers. Many French fear that a more powerful EU would ultimately result in lost job security and social benefits (a huge issue in France).

French national politics are complex but fascinating. France has seven major political parties and several smaller ones. From left to right, the major parties include the Nouveau Parti Anti-Capitaliste (NPA, the new anti-capitalist party), which is as far left as you get in France; the more moderate reformed Communists (PCF); the environmental party (Les Verts, "The Greens"); the middle-of-the-road Socialists (PS); the centrist MoDem party; the center-right Popular Movement (UMP); and the racist, isolationist Front National (FN). In general, the two parties with the most support are UMP and the Socialists—they offered the top two candidates in the last presidential election. But in France, unlike in the US, informal coalitions are generally necessary for any party to "rule."

The Front National party, led by Jean-Marie Le Pen, campaigns on a "France for the French" platform—calling for expulsion of ethnic minorities, restoration of the French franc, and broader police powers. The situation in the country became especially tense in the fall of 2005, when disadvantaged youths (a large percentage of North African descent) rioted in Parisian suburbs, protesting discrimination. Although the Front Nationalists have a staunch voter base of about 13 percent, rising unemployment and globalization worries have increased its following, allowing Le Pen to nudge the political agenda to the right.

On the left, the once-powerful Communists (PCF) draw only about 5 percent of the popular vote, forcing them to work more flexibly with the less-radical Socialists and Greens. This left end of the political spectrum in France tends to see its popularity rise when the economy is strong, and fall when it's weak.

The French president is elected by popular vote every five

years. The prime minister is chosen by the president, then confirmed by the parliament (Assemblée Nationale), and is a very powerful position when the president's party loses its majority in parliament. With seven major parties, a single majority is rare, so it takes a coalition to confirm a prime minister. Over the past 12 years, the right has been more successful than the left in marshaling supporters. Previous President Jacques Chirac (who served two terms) and current President Nicolas Sarkozy (elected in 2007) are both conservatives.

Sarkozy is pro-American (though he doesn't speak English) and pro-EU. He is tough on crime and on unchecked immigration. To address a sluggish economy, he proposes a tough-love, carrot-and-stick approach—limiting the power of unions and cutting workers' benefits, while offering tax incentives to workers who work overtime (above the current 35–39-hour workweek). His policies are generating predictable resistance from unions: Expect at least one major strike somewhere in France during your trip.

More French eyebrows have been raised by Sarkozy's personal life. Within a year of becoming president, he divorced his wife of 11 years and married sexy Italian model-turned-singer Carla Bruni (who has been linked romantically with Mick Jagger, Eric Clapton, and one of your co-authors). Sarkozy likes to jog, and even wears sweats when relaxing *(quelle horreur!)*. The press has nicknamed Sarkozy "Président Bling Bling" for his love of shiny things (Ray-Ban sunglasses, expensive watches, yachts), his jet-set lifestyle, and consorting with celebrities.

APPENDIX

Contents

Tourist Information

The French national tourist office **in the US** is a wealth of information. Before your trip, scan their website: www.franceguide.com. You can contact them to describe your trip (briefly) and request any information (such as city maps and schedules of upcoming festivals). To ask questions and request tourist materials (for a small shipping fee), email info.us@franceguide.com or call 514/288-1904. You can download many brochures free of charge at their website.

In France your best first stop in a new city is generally the tourist information office (remember that these are abbreviated as **TI** in this book). A TI is a great place to get a city map and advice on public transportation (including bus and train schedules), special events, and recommendations for nightlife. Many TIs have information on the entire country or at least the region, so try to pick up maps for towns you'll be visiting later in your trip.

Unfortunately, Paris' network of TIs—scattered at key locations throughout the city—are not always very helpful (for details, see page 25). Paris' TIs share an official **website** (www.paris info.com) offering practical information on hotels, special events, museums, children's activities, fashion, nightlife, and more.

Two other entertaining and useful websites are www.bonjour paris.com (which claims to offer a virtual trip to Paris—featuring interactive French lessons, tips on wine and food, and news on the latest Parisian trends) and the similar www.paris-anglo.com (with informative stories on visiting Paris, plus a directory of over 2,500 English-speaking businesses). For a preview of special art exhibitions in Paris, check www.rmn.fr.

Communicating

Telephones

Smart travelers get comfortable using the telephone system to reserve or reconfirm rooms, get tourist information, reserve restaurants, confirm tour times, or phone home. When spelling out your name on the phone, you'll find that some letters are pronounced differently in French: *a* is pronounced "ah," *e* is pronounced "uh," and *i* is pronounced "ee." To avoid confusion, say "*a*, Anne," "*e*, euro," and "*i*, Isabelle."

Generally the easiest, cheapest way to call home is to use an international phone card purchased in France. This section covers dialing instructions, phone cards, and types of phones (for more in-depth information, see www.ricksteves.com/phones).

How to Dial

Calling from the US to France, or vice versa, is simple—once you break the code. The European Calling Chart in this chapter will walk you through it.

Dialing Domestically Within France

France has a direct-dial 10-digit phone system (no area codes). To make domestic calls anywhere within France, just dial the number. All Paris numbers start with 01.

For example, the number of one of my recommended hotels in Paris (the Grand Hôtel Lévêque) is 01 47 05 49 15. That's the number you dial whether you're calling it from across the street or across the country.

Dialing Internationally to or from France

If you want to make an international call, follow these steps:

1. Dial the international access code (00 if you're calling from Europe, 011 from the US or Canada).

2. Dial the country code of the country you're calling (see European calling chart in this chapter).

3. Dial the local number. If you're calling France, drop the initial zero of the phone number (the European calling chart lists specifics per country).

Calling from the US to France: To call from the US to a recommended Paris hotel, dial 011 (the US international access code), 33 (France's country code), then 1 47 05 49 15 (the Paris hotel's number without its initial zero).

Calling from France to the US: To call from Paris to my office in Edmonds, Washington, I dial 00 (Europe's international access code), 1 (the US country code), 425 (Edmonds' area code), and 771-8303.

Note: You might see a + in front of a European number. When dialing the number, replace the + with the international access code of the country you're calling from (00 from Europe, 011 from the US or Canada).

Public Phones and Hotel-Room Phones

To make calls from public phones you'll need a prepaid phone card. There are two different kinds of phone cards: international and insertable. (Coin-op phones are virtually extinct.) Both types of phone card work only in France. If you have a live card at the end of your trip, give it to another traveler to use up.

International Phone Cards: Called "code cards"(*cartes à code*, cart ah code), these are the cheapest way to make international calls from Europe—with the best cards, it costs literally pennies a minute. They also work for local calls.

You can use international phone cards from any type of phone, even the one in your hotel room (but ask at the front desk if there are any fees for toll-free calls). The cards are sold all over; look for them at newsstand kiosks, tobacco shops *(tabacs)*, and hole-in-the-wall long-distance shops. Ask the clerk which of the various brands has the best rates for calls to America. Because cards are occasionally duds, avoid the more expensive denominations. Some shops also sell cardless codes, printed right on the receipt.

To use the card, scratch to get your code, then dial the free (usually 4-digit) access number. If access code on the card doesn't work from your hotel-room phone, try the card's 10-digit, toll-free code that starts with 08. A voice in French (followed by English) tells you to enter your code. Before or after entering your code, you may need to press (or "*touche*," pronounced toosh) the pound key (#, *dièse*, dee-ehz) or the star key (*, *étoile*, eh-twahl). At the next message, dial the number you're calling (possibly followed by pound or star key; you don't have to listen to the entire sales pitch).

Remember that you don't need the actual card to use a card

European Calling Chart

Just smile and dial, using this key:
AC = Area Code, LN = Local Number.

European Country	Calling long distance within ...	Calling from the US or Canada to ...	Calling from a European country to ...
Austria	AC + LN	011 + 43 + AC (without the initial zero) + LN	00 + 43 + AC (without the initial zero) + LN
Belgium	LN	011 + 32 + LN (without initial zero)	00 + 32 + LN (without initial zero)
Bosnia-Herzegovina	AC + LN	011 + 387 + AC (without initial zero) + LN	00 + 387 + AC (without initial zero) + LN
Britain	AC + LN	011 + 44 + AC (without initial zero) + LN	00 + 44 + AC (without initial zero) + LN
Croatia	AC + LN	011 + 385 + AC (without initial zero) + LN	00 + 385 + AC (without initial zero) + LN
Czech Republic	LN	011 + 420 + LN	00 + 420 + LN
Denmark	LN	011 + 45 + LN	00 + 45 + LN
Estonia	LN	011 + 372 + LN	00 + 372 + LN
Finland	AC + LN	011 + 358 + AC (without initial zero) + LN	999 + 358 + AC (without initial zero) + LN
France	LN	011 + 33 + LN (without initial zero)	00 + 33 + LN (without initial zero)
Germany	AC + LN	011 + 49 + AC (without initial zero) + LN	00 + 49 + AC (without initial zero) + LN
Gibraltar	LN	011 + 350 + LN	00 + 350 + LN
Greece	LN	011 + 30 + LN	00 + 30 + LN
Hungary	06 + AC + LN	011 + 36 + AC + LN	00 + 36 + AC + LN
Ireland	AC + LN	011 + 353 + AC (without initial zero) + LN	00 + 353 + AC (without initial zero) + LN
Italy	LN	011 + 39 + LN	00 + 39 + LN

European Country	Calling long distance within ...	Calling from the US or Canada to ...	Calling from a European country to ...
Montenegro	AC + LN	011 + 382 + AC (without initial zero) + LN	00 + 382 + AC (without initial zero) + LN
Morocco	LN	011 + 212 + LN (without initial zero)	00 + 212 + LN (without initial zero)
Netherlands	AC + LN	011 + 31 + AC (without initial zero) + LN	00 + 31 + AC (without initial zero) + LN
Norway	LN	011 + 47 + LN	00 + 47 + LN
Poland	LN	011 + 48 + LN (without initial zero)	00 + 48 + LN (without initial zero)
Portugal	LN	011 + 351 + LN	00 + 351 + LN
Slovakia	AC + LN	011 + 421 + AC (without initial zero) + LN	00 + 421 + AC (without initial zero) + LN
Slovenia	AC + LN	011 + 386 + AC (without initial zero) + LN	00 + 386 + AC (without initial zero) + LN
Spain	LN	011 + 34 + LN	00 + 34 + LN
Sweden	AC + LN	011 + 46 + AC (without initial zero) + LN	00 + 46 + AC (without initial zero) + LN
Switzerland	LN	011 + 41 + LN (without initial zero)	00 + 41 + LN (without initial zero)
Turkey	AC (if no initial zero is included, add one) + LN	011 + 90 + AC (without initial zero) + LN	00 + 90 + AC (without initial zero) + LN

- The instructions above apply whether you're calling a land line or mobile phone.
- The international access codes (the first numbers you dial when making an international call) are 011 if you're calling from the US or Canada, or 00 if you're calling from virtually anywhere in Europe (except Finland, where it's 999).
- To call the US or Canada from Europe, dial 00, then 1 (the country code for the US and Canada), then the area code and number. In short, 00 + 1 + AC + LN = Hi, Mom!

The Language Barrier and That French Attitude

You've no doubt heard that Parisians are "mean and cold and refuse to speak English." This is an out-of-date preconception left over from the days of Charles de Gaulle. Parisians are as friendly as any other people, and no more disagreeable than New Yorkers. Like many big cities, Paris is a massive melting pot of international cultures; your evening hotel receptionist is just as likely to speak French with an accent as not. Without any doubt, Parisians speak more English than Americans speak French. Be reasonable in your expectations: Waiters are paid to be efficient, not chatty. And Parisian postal clerks are every bit as speedy, cheery, and multilingual as ours are back home.

The biggest mistake most Americans make when traveling in France is trying to do too much with limited time. Hurried, impatient travelers who miss the subtle pleasures of people-watching from a sun-dappled café often misinterpret French attitudes. By slowing your pace and making an effort to understand French culture, you're much more likely to have a richer experience. With five weeks' paid time off each year, your hosts can't comprehend why anyone would rush through a vacation.

Parisians take great pride in their customs, clinging to their belief in cultural superiority. Let's face it: It's tough to keep on smiling when you've been crushed by a Big Mac, Mickey-Moused by Disney, and drowned in instant coffee. Your hosts are cold only if you decide to see them that way. Polite and formal, the French respect the fine points of culture and tradition. In Paris, strolling down the street with a big grin on your face and saying

account, so it's shareable. You can write down the access number and code in your notebook and share it with friends.

Insertable Phone Cards: Called a *télécarte* (tay-lay-kart), this type of card can be used only at pay phones. It's handy and affordable for local and domestic calls, but more expensive for international calls. To use the card, insert it into a slot in the pay phone. They're sold in two denominations—*une petite* costs about €7.50; *une grande* about €15—at *tabacs*, newsstands, post offices, and train stations. Though you can use a *télécarte* to call anywhere in the world, it's only a good deal for making quick local calls from a phone booth.

Hotel-Room Phones: Phoning from your room can be cheap for local calls (ask for the rates at the front desk first), but is often a rip-off for long-distance calls (unless you use an international phone card, explained earlier). Incoming calls are free, making this a cheap way for friends and family to stay in touch (provided they

hello to strangers is a sign of senility, not friendliness (seriously). Parisians think that Americans, while friendly, are hesitant to pursue more serious friendships. Recognize sincerity and look for kindness. Give them the benefit of the doubt.

Communication difficulties are exaggerated. To hurdle the language barrier, bring a phrase book (or use the French Survival Phrases—later in this appendix), a small English/French dictionary, a menu reader, and a good supply of patience. In transactions, a small notepad and pen minimize misunderstandings about prices; have vendors write the price down.

Though many French people—especially those in the tourist trade, and in big cities—speak English, you'll get better treatment if you learn and use the French pleasantries. If you learn only five phrases, choose these: *bonjour* (good day), *pardon* (pardon me), *s'il vous plaît* (please), *merci* (thank you), and *au revoir* (good-bye). The French place great importance on politeness. Begin every encounter with *"Bonjour, madame* or *monsieur,"* or *"s'il vous plaît"* and end every encounter with *"Au revoir, madame* or *monsieur."*

The French are language perfectionists—they take their language (and other languages) seriously. Often they speak more English than they let on. This isn't a tourist-baiting tactic, but timidity on their part to speak another language less than fluently. Start any conversation with, *"Bonjour, madame* or *monsieur. Parlez-vous anglais?"* and hope they speak more English than you speak French.

have a good long-distance plan for calls to Europe—and a list of your hotels' phone numbers).

US Calling Cards: These cards, such as the ones offered by AT&T, Verizon, or Sprint, are the worst option. You'll nearly always save a lot of money by using a local phone card instead.

Mobile Phones

Many travelers enjoy the convenience of traveling with a mobile phone.

Using Your Mobile Phone: Your US mobile phone works in Europe if it's GSM-enabled, tri-band or quad-band, and on a calling plan that includes international calls. For example, with a T-Mobile phone, you'll pay $1 per minute to make or receive a call, and about $0.35 apiece for text messages.

You can save money if your phone is electronically "unlocked"—then you can simply buy a **SIM card** (a fingernail-sized chip that stores the phone's information) in Europe. SIM cards, which give you a European phone number, are sold at mobile-phone stores and some newsstand kiosks for about $5–10. When you buy the card you'll also buy some prepaid calling time (€25 buys about 30 minutes). Simply insert the SIM card in your phone (usually in a slot behind the battery), and it'll work like a European mobile phone. When buying a SIM card, always ask about fees for domestic and international calls, roaming charges, and how to check your credit balance and buy more time.

Many **smartphones**, such as the iPhone or BlackBerry, work in Europe—but beware of sky-high fees, especially for data downloading (checking email, browsing the Internet, watching videos, and so on). Ask your provider in advance how to avoid unwittingly "roaming" your way to a huge bill. Some applications allow for cheap or free smartphone calls over a Wi-Fi connection (see "Calling over the Internet," below).

Using a European Mobile Phone: Local mobile-phone shops all over Europe sell basic phones for around $50–100. You'll also need to buy a SIM card (explained above) and prepaid credit for making calls. If you remain in the phone's home country, domestic calls are reasonable and incoming calls are free. You'll pay more if you're "roaming" in another country. If your phone is "unlocked," you can swap out its SIM card for a new one in other countries.

For more information on mobile phones, see www.ricksteves.com/phones.

Calling over the Internet

Some things that seem too good to be true...actually are true. If you're traveling with a laptop, make calls using VoIP (Voice over Internet Protocol). With VoIP, two computers act as the phones, and the Internet-based calls are free (or you can pay a few cents to call from your computer to a telephone). The major providers are Skype (www.skype.com) and Google Talk (www.google.com/talk).

Useful Phone Numbers

Understand the various prefixes. France's toll-free numbers start with 0800 (like US 800 numbers, though in France you don't dial a 1 first). In France these 0800 numbers—called *numéro vert* (green number)—can be dialed free from any phone without using a phone card. But you can't call France's toll-free numbers from America, nor can you count on reaching America's toll-free numbers from France.

Any 08 number that does not have a 00 directly following is a toll call, generally costing €0.10–0.50 per minute.

Embassies and Consulates
US Consulate and Embassy: tel. 01 43 12 22 22, passport services available Mon–Fri 10:00–11:00, online appointments possible, closed Sat–Sun (4 avenue Gabriel, to the left as you face Hôtel Crillon, Mo: Concorde, http://france.usembassy.gov)
Canadian Consulate and Embassy: tel. 01 44 43 29 00, reception open daily 9:00–12:00 & 14:00–17:00 (35 avenue Montaigne, Mo: Franklin D. Roosevelt, www.amb-canada.fr)
Australian Consulate: tel. 01 40 59 33 00, Mon–Fri 9:00–17:00, closed Sat–Sun (4 rue Jean Rey, Mo: Bir-Hakeim, www.france .embassy.gov.au)

Emergency Needs
Police: tel. 17
Emergency Medical Assistance: tel. 15
American Hospital: tel. 01 46 41 25 25 (63 boulevard Victor Hugo, in Neuilly suburb, Mo: Porte Maillot, then bus #82)
Ambulance: tel. 01 45 67 50 50 (message asks for your address and name)
English-Speaking Pharmacy (Pharmacie les Champs): tel. 01 45 62 02 41, open 24 hours every day of the year (84 avenue des Champs-Elysées, Mo: Georges V)
SOS Doctors: tel. 01 47 07 77 77 or toll tel. 08 20 33 24 24
SOS Help: tel. 01 46 21 46 46 (anonymous telephone hotline with crisis/suicide prevention listening service in English, daily 15:00–23:00)
SOS Dentist: tel. 01 43 37 51 00
Chiropractic Centers: tel. 01 43 54 26 25 or 01 43 87 81 62
Lost Property (Bureau des Objets Trouvés, at police station): tel. 08 21 00 25 25, €0.12/min, open Tue and Thu 8:30–20:00 (36 rue des Morillons, Mo: Convention)

Travel Advisories
US Department of State: tel. 202/647-5225, www.travel.state.gov
Canadian Department of Foreign Affairs: Canadian tel. 800-267-6788, www.dfait-maeci.gc.ca
US Centers for Disease Control and Prevention: tel. 800-CDC-INFO (800-232-4636), www.cdc.gov/travel

Directory Assistance
Directory Assistance for Paris and France (some English spoken): tel. 12
Collect Calls to the US: tel. 00 00 11

Tourist Info, Transportation, and Banking
Paris Tourist Information: toll tel. 08 92 68 30 00 (recorded info

with long menu, €0.34/min)

Ile de France Tourist Information (covers Paris area, including Fontainebleau, Vaux-le-Vicomte, and Chantilly): tel. 01 42 60 28 62

Booking Service (for hotels, transportation, restaurants, and other tourist activities): tel. 01 53 62 02 29 for **Paris Webservices** (111 avenue Victor Hugo, www.pariswebservices.com, contactpws @pariswebservices.com, helpful Gérard)

Taxis: tel. 01 47 39 47 39

Airports
Charles de Gaulle and Orly: toll tel. 3950 (€0.34/min), www.adp .fr

Beauvais: toll tel. 08 92 68 20 66, www.aeroportbeauvais.com

Airlines
Aer Lingus: toll tel. 08 21 23 02 67

Air Canada: toll tel. 08 25 88 08 81

Air France: tel. 3654 or toll tel. 08 20 82 36 54

Alitalia: toll tel. 08 20 31 53 15

American Airlines: tel. 01 55 17 43 41

Austrian Airlines: toll tel. 08 02 81 68 16

BMI British Midlands: toll tel. 08 90 71 00 81

British Airways: toll tel. 08 25 82 54 00

Continental: tel. 01 71 23 03 35

Delta: toll tel. 08 11 64 00 05

Easy Jet: toll tel. 08 26 10 33 20

Iberia: toll tel. 08 25 80 09 65

Icelandair: tel. 01 44 51 60 51

KLM: toll tel. 08 92 70 26 08

Lufthansa: toll tel. 08 92 23 16 90

Northwest: toll tel. 08 92 70 26 08

Olympic: tel. 01 44 94 58 58

Royal Air Maroc: toll tel. 08 20 82 18 21

SAS: toll tel. 08 25 32 53 35

Swiss International: toll tel. 08 92 23 25 01

United: toll tel. 08 10 72 72 72

US Airways: toll tel. 08 10 63 22 22

Hotel Chains
Huge Chain of Hotels: www.accorhotels.com (handles Ibis, Mercure, and Novotel hotels), US tel. 800-221-4542

Ibis Hotels: www.ibishotel.com, tel. 08 92 68 66 86, US tel. 800-221-4542

Mercure Hotels: www.mercure.com, toll tel. 08 25 88 33 33, US tel. 800-221-4542

Kyriad Hotels: www.kyriad.com, toll tel. 08 25 02 80 38; from US, dial 011 33 1 64 62 59 70
Best Western Hotels: www.bestwestern.com, tel. 08 00 90 44 90, US tel. 800-780-7234
Country Home Rental: www.gites-de-france.fr/eng or www.gite.com

Youth Hostels
Hostelling International, US Office: www.hiayh.org
Hostelling International, Canada Office: www.hostellingintl.ca

English-Language Churches in Paris
American Church (interdenominational): tel. 01 40 62 05 00, reception open Mon–Sat 9:30–13:00 & 14:00–22:30, Sun 9:00–14:00 & 15:00–19:00 (65 quai d'Orsay, Mo: Invalides, www.acparis.org; for more information, see page 25)
American Cathedral (Episcopalian): tel. 01 53 23 84 00 (23 avenue George V, Mo. George V, www.americancathedral.org)
Unitarian Universalist Fellowship: tel. 01 30 82 75 33 (7 bis rue du Pasteur Wagner, Mo: Bastille, www.uufp.info)
Scots Kirk (Church of Scotland): tel. 01 40 70 09 59 (17 rue Bayard, Mo: Franklin D. Roosevelt, www.scotskirkparis.com)
St. George's Anglican Church: tel. 01 47 20 22 51 (7 rue Auguste Vacquerie, www.stgeorgesparis.com)
St. Joseph's Church (Roman Catholic): tel. 01 42 27 28 56 (50 avenue Hoche, www.stjoeparis.org)
St. Michael's Church (Anglican): tel. 01 47 42 70 88 (5 rue d'Aguesseau, Mo: Concorde or Madeleine, www.saintmichaelsparis.com)

Multi-Subject Classes in English
WICE: tel. 01 45 66 75 50, offers a variety of well-run short- and longer-term classes in English on art, food, and more (20 boulevard du Montparnasse, www.wice-paris.org)

French-Language Classes
Ecole France Langue: tel. 01 45 00 40 15, provides intensive classes on weekly basis with business-language options (www.france-langue.fr)
Institut Parisien: tel. 01 40 56 09 53, offers general conversational courses (www.institut-parisien.com)
OISE: tel. 01 42 22 01 98, has total-immersion French classes (www.oise.com/paris)
Le Français Face à Face: tel. 06 66 60 00 63, runs intensive French courses with total immersion and full-board options (www.lefrancaisfaceaface.com)

Cooking Schools

These schools have demonstration courses:

Le Cordon Bleu: tel. 01 53 68 22 50 (8 Rue Léon Delhomme, www.lcbparis.com)

Ritz Escoffier Ecole de Gastronomie: tel. 01 43 16 30 50 (15 place Vendôme, Mo: Madeleine, www.ritzparis.com)

Ecole Superieure de Cuisine Francaise: tel. 01 45 27 09 09 (www .escf.ccip.fr)

These schools are more relaxed:

Marguerite's Cooking Courses: tel. 01 42 04 74 00 (www .elegantcooking.com)

Cook'n with Class: Convivial cooking and wine-and-cheese classes with a maximum of six students, tasting courses offered as well (tel. 06 31 73 62 77, www.cooknwithclass.com)

Wine Tasting

Ô Château: tel 08 00 80 11 48 (fun and informative, €20 one-hour class, €65 for wine-and-cheese lunch, at private apartment in Paris, www.o-chateau.com, young and enthusiastic Olivier Magny)

The Internet

The Internet can be an invaluable tool for planning your trip (researching and booking hotels, checking train schedules, and so on). It's also useful to get online periodically as you travel— to reconfirm your trip plans, check the weather, catch up on email, blog or post photos from your trip, or call folks back home (explained earlier, under "Calling over the Internet").

Many hotels offer a computer in the lobby with Internet access for guests. Smaller places may sometimes let you sit at their desk for a few minutes just to check your email, if you ask politely. For those traveling with a laptop, your hotel may have Wi-Fi (wireless Internet access, pronounced "wee-fee" by the French) or a port in your room for plugging in a cable to get online. Some hotels offer internet access an/or Wi-Fi for free; others charge a fee.

If your hotel doesn't have access, ask your hotelier to direct you to the nearest place to get online. Paris has plenty of coffee shops offering Wi-Fi to travelers with laptop computers. Little hole-in-the-wall Internet-access shops, though common in the rest of Europe, are not prevalent in France. Post offices are a good solution in smaller towns offering Internet access *(cyberposte)*; buy a chip-card (for about same prices as phone cards) and you're in business.

Mail

French post offices are sometimes called PTT, for "Post, Telegraph, and Telephone"—look for signs for *La Poste*. Hours vary, though most are open weekdays 8:00–19:00 and Saturday morning 8:00–12:00. Stamps and phone cards are also sold at *tabac* (tobacco) shops. It costs about €1 to mail a postcard to the US. Federal Express makes pricey two-day deliveries. One convenient, if pricey, way to send packages home is by using the PTT's Colissimo XL postage-paid mailing box. It costs about €33 for the International version, which allows you to send home all the goodies you can stuff into an 18" × 12" × 8" box (no weight limit).

You can arrange for mail delivery to your hotel (allow 10 days for a letter to arrive), but phoning and emailing are so easy that I've dispensed with mail stops altogether.

Resources

Resources from Rick Steves

Rick Steves Paris 2010 is one of more than 30 titles in a series of **books** on European travel, which includes country guidebooks

(including France), city and regional guidebooks (including Provence and the French Riviera), and my budget-travel skills handbook, *Rick Steves' Europe Through the Back Door.* My phrase books—for French, Italian, German, Spanish, and Portuguese—are practical and budget-oriented. My other books are *Europe 101* (a crash course on art and history, newly expanded and in full color), *Travel as a Political Act* (a travelogue sprinkled with tips for bringing home a global perspective), *European Christmas* (on traditional and modern-day celebrations),

and *Postcards from Europe* (a fun memoir of my travels). For a complete list of my books, see the inside of the last page of this book.

My **TV series,** *Rick Steves' Europe,* covers European destinations in 100 shows, with nine episodes on France. My weekly public **radio show,** *Travel with Rick Steves,* features interviews with travel experts from around the world, including several hours on France and French culture. All the TV scripts and radio shows (which are easy and free to download to an iPod or other MP3 player) are at www.rick steves.com.

Take advantage of my free, self-guided **audio tours** of the Louvre, Orsay, Versailles, and Historic Paris. Simply download them from www.rick steves.com or iTunes (search for "Rick Steves' tours" in the iTunes Store), then

Begin Your Trip at www.ricksteves.com

At our travel website you'll find a wealth of free information on European destinations, including fresh monthly news and helpful tips from thousands of fellow travelers. You'll also find my latest guidebook updates (www.ricksteves.com/update) and my travel blog.

Our **online Travel Store** offers travel bags and accessories specially designed by Rick Steves to help you travel smarter and lighter. These include Rick's popular carry-on bags (roll-aboard and rucksack versions), money belts, totes, toiletries kits, adapters, other accessories, and a wide selection of guidebooks, planning maps, and DVDs.

Choosing the right **railpass** for your trip—amidst hundreds of options—can drive you nutty. We'll help you choose the best pass for your needs, plus give you a bunch of free extras.

Rick Steves' Europe Through the Back Door travel company offers **tours** with more than three dozen itineraries and more than 300 departures reaching the best destinations in this book...and beyond. We offer several tours that include Paris, such as our 7-day in-depth Paris city tour, our 11-day Paris and the Heart of France tour (focusing on the best of the north), our 13-day Villages and Vineyards of Eastern France tour, and our 15-day Paris and the South of France tour. You'll enjoy great guides, a fun bunch of travel partners (with small groups of around 28), and plenty of room to spread out in a big, comfy bus. You'll find European adventures to fit every vacation length. For all the details, and to get our Tour Catalog and a free Rick Steves Tour Experience DVD (filmed on location during an actual tour), visit www.ricksteves.com or call the Tour Department at 425/608-4217.

transfer them to your iPod or other MP3 player. If your travels take you beyond Paris, we also offer audio tours of the major sights in Florence, Rome, Venice, and London.

Interactive versions of my favorite Paris tours are for sale as iPhone apps on iTunes (for details, see www.ricksteves.com /iphonesupport).

Maps

The black-and-white maps in this book, drawn by Dave Hoerlein, are concise and simple. Dave is well-traveled in Paris and has designed these maps to help you get oriented quickly. The color city maps and Métro map at the front of this book are also useful.

Though Paris is littered with free maps, they don't show all the streets. For an extended stay, I prefer the pocket-size, street-indexed *Paris Pratique* or Michelin's *Paris par Arrondissement* (each about €6, sold at newsstands and bookstores in Paris). Before you buy a map, look at it to be sure it has the level of detail you want.

Other Guidebooks

If you're like most travelers, this book is all you need. But if you'll be exploring beyond my recommended neighborhoods and destinations, $30 for extra maps and books can be money well spent.

The following books are worthwhile, though are not updated annually; check the publication date before you buy. The readable *Paris Access* guide and the more scholarly *Michelin Green Guide* are informative. Also recommended are *Paris: The Collected Traveler* (Barrie Kerper) and *The Paris Mapguide* (Michael Middleditch). Of the multitude of other guidebooks on France and Paris, many are high on facts and low on opinion, guts, or personality.

If you'll be traveling elsewhere in France, consider *Rick Steves' France 2010* or *Rick Steves' Provence and the French Riviera 2010*.

Recommended Books and Movies

To get the feel for Paris past and present, check out a few of these books or films.

Nonfiction

For a better understanding of French politics, culture, and people, check out *Sixty Million Frenchmen Can't Be Wrong* (Nadeau and Barlow), *Culture Shock: France* (Taylor), *French or Foe*, and *Savoir-Flair!* (both by Polly Platt). *The Course of French History* (Goubert) provides a basic summary of French history, while *The Cambridge Illustrated History of France* (Jones) comes with coffee-table-book pictures and illustrations.

A Moveable Feast is Ernest Hemingway's classic memoir of 1920s Paris. In *I'll Always Have Paris*, Art Buchwald meets

Hemingway, among others. *Suite Française* (Nemirovsky) is by a Jewish writer who eloquently describes how life changed after the Nazi occupation. *Is Paris Burning?* (Collins) brings late-WWII Paris to life on its pages. *Americans in Paris: Life and Death under Nazi Occupation* is a fascinating read (Glass). *Paris Noir: African Americans in the City of Light* (Stovall) explains why African Americans found Paris so freeing in the first half of the 20th century.

Paris to the Moon is Adam Gopnik's charming collection of stories about life as a New Yorker in Paris (his literary anthology, *Americans in Paris*, is also recommended). *A Corner in the Marais* (Karmel) is a detailed account of one Parisian neighborhood; Diane Johnson's *Into a Paris Quartier* tells tales about the sixth arrondissement. The memoir *The Piano Shop on the Left Bank* (Carhart) captures Paris' sentimental appeal. *Almost French* (Turnbull) is a funny take on living as a Parisian native. Reading *The Flaneur* is like wandering with author Edmund White through his favorite finds. *The Authentic Bistros of Paris* (Thomazeau), a pretty picture book, will have you longing for a *croque monsieur*. A mix of writers explore Parisian culture in *Travelers Tales: Paris* (O'Reilly).

Fiction

Dickens' *A Tale of Two Cities* shows the pathos and horror of the French Revolution, as does Victor Hugo's *Les Misérables* (his *The Hunchback of Notre-Dame* is also set in Paris).

The anthology *A Place in the World Called Paris* (Barclay) includes essays by literary greats from Truman Capote to Franz Kafka. The characters in Marge Piercy's *City of Darkness, City of Light* storm the Bastille. And though it relies on some stereotypes, *A Year in the Merde* (Clarke) is a lighthearted look at life as a *faux* Parisian.

Georges Simenon was a Belgian, but he often set his *Inspector Maigret* detective series in Paris; *The Hotel Majestic* is particularly good. Mystery fans should also consider *Murder in Montparnasse* (Engel), *Murder in the Marais* (Black), and *Sandman* (Janes), set in Vichy-era Paris. Alan Furst writes gripping novels about WWII espionage that put you right into the action in Paris.

For children, there's the beloved *Madeline* series (Bemelmans), where "in an old house in Paris that was covered with vines, lived twelve little girls in two straight lines." Kids of all ages enjoy the whimsical and colorful impressions of the city in Miroslav Sasek's classic picture-book *This Is Paris*.

Films

Children of Paradise (1946), a melancholy romance, was filmed during the Nazi occupation of Paris. In *The Red Balloon* (1956), a small boy chases his balloon through the city streets, symbolizing that beauty can be found even in the simplest toy. *The 400 Blows* (1959) and *Jules and Jim* (1962) are both classics of French New Wave cinema by director François Truffaut. *Charade* (1963) combines a romance between Audrey Hepburn and Cary Grant with a crime story.

Blue/White/Red (1990s) is a stylish trilogy of films, each featuring a famous French actress as the lead (*Blue*, with Juliette Binoche, is the best of the three). *Ridicule* (1996), set in the opulent court of Louis XVI, shows that survival then depended on a quick wit and an acid tongue. In the crime caper *Ronin* (1998), Robert De Niro and Jean Reno lead a car chase through the city.

Moulin Rouge! (2001) is a fanciful musical set in the legendary Montmartre night club. *Amélie* (2001), a crowd-pleasing romance, features a charming young waitress searching for love and the meaning of life. No Disney flick, *The Triplets of Belleville* (2003) is a surreal, creepy-yet-heartwarming animated film that begins in a very Parisian fictional city.

For over-the-top, schlocky fun, watch *The Phantom of the Opera* (2004), about a disfigured musical genius hiding in the Paris Opera House, and *The Da Vinci Code* (2006), a blockbuster murder mystery partly filmed inside the Louvre.

If you'll be heading to Versailles, try *Marie Antoinette* (2006), a delicate little bonbon of a film about the misunderstood queen.

Holidays and Festivals

Holidays and Festivals in Paris

Paris is lively with festivals throughout the summer and fall. Kicking off the season in late May is the month-long **Festival of St. Denis** in that Parisian suburb, featuring musicians from around the world at various venues (tel. 01 48 13 06 07, www.festival-saint -denis.fr).

Paris celebrates the solstice (June 21) with its **Music Festival** (Fête de la Musique), staging concerts throughout the city.

In late July the **Tour de France** bicycle race ends on the Champs-Elysées (www.letour.fr). **Bastille Day,** France's National Day (July 14), brings fireworks, dancing, and revelry countrywide (see sidebar on page 283).

From mid-July to mid-August, the **Paris Neighborhoods Festival** features theater, dance, and concerts around the city. At the same time, the fun **Paris Plage,** a riverside ersatz beach, is set up in the middle of the city (see page 50).

La Villette Jazz Festival brings a week of outdoor jazz concerts to this Parisian park in early- to mid-September. The first Saturday of October Montmartre celebrates the **grape harvest**

2010

JANUARY
S	M	T	W	T	F	S
					1	2
3	4	5	6	7	8	9
10	11	12	13	14	15	16
17	18	19	20	21	22	23
24/31	25	26	27	28	29	30

FEBRUARY
S	M	T	W	T	F	S
1	2	3	4	5	6	
7	8	9	10	11	12	13
14	15	16	17	18	19	20
21	22	23	24	25	26	27
28						

MARCH
S	M	T	W	T	F	S
	1	2	3	4	5	6
7	8	9	10	11	12	13
14	15	16	17	18	19	20
21	22	23	24	25	26	27
28	29	30	31			

APRIL
S	M	T	W	T	F	S
				1	2	3
4	5	6	7	8	9	10
11	12	13	14	15	16	17
18	19	20	21	22	23	24
25	26	27	28	29	30	

MAY
S	M	T	W	T	F	S
						1
2	3	4	5	6	7	8
9	10	11	12	13	14	15
16	17	18	19	20	21	22
23/30	24/31	25	26	27	28	29

JUNE
S	M	T	W	T	F	S
		1	2	3	4	5
6	7	8	9	10	11	12
13	14	15	16	17	18	19
20	21	22	23	24	25	26
27	28	29	30			

JULY
S	M	T	W	T	F	S
				1	2	3
4	5	6	7	8	9	10
11	12	13	14	15	16	17
18	19	20	21	22	23	24
25	26	27	28	29	30	31

AUGUST
S	M	T	W	T	F	S
1	2	3	4	5	6	7
8	9	10	11	12	13	14
15	16	17	18	19	20	21
22	23	24	25	26	27	28
29	30	31				

SEPTEMBER
S	M	T	W	T	F	S
			1	2	3	4
5	6	7	8	9	10	11
12	13	14	15	16	17	18
19	20	21	22	23	24	25
26	27	28	29	30		

OCTOBER
S	M	T	W	T	F	S
					1	2
3	4	5	6	7	8	9
10	11	12	13	14	15	16
17	18	19	20	21	22	23
24/31	25	26	27	28	29	30

NOVEMBER
S	M	T	W	T	F	S
	1	2	3	4	5	6
7	8	9	10	11	12	13
14	15	16	17	18	19	20
21	22	23	24	25	26	27
28	29	30				

DECEMBER
S	M	T	W	T	F	S
		1	2	3	4	
5	6	7	8	9	10	11
12	13	14	15	16	17	18
19	20	21	22	23	24	25
26	27	28	29	30	31	

with a parade and festivities. The **Festival of Autumn** (www .festival-automne.com) runs through autumn, with theater, dance, film, and opera performances.

For more information, check the websites www.parisinfo.com and www.franceguide.com.

French Holidays in 2010

These national holidays (when many sights close) are observed throughout France. Note that this isn't a complete list; holidays can strike without warning.

Jan 1	New Year's Day
Jan 6	Epiphany
April 4	Easter Sunday
April 5	Easter Monday
May 1	Labor Day
May 8	V-E Day

May 13	Ascension
May 23	Pentecost
July 14	Bastille Day
Aug 15	Assumption of Mary
Nov 1	All Saints' Day
Nov 11	Armistice Day
Dec 25	Christmas Day

Conversions and Climate

Numbers and Stumblers

- Europeans write a few of their numbers differently than we do. 1 = 1, 4 = 4, 7 = 7.
- In Europe dates appear as day/month/year, so Christmas is 25/12/10.
- Commas are decimal points and decimals commas. A dollar and a half is 1,50, and there are 5.280 feet in a mile.
- When pointing, use your whole hand, palm down.
- When counting with fingers, start with your thumb. If you hold up your first finger to request one item, you'll probably get two.
- What Americans call the second floor of a building is the first floor in Europe.
- On escalators and moving sidewalks, Europeans keep the left "lane" open for passing. Keep to the right.

Metric Conversions (approximate)

A kilogram is 2.2 pounds, and 1 liter is about a quart, or almost four to a gallon. A kilometer is six-tenths of a mile. I figure kilometers to miles by cutting them in half and adding back 10 percent of the original (120 km: 60 + 12 = 72 miles, 300 km: 150 + 30 = 180 miles).

1 foot = 0.3 meter	1 square yard = 0.8 square meter
1 yard = 0.9 meter	1 square mile = 2.6 square kilometers
1 mile = 1.6 kilometers	1 ounce = 28 grams
1 centimeter = 0.4 inch	1 quart = 0.95 liter
1 meter = 39.4 inches	1 kilogram = 2.2 pounds
1 kilometer = 0.62 mile	32°F = 0°C

Clothing Sizes

When shopping for clothing, use these US-to-European comparisons as general guidelines (but note that no conversion is perfect):

- Women's dresses and blouses: Add 30 (US size 10 = European size 40)
- Men's suits and jackets: Add 10 (US size 40 regular = European size 50)

- Men's shirts: Multiply by 2 and add about 8 (US size 15 collar = European size 38)
- Women's shoes: Add about 30 (US size 8 = European size 38½)
- Men's shoes: Add 32–34 (US size 9 = European size 41; US size 11 = European size 45)

Paris' Climate

First line, average daily high; second line, average daily low; third line, days of no rain. For more detailed weather statistics for destinations in this book (as well as the rest of the world), check www.worldclimate.com.

J	F	M	A	M	J	J	A	S	O	N	D
43°	45°	54°	60°	68°	73°	76°	75°	70°	60°	50°	44°
34°	34°	39°	43°	49°	55°	58°	58°	53°	46°	40°	36°
14	14	19	17	19	18	19	18	17	18	15	15

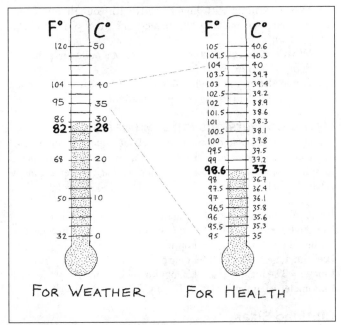

FOR WEATHER   FOR HEALTH

Temperature Conversion: Fahrenheit and Celsius

Europe takes its temperature using the Celsius scale, while we opt for Fahrenheit. For a rough conversion from Celsius to Fahrenheit, double the number and add 30. For weather, remember that 28°C is 82°F—perfect. For health, 37°C is just right.

Essential Packing Checklist

Whether you're traveling for five days or five weeks, here's what you'll need to bring. Remember to pack light to enjoy the sweet freedom of true mobility. Happy travels!

- ❑ 5 shirts
- ❑ 1 sweater or lightweight fleece jacket
- ❑ 2 pairs pants
- ❑ 1 pair shorts
- ❑ 1 swimsuit (women only—men can use shorts)
- ❑ 5 pairs underwear and socks
- ❑ 1 pair shoes
- ❑ 1 rainproof jacket
- ❑ Tie or scarf
- ❑ Money belt
- ❑ Money—your mix of:
  - ❑ Debit card for ATM withdrawals
  - ❑ Credit card
  - ❑ Hard cash in US dollars ($20 bills)
- ❑ Documents (and back-up photocopies)
- ❑ Passport
- ❑ Printout of airline e-ticket
- ❑ Driver's license
- ❑ Student ID and hostel card
- ❑ Railpass/car rental voucher
- ❑ Insurance details
- ❑ Daypack
- ❑ Sealable plastic baggies
- ❑ Camera and related gear
- ❑ Empty water bottle
- ❑ Wristwatch and alarm clock
- ❑ Earplugs
- ❑ First-aid kit
- ❑ Medicine (labeled)
- ❑ Extra glasses/contacts and prescriptions
- ❑ Sunscreen and sunglasses
- ❑ Toiletries kit
- ❑ Soap
- ❑ Laundry soap
- ❑ Clothesline
- ❑ Small towel
- ❑ Sewing kit
- ❑ Travel information
- ❑ Necessary map(s)
- ❑ Address list (email and mailing addresses)
- ❑ Postcards and photos from home
- ❑ Notepad and pen
- ❑ Journal

If you plan to carry on your luggage, note that all liquids must be in three-ounce or smaller containers and fit within a single quart-size baggie. For details, see www.tsa.gov/travelers.

Hotel Reservation

To: _____   _____
                hotel   *email or fax*

From: _____   _____
                name   *email or fax*

Today's date: _____ /_____ /_____
                    day   *month*   *year*

Dear Hotel _____ ,
Please make this reservation for me:

Name: _____

Total # of people: _____   # of rooms: _____   # of nights: _____

Arriving: _____ /_____ /_____   My time of arrival (24-hr clock): _____
              day *month* *year*   (I will telephone if I will be late)

Departing: _____ /_____ /_____
                day *month* *year*

Room(s): Single____   Double ____   Twin ____   Triple ____   Quad____

With: Toilet ____   Shower____   Bath ____   Sink only____

Special needs: View____   Quiet____   Cheapest ____   Ground Floor____

Please email or fax confirmation of my reservation, along with the type of room reserved and the price. Please also inform me of your cancellation policy. After I hear from you, I will quickly send my credit-card information as a deposit to hold the room. Thank you.

_____
Name

_____
Address

_____
City   *State*   *Zip Code*   *Country*

Before hoteliers can make your reservation, they want to know the information listed above. You can use this form as the basis for your email, or you can photocopy this page, fill in the information, and send it as a fax (also available online at www.ricksteves.com/reservation).

French Pronunciation Guide for Paris

Nasalize the underlined "n" if you can (let the sound come through your nose).

Arc de Triomphe ark duh tree-oh<u>n</u>f

arrondissement ah-roh<u>n</u>-dees-moh<u>n</u>

Art Nouveau art noo-voh

Auvers-sur-Oise oh-vehr-sur-wahz

Bateaux Mouches bah-toh moosh

Bon Marché boh<u>n</u> mar-chay

boulangerie boo-lah<u>n</u>-zheh-ree

Carnavalet kar-nah-val-eh

Champ de Mars shah<u>n</u> duh mar

Champs-Elysées shah<u>n</u>-zay-lee-zay

Chantilly shah<u>n</u>-tee-yee

charcuterie shar-koo-tuh-ree

Chartres shar-truh

château(x) shah-toh

Cité see-tay

Cité des Sciences see-tay day see-ah<u>n</u>s

Conciergerie kon-see-ehr-zhuh-ree

Contrescarpe koh<u>n</u>-truh-scarp

droguerie droh-guh-ree

Ecole Militaire eh-kohl mee-lee-tehr

Egouts ay-goo

Fauchon foh-shoh<u>n</u>

Fontainebleau foh<u>n</u>-tehn-bloh

fromagerie froh-mah-zhuh-ree

Galeries Lafayette gah-luh-ree lah-fay-yet

gare gar

Gare d'Austerlitz gar doh-stehr-leets

Gare de l'Est gar duh lest

Gare de Lyon gar duh lee-oh<u>n</u>

Gare du Nord gar dew nor

Gare St. Lazare gar sah<u>n</u> lah-zar

Garnier gar-nee-ay

Giverny zhee-vehr-nee

Grand Palais grah<u>n</u> pah-lay

Grande Arche de la Défense grah<u>n</u>d arsh duh lah day-fah<u>n</u>s

Hôtel de Sully oh-tehl duh soo-lee

Hôtel Salé oh-tehl sah-lay

Ile de la Cité eel duh lah see-tay

Ile St. Louis eel sah<u>n</u> loo-ee

Jacquemart-André zhahk-mar-ah<u>n</u>-dray

jardin zhar-da<u>n</u>

Jardin des Plantes zhar-da<u>n</u> day plahnt

Jeu de Paume juh duh pohm

La Madeleine lah mah-duh-lehn

La Marseillaise lah mar-seh-yehz

Le Hameau luh ah-moh

Les Halles lay ahl

Les Invalides lay-za<u>n</u>-vah-leed

Loire lwar

L'Orangerie loh-rah<u>n</u>-zhuh-ree

Louvre loov-ruh

Marais mah-ray

marché aux puces mar-chay oh poos

Marmottan mar-moh-tah<u>n</u>

Métro may-troh

Monge moh<u>n</u>zh

Montmartre moh<u>n</u>-mart

Montparnasse moh<u>n</u>-par-nas

Moulin Rouge moo-la<u>n</u> roozh

musée mew-zay

Musée de l'Armée mew-zay duh lar-may

Musée d'Orsay mew-zay dor-say

Notre-Dame noh-truh-dahm

orangerie oh-rah<u>n</u>-zhuh-ree

Orsay or-say

palais pah-lay

Palais de Justice pah-lay duh zhew-stees

Palais Garnier pah-lay gar-nee-ay

Palais Royal pah-lay roh-yahl
Parc de la Villette park duh la vee-leht
Parc Monceau park mohn-soh
Père Lachaise pehr lah-shehz
Petit Palais puh-tee pah-lay
Pigalle pee-gahl
place plahs
Place Dauphine plahs doh-feen
Place de la Bastille plahs duh lah bah-steel
Place de la Concorde plahs duh lah kohn-kord
Place de la République plahs duh lah ray-poo-bleek
Place des Vosges plahs day vohzh
Place du Tertre plahs dew tehr-truh
Place St. André-des-Arts plahs sahn tahn-dray day zart
Place Vendôme plahs vahn-dohm
Pompidou pohn-pee-doo
pont pohn
Pont Alexandre III pohn ah-leks-ahn-druh twah
Pont Neuf pohn nuhf
Promenade Plantée proh-mehn-ahd plahn-tay
quai kay
Rive Droite reeve dwaht
Rive Gauche reeve gohsh

Rodin roh-dan
rue rew
Rue Cler rew klehr
Rue Daguerre rew dah-gehr
Rue des Rosiers rew day roz-ee-ay
Rue Montorgueil rew mohn-tor-goy
Rue Mouffetard rew moof-tar
Rue de Rivoli rew duh ree-voh-lee
Sacré-Cœur sah-kray-koor
Sainte-Chapelle sahnt-shah-pehl
Seine sehn
Sèvres-Babylone seh-vruh-bah-bee-lohn
Sorbonne sor-buhn
St. Germain-des-Prés sahn zhehr-man-day-pray
St. Julien-le-Pauvre sahn zhew-lee-an-luh-poh-vruh
St. Séverin sahn say-vuh-ran
St. Sulpice sahn sool-pees
Tour Eiffel toor ee-fehl
Trianon tree-ahn-ohn
Trocadéro troh-kah-day-roh
Tuileries twee-lay-ree
Vaux-le-Vicomte voh-luh-vee-kohnt
Venus de Milo vuh-news duh mee-loh
Versailles vehr-"sigh"

APPENDIX

French Survival Phrases

When using the phonetics, try to nasalize the <u>n</u> sound.

Good day.	**Bonjour.**	boh<u>n</u>-zhoor
Mrs. / Mr.	**Madame / Monsieur**	mah-dahm / muhs-yur
Do you speak English?	**Parlez-vous anglais?**	par-lay-voo ah<u>n</u>-glay
Yes. / No.	**Oui. / Non.**	wee / noh<u>n</u>
I understand.	**Je comprends.**	zhuh koh<u>n</u>-prah<u>n</u>
I don't understand.	**Je ne comprends pas.**	zhuh nuh koh<u>n</u>-prah<u>n</u> pah
Please.	**S'il vous plaît.**	see voo play
Thank you.	**Merci.**	mehr-see
I'm sorry.	**Désolé.**	day-zoh-lay
Excuse me.	**Pardon.**	par-doh<u>n</u>
(No) problem.	**(Pas de) problème.**	(pah duh) proh-blehm
It's good.	**C'est bon.**	say boh<u>n</u>
Goodbye.	**Au revoir.**	oh vwahr
one / two	**un / deux**	uh<u>n</u> / duh
three / four	**trois / quatre**	twah / kah-truh
five / six	**cinq / six**	sa<u>n</u>k / sees
seven / eight	**sept / huit**	seht / weet
nine / ten	**neuf / dix**	nuhf / dees
How much is it?	**Combien?**	koh<u>n</u>-bee-a<u>n</u>
Write it?	**Ecrivez?**	ay-kree-vay
Is it free?	**C'est gratuit?**	say grah-twee
Included?	**Inclus?**	a<u>n</u>-klew
Where can I buy / find...?	**Où puis-je acheter / trouver...?**	oo pwee-zhuh ah-shuh-tay / troo-vay
I'd like / We'd like...	**Je voudrais / Nous voudrions...**	zhuh voo-dray / noo voo-dree-oh<u>n</u>
...a room.	**...une chambre.**	ewn shah<u>n</u>-bruh
...a ticket to ___.	**...un billet pour ___.**	uh<u>n</u> bee-yay poor
Is it possible?	**C'est possible?**	say poh-see-bluh
Where is...?	**Où est...?**	oo ay
...the train station	**...la gare**	lah gar
...the bus station	**...la gare routière**	lah gar root-yehr
...tourist information	**...l'office du tourisme**	loh-fees dew too-reez-muh
Where are the toilets?	**Où sont les toilettes?**	oo soh<u>n</u> lay twah-leht
men	**hommes**	ohm
women	**dames**	dahm
left / right	**à gauche / à droite**	ah gohsh / ah dwaht
straight	**tout droit**	too dwah
When does this open / close?	**Ça ouvre / ferme à quelle heure?**	sah oo-vruh / fehrm ah kehl ur
At what time?	**À quelle heure?**	ah kehl ur
Just a moment.	**Un moment.**	uh<u>n</u> moh-mah<u>n</u>
now / soon / later	**maintenant / bientôt / plus tard**	ma<u>n</u>-tuh-nah<u>n</u> / bee-a<u>n</u>-toh / plew tar
today / tomorrow	**aujourd'hui / demain**	oh-zhoor-dwee / duh-ma<u>n</u>

APPENDIX

In the Restaurant

English	French	Pronunciation
I'd like / We'd like...	Je voudrais / Nous voudrions...	zhuh voo-dray / noo voo-dree-ohn
...to reserve...	...réserver...	ray-zehr-vay
...a table for one / two.	...une table pour un / deux.	ewn tah-bluh poor uhn / duh
Non-smoking.	Non fumeur.	nohn few-mur
Is this seat free?	C'est libre?	say lee-bruh
The menu (in English), please.	La carte (en anglais), s'il vous plaît.	lah kart (ahn ahn-glay) see voo play
service (not) included	service (non) compris	sehr-vees (nohn) kohn-pree
to go	à emporter	ah ahn-por-tay
with / without	avec / sans	ah-vehk / sahn
and / or	et / ou	ay / oo
special of the day	plat du jour	plah dew zhoor
specialty of the house	spécialité de la maison	spay-see-ah-lee-tay duh lah may-zohn
appetizers	hors-d'oeuvre	or-duh-vruh
first course (soup, salad)	entrée	ahn-tray
main course (meat, fish)	plat principal	plah pran-see-pahl
bread	pain	pan
cheese	fromage	froh-mahzh
sandwich	sandwich	sahnd-weech
soup	soupe	soop
salad	salade	sah-lahd
meat	viande	vee-ahnd
chicken	poulet	poo-lay
fish	poisson	pwah-sohn
seafood	fruits de mer	frwee duh mehr
fruit	fruit	frwee
vegetables	légumes	lay-gewm
dessert	dessert	duh-sehr
mineral water	eau minérale	oh mee-nay-rahl
tap water	l'eau du robinet	loh dew roh-bee-nay
milk	lait	lay
(orange) juice	jus (d'orange)	zhew (doh-rahnzh)
coffee	café	kah-fay
tea	thé	tay
wine	vin	van
red / white	rouge / blanc	roozh / blahn
glass / bottle	verre / bouteille	vehr / boo-teh-ee
beer	bière	bee-ehr
Cheers!	Santé!	sahn-tay
More. / Another.	Plus. / Un autre.	plew / uhn oh-truh
The same.	La même chose.	lah mehm shohz
The bill, please.	L'addition, s'il vous plaît.	lah-dee-see-ohn see voo play
tip	pourboire	poor-bwar
Delicious!	Délicieux!	day-lee-see-uh

For more user-friendly French phrases, check out *Rick Steves' French Phrase Book and Dictionary* or *Rick Steves' French, Italian & German Phrase Book*.

INDEX

INDEX

MAP INDEX

▶ Plan Your Trip

Browse thousands of articles and a wealth of money-saving tips for planning your dream trip. You'll find up-to-date information on Europe's best destinations, packing smart, getting around, finding rooms, staying healthy, avoiding scams and more.

▶ Eurail Passes

Find out, step-by-step, if a rail pass makes sense for your trip—and how to avoid buying more than you need. Get a bunch of free extras!

▶ Graffiti Wall & Travelers' Helpline

Learn, ask, share—our online community of savvy travelers is a great resource for first-time travelers to Europe, as well as seasoned pros.

Rick Steves' Europe Through the Back Door, Inc.

Rick Steves.

www.ricksteves.com

TRAVEL SKILLS
Europe Through the Back Door

EUROPE GUIDES
Best of Europe
Eastern Europe
Europe 101
European Christmas
Postcards from Europe

COUNTRY GUIDES
Croatia & Slovenia
England
France
Germany
Great Britain
Ireland
Italy
Portugal
Scandinavia
Spain
Switzerland

CITY & REGIONAL GUIDES
Amsterdam, Bruges & Brussels
Athens & The Peloponnese
Budapest
Florence & Tuscany
Istanbul
London
Paris
Prague & The Czech Republic
Provence & The French Riviera
Rome
Venice
Vienna, Salzburg & Tirol

PHRASE BOOKS & DICTIONARIES
French
French, Italian & German
German
Italian
Portuguese
Spanish

RICK STEVES' EUROPE DVDs
Austria & The Alps
Eastern Europe
England
Europe
France & Benelux
Germany & Scandinavia
Greece, Turkey, Israel & Egypt
Ireland & Scotland
Italy's Cities
Italy's Countryside
Rick Steves' European Christmas
Spain & Portugal
Travel Skills & "The Making Of"

PLANNING MAPS
Britain, Ireland & London
Europe
France & Paris
Germany, Austria & Switzerland
Ireland
Italy
Spain & Portugal

JOURNALS
Rick Steves' Pocket Travel Journal
Rick Steves' Travel Journal

NOW AVAILABLE

RICK STEVES APPS FOR THE iPHONE OR iPOD TOUCH

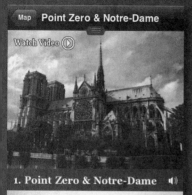

With these apps you can:

▸ Spin the compass icon to switch views between sights, hotels, and restaurant selections—and get details on cost, hours, address, and phone number.

▸ Tap any point on the screen to read Rick's detailed information, including history and suggested viewpoints.

▸ Get a deeper view into Rick's tours with audio and video segments.

Go to iTunes to download the following apps:

Rick Steves' Louvre Tour

Rick Steves' Historic Paris Walk

Rick Steves' Orsay Museum Tour

Rick Steves' Versailles

Rick Steves' Colosseum & Roman Forum Tour

Rick Steves' St. Peter's Basilica Tour

Once downloaded, these apps are completely self-contained on your iPhone or iPod Touch, so you will not incur pricey roaming charges during use overseas.

Rick Steves' Guidebook Series

Country Guides

Rick Steves' Best of Europe
Rick Steves' Croatia & Slovenia
Rick Steves' Eastern Europe
Rick Steves' England
Rick Steves' France
Rick Steves' Germany
Rick Steves' Great Britain
Rick Steves' Ireland
Rick Steves' Italy
Rick Steves' Portugal
Rick Steves' Scandinavia
Rick Steves' Spain
Rick Steves' Switzerland

City and Regional Guides

Rick Steves' Amsterdam, Bruges & Brussels
Rick Steves' Athens & the Peloponnese
Rick Steves' Budapest
Rick Steves' Florence & Tuscany
Rick Steves' Istanbul
Rick Steves' London
Rick Steves' Paris
Rick Steves' Prague & the Czech Republic
Rick Steves' Provence & the French Riviera
Rick Steves' Rome
Rick Steves' Venice
Rick Steves' Vienna, Salzburg & Tirol

Rick Steves' Phrase Books

French
French/Italian/German
German
Italian
Portuguese
Spanish

Other Books

Rick Steves' Europe 101: History and Art for the Traveler
Rick Steves' Europe Through the Back Door
Rick Steves' European Christmas
Rick Steves' Postcards from Europe
Rick Steves' Travel as a Political Act

Avalon Travel
a member of the Perseus Books Group
1700 Fourth Street
Berkeley, CA 94710

Text © 2009, 2008, 2007, 2006, 2005 by Europe Through the Back Door.
All rights reserved.
Maps © 2009 by Europe Through the Back Door. All rights reserved.
Paris Métro map © 2009 La Régie Autonome des Transports Parisiens (RATP).
Used with permission.
Printed in the United States of America by Worzalla
Second printing December 2009

Portions of this book were originally published in *Rick Steves' Mona Winks*, © 2001, 1998,
1996, 1993, 1988 by Rick Steves and Gene Openshaw; *Rick Steves' France, Belgium & the
Netherlands* © 2002, 2001, 2000, 1999, 1998 by Rick Steves and Steve Smith; and in *Rick
Steves' France* © 2008, 2007, 2006, 2005 by Rick Steves and Steve Smith.

ISBN 978-1-59880-287-0
ISSN 1522-3299

For the latest on Rick's lectures, guidebooks, tours, public radio show, and public television
series, contact Europe Through the Back Door, Box 2009, Edmonds, WA 98020, tel.
425/771-8303, fax 425/771-0833, www.ricksteves.com, or rick@ricksteves.com.

Europe Through the Back Door Managing Editor: Risa Laib
ETBD Senior Editor: Jennifer Madison Davis
ETBD Editors: Cathy Lu, Gretchen Strauch, Tom Griffin, Cathy MacDonald
Avalon Travel Senior Editor and Series Manager: Madhu Prasher
Avalon Travel Project Editor: Kelly Lydick
Copy Editor: Jennifer Malnick
Proofreader: Becca Freed
Indexer: Stephen Callahan
Production & Typesetting: McGuire Barber Design
Cover Design: Kimberly Glyder Design
Graphic Content Director: Laura VanDeventer
Maps & Graphics: David C. Hoerlein, Laura VanDeventer, Lauren Mills, Barb Geisler,
  Mike Morgenfeld
Photography: Rick Steves, Steve Smith, David C. Hoerlein, Gene Openshaw, Laura
  VanDeventer, Barb Geisler, Rob Unck, Carol Ries, Rich Earl
Front Cover Image: The Latin Quarter © Laura VanDeventer
Front Matter Color Photos: p. i, The Louvre at Night © Laura VanDeventer; p. viii, Place
  du Tertre © FOLIO, Inc.